STUDIES IN BAPTIST HISTORY AND THOUGHT
VOLUME 32

Counter-Cultural Communities

Baptistic Life in Twentieth-Century Europe

STUDIES IN BAPTIST HISTORY AND THOUGHT
VOLUME 32

A full listing of all titles in this series
appears at the close of the book

This volume is published in co-operation with the
International Baptist Theological Seminary, Prague, Czech Republic,
where the original studies that comprise this volume were researched.

STUDIES IN BAPTIST HISTORY AND THOUGHT
VOLUME 32

Counter-Cultural Communities

Baptistic Life in Twentieth-Century Europe

Edited by
Keith G. Jones and Ian M. Randall

Foreword by John Briggs

WIPF & STOCK · Eugene, Oregon

Wipf and Stock Publishers
199 W 8th Ave, Suite 3
Eugene, OR 97401

Counter-Cultural Communities
Baptistic Life in Twentieth-Century Europe
By Jones, Keith G. and Randall, Ian M.
Copyright©2008 Paternoster
ISBN 13: 978-1-60608-316-1
Publication date 11/03/2008
Previously published by Paternoster, 2008

STUDIES IN BAPTIST HISTORY AND THOUGHT

Series Preface

Baptists form one of the largest Christian communities in the world, and while they hold the historic faith in common with other mainstream Christian traditions, they nevertheless have important insights which they can offer to the worldwide church. Studies in Baptist History and Thought will be one means towards this end. It is an international series of academic studies which includes original monographs, revised dissertations, collections of essays and conference papers, and aims to cover any aspect of Baptist history and thought. While not all the authors are themselves Baptists, they nevertheless share an interest in relating Baptist history and thought to the other branches of the Christian church and to the wider life of the world.

The series includes studies in various aspects of Baptist history from the seventeenth century down to the present day, including biographical works, and Baptist thought is understood as covering the subject-matter of theology (including interdisciplinary studies embracing biblical studies, philosophy, sociology, practical theology, liturgy and women's studies). The diverse streams of Baptist life throughout the world are all within the scope of these volumes.

The series editors and consultants believe that the academic disciplines of history and theology are of vital importance to the spiritual vitality of the churches of the Baptist faith and order. The series sets out to discuss, examine and explore the many dimensions of their tradition and so to contribute to their on-going intellectual vigour.

A brief word of explanation is due for the series identifier on the front cover. The fountains, taken from heraldry, represent the Baptist distinctive of believer's baptism and, at the same time, the source of the water of life. There are three of them because they symbolize the Trinitarian basis of Baptist life and faith. Those who are redeemed by the Lamb, the book of Revelation reminds us, will be led to 'fountains of living waters' (Rev. 7.17).

Series Editors

Anthony R. Cross, Fellow of the Centre for Baptist History and Heritage, Regent's Park College, Oxford, UK

Curtis W. Freeman, Research Professor of Theology and Director of the Baptist house of Studies, Duke University, North Carolina, USA

Stephen R. Holmes, Lecturer in Theology, University of St Andrews, Scotland, UK

Elizabeth Newman, Professor of Theology and Ethics, Baptist Theological Seminary at Richmond, Virginia, USA

Philip E. Thompson, Assistant Professor of Systematic Theology and Christian Heritage, North American Baptist Seminary, Sioux Falls, South Dakota, USA

Series Consultant Editors

David Bebbington, Professor of History, University of Stirling, Scotland, UK

Paul S. Fiddes, Professor of Systematic Theology, University of Oxford, and Principal of Regent's Park College, Oxford, UK

† Stanley J. Grenz, Pioneer McDonald Professor of Theology, Carey Theological College, Vancouver, British Columbia, Canada

Ken R. Manley, Distinguished Professor of Church History, Whitley College, The University of Melbourne, Australia

Stanley E. Porter, President and Professor of New Testament, McMaster Divinity College, Hamilton, Ontario, Canada

Contents

Contributors xi

Foreword by John Briggs xiii

Introduction by Keith G. Jones and Ian M. Randall xv

Chapter 1: The State and the Baptist Churches in the USSR (1960-1980) 1
Constantine Prokhorov
    The Communist Party and State Policy on Religion in the Early
        1960s 2
    Historical Background 2
    Communism as a Goal: Intensified Atheistic Pressure 4
    The Official Baptist Union and Underground Communities in
        the Early 1960s 8
    The Crisis in the Baptist Union 8
    The Conflict between the AUCECB and Initsiativniki 9
    A Point of Comparison: The Orthodox Church 15
    The State and Baptist Churches (1960s-1970s) 19
    Legislation and Propaganda 19
    Creating Atheistic Stereotypes 20
    Apostates 24
    Statistical Data and General Tendencies 26
    The Personality of Gennady Kryuchkov 28
    Baptist Extremism 31
    Trials of the Baptists 36
    The About-faces of the Second Half of the 1970s 39
    Baptist Survival in an Atheistic Context 41
    Summary of Testimonies of the Witnesses 41
    Personal Spirituality 42
    Councils and Courses 43
    Local Church Life 44
    The Baptist Family as a Household Church 45
    Christian and Communist Outlooks 47
    God's and Caesar's Kingdoms 49
    Conclusion 53

Bibliography 54

Chapter 2: Separation or Co-operation? Moldavian Baptists (1940-1965) 63
Irina Bondareva-Zuehlke
    Political Pressure on Baptist Churches in Post-War Moldavia 67
    Formation of the Moldavian Soviet Socialist Republic 68
    Decline in Membership and Fragmentation 69
    Famine and Migration 72
    Applying Soviet Religious Laws in Moldavia 72
    Council for the Affairs of Religious Cults: Registration and
        Closure of Churches 74
    CARC and the AUCECB Commissioner in Moldavia 75
    Registration of Baptist Churches 76
    Underground Work as an Option 79
    Closing the Churches 80
    Khruschev's Campaign against the Believers 82
    The AUCECB in Moldavia: 'Big Brother', Agent of State
        Pressure, or Partner? 84
    'To Restore God's Work in Moldavia' 85
    Office of Senior Presbyter in Moldavia 87
    'Struggle for Freedom?'—Opposition to the AUCECB's
        Statutes 89
    Towards Separation: A Split among Moldavian Baptists 91
    The Division in the Kishinev ECB Church at Vokzal'naya
        Street 92
    Grigoriy Rudenko's Separatist Group 93
    The Council of Churches of the ECB and the Movement of
        Independent ECB Churches in Moldavia 94
    Broken Fellowship 96
    Attempts to Foster Unity 98
    Attempts to Restore Unity by Congresses 98
    Attempts to Find Unity in Fellowship and Worship 100
    Baptism as a Theological-ecclesiological Centre for
        Moldavian Baptists 102
    Attempts to Unify the Theology of Moldavian Baptist
        Believers 104
    Conclusion 106
    Bibliography 109

Contents

Chapter 3: August Jauhiainen and the Pentecostal Dilemma in the Finnish Baptist Union (1930-1953) 115
Anneli Lohikko
    Baptists and Other Free Churches in Finland 120
    A New Leader for the Union 128
    Jauiainen's Theology of the Holy Spirit and Pentecostal
        Teaching 134
    Trying to Re-build Baptist Identity (1930s) 142
    The 1940s: A New Wave of Pentecostalism 150
    The Beginning of the 1950s and the Final Conflict 157
    Jauhiainen's Dismissal 162
    Conclusion 166
    Bibliography 169

Chapter 4: The Theology of Baptist Believers in Bulgaria as Reflected in the Publication *Evangelist* (1920-1939) 173
Teodor B. Oprenov
    The Foundation of Early Baptist Theology and Practice in
        Bulgaria 176
    Evangelist's Role in Shaping the Theological Identity of Early
        Bulgarian Baptists 183
    The Birth of Evangelist 183
    Historical Identity: Search for Spiritual Roots 186
    *Theological Identity: Defining the Basics of Christian Life
        and Belief* 188
    The Church and its Mission as Reflected by *Evangelist* 198
    Church 198
    Mission and Evangelism 202
    Baptists and Others 205
    Bulgarian Baptist Theology in the Making: Internal
        Convictions, External Influences 211
    Conclusion 217
    Bibliography 219

Chapter 5: Baptist Mission Efforts in Bosnia-Herzegovina: 150 Years of Discontinuity and Struggle 227
Oksana Raychynets
    The Beginnings: The Baptist Church under Austro-Hungarian
        Rule (1878-1918) 228
    *The First Baptist Group in Sarajevo: Under Turkish
        Occupation* 228

Baptist Mission under Austro-Hungarian Rule: Possibilities and Difficulties 233
Political, Economic, Social and Religious Circumstances 239
The 'Golden Age': Between Two World Wars (1919-1945) 243
The Revitalisation of Baptist Mission 243
MISSION OF THE SOUTHERN BAPTIST CONVENTION, USA 245
MISSION OF THE SOUTH-EASTERN EUROPEAN GERMAN
    MISSION COMMITTEE 251
Political, Religious, Economic and Social Circumstances 256
Stagnation: Baptist Mission in Bosnia-Herzegovina in
    Communist Times (1946-1994) 258
The Baptist Union: Emerging Hope 258
MISSION 262
SUNDAY SCHOOL AND YOUTH MINISTRY 264
THEOLOGICAL EDUCATION 264
Mission Work in Bosnia-Herzegovina: Stagnation 266
SARAJEVO BAPTIST CHURCH 267
Political, Religious, Social and Economic Circumstances 270
The Revitalisation of the Baptist Mission in Independent
    Bosnia-Herzegovina 273
Conclusion 277
Bibliography 279

Chapter 6: 'The Practical, Visible Witness of Discipleship': The Life and Convictions of Hans Meier (1902-1992) 285
Dejan Adam
'The Way of Discipleship' 288
'To Follow the Holy Spirit's Promptings' 296
'A State which Claims Absolute Power' 303
'Seriously Seeking People' 312
'We, Like They, Wanted to Live in Community' 319
'The Forgiveness of the Church' 328
Conclusion 335
Bibliography 336

General Index 343

Contributors

Dejan Adam is a native of Serbia. He came to the International Baptist Theological Seminary (IBTS) and completed a Magister (Czech) degree, specialising in Baptist and Anabaptist history.

Irina Bondareva-Zuehlke came to IBTS to study for her MTh from Moldova, where she was lecturer in church history at the Baptist seminary in Kishenev. Her Bachelor's level study in theology was in Ukraine. She is currently working in the USA.

Anneli Lohikko has been deeply involved in Finnish Baptist life as the administrator of the Finnish (Finnish-speaking) Baptist Union. She did her MTh at IBTS. She has done extensive research on Finnish Baptist history and is now their primary historian.

Teodor Oprenov is pastor of the Evangelical Baptist Church in Sofia, Bulgaria. Teodor studied at Spurgeon's College, London, for his Bachelor's degree. He then did his MTh through IBTS. He has been the General Secretary of the Bulgarian Baptist Union, has overseen the development of Baptist theological education in the country and has taught at the Baptist Theological Institute and Evangelical Biblical Institute in Sofia.

Constantine Prokhorov is a Russian, who taught for a number of years in Kazhakstan. He has published several books in Russian. His Bachelor's degree in theology was obtained in Ukraine. He now teaches at a seminary in Omsk, Russia. He completed his MTh with distinction at IBTS and is now studying part time through IBTS for a PhD.

Oksana Raychynets is a native of Ukraine. She studied at the Evangelical Theological Seminary in Osijek, Croatia, for her Bachelor's degree in theology. She then came to IBTS and obtained her MTh. She and her husband are missionaries in Sarejeva, Bosnia, where they lead a church and help to oversee a Bible school.

Foreword

It is with great pleasure that I write a foreword to this volume, some of the contents of which I have previously only read with an examiner's eye! Common themes and emphases run through the essays. All the writers, for example, experience the need to engage in extended contextual analysis in order to situate the particular studies offered. All confront the lack of both primary sources and earlier scholarly studies, making the task of critical reconstruction more difficult. Language is an important factor, with Baptist work often starting in German-speaking communities before spreading to the local Slavic population; but other linguistic divisions also intrude into the story. The essays also illustrate the need for appropriate emphasis on the ecclesiastical and political environment—the different faces of the Orthodox Church, and of the State, with its moving boundaries and changing ideology of left and right, repression and greater freedom. The importance of leadership necessarily leads to the need to engage biography. Although the authors and their families are sometimes part of the story they have to tell, they all manage to handle their sources with admirable critical discipline.

The separation of church and state has been something of a sacred cow in Baptist circles but only rarely have the theory and the practice been consonant the one with the other. Even John Clifford, famed as the genius of the Passive Resistance Movement which persuaded Free-churchmen in early twentieth-century Britain to refuse to pay an educational rate part of which was to be used to support Anglican and Catholic schools, accepted a government grant for the support of the Westbourne Park Institute, the adult educational arm of his church. Just how problematical were relations between church and state in the former Soviet Union in the 1960s and 1970s is skilfully probed by Constantine Prokhorov in his substantial article with its magisterial catalogue of sources. This is just the topic on which such a carefully documented and subtly assessed argument serves to illuminate every aspect of those two decades and the legacy they left for subsequent years. Relations between church and state also form the backcloth for Irina Bondareva-Zuehlke's study of the situation in Soviet Moldavia for a rather earlier period in what the author confesses is 'the first systematic attempt in English to introduce the story of the post-war Moldavian Baptists and their relationships with the Soviet State'. As in Russia relating to the demands of the state became a cause of painful division amongst Baptists at a time of costly witness.

The internal life of the churches is also studied, analysing how sensitively to handle the Pentecostal challenge and the way in which periodical literature was used to root a people's discipleship in an orderly and sustaining theology. Accordingly Anneli Lohikko's examination of the Pentecostal Dilemma in the Finnish Baptist Union (1930-1953) is a study of internal tensions amongst

Baptists in Finland which continues a story begun in Norway and Sweden. In particular it seeks to assess the leadership of August Jauhiainen, president of the Finnish Baptists from 1931 until his dismissal in 1953 because of his failure to follow the majority of Finnish Baptists in adopting a Pentecostal understanding of the work of the Holy Spirit. The Finnish Union was not the only one which found some difficulty in handling the Pentecostal challenge, both within and outside Baptist structures, for a common evangelicalism did not always ensure good relations between the two groups.

Deducing a denomination's theology from its periodical literature, so often concerned with the immediacy of news, the recording of memoirs and devotional nurture, is no easy task, but it is this that Teodor Oprenov achieves with systematic distinction in 'The Theology of Baptist Believers in Bulgaria as Reflected in the Publication Evangelist (1920-1939)'. Oksana Raychynets' 'Baptist Mission Efforts in Bosnia-Herzegovina: 150 Years of Discontinuity and Struggle' offers a wider chronological perspective with a more restricted geographical focus, since, to date, the literature has embraced the whole of the former Yugoslavia. However, this detailed study of Bosnia-Hercegovina also demonstrates how the mission there was part of a larger strategy addressing all Slavic peoples as well as the many German settlers in the area, particularly in the period of Austro-Hungarian rule, and its imperial legacy. In this chapter the interplay between national and expatriate personnel is clearly shown.

In the final chapter Dejan Adam moves outside strictly Baptist circles to consider 'The Practical, Visible Witness of Discipleship: The Life and Convictions of Hans Meier (1902-1992)', a consideration of Meier's contribution to the Bruderhof movement, an exciting attempt to re-interpret the Anabaptist praxis in the context of twentieth-century life. In this study the collection comes back to its starting point for the fragile life of the Bruderhof represents another, even more radical way, of dealing with the church-state tension. The life of the separated community was to prove no easier than that of the valorous path of challenging the state, or indeed the way of discretion, buying pastoral opportunity by conforming to state demands.

The publication of these essays is a testimony to the excellent work done by the Department of Baptist and Anabaptist Studies at IBTS, Prague. It is also an enormously useful tool in providing critical scholarship in English which gives an assessment of aspects of East European Baptist thought and activity hitherto not known outside the literature of the different East European languages. In this sense this collection of essays is excitingly pioneering.

John Briggs
Senior Research Fellow and Director of the Centre for Baptist History and Heritage, Regent's Park College, University of Oxford
Research Professor in Baptist and Anabaptist Studies, IBTS

Introduction

The essays in this volume arise out of an interest in Anabaptist and Baptist history and identity across Europe which has flourished over the past twenty-five years. A key stimulus to the growth of these studies and to wider reflection on baptistic life in Europe was the establishment in 1984 of the Institute of Baptist and Anabaptist Studies by H. Walker W. Pipkin at the International Baptist Theological Seminary, then in Rüschlikon, Switzerland. The later development of the Hughey Lectures in Baptist and Anabaptist history and identity was a further factor awakening interest within Europe in this important topic.

Further energy was unleashed with the establishment of an Anabaptist study group in the United Kingdom in the 1980s, linked with the vision of Mennonites based in London, Alan and Eleanor Kreider, and then later the Anabaptist Network, which spawned further local groups. This was followed by the creation of specialist Master's programmes in Baptist and Anabaptist studies, firstly at Spurgeon's College in the early 1990s and then later in the decade at the International Baptist Theological Seminary (IBTS), by now located in Prague. The essays included here are all from students who have obtained Master's degrees at IBTS.

Over the past decade IBTS has used both the Master's degrees and the Institute of Baptist and Anabaptist Studies to develop enquiry into and analysis of baptistic history and identity in Europe, seeking to understand the distinctives of these 'gathering' churches. An important element of the work of the Institute has been the holding of annual conferences in Prague on key themes of our heritage and identity, in order to encourage a new generation of scholars to undertake research and share their work. We make no apology for the evangelical fervour with which we have pursued this vision on behalf of European Baptists. We are very conscious that in the past much of the conference and publication activity in the area of Baptist studies has been located in North America.

Research and reflection, however, need primary sources, and with the collapse of the Soviet Empire in 1989 there has been freedom for baptistic communities throughout central and eastern Europe to gain access to archives previously closed to them. This has produced a heady mix: an increasing number of younger baptistic historians and the ability to access key primary resources. The result has been a flowering of original research and reflection, especially during the past decade. This volume is one evidence of that process. The history and identity of many baptistic communities in the geographical area from the Pacific to the Latin/Slavic confluence in central Europe and from the Arctic Circle to the emerging nations of north/central Asia is almost unknown and uncharted in the wider world—and we are much the poorer for this lack.

Indeed these communities have often not been adequately aware of their own stories. They have had to rely on oral tradition, without knowledge of the kind of documents being used by the writers in this collection. As this situation is gradually addressed, not only can these communities review afresh their own histories, but a wider public can be enlightened.

As we approach the four hundredth anniversary of the establishment of the Baptist congregation developed out of the English separatist congregation of John Smyth and Thomas Helwys, meeting in a bake-house owned by a member of the Dutch Mennonite community in Amsterdam, it is entirely appropriate to invest in thorough investigation of the European Baptist story. Monographs and collections such as this are emerging and will do so in greater numbers as a new generation of qualified historians uncovers much original material. This helps our European family, the wider scholarly community, and even the wider societies of the region, to have a better understanding of, and respect for, the rich ecclesial life of baptistic churches in the region.

We feel immense satisfaction in the role that IBTS has been able to play since the 1990s in this important enterprise. A steady stream of highly competent younger scholars has been emerging from this venture in European academic collaboration. We are also grateful to those who have helped to mentor such students and want to express particular thanks to Professor John Briggs, who has kindly written the foreword to this volume, Dr Toivo Pilli, Rector of the Estonian Baptist Seminary, and Dr Ruth Gouldbourne, minister of Bloomsbury Baptist Church, London. We also wish to thank Jennifer Thomas for her careful sub-editing, Philip Alexander for formatting, and Bill Lively for the index. The sense of a research community engaging in a common enterprise together is inspiring.

In our opinion there can be no doubt that the field of studies represented in this volume is emerging out of the shadows to take its place as a fruitful exercise not simply in uncovering and telling previously unknown stories, but (more importantly) in stimulating baptistic communities to understand their histories and identity better within the context of the Christian world communions and within society. In exploring our distinctive identity we believe there is a stimulus to mission. IBTS remains committed to this missional task. We have greatly enjoyed participating in the production of these essays and it is our hope that they will provide a better understanding of the variety and quality of counter-cultural baptistic life in Europe in the twentieth century.

Keith G. Jones
Rector, IBTS
Ian M. Randall
Senior Research Fellow, IBTS
Lent 2008

CHAPTER 1

The State and the Baptist Churches in the USSR (1960-1980)

Constantine Prokhorov

Traditionally, the relationship between State and Church has not been an easy one. Throughout the centuries, the values and interests of Caesar's kingdom have often been in opposition to God's kingdom. The early church experienced persecution at the hands of the Roman authorities. The medieval Inquisition in Europe was an extreme example of another phenomenon—the close links that can exist between Church and State. Many Christian thinkers, in reaction to this, have defended strict separation between Church and State, but this is easier said than done. The former Soviet Union is an example of the problematic relationship between Church and State. The specific situation there was a combination of 'State interests' with militant atheism and faith in communism. This combination can be considered a powerful rival religion rather than as atheism proper.

The focus of this study is the Baptist communities in the Soviet Union in the 1960s and 1970s. At the beginning of this period, when the Soviet State oppressed all religions and denominations in the Soviet empire, the Soviet Baptists offered such serious resistance to authority that they became the recognized leaders among religious dissidents in the USSR. This standing had some obvious advantages and disadvantages. To analyse the situation, it is necessary to look at the political reality and the causes of the severe persecution against believers at that time; the position of the official Baptist Union and the underground Baptist communities; and the painful split of the Russian Baptists between the All-Union Council of Evangelical Christians–Baptists (AUCECB) and the radical *Initsiativniki* (the Initiative Group—later known as the Council of Churches of the Evangelical Christians–Baptists, the CCECB). It is important to compare divergent points of view of the events: from the perspective of atheists, the moderates of the official Baptist Union, the radicals of the unregistered Baptist movement, and Western and Russian historians. Unpublished documents of that time from the Archives of the All-Union Council of Evangelical Christians–Baptists in Moscow and some local Siberian and Central Asian sources will help to reveal the tension in the situation and the causes of the radicalism in a faction of Soviet Baptists.

In this study, the established English spellings of common Russian names and terms, as found in dictionaries, will be used. Other Cyrillic words will be transliterated by the following system:

А—*A*; Б—*B*; В—*V*; Г—*G*; Д—*D*; Е—*E*; Ё—*YE*; Ж—*ZH*; З—*Z*; И—*I*; Й –*Y*; К—*K*; Л—*L*; М—*M*; Н—*N*; О—*O*; П—*P*; Р—*R*; С—*S*; Т—*T*; У—*U*; Ф—*F*; Х—*KH*; Ц—*TS*; Ч—*CH*; Ш—*SH*; Щ—*SHCH*; Ъ—``; Ы—*Y*; Ь—`; Э—*E*; Ю—*YU*; Я –*YA*.

The Communist Party and State Policy on Religion in the Early 1960s

Historical Background

The nearly total destruction of all religious confessions in the USSR in 1918–1938 as a result of the militant, atheistic roots of Communist ideology, was followed by an enigmatic partial restoration of religion by Joseph Stalin from 1943[1] to his death in 1953, and this brought a great revival for the Russian Orthodox and Protestant Churches. For instance, the Russian Evangelical Christians-Baptists (ECB) had only four official churches at the beginning of the 1940s,[2] but approximately 4,000 congregations with 400,000 members by 1948,[3] and about 5,400 congregations with more than 500,000 members in the mid-1950s; though, of course, not all of those churches and groups were

---

[1] In September of that year, Stalin suddenly invited Metropolitan Sergy (Stragorodsky) to the Kremlin, acquainted him with the new policy on religion in the USSR, and demanded 'to show Bolshevik speed' to summon the Episcopal Council of the Russian Orthodox Church in order to normalize Church life as soon as possible. Funds were given and even military airplanes provided to transport the participants of the Council to Moscow. (M.I. Odintsov, *Put Dlinoyu v Sem Desyatilety* in D. Furman ed., *Na Puti k Svobode Sovesti* (On the Way to Liberty of Conscience) (Moscow: Progress, 1989), p. 60; D. Pospelovsky, *Pravoslavnaya Tserkov v Istorii Rusi, Rossii i SSSR* (The Orthodox Church in the History of Old Russia, Russia and the USSR) (Moscow: Bibleysky Institut Sv. Apostola Andreya, 1996), p. 298.

[2] See Supplement 6 in S.N. Savinsky, *Istoria Evangelskikh Khristian-Baptistov Ukrainy, Rossii, Belorussii, 1917-1967* (The History of the Evangelical Christian-Baptists of Ukraine, Russia, and Byelorussia, 1917-1967) (Saint Petersburg: Biblia Dlya Vsekh, 2001), p. 355.

[3] S. Bolshakoff, *Russian Nonconformity* (Philadelphia: Westminster Press, 1950), p. 128. Of course, such progress was not founded on nothing. In 1928, before Stalin's terror, the Evangelical Christians and Baptists already had nearly 4,000 congregations with approximately 800,000 members in the USSR. (V. Zavatski, *Evangelicheskoe Dvizhenie v SSSR Posle Vtoroy Mirovoy Voyny* (Soviet Evangelicals Since World War II) (Moscow: n.p, 1995), p. 42; Savinsky, *Istoria Evangelskikh*, p. 12.

registered.⁴ The majority of historians have connected the religious restoration in the USSR with the burdens of the war period and patriotic support of the Soviet authorities by the believers at that time.⁵ However, something serious was lacking—the relative religious freedom in the country was not based on any official law, but on the individual decision of the great 'defender of the faith', Joseph Stalin. Members of the governing body and the Communist Party leaders (V. Molotov, G. Malenkov, K. Voroshilov, L. Beriya, N. Khrushchev, etc.) were primarily strict atheists who felt bewilderment and hostility toward the reinstatement by Stalin of churches in the Soviet Union. Thus, the rapid change of policy immediately following Stalin's death, under the leadership of Nikita Khrushchev, was not a surprise for observers who knew the Soviet system well. It was not necessary to create any new laws for the persecution of believers in the country. The simple re-enforcement of the RSFSR⁶ Law on Religious Associations of 8 April 1929 was enough to solve the problem.⁷

The first half of the period of the leadership of Nikita Khrushchev saw the denunciation of the personality cult of Stalin (at the twentieth Congress of the Communist Party in 1956) and the general liberalization of Soviet society. But Krushchev combined bold criticism of Stalin's terrible regime with the suppression of religious life in the USSR.⁸ Khrushchev's popular reforms, popular both within the country and abroad (the famous Khrushchev Thaw), went along with his initiation of his severe struggle against Soviet believers (the new *Zamorozki*—Late Frosts).⁹

The first indications of a change in official policy relative to religion in the USSR were already evident in 1954 when two decrees were issued at the same time by the Central Committee of the CPSU (Communist Party of the Soviet Union). Even the titles of the decrees put people on their guard: *On the Grave Shortcomings of the Scientific and Atheistic Propaganda and Measures for Its Improvement* (of 7 July) and *On the Errors in the Realization of Scientific and Atheistic Propaganda among the Population* (of 10 November). 'I remember well', wrote L. Mitrokhin, former Soviet critic of the Baptist churches,

---

⁴ Savinsky, *Istoria Evangelskikh*, p. 195.
⁵ For example, Zavatski, *Evangelicheskoe Dvizhenie v SSSR*, p. 50.
⁶ The Russian Soviet Federal Socialist Republic.
⁷ This forbade religious communities to have any kind of social, charitable, missionary, or educational activity. Local authorities could close churches and prayer houses because of any minor violation. Indeed, many Orthodox and almost all Protestant churches were closed in the 1930s. The law was not abrogated in full until 1990. (See text of the law in A. Nikolin, *Tserkov i Gosudarstvo* (Church and State) (Mosow: Sretensky Monastyr, 1997), pp. 382-93).
⁸ Many people did not agree with Khrushchev's antireligious course. It is notable that Svetlana Allilueva, Stalin's daughter, was baptized in a Moscow Orthodox church in 1962. (M.V. Shkarovsky, *Russkaya Pravoslavnaya Tserkov pri Staline i Khrushcheve* (The Russian Orthodox Church under Stalin and Khrushchev) (Moscow: Krutitskoe Patriarshee Podvor'e, 1999), p. 268).
⁹ Ibid., pp. 359-360, 389.

The decree directed them to fight against religion in the form of the scientific and materialistic outlook struggling with the anti-scientific religious notions. It was interesting to watch as the former investigators and 'red professors' assumed the delicate work of spreading all kinds of knowledge.[10]

The first decree also directed Party organizations to increase the quantity and quality of atheistic lectures, articles, books, films and broadcasts.[11] The second decree cautioned against some extreme anti-religious offensives in the country[12] and, in particular, proclaimed a remarkable interpretation of the principle of Church-State separation:

> Though religion is a private affair in relation to the State, and the church is disestablished, the Communist Party, which is based on the only true scientific outlook, Marxism-Leninism, and its theoretical basis—dialectical materialism—cannot be indifferent to religion as the ideology which has nothing in common with science... The Party considers it necessary to conduct deep systematic scientific and atheistic propaganda, though not permitting insults against the religious feelings of believers and ministers.[13]

Later the general secretary of the AUCECB, A. Karev, would more clearly define the situation in the USSR: 'The Church is separated from the State, but the State is not separated from the Church.'[14] How the atheists in the Soviet Union held to the official Party call to 'not insult the religious feelings of believers' will be shown in a subsequent section of this study. For now, it is important to show the main cause of the increasingly severe treatment of all kinds of believers in the country at that time.

Communism as a Goal: Intensified Atheistic Pressure

The second half of Khrushchev's leadership opened the way for the building up of the communist society in the USSR. In January 1959, the twenty-first Congress of the Communist Party solemnly declared,

---

[10] L. Mitrokhin, *Baptism: Istoriya i Sovremennost* (Baptists: History and the Present) (Saint-Petersburg: Russky Khristiansky Gumanitarny Institut, 1997), p. 56.

[11] See *O Religii i Tserkvi:S Sbornik Dokumentov* (On Religion and Church: Collected Documents) (Moscow: Politizdat, 1965), pp. 71-77.

[12] Undoubtedly, it was an old communist trick to show the Party leaders in Moscow as wise and patient, by contrast with 'some impatient provincial leaders' who 'carry everything to extremes'. In practice, both kinds of leaders always worked in close co-operation.

[13] *O Religii i Tserkvi: Sbornik Dokumentov*, pp. 80-81.

[14] See Supplement 6 in Savinsky, *Istoria Evangelskikhh*, p. 356.

> The Soviet people, under the leadership of the Party...accomplished such grandiose transformations of all spheres of economic and social-political life, which gave our country an opportunity to enter the new and the most important period of its development—the period of large-scale building of the communist society.15

At that time, it was considered that there were two world social systems: capitalism, which was waning, and socialism, which was increasing in vitality.[16] The promising economic growth of the USSR at that time gave Khrushchev's government the confidence to make the following plans: in seven years, 'the socialist countries will produce more than half of all the world's industrial production'[17] and will overtake and surpass the USA, 'leaving it on the slow-track. [Storm of applause].'[18] The twenty-second Congress of the Communist Party continued and strengthened this political course in 1961: 'We are guided by strict scientific calculations, and these calculations show that we will build the core of communist society in twenty years.'[19] 'The Party solemnly declares: the present generation of Soviet people will live in Communism!'[20]

Besides the fascinating political and economic aspects of Soviet society, there was, of course, a moral aspect to it, dubbed 'the rise of the new man', who would be 'the active builder of Communism'.[21] This goal was in a sense religious, reminding one of the Christian doctrine of 'new birth'. Indeed, many of the above-mentioned Communist Congress messages could be stylistically defined as 'sermonic' or 'religious exhortation'; for example, the following famous 'Moral Code for the Builder of Communism' which was a part of the Programme of the Communist Party approved by the twenty-second Congress.

- Dedication to Communism, love for the Socialist Fatherland and the other socialist countries
- Conscientious labour for the good of society; he who does not work, shall not eat
- The concern of each man for the preservation and augmenting of community property
- Deep awareness of public duty and intolerance of infringements on public interests
- Cooperative and friendly mutual assistance: one for all, all for one

---

[15] The Materials of the Special Twenty-first Congress of the Communist Party of the Soviet Union (Moscow: Politizdat, 1959), p. 11.
[16] Ibid., p. 97.
[17] Ibid., p. 59.
[18] Ibid., p. 87.
[19] The Materials of the Twenty-second Congress of the Communist Party of the Soviet Union (Moscow: Politizdat, 1961), p. 140.
[20] Ibid., pp. 319, 428.
[21] Ibid., pp. 86, 111.

- Humane treatment and mutual respect among people: each one treats the other as a friend, comrade and brother
- Honesty and justice, moral purity, simplicity and modesty in public and private life
- Mutual respect in the family and care for the upbringing of children
- Relentless animosity towards injustice, parasitism, dishonesty and self-seeking
- Friendship and fraternity of all peoples of the USSR and intolerance of national and racial prejudices
- Relentless animosity towards the enemies of Communism, peace and the freedom of nations
- Fraternal solidarity with the workers of all countries and with all nations.[22]

Though these twelve commandments of the 'Bolshevik paradise' were not unlike the biblical Ten Commandments,[23] none of the believers in the USSR were recognized as 'fit for' (Luke 9:62) the communist kingdom.[24] Even the large population of Soviet criminals and labour camp prisoners, who were traditionally, from Stalin's time, another section of the population unlikely to be able to cultivate the ability to become the 'new man' of the 'radiant future', did not worry the authorities too much.

> We have quite a few breaches of the peace, and we need to resolutely struggle with such a position. Have not the Soviet people managed those who commit a breach of socialist law and order? Of course, we have.[25]

> At the present stage of the development of communism, we need to struggle more resolutely with such remnants of capitalism as idleness and sponging, hard drinking and hooliganism, sharp practice and money-grubbing... These weeds should not have room in our life.[26]

It is remarkable that faith in God was also named a 'remnant of capitalism' in the USSR at that time. Believers were usually mentioned side by side with criminals, although the former caused more alarm to the communist leaders. In 1961, the Communist Party Congress warned against 'religious prejudices':

---

[22] Ibid., p. 410-411.

[23] The majority of the Russian rulers of that time were born before the Bolshevik revolution of 1917 and studied, as a required subject, *God's Law*, in tsarist schools. For example, Nikita Khrushchev, who was born in 1894, liked to remember his studies at a parish school. (R. Medvedev, *N.S. Khrushchev: Politicheskaya Biografiya* (N.S. Khrushchev: Political Biography) (Moscow: Kniga, 1990), pp. 14-15).

[24] The bases of the two types of commandments were, nevertheless, absolutely different: dedication to God alone or to the Communist idea. As rival religions, they were irreconcilable. (See: M. D'Arcy, *Communism and Christianity* (Aylesbury: Penguin Books, 1956), p. 126ff).

[25] *Materials of Twenty-first Congress*, p. 94.

[26] *Materials of Twenty-second Congress*, p. 111.

> Religious prejudices and superstitions are firm, and they are still spread among a part of the population. First of all, a communist must explain the anti-scientific nature of religious notions.[27]

Traditionally, the communists fought against all foreign enemies and Soviet dissidents, as well as their allies and comrades-in-arms, with the sharp 'proletarian' sword. However, to write about such things in the official documents was not done, even more so after the public denunciation of Stalin's period of terror. Therefore, the communist Congresses said more about the ideological struggle with religion and the special tasks of the Soviet educational system.

> The Soviet school has a special place in the process of the communist education of the growing generation.[28]

> The upbringing of the new man is a difficult and long process. It is impossible to automatically resettle people from the kingdom of capitalism to the kingdom of communism. We cannot take a man overgrown with the moss of capitalist prejudices into communism. We must see to it beforehand that he is freed from the burden of the past... Communist education proposes the liberation of consciousness from religious prejudices and superstitions... We need a considered and harmonious system of scientific and atheistic education, which would involve all levels and groups of the population and prevent dissemination of religious views, especially among children and teenagers.[29]

The specific character of the anti-religious campaigns of both the Khrushchev and later the Brezhnev eras were, more or less, a successful combination of both of the mainstream communist methods of struggling with religion in the USSR: criminal punishment of and discrimination against adult believers, and the obligatory atheistic education of their children at Soviet schools. The goals of such policies were the 'gradual withering of religion'; moral separation of children from parents in religious families; and training the children to be in a sense atheistic *janissaries* who would fight against their believing relatives. It is remarkable that even Stalin's campaign against believers in the USSR was not very successful. For instance, for all the evangelicals who were killed or died in the gulag, approximately the same number of new believers came to both official and underground communities of the Evangelical Christians and Baptists by the middle of the 1950s.[30] However, the second communist method used in the following years—the atheistic education of children—was much more effective. Even many of the famous

---

[27] Ibid., p. 292.
[28] *Materials of Twenty-first Congress*, p. 49.
[29] *Materials of Twenty-second Congress*, pp. 111-12.
[30] The known comparative figures were already mentioned above.

Christian ministers had unbelieving children during this period.[31] There was a tendency towards an 'aging of all religious communities' and some decrease in their numbers in the Soviet Union during 1960s and 1970s. More details on this point will be mentioned later.

The Official Baptist Union and Underground Communities in the Early 1960s

The Crisis in the Baptist Union

After the short-lived religious revival that took place late in Stalin's time, the evangelical movement undoubtedly went through an increasing crisis in the second half of the 1950s. The official account, *History of the Evangelical Christians–Baptists in the USSR* (1989), mentions the following indications of the crisis: a lack of ministers, prayer houses and spiritual literature; the underground movement of 'pure Baptists';[32] numerous 'unregistered' communities which were refused official registration; dictatorship and oppression of the local communities by regional senior presbyters who were not even elected by the churches; the declining authority of the AUCECB because of its approval and support of the more 'bureaucratic' rather than spiritual activity of such 'elder brothers'; and many local splits due to disagreements among senior presbyters who often tried to appoint church ministers without the usual Baptist practice of election.[33] Instead of the traditional congregationalism of the Russian Baptist churches, the AUCECB, under pressure from the state in the Council for Religious Affairs, spread the Episcopalian system, which was easier to control. This situation was aggravated by the increasingly intolerant atheistic propaganda in all the Soviet mass media and work collectives. As a result, the dissatisfaction of many Baptist church members increased.

These were not Stalinist times any longer. People, especially young people, were not particularly afraid of the authorities. After the denunciation of the

---

[31] G. Vins, *Evangelie v Uzakh* (The Gospel in Bonds) (Elkhart: Russian Gospel Ministries, 1991), p. 48; A. Belov, *Lzhenastavniki Yunoshestva: O Deyatel'nosti Khristianskikh Sekt* (False Teachers of the Young People: On the Activity of Christian Sects) (Moscow: Pedagogika, 1973), p. 96.

[32] The 'pure Baptists' (the third Baptist movement of that time) strove for the separation of Baptists from Evangelical Christians and Pentecostals who had been joined by the authorities into one union (AUCECB) since 1944-1945. (Yu. Reshetnikov and S. Sannikov, *Obsor Istorii Evangelsko-Baptistskogo Bratstva na Ukraine* (The Historical Review of the Ukrainian Evangelical-Baptist Brotherhood) (Odessa: Bogomyslie, 2000), p. 190).

[33] *Istoriya Evangelskikh Khristian-Baptistov v SSSR* (History of Evangelical Christians–Baptists in the USSR) (Moscow: VSEHB, 1989), pp. 238-40.

personality cult of Stalin, the idea of 'returning to Lenin's Socialist law' was widespread and popular. Such an illusion ('Lenin was kind and wise, but Stalin was terrible and led us the wrong way.') could not be escaped by the Soviet Baptists either. They probably believed this myth even more than unbelievers did; since many Baptists still remembered the 'blessed 1920s', a period when Baptist churches in the USSR were growing quickly. 'Life under Lenin's rule was better', said a rural Baptist preacher from the Novosibirsk region.

> Lenin was good, but the Leninists [in the original: 'Leninyata', a contemptuous word] are not so good; there are drunkards among them; the Baptists are the opposite, they do not smoke or drink, and they work honestly everywhere.[34]

Another preacher from Kazakhstan compared Lenin with Moses, who 'led the peoples of our country from slavery and oppression out into the kingdom of justice and happiness'.[35] The Baptist periodical, the *Bratsky Vestnik* (Fraternal Bulletin), wrote on the 100th anniversary of Lenin's birthday, 'As Everest [is the highest] among all mountains of the world, there was our great sociologist-humanist Vladimir Il'ich Lenin... There is no exploitation in the Soviet State founded by the genius of Lenin.'[36] Even during the hearings of 'Baptist cases' in Soviet courts, it was a common argument in their self-justification that, 'There is Lenin's law of liberty of conscience for believers...'[37] There was a sad irony in such naïve words, just as in the old parable about a kind landowner and his vicious dogs.[38]

The Conflict between the AUCECB and Initsiativniki

In 1960 the AUCECB published documents about Baptist life in relation to the State that became famous, or infamous—the *New Statutes* and *Letter of*

---

[34] Cited in A. Pakina, *Raskol Evangelskikh Khristian-Baptistov 1961 g. i Ego Vliyanie na Obshchiny Novosibirskoy Oblasti* (The 1961 Split of the Evangelical Christians–Baptists and Its Influence on the Communities of the Novosibirsk Region), Diplomnaya Rabota (Novosibirsk: Novosibirsky Gosuniversitet, 2000), p. 28.

[35] A. Nikiforov and F. Sim, *'Podryazhayutsya Voyti Skvoz' Tesnye Vrata'* (They 'Make Every Effort to Enter Through the Narrow Door') (Petropavlovsk, 1985), p. 27.

[36] *Bratsky Vestnik* (Fraternal Bulletin) 2 (1970), pp. 6-7.

[37] *Vestnik Spaseniya* (Bulletin of Salvation) 1 (1973), pp. 24-25. See also *Byulleten' Soveta Rodstvennikov Uznikov Evangelskikh Khristian-Baptistov v SSSR* 17 (Bulletin of the Council of Prisoners' Relatives of the Evangelical Christians–Baptists of the USSR 17) (Moscow, 1974), p. 4.

[38] In a year of bad harvest, a few hungry peasants asked their master to give them some grain. 'Surely, my dear servants, please come tomorrow with your bags!' he answered smiling. The next day, when the peasants came to the barn, the landowner ordered the vicious dogs to be unchained. The frightened servants ran and said later, 'Our master is very kind, but his dogs are wicked...'

Instructions. These documents became a formal and visible cause of the great split among the Soviet Baptists between the AUCECB and the radicals of the *Initsiativniki*—the Initiative Group. It is wrong, however, to think that the documents of 1960 really contained anything new. The State policy on religion in the USSR, not excluding the relatively favourable post-war period, always had numerous restrictions on church activity. For example, the following sentences from the earlier *Instructions for the Senior Presbyters* by the AUCECB of 1950 were very similar to the aforementioned documents of 1960:

> Pay special attention so that only the official preachers chosen for this ministry preach in the communities of your region. Any preachers coming from other places (churches) cannot be invited to preach in your communities. Also, pay attention so that no community in your region practises recitations of verses, solos and other songs, excluding the general congregational and choral singing. We remind you again that...students cannot be choir members... No communities can celebrate the Harvest Day with meals as well as meetings of visitors from other communities... We advise the reduction of the number of the baptisms among the 18-25 age group as much as possible... Students cannot be baptized at all... P.S. This letter is intended for you personally, and not for circulation among the communities.[39]

Of course, it is easy to charge the AUCECB with servility before the communist authorities, and 'friendship with the world'. The unpopularity of the senior presbyters, who needed to correlate their work with semi-secret instructions from the centre, is also clear. However, critics must remember the severe political context of those times, and that, in spite of everything, the evangelical communities were alive and increasing by thousands of members every year. That was the priority. That was worth the sacrifice of some good traditional elements of Baptist services. The position 'all or nothing' was never wise. Let us also try to understand another remarkable example of the 'moderate' policy of the AUCECB shortly before the 'revolutionary events', as they can be termed, of the beginning of the 1960s.

> To the senior presbyter... Dear brother in the Lord, peace be with you! We were told that some communities of your region use string orchestras, engage in the singing of solos and duets, as well as an unlimited number of preachers, sometimes unknown and from other communities. We ask you, dear brother, to check such information... We understand that there are some ministers who do not fully agree with the approved Statutes of the Communities of the ECB... You should patiently explain to them the need to act properly, because the above-mentioned violation may not do them good. We are praying to the Lord that He

---

[39] Cited in *Vestnik Istiny* (Bulletin of the Truth) 3 (2001), pp. 2-3.

helps you with the improvement of your communities' life. With our fraternal greetings, Ya. Zhidkov and A. Karev (March of 1957).[40]

Such documents were and are undoubtedly 'criminal' for the radical wing of Russian Baptists. However, official letters of that time, with the obligatory copies sent to the Council for Religious Affairs, could not be different. An analysis of the text shows the 'wisdom of the elders'[41] rather than the 'justice of the youth'.[42] Of course, the brothers of the *Initsiativniki* (the Initiative Group was also often known in the West as Reform Baptists or 'underground' congregations) were bold people who dared, in 1961, to struggle for the purity of the Baptists. This was the year of the twenty-second Congress of the Communist Party and the official proclamation that the Communist society was imminent,[43] when the 'last priest in the Soviet Union' [in the original: 'pop', a term of contempt] would be shown as a wonder on central TV (a promise by Khrushchev).[44] The radicals' zealous vigilance and readiness to suffer were worthy of respect. However, at the same time, the cautious position of the AUCECB was important for mediation between the state authorities and the thousands of evangelical communities, in order to present regularly the believers' needs. It is interesting that both lines of conduct can be found in the Bible. There were those in the Bible who cast down idols, destroyed heathen sacred places and bravely condemned kings; and there were those who patiently prayed, and with humility pleaded before the pagan kings for the believers. Each wing of the Russian Baptists pointed to their favourite biblical texts. So, which actions were most appropriate for the situation at the beginning of the 1960s? This was the question many asked.

---

[40] Ya. Zhidkov, A. Karev, 'O Nedopustimosti na Bogosluzheniyakh Strunnykh Orkestrov, Peniya Solo, Duetov, a Takzhe Neogranichennogo Chisla Propovednikov' (On the Inadmissibility of Using String Orchestras, Solo and Duet Singing as Well as Many Preachers during Worship). *Arkhiv Rossiyskogo Soyuza Evangel'skikh Khristian-Baptistov, Arkhiv VSEHB* (The Archives of the Russian Union of the Evangelical Christian-Baptists, the AUCECB Archives), papka 1\1, document 33.

[41] At the beginning of the 1960s, the average age of the members of the presidium of the AUCECB was over 60; the majority of them were imprisoned, because of their faith in God, in Stalin's time. (See Savinsky, *Istoria Evangelskikh,* p. 154).

[42] At the same period of time, the average age of the leaders of the dissident Russian Baptists was slightly more than 30; they were children of *Khrushchev's Thaw.* (See Zavatski, *Evangelicheskoe Dvizhenie*, p. 186).

[43] At that time, Communism had already started to use Party nomenclature. The enthusiasm and pathos come from that. See detailed research of this theme in: M. Voslensky, *Nomenklatura: Gospodstbuyushchy Klass Sovetskogo Soyuza* (Nomenclature: The Ruling Class of the Soviet Union) (Moscow: Sovetskaya Rossiya, 1991).

[44] Shkarovsky, *Russkaya Pravoslavnaya Tserkov,* p. 382. This expression by the Soviet leadership was widely spread among the evangelical churches with the following variation: 'to show the last Baptist on TV', and that expression was not very different from the wishes of the Party leaders of the country.

When the members of the AUCECB (Ya. Zhidkov, A. Karev, I. Ivanov, and others) and the members of the Initiative Group (G. Kryuchkov, S. Evlakov, Samsakov, and others) met in Moscow at the end of 1961, two short sentences defined the motivations of each party very well. Kryuchkov, for the Initiative Group, asked, 'What do you think about the basis of our messages?[45] Have our strivings pleased the Lord?' Karev, for the AUCECB, answered, 'Yes, they have, brother, but if the Lord wants to give us freedom, he will give it without the struggling of the Church'.[46] The majority of the Russian Baptists followed the AUCECB line in rejecting a 'revolutionary' struggle. It did not mean that there was not any struggle at all. There was the daily spiritual resistance to the militant atheism in the country, and the 'moderate' Baptists also taught their children to pray to God and read the Gospel, but did not encourage them, for instance, to tear up the 'young pioneers' [the communist youth organisation] red neckerchiefs'.[47] Since the preaching of brethren from other communities was forbidden, visitors just gave 'greetings' which sometimes lasted for 15-20 minutes and which exhorted the churches. The members of the registered communities also testified about God to unbelievers, but usually did it in private, and never loudly in public places such as parks, streets, trains, buses, as the radicals did sometimes, breaking Soviet law and even resisting the militia.[48] One elderly member of my own home church, resistant to such radical trends at that time said, 'I do not have military factories to fight against the State... But the Scripture says, "A king's wrath is a messenger of death, but a wise man will appease it." (Prov. 16:14)'.

Meanwhile, the State policy of pressure upon the churches in the USSR was gaining strength. In December of 1959, the Plenum[49] of the AUCECB was

---

[45] The first messages of the Initiative Group about the calling of the extraordinary Congress of the Evangelical Christians–Baptists of the USSR condemned the AUCECB and pointed to the Congress as the only authoritative body under the circumstances.

[46] *Po Puti Vozrozhdeniya* (On the Way of the Revival) (Sovet Tserkvey Evangelical Christian Bretheren (ECB): 1989), p. 35.

[47] Some young Orthodox Christians who had similar problems in the USSR made an interesting decision about the red neckerchiefs: they were consecrated by holy water before being worn. 'Since you force us, we will wear [the red neckerchiefs], but will consecrate them first.' (Father D. Dudko, *O Nashem Upovanii* (On Our Hope) (Svet na Vostoke, 1974), p. 96).

[48] *Vestnik Istiny* 2 (2001), pp. 26-27; 1 (2000), p. 9. Public evangelism in the 1960s and 1970s shocked the average Soviet citizen, and strengthened the anti-religious mood of the population. It was a weak and dangerous game against Soviet power.

[49] The close contacts between the AUCECB and the Soviet State had, of course, their nuances. For example, the structure of the official Baptist Union was an exact copy of the Soviet Communist Party structure including the main terminology. The AUCECB was an analogue of the Central Committee of the CPSU. The General Secretary and Presidium were in both the AUCECB and the Central Committee of the Party. Each region had a senior presbyter (first secretary of the Party). Communities/Party cells had their 'executive organs', 'inspection committees', and so on. (See *Bratsky Vestnik*, 6 (1966), p. 33) These main features of the structure of the Baptist Union still persist

forced to approve the aforementioned *New Statutes* and *Letter of Instructions*, which were then sent to the senior presbyters in the provinces at the beginning of 1960. During the presentation of the documents, A. Karev said,

> Our movement has had different periods in the past: the legal and underground stages. Today's situation is a combination of both standings... We have experienced an overflow [in our communities] recently. People of a different ideology cannot countenance it... The Council for Religious Affairs has made us understand that we must return to the banks... These documents are born with torment... We have responsibility before the churches, and we can lose our authority; but we have responsibility before the government bodies, too. We can make some reasonable suggestions...[50]

A. Sinichkin, archivist of The Russian Union of the ECB Archives in Moscow, notes regarding the original paper of the *Statutes of the Union of ECB* (of 1960):

> On the cover of this document, which is kept in the AUCECB Archives, was written a Bible reference—*Ecclesiastes 8:5*. This verse says, 'Whoever obeys his command will come to no harm, and the wise heart will know the proper time and procedure.'[51] It seems, the authors of this document expected to use it wisely.[52]

The most disagreeable points of the new *Statutes of the Union of ECB* were the following (in parentheses and in italics there are the alternative points from the underground *Statutes of the Union of ECB* written by the Initiative Group (1961) and signed by A. Prokof'ev and G. Kryuchkov):

> 12. The AUCECB members and the senior presbyters follow the rule not to officiate at any church offices, but to be only chief spiritual supervisors in order to maintain the established order in the communities according to the AUCECB

---

today. Russian Baptist leaders were more afraid of another contemporary tendency—to copy the Russian Orthodox Church structure—and so chose 'the lesser of two evils'. The term 'plenum' is from this context.

[50] 'Zapis' 63, Zasedanie Malogo Plenuma VSEHB (26.12.1959)' (Record of Proceeding 63, The Meeting of the Closed Plenum of the AUCECB of 26.12.1959), *The AUCECB Archives*, papka 22, doc. 11.

[51] There are 'statutes' instead of 'procedures' in the Russian Bible. It is interesting to look at the context of the verse, 'Since a king's word is supreme, who can say to him, "What are you doing?". "Whoever obeys his command will come to no harm, and the wise heart will know the proper time and procedure".' (Ecclesiastes 8:4-5, NIV).

[52] A. Sinichkin, *Istoria ECB v SSSR s 1959 po 1966* (The History of the ECB in the USSR from 1959 to 1966), Diplomnaya Rabota (Moscow: Moskovskaya Bogoslovskaya Seminariya ECB, 2001), p. 38.

statutes and Soviet law on religious affairs.[53] *(The AUCECB members and the senior presbyters follow the rule to be only the chief spiritual supervisors to keep the established order of God's Word (1 Pet. 5:1-3). All decisions and documents of the chief ministers, including the ministers of the AUCECB, should be accepted by the Church only if they do not contradict the Holy Scripture (Gal. 1:8-9)).*[54]

18. The members of the AUCECB are elected by simple majority during the special meetings of the executive workers of the Union.[55] *(The members of the AUCECB are elected by simple majority during the All-Union Congresses).*[56]

26. Only persons who are of age and have had a probationary period of not less than two-three years can become members of the communities of the Evangelical Christians–Baptists.[57] *(Persons who were baptized by faith and accepted by the Church can become members of the communities of the Evangelical Christians–Baptists (Acts 8:12)).*[58]

34. Only persons who are the members of the executive organ of the community can preach in services. No other persons, either from the community or other churches, can preach.[59] *(The community decides which church members should preach in services).*[60]

The second document, the *Letter of Instructions for the Senior Presbyters* by the AUCECB, added more severe restrictions to Baptist services:

I.3 ...the main goal of today's services is not the calling of new people, but satisfying the spiritual needs of believers.

I.4. The Senior presbyter must stop unhealthy missionary activity...

VII.3 ...to reduce the number of baptisms among the 18-30 age group as much as possible... No students or servicemen should be baptized at all.

VIII.6. Children, both under school age and of school age, as a rule, cannot be allowed to visit services.

---

[53] 'Polozhenie o Soyuze Evangelskikh Khristian-Baptistov v SSSR (VSEHB)' (Statutes of the Union of Evangelical Christians–Baptists in the USSR: the AUCECB), *The AUCECB Archives*, papka 28, doc. 52.

[54] 'Polozhenie o Soyuze Evangelskikh Khristian-Baptistov v SSSR (Initsiativnaya Gruppa)' (Statutes of the Union of Evangelical Christians–Baptists of the USSR: the Initiative Group), *The AUCECB Archives*, papka 28, doc. 2-5.

[55] *The AUCECB Archives*, papka 28, doc. 52.

[56] Ibid., doc. 2-5.

[57] Ibid., doc. 52.

[58] Ibid., doc. 2-5.

[59] Ibid., doc. 52.

[60] Ibid., doc. 2-5.

Extract of the Conclusion: It is a necessity to submit church life to the Soviet law on religious affairs and give up the following 'violations': a variety of musical instruments, baptism of young people, financial support of church members, any church gatherings besides worship services, Christian education, evangelism...[61]

The Initiative Group publicized these documents among the Baptist communities in 1961 and condemned the leaders of the AUCECB because of their 'diligence in putting into practice the program of the destruction of the church by the church members' hands' (*The First Letter to the Whole Church of ECB*).[62] Of course, the radical position had some substance at that time, but it seems it was too short-sighted a position. The dissident Baptists saw only the weakness of the AUCECB, but they shut their eyes to the real root causes of the situation—the State policy of severe pressure on the religious associations in a country on the threshold of becoming a communist society. The Initiative Group had even created the illusion that it was possible to have a legal, free, Baptist Congress at that time.[63] There were two extreme positions among the Russian Baptists; but, unfortunately, there was no powerful centre. The leaders of the AUCECB themselves, of course, were unhappy because of the new restrictions and the closures of prayer houses in the provinces.[64] Though perhaps, as is often said today, the 'moderates' tended to be servile before the Soviet power, the 'radical' activity of the Initiative Group had a tendency toward impudence before the authorities and even 'Christian extremism'.

A Point of Comparison: The Orthodox Church

Since there was also a similar situation in the Russian Orthodox Church at that time,[65] it would be helpful to compare their discussion of the problem with the Baptist debates. The climax of the Orthodox controversies came about ten years later than the Baptists'—at the beginning of the 1970s[66] but its essence was, of

---

[61] 'Letter of Instructions for the Senior Presbyters', *Novosibirsk Baptist Church Archives* (1960).

[62] 'Po Puti Vozrozhdeniya', p. 30.

[63] Though there was a Congress of the AUCECB (in 1963), it was permitted to ease tension among the Baptists and passed under strict State control. (*Podrazhayte Vere Ikh, 40 Let Probuzhdyennomu Bratstvu* (Imitate Their Faith: The Fortieth Anniversary of the Revival Brotherhood) (Sovet Tserkvey ECB, 2001), p. 18).

[64] See Supplement 6 in Savinsky, *Istoria Evangelskikh*, p. 353-354.

[65] In 1961, the Russian Orthodox clergy received the *Instruction on the Application of the Law on Religious Affairs*, which was a copy of the *Letter of Instructions* for the Baptists but using Orthodox terminology. It was also forbidden to have: charities, pilgrimages, church gatherings besides worship services, Christian education, evangelism... (See Shkarovsky, *Russkaya Pravoslavnaya Tserkov*, p. 375).

[66] The priests of the Moscow Patriarchate, G. Yakunin and N. Eshliman, wrote their two famous open letters of protest against State pressure on the Church in 1965.

course, very similar. In 1972, the dissident writer and Orthodox Christian, Alexander Solzhenitsyn, wrote his famous *Lenten Letter* to Pimen, the Patriarch of All Russia.[67] It was a remarkable piece of Orthodox radicalism. The following few sentences are enough to understand the spirit of the author.

> Why, when I come to church to have my son baptized, should I have to produce my identity card? Under what canonical obligations does the Moscow Patriarchate need to register those who are baptized?...
>
> The Church is ruled dictatorially by atheists—a sight never before seen in two millennia!...
>
> By what reasoning is it possible to convince oneself that the planned *destruction* of the spirit and body of the Church under the guidance of atheists is the best way of *preserving* it? Preserving it for *whom*? Certainly not for Christ? Preserving it *by what means*? By *falsehood*? But after the falsehood by whose hands are the holy mysteries to be celebrated?...
>
> Things were no easier at the birth of the Christian faith; nevertheless it held out and prospered. It showed us the way: *sacrifice*... Within our own living memory many of our priests and fellow-believers have accepted such a martyrdom, worthy of the early Christians. But in those days they were thrown to the *lions*, whereas today you can lose only your material well-being.[68]

Among the many reactions to Solzhenitsyn's letter, the *Easter Message* (1972) of Father Sergi (Zheludkov) was probably the most significant. Below are the main arguments of the 'moderate' wing of Russian Orthodoxy as set out by Father Sergi:

> You have made a written accusation that has been publicized throughout the world against...[Patriarch Pimen] who, as everyone knows, has no possible chance of replying to you...

(Shkarovsky, *Russkaya Pravoslavnaya Tserkov*, p. 276). In addition, the radicals from the underground movements, The True Orthodox Church and The True Orthodox Christians, had separated from the Patriarchate of Moscow as far back as the 1920s to become similar to the Protestant communities in many respects. (W. Fletcher, *The Russian Orthodox Church Underground, 1917-1970* (London: Oxford University Press, 1971), p. 282).

[67] It was immediately published in the West and was widespread in the USSR in *Samizdat*.
[68] A. Solzhenitsyn, *Velikopostnoe Pismo Patriarhu Pimenu in Russkaya Pravoslavnaya Tserkov v Sovetskoe Vremya (1971-1991)* (The Russian Orthodox Church in the Soviet Times (1971-1991), G. Shtrikker, ed. (Moscow: Propilei, 1995), pp. 110-113.

You did not tell the whole truth, you gave half-truths... The *full truth* is that the legal Church organization cannot be an *island of freedom* in our strictly unified society, directed from a single Centre...

We are *not permitted* to work at the religious education of children, or of adults, just as we are not permitted to do many other things necessary for the existence of real church life. *We are permitted only one thing*—to conduct divine worship in our churches...

Should we try to go underground, which in the present system is unthinkable? Or should we try somehow to accept the system and for the present make use of those opportunities that are permitted? The Russian hierarchy took the latter decision...

By what deed do you suppose...[Patriarch Pimen] could answer you? Only by giving up his position. But there is no one better to take his place. And anyway one man cannot change anything. So everything would stay the same.[69] One of the consequences of your accusatory letter will be a still greater discrediting of the Church hierarchy in the eyes of those who do not understand the whole truth.[70]

In the light of such arguments, the traditional charges of the radicals (both Baptist and Orthodox) against the moderate church leaders, was misdirected. The State, not fellow Christians, should have been recognized as the real opponent. Like the Patriarch, the ministers of the AUCECB could not answer their accusers publicly and explain the 'whole truth' of the situation in the brotherhood to the thousands of Baptist communities. However, they at least showed courage in saying this during the closed meetings with the brothers of the radical Initiative group—increasingly called the Council of Churches of ECB.[71] For instance, in March 1966 during one such meeting in Moscow, Alexander Karev openly said that Soviet power was the cause of the separation of Baptist churches and that the atheists had wanted to embroil the brothers of both camps: 'they want to blacken our reputation'. V. Koval'kov expressed the same opinion in the meeting.[72] However, the dissident Baptists did not want to make distinctions between the State and the official Baptist Union. 'To

---

[69] Similar reasons were given by A. Karev in response to G. Kryuchkov's call to protest in 1961: 'I cannot do this. And in general, it would be useless... If I set out...I will be removed. Another person will be posted in my office and rule in the same way or even worse than me.' (G. Kryuchkov, '20 Let po Puti Vozrozhdeniya' in *Po Puti Vozrozhdeniya*, p. 15).

[70] See *Documents* in G. Simon, *Church, State and Opposition in the USSR* (London: C. Hurst & Company, 1974), pp. 206-207.

[71] The Initiative Group (since 1961), the *Orgkomitet* (since 1962), and the Council of Churches of ECB (since 1965) were the three names or steps of development of the same movement of the dissident Baptists in the USSR.

[72] See Supplement 6 in Savinsky, *Istoria Evangelskikh*, pp. 354, 360-361.

collaborate with the AUCECB means to collaborate with the atheists', pronounced G. Kryuchkov.[73] The split within Russian Baptists was irreversible after a series of mutual excommunications.[74] In 1961–1962, the AUCECB influence submitted churches of the active followers of the Initiative Group for excommunication.[75] In June of 1962, the radicals' *Orgkomitet* declared the excommunication of all leaders of the AUCECB and many regional senior presbyters (firstly twenty-seven people) from the so-called (Episcopal) 'Church ECB', and *agreed* 'to take leadership of the ECB in the USSR until the Congress'.[76] During the Baptist Congress in 1963 the revocation of both compromised documents of the AUCECB of 1960 was announced, but this step could not change the situation of division.[77]

To conclude this section, it is arguable that both main groups of Soviet Baptists played their mysterious part in the 1960s in the survival of the Church under the communist regime. The radical Baptists, by their numerous acts of protest, led the authorities to the view that to close the majority of official Baptist churches would give more space for the underground communities, led by 'uncontrolled' people hostile to the government, and would be much more dangerous for the Soviet ideological system.[78] Thus, unintentionally, the radicals helped the moderate Baptists. The moderates, for their part, bore much humiliation from Soviet power, but they saved congregations by preventing them from scattering into many small, unrecognized groups which could easily have led to further degeneration and sectarianism under the climate of totalitarianism.[79]

---

[73] Ibid., p. 242.

[74] Church history has had many similar events. The most famous was in 1054, when legates of Pope Leo IX declared the excommunication of Mikhail, Patriarch of Constantinople, and all of his followers; and Mikhail, in his turn, anathematized the Pope of Rome and his hierarchy. (E. Kerns, *Dorogami Khristianstva* (Christianity through the Centuries) (Moscow: Protestant, 1992), p. 162).

[75] Savinsky, *Istoria Evangelskikh*, p. 212.

[76] Reshenie 'Orgkomiteta po Voprosu Protivotserkovnoy Deyatel'nosti VSEHB' (Decision of the Orgkomitet Regarding the Anti-Church Activity of the AUCECB), *The AUCECB Archives*, papka 28, doc. 77; 'Protokol 7; (Soveshchanie Orgkomiteta Tserkvey ECB 23.06.1962)' (Record of Proceedings 7, The Meeting of the *Orgkomitet* of Churches of ECB of 23.06.1962), *The AUCECB Archives*, papka 28, doc. 78; *Vestnik Istiny* 3 (2001), p. 13.

[77] *Bratsky Vestnik* 6 (1966), p. 10; 5 (1970), pp. 72, 76.

[78] About 2,000 brothers and sisters from both Baptist Unions (mainly from the Council of Churches of ECB) were imprisoned in the USSR from 1961 to the middle of the 1980s. It seems their resistance helped to save not only Baptist communities, but also (indirectly) Orthodox churches. Russian Orthodoxy had appreciably fewer radical priests and laymen in that period. (A. Rudenko, 'Evangelskie Khristiane-Baptisty i Perestroyka v SSSR' in *Na Puti k Svobode Sovesti*, p. 353; *Vestnik Istiny* 3 (2001), p. 36; Shkarovsky, *Russkaya Pravoslavnaya Tserkov*, pp. 269-83).

[79] Small groups usually do not have a defence mechanism to resist the dictatorship of their leaders or false teaching which penetrates into the community. (See K. Prokhorov,

The State and Baptist Churches (1960s-1970s)

Legislation and Propaganda

The fierce struggle of the Communist Party against religion in the USSR had many implications for Soviet society. First of all, it was manifested in what was termed the 'improvement' of the judicial legislation and the increase of atheistic propaganda in the country. Although Stalin's time had come to an end, the Soviet government continued to show its military force both within the State[80] and in neighbouring countries.[81] Article 70 of the RSFSR criminal code ('anti-Soviet propaganda') was the successor of the notorious article 58 of Stalin's code, which was traditionally used against active religious leaders.[82] Additional articles created included: article 142 (*Violation of the Laws on the Separation of Church from State and School from Church*, punishable by up to three years imprisonment) in 1960; and in 1962, article 227 (*Encroachment on Personality and Rights of Citizens under the Pretence of Discharge of Religious Rites*, punishable by up to five years imprisonment).[83] The aforementioned articles of the RSFSR code had their equivalent articles in the criminal codes of the other Soviet republics.[84]

There was an additional law in the Central Asian Soviet republics that allowed imprisonment for up to three years for 'deception by using religious superstitions': article 143 of the criminal code of Kirghiz SSR, 153–Tajik SSR, 262–Turkmen SSR, 147–Uzbek SSR.[85]

Also, it should be noted that there was the RSFSR criminal code article 143, which provided punishment of up to six months community work or public reprimand for 'hindering of discharge of religious rites' when the rites had a

---

'Bozh'i Puti' (God's Ways) in *Sektantskie Rasskasy* (Sectarian Stories) (Idar-Oberstein: Titel-Verlag, 2002), p. 147).

[80] In 1962 in Novocherkassk, there was a terrible shooting of workers who were demonstrating for economic demands. Dozens of people were killed and wounded, and more than 100 workers were imprisoned. (*Literaturnaya Gazeta* (Literary Newspaper), (21 June 1989); *Komsomol'skaya Pravda* (The Komsomol Truth) (2 June 1989)).

[81] The government of Khrushchev used the Soviet army against the revolt in Budapest, Hungary, in 1956 and brought Russian rockets with nuclear war-heads to Cuba in 1962. The government of Brezhnev also used the army against the popular uprising in Prague, Czechoslovakia, in 1968 and started the Soviet intervention in Afghanistan in 1979. (Medvedev, *N. S. Khrushchev: Politicheskaya Biografiya* (Moscow: Kniga, 1990), pp. 108-110, 203-212; Yu. Aksyutin, ed., *L.I. Brezhnev: Materialy k Biografii* (L.I. Brezhnev: Materials to His Biography) (Moscow: Politizdat, 1991), pp. 307-311, 332-335).

[82] *Podrazhayte Vere Ikh*, p. 173.

[83] *O Religii i Tserkvi. Sbornik Dokumentov* (On Religion and Church: Collected Documents) (Moscow: Politizdat, 1981), pp. 161-3.

[84] Ibid., p. 162.

[85] Ibid., p. 165.

legal basis. That punishment, compared to the Soviet measures against religion, could not be called severe; and, in addition, there was no known application of it. Though the article had its equivalents in the criminal codes of all Soviet republics, they probably did not work 'in a friendly manner' for believers. It was a so-called abortive communist law; in reality many old believers testified about the unpunished intimidations of ministers, beatings of preachers and choir members, and breaking of prayer house windows with stones in the 1960s and 1970s.[86]

Atheistic propaganda, especially from the beginning of the 1960s, became very aggressive. Approximately 660,000 atheistic lectures were given in the USSR by the *Znanie* (Educational) Society in 1963 alone. Also, in 1957, 102 new atheistic books were published in the country; in 1958, another 264 such volumes; and in 1962, 336 anti-religious books with a total circulation in that year alone of 5,845,000.[87] All of these were proclaimed, of course, to be meeting the basic needs and wishes of the Soviet people themselves. A 1960 picture from *Krokodil*, a popular Soviet satirical magazine, was significant. It depicted some believers dreaming of deserting religion, down on their knees appealing to heaven, 'Dear Lord, send to us at least one lecturer of atheism!'[88] At that time, many atheistic institutions and schools started their activities. The following is a partial list of those in Moscow alone: the Anti-Religious Faculty of Moscow University of Marxism-Leninism; the Anti-Religious Sector of the Institute of Philosophy; the Department of Scientific Atheism in the Faculty of Philosophy at Moscow State University (and many high schools); the House of Scientific Atheism; the offices of the journal *Nauka i Religiya* (Science and Religion); the Scientific Atheistic Editorial Board of the State Publishing House of Political Literature; the Scientific Atheistic Section at the Moscow Planetarium; the Scientific Atheistic Section attached to the Board of the All-Union *Znanie* Society; and the Sector of the History of Religion and Atheism of the USSR Academy of Sciences' Institute of History.[89]

Creating Atheistic Stereotypes

All of this great power of the State machine pressed down hard on Soviet Christian believers, and upon Baptists in particular. The following are some of the titles of the popular anti-sectarian books, representing the spirit of that time:

---

[86] One such incident is described in a book by S. Savinsky. A Baptist community was forced to have their services with the wood shutters closed because some unpunished hooligans, usually active members of Komsomol, with the connivance of the militia, regularly broke their prayer house windows with stones. (See Supplement 3 in Savinsky, *Istoria Evangelskikh*, p. 317).

[87] R. Conquest, *Religion in the USSR* (London: Bodley Head, 1968), p. 48.

[88] *Krokodil* (Crocodile), 29 February 1960.

[89] Conquest, *Religion in the USSR*, pp. 48-9.

We Were Baptists;[90] *Sectarians and Their Preaching;*[91] *Obscurants Without Masks;*[92] *Under the Mask of Holiness;*[93] *The Truth about Sectarianism;*[94] *Among Sectarians;*[95] *Sects, Their Beliefs and Deeds;*[96] *The Reactionary Character of Mysticism in Contemporary Christian Sectarianism;*[97] *Sham Brotherhood;*[98] *Sectarianism and Family;*[99] *Baptism and Humanism;*[100] *Religious Illusions on the Threshold of Life.*[101] The majority of such books portrayed Russian Baptists as terrible fanatics, reinforcing traditional pagan stereotypes about Christians. Here is an example:

> When a young beautiful woman...mounts [the pulpit of the Baptist prayer house] and raises her hand with burned fingers, I stand still. Who is she? Maybe, she is a foundry worker? Undoubtedly, she is a worker!... She cannot say anything else except the word 'comrades'...'Brothers and sisters,' she exclaims, 'let us praise God for everything He gave us by His great mercy!'... Maybe, I am just having a bad dream... Is it possible that these three hundred people—the old, young, average age, men, women, boys, and girls—can really believe in a kind of god, who is ether the biblical old man wearing a white long while robe, snub-nosed and weak-sighted, or another of his variations... Is it possible they are really convinced that this god gave them everything they have, not that they themselves earned it by their hands? That is gibberish!*[102]

---

[90] *My Byli Baptistami (Sbornik)* (We were Baptists (Collection of life stories)) (Moscow: n.p., 1960).

[91] E. Tsvetogorov, *Sektanty i Chto Oni Propoveduyut* (Sectarians and Their Preaching) (Novosibirsk: n.p., 1960).

[92] A. Komm, *Mrakobesy bez Maski* (Obscurants without Masks) (Maykop: n.p., 1960).

[93] O. Antonova, *Pod Maskoy Svyatosti* (Under the Mask of Holiness) (Omsk: n.p., 1962).

[94] *Pravda o Sektantstve (Sbornik)* (The Truth about Sectarianism (Collection of life stories)) (Leningrad: n.p., 1963).

[95] A. Terskoy, *U Sectantov* (Among Sectarians) (Moscow: Politizdat, 1965).

[96] F. Fedorenko, *Sekty, Ikh Vera I Dela* (Sects, Their Beliefs and Deeds) (Moscow: Politizdat, 1965).

[97] N. Safronova, *Reaktsionnoct' Misticheskikh Idey Sovremennogo Christianskogo Sektantstva* (Reactionary Character of Mysticism of Contemporary Christian Sectarianism) (Lvov: n.p., 1975).

[98] A. Belov, *Mnimoe Bratstvo* (Sham Brotherhood) (Moscow: n.p., 1976).

[99] L. Serdobol'skaya, *Sektantstvo i Sem'ya* (Sectarianism and Family) (Leningrad: Znanie, 1976).

[100] E. Filimonov, *Baptizm i Gumanizm* (Baptists and Humanism) (Moscow: Mysl', 1978).

[101] A. Budov, *Religioznye Illuzii na Poroge Zhizni* (Religious Illusions on the Threshold of the Life) (Moscow: Molodaya Gvardiya, 1980).

[102] Terskoy, *U Sectantov*, p. 99.

One of the sectarian women...once nearly cut her children with an axe 'according to a command of the Lord God'... It was merely the waking of one daughter that saved the children. The sacrifice of children to god...is not an isolated instance.[103] Children who are nurtured in permanent fear before the all-seeing god, who may punish them any time because of...a small fault, live with nervous tension; they are cowed permanently. [That is] sectarian 'pedagogy'...[104]

[From a dialogue between a mature atheist and a 17 year old Baptist girl] 'Have you heard about space flights?'... 'It is not true.' 'Is it true that airplanes are flying?' 'That is true, but we do not use them. That is from Satan...' 'You came here by bus. Is it also from Satan?' She remains silent. We suggest she read a book of fiction. She says, 'Don't! I have my own books. I will not read any worldly works. They are lies.' 'Did you read them in school?' 'Yes, I did; Pushkin, for instance. But it is nothing. Since I became a believer I do not read such books.'[105]

Sectarian theology carries the Christian ideas of self-abasement, rejection of civilization, and withdrawal from society to their logical end; because of this, Lenin...called religion 'ideological necrophilia'.[106]

According to research from the Sector of Scientific Atheism of the Institute of Philosophy of the Ukrainian SSR Academy of Sciences, among the interrogated members of sectarian communities, there are 10 *fanatics* out of 168 Evangelical Christians–Baptists...113 [of them] are *firm believers*.[107]

Atheistic propaganda created public stereotypes that showed Baptists in a very unfavourable light. The following are some stereotypes of Soviet Baptists at that time, which the communists remarkably copied—consciously or unconsciously—from the ancient Roman charges against the Christians.[108]

1. *Immorality*. The grounds for such charges were the semi-closed character of the Christian services (especially, during persecutions) as well as the rumours about 'agape-feasts' and 'holy kisses' of believers.[109]

---

[103] Ibid., p. 117.

[104] A. Belov, *Lzhenastavniki Yunoshestva*, p. 43.

[105] M. Pismannik, *Lichnost' i Religiya* (Personality and Religion) (Moscow: n.p., 1976), p. 113.

[106] Fedorenko, *Sekty, Ikh Vera I Dela*, p. 217.

[107] Such names were usually synonyms for atheistic writers. See A. Belov, *Sekty, Sektantstvo, Sektanty* (Sects, Sectarianism; Sectarians) (Moscow: Nauka, 1978), p. 113; N. Safronova, *Reaktsionnoct' Misticheskikh*, pp. 98-9.

[108] Bolotov, *Lektsii po Istorii Drevney Tserkvi* 2 (Moscow: Spaso-Preobrazhensky Valaamsky Stavropigialny Monastyr', 1994), pp. 10-12; V. Leont'ev, 'Nozhi v Spinu Otechestvennogo Baptizma', *Slovo Very* (Word of Faith) 2 (2002), pp. 19-23.

[109] G. Suglobov, *Venchaetsya Raba Bozhiya* (The Servant of God Is Wedding) (Moscow: Politizdat, 1959), p. 29ff.

2. *Sacrifices of children to God and cannibalism.* This was due to the misunderstanding of the biblical story of Abraham's readiness to offer Isaac as a sacrifice to the Lord, as well as the semi-true information about the eating of a 'body' and drinking 'blood' during Christian services.[110]
3. *Disloyalty to the State.* The Christians were often considered unreliable citizens of the country, and their communities as 'a state within the State', with dubious laws and traditions. The situation was aggravated because of the pacifism and internationalism of some believers.[111]
4. *Lack of faith in the generally accepted 'spiritual' values.* The 'state religion' was always perceived by Christians as unacceptable. The communist trinity (Marx, Engels, Lenin), their icons (portraits), statues (monuments), relics (Lenin's body in the mausoleum), and their eschatological teaching on the final worker's happiness and the inevitable victory of communism around the world, were very much outside of the limits of Christian beliefs.[112]
5. *Sectarianism.* Just as the first Christian movement was considered a new sect of Judaism in the beginning, the Russian Baptists were scornfully named 'sectarians', first by the Orthodox clergy in the nineteenth century in Russia and then by the militant Soviet atheists who struggled against Orthodoxy as well, but sometimes gladly used its terminology. It is also remarkable that the Bolsheviks themselves were usually considered sectarians among the Russian Social Democracy.[113]
6. *Lack of education.* The Baptists in the USSR were very often 'unschooled' ('ordinary fishermen'), but such a situation was mainly because, with rare exceptions, only the members of Komsomol and the Communist Party could study at Soviet colleges and universities at that time.[114]

---

[110] 'Otvet na Antireligioznuyu Stat'yu "Ne Bud'te Trupom Sredi Zhivykh"' (Answer to the Antireligious Article "Do Not Be Dead Among the Alive"), *The AUCECB Archives*, papka 28, doc. 61, p. 12.

[111] That was manifested by the traditional refusal on the part of the Russian Baptists to serve in the army, take up arms, take oaths, and so on. See on the subject: 'Pis'mo Prezidiuma VSEHB Vsem Presviteram Obshchin EHB v SSSR (1953)' (Letter of the Presidium of the AUCECB to All Presbyters of Baptist Communities of the USSR, 1953), *The AUCECB Archives*, papka 1, doc. 1/64; I. Plett, 'Istoriya Bratstva EHB s 1905 po 1944 Gody' (The History of the Baptist Brotherhood from 1905 to 1944), *Kazakhstan's Baptist Union Archives* (2001), p. 103; *Bratsky Vestnik* 2 (1968), p. 51; 3 (1971) pp. 66-71, etc.

[112] A. Klibanov, *Religioznoe Sektantstvo v Proshlom i Nastoyashchem* (Religious Sectarianism in the Past and Present) (Moscow: Nauka, 1973), p. 225; N. Gordienko, *Osnovy Nauchnogo Ateizma* (The Principles of Scientific Atheism) (Moscow: Prosveshchenie, 1988), pp. 89, 125-137.

[113] A. Solzhenitsyn, *Lenin: Tsyurikh–Petrograd (Lenin: Zurich–Petrograd)* (Ekaterinburg: U-Faktoriya, 2001), pp. 43-44, 117.

[114] See *Byulleten' Soveta Rodstvennikov Uznikov Evangelskikh Khristian-Baptistov v SSSR* 22 (Moscow: Samizdat, 1975), p. 14.

7. *Fanaticism*. The more the atheists oppressed religion in the country, the more believers resisted them. Who were the greater fanatics then?[115]

Taking into account these public stereotypes, which were spread by millions of copies of various forms of atheistic media, it is clear why ordinary Soviet people felt no love for Baptists. Some Soviet people were even perplexed at how such terrible 'obscurants' still had their prayer houses in many towns and villages of the USSR. 'Our government is too kind and tolerant,' they supposed.[116] An interesting exception among such pictures of the Baptists at that time was the positive image of the Baptist, Alyeshka, from the famous story *A Day in the Life of Ivan Denisovich* by A. Solzhenitsyn, published in the best Soviet fiction periodical, *Novy Mir*, in 1962.[117] This exception was probably a result of the tension between the two important ideological tendencies in Soviet society at that time: to show some of the truth about Stalin's repressions (which were in the past) and yet to fight against religion (in the present). Solzhenitsyn's great service to truth was that he refused to let the text of his story be considerably edited.

Apostates

Among other propagandist methods widely used at that time were the public 'penitential testimonies' of former priests and active members of religious communities that had apostasized under the State pressure of threats and bribery. By the middle of the 1960s, about 200 Orthodox priests had denied their calling.[118] They wrote many anti-religious books and articles, vividly describing how they had 'deceived common people' in the past. A similar process of apostasy, of course, took place among the Soviet Protestants and the Baptists. Some former Baptist ministers also wrote their emotional atheistic treatises.

> I am sure that all gospel preaching is a myth and falsehood from the beginning to the end... Do not trust the gospel promises! I know their falsity by my own experience. We have the real human life today in our kolkhoz and Soviet State.[119]

---

[115] G. Vins described an incident when the chief of a labour camp threatened a Baptist prisoner, 'Deny your Christ-God and believe in communism!' He announced that there was only one true religion—communism, and only one god—Lenin! (G. Vins, *Gorizonty Very* (Horizons of Faith) (Elkhart: Russian Gospel Ministries, 1994), p. 33).

[116] *Otvet na Antireligioznuyu Stat'yu*, p. 12.

[117] *Novy Mir* (New World) 11 (1962); A. Solzhenitsyn, *Odin Den' Ivana Denisovicha* (A Day in the Life of Ivan Denisovich) (Moscow: Novy Mir, 1990), pp. 17, 19, 69, 109-112.

[118] Shkarovsky, *Russkaya Pravoslavnaya Tserkov*, p. 370.

[119] Cited in Fedorenko, *Sekty*, p. 244. A *kolkhoz* is a collective farm.

I am conscience-stricken when I remember the boys and girls whom I inveigled into the sect. Where are you now?... Are you singing psalms as before...or are you already awake from the bad dream and merrily working in constructing the new buildings in Siberia and in the virgin lands of Kazakhstan? I am ashamed, my dear friends...[120]

An attentive reader of such 'testimonies' can easily find indications of the conversion of the authors to a *new faith* (atheism). There was not so much a disappointment with religion proper, as happiness at the discovery of what they perceived as the best kind of religion. 'My atheism is the light of my life,' wrote another apostate, 'I will be faithful to it until I can no longer see and breathe.'[121] Fedor Dostoevsky once said that a Russian man becomes an atheist very easily because without fail he starts to 'believe in' atheism. With the zeal of new converts, the former Christians sought to help their new religion win victories over the old one, for instance, by public disclosure of some secrets about the survival of the latter. For example, a former Baptist from Kazakhstan wrote a book in which he gave advice on the atheistic education of believers' children at school and informed Soviet teachers about a 'Baptist ruse': to listen to teachers and to study textbooks at school, but in order only to know the subjects, not to trust the knowledge acquired.[122] Another former preacher wrote indignantly about the brethren who were illegally travelling from place to place to preach and encourage communities.[123] Of course, nobody liked informers. At that time, the Russian Baptists even created the following interesting 'syllabic' pronunciation of a biblical name familiar to believers, *Na-vukho-donosor*, to describe such people.[124]

At the same time, not all the apostates became like Judas. There were some who could be considered more like St. Peter denying Christ. For instance, there is the example of a believing family which was oppressed by the local authorities. As a result, the head of the family denied his faith in Christ, but his daughter-in-law, who lived separately without her husband but with her two children, showed courage, and confessed her faith to the oppressors and was ultimately imprisoned. Then the father (the 'apostate') took the children into his

---

[120] Cited in A. Moskalenko, *Ideologiya i Deyatel'nost' Khristianskikh Sekt* (Ideology and Activity of Christian Sects) (Novosibirsk: Nauka, 1978), p. 402.

[121] *Nauka i Religiya* (Science and Religion) 1 (1968), p. 58.

[122] Yu. Gutsalov, *Ya Otvergayu* (I Reject) (Alma-Ata: n.p., 1962), p. 8.

[123] Komm, *Mrakobesy bez Maski*, pp. 19-20.

[124] This is the Russian pronunciation of the name of the Babylonian king Nebuchadnezzar and in Russian means: 'the one who informs in somebody's ear'. In general, biblical allusions were widespread among the Baptists as a form of Aesopian language in the atheistic context. For instance, church members who kept children out of the prayer house (to follow the *Letter of Instruction* of 1960) were sometimes named the 'Egyptian midwives' (Exodus 1); Soviet power was the 'red dragon' (Rev. 12:3); V.I. Lenin—VIL in abbreviation—was the Babylonian god Bel (Jer. 51:44—*Vil* in the Russian Bible), and so on.

house and reared them.[125] Several stories show that the atheistic propaganda in the USSR was not very effective. A remarkable saying of one university professor of Marxist-Leninist philosophy reveals this: 'The longer I teach atheism, the more I begin to believe in God.'[126] Communist ideas and the Christian faith often paradoxically mixed in Soviet mentality. 'Mamma, I became a communist... Please, pray for me,' wrote a Russian soldier from the front of World War II.[127] There was a similar mixing of ideas in Soviet society in Khrushchev's and Brezhnev's times. It can be seen, for example, in the baptism of the children of communists;[128] the spread of the Christian *samizdat* books among both the intelligentsia and common people;[129] and the 'God-seeking' motifs in works of literature by the best Soviet writers and poets.[130] The idea was artistically expressed in the *Soviet Easter Song* in the 1960s by dissident writer Y. Aleshkovsky

> I love this Day as Miner's Day and the anniversary of our Army. There is the breaking of eggs today, my soul is glad because of joyful bells. And 'workers of the world' are uniting around the Easter table.[131]

Statistical Data and General Tendencies

Returning to the theme of atheistic propaganda, it is important to add that there was also some more serious and scientific Soviet research on the Russian Baptists, such as work by A. Klibanov,[132] L. Mitrokhin,[133] and G. Lyalina,[134]

---

[125] Author's interview with V. Kulyaev (Bishkul', Kazakhstan, 2003).

[126] It was said that he recently died a good Catholic.

[127] Shkarovsky, *Russkaya Pravoslavnaya Tserkov*, p. 124.

[128] Ibid., p. 383.

[129] Unlike the varied Orthodox *samizdat* (hand- and type-written books, articles, petitions, open letters), Baptist *samizdat* was distinguished by often being *typographical* (though there were also many hand- and type-written papers) and also by the mass production of spiritual periodicals, books and Holy Scriptures; especially after 1971, when the underground publishing house *Christian* (of the Council of Churches ECB) was founded. (*Vestnik Istiny* 3 (2001), pp. 34-35).

[130] There were the writings by V. Soloukhin, O. Gonchar, A. Solzhenitsyn, V. Maksimov, E. Evtushenko, G. Vladimov, S. Aleshin, and some others.

[131] Yu. Aleshkovsky, *Antologiya Satiry i Yumora Rossii 20 Veka* (Anthology of the 20th Century Russian Satire and Humor) (Moscow: Eksmo-Press, 2000), p. 524.

[132] A. Klibanov, *Religioznoe Sectantstvo i Sovremennost'* (Religious Sectarianism Today) (Moscow: Nauka, 1969); *Problemy Izucheniya i Kritiki Religioznogo Sektantstva* (The Problems of Studies and Criticism of Religious Sectarianism) (Moscow: Nauka, 1971); A. Klibanov, L. Mitrokhin, *Krizisnye Yavleniya v Sovremennom Baptizme* (The Crisis of the Modern Baptists) (Moscow, 1967).

[133] L. Mitrokhin, *Baptizm i Sovremennost'* (Baptists Today) (Moscow: Politizdat, 1964); L. Mitrokhin, *Baptizm* (Baptists) (Moscow: Politizdat, 1966).

who looked at the Baptists from the perspective of scholars, rather than as Party propagandists. They carried out some important sociological research on Soviet Baptist communities, which the believers of those times could not do themselves. Lyalina found:

> The Baptist communities, followers of the AUCECB, who were located in 49 oblasts of the country, had 20.8% men and 79.2% women in 1965-1996. Their age range was as follows: up to 30—3%, from 31-40—10%, from 41-50—11%, from 51-60—16%, over 60—60%. Among them were employees—37%, pensioners—29%, housewives—32% (the rest were dependants and invalids). Their educational level was as follows: higher education—0.5%, secondary—2.3%, incomplete secondary—12.1%, primary—43.1%, and semi-literate—42%.[135]

Of course, such results cannot be used uncritically. The research was carried out in an unfavourable time for honest statistics. On the face of it, the figures make Baptists look insignificant, but it does not mean that they are entirely wrong. It is important to remember that Baptist children and teenagers, since they were not church members, could not be included in these statistics, and this fact made the quoted figures only half-truths. This should be seen as valuable information on the history of the Baptist community, especially as the trend toward the ageing of the Baptist communities under the heavy State pressure was undoubtedly right. At the same time, the communities of the Initiative Group, the Council of Churches of the ECB (CCECB), had more Christian youth than the average churches of the AUCECB. This is usually accounted for by the age-related radicalism of Baptist 'children' in comparison with Baptist 'fathers'.[136]

The causes for the lack of education of Baptists in the USSR have already been mentioned. This was bound up with the problem of believers finding good jobs. As a result of their convictions, Russian Baptists were often discharged from even common office work, and sometimes after that they were unable to find any job, though there was always a lack of workers in the USSR.[137]

The fact that women outnumbered men by about four to one was near to the norm which was historically found in the Russian evangelical communities and which still exists today. There was also a similar situation in Russian Orthodox

---

[134] G. Lyalina, *Baptizm: Illuzii i Real'nost'* (Baptists: Illusions and Reality) (Moscow: Politizdat, 1977).

[135] Ibid., p. 13. Cf. Klibanov, *Religioznoe Sectantstvo i Sovremennost'*, pp. 73-76; Mitrokhin, *Baptizm*, pp. 252-253.

[136] *Vestnik Spaseniya* 3 (1965), p. 2ff.; Reshetnikov and Sannikov, *Obsor Istorii Evangelsko-Baptistskogo*, p. 199.

[137] L. Kovalenko, *Oblako Svideteley Khristovykh* (The Cloud of Witnesses of Christ) (Kiev: Tsentr Hristianskogo Sotrudnichestva, 1997), p. 209; *Byulleten' Soveta Rodstvennikov Uznikov Evangelskikh Khristian-Baptistov v SSSR* 24 (Moscow, 1975), p. 13.

parishes.[138] It seems that to be religious in these communities was primarily a distinctive feature of women's natures rather than men's, though only the 'brothers' were the spiritual leaders and ministers in Russian churches. G. Kryuchkov, leader of the dissident Baptists, had this to say about the demographic situation in the community of the ECB in the beginning of the 1960s:

> Our brotherhood was aging and dying out. Look at the former membership of our communities. They were 80 percent sisters, mainly old women! They were a grey-haired and wrinkled church. We were more a sisterhood, than a brotherhood.[139]

This is an interesting and independent confirmation of some of the aforementioned information from Soviet secular scholars. Kryuchkov was too extreme a Baptist radical to use any 'worldly' or 'Soviet' sources. He knew the situation in the Baptist communities well enough to generalize and to come to the same conclusion. It is remarkable that he did not also mention the unbaptized Christian youth of the communities, but this was probably to strengthen his criticism of the policy of the AUCECB. An average Baptist family of those times had 4-5 children. Even taking into account the atheistic influence in Soviet schools, and the known restrictions on attending church meetings, the Baptist youth made up much more than the secularly attested 'quota' of 3% of the total number of church members.[140] In addition, the contemporary gender proportion of the congregations of the radical Council of Churches itself is hardly much different from the traditional (to use G. Kryuchkov's term) 'sisterhood'.

The Personality of Gennady Kryuchkov

More attention needs to be given to the personality of Gennady Kryuchkov, the leader of the Council of Churches of the ECB and undoubtedly an outstanding and enigmatic person. Looking at centuries-old Russian history, some interesting parallels can be found between G. Kryuchkov and the Orthodox Protopope (chief pope) Avvakum, who resolutely denied Patriarch Nikon's reform of Russian Orthodoxy and became the famous leader of the Old Russian Orthodox Church in the seventeenth century. Avvakum resisted both the official Church, in the person of the Patriarch Nikon and his entourage, and the

---

[138] S. Skazkin ed., *Nastol'naya Kniga Ateista* (The Handbook of Atheists) (Moscow: Politizdat, 1983), p. 435.

[139] *Bratsky Listok* (Fraternal Leaflet) 4 (1981).

[140] When I see the pictures of the official Baptist churches of the 1960s and 1970s of Kazakhstan in general, I find there at least 20-25% younger faces. Yet it is unlikely that Kazakhstan was the best place for the multiplication of Soviet Baptists.

State, in the person of Tsar Aleksey Mikhaylovich, who together installed the new, revised worship books and liturgical texts in Russia from 1652.[141] In the early 1960s in the Russian Baptist community, there was a similar attempt from the State and the leaders of the AUCECB to dictate to the communities the new and unpopular restrictions on church activity (the *New Statutes* and *Letter of Instructions*) which touched upon some 'liturgical' aspects of the Baptist worship rather than the Christian faith itself. The following are parallel quotations from works by Avvakum and Kryuchkov, perhaps indicating some continuity in Russian religious tradition.

This was the reaction of Avvakum and his like-minded traditionalist believers in Moscow to Nikon's books:

> We, meeting with the fathers, fell to thinking. We saw that the 'winter' was coming; our hearts froze and legs shivered... There was a voice from the holy image during the prayer, 'That is the time of suffering, you must suffer assiduously!' He told me crying... We...wrote the extracts from the [old] books...and gave them to His Majesty. A great deal was written, but he hid it somewhere...[142]

The following was the reaction of Kryuchkov and his like-minded believers in the Tula region to the new documents of the AUCECB:

> Together with the brothers...we began to reason with the whole church, 'What shall we do? All nearby communities are closed... Let us firstly repent and pray...' All the community was in tears... The Lord...seeing our repentance...said, 'I am with you now!'... We wrote the appeal to the leaders of the AUCECB... We tried to convince them of the necessity to change their attitude toward God. The AUCECB did not answer us.[143]

The following are some memorable utterances of Protopope Avvakum and G. Kryuchkov about the 'new beliefs', about suffering and about the role of the State in the Church conflict:

> Nikon's beliefs and statutes are not from God, but from man.[144] (Avvakum)

> The AUCECB's origin does not have any relationship to God.[145] (Kryuchkov)

---

[141] S. Solov'ev, *Chteniya i Rasskazy po Istorii Rossii* (Lecturing on Russian History) (Moscow: Pravda, 1990), pp. 385-395.

[142] Avvakum, *Zhitie Avvakuma i Drugie Ego Sochineniya* (Life of Avvakum and His Other Writings) (Moscow: Sovetskaya Rossiya, 1991), p. 36.

[143] G. Kryuchkov, 'Ya s Vami, Govorit Gospod' in *Vestnik Istiny* 3-4 (1991), pp. 12-13.

[144] Avvakum, *Zhitie*, p. 101.

[145] G. Kryuchkov, '20 Let po Puty Vozrozhdeniya' in *Po Puty Vozrozhdeniya*, p. 11.

I was brought to the Eastern Patriarchs...[146] I said much to the Patriarchs from the Scripture. God opened my sinful mouth, and Christ disgraced them by my mouth... I reproved them...and said as written, 'Better one man doing the will of God than thousands upon thousands of wicked men!'... They laughed, 'The protopope is foolish. He does not honour even the Patriarchs.' But I told them, 'We are fools for Christ's sake! Ye are honourable, but we are despised! Ye are strong, but we are weak.'[147] (Avvakum)

We have not greeted you...[148] We...do not consider you our brothers... We believe that God is almighty, despite what you ironically spoke about our trust... We know you can set out to oppose the work of God with bigger frantic zeal...but know that...nothing can depose the Church of Christ. 'I will build my Church, and the gates of hell shall not prevail against it'... This is a display of your extreme unfaithfulness to God and His Church. The Word of God calls believers to be faithful, because only such ones will receive the 'crown of life' (Rev. 2:10).[149] (Kryuchkov)

Stop, Your Majesty,[150] shedding the blood of the innocents. Shed tears... Stop tormenting us! Catch the heretics who ruined your soul, and burn them, foul dogs... And release us, your own people. That would be good.[151] If you, Your Majesty,[152] set me free, I would at once cut [the 'heretics'] into pieces as the prophet Elijah did... Firstly, Nikon would be cut...and then—the Nikonians... God is the Judge between me and the tsar Aleksey. He is in the [eternal] tortures now; I heard this from the Saviour.[153] (Avvakum)

If it were not for the interference of the State[154] in the Church affairs with the new repressions against the believers...the Church would shortly restore due order without any problems and make the unrepentant ministers-traitors (leaders of the AUCECB) leave... We, as witnesses of God, want to remind you once again that God's Judgment will be for all doing unlawful actions, and you as the head of the

---

[146] In 1667, Paisy, Patriarch of Alexandria, and Makary, Patriarch of Antioch and many Greek hierarchs took part in the Russian Orthodox Moscow Council. (Smirnov, *Istoriya Khristianskoy Pravoslavnoy Tserkvi*, p. 193.)

[147] Avvakum, *Zhitie*, pp. 60-61.

[148] This was said during the meeting of some leaders of the Council of Churches, headed by Kryuchkov, with all the main leaders of the AUCECB present in Moscow in 1966.

[149] See Supplement 6 in Savinsky, *Istoria Evangelskikh*, pp. 352f.

[150] Appeal to the Russian Tsar, Aleksey Mikhaylovich.

[151] Avvakum, *Zhitie*, pp. 272, 274.

[152] Appeal to the Russian Tsar, Feodor Alekseevich (who succeeded Aleksey Mikhaylovich).

[153] Avvakum, *Zhitie*, p. 99.

[154] Appeal to the Soviet State leader, Nikita Khrushchev (1963).

Soviet government have the main responsibility because of this... God is Witness between us and you.[155] (G. Kryuchkov, A. Shalashov)

Both Avvakum and Kryuchkov are examples of a Russian religious phenomenon with old national roots. It would be easy to add other persons and parallels from Russian history. Maybe Avvakum, at first sight, seems a bit more radical than Kryuchkov. Avvakum dreamed of killing his enemies and encouraged his followers to suffer for the 'old beliefs' to the point of self-immolation and starvation. He is quoted as saying, 'Those who burn themselves to save their piety...as well as those who die because of fasting, do good works.'[156] But many conflicts between the Council of Churches of the ECB and the State in the second half of the 1960s and 1970s showed clearly that it was a similar type of religious radicalism.

Baptist Extremism

After the dismissal from power of Khrushchev in the end of 1964, the new leadership of the USSR headed by Leonid Brezhnev started a more cautious religious policy. For instance, many Baptists arrested in Khrushchev's times were discharged and even rehabilitated in 1965.[157] In spite of some local discrimination against believers, the central authorities let the Russian religious communities understand their readiness to open a new stage of the relationship between the Church and the State. But the Baptist radicals were not satisfied. About fifty brethren were still in prison.[158] The radicals of the Council of Churches of the ECB wanted more concessions from the government, as always: all or nothing. For this, they arranged the famous protest demonstration of 400-500 of their followers[159] near the Kremlin in Moscow on 16-17 May 1966. During that event, these radical Baptist leaders asked in the hearing of the chiefs of the KGB, 'Brothers and sisters, will we leave here or die?' and the Baptist demonstrators screamed all together, 'We will die!'[160] Then the Baptists actively resisted their dispersal and arrest. One of the participants in that protest action was the former executive minister of the Council of Churches of the ECB in the Central Asian region, Yu. Kuksenko,[161] who said, 'It was not a

---

[155] *Vestnik Istiny* 3 (2001), p. 16.

[156] Avvakum, *Zhitie*, p. 226.

[157] Podrazhayte Vere Ikh, pp. 84, 173.

[158] Ibid.

[159] N. Baturin mentioned about 500 people (Vestnik Istiny 4 (1988), p. 23), Yu. Reshetnikov and S. Sannikov mentioned 400 people (*Obzor Istorii*, p. 207).

[160] Yu. Kuksenko, 'Nashi Besedy' (Our Conversations), *Kazakhstan's Baptist Union Archives* (2002), p. 55.

[161] After that he was the pastor of a registered Baptist church in Taraz (Kazakhstan) until his death in 2003.

delegation [to the government], but a demonstration of force... It was not difficult to inspire the believers to cry, 'We will die!'... It was like...the people who poured gasoline over themselves and burned...as a token of protest...against the war in Vietnam. I think that some of our demonstrators would have done this, if the command had been given.'[162]

Fasting to the verge of starvation was also used widely by the members of the Council of Churches. Two sisters from the Uzlovaya community (the 'mother-church' of the Initiative Group) once fasted, or perhaps better, had a hunger strike, for twenty-four days as a token of protest against the pressure of the authorities upon their church.[163] Brothers and sisters acted so because their ministers set the example. G. Vins, one of the most respected and less radical representatives of the movement, nevertheless wrote, 'There were about thirty believers at Lefortovo [a prison in Moscow]. Many of them refused food, asking for permission to have a Bible. I also did not eat for six days, asking for a Bible. We received the Bibles, though probably not all of us did.'[164] Another leader of the Council of Churches, N. Baturin, said, 'During one year of transportation under guard from prison to prison, I spent approximately half a year in fasting... I did not eat and drink for three days and nights and was praying that my Bible and writing-books would not be taken away. The Lord heard me and all remained with me...'[165] G. Kryuchkov and his assistant P. Peters also had ten to twenty day strict fasts in prison in order to have a Bible or to receive permission to meet with relatives.[166] It is notable that the radical Baptists were able to put pressure on the Soviet authorities in Brezhnev's times. They received their Bibles, papers and other things. It was considered a weakness in the authorities, and the demands of the radicals were growing.

The following are some more examples of 'Baptist extremism' in the 1960s and 1970s. In 1963, there was a meeting of a committee of ministers—the *Orgkomitet*—in Prokop'evsk, Siberia. The house where they met was encircled by militia and officers of the KGB. The brethren decided to have a prayer service throughout the night. This did not prevent them from resisting the militiamen when the latter tried to arrest one of the ministers. The brethren 'encircled the dear brother in a strong circle and did not allow him to be led away'. After that, the militia decided to arrest the brothers on the street when they began to go away, but some of the believers helped the ministers to escape

---

[162] Kuksenko, 'Nashi Besedy', p. 56. The author testifies also that a chief of the KGB said to the demonstrators before the dispersal the following remarkable words, 'We have only to call the Ball-bearing plant and the workers will come and grind you into dust!' (Ibid., p. 55). Remembering the widespread Soviet stereotypes about Baptists, it was not an empty threat.
[163] Ibid., p. 41.
[164] G. Vins, *Evangelie v Uzakh*, p. 195; See also his book *Gorizonty Very*, p. 15.
[165] Cited in Kovalenko, *Oblako Svideteley Khristovykh*, p. 214.
[166] Kuksenko, 'Nashi Besedy', p. 58.

miraculously, as it was understood, 'through the hills and forest' to another town.[167]

In 1965, a group of radical Baptists of the Novosibirsk community, Siberia, demanded that the town authorities provide a public building for the 'Day of the Prisoner' (a meeting in honour of the Baptist prisoners of Khrushchev's times). Otherwise, they threatened to hold the meeting on the streets of Novosibirsk. The authorities were indignant with the ultimatum and warned these radical Baptists about the criminal penalties for disturbing the peace. Finally, the radicals had their 'Day of the Prisoner' somewhere in the forest.[168]

In the first half of the 1970s, the militia arrested a Baptist pastor in Frunze, Kirghizia. About twenty young believers went to the office of the city prosecutor and demanded that he discharge their presbyter. The prosecutor said that he needed to know more about the arrest before it would be possible to make a decision. The young Christians insisted that the prosecutor immediately order the discharge, and they started singing psalms in his room. When the poor prosecutor tried to leave the room, he was knocked down. He shouted, and his guard came and arrested the delegation. One of the brethren was convicted of hooliganism according to an article in the criminal code.[169]

In the first half of the 1970s, groups of Baptists in Barnaul (Altai) and Dzhambul (Kazakhstan), as a token of protest against the persecutions of believers, denied their Soviet citizenship and sent their passports to the government.[170] The same action was also taken by the members of Issyk's Baptist community in Kazakhstan, but they soon found that they could not get a job or go for a journey without passports, so they were forced to go to the militia office and ask to be given back their passports.[171]

In 1976, there was a trial against three Baptists in Dzhambul. A brother who sat among the listeners tried to take down in shorthand the interrogation of the accused. Seeing this, the agents of the KGB caught him and led him away. Y. Skornyakov continues, 'Some young brothers, including me, burned with the desire to free the brother. Of course, it was boyish behaviour, but we did it: the brother escaped...'[172]

In 1977, there was a large, unsanctioned meeting of the young believers of the Council of Churches in Rostov-on-Don, Russia. About 2,000 young Baptists met on the outskirts of the town and started their service. The local authorities were horrified and tried to force them out of the city. But the result was exactly the opposite: at the call of the ministers, the brothers and sisters

---

[167] *Podrazhayte Vere Ikh*, p. 171-2.

[168] Pakina, *Raskol Evangelskikh Khristian-Baptistov*, p. 28.

[169] Kuksenko, 'Nashi Besedy', p. 54.

[170] *Byulleten' Soveta Rodstvennikov Uznikov Evangelskikh Khristian-Baptistov v SSSR* 21 (Moscow, 1975), p. 46.

[171] Kuksenko, 'Nashi Besedy', p. 113.

[172] *Vestnik Istiny* 1 (2000), p. 9.

moved downtown. All the attempts of the militia to stop the column of marchers, even using cars to block the streets, were in vain. G. Nikita writes,

> [The leaders of the town]...were indignant with each other, 'I said to you: let them pray here. They will finish singing their songs and go away... Who can stop them now?'... The brothers decided to stop and have worship there. The surroundings were good: the high-rise buildings, a mass of passers-by... They quickly built a Dais using some stones and started the service... The trams and trolleybuses stopped, the crowd of listeners increased each minute. The ministers of the Council of Churches and the brothers from Rostov's community preached, the young Christians recited poetry, the choir...sang... The leaders of the town came... Their suggestion was acceptable: to go back to the former place and 'to pray there as long as you want! We guarantee that nobody will touch you; but please leave the square!'... All the people moved to the former place... The sermons, singing, and declamation of verses rang out for two days... It is impossible to forget such meetings.[173]

In 1978, some members of the unregistered Dzhetysay Baptist community in Kazakhstan tried to heal a seriously ill boy, but there and then he died. Then the healers promised the parents that they would raise their child from the dead. The brethren proclaimed three days of fasting and prayer for the resurrection of the boy. The news of this spread throughout the town. Many people came to look at the miracle. But it was, as is easy to guess, a time of shame for the wonder-workers. In addition, they were arrested. The local authorities arranged an open criminal trial where Baptists as a whole were discredited.[174] It must be admitted that the previously mentioned communist stereotypes about Baptists could have been partly based on such outrageous incidents, which could have indirectly harmed other Christian denominations in the USSR.

Of course, not all members of the Council of Churches would approve of such 'fights of faith', but, as a whole, the direction of this unregistered Baptist Union was, and still remains, staunchly radical. That is true not only for its 'internal', but also its 'foreign' policy. When G. Vins was deported from the USSR in 1979[175] and began his press campaign against religious persecution in the Soviet Union in the West, G. Kryuchkov learned about his visit to the President of the United States and rebuked him. G. Vins himself reminisced about this, 'When G.K. Kryuchkov...said, 'That is politics: stop going to presidents', I did not go to them anymore, though I had another opinion and I

---

[173] *Vestnik Istiny* 2 (2001), pp. 26-27.

[174] Kuksenko, 'Nashi Besedy', p. 66.

[175] Vins was one of five Soviet prisoners of conscience who were exchanged for two Russian spies caught in the West. (*Religion in Communist Dominated Areas* XVIII: 7, 8, and 9 (1979), pp. 115-116).

could have easily gone. I visited Reagan in 1982; and then Reagan invited me several more times, and Bush also invited me, but I did not go again.'[176]

In addition to their extreme actions, the radicals of the Council of Churches often publicly condemned, and indeed are still condemning, those who did not act as they did in communist times, by which they primarily mean the moderate leaders of the AUCECB. Verdicts have even been brought as recently as 2003 against AUCECB ministers who have already passed into eternity, 'The people who were leaders of the AUCECB in 1961 are already in hell'.[177]

Taking into account the aforementioned acts of the radicals, it is not easy for a contemporary historian to judge categorically the 'communist severity' regarding the same Baptists, at least during Brezhnev's time. L. Brezhnev himself was by no means a cruel man. An unbiased assessment of him written by people who used to know him said, "He fell short in education, culture and refinement, in general. He would have been a good landowner with a big hospitable house in Turgenev's time [in the nineteenth century]. I remember an incident...in Ul'yanovsk... There were the local communist leaders at the table. Brezhnev said, 'I am like the tsar now. Only the tsar could give someone a village, but I cannot...but on the other hand I can give an order.'"[178] During the 25th Congress of the Communist Party, Brezhnev interpreted what democracy means this way:

> One remembers Lenin's words, that all things which serve the cause of building communism are moral in our society. In the same way, we may say that all things which serve the cause of our people, the cause of building communism, are democratic for us. We deny what contradicts the cause; and nobody can convince us that it is the wrong approach.[179]

Such a policy always included a certain severity towards all nonconformists. But was it reasonable to expect from the 'godless' Soviet power more humility than from the Christians? Only extreme anti-communism can fully defend the extremist actions of the 'Christian' revolutionaries from the Council of Churches (as well as of some brethren from 'registered' communities). About

---

[176] From the recording of the meeting of the ministers of the Council of Churches of 17 December 1991. Cited in Kuksenko, 'Nashi Besedy', pp. 71-72. See also Reshetnikov and Sannikov, *Obzor Istorii*, pp. 217-218.

[177] *Khristianskaya Gazeta Kuzbassa* (The Christian Newspaper of Kuzbass) 1 (2003), p. 9. Compare: 'God is the Judge between me and the Tsar Aleksey. He is in the [eternal] tortures now; I heard this from the Saviour...' (Avvakum, *Zhitie*, p. 99).

[178] A. Bovin, 'Kurs na Stabil'nost' Porodil Zastoy', in *L.I. Brezhnev: Materialy k Biografii* (Moscow: Politizdat, 1991), pp. 93-94. On May Day 1966, when there were protests by the CCECB in Moscow, the demonstrators were told that L. Brezhnev was not able to receive them because he had flown to decorate someone with the Order of Lenin. (Kuksenko, 'Nashi Besedy', p. 55).

[179] *The Materials of the 25nd Congress of the Communist Party of the Soviet Union* (Moscow: Politizdat, 1976), p. 85.

2,000 Baptists, mainly from the Council of Churches, were imprisoned in the Soviet Union during Khrushchev's and Brezhnev's times.[180] Dozens of them were killed or died in labour camps (N. Khmara, I. Moiseev, N. Kucherenko, and others).[181] On no account should we forget these crimes of the communist regime against Christians in the USSR. At the same time, we should also not forget the bitter truth about Baptist radicalism, which is that it was often only very remotely connected with the Gospel and often provoked the authorities to extreme force.

Trials of the Baptists

The Soviet State tried many Baptists in court, using these occasions both to attack them and defend itself because of their provocations. Many such trials were striking examples of traditional misunderstandings between believers and unbelievers, illustrating different approaches to civic duties, and including much pathos, sarcasm and irony from both sides. The following is from the interrogation of a few Baptists (*B.*) by a Prosecutor (*P.*) in Fergana in 1971

> *P.*: 'One of your psalms has the following words, 'It is worth working, it is worth struggling'. Tell us: to work—with whom; to struggle—against whom?'
> *B.*: 'We wrestle not against flesh and blood, but against spiritual wickedness in high places'...
> *P.*: 'You must have an official certificate confirming that you are a presbyter'
> *B.*: 'A presbyter should work not by certificate, but by inspiration'...
> *P.*: 'Where is your literature: '*Vestnik Spaseniya*', '*Bratsky Listok*' printed?
> *B.*: 'I do not know'...
> *P.*: 'Why is your literature spreading illegally? Why is it not in bookstalls?'...
> *B.*: 'Is the Bible a legal book?'
> *P.*: 'Yes, it is. It was even printed on State presses.'
> *B.*: 'If so, why is it not in the bookstalls?'...
> *P.*: 'What do you know about the accused?'
> *B.*: 'I know that their names are written in the Book of Life'...
> *P.*: 'Show us this book, we need documents!'...
> [From a speech for the prosecution] 'Baptism stands for bourgeoisie...American Baptists bombed Hiroshima and Nagasaki... The Rockefellers grabbed all capital... The [Russian] Baptists have strong propaganda... 'I want to lead to Jesus, if only one soul,' the Baptists sing'.[182]

In 1967, a young Baptist woman was tried in Novosibirsk. Much underground literature of the Council of Churches, as well as machines for

---

[180] A. Rudenko, *Evangelskie Khristiane-Baptisty i Perestroyka v SSSR*, p. 353; *Vestnik Istiny*, 3 (2001), p. 36.

[181] *Podrazhayte Vere Ikh*, pp. 278-86, 340-58; *Vestnik Istiny*, 3 (2001), p. 36.

[182] *Vestnik Spaseniya* 1 (1973), pp. 22-27.

copying and home printing, were found in her apartment. When the judge asked who her chief was and who had managed the process of printing, the woman answered, 'Christ', and she said nothing more on the point.[183] N. Struve wrote about a similar incident involving another Soviet 'sectarian'. This man refused to serve in the army, and burnt his identity card, saying that he 'shall never accept any papers from the devil'. When, standing trial, he was asked his name, and he answered, 'God knows it'. When he was asked 'Who are you?' he replied, 'God's servant'. The next question 'But you are also a citizen of the USSR?' was answered, 'No, I belong to God'.[184]

A Baptist girl, who with some brethren was led to the militia office in the 1960s, protested against the prohibition of private prayer meetings with these noteworthy words, 'If we had some vodka on our table and our hands held, instead of the Bible, glasses with wine, nobody would disturb us... You have an army of thousands upon thousands of propagandists and agitators printing millions of copies of anti-religious literature and, at the same time, you are afraid when a few believers meet together to pray and read the Gospel.'[185]

It was really a problem in a country which was building a communist society. Ordinary Baptists, as well as other believers in the USSR, simply met together, prayed and read the Scriptures, but that was a real threat that could have derailed the Soviet locomotive. 'Our steam-engine runs at full; the stop will be in communism,' a popular Soviet song said. Josef Brodsky, who was deported from the USSR in 1972, remembered his native land in these melancholy verses from 1977:

> The puddle in the yard there is like the area of two Americas...
> And pouring some tea, someone's tooth is broken by spice-cake there...
> The train leaving point 'A' there...
> Speeds to point 'B' which does not exist...[186]

Another Russian classical writer, A.P. Chekhov, wrote a story called *Malefactor* (1885), which could be a useful illustration for a better understanding of some important psychological nuances of the aforementioned

---

[183] Pakina, *Raskol Evangelskikh Khristian-Baptistov*, p. 33.

[184] N. Struve, *Christians in Contemporary Russia* (New York: Charles Scribner's Sons, 1967), p. 248.

[185] *Otvet na Antireligioznuyu Stat'yu 'Ne Bud'te Trupom Sredi Zhivykh'*, p. 2. Another Baptist, who was publicly tried in the late 1950s because of his adherence to 'harmful' religious views argued against the judges having frequent smoking breaks with the argument: 'Is it unhealthy to smoke? Yes or no? Everybody knows that it is harmful. There is much written in the media (as well as against religion) about this. Nevertheless, you are smoking. So, you also hold a socially harmful position and propagandize it your own way.' (Author's interview with I. Shatokhin, Petropavlovsk, Kazakhstan, 2002).

[186] I. Brodsky, *Pis'ma Rimskomu Drugu* (Letters to a Roman Friend) (Saint Petersburg: Azbuka-klassika, 2001), pp. 219-220.

Soviet trials against the radical Baptists who, in spite of the common Western delusion that they were anti-communists,[187] were mainly indifferent to politics. The story is also on the railway theme. A Russian villager, Denis Grigor'ev, is caught unscrewing a nut from the rail. The investigator asks him about the purpose of such dangerous work, to which he replies, 'If I did not need it, I would not unscrew it,' adding, 'We make weights [for fishing]... When you are baiting live bait it does not sink without a weight.' The nut is to be used as a weight for fishing. The investigator is shocked. He asks if the 'malefactor' understands that it could make the train crash, resulting in many victims. Grinning, Denis responds, 'What! The whole village has been unscrewing the nuts for many years, and the Lord has saved us, but you say: the 'crash', 'many victims'... If I take a rail away or put a log across the way, maybe the train will crash, but it is...pah! a nut!'[188]

Charging the Soviet Baptists, even the most radical of them, with 'anti-Soviet activity' or 'anti-communist propaganda', and with threatening the State system, looked a little like charging Chekhov's Denis Grigor'ev and his fellow-villagers with acts of terrorism. They collected the screw-nuts for their weights and that was all. They could not even imagine that the huge train could crash because of such a small thing. In the same way, the Soviet Baptists met together only for prayers (including prayers for the Soviet government so long as it was established by God—Rom. 13:1) and for peaceful evangelical preaching. They could not know that the gigantic communist 'steam-engine', which seemed to be almost at the terminal, was derailing because of their unbelief in the famous point 'B'... It was not the Baptists' business to derail the government, but after the great crash of communism they were found to have been players—and not insignificant players—in that surrealistic game.

In 1974, G. Vins was asked by an officer of the KGB about the prospects of adjusting the relationships between the Council of Churches and the Soviet State. Vins said that the position of his brotherhood at that time was that the State must:

> abrogate the Law on Religious Associations of 1929; give freedom to preach the Gospel in the country; dismiss all Christians from the prisons, camps and exiles[189] who are there because of their religious activity; give back all confiscated prayer houses and Christian literature...and give back to their parents the children, taken

---

[187] J. Pollock, *The Faith of the Russian Evangelicals* (New York: McGraw-Hill Book Company, 1964), pp. 142-143; J. Hebly, *Protestants in Russia* (Belfast: Christian Journals Ltd, 1976), pp. 155-156.

[188] A. Chekhov, *Izbrannye Sochineniay* (Selected Works) 1, (Moscow: Khudozhestvennaya Literatura, 1986), pp. 83-84.

[189] Besides such types of imprisonment, some Baptists were forcibly interned in mental hospitals because of their beliefs. (M. Bourdeaux, *Faith on Trial in Russia* (New York: Harper & Row, Publishers, 1971), p. 140; *Podrazhayte Vere Ikh*, pp. 303, 317; See also Supplement 8 in Savinsky, *Istoria Evangelskikh*, pp. 391-397).

by the State[190] because of their Christian education in the family... 'That is impossible! That is an ultimatum!' [the officer of the KGB said] 'No, that is not an ultimatum, but the only possible judicious way... I'm talking about the *minimum* terms which would return the confidence of the believers to...the governing body. There is no other way!'[191]

To be sure, such proposals were not constructive at the time. The radical hand of Kryuchkov was felt here. On the other hand, since 1917, the Soviet State had tried at various times to eradicate 'religious prejudices' in the USSR, but without result. So, the communist authorities were seeking a compromise settlement. In addition to the permanent religious resistance within the country, there was also the strong external pressure of Western public opinion, with the constant unpleasant accusations about the USSR's disregard of human rights in general, and liberty of conscience in particular, as well as its non-observance of many international commitments in the humanitarian sphere.[192] Taking into account this situation, the Soviet government made some serious decisions on these issues in 1975. The following 'about-faces' will be examined: the changing of the Law of 1929 on Religious Associations; the signing by the USSR of the Helsinki Final Act; and the issuing of the decree of the Council for Religious Affairs on the German religious communities.

The About-faces of the Second Half of the 1970s

The old Law on Religious Associations of 1929 was redefined by some important changes in June of 1975. Some articles were completely removed. In fact, religious communities obtained the status of a juridical person, which was necessary for them to have a place in the society. This status had been forfeited as far back as 1918, according to Lenin's decree *On Separation of Church from State and School from Church*[193]. Article 3 of the law of 1929, 'Religious communities and groups of believers do not have the status of a juridical

---

[190] It was known that there were some terrible incidents where local courts decided to take the children of Baptists for atheistic education in Soviet children's homes. (*Byulleten' Soveta Rodstvennikov Uznikov Evangelskikh Khristian-Baptistov v SSSR* 23 (Moscow: Samizdat, 1975), pp. 11-12; *Podrazhayte Vere Ikh*, pp. 266-267).

[191] Vins, *Evangelie v Uzakh*, p. 121.

[192] In the second half of the 1950s, the USSR signed some important international pacts and conventions on human rights, but the realisation of them in the country was always a problem. (*Prava Cheloveka: Osnovnye Mezhdunarodnye Dokumenty* (Human Rights: the Fundamental International Documents) (Moscow: Mezhdunarodnye Otnosheniya, 1989), pp. 4-5, 20, 35, 151).

[193] Article 12 of the decree said, 'No church or religious community has the right to possess property. They do not have the status of a juridical person'. (See text of the decree of 1918 in *O Religii i Tserkvi* (Moscow: Politizdat, 1965), p. 96.

person',[194] was changed in 1975 to: 'Religious communities have the right to purchase church plates, religious items, means of transport, as well as to rent, build and buy buildings for their needs according to that established by the legal order'.[195] At the same time, many restrictions on the religious activity of communities of believers were retained (especially articles 17-20).[196]

In August 1975, the Soviet Union, following the lead of the democratic countries, signed the Helsinki Final Act, which dealt with human rights.[197] The atmosphere of the Soviet society was changing step by step towards more liberalization. According to the Helsinki agreements, independent committees were established in different countries for the observance of the realization of citizens' rights. In the USSR, such committees were dispersed and soon some of their activists were even imprisoned.[198] Expecting more from the communist authorities at that time was probably much too optimistic. At the same time it seemed that believers had made much progress (especially in comparison with the period of Stalin's terror). The 1970s was a period of political détente. The USSR and the USA signed important treaties on the restriction of the production of weapons of mass annihilation; the frontiers of post-war Europe were recognized as inviolable; and trade relations between the 'capitalist West' and the 'socialist East' increased greatly.[199]

Also, in August of 1975, the Council for Religious Affairs issued the decree: *On the Measures of the Regulation of the Network of Religious Communities Consisting of Citizens of German Nationality and Strengthening of the Control of Its Activities.* As a result of the implementation of this document, many underground Lutheran, Catholic, Mennonite, and Baptist German communities in the USSR were registered and received the official right to exist.[200] But the normalization of relations between the State and the religious communities of Soviet Germans was too late in coming. Some of them, including the Baptists, had, during the first half of the 1970s, started to protest the discrimination against Germans in the USSR, remembering their experiences since Stalin's

---

[194] See text of the law of 1929 in Nikolin, *Tserkov i Gosudarstvo*, p. 382.

[195] See text of the law of 1975 in *O Religii i Tserkvi* (Moscow: Politizdat, 1981), p. 127.

[196] Ibid., p. 130.

[197] *Prava Cheloveka*, p. 66; P. Walters, 'A Survey of Soviet Religious Policy' in *Religious Policy in the Soviet Union*, S. Ramet, ed. (Cambridge: Cambridge University Press, 1993), p. 27.

[198] Zavatski, *Evangelicheskoe Dvizhenie*, p. 487; *Amnesty International Report 1980* (London: Amnesty International Publications, 1980), p. 302.

[199] A. Prokhorov, ed., *Sovetsky Entsiklopedichesky Slovar* (The Soviet Encyclopedia) (Moscow: Sovetskaya Entsiklopediya, 1982), p. 1095.

[200] O. Nikolaev, *Protestantskie Ob"edineniya Orenburzh'ya: Istoriya, Sovremennoe Sostoyanie, Vzaimootnosheniya s Gosudarstvom* (The Protestant Associations of the Orenburg Region: History, the Present, and Their Relationship with the State), Diplomnaya Rabota (Moscow: Rossiyskaya Akademiya Gosudarstvennoy Sluzhby pri Prezidente Rossiyskoy Federatsii, 1999), pp. 15-16.

time, and had asked the authorities for permission to emigrate. In the second half of the 1970s, demands for emigration were common: German Baptists asked to be allowed to leave the 'country of victorious socialism' to go to Western Germany;[201] Russian Baptists asked to go to the USA;[202] Ukrainian Baptists asked to go to Canada;[203] and sometimes multinational groups of Soviet Baptists even asked to be allowed to go to 'any foreign country'.[204]

Public opinion polls indicated a real increase in the religious mood in the society in the 1970s. For instance, workers in Leningrad, (the model 'proletariat' from the 'cradle of the Bolshevik revolution'), thought of religion in 1970 in the following way: negatively—44%, positively—11%, vacillating—7.4% (the rest did not want to answer the question). By 1979, the workers' opinion had changed appreciably: only 14% of the responses were negative towards religion; positive—19%; vacillating—8.8% (the rest did not want to answer the question).[205] Such a large percentage of 'abstentions' under the circumstances of Soviet life did not testify to strong atheism. It could be said that the climax of the liberalization of Russian religious life during the détente period, before the Soviet intervention in Afghanistan in 1979 and the general changes in the political situation within the country and all over the world connected with that event, was the new Constitution of the USSR of 1977. The fifty-second article of that Constitution proclaimed guarantees of 'liberty of conscience' to all citizens. In the Soviet understanding, it was, 'the right to confess any religion or to confess none of them, to conduct religious worship or to carry on atheistic propaganda'.[206] Of course, there was no real equality of believers and atheists in the country so long as religious 'propaganda' was not permitted, but the Russian believers were happy to have even this official confirmation of their right to exist in the USSR.

Baptist Survival in an Atheistic Context

Summary of Testimonies of the Witnesses

The radicals have already been dealt with adequately in this study, but not much has yet been said about the moderate groups which constituted the

---

[201] *Byulleten' Soveta Rodstvennikov Uznikov Evangelskikh Khristian-Baptistov v SSSR* 23 (Moscow: Samizdat, 1975), p. 7.

[202] Kuksenko, 'Nashi Besedy', pp. 150-151.

[203] *Byulleten' Soveta Rodstvennikov Uznikov Evangelskikh Khristian-Baptistov v SSSR* 24 (Moscow: Samizdat, 1975), pp. 1-2.

[204] *Byulleten' Soveta Rodstvennikov Uznikov Evangelskikh Khristian-Baptistov v SSSR* 21 (Moscow: Samizdat, 1975), p. 20.

[205] See Pospelovsky, *Pravoslavnaya Tserkov*, p. 341.

[206] *Konstitutsiya (Osnovnoy Zakon) Soyuza Sovetskikh Sotsialisticheskikh Respublik* (The Constitution of the USSR) (Moscow: Politizdat, 1977).

majority of Russian Baptists. It was previously mentioned that their 'gentle resistance' was the basis of the survival of the communities of Baptist believers during communism. To seek to investigate this subject, I interviewed some older members of my home church as well as several established ministers from other churches.[207] In summarizing the testimonies of the witnesses of that period, the following 'survival' methods of Baptists living among the Soviet atheists are notable. They give insights into the life of the moderate Baptists of the time.

Personal Spirituality

It is remarkable that the majority of the moderate members of the Baptist churches during communism speak first about God's help in surviving under the pressure of Soviet atheism. It shows how their humility and their faith provided an inexhaustible source of consolation during suffering. Much prayer and fasting—usually for one day, and not for more than three days running—was a distinctive feature of the Soviet Baptists. Their lack of theological knowledge was often compensated for by their thorough reading of the Bible. An interesting paradox may be noted: the fewer the copies of the Bible there were among the Baptists in the USSR, the better their knowledge of it. Whole books of the Bible were handwritten and memorizing numerous Scriptural passages and chapters was very common. As an echo of such pious practices, an occurrence at the Odessa Theological Seminary of the ECB[208] in the beginning of the 1990s is noteworthy. Among the first group of Russian students, a Western teacher of the Pauline epistles without thinking offered 100 American dollars to any person who would be able to memorize the Epistle to the Galatians in two weeks. The teacher was surprised that one student was ready to recite the epistle immediately and some other brothers said that they would do it in one or two days. There was a healthy tradition of daily Bible reading and study by the Soviet Baptists which comforted them and helped them to survive under the pressure of atheistic ideology. However, the analysis must range more broadly to look at wider church life, local congregations and the family.

---

[207] In 1999-2003, valuable recollections were shared with me by Y. Meleshkevich, V. Hot'ko, and V. Frisen (Petropavlovsk), I. Fast (Shchuchinsk), V. Alperov (Almaty), N. Kolesnikov (Moscow), and others.

[208] This was the first full-time Baptist school in the territory of the former Soviet Union and it was where the author of this paper had the privilege of studying.

Councils and Courses

Many 'official' Baptist authors have a tendency to describe the history of the Baptist community since 1963 as a simple chronicle of regular All-Union Councils. Another extreme is the tendency of the writers of the radical Council of Churches to disregard completely the Councils of the Soviet times, as 'controlled by the comrades from without', and not to ascribe any importance to them. Of course, to find the golden mean between these poles would be desirable. There were five All-Union Councils of the ECB in the period of time examined here: in 1963, 1966, 1969, 1974 and 1979.[209] All of them were in Moscow. The average number of their delegates was approximately 500. All of the Councils spent significant time discussing the theme of separation and seeking ways to build unity. It is notable that the Councils of the 1960s spent much more time on this subject than the Councils of the 1970s, when the Council of Churches was already rather unpopular among the Russian Baptists (the CCECB had about 18,000 believers on 1 January 1972[210]). Instead of their discredited documents of 1960, the AUCECB of 1963 approved new Statutes for the ECB, which were then changed and augmented many times in the Councils of 1966, 1969 and 1979.[211] The Council of 1966 started work on approving the Confession of Faith of the ECB, which was finally finished during *Perestroika*.[212] The Councils tried to change the AUCECB into a more democratic structure by electing its leaders and increasing their numbers: instead of the former 10 members, 15 brothers were elected in 1963 and 25 leaders plus 8 candidate-members in 1966. In subsequent years this practice became the norm.[213] At the end of the 1960s and the beginning of 1970s, there was a major 'changing of generations' among Russian Baptist leaders. Many new individuals assumed leadership at that time: A. Bychkov, A. Klimenko, V.

---

[209] *Istoriya Evangelskikh Khristian-Baptistov v SSSR*, pp. 243-253.

[210] Ibid., p. 251. It seems the membership of the CCECB peaked in the middle of the 1960s when there may have been about 20,000-25,000 members. V. Zavatsky's estimate of 155,000 followers of the CCECB in 1966 (V. Zavatsky, *Evangelicheskoe*, pp. 211, 222, 551) is not corroborated. Zavatsky referred to G. Lyalina ('Baptizm: Illuyzii i Realnost', pp. 42, 51), who could not have been a good source because she did not write any actual numbers, but only enigmatic 'percentages'. Even the contemporary total number of members of the CCECB, after the great revival of all denominations in the former USSR during Perestroika, is little more than 60,000 members (*Vestnik Istiny* 1 (2001), p. 3). See also the following sources on the subject: 'Mesta Naibol'shego Vliyaniya Orgkomiteta' (The Districts Come under the Great Influence of the Orgkomitet), *The AUCECB Archives*, papka 28, doc. 67; Savinsky, *Istoria Evangelskikh*, p. 230; *Istoriya Evangelskikh Khristian-Baptistov v SSSR*, pp. 245, 247-249; Reshetnikov, Sannikov, *Obsor Istorii Evangelsko-Baptistskogo*, p. 221.

[211] *Istoriya Evangelskikh Khristian-Baptistov v SSSR*, pp. 244, 246, 248-249, 253.

[212] Ibid., pp. 246, 253-254.

[213] Ibid., pp. 244, 247, 252.

Logvinenko, Y. Tervits, N. Kolesnikov, and others.[214] This was an important factor for the renewal of the community of the AUECB and the continuation of dialogue with the CCECB.

The first official part-time Bible courses to take place after World War II began in Moscow when permission for this was granted by the Council for Religious Affairs. The first group had 100 students from various regions of the country. The teachers were mainly Russian. The executive minister of the courses was A. Mitskevich, who was also a member of the leadership of the AUECB.[215] Originally, the following disciplines were studied in the courses: Dogmatics, Biblical Theology, Homiletics, Exegetics, Pastoral Theology, History of Christianity, History of the Evangelical Christians–Baptists, and the Constitution of the USSR. The last subject, to be sure, gave the CCECB opportunity to criticise the courses.[216] However, the Moscow Bible Courses were a very important event in the Baptist community's life. It is well known that the majority of the students who graduated at that time became teachers of the unofficial courses for preachers in their regions and local churches through the 1970s. The courses provided significant help in the spiritual growth of many communities. Though the theological level of the courses was relatively modest, holding the traditional practical direction, they were exactly what was needed at that time. Also, in 1979, the first group of choir directors started their important studies as a division of the Moscow Bible Courses.[217]

Local Church Life

As a rule, the old believers remember their Baptist communities during the atheistic times as more pure and more zealous for God's work than is the case with contemporary churches. Among the causes of this zeal could be the following: the natural refinement of the communities under the heavy State pressure, where nominal believers could not survive; strict discipline, through which Baptists usually did not let the very common features of Soviet society (drunkenness, theft, etc.) come into their circles; and finally, the psychological tendency of the elderly to recall their youth as a time that was much better than 'these days' (see Ecclesiastes 7:10).

Russian Baptist community disciplines historically included: corporate adherence to evangelical faith in God; regular church attendance 2-3 times a week; studying the Bible; faithfulness to one's spouse; a modest appearance

---

[214] Ibid., pp. 250-253.

[215] Reshetnikov, Sannikov, *Obsor Istorii Evangelsko-Baptistskogo*, p. 211.

[216] V. Kuz'min, 'Chastichny Analiz "Bratskogo Listka" za 1975 g. po Sluchayu Desyatiletiya so Dnya Vypuska' (Partial Analysis of 'Fraternal Leaflet' of 1975 on the Occasion of The 10th Anniversary of its Issue), *The AUCECB Archives*, papka 28, doc. 46, list 26; *Vestnik Istiny* 1 (1984), p. 5.

[217] *Istoriya Evangelskikh Khristian-Baptistov v SSSR*, p. 253.

manifested by a simple haircut, inexpensive clothes and a lack of adornment; total abstention from alcohol and tobacco (drugs were not even mentioned since they were considered a Western, not a Soviet problem); and active assistance in any church needs. Any serious violation of discipline was punished during church meetings by public denunciation or excommunication. If either of these things happened, the guilty person lost the right to take part in the Lord's Supper. It seems possible that such a ban mainly proved its value in the context of militant atheism by showing the evident moral superiority of Baptists in comparison with the average Soviet citizen. It has to be said that excommunications were often not used for the purification of church members, but rather were connected to the pursuit of personal agendas and were thus a simple abuse of power.[218]

In Russian Baptist preaching, although there was a range of traditional Baptist sermon themes the subjects of the chosen status of the children of God and a daily waiting for the Second Coming of Christ were especially important in opposing the secular and communist values of those times. It would be wrong to understand the theme of being chosen in the sense of Calvinistic election to salvation. The majority of Russian Baptists were always Arminian, according to the Western classification; or rather they were influenced, I would argue, by Orthodox soteriology. The 'chosen' status of the Baptists was understood in terms of the many spiritual privileges of believers in comparison with unbelievers. The preachers often stressed, using biblical imagery, how terrible it was 'to sell our birthright' or go back to the world 'to eat the husks with swine'.

The Second Advent was a favourite theme of the Russian preachers. The actual sufferings of the Christians of those times were perceived as connected with the sufferings of the Church of the Last Days, after which the Redeemer will come from heaven and 'wipe away all tears from their eyes'. The Church was to be ready to meet her Bridegroom. The Bride of Christ had to have a snow-white dress without any spots, which was an allusion to holiness and to avoiding sins. Those who were not fully ready to meet Christ at his return would stay on earth when believers were taken away. Eschatological schemes were not worked out in any systematic way. Rather, such reflections, regularly repeated and thoroughly discussed, strengthened the resolve of Baptist communities to endure the 'temptations of atheism' to the end.

The Baptist Family as a Household Church

Since the world around dealt harshly with Baptists, they longed for Christian fellowship, comfort and encouragement, and were not satisfied by attending official church services. Older church members testify that Baptist communities

---

[218] *Bratsky Vestnik* 5 (1970), pp. 50ff; 1(1975), p. 48.

survived the darkest periods of Soviet history because of the existence of the 'household churches' which were made up of the believers' families. Fortunately, State control could not penetrate all believers' houses at the same time. In addition, an average Baptist community with about 50-100 people had the legal right to celebrate one or two birthdays of its members each week. Meeting together at the home of someone celebrating a birthday, it was necessary only to keep the passport of the person near at hand to show the date of birth to militiamen if they came to check the cause of the crowded gathering. Due to these common practices, sizable families of believers, or 'clans', with many children, enjoyed authority within the community and became, in a sense, independent 'household churches'.[219]

The Christian education of children was done exclusively in the home. Besides acquiring basic biblical knowledge, children were usually taught how to behave at Soviet schools; to refrain from discussing with others their Baptist context; and to say nothing about their beliefs in public, since no good would come of it. There were also numerous meetings of Baptist youth in homes, as well as youth choir practices, spiritual poetry readings, rehearsals of string orchestras and plays acting out various biblical scenes. Household meetings were also important for the formation of new Christian families. Boys and girls knew from childhood that godly marriages were marriages between believers. This firm rule was based on the Scriptures (mainly 2 Corinthians 6:14-18) and also on the unfavourable experiences of mixed families, which often resulted in the apostasy of the believer rather then the unbelieving spouse coming to the church. There were many instructive Baptist verses and stories on this subject. For example, one poem told about a bird with a wonderful voice which was placed in a cage with street sparrows to teach them to sing, but the result was exactly opposite: soon the song-bird started to twitter crudely with the sparrows.

In the 1960s and 1970s, many Baptist families started to listen to the Russian religious broadcasts produced by some Western radio stations: such as the *BBC*, *Voice of America*, *Liberty*, *German Wave*, *Monte-Carlo*, and *Voice of the Andes*. The image of a Soviet Baptist with a radio receiver in his arms became a distinctive mark of that time. However, the habit of listening to foreign radio stations was widespread among all levels of Soviet people. There was even a famous saying: 'There is a habit in Russia to listen to the BBC in the night' (it rhymes nicely in Russian). Some older Baptist families fell into the habit so much that today they still regularly listen to religious broadcasts and testify about the important role of radio-preaching in their spiritual life.

---

[219] Similar practices are described using the foreign term 'cell-churches' in Russia today.

Christian and Communist Outlooks

It has already been mentioned that it would be wrong to consider Russian Baptists as anti-communists, so the clash between the State and the believers usually had, on the believers' side, a peaceful character. The Soviet Baptists created, to some degree, an apologetic for Russian Baptist belief that used the following line of argumentation: we are also Soviet citizens, faithful to our country[220] and honestly working in Soviet enterprises;[221] the founder of our Christian faith was Jesus Christ, who in his life on earth was from a poor carpenter's family;[222] Jesus Christ's disciples were also common fishermen, and they were the first to proclaim the famous socialist slogan, 'he who does not work, shall not eat'; our beliefs are similar to the 'Moral Code for the Builder of Communism';[223] V. Lenin and the Soviet Constitution gave freedom for all religions in our country,[224] so we have the full right to live in the USSR. Of course, such speeches did not always work, but to set out the arguments was better than weakly agreeing with the common charge against the Baptists of 'obscurantism'.

However the best arguments of the Baptists were not their words, though a few of them were eloquent orators and could rival the professional Party propagandists, but their deeds. Quite often Baptists had a good reputation in the work collectives.[225] It was an amusing paradox: many leaders, as members of the communist party, were *de jure* against religion, but *de facto* respected their subordinates who were Baptists and even entrusted them with responsibility. They knew by experience that believers were, as a rule, more reliable than unbelievers, including the communist employees.[226] Today, this theme is often included in the reminiscences of older believers as a kind of *consensus patrum* in Baptist churches. In addition, some former communists who became Baptists

---

[220] In 1969, A. Karev wrote his popular essay, *A Christian and Native Land*, in which he said, 'Every Christian should know that God gave him not only the heavenly fatherland, but also the earthly native land. Jesus Christ loving all the world...had a special love for His own nation... [Our] native land is the country with the State power and laws, and each Christian should have the correct position towards the authorities.' (*Nastol'naya Kniga Presvitera* (The Handbook of a Presbyter) (Moscow: VSECB, 1982), pp. 194-195.) There was a caustic remark about this from the Council of Churches, 'There was written the famous essay *A Christian and Native Land* where love of the native land practically came to the necessity to observe the laws on religious affairs.' (*Bratsky Listok* 1-3 (1975), p. 4; *Vestnik Istiny* 1 (1984), p. 5).

[221] *Bratsky Vestnik* 1 (1963), p. 51.

[222] *Bratsky Vestnik* 3-4 (1955), p. 64.

[223] Belov, *Sekty, Sektantstvo, Sektanty*, p. 120.

[224] *Bratsky Vestnik* 2 (1970), p. 7.

[225] J. Lawrence, *Russians Observed* (London: Hodder and Stoughton, 1969), p. 61.

[226] This was especially true regarding the commandment 'Thou shalt not steal', which was rarely observed in wider Russian life.

in the 1960s and 1970s[227] furthered this perception by approaching the subject from the vantage point of their previous beliefs, thus greatly strengthening the Christian position. I remember the words of one preacher in Siberia, 'When, in the past, I visited an unfamiliar town, I could not even imagine going to nearby houses to ask where communists live or to say to them, 'Dear comrades, please let me in to spend the night. I am a member of the communist party, too!' I would be considered mentally ill. But now I have real brothers and sisters in almost every town in the country and I can expect their hospitality, and they mine.'

Since there was strong atheistic ('scientific') pressure brought to bear on the religious outlook in Khrushchev's and Brezhnev's times, the Baptists tried to respond to the important current events with their own version of science. For example, the famous jokes of the Soviet cosmonauts that they had not seen either the garden of Eden nor the Lord God in space[228] were countered by words of firm faith, similar to Tertullian's *credo, quia absurdum* but confessed this time by ordinary Baptist members: 'The Bible says Paradise is located in the 'third heaven' (2 Cor. 12:2-4); it seems, the cosmonauts flew too low!'

In general, Russian Baptists found testimonies about the Lord everywhere, even among the writings of atheists. Many old preachers recalled that they read atheistic books to know more about theology, since the Soviet authors needed to quote some Christian sources in order to criticize them. Some sisters cut out the Scripture passages published in anti-religious literature and then glued them in their hidden writing-books with their poems and devotions. Even a Sunday was a permanent testimony for Russian believers about Christ's rising from the dead, since the word 'Sunday' means 'resurrection' in Russian. Preachers never tired of reminding their communities about this. Public events, even the proposed completion date of the building of the communist society in the USSR in 1980, found an answering interpretation from Baptist preachers: 'What is the starting-point of the date? That is the Anno Domini! That is a confirmation by unbelievers themselves that our Lord Jesus Christ really lived on the earth!' The spiritual poetry and hymnology of the Baptist communities were developing independent creative work and this involved some imitation of Russian and even Soviet classics. Besides some genuine Christian poets (V. Ozhevskaya, M. Kozubovsky, Y. Buzinny, L. Vasenina, etc.) and composers (N. Vysotsky, V. Kreiman, L. Tkachenko, E. Goncharenko), there were always numerous non-professional authors and performers in the churches whose naive but sincere works became a distinctive feature of the worship services of Evangelical Christians–Baptists. The best Russian hymns had texts with deep meaning, 'sermons in verses', encouraging believers to think about what they

---

[227] I.e., there were 'apostates' not only among Christians, but also communists; see, for instance C. de Grunwald, *The Churches and the Soviet Union* (New York: Macmillan, 1962), p. 169; Pakina, *Raskol Evangelskikh Khristian-Baptistov*, p. 27.

[228] *Izvestiya* (News) (6 July 1963); Conquest, *Religion in the USSR*, p. 49.

were singing, and their typically minor key reflected the historical difficulties of the community.

All the aforementioned features of the Soviet Baptist mode of life formed a very effective and practical 'survival theology', much of which was found in the moderate Baptist communities of the AUCECB. The outworking of this in personal life, wider church life, in local congregations and in families all helped to ensure the preservation of thousands of evangelical communities in the officially atheistic USSR.

God's and Caesar's Kingdoms

The Soviet Baptists, in defending their faith and churches, not only operated in legal ways, but also quite often in a way that infringed upon Soviet legislation. This raises the difficult question: how far can a Christian submit to atheistic State laws? It seems that both the moderate and radical lines of Baptist resistance were important in the early 1960s. After the dismissal of Khrushchev at the end of 1964, the situation relating to religion in the country changed appreciably. By 1966, the fact that there were only fifty Baptists in prison indicated a better situation. One should remember that there were several hundred thousand Soviet Baptists at that time. Comparison needs to be made with Stalin's reign of terror; his millions of victims included many thousands of Baptist activists. The government of Leonid Brezhnev started a more pragmatic religious policy in the USSR. Under the new circumstances, the radicalism, and even extremism, of a part of the Russian Baptists became a significant obstacle in the way of a reasonable adjustment of the relationship between the State and the churches. If during a delicate armistice with an enemy, some soldiers refuse the call to display self-control and try to pick a quarrel, provoking the enemy to continue fighting, such soldiers are usually punished and not named as heroes—even if they were brave. It seems that the religious situation in Brezhnev's period of Soviet history was relatively good; indeed it could be compared with the 1920s when the majority of evangelical Christians enjoyed even more liberties than in Tsarist Russia.

Looking at the history of the relationships between the Church and earthly kingdoms from the apostolic age onwards, it is possible to conclude that a system of government, however flawed, is a lesser evil than anarchy. So, the Baptist commitment to the strict separation of Church and State, which was a feature of the Soviet Baptists, is doubtless not as harmless as it seems at first sight. Throughout Church history, this view has often opened the door to sectarianism and 'Christian' extremism. Churches can collaborate positively with the authorities in solving many social and humanitarian problems. Of course this can also run the danger of the so-called Constantinian relationship between the powers-that-be and the Church, where the latter becomes only an appendage of the State.[229] To prevent this, it is arguable that the Church should pursue a 'moderate' and relatively independent course between the extremes. Freedom on earth, including the freedom of the Church, cannot be absolute; it is always restricted by the freedom of our neighbour.

Of course, when the atheistic State in the USSR meddled tactlessly in Church affairs, the blood of some Baptists, and not just young people, started to boil.[230] At the beginning of the 1930s, the famous Russian minister and theologian, I. Kargel, who was then 80 years of age, wrote to the board of the Leningrad community of Evangelical Christians, who were asking him to fill in a form demanded by the authorities:[231]

> Let us look attentively to the form... The whole of it is conformed to this world... It would...be terrible for you if your father were an officer in the tsarist army, and on the contrary you were blessed if your father were in the Red Army. And the biggest sorrow is if your parents or you, yourself, were landowners. That is the unpardonable sin... I imagine with horror how the Leningrad [church] community comes to break bread with membership cards received after the filling of the forms.[232]

Such feelings on the part of Soviet believers are completely understandable. But the question arises again: what was the alternative to humiliating submission to the authorities during the periods of persecution? To be sure, there was martyrdom. But can every church member be a martyr or can a very large church exist underground? The conflict of the Soviet State with the Baptists revolved around the problem of the observance of legislation on religious affairs. The laws themselves were not all repressive. But, as always, there were problems with their interpretation. G. Vins quoted the following involuntary communist admission: 'There are written and unwritten laws. We live mainly by the unwritten laws. These are laws of communism and materialism... The written laws...are not for you, Baptists, but for the foreign

---

[229] In this sense, the words of the pre-revolutionary Russian national anthem *God, Save our Tsar* were remarkable. D. Pospelovsky describes the Russian 'symphony': the State punished citizens because of their religious crimes, and the Church anathematized the enemies of the Tsar. (D. Pospelovsky, *Totalitarizm i Veroispovedanie* (Totalitarianism and Religion) (Moscow: Bibleysky Institut Sv. Apostola Andreya, 2003), p. 634).

[230] See, for instance, some resolute expressions on the subject in *Ob Osvyashchenii* (On Sanctification) (Sovet Tserkvey ECB: 1990), p. 75; G. Kryuchkov, 'Ya s Vami, Govorit Gospod' in *Vestnik Istiny* 3-4 (1991), p. 15.

[231] This famous *Letter of Kargel to Zhidkov* was used widely by radical Baptists in the 1960s. See, for instance: 'Reshenie Orgkomiteta po Voprosu Protivotserkovnoy Deyatel'nosti VSEHB', *The AUCECB Archives*, papka 28, doc. 77; Kovalenko, *Oblako Svideteley Khristovykh*, p. 53.

[232] See text of the letter in Supplements to Kovalenko, *Oblako Svideteley Khristovykh*, pp. 229-230.

countries... Let them read our Constitution and wonder how much liberty of conscience we have!'[233] The radicals of the CCECB refused to obey Soviet anti-religious laws: 'We need freedom to preach the Gospel. We need independence of the churches.'[234] That was practically impossible in the 1960s and 1970s, but the CCECB was stubborn, fighting against both the State religious laws and the AUCECB due to its submission to the legislation. The radicals stated: "We must obey God rather then men' (Acts 5:29)... The answer of Peter to the Sanhedrin must be the basis of our attitude towards the authorities... If all believers did this, including the ministers of the AUCECB, they would not find themselves in today's sad condition.'[235] The defenders of the AUCECB responded, "Who are we? You are not grumbling against us, but against the Lord' (Ex. 16:8)... The brothers from the AUCECB...have no power to change the State laws. They were not invited to the legislatures. Nobody asked their advice.'[236]

The majority of the Soviet Baptists in this period of great internal strain backed the moderate line of the AUCECB. By 1970, more than 10,000 brethren had left the CCECB and had returned to the official Union.[237] The improvement of relationships between the State and the religious communities since 1965 helped to foster this process. At the same time, the gentle policy of the AUCECB recognized all ordinations of deacons and presbyters that had been made in the CCECB, as the ancient Church did with the Donatist priests,[238] promoting the return of all churches and groups associated with the radical Baptists to the official Union.[239]

Unfortunately, besides the rejection of religious legislation, some doubtful theological innovations had appeared in the CCECB:

1. There was a distinction between the 'saved churches' (the unregistered communities of the CCECB) and 'perishing churches' (the registered communities of the AUCECB), which undermined the evangelical teaching that personal salvation is by faith in Christ.[240]

---

[233] Vins, *Gorizonty Very*, p. 18.

[234] G. Kryuchkov, 'Ya s Vami, Govorit Gospod' in *Vestnik Istiny* 3-4 (1991), p. 16. A picturesque preacher from the radicals once gave me the following reason against registration: 'Christ comes to take His Church, but she has already registered her marriage with the State... Of course, He will repudiate such a church! Would you be pleased if your bride registered her marriage with another man?'

[235] *Vestnik Spaseniya* 2 (1966), pp. 33-34.

[236] Kuz'min, *Chastichny Analiz 'Bratskogo Listka' za 1975 g. po Sluchayu Desyatiletiya so Dnya Vypuska,* lists 35-36.

[237] *Istoriya Evangelskikh Khristian-Baptistov v SSSR,* p. 249.

[238] See rule 68 of the Carthaginian Council (V c.). (*Pravila Pravoslavnoy Tserkvi* (Moscow: Otchy Dom, 2001) II, pp. 220-221).

[239] *Bratsky Vestnik* 6 (1966), p. 71.

[240] *Bratsky Vestnik* 5 (1971), pp. 70-71; *Istoriya Evangelskikh Khristian-Baptistov v SSSR,* p. 243.

2. The CCECB had a kind of Episcopal system instead of traditional Baptist congregationalism with its affirmation of the role of independent communities.[241]
3. The CCECB had a perfectionist teaching on holiness and a practice of 'purifying' the communities with mass excommunications when there was disloyalty to the CCECB.[242]
4. Connected with the previous point, the CCECB introduced confession to a minister ('spiritual father'), a practice taken from the Orthodox Church but without the strict observance of the confidentiality of the confession obligatory for Orthodox priests.[243]

Unfortunately, such teachings pushed the Russian Baptist Unions towards forming two different denominations rather than towards the desired unity. In this sense, the Baptists were weakened by the Soviet communists.

The last wave of repression against the believers in the USSR started in 1979, when all 'East-West' policies of détente were renounced and the notable decree of the Central Committee of the Communist Party of the Soviet Union, *On the Further Improvement of Ideological and Political-Educational Works*,[244] was issued in April of that year. The decree again called the members of the Communist Party and Komsomol to struggle against the 'religious prejudices' in Soviet society.[245] As always, some of the lines of the Party decree written in Moscow created sizable troubles in the provinces: hundreds of religious activists (including Baptists) were imprisoned in Brezhnev's last years and during the short periods of the leadership of Y. Andropov (1982-1984) and K. Chernenko (1984-1985).[246] The repression ceased in 1985-1986 when the new Soviet leader M. Gorbachev began his memorable policies of *Glasnost'* and *Perestroika*. In 1988, the Soviet government welcomed the splendid celebration of the Millennium of the first baptisms in Russia, and that event apparently signified the end of the 'seventy year captivity' of Christianity in the USSR.

---

[241] This was the assessment made by the 'moderate camp' (See Savinsky, *Istoria Evangelskikh*, p. 221) and also some radical leaders themselves, including G. Vins (See Kuksenko, 'Nashi Besedy', pp. 48-49, 70). It is remarkable that the AUCECB was criticised by the Initiative Group because of the violation of the principle of the independence of communities at the beginning of the 1960s; but when the situation in the official Union took a turn for the better, CCECB leadership came to exert an even stricter dictatorship over its churches.

[242] *Ob Osvyashchenii*, p. 57; Kuksenko, 'Nashi Besedy', pp. 50-51.

[243] Kuksenko, 'Nashi Besedy', pp. 50-51; A. Koni, 'Tayna Ispovedi', in *Hristianstvo* (Encyclopaedia of Christianity) 3, (Moscow: Bol'shaya Rossiyskaya Entsiklopediya, 1995), pp. 7-8.

[244] *Nastol'naya Kniga Ateista*, p. 433.

[245] Ibid.

[246] *Amnesty International Report 1982* (London: Amnesty International Publications, 1982), p. 298; Walters, *A Survey of Soviet Religious Policy*, p. 27.

Conclusion

This study has attempted to look at some aspects of the history of the relationship of the Soviet State and Baptist communities in the period of leadership of the country by N. Khrushchev and L. Brezhnev, a crucial period in Soviet Baptist life. The government of Khrushchev, pursuing the cause of building the communist society in the near future, tried to do what it could to eradicate religious communities in the USSR. The Soviet Baptists, directly or indirectly, in moderate and in more radical ways, seriously resisted the official atheistic pressure and the activities of the Baptists were seen by the authorities as constituting a reason for stopping widespread persecution against believers. It was against this background that the next Soviet government (of Brezhnev) mainly avoided adopting violent means of acting against believers, focusing rather on the atheistic education of children in Soviet schools. But a strain of Baptist radicalism continued during Brezhnev's period, hindering a reasonable adjustment of the relationship between the State and the churches. In analyzing the situation, this study has examined the political realities of the 1960s and 1970s in the USSR, as well as the peculiarities of the position of the official Baptist Union and the underground communities, the Initiative Group, which responded in different ways to the official State policy on religion. The painful split of the Russian Baptists, in which the AUCECB lost members to the CCECB, has been analysed by including the atheistic point of view, the perspective of the official Baptist Union, the thinking of the unregistered Baptists, and comments from Western and Russian historians, have all been included. Information from different sources helps to depict this complicated picture, a picture which is not always favourable for the Soviet Baptists. Some unpublished documents from the archives of the All-Union Council of Evangelical Christians-Baptists in Moscow and some previously unknown local Central Asian and Siberian sources have been used. These have helped to achieve a better understanding of the tension of the situation and the causes of radicalism on the part of Soviet Baptists. The conflict of the State with Baptists in the 1960s and 1970s was chiefly based on the negative reaction of the latter to Soviet legislation on religious affairs. Both main groups of Soviet Baptists played an important part, it has been argued, although in different ways, in the survival of the churches. However, the radicals opened the door to sectarianism and 'Christian' extremism. The policy of the moderate majority of evangelical communities in the atheistic context, which allowed them to survive as they did, has been seen in this study to be an alternative to Baptist radicalism.

Bibliography

Unpublished

'80-letniy Jubiley Pervoy Almatynskoy Tserkvi EHB 'Golgofa' (The 80th Anniversary of the First Almaty Church of ECB 'Calvary'). *Almaty Baptist Church Archives* (1997).

Alperov, V., 'Istoricheskiy Ocherk Vtoroy Almatynskoy Tserkvi' (Historical Essay on the Second Almaty Church). *Almaty Baptist Church Archives* (1996).

Borisov, I., 'Istoria Tserkvi g. Osh' (History of the Osh Church). *Osh Baptist Church Archives* (2001).

Kondratiev, V., 'Voin Hristov' (Warrior of Christ). *Diplomnaya Rabota* (Almaty: Almaty Bible Institute, 2001).

Nikolaev, O., 'Protestantskie Ob'edineniya Orenburzh'ya: Istoriya, Sovremennoe Sostoyanie, Vzaimootnosheniya s Gosudarstvom' (The Protestant Associations of the Orenburg Region: History, the Present, and Their Relationship with the State). *Diplomnaya Rabota* (Moscow: Rossiyskaya Akademiya Gosudarstvennoy Sluzhby pri Prezidente Rossiyskoy Federatsii, 1999).

Pakina, A., 'Raskol Evangelskikh Khristian-Baptistov 1961 g. i Ego Vliyanie na Obshchiny Novosibirskoy Oblasti' (The 1961 Year Split of the Evangelical Christians–Baptists and Its Influence on the Communities of the Novosibirsk Region). *Diplomnaya Rabota* (Novosibirsk: Novosibirsky Gosuniversitet, 2000).

Plett, I., 'Istoriya Bratstva EHB s 1905 po 1944 Gody' (The History of the Baptist Brotherhood from 1905 to 1944). *Kazakhstan's Baptist Union Archives* (2001).

Sinichkin, A., 'Istoriya ECB v SSSR s 1959 po 1966' (The History of the ECB in the USSR from 1959 to 1966). *Diplomnaya Rabota* (Moscow: Moskovskaya Bogoslovskaya Seminariya ECB, 2001).

Sysoev, B., 'Istoria Evangelskogo Dvishenia v Karagande i Karagandinskoy Oblasti' (The History of the Evangelical Movement in Karaganda and Karaganda Region). *Kazakhstan's Baptist Union Archives* (2001).

Primary

Arkhiv Rossiyskogo Soyuza Evangel'skikh Khristian-Baptistov, Arkhiv VSEHB (The Archives of the Russian Union of the Evangelical Christian-Baptists (*The AUCECB Archives*)).

Avvakum, *Zhitie Avvakuma i Drugie Ego Sochineniya* (Life of Avvakum and His Other Writings) (Moscow: Sovetskaya Rossiya, 1991).

Istoriya Kostanayskoy Tserkvi EHB (Chronicle of the Baptist Church of Kostanay) (Kostanay: n.p., 1998).

Istoriya Petropavlovskoy Tserkvi EHB (Chronicle of the Baptist Church of Petropavlovsk) (Petropavlovsk: n.p., 1998).

Istoriya Vozniknoveniya i Rosta Hkristianskihk Obshchin v Omskoy Oblasti (The History of Origin and Development of Christian Communities of the Omsk Region) (Omsk: n.p., 1993).

Konstitutsiya (Osnovnoy Zakon) Soyuza Sovetskikh Sotsialisticheskikh Respublik (The Constitution of the USSR) (Moscow: Politizdat, 1977).

Kuksenko, Yu., 'Nashi Besedy' (Our Conversations). *Kazakhstan's Baptist Union Archives* (2002).

Kuz'min, V., 'Chastichny Analiz 'Bratskogo Listka' za 1975 g. po Sluchayu Desyatiletiya so Dnya Vypuska' (Partial Analysis of 'Fraternal Leaflet' of 1975 on the Tenth Anniversary of its Issue). *The AUCECB Archives*, papka 28, document 46.

'Letter of Instructions for the Senior Presbyters'. *Novosibirsk Baptist Church Archives* (1960).

Materials of the Special Twenty-first Congress of the Communist Party of the Soviet Union (Moscow: Politizdat, 1959).

Materials of the Twenty-second Congress of the Communist Party of the Soviet Union (Moscow: Politizdat, 1961).

Materials of the Twenty-fifth Congress of the Communist Party of the Soviet Union (Moscow: Politizdat, 1976).

'Mesta Naibol'shego Vliyaniya Orgkomiteta' (The Districts Come under the Great Influence of the Orgkomitet). *The AUCECB Archives*, papka 28, document 67.

'O Nedopustimosti na Bogosluzheniyakh Strunnykh Orkestrov, Peniya Solo, Duetov, a Takzhe Neogranichennogo Chisla Propovednikov' (On Inadmissibility of Using String Orchestras, Solo and Duet Singing as Well as Many Preachers during Worship). *The AUCECB Archives*, papka 1\1, document 33.

O Religii i Tserkvi. Sbornik Dokumentov (On Religion and Church: Collected Documents) (Moscow: Politizdat, 1965).

O Religii i Tserkvi. Sbornik Dokumentov (On Religion and Church: Collected Documents) (Moscow: Politizdat, 1981).

Ob Osvyashchenii (On Sanctification) (Sovet Tserkvey ECB: 1990).

'Otvet na Antireligioznuyu Stat'yu 'Ne Bud'te Trupom Sredi Zhivykh'' (Answer to the Antireligious Article 'Do Not Be Dead Among the Living'). *The AUCECB Archives*, papka 28, document 61.

'Pis'mo Prezidiuma VSEHB Vsem Presviteram Obshchin EHB v SSSR, 1953' (Letter of the Presidium of the AUCECB to All Presbyters of Baptist Communities of the USSR, 1953). *The AUCECB Archives*, papka 1, document 1/64.

'Polozhenie o Soyuze Evangelskikh Khristian-Baptistov v SSSR: Initsiativnaya Gruppa' (Statutes of the Union of Evangelical Christians–Baptists of the USSR: the Initiative Group). *The AUCECB Archives*, papka 28, document 2-5.

'Polozhenie o Soyuze Evangelskikh Khristian-Baptistov v SSSR: VSEHB' (Statutes of the Union of Evangelical Christians–Baptists of the USSR: the AUCECB). *The AUCECB Archives*, papka 28, document 52.

'Protokol 7, Soveshchanie Orgkomiteta Tserkvey ECB 23.06.1962' (Record of Proceedings 7, The Meeting of the Orgkomitet of Churches of ECB of 23.06.1962). *The AUCECB Archives*, papka 28, document 78.

Po Puti Vozrozhdeniya (On the Way of the Revival) (Sovet Tserkvey ECB: 1989).

Podrazhayte Vere Ikh, 40 Let Probuzhdyennomu Bratstvu (Imitate Their Faith: The Fortieth Anniversary of the Revival Brotherhood) (Sovet Tserkvey ECB: 2001).

Prava Cheloveka. Osnovnye Mezhdunarodnye Dokumenty (Human Rights: the Fundamental International Documents) (Moscow: Mezhdunarodnye Otnosheniya, 1989).

'Reshenie Orgkomiteta po Voprosu Protivotserkovnoy Deyatel'nosti VSEHB' (Decision of the Orgkomitet Regarding the Anti-Church Activity of the AUCECB). *The AUCECB Archives*, papka 28, document 77.

'Zapis' 63, Zasedanie Malogo Plenuma VSEHB 26.12.1959' (Record of Proceeding 63, The Meeting of the Closed Plenum of the AUCECB of 26.12.1959). *The AUCECB Archives*, papka 22, document 11.

Author's Interviews With

Fast I. (Shchuchinsk, Kazakhstan, 2003).
Frisen V. (Petropavlovsk, Kazakhstan, 2000).
Hot'ko V. (Petropavlovsk, 2001).
Kolesnikov N. (Moscow, 2001).
Kulyaev V. (Bishkul', Kazakhstan, 2003).
Meleshkevich Ya. (Bishkul', 2002).
Shatokhin I. (Petropavlovsk, 2002).

Reference

Bercot, D. (ed.), *A Dictionary of Early Christian Beliefs* (Peabody: Hendrickson Publishers, 1998).

Hristianstvo, Entsyklopedichesky Slovar' (Encyclopedia of Christianity), 3 vols. (Moscow: Bol'shaya Rossiyskaya Entsiklopediya, 1995).

Pravila Pravoslavnoy Tserkvi (The Rules of The Orthodox Church), 2 vols. (Moscow: Otchy Dom, 2001).

Prokhorov, A. (ed.), *Sovetsky Entsiklopedichesky Slovar* (The Soviet Encyclopedia) (Moscow: Sovetskaya Entsiklopediya, 1982).

Secondary

Aksyutin, Yu. (ed.), *L.I. Brezhnev: Materialy k Biografii* (L.I. Brezhnev: Materials to His Biography) (Moscow: Politizdat, 1991).

Aleshkovsky, Yu., *Antologiya Satiry i Yumora Rossii 20 Veka (Anthology of Twentieth Century Russian Satire and Humour)* (Moscow: Eksmo-Press, 2000).
Antonova, O., *Pod Maskoy Svyatosti* (Under the Mask of Holiness) (Omsk: n.p., 1962).
Bach, M., *God and the Soviets* (New York: Thomas Y. Crowell, 1958).
Baker, A., *Religion in Russia Today* (Nashville: Southern Publishing Association, 1967).
Beeson, T., *Discretion and Valour: Religious Conditions in Russia and Eastern Europe* (Glasgow: William Collins Sons, 1974).
Belov, A., *Lzhenastavniki Yunoshestva. O Deyatel'nosti Khristianskikh Sekt* (False Teachers of the Young People: On the Activity of Christian Sects) (Moscow: Pedagogika, 1973).
_____, *Mnimoe Bratstvo* (Sham Brotherhood) (Moscow: n.p., 1976).
_____, *Sekty, Sektantstvo, Sektanty* (Sects, Sectarianism, and Sectarians) (Moscow: Nauka, 1978).
_____, Shilkin, A., *Religiya v Sovremennoy Ideologicheskoy Bor'be* (Religion in the Contemporary Ideological Struggle) (Moscow: Politizdat, 1971).
Bolotov, V., *Lektsii po Istorii Drevney Tserkvi* (Lectures on the History of the Ancient Church), 4 vols. (Moscow: Spaso-Preobrazhensky Valaamsky Stavropigialny Monastyr', 1994).
Bolshakoff, S., *Russian Nonconformity* (Philadelphia: Westminster, 1950).
Bourdeaux, M., *Faith on Trial in Russia* (New York: Harper & Row, 1971).
_____, *Opium of the People: The Christian Religion in the USSR* (London: Faber and Faber, 1965).
_____, *Religious Ferment in Russia: Protestant Opposition to Soviet Religious Policy* (London: Macmillan, 1968).
Bourdeaux, M. and H. Hebly, (eds.), *Religious Liberty in the Soviet Union* (Keston Book 7, n.d.).
Bourdeaux, M. and K. Murray, *Young Christians in Russia* (London: Lakeland, 1976).
Brodsky, I., *Pis'ma Rimskomu Drugu* (Letters to Roman Friend) (Saint Petersburg: Azbuka-klassika, 2001).
Budov, A., *Religioznye Illuzii na Poroge Zhizni* (Religious Illusions on the Threshold of the Life) (Moscow: Molodaya Gvardiya, 1980).
Chekhov, A., *Izbrannye Sochineniay* (Selected Works), 2 vols. (Moscow: Khudozhestvennaya Literatura, 1986).
Conquest, R., *Religion in the USSR* (London: The Bodley Head, 1968).
D'Arcy, M., *Communism and Christianity* (Aylesbur: Penguin Books, 1956).
De Grunwald, C., *God and the Soviets* (London: Hutchinson & Co, Ltd, 1961).
_____, *The Churches and the Soviet Union* (New York: Macmillan, 1962).
Dudko, D., *O Nashem Upovanii* (On Our Hope) (Korntal: Svet na Vostoke, 1974).
Fast, V., *Ya s Vami Vo Vse Dni do Sconchaniya Veka* (I Am With You Always, To the Very End of the Age) (Karaganda—Steinhagen, n.p., 2001).
Fedorenko, F., *Sekty, Ikh Vera I Dela* (Sects, Their Beliefs and Deeds) (Moscow: Politizdat, 1965).
Filimonov, E., *Baptizm i Gumanizm* (Baptists and Humanism) (Moscow, 1978).

_____, *Hkristianskoe Sektantstvo i Problemy Ateisticheskoy Raboty* (Christian Sectarianism and the Problems of Atheistic Work) (Kiev: Politizdat Ukrainy, 1981).

Fletcher, W., *The Russian Orthodox Church Underground, 1917-1970* (London: Oxford University Press, 1971).

_____, *Religion and Soviet Foreign Policy, 1945-1970* (London: Oxford University Press, 1973).

Fletcher, W. and A. Strover, (eds.), *Religion and the Search for New Ideals in the USSR* (New York: Praeger, 1967).

Furman, D., (ed.), *Na Puti k Svobode Sovesti* (On the Way to Liberty of Conscience) (Moscow: Progress, 1989).

Gordienko, N., *Osnovy Nauchnogo Ateizma* (The Principles of Scientific Atheism) (Moscow: Prosveshchenie, 1988).

Gutsalov, Yu., *Ya Otvergayu* (I Reject) (Alma-Ata: n.p., 1962).

Hebly, J., *Protestants in Russia* (Belfast: Christian Journals Ltd, 1976).

Hutten, K., *Iron Curtain Christians: The Church in Communist Countries Today* (Minneapolis: Augsburg, 1967).

Istoriya Evangelskikh Khristian-Baptistov v SSSR (History of Evangelical Christians-Baptists of the USSR) (Moscow: VSEHB, 1989).

Iwanow, B., (ed.)., *Religion in the USSR* (Munich: Institute for the Study of the USSR, 1960).

Kalinicheva, Z., *Sotsial'naya Sushchnost' Baptizma* (Social Nature of Baptist Life) (Leningrad: n.p., 1972).

Kerns, E., *Dorogami Khristianstva* (Christianity through the Centuries) (Moscow: Protestant, 1992).

Klibanov, A. and L. Mitrokhin, *Krizisnye Yavleniya v Sovremennom Baptizme* (The Crisis of the Modern Baptists) (Moscow: n.p., 1967).

_____, *Religioznoe Sectantstvo i Sovremennost'* (Religious Sectarianism Today) (Moscow: Nauka, 1969).

_____, *Religioznoe Sektantstvo v Proshlom i Nastoyashchem* (Religious Sectarianism in the Past and Present) (Moscow: Nauka, 1973).

Kolyvantsev, A., *V chem Zhivuchest' Baptizma* (Why Baptist Life is Still Alive), in *Razum Protiv Religii* (Mind Against Religion) (Leningrad: n.p., 1965).

Komm, A., *Mrakobesy bez Maski* (Obscurants without Masks) (Maykop: n.p., 1960).

Kosukha, P., *Modernizatsiya Sovremennogo Khristianskogo Sektantstva* (Modernization of Contemporary Christian Sectarianism) (Kiev: n.p., 1967).

Kovalenko, L., *Oblako Svideteley Khristovykh* (The Cloud of Witnesses of Christ) (Kiev: Tsentr Hristianskogo Sotrudnichestva, 1997).

Kuroedov, V., *Religiya i Zakon* (Religion and the Law) (Moscow: Znanie, 1970).

Lawrence, J., *Russians Observed* (London: Hodder and Stoughton, 1969).

Lyalina, G., *Baptizm: Illuzii i Real'nost'* (Baptists: Illusions and Reality) (Moscow: Politizdat, 1977).

Medvedev, R., *N.S. Khrushchev: Politicheskaya Biografiya* (N.S. Khrushchev: Political Biography) (Moscow: Kniga, 1990).

Mitrokhin, L., *Baptism: Istoriya i Sovremennost'* (Baptists: History and the Present) (Saint-Petersburg: Russky Khristiansky Gumanitarny Inst., 1997).

_____, *Baptizm* (Baptists) (Moscow: Politizdat, 1966).

_____, *Baptizm i Sovremennost'* (Baptists Today) (Moscow: Politizdat, 1964).

Moskalenko, A., *Ideologiya i Deyatel'nost' Khristianskikh Sekt* (Ideology and Activity of Christian Sects) (Novosibirsk: Nauka, 1978).

My Byli Baptistami (Sbornik) (We were Baptists (Collection of life stories)) (Moscow: n.p., 1960).

Nastol'naya Kniga Presvitera (The Handbook of Presbyter) (Moscow: VSECB, 1982).

Nikiforov, A. and F. Sim, *'Podryazhayutsya Voyti Skvoz' Tesnye Vrata'* (They Make Every Effort to Enter Through the Narrow Door) (Petropavlovsk, 1985).

Nikolin, A., *Tserkov i Gosudarstvo* (Church and State) (Moscow: Sretensky monastyr', 1997).

Ogryzko, I., *Deti i Religiya* (Children and Religion) (Leningrad, 1970).

Pascal, P., *The Religion of the Russian People* (London: Mowbrays, 1976).

Pismannik, M., *Lichnost' i Religiya* (Personality and Religion) (Moscow, 1976).

Pollock, J., *The Faith of the Russian Evangelicals* (New York: McGraw-Hill, 1964).

Pospelovsky, D., *Pravoslavnaya Tserkov v Istorii Rusi, Rossii i SSSR* (The Orthodox Church in the History of the Old Russia, Russia and the USSR) (Moscow: Bibleysky Institut Sv. Apostola Andreya, 1996).

_____, *Totalitarizm i Veroispovedanie* (Totalitarianism and Religion) (Moscow: Bibleysky Institut Sv. Apostola Andreya, 2003).

Pravda o Sektantstve (The Truth about Sectarianism) (Leningrad: n.p., 1963).

Problemy Izucheniya i Kritiki Religioznogo Sektantstva (The Problems of Studies and Criticism of Religious Sectarianism) (Moscow: Nauka, 1971).

Prokhorov, K., 'Bozh'i Puti' (God's Ways) in *Sektantskie Rasskasy* (Sectarian Stories) (Idar-Oberstein: Titel-Verlag, 2002).

Prokoshina, E. and M. Lensu, (eds.), *Baptizm i Baptisty: Sotsiologichesky Ocherk* (Baptism and Baptists: Sociological Essay) (Minsk: Nauka i Tehknika, 1969).

Reshetnikov, Yu. And S. Sannikov, *Obsor Istorii Evangelsko-Baptistskogo Bratstva na Ukraine* (The Historical Review of the Ukrainian Evangelical-Baptist Brotherhood) (Odessa: Bogomyslie, 2000).

Safronova, N., *Reaktsionnoct' Misticheskikh Idey Sovremennogo Christianskogo Sektantstva* (Reactionary Character of Mysticism of Contemporary Christian Sectarianism) (Lvov: n.p., 1975).

Savinsky, S., *Istoria Evangelskikh Khristian-Baptistov Ukrainy, Rossii, Belorussii, 1917-1967* (The History of the Evangelical Christian-Baptists of Ukraine, Russia, and Byelorussia, 1917-1967) (Saint-Petersburg: Biblia Dlya Vsekh, 2001).

Serdobol'skaya, L., *Sektantstvo i Sem'ya* (Sectarianism and Family) (Leningrad: Znanie, 1976).

Shkarovsky, M., *Russkaya Pravoslavnaya Tserkov pri Staline i Khrushcheve* (The Russian Orthodox Church under Stalin and Khrushchev) (Moscow: Krutitskoe Patriarshee Podvor'e, 1999).
Simon, G., *Church, State and Opposition in the USSR* (London: C. Hurst & Company, 1974).
Skazkin, S. (ed.), *Nastol'naya Kniga Ateista* (The Handbook of Atheists) (Moscow: Politizdat, 1983).
Smirnov, P., *Istoriya Khristianskoy Pravoslavnoy Tserkvi* (The History of the Christian Orthodox Church) (Moscow: Krutitskoe Patriarshee Podvor'e, 1998).
Sneider, I., *O Tserkvi Dorogoy, Sobranii Dush Shivyh* ('About Dear Church, the Meeting of the Alive Souls') (Herford: Aktuell Druck GmbH, 1996).
Solov'ev, S., *Chteniya i Rasskazy po Istorii Rossii* (Lecturing on the Russian History) (Moscow: Pravda, 1990).
Solzhenitsyn, A., *Lenin: Tsyurikh—Petrograd (Lenin: Zurich—Petrograd)* (Ekaterinburg: U-Faktoriya, 2001).
_____, *Odin Den' Ivana Denisovicha* (One Day in the Life of Ivan Denisovich) (Moscow: Novy Mir, 1990).
_____, 'Velikopostnoe Pismo Patriarhu Pimenu' (The Lenten Letter to Patriarch Pimen) in *Russkaya Pravoslavnaya Tserkov v Sovetskoe Vremya, 1971-1991* (The Russian Orthodox Church at the Soviet Times, 1971-1991), G. Shtrikker (ed.) (Moscow: Propilei, 1995).
Soplyakova, L., *Slova i Dela Evangelskikh Khristian-Baptistov* (Words and Deeds of the Evangelical Christians–Baptists) (Tashkent: n.p., 1961).
Struve, N., *Christians in Contemporary Russia* (New York: Charles Scribner's Sons, 1967).
Suglobov, G., *Venchaetsya Raba Bozhiya* ('The Servant of God Is Wedding') (Moscow: Politizdat, 1959).
Terskoy, A., *U Sectantov* (Among Sectarians) (Moscow: Politizdat, 1965).
Thrower, J., *Marxist-Leninist 'Scientific Atheism' and the Study of Religion and Atheism in the USSR* (Berlin: Mouton Publisher, 1983).
Tsvetogorov, E., *Sektanty i Chto Oni Propoveduyut* (Sectarians and Their Preaching) (Novosibirsk: n.p., 1960).
Vins, G., *Evangelie v Uzakh* (The Gospel in Bonds) (Elkhart: Russian Gospel Ministries, 1991).
_____, *Gorizonty Very* (Horizons of Faith) (Elkhart: Russian Gospel Ministries, 1994).
Voprosy Istorii i Teorii Ateizma: Sovremennoe Sektantstvo (Studies on the History and Theory of Atheism: Contemporary Sectarianism) (Moscow: AN SSSR, 1961).
Voslensky, M., *Nomenklatura: Gospodstbuyushchy Klass Sovetskogo Soyuza* (Nomenclature: The Ruling Class of the Soviet Union) (Moscow: Sovetskaya Rossiya, 1991).
Walters, P., *A Survey of Soviet Religious Policy* in *Religious Policy in the Soviet Union*, S. Ramet, (ed.) (Cambridge: Cambridge Univ. Press, 1993).
Zavatski, V., *Evangelicheskoe Dvizhenie v SSSR Posle Vtoroy Mirovoy Voyny* (Soviet Evangelicals Since World War II) (Moscow: n.p., 1995).

Yakovlev, V., *Formirovanie Nauchnogo Mirovozzreniya i Khristianskoe Sectantstvo* (Forming of the Scientific Outlook and Christian Sectarianism) (Alma-Ata: n.p., 1965).

Periodicals

Bratsky Listok (Fraternal Leaflet) 1-3 (1975).
_____ 4 (1981).
Bratsky Vestnik (Fraternal Bulletin) 3-4 (1955).
_____ 1 (1963).
_____ 5 (1966).
_____ 6 (1966).
_____ 2 (1968).
_____ 2 (1970).
_____ 5 (1970).
_____ 3 (1971).
_____ 5 (1971).
_____ 6 (1972).
_____ 4 (1974).
_____ 5 (1974).
_____ 1 (1975).
_____ 1 (1979).
Byulleten' Soveta Rodstvennikov Uznikov Evangelskikh Khristian-Baptistov v SSSR 17 (Bulletin of the Council of Prisoners' Relatives of the Evangelical Christians-Baptists of the USSR 17) (Moscow, 1974).
_____ 21 (Moscow, 1975).
_____ 22 (Moscow, 1975).
_____ 23 (Moscow, 1975).
_____ 24 (Moscow, 1975).
Ezegodnik Muzeya Istorii Religii i Ateizma (The Year-book of the Museum of History of Religion and Atheism) 6 (1962).
Izvestiya (*News*). (20 December 1959).
Izvestiya (6 July 1963).
Khristianskaya Gazeta Kuzbassa (The Christian Newspaper of Kuzbass) 1 (2003).
Komsomol'skaya Pravda (The Komsomol Truth). (2 June 1989).
Krokodil (Crocodile) (20 February 1960).
Literaturnaya Gazeta (Literary Newspaper) (21 June 1989).
Nauka i Religiya (Science and Religion) 7 (1966).
_____ 9 (1966).
_____ 1 (1968).
_____ 6 (1971).
Novy Mir (New World) 11 (1962).
Poslednie Dni (The Last Days) 1 (2000).
Pravda (The Truth) (6 December 1959).
Religion in Communist Dominated Areas IX:23-24 (1970).
_____, XIV:7, 8, and 9 (1975).

_____, XVIII:7, 8, and 9 (1979).
Slovo Very (Word of Faith) 1 (2001).
_____ 2 (2002).
Vestnik Istiny (Bulletin of the Truth) 1 (1984).
_____ 4 (1988).
_____ 3-4 (1991).
_____ 1 (2000).
_____ 1 (2001).
_____ 2 (2001).
_____ 2 (2002).
_____ 3 (2001).
Vestnik Spaseniya (Bulletin of Salvation) 3 (1965).
_____ 2 (1966).
_____ 1 (1973).
Voprosy Filosofii (Studies on Philosophy) 2 (1964).
_____ 10 (1964).
Voprosy Istorii Religii i Ateizma (Studies on History of Religion and Atheism) 11 (1963).
Voprosy Nauchnogo Ateizma (Studies on Scientific Atheism) 3 (1967).
_____ 4 (1967).
Zhizn' Very (Life of Faith) 3 (2001).

CHAPTER 2

Separation or Co-operation?
Moldavian Baptists (1940-1965)

Irina Bondareva-Zuehlke

The period since the end of the 1980s has been a period of new freedom in post-Soviet countries. Newly formed independent republics of the former USSR have been looking for a new identity. This process directly relates to religious institutions as they, too, search for their identity. However, this process involves not only new challenges, but also an understanding of the historical dimension. The records that enable an understanding of the history of the Moldavian Union of Evangelical Christians–Baptists are only now being analysed. The present study is an attempt to explore and understand more fully the complicated situation of the Baptist churches in Bessarabia/Moldavia, and specifically in the Moldavian Soviet Socialist Republic (MSSR). This was the name during the years of the USSR while—roughly speaking—before 1940 the area had another name: Bessarabia.[1] The study concentrates on the period 1940-1965, from World War II until the years of the emergence of the Reform Baptists (known as *Initsiativniki*—the Initiative Group) and the split in the All-Union Council of Evangelical Christians–Baptists in the USSR in the early 1960s.

The Moldavian Baptists had similar experiences to Baptists in many other newly formed Soviet Republics after World War II. They faced the urgent need to adjust their life and their practices to the new political situation. All the changes that took place—political, social, demographic and religious—shaped Moldavian Baptist life in general and the local churches in particular; including their teaching, practices, and everyday Christian living. The new socio-political circumstances constituted a powerful factor in determining the life of the nation and of the evangelical churches within it. The purpose of this work is to analyse the circumstances that helped to shape the Baptist movement in Moldavia

---

[1] I will be using the name Moldavia which was the name throughout the period covered in this study. Today the country has the name Moldova.

during the above mentioned period and to show in detail the influence of these circumstances on Moldavian Baptists.

The political situation has played a considerable role in the development of the life and theology of the Evangelical Christian-Baptist (ECB) churches in Moldavia from their beginnings. The story of Bessarabia/Moldavia is the story of 'going back and forth' between Russia and Romania.[2] For a long period, Bessarabia was a province of the Russian empire (1812–1918), then it was under the Romanian king (1918–1940), and then once more it was under the Soviet Union (1940–1941). During the period of World War II it was under the Romanians again, and from 1944 until 1991 it was one of the Soviet Republics. Since 1991 the country has manifested independence and is called Moldova. For Baptists in Bessarabia/Moldavia relationships with the state have been complicated. In 1944 Evangelical Christians and Baptists were merged into the All-Union Council of Evangelical Christians–Baptists (AUCECB) and this raised the question of what policy should be adopted towards the USSR: 'strict separation' or 'co-operation between church and state?' Moldavian Baptists were brought into deep conflict over this issue.

The study discusses the constant political pressure that was exerted on Moldavian Baptist churches in the period 1940-1965 through state repression, restrictive religious laws, and work of the Council for the Affairs of Religious Cults (CARC), represented in Moldavia by its Commissioner. As a result of these pressures, there was considerable decline in Baptist churches. For example, in 1933 the Bessarabian Baptist Union had 238 churches.[3] In 1940, the Moldavian Evangelical Christians-Baptists (the successor body—to be referred to as Baptists) had only 108 churches,[4] and in 1949 the authorities registered only 83.[5] Fourteen years later, in 1963, the number of churches was even smaller—only 71.[6] One of the tasks of the present work is to point out the causes for the diminished numbers of Baptist churches. An evaluation of the relationships between the AUCECB and Moldavian Baptists will also be offered. A key question to be considered is whether the AUCECB was seen by Moldavians as an agent of state pressure or as a genuine Baptist partner.

While gathering the material and investigating the documents the author encountered some specific difficulties. Baptists in present-day Moldova do not have any archive in the formal sense of the word. Many documents have been lost. Fortunately, the present bishop of the Baptist Union, Valeriu Giletchi, has

---

[2] See Irina Bondareva, 'Baptist Origins and Early Development in Moldova', *Journal of European Baptist Studies*, 2:3 (2002), pp. 31-44.

[3] Walter Craighead, 'The Gospel in Bessarabia', *Home and Foreign Fields* (April 1935), p. 10.

[4] V. Pasat, ed., *Trudnye Stranitsy Istorii Moldavii 1940-1950-e gody* (Hard Pages in the History of Moldavia) (Moscow: Terra, 1994), p. 601.

[5] Ibid.

[6] *National Archives of the Republic of Moldova* [hereafter *NARM*], File [hereafter F] 3305, Inv. 1, D. 90, pp. 210-213.

gathered some documents, memoirs and manuscripts that will, it is hoped, be the beginning of a Union archive. Another obstacle has been that in some cases the information gathered through interviews conducted with old members of the Baptist churches included contradictory statements. These had to be evaluated in the light of other sources and of data relating to the general situation. Also, I myself have a mixed spiritual background: I was converted in a Baptist Union (AUCECB) church, but was baptised in an Independent Baptist church (formerly a Reform Baptist church). Thus, maintaining objectivity has been challenging.

My research has made extensive use of the archive materials of the Commissioner of the Council for the Affairs of Religious Cults in the Moldavian SSR, now available at the National Archives. A mass of statistical data about the number of Baptist churches and their membership, and about closed churches, as well as numerous senior presbyters' reports sent to the CARC, are found in these files, which are open to researchers for the first time. Not all of that data could be utilised here; only the most interesting and important items for the present study. In addition, the oral history project that was started in areas of the former Soviet Union (including the Republic of Moldova) in 1996 by Walter Sawatsky provided me with some interviews conducted with those who lived through the events explored here. A project initiated by the professors of Church History of the College of Theology and Education in Chisinau (the capital of Moldova) was also very helpful for this research. Within the framework of this project, the college students were encouraged to gather information about their local churches. It should also be mentioned that Valeriy Pasat, a Moldovan historian, has edited a collection of archive documents, gathered at the main KGB archives in the Russian Federation and the Republic of Moldova, that directly relate to the years 1940-1965 in Moldavian history. Most of these documents were used in the present work.

The number of secondary sources written on Baptist history in Moldavia is very limited. This work is probably the first systematic attempt in English to introduce the story of the post-war Moldavian Baptists and their relationships with the Soviet State. However, there were some volumes that contained valuable insights and comments relevant to the present work. In Russian, the history of the Moldavian 'Baptist brotherhood' has been described to a certain extent in *Istoriya Evangel'skikh Khristian-Baptistov v SSSR*.[7] V. Schemchischin, in his dissertation *Zarozhdenie I Razvitie Evangel'sko*

---

[7] *Istoriya Evangel'skikh Khristian-Baptistov v SSSR* (A History of Evangelical Christians-Baptists in the USSR) (Moscow: All-Union Council of Evangelical Christians-Baptists, 1989).

Baptistskogo Dvizheniya v Bessarabii,[8] partially touches upon the issue of Moldovan Baptist development in the first years after World War II. Also, *Evangelicheskoe Dvizhenie v SSSR posle Vtoroy Mirovoy Voyny* by Walter Sawatsky,[9] first published in English, provided valuable information, as well as *Obzor Istorii Evangel'sko-Baptistskogo Bratstva na Ukraine* by Y. Reschetnikov and S. Sannikov.[10] The early stages of Baptists in Moldavia have been covered in my article 'Baptist Origins and Early Development in Moldova' in the *Journal of European Baptist Studies*. Some chapters from Charles King's work, *The Moldovans*,[11] insightfully explain the social, political and economical difficulties that Moldavia went through after its forced unification with the USSR. Additionally, Trevor Beeson's volume *Discretion and Valour* is helpful in offering a perspective on Soviet Evangelicals.[12] Antireligious materials published in the 1940s and the 1950s have helped to create a fuller picture of the relationship between Baptists and Soviet society. These documents are eloquent and often speak volumes in themselves.

This study analyses the tensions created by different approaches among Moldavian Baptists towards church-state relationships, touches upon the state pressure on the churches to conform to Soviet restrictive religious policies and explores the role of the Baptist headquarters in Moscow in the processes that took place in Moldavia. There were attempts to maintain unity between Moldavian Baptists as a whole and the AUCECB, as well as between registered and unregistered churches; however, the atheistic measures taken by state authorities, the authoritarian leadership style that became characteristic of Baptist leaders and the inability of those with different viewpoints about 'co-operation or separation' in relation to the Soviet State to resolve their differences caused major problems for Baptist churches in post-war Moldavia. As well as investigating the wider picture, this study also looks at the issue of 'unity and diversity' at the local church level, as local churches were inevitably affected by the wider issues that produced such serious tensions.

---

[8] V. P. Schemchishin, *Zarozhdenie I Razvitie Evangel'sko-baptistskogo Dvizheniya v Bessarabi* (The Origins and Development of Evangelical Baptist Movement in Bessarabia) (unpubl. PhD thesis, Kiev: Kiev Theological Seminary, 1998).

[9] W. Sawatsky, *Evangelicheskoe Dvizhenie v SSSR Posle Vtoroy Mirovoy Voyny* (Soviet Evangelicals Since World War II), N.A. Kornylov, trans. (first published in Kitchener, Ontario: Herald Press, 1981; republished in Moscow, 1995).

[10] Y. Reschetnikov and S. Sannikov, *Obzor Istorii Evangel'sko-Baptistskogo Bratstva na Ukraine* (A Review of the History of the Evangelical Baptist Brotherhood in Ukraine) (Odessa: Bogomyslie, 2000).

[11] C. King, *The Moldovans: Romania, Russia and the Politics of Culture* (Stanford, Calif.: Hoover Institution Press, 1999).

[12] T. Beeson, *Discretion and Valour, Religious Conditions in Russia and Eastern Europe* (Glasgow: Collins, 1974).

Political Pressure on Baptist Churches in Post-war Moldavia

During the period 1918 to 1940 Moldavian Evangelical Christian-Baptist churches saw considerable growth. The publication *Link* states that during this period the number of Baptists grew from 42 persons to almost 14,000.[13] Before World War II, the Evangelical Christians–Baptists in Bessarabia had a strong Union. This was formed in 1918,[14] when Moldavia moved from being under Russia to being under the Romanian king, though officially the Union began to function in 1920.[15] This Union was a member of the All-Romanian Union of Baptist Churches, but it worked fairly independently.[16] In 1921 it became a part of the Baptist World Alliance.[17] Though Baptists experienced difficulties and even severe persecution during this Romanian era, the Russian re-conquest of Moldavia, in which it was taken from the Nazis by the USSR in 1944, introduced a period of constant political pressure. Baptists in the Moldavian Republic suffered, as Albert Wardin notes, the same restrictions and atheistic pressures as other religious groups in the USSR.[18] Moldavian ECB churches had to join the All-Union Council of Evangelical Christian-Baptists, with its headquarters in Moscow. Though opposed by the State and Orthodox Church authorities before World War II, the Moldavian Baptists had maintained relative freedom. Now they had almost completely lost their autonomy. But joining the AUCECB was the only option if they were to function legally.

However, political pressure meant much more than losing autonomy; it meant living with atheistic measures, imprisonment of church members, restricted rights for believers and deportation. Evangelical believers were affected by several deportations: the eviction of Germans to Germany in 1940, and the deportation of 'anti-Soviet elements' and *kulaks* (the Russian term for a peasant who could afford to hire labour and often acted as village money-lender) in 1941 as well as in 1945-1948. In 1949 the eviction of 'undesirable elements' was carried out under the code name 'Operation South', and in 1951 'sectarian elements' were expelled from Moldavia. Also, the famine of the years 1946-1947 and the collapse of old traditional ways of life and values[19]

---

[13] 'Bessarabia', *Link* 24 (1940), p. 3.

[14] C.A. Brooks and J.H. Rushbrooke, *Baptist Work in Europe*, Report of Commissioners of the Baptist World Alliance, presented at the Conference in London, 19 July 1920 (London: Baptist Union Publication Department, 1920), p. 51.

[15] *Istoriya Evangel'skikh*, p. 383.

[16] Peter Trutza, 'A Short History of Romanian Baptists', *The Chronicle* 5:1 (1942), p. 13.

[17] Craighead, 'Gospel in Bessarabia', p. 10.

[18] A.W. Wardin, ed., *Baptists Around the World* (Nashville: Broadman and Holman, 1995), p. 228.

[19] See V. Pasat, *Golod v Moldove* (Hunger in Moldova) (1946-1947) (Kishinev, 1993); 'Deportatsii iz Moldovy' (Deportations from Moldova), *Svobodnaya Mysl'* (Free Thought) 3 (1993).

caused both membership losses and a loss of morale for Moldavian Baptists. Baptists suffered not only a loss of freedom as believers, but also a loss of identity as members of Moldavian society. In the 1940s, the region was converted into one of the Soviet Socialist Republics, with a political leadership that supported the line of Moscow. Thus the whole nation had to submit to new legislation and new orders, and experience the violent tensions of political change. Baptist believers were among those groups of people that the Soviet system considered 'alien' and on the other hand the Soviet system was alien to the Baptists of Moldavia. This double alienation was to have far far-reaching consequences.

Formation of the Moldavian Soviet Socialist Republic

The Soviet period in Moldavia had, in some ways, already begun in August 1939 when Germany and the Soviet Union signed the so-called Molotov-Ribbentrop pact. In the secret protocols of the pact 'Germany declared its lack of political interest with respect to the fate of Bessarabia and implicitly acknowledged the Soviet Union's claims on the region'.[20] Less than a year later, on 26 June 1940, the Soviet government issued an ultimatum to the Romanian minister in Moscow demanding the immediate cession of Bessarabia to the USSR, for 'Bessarabia had a population that was "for the most part Ukrainian"'.[21] That was not true. Nevertheless, the Romanian King Carol II, urged on by Italy and Germany, accepted Moscow's demands. Two days later 'Soviet troops crossed the Dnester River and occupied Bessarabia'.[22]

Formally the MSSR was formed on 2 August 1940.[23] The Soviet government wanted to show this as an act of liberation of the Moldovans, or as the newspaper *Izvestiya* argued at the time, it was the 'peaceful policy of the USSR' that had 'liquidated the Soviet-Romanian conflict' from Bessarabia forever.[24] Some evangelical believers, such as Vasily Davny, agreed with the view that 'Bessarabia was joined to the Soviet Union peacefully'.[25] This was

---

[20] King, *Moldovans*, p. 91.
[21] Ibid., p. 92.
[22] Ibid.
[23] The Republic included Kishinev city as well as Beltsky, Bendersky, Cahulsky, Kishinevsky, Orgeevsky and Soroksky counties. In additon the Grigoryopolsky, Dubossarsky, Camensky, Rybnitsky, Slobodzeisky and Tiraspolsky regions were added to the Republic, and also Tiraspol city. A narrow strip of territory east of the Dnestr that had never been part of Bessarabia was added to the new MSSR.
[24] Quoted in King, *Moldovans*, p. 93.
[25] V. Davnyy, *Istoriya Vozniknoveniya I Razvitiya Evangel'sko-baptistskogo Dvizheniya v Moldove* (A History of the Origins and Development of the Evangelical Baptist Movement in Moldova) (unpubl. memoirs, Chisinau, 2000). On the whole I have made my own translation of Russian language sources.

also the opinion of *Bratskiy Vestnik* (Brotherly Messenger), the periodical of the AUCECB.[26] It was not, however, the case. According to King's research 'as many as 90,000 fell in the wave of repression and deportations that immediately followed the annexation'.[27] Among them were many Baptists and other evangelical believers. Baptists in Moldavia were drawn into unprecedented turmoil and confusion. Turmoil continued: in late July 1941, Romanian and German troops took Bessarabia and Bukovina, and the area was joined with Romania once again. However, this proved to be a short interlude of three years. In August 1944 both Bessarabia and northern Bukovina came under Soviet occupation, and the peace treaty established the Soviet-Romanian border along the Prut River. The re-established Moldavian Socialist Republic had a population of 2.4 million, of which 68.8 percent were Moldavians.[28]

The Soviet Constitution promised '*equal* and guaranteed political, economical and personal rights' to *all* citizens.[29] However, the reality was that believers were often deprived of personal rights and were restricted politically and economically. For example, pastors and other church workers had to pay higher taxes than did other citizens.[30] They could not be members in collective farms (*kolkhoz*).[31] Pastors were not allowed to work outside the churches, because of the state's fear of religious propaganda in the work place. The formation of the MSSR brought Moldovan Baptists into a new era. The Soviet authorities established strict control over churches, and the state's policy was oriented toward reducing church membership numbers. The war and the political changes broke up the normal relationships between churches and even between church members. Migration of Baptist members took place and imprisonment added to the problems Baptists faced. Membership numbers declined drastically.

Decline in Membership and Fragmentation

During the first ten years of the Sovietisation of Moldavia the membership of Baptist churches declined by approximately two-thirds. As has already been mentioned, in 1940 there were 14,000 Baptists and by 1949 the number had

---

[26] A.I. Mitskevich, 'Vospominaniya o Vozniknovenii Dela Gospodnego v Moldavii' (Remembering the Origins of God's Work in Moldavia), *Bratskiy Vestnik* 2 (1955), pp. 53-57. *Bratskiy Vestnik* included news as well as articles about life in local churches and unions, spiritual and worship materials, sermons, and historical information.

[27] King, *Moldovans*, p. 93.

[28] Ibid.

[29] Pasat, ed., *Trudnye Stranitsy*, pp. 9-10.

[30] NARM, F. 3305, Inv. 1, D. 82, p. 84.

[31] NARM, F. 3305, Inv. 1, D. 55, pp. 28-31, 37, 46-48; NARM, F. 3305, Inv. 1, D. 40, pp. 75-78.

fallen to just 4,795 members in total.[32] There were several reasons why membership numbers began to decline immediately after the Soviet period began. Most of these causes are related to the repressive Soviet policies toward minority social and ethnic groups. Valeriy Pasat, in attempting to explain why the Soviet authorities carried out deportations and other forms of repression in Moldavia, has emphasised that the Soviet authorities were led by their idea of social 'selection'. He states: 'In the social practice of the Soviet government it meant cleansing the society from *alien elements* which prevent or could prevent the building of a 'pure' socialist society'.[33]

Many evangelical believers were condemned as *kulaks* or were portrayed as *alien elements* in the society—people who, it was alleged, held to anti-Soviet ideology. Often believers were exiled to Siberia. The authorities left the population in no doubt about their goals. According to Marxist atheistic ideology, 'religion, whatever its limited past virtues, is one aspect of man's lack of freedom. It is one of the unfortunate consequences of a corrupt economic order which, at many different levels, binds men in chains'.[34] This was the kind of atheistic rhetoric that was used to justify the repression of believers. Moreover, the Moldavian SSR was a frontier region of the USSR that had to be especially 'clean', to avoid any possible collaboration with outside agencies that might aid the intervention of the enemies of the USSR.

Unfortunately we only know a few names of Baptist believers who were subjected to suppression. Grigoriy Tentiuc, a Baptist writing in 1998, has pointed out that many Christians in Bessarabia were trying to deal with the Soviet authorities at a time when they were already feeling worn down by pressures they had been under during the period of Romanian rule. For example, there was a fully-functioning Romanian concentration camp in the village of Onesti during World War II. But compared to the Romanian policy, Soviet repression in the 1940s was more wide-scale and systematic. Tentiuc notes that 'Soviet authorities deported entire families of believers to Siberia'.[35] As early as June 1941 the Soviets made mass arrests of Moldavian Baptists, accusing them of being 'anti-Soviet elements'.[36] Baptists lost many of their pastoral leaders, such as Andrey Ivanov, Lidia Caldararu, Mihail Tarlev, and others. Also, Boris Bushilo (1893-1942), a pastor in Kishinev, and for many years the Executive Secretary of the Bessarabian Baptist Union, was arrested. They were usually sentenced to ten years imprisonment and exiled to the Tumen region. Before his arrest, Bushilo was advised to leave for Romania, but he refused, saying: 'I am a pastor and how will I answer to God if I leave my

---

[32] *NARM*, F. 3305, Inv. 1, D. 5, pp. 63-99.
[33] Pasat, ed., *Trudnye Stranitsy*, p. 11.
[34] Beeson, *Discretion and Valour*, p. 19.
[35] Grigoriy Tentiuc, 'Tropoyu Muzhestva', *Svet Zhizni* 4 (1998), p. 10.
[36] Schemchishin, 'Zarozhdenie I Razvitie', p. 51.

flock and escape?'[37] In 1942, Peter Trutza reported: 'Our brethren were scattered in 1940 by the Soviets, being sent into interior Russia...'[38]

In 1940 the Soviet government organised the forced departure of Germans from Moldavia to Germany.[39] The communists took these measures in agreement with the German government. According to the published documents, more than 124,000 Germans from 161 colonies were sent out of Moldavia and northern Bucovina. It was in fact the forced departure of a whole nation, carried out by the Soviet secret service forces (NKVD), though it was called an evacuation or a migration.[40] The Germans who somehow managed to remain in Moldavia were deported to the Asian or the northern parts of the USSR in 1941, as far as possible from the Soviet borders. The number of evangelical churches decreased considerably because of the migration of thousands of Germans. In Bessarabia, as Trutza notes, 'by 1940 these [German] churches had grown to thirty with 1,185 members, including the children of actual members'.[41] Now most of these German church buildings were empty.

In 1949 there was another wave of repression. A contemporary witness said: '...from our village 19 families were taken away, in Milesti, 21 families. Women and children were taken too. Houses are empty. They [the authorities] have said that these people were *kulaks*, but they did not have even a cat... No one is sleeping at home now, every house is closed, the village is empty, no one is singing...a real desert...'[42] The eviction of anti-Soviet contingents touched also the so-called 'sectarians'. Among 'illegal sects' there were unregistered Baptist groups.[43] Their continued presence proves that persecution could not totally destroy the Baptist movement in Moldavia. However, Baptists were scattered around the country and Baptist groups became more fragmented. For example, in the Ceadir-Lunga church, Constantin Ivancev served as a pastor from 1936 till 1949.[44] In 1949 he was banished to the Curgan region with his entire family.[45] Sometimes believers, under the fear of persecution, moved to other locations. A Baptist inhabitant of Romanovca village, Vasiliy Izikhovich, declared: 'It is necessary to change my place of residence, I am selling my property...'[46] The Baptist movement was suffering decline and fragmentation.

---

[37] Ibid., p. 52
[38] Trutza, 'Short History', pp. 12-13.
[39] See Pasat, ed., *Trudnye Stranitsy*, pp. 65-138.
[40] Germans understood that to stay in Bessarabia meant to suffer as a member of a foreign nation.
[41] Trutza, 'Short History', pp. 12-13.
[42] Pasat, ed., *Trudnye Stranitsy*, p. 499.
[43] 'Bessarabia', *Link*, p. 3.
[44] *Svet Zhizni* 3 (1997), p. 5.
[45] *NARM*, F. 3305, Inv. 1, D. 39, p. 32.
[46] Pasat, ed., *Trudnye Stranitsy*, p. 508.

Famine and Migration

There was another factor that aggravated the situation. In 1945-1947 catastrophic starvation tested the ability of the country to survive. This situation was partly created by the new Soviet authorities since they opened hundreds of commercial centres of their own and took all the supplies of farm production away from the Moldavian population. In addition, these were years of drought and bad harvest. The food situation was extremely severe and affected especially the peasant population. People were dying in villages, on the roads and in the cities and the human toll from the famine was estimated as between 150,000 and 200,000 persons dead.[47] King comments: 'The Soviet invasion of 1940, the Romanian and German operation of 1941, and the Soviet reconquest in 1944 had laid waste to the Bessarabian countryside and uprooted hundreds of thousands of average Bessarabians'.[48] The famine worsened the situation.

Some Baptist churches were weakened or ceased to function altogether because of the migration of their members to better regions in search of food. For example, due to starvation, the Baptist church in Chislita-Prut disintegrated and later the congregation joined the Giurgiulesti church.[49] As a result of Soviet repression and the famine of 1945-1947 Moldavian Baptists not only lost many of their church members but also many of their leaders who had given a sense of unity to the Baptist movement in the country. All this increased the fragmentation among Baptists. This certainly was in accordance with the intentions of Soviet religious policy, and it seemed that the churches did not have a way of coping.

Leonid Brezhnev, who served as first secretary of the Communist Party in the MSSR during 1950-1952, later reflected that in the new republic of Moldavia the Sovietisation process had to take place within a much shorter period of time than in republics that had been part of the Soviet Union since the 1920s. 'These remote *raions* [districts] lying along the Dnestr,' he wrote, 'had to break through to socialism by the shortest possible path.'[50] Translated into blunt language, this meant drastic measures against the local population. These measures, coupled with the factors outlined, meant that in Moldavia there were fewer churches within the Baptist community with each succeeding year.

Applying Soviet Religious Laws in Moldavia

The Soviet legislative system concerning religion was adopted in Moldavia in a very short period. Two of the central documents that controlled religious life all

---

[47] Ibid., p. 31.
[48] King, *Moldovans*, pp. 95-96.
[49] *NARM*, F. 3305, Inv. 1, D. 5, p. 71.
[50] King, *Moldovans*, p. 95.

over the USSR were 'The Separation of the Church from the State and Schools from the Church' (1918) and 'About Religious Societies' (1929). On 1 March 1929 the All-Union Central Soviet of Trade Unions issued a Circular Letter 53, 'About the Reinforcement of Antireligious Propaganda' that pointed to the 'necessity of reinforcement of ideological struggle with religious ideology', and that referred specifically to the problematic issue of 'the development of the Baptist church, and evangelical teaching...'[51] The evidence is that this directive received the same rigid interpretation in the MSSR in the 1940s as had previously been the case in other parts of the USSR in the 1930s, a period which is considered one of the most severe in terms of atheistic pressure.

The law prohibited mission and religious propaganda by the churches, as well as the sharing of material help among co-religionists, the formation of mutual aid funds, cooperatives and communes, and religious meetings of children, youth and women.[52] One of the characteristics of Moldavian Baptist churches was their passion to help others, thus supporting an atmosphere of fellowship and building bridges to their fellow countrymen. Baptists had nursing homes, for example. In the new political situation they were not allowed to do this—at least not in any organised form. Atheistic policies, which were often carried out by the Baptist leadership under pressure from the state, marginalised Baptists even more than they were marginalised before World War II. In Mikhailovka village, Singerei district, for example, Baptist church members were instructed by Senior Presbyter, Frol Astakhov, not to continue collecting 'freewill offerings for the needs of the poor and orphans'.[53] Also, preaching outside of church walls was considered to be a violation of the law.

It should be noted that based on and connected with the above mentioned laws there were many other regulations and orders: the Order for Opening the Churches (1943), The Order for the Opening of Prayer Houses of Religious Cults (1944), the Order for Taxation of Ministers of Religious Cults (1946).[54] All of these regulations changed many times during the years but the repressive aim of the regulations remained unchanged. In many cases, the state authorities tried to use the AUCECB and its representatives in Moldavia to force these restrictive laws on believers and control the religious situation. Evangelical Christians-Baptists especially felt the pressure when the Communist Party began to emphasize new strategic aims at the end of the 1950s and at the beginning of the 1960s. The Soviet power openly charted a course for overcoming religion and applied additional administrative measures. In 1961

---

[51] V. I. Lubaschenko, *Istoriya Protestantizmu v Ukraine: Kurs Lektsiy* (Kiev: Polys, 1995), from Electronic Christian Library 'History of the Euro-Asian Evangelical Movement: Primary Sources' (EAAA: 2001).

[52] 'O Religioznykh Ob'edineniyakh' in section 'Normativnye Akty po Voprosam Deyatel'nosti Religioznykh Organizatsiy', from Electronic Christian Library 'History of Euro-Asian Evangelical Movement: Primary Sources' (EAAA: 2001).

[53] *NARM*, F. 3305, Inv. 1, D. 40, p. 75.

[54] *NARM*, F. 3305, Inv. 1, D. 82, p. 84.

the Council for the Affairs of Religious Cults approved 'Instruction According to the Application of Legislation of Cults'.[55] Among numerous prohibitive steps, the registration of several 'sects' was clearly refused. These groups— Jehovah's Witnesses, Pentecostals, Seventh-Day Adventists 'and so forth'— were accused of 'activities of an anti-state and fanatical character'. This indefinite wording, 'and so forth', allowed the instruction to be applied to Baptists.

Regarding religious law, the Moldavian SSR simply followed the legislation of the USSR. The Presidium of the Supreme Council or the Council of Ministers of the Moldavian SSR 'did not issue any legal statements regulating the status of religious cults'.[56] However, the laws issued in Moscow were followed strictly, without any attempt being made to adjust these for the local situation. These restrictive laws were aimed, among other things, at isolating Christians from the rest of the society and helping the state to control religious life. A special organisation, the Council for the Affairs of Religious Cults, was created by the Soviet government in order to keep an eye on churches. New registration of churches, accompanied by the wave of church closures, was to aid the state in achieving its atheistic goals. The political pressures on the Baptists were intense, and the Baptist churches found that to a large extent they were unable to cope.

Council for the Affairs of Religious Cults: Registration and Closure of Churches

In July 1944 the Soviet government formed the Council for the Affairs of Religious Cults (CARC) in order to regulate the relationships between the State and religious organisations, with the exception of the Orthodox Church. For Orthodox Church affairs another organisation was formed. The Council for the Affairs of Religious Cults also had control of the application of Soviet policies regarding religion.[57] The first chairman of the CARC was Ivan Polyanskiy. He oversaw the work of Commissioners who worked in the Soviet Republics and the larger regions. The Commissioners were often professional Soviet security service officers.[58] In addition, CARC had to prepare religious laws and issue decrees and instructive letters to help resolve questions in the field of religion at

---

[55] Schemchishin, 'Zarozhdenie I Razvitie', p. 64.
[56] *NARM*, F. 3305, Inv. 1, D. 64, p. 22.
[57] 'Polozhenie o Sovete po Delam Religiy pri Sovete Ministrov SSSR' in section 'Normativnye Akty po Voprosam Deyatel'nosti Religioznykh Organizatsiy', *SALR*, F. 1332, Inv. 1, D. 37, p. 32; retrieved from the Electronic Christian Library 'History of the Euro-Asian Evangelical Movement: primary sources' (EAAA: 2001).
[58] Tat'yana Nikol'skaya, 'Kto Takie 'Otdelennye?', *Mirt* 5:30 (September-October, 2001).

the highest level, the level of the Council of Ministers.[59] However, CARC increasingly began to function as a means for applying the state policy of 'divide and rule' towards religious communities.

CARC and the AUCECB Commissioner in Moldavia

Sergey Desyatnikov began to work as the Commissioner of CARC in the Moldavian SSR. His chief task was to organise the process of the legalisation and registration of the ECB churches. In several cases he suggested leadership changes in local churches. As S. Savinsky writes:

> The assignment and approval of presbyters or their dismissal was carried out according to the approval by the authorities (the Commissioners of CARC). The affirmation or dismissal of senior presbyters of AUCECB was held in that way, too. That was the direct interference of the state in internal affairs of the church. The interference in the affairs of the church seemed to run into absurdity, such as inserting amendments into the text of festive congratulations, in texts of spiritual songs, in repertoires of songs that were performed in worship meetings and in the spiritual articles published in *Bratskiy Vestnik*.[60]

In one of his reports, Desyatnikov emphasised the results of his work:

> At the present time the leadership of local churches has been renewed to a considerable extent: most reactionary presbyters were removed from office and replaced by followers of the 'new' course of the All-Union Council of Evangelical Christians-Baptists, controlled by the Council for the Affairs of Religious Cults.[61]

However, in many cases when a growing number of conformist presbyters began to work in local churches, the inner trust within these church communities was damaged.

The Commissioner of the CARC, Sergey Desyatnikov, worked closely with the Commissioner of the AUCECB, Ilia Ivanov, who first visited Moldavia in 1946. Ivanov gave detailed descriptions about the situation of the Moldavian churches to Sergey Desyatnikov. Some of these reports are quite shocking. In some cases Ivanov suggested changing the presbyters, in some cases he proposed refusing a church registration and in other cases recommended merging a church with a nearby community that would receive registration.[62]

---

[59] 'Polozhenie o Sovete po Delam Religiy'.
[60] Savinsky, *Istoriya Russko-Ukrainskogo Baptizma* (A History of Russian-Ukrainian Baptist Movement) (Bogomyslie: Odessa Theological Seminary, 1995), pp. 120-121.
[61] Pasat, ed., *Trudnye Stranitsy*, p. 602.
[62] See *NARM*, F. 3305, Inv. 1, D. 5, pp. 16-18, 38.

Some scholars, such as Trevor Beeson, have expressed surprise about 'the uncomfortably close relationship between the new All-Union Council and the body set up by the State to oversee the activities of all non-Orthodox religious bodies—the Council for the Affairs of Religious Cults'.[63] In 1948, Ivanov wrote to Desyatnikov:

> Slobozia [church] needs the same change of apparatus as in Kishinev in order to avoid further complications. Having this in view, I do not have the opportunity [i.e. I am not willing] to give sanction for registration of F. K. Verebchan as a minister of the cult.[64]

Ivanov's suggestion was intended to control more completely the local church and also to diminish the influence of Silvester Tsurkan, who was one of the active Moldavian pastors and whom Verebchan respected. Tsurkan's influence spread throughout the churches in the southeastern part of Moldova. Moreover, the Slobozia church was one of the most active churches in Moldavia. So Ivanov's suggestion is clearly orientated towards diminishing the influence of the church and its leadership role in the region. He was successful in weakening relationships between local churches. In the long-term perspective, the undermining of the authority of respected Baptist leaders also resulted in weakened spiritual and theological unity among Moldavian Baptists. This was to have dire consequences.

Registration of Baptist Churches

The registration of ECB churches began in the Moldavian SSR in 1946. Only properly registered churches could continue their existence legally. In spite of Soviet atheistic pressure, for many evangelical believers in the wider Soviet Union the two or three years immediately after the war were years of new hope, especially when compared to the 1930s. During the Stalinist pressure before the war almost all evangelical churches were closed. Now a Union of ECB churches in the USSR had been formed and it seemed that at local level a door for the congregational registration was opened. In some areas there were spiritual revivals. Savinsky, referring to the situation in Russia, writes: 'Joyful news was shared about new souls joining to the churches through baptism; the celebration of Easter, Whitsunday and Christmas were performed solemnly.'[65]

In Moldavia the situation was different. Before the war in Bessarabia more then two-hundred Baptist churches, with several hundreds of groups of believers, functioned even under the rigid Romanian pressure.[66] So, for

---

[63] Beeson, *Discretion and Valour*, p. 97.
[64] *NARM*, F. 3305, Inv. 1, D. 5, p. 38.
[65] Savinsky, *Istoriya*, p. 118.
[66] 'Bessarabia', *Link*, p. 3.

Moldavian Baptists the beginning of the socialist era was a turn for the worse, not the better. Under Romanian rule the ECB churches could meet freely if they had received registration at the Ministry of Religion in Bucharest. In order to receive this registration a church needed to give the surname, name and the father's name of the leader of the church. Thus the registration was not complicated. Registration after World War II was a far more difficult process and became a vicious circle. Multiple documents were demanded and church leaders often did not understand registration procedures. Moreover, several unregistered groups and churches were immediately closed by local authorities, though according to the official instructions 'the liquidation of religious societies is made...according to the resolutions of the Council of Ministers of the Republics, and coordinated in conformity with...the Council for the Affairs of Religious Cults'.[67] Years later, A. Mitskevich, the former member of the Presidium of the AUCECB in Moscow, who visited Moldavia on several occasions, concluded: 'Surely, those people had a determined program—not to develop, but somehow to extinguish.'[68]

According to the law, a religious society had to have at least 20 members, all at least 18 years old.[69] This minimum of 20 members came to be called *dvadtsatka*. Registration documents had to be signed by the *dvadtsatka*. Beside this, a great deal of additional information about church members and church leadership had to be sent to Kishinev in order to register the church.[70] For the opening of a house of worship, the documents were first sent to the local government, and then the papers moved forward to the Council of Ministers of Moldavian Republic.[71] In the end, all applications were sent to the CARC in Moscow, from where the local Commissioner received instructions. While the registration was in process believers were not allowed to come together. In this way the regular worship patterns, so important for Baptists, were destroyed. Some believers, however, continued to meet, even though it was illegal. Strict regulations and restrictions gave too many believers an impression that following Soviet laws and maintaining their religious identity was incompatible. They faced the dilemma: to choose to obey the regulations and compromise their faith or to disobey and keep their inner integrity?

---

[67] *NARM*, F. 3305, Inv. 1, D. 82, p. 73.
[68] N.A. Kornilov, 'Interview with Mitskevich', Project of Oral History 'Protestantism in the Former Soviet Union'; retrieved from the Electronic Christian Library 'History of the Euro-Asian Evangelical Movement: Primary Sources' (EAAA: 2001).
[69] 'O Religioznykh Ob'edineniyakh' in section 'Normativnye Akty po Voprosam Deyatel'nosti Religioznykh Organizatsii', *SALR*, F. 1332, Inv. 1, D. 37, p. 50; retrieved from the Electronic Christian Library 'History of the Euro-Asian Evangelical Movement: Primary Sources' (EAAA: 2001).
[70] *NARM*, F. 3305, Inv. 1, D. 71, pp. 75-76.
[71] 'O Religioznykh Ob'edineniyakh'.

Registration of the church and the use of a prayer house were linked with each other. If the church had no registration, it could not use the prayer house.[72] Or there could be another scenario: in the city of Bender, local authorities confiscated the prayer house and because of that church members were not allowed to gather.[73] After registration of the church, the prayer house and other property had to be handed over to the City or District Executive Soviet, as religious organisations were not allowed to own property. The property was then—in ideal cases—given back to the religious community to use on a rent-free basis with no fixed term.[74] Practically speaking, this was the nationalisation of all church property. It began in 1940, though it seems to have been delayed in Moldavia. In February 1946 the Commissioner Sergey Desyatnikov reported to the Chairman of CARC: 'After checking all documentary material...for 1940-1941, there is no data concerning the question of nationalization of the prayer houses...'[75] The Commissioner of CARC in the MSSR wrote in August 1945, referring to the early 1940s: '...for the nationalization of churches and prayer houses did not take place in Moldavian SSR'.[76] Nevertheless, after World War II this task was taken seriously. The prayer houses of ECB communities became state property. Often the congregations were not allowed to use their buildings, and the authorities suggested renting halls for meetings. Many local authorities ignored the formal requirement that questions related to the closing of church buildings should be decided at government level.

The authorities tried to legalise existing churches—at least to a certain extent. But the door was not open for new churches or new church buildings to emerge. The Commissioner of CARC received the following instruction:

> Take into account...that the existing network of the opened prayer houses can supply all believers and satisfy their religious needs, on account of that, the opening of new prayer houses...is not called by necessity and not dictated by political expediency.[77]

In cases where applications for opening new prayer houses were handed in, the registration procedure was especially dragged out by local authorities or by government bodies. This was done despite the fact that according to law, during a one-month period after the receipt of application, the Council of Ministers along with CARC had to register the community or to report news of the official rejection.[78] In cases where the application was delayed Baptists sent appeals to senior presbyters, local government officials, to the CARC, to the

---

[72] *NARM*, F. 3305, Inv. 1, D. 84, pp. 2, 5, 19, 21.
[73] *NARM*, F. 3305, Inv. 1, D. 83, pp. 11-13, 16-20.
[74] 'O Religioznykh Ob'edineniyakh'.
[75] *NARM*, F. 3305, Inv. 1, D. 2, p. 6.
[76] *NARM*, F. 3046, Inv. 1, D. 2, p. 50.
[77] Pasat, ed., *Trudnye Stranitsy*, p. 600.
[78] 'O Religioznykh Ob"edineniyakh'.

AUCECB, and even to the Council of Ministers. It seldom happened, however, that these churches were granted the desired registration. Growth was effectively stifled.

Underground Work as an Option

In addition to the fully-constituted ECB churches in Moldavia after World War II there were about four-hundred small groups,[79] often consisting of less than twenty people. These groups had two choices: legally to continue to function by joining a registered community (some ECB village churches included people from nine or ten villages[80]), or to gather without registration, i.e. illegally. As an example of those who chose the second option, believers in the villages of Kotovsk and Hirtop gathered without registration until 1950, when they finally decided to join the Sarata Mereseni church.[81] With rigid criteria for registration, the dragging out of the registration process and consistent refusal to register new churches, the government practically declared many Baptist churches and groups non-existent. This increased the number of illegal churches.

Ilia Ivanov personally played an important role in the registration of Baptist churches. He was a controversial figure: in some cases he suggested that churches should not be registered, while in other cases he protected existing churches. For example, when the registration of the church in Chioselia Mica was postponed, Ivanov reminded the Commissioner that:

> these facts distort the meaning of the Constitution of the USSR, especially in the attitude to the believers, who already were subjected to rigid repressions under Romanians and who were beaten and called communists. Informing you about the foregoing violations against freedom of religious cults, I am asking you to take urgent measures to influence the violators of the Constitution.[82]

Unfortunately, the AUCECB and its commissioner could not help every local Baptist church, and formally had no right to influence the decision-making process. It is also possible that in the 1940s the AUCECB did not foresee the backlash that was created against these processes due to the fact that many viable Baptist communities were deprived of the possibility to operate legally. In the majority of cases, these church communities did not choose 'underground life' themselves, but were forced to go this way.

At the same time, the difficulties of the registration processes diminished the number of legally operating churches. In addition, the Izmail region of Bessarabia, which in 1945 had approximately fifty Baptist churches with a total

---

[79] 'Bessarabia', *Link*, p. 3.
[80] *NARM*, F. 3305, Inv. 1, D. 50, p. 72.
[81] *NARM*, F. 3305, Inv. 1, D. 50, p. 40.
[82] *NARM*, F. 3305, Inv. 1, D. 5, pp. 7-8.

membership of two-thousand, was joined with the Ukrainian SSR.[83] They were thus 'cut off' from Moldavia and Moldavian Baptist life, even if some personal relationships continued. According to the present author's estimation, in 1945 the Moldavian Baptist Churches (without the Izmail region) numbered about 110 churches, not all of them registered.[84] In the archive files of the Commissioner of the CARC the official data is not given, though based on the reports of the Commissioner of the AUCECB in Moldavia, it is possible to calculate up to 115 churches.[85] However, there were many groups of Baptist believers that had not been organised as churches. In the *Istoriya Evangel'skikh Khristian-Baptistov v SSSR* it is said that in February 1946 there were eighty-eight registered Baptist Churches in Moldavia.[86] In 1950, Senior Presbyter Astakhov reported about seventy-eight Baptist church communities that had fifty-two presbyters, forty-one prayer houses and thirty-three choirs.[87]

Thus, at the end of the registration process in Moldavia, about eighty to eighty-five ECB churches had received legal status. Other churches and groups were either joined to registered churches or entered the category of illegal churches. With total disregard for the historical development and context of Moldavian Baptist communities, the state authorities either forced formal unity upon churches or created separation. After losing the Izmail region churches to Ukraine, the Moldavian Evangelical Christians-Baptist movement was weakened significantly. The AUCECB in many cases appeared to be helpless in supporting local churches. This diminished the AUCECB's influence and authority among Moldavian Baptists. The registration of churches practically came to a halt in Moldavia in 1948. Despite this, many 'underground' believers hoped that sooner or later their group would be registered, and in the 1950s many of them again tried to start an application process with CARC.

Closing the Churches

When the legalisation process for churches stopped in 1948, the reverse process had already begun. Or to put this in another way: when the registration of churches stopped, the closing of churches, which had already begun, continued. For example, in 1949 some of the Moldavian Baptist churches were closed without any reasons being given. In Tiraspol the prayer room was taken away

---

[83] Schemchishin, 'Zarozhdenie I Razvitie', p. 55. In 1939, there were approximately 120 Baptist churches in the Izmail region with a total membersip of nearly six thousand. During the war these numbers diminished significantly. The Izmail region was joined to Ukraine in May 1945.

[84] The information about these churches can be found in the archive files of the Commissioner of CARC. I have also used information received from oral history.

[85] *NARM*, F. 3305, Inv. 1, D. 5, pp. 7-55.

[86] *Istoriya Evangel'skikh*, p. 327.

[87] *NARM*, F. 3305, Inv. 1, D. 50, p. 61.

from the church. The church was deprived of registration and closed.[88] By 5 April 1949 the Moldavian SSR had eighty-three registered ECB churches.[89] If in 1945 there were approximately 115 Baptist churches,[90] then within four years more than thirty Baptist churches had either been refused registration, had closed, or had merged with some nearby registered churches. This was the case in the villages of Cairaclia, Cazaclia, Cubara, Falesti Noi, Clococeni de Jos, Tiraspol, and others. In September 1949 Emilian Bucov, the Vice-chairman of the Council of Ministers of Moldavian SSR, wrote a letter to the Chairman of CARC, accusing the Baptist church in Tataresti village of breaking Soviet legislation. He wrote:

> ...taking into account the fact that Tataresti village is the frontier, the Council of Ministers of MSSR considers it necessary to cancel the registration of the religious community of ECB in Tataresti village and to close the house of prayer.[91]

There are other examples of prayer houses being closed. One comes from the village of Novye Zazuleny. Older members remember:

> New local authorities came to the leadership of the church with a resolution to take away the building of the prayer house for a school. Local officials added: 'and your children [too] will study there, but [now] we do not have a school in the village'... So, the leadership of the church with pain in their hearts gave away the house of prayer.[92]

In a Bulgarian community in the village of Tarakliya the district executive committee took the prayer house and passed it on to a local barrel-maker's workshop.[93] Many appeals sent from church communities to the Commissioner of CARC show that Baptists were asking for help in getting back the houses of prayer taken by local authorities. Usually they got a refusal from CARC.[94] In the late 1940s, in the face of this policy, two kinds of churches appeared: registered and unregistered. Later, it was the unregistered groups that especially stood in opposition to the AUCECB.

---

[88] *NARM*, F. 3305, Inv. 1, D. 59, p. 11.
[89] Pasat, ed., *Trudnye Stranitsy*, pp. 601-602.
[90] *NARM*, F. 3305, Inv. 1, D. 5, pp. 7-55.
[91] Pasat, ed. *Trudnye Stranitsy*, p. 605.
[92] Denis Schuparsky, 'History of the ECB Church in Novye Zazuleny village' (unpubl. paper, Chisinau: College of Theology and Education, 2001).
[93] *NARM*, F. 3305, Inv. 1, D. 5, pp. 7-8.
[94] *NARM*, F. 3305, Inv. 1, D. 69, pp. 17-20. A church community in Maramonovca village appealed to the Council of Ministers of the USSR to get back their house of prayer which was illegally taken away by the village soviet authorities in 1947. The appeal was not granted.

It should be noted that in an atmosphere of general hostility, some local officials were friendly to believers, sometimes even trying to help them. For instance, in Congaz, in 1962, an ECB community could not obtain land on which to build a house for meetings. An official told the presbyter that their request would never be granted, but he tried to help, advising believers to build a house for a young family and to include a hall for worship services.[95] In the time of Nikita Khrushchev, however, 'many church buildings were closed or turned into store-rooms or museums...'[96] Dmitriy Ponomarchuk, the Senior Presbyter of the ECB in Moldavia from 1957, in his report to the Commissioner of CARC gives the exact number of Baptist churches closed in the years 1958-1961. According to this data, none of the ECB houses of prayer were closed in 1958; in 1959 a prayer house in Bender city was closed; in 1960 prayer houses in the villages of Suvorovka, Brejeni and Radoia were closed; and in 1961 four more prayer houses in the villages of Beshgioz, Semenovka, Hirtop and Pirlita were closed.[97] In addition to this, four rented meeting places that had been used by ECB groups were closed in 1960-1961 in the villages of Valeni, Ciuluk, Iscalau and Slobozia Mare.[98] As a result, feelings of helplessness and protest emerged in Baptist relationships with the authorities.

Khruschev's Campaign against the Believers

More should be said about Nikita Khrushchev's atheistic campaign and its influence in Moldavia. This 'brutal anti-religious campaign'[99] began in 1959 and was connected with fresh political hopes of building communism in the USSR. Anti-religious activities were intensified, since religion was seen as one of the main hindrances standing in the way of the society's march to communism. Sannikov asserts that the main ideological leader of the campaign was L. Ilichiov, who was the head of the Department of Propaganda and Agitation in the Central Committee of the Communist Party 1958-1959, and who from 1961 to 1965 occupied the post of Secretary of the Central Committee of ideological affairs.[100]

---

[95] Ivan Donchev, 'The Brief Historical Sketch of the Church in Kongaz Village' (unpubl. paper, Chisinau: College of Theology and Education, 2001).
[96] D.S. Russell, 'Church-State Relations in the Soviet Union: Recollections and Reflections on the "Cold War" Years', *The Baptist Quarterly* 36 (1995-1996), pp. 21-22.
[97] There are some more notes made in pencil on this document. The notes refer to five other prayer houses that were closed in 1961: in Suvorovka, Antonovka, Chobruchy, Slobodzeya and Talmazy.
[98] *NARM*, F. 3305, Inv. 1, D. 90, p. 193.
[99] Beeson, *Discretion and Valour*, p. 98.
[100] S.V. Sannikov, *Dvadtsat' Vekov Khristianstva* (Twenty Centuries of Christianity) 2 (Odessa, Saint Petersburg, 2001), p. 522.

The atheistic campaign was launched throughout the Soviet Union; and Moldavia was no exception. Besides communist party and government efforts, the KGB was also involved, using different techniques 'to struggle with the hostile activity of clerics and sectarians...' [101] On 8 January 1960, I. Savchenko, Chairman of the KGB in Moldavia, reported in his 'strictly confidential' report to Moscow:

> The Committee of State Security (KGB) at the Council of Ministers of Moldavian SSR in 1958-1959 carried out the agency-operative and prophylactic measures to stop the hostile activity of clerics and sectarians according to the orders of KGB at Council of Ministers of the USSR, the resolutions of party bodies and according to the concrete and operative situation in the republic.[102]

The document states that much attention was paid to measures limiting the work of 'clerics and sectarians'. The influence of 'sectarians'—which Baptists were considered to be—was diminished not only by closing prayer houses but also by attempts to break the local churches with the help of secret agents who carried out individual work with believers, for example by exerting pressure on them to become informers. More widely, radio, press and cinema were also used for atheistic propaganda.

The KGB document states that there were four tactical goals in Moldavia at the beginning of the 1960s for 'paralysing the influence of sectarians': (1) to infiltrate circles of church leadership and to destroy the organisational structure of 'sects' as well as to pull out groups of believers and corrupt them separately; (2) to use various methods to compromise the leaders of the churches and entire groups of believers; to create uncertainty, conflicts and suspicions; (3) to appeal to the wider society in the fight against sectarians; to work on believers on an individual basis; to condemn religious belief at the meetings of *kolkhoz* people as well as in factories and other institutions; and (4) in crucial matters to bring the leaders of sectarians to court.[103] The government's goal was to create tension and fragmentation inside the churches. This only proves the popular saying that in the Soviet Union the church was separate from the state, but the state was not separate from the church.

Many Moldavian Baptists saw and would still see the state pressure in spiritual terms. This was, for them, a spiritual battle. Many of them would have agreed with Walter Craighead, who in 1940 said that Moldavian Baptists would go through a struggle with the forces of atheism that 'at its worst will be fierce, but final victory to God's children is certain'.[104] The Bessarabian Baptists, who had endured Romanian persecution and had remained steadfast, would, the

---

[101] Pasat, ed., *Trudnye Stranitsy*, p. 651.
[102] Ibid.
[103] Ibid., pp. 651-658.
[104] Walter Craighead, 'The Soviet Invasion', *The Commission* 3:9 (October, 1940), p. 275.

believers considered, 'stand up to the next test of discipleship'.[105] What was not apparent was that 'the test of discipleship' would not only include state pressure, with which Baptists were familiar, but would also include pressure which some saw as compromise coming from within their own Baptist ranks. It is to the complicated relations between Moldavian Baptists and the All-Union Council of Evangelical Christians-Baptists that we now turn.

The AUCECB in Moldavia: 'Big Brother', Agent of State Pressure, or Partner?

In 1943-1944 the government of the Soviet Union permitted Evangelicals to re-establish their church structures and the suppressed and scattered ECB churches in the Soviet Union organised themselves once again. But the government demanded obedience and collaboration in return for this permission. In October 1944 the unification of the Soviet Evangelical Christians-Baptists took place at a meeting in Moscow, and the first promulgation of AUCECB statutes was accepted. From that point on, the activities of local ECB churches were directed in accordance with AUCECB regulations. Though it initially seemed as if the Evangelical Christians-Baptists gained more freedom with the formation of their own Union, believers discovered that the State policy was to put pressure on the churches by using the Union as its tool. According to AUCECB statutes, congresses were not allowed. In August 1945 Christians of the Evangelical Faith (Pentecostals) joined the AUCECB. The formal unification of several evangelical movements into one union was certainly in the state's favour. However, it did not follow that the Baptist movement was united at a deeper level.

The Moldavian Evangelical Christians–Baptists joined the All-Union Council of Evangelical Christians–Baptists. The central headquarters of the AUCECB, in Moscow, began to function as the supreme governing structure for the whole of the umbrella organisation. The Moldavian ECB churches might, in theory, have been faced with a choice in respect of their relationship with the AUECECB, but in reality there was no choice. There was simply the fact that they had to be part of the AUCECB, whether or not they wished to do so, since only this organisation was granted legal recognition from the State. It would have been impossible for evangelical churches in Moldavia to exist and function legally without having membership in the AUCECB. This merger was, therefore, made automatically. There is no evidence that Moldavian Baptists were the initiators of this move. The Soviet government worked out its policy concerning ECB churches through the AUCECB as the supreme organ of the

---

[105] Craighead, 'The Soviet Invasion', p. 275.

Evangelical Christians–Baptists in the USSR in collaboration with the Council for the Affairs of Religious Cults (CARC).[106]

'To Restore God's Work in Moldavia'

The AUCECB sent their representative, the Commissioner, Ilia Ivanov to Moldavia. He arrived in Kishinev in January 1946. The official history of the AUCECB from 1989 states: 'The All-Union Council of Evangelical Christians-Baptists sent Ivanov...to organize and restore God's work in Moldavia.'[107] However, according to Ivanov's reports to the Commissioner of CARC in Moldavia, it would be more appropriate to say that his main task was to put the regulations of the AUCECB into practice and to acquaint the Moldavian 'brotherhood' with Soviet religious laws. The fact that the Moldavian ECB had no choice in the matter, and was not a real partner, was to have far-reaching implications. On the other hand, Ivanov's work could be interpreted more positively way, since he did assist in the registration process of the ECB churches, allowing them some freedom to continue their congregational life.

From 15-25 February 1946 Ivanov organised a ten-day meeting in Kishinev for the representatives from all the Moldavian Evangelical Christian–Baptist churches. Many distinguished Baptist leaders of that time participated in this meeting, which was later proclaimed to have been the thirteenth Congress of the ECB churches of Moldavia. At the beginning, Moldavian Baptists perceived the role of the AUCECB as constructive. There are good reasons to assume that the atmosphere during this meeting was friendly. The main goal of the meeting was to get to know the situation of the local churches better, as well as their leaders, and to discover what kind of ministries were practised in the churches. The war and Soviet annexation had scattered many church leaders and church members and it was important to renew contacts and friendships. Among the participants were Ivan Slobodchikov[108] (Balti, pastor), Mikhail Belousov (Kishinev, evangelist), Tikhon Hijniacov (Kishinev), Grigoriy Rudenco (Kishinev, pastor), Silvestr Tsurkan (Slobozia, pastor), and many others. But times had changed.

Starting in 1946, Moldavian church life came under the control of the Commissioner of the AUCECB.[109] CARC in turn kept a close eye on the AUCECB and its commissioner. It took some time before Moldavian believers realised the gravity of the situation. A critical attitude towards the AUCECB

---

[106] In July 1945 CARC began its activity in MSSR.

[107] *Istoriya Evangel'skikh*, p. 327.

[108] In 1948, Ivan Slobodchikov was removed from his position of senior presbyter by the AUCECB because he was reluctant to collaborate with the CARC. *NARM*, F. 3305, Inv. 1, D. 40, p. 16.

[109] *NARM*, F. 3305, Inv. 1, D. 5, p. 15.

and its commissioner began to grow in Moldavia from the second part of 1947. The friendly atmosphere of the 1946 congress was not maintained. Because of their disagreement with some AUCECB regulations, Moldavian Baptist critics had to suffer. Some of them were imprisoned or exiled, such as Grigoriy Rudenco[110] and Pastor Ivancev[111] from Ceadir-Lunga. Some were deprived of pastoral ministry and some hid to avoid imprisonment,[112] running from place to place.

Tensions grew. Trevor Beeson states that Moldavian Baptist congregations made attempts to develop a variety of activities, including musical evenings, youth clubs and mutual aid societies.[113] But according to reports sent by Ivanov to the Commissioner of CARC, and now available in the National Archives, many of these methods were 'faults'. The only permitted activities were choir ministry, preaching, and sporadic poetry reading.[114] After a meeting with church leaders in March 1946, Ivanov reported: '...there are Sunday schools, youth groups and women's auxiliaries in a number of the communities... Such forms of activity have been discovered in 24 churches.'[115] All in all there were twenty-one Sunday schools with a total of 604 children, fifteen youth groups which included 361 young men, and five women's auxiliaries with a total of 180 women. In some communities, Ivanov said, 'it looks as if they do not have open youth groups but they do have choirs chiefly consisting of young people'.[116] To stop such activities Ivanov sent instructions to all the ECB communities. After several months he reported to the Commissioner of CARC that the work in Moldavia was generally normalised. Only some Baptist communities still had shortcomings such as 'loud meetings with crowds', 'brass bands' and 'youth groups' (as in the village of Busdugani), but 'as a rule children's and youth ministry has been stopped everywhere'.[117]

The AUCECB and its commissioner gradually began to lose its authority in Moldavia. Why was this? One reason was the AUCECB's extremely close relationship with the State. Another important reason was that the AUCECB, under powerful pressure from the CARC, was frequently incapable of helping local churches to protect their members from oppression at work, at school or in institutes of higher education. This was true even in the case of registered

---

[110] See also *NARM*, F. 3305, Inv. 1, D. 5, pp. 79, 92.

[111] Ivanchev was deported to the Kurgan region in spring 1949. 'Yuzhnoe Nasledie', *Svet Zhizni* 3 (1997), p. 5; *NARM*, F. 3305, Inv. 1, D. 50, p. 59.

[112] Silvestr Tsurkan, after he had severely criticised the work of the AUCECB and its Chairman Zhidkov, escaped from his church and home because of expected arrest and hid from the KGB until the end of the 1950s. *NARM*, F. 3305, Inv. 1, D. 5, p. 92.

[113] Beeson, *Discretion and Valour*, p. 98.

[114] *NARM*, F. 3305, Inv. 1, D. 5, pp. 37-38. The report of Ivanov was sent to CARC on 6 September 1948.

[115] Ibid., p. 11.

[116] Ibid.

[117] Ibid., p. 16-18.

churches and their members, to say nothing of non-registered communities. A further reason is that those Baptist communities which were refused registration or did not wish to register felt deeply alienated. Such communities, according to the repeated declarations of the CARC, simply did not exist.[118]

Office of Senior Presbyter in Moldavia

Starting in 1947, 'for the observance of the correct activity of Evangelical Christians–Baptists at the big regions, territories and republics of USSR',[119] senior presbyters were nominated by the AUCECB. These senior presbyters lived in the central cities of various regions or in the capitals of republics. The first senior presbyter among the Moldavian Baptists was Ivan Slobodchikov, who served from 1947-1949, when he was dismissed by an AUCECB resolution. Years later he remembered: 'I was immediately dismissed from work for badly teaching the presbyters.'[120] The AUCECB commissioner Ivanov described Slobodchikov's work as 'abnormal', because of 'the absence of close connection between the Senior Presbyter Ivan Slobodchikov and the Commissioner of CARC that leads to the detection of the shortcomings only when I arrive. This gives a blow to my prestige as well as to the AUCECB's authority.'[121] In February 1949 the Commissioner of CARC, Desyatnikov, sent the chairman of CARC, Ivan Polyanskiy, information that the 'senior presbyter over Moldavian SSR Ivan Slobodchikov was dismissed from his post by the AUCECB and instead of him Frol Astakhov was appointed'.[122] Slobodchikov continued to serve as a presbyter in Kishinev. Not much is known about his work as a senior presbyter. He did not send many reports to the authorities, as Astakhov later did. It seems that Slobodchikov tried to keep his distance from the Commissioner of CARC, and this was why he was dismissed. It is difficult to say if Slobodchikov consciously used the method of non co-operation, or if this was simply because of his character or leadership style.

Frol Astakhov, Slobodchikov's successor in the senior presbyter's position, was a different kind of person. He can be considered one of the most 'zealous' senior presbyters for co-operation—or rather collaboration—with the Commissioner of CARC. In 1949, the AUCECB sent Astakhov to Moldavia from Novosibirsk, Western Siberia, where he had already served as a senior presbyter. Astakhov was put in 'from the outside', although the Moldavian brotherhood undoubtedly had enough worthy and trusted presbyters who could

---

[118] Savinsky, *Istoriya*, pp. 120-121.
[119] *NARM*, F. 3305, Inv. 1, D. 50, p. 47.
[120] 'Interview with Ivan Slobodchikov', Project of Oral History, 'Protestantism in the former Soviet Union'; retrieved from the Electronic Christian Library 'History of the Euro-Asian Evangelical Movement: Primary Sources' (EAAA: 2001).
[121] *NARM*, F. 3305, Inv. 1, D. 5, pp. 37-38.
[122] *NARM*, F. 3305, Inv. 1, D. 40, p. 16.

have been appointed to this position.[123] Astakhov brought many problems to the Moldavian brotherhood. As the Kishinev church in its appeal to the presidium of AUCECB wrote: 'It is already the ninth year that you left us to the mercy of fate. You have completely entrusted us into the hands of Astakhov. He is telling you that everything is well here, but under such oppression and dictatorship we cannot continue spiritual living.'[124]

Even today the attitude towards Astakhov is contradictory. Some have described him as a leader sent by the KGB. Slobodchikov, in his interview, stated that 'this person was completely devoted to the KGB. The KGB authorities sent him.'[125] Some others have suggested that Astakhov had a complicated relationship with his son, and the latter talked slanderously about his father. The slander was that a Communist Party membership card was found in their home. However, these are only legends today. The evidence of Astakhov's unfavourable influence on Baptist work in Moldavia is contained in a huge file in the National Archives. This file includes Astakhov's reports to CARC and his correspondence with the AUCECB as well as with local presbyters. Ivan Slobodchikov remembered:

> Brothers came to the Commissioner [of CARC] and asked, 'Could we sing at the wedding?' And he said, 'How could there be the wedding without songs? Sure, you can.' Then brothers came to Astakhov and said, 'We had an appointment with the Commissioner and he gave permission to sing at weddings.' But Astakhov slammed his fist on the table and said: 'But I do not permit singing.'[126]

Finally, the central church of Kishinev wrote a letter of protest to the AUCECB and demanded the excommunication and dismissal of Astakhov from the post of senior presbyter in the MSSR. In February 1957, the AUCECB replaced Frol Astakhov with Dmitriy Ponomarchuk. Astakhov was sent to the Caucasuses as an AUCECB representative, though questions about his integrity were also raised in the Caucasuses.

Dmitriy Ponomarchuk, who was from Kiev, was a former leader of the Pentecostal movement in Ukraine, and was the member of the revision commission of the AUCECB. He served in Moldavia until 1965. The older generation of Moldavian believers have said that 'he was one who loved "remuneration"'.[127] It is significant that the presidium of AUCECB had again chosen a senior presbyter from outside Moldavia. This 'big brother mentality' did not help Moldavian Baptists to integrate into the All-Union Baptist work, nor did it give them any self-confidence to rebuild their church work. It can also be asked, from the Moldavian point of view, if it was the best solution to

---

[123] *NARM*, F. 3305, Inv. 1, D. 71, p. 121.
[124] Ibid., p. 124.
[125] 'Interview with Ivan Slobodchikov'.
[126] Ibid.
[127] According to Vasiliy Davniy, Vasiliy Dubchak, and Ivan Slobodchikov.

have a former Pentecostal leader as a senior presbyter for the Moldavian ECB churches, as the Pentecostals had created some tensions in these churches. As with the eight years when Astakhov was senior presbyter, so the eight years when Ponomarchuk was in the post were years when the AUCECB was not seen in a very positive light by the ECB communities in Moldavia.

For most of the period from 1940-1965, therefore, the Moldavian Baptist brotherhood did not have any senior presbyters who could act as respected leaders with spiritual authority. Most behaved like stepfathers sent to Moldavia by an outside body, the AUCECB. The situation changed for the better in 1965 when one of the most significant leaders from the Moldavian Baptists, Sergey Malanchuk, was chosen as the senior presbyter for Moldavia. Had the Moldavians had their own leader earlier, perhaps some of the painful conflicts could have been resolved and some common ground for spiritual work could have been more readily found. But the reality was different. Moldavia became one of the regions where opposition to AUCECB policies gradually grew and where tensions between registered and non-registered churches in the 1960s produced painful wounds and long-lasting scars.

'Struggle for Freedom?'—Opposition to the AUCECB's Statutes

Most of the significant leaders of the ECB churches in Moldavia could not remain indifferent to the goal of the state in seeking to destroy the freedom of local churches and centralising the decision-making powers in the AUCECB headquarters in Moscow. Early in 1948 in the MSSR, voices were raised against the statutes of the AUCECB. The reason was quite obvious. In 1949 the Moldavian SSR had eighty-three registered ECB churches. After the war, at least thirty-two Baptist churches were closed or joined to other registered churches.[128] Several churches continued to exist illegally.[129] It was only to be expected that the unregistered Baptist communities would one day rise against their 'big brother' who did not provide much support even for registered communities and who often kept silent about the unjust situation faced by all the ECB communities in Moldavia.

New 'Statutes' and 'Instructions' of the AUCECB, which restricted Baptist activity severely, were published in 1960. These documents, about Baptist life in relation to the State—the *New Statutes* and *Letter of Instructions*—have been called 'a bomb of delayed reaction'.[130] The explosion happened in the

---

[128] *NARM*, F. 3305, Inv. 1, D. 40, p. 68.

[129] According to official statistics, in 1953 there were twelve unregistered groups of ECB communities with 267 members in Moldavia. *NARM*, F. 3305, Inv. 1, D. 65, p. 21. The actual number was probably higher.

[130] Y. Reschetnikov and S. Sannikov, *Obzor Istorii Evangel'sko-Baptistskogo Bratstva na Ukraine* (A Review of the History of the Evangelical Baptist Brotherhood in Ukraine) (Odessa: Bogomyslie, 2000), p. 183.

beginning of the 1960s, causing deep division among Baptists, but the first sparks were seen years earlier, particularly in Moldavia. The first evidence of this was contained in the reports of Ilia Ivanov[131] and Frol Astakhov. According to Ivanov and Astakhov, in 1949 'some members of the ECB church in Tolmazy village were excommunicated because of their non-recognition of the statutes of the AUCECB...'[132] This was not an isolated instance. In 1953-1955, revoking a church's registration or depriving a pastor of pastoral office were typical measures taken by the authorities in response to the negative attitude of local churches toward the statutes of the AUCECB, which severely restricted local church autonomy. However, critical Baptist voices were hard to silence.

Even the central church of the Moldavian 'brotherhood', the Baptist church in Kishinev, did not support all the points of the AUCECB policies. The reports of Ivanov criticised the democratic leadership style in the Kishinev church that, according to Ivanov, needed urgently to be changed. In Kishinev, church decisions were made collectively, instead of limiting decision-making only to the executive council of the church.[133] As the result of the church's non-compliance, the KGB took Pastor Grigorii Rudenko away from the meeting house immediately after a church service on 24 November 1948. Without examination at the People's Court, the Supreme Court sentenced Rudenko to ten years of imprisonment and penal servitude in the small town of Molotovsk in the Arkhangelsk region. After his term of imprisonment, he and his wife together with their children were exiled to the Kemerovo region and returned to Moldavia only after his liberation many years later.[134]

Another factor that influenced the mood among some ECB communities in Moldavia was the fact that Ivanov as Commissioner of the AUCECB and later the senior presbyters, such as Astakhov and Ponomarciuk, had close ties to the Commissioner of CARC. Ivanov's reports to CARC give detailed information on the 'shortcomings' of the churches. These opened the way for the closing of these prayer houses, and the interrogation of presbyters and other leaders by the Commissioner of CARC, by the KGB, or by local Executive Committees. In many cases the *kolkhoz* meetings on the collectives publicly condemned the 'troublemakers' and mocked their faith.[135] Archive documents give a clear picture of the situation. It is hard to understand the motives of those Christian leaders who wrote the reports. In some cases even the names of the 'troublemakers' were given:

> The second considerable shortcoming is strong activity at these places through the arrangements of meals and noisy meetings with participation of choirs and

---

[131] *NARM*, F. 3305, Inv. 1, D. 5, pp. 37-38.
[132] *NARM*, F. 3305, Inv. 1, D. 40, pp. 69-70.
[133] *NARM*, F. 3305, Inv. 1, D. 5, pp. 37-38.
[134] Vasiliy Davniy, 'Grigoriy Antonovich Rudenko' (unpubl. memoirs, Chisinau, 2000).
[135] *NARM*, F. 3305, Inv. 1, D. 5, pp. 37-38.

orchestras from other communities. Especially involved in this were the distinguished presbyters Grigoriy Malay...Yakov Burlak...and Burdeiny from Baltsaty village, who during the baptism service in August 1948, ventured to arrange noisy meals in the open air where several hundreds of persons not belonging to the ECB participated.[136]

In some cases the Moldavian Baptist leaders sharply criticised the concessions made by the AUCECB headquarters in Moscow. For example, Silvestr Tsyrkan from Slobozia in the Olonesti district criticised Jakov Zhidkov as the leader of AUCECB, because in 1947 *Bratskiy Vestnik*, the official herald of the Soviet ECB churches, published an article that was devoted to the thirty year anniversary of the October Revolution.[137] The opposition to the AUCECB intensified in Moldavia after the *New Statutes* and *Letter of Instructions* were issued by the AUCECB. The close relationship to the state authorities and the compromises made by the AUCECB leadership caused tensions and increased the atmosphere of opposition to the AUCECB in Moldavia. The tensions, however, were not only between some Moldavian churches and the AUCECB. Divisions also reached local churches in Moldavia. Positions over the issues of co-operation and separation became more rigid, the solutions came to be seen in black and white and those involved in the tensions related to church-state issues were apt to take sides in a fairly uncompromising way.

Towards Separation: A Split among Moldavian Baptists

It was after the new anti-religious campaign unleashed by Khrushchev in 1959 that AUCECB altered the ECB statutes by which it governed itself. Under the new directions given to the churches, which were even more restrictive than those previously in place, the churches were, in effect, made instruments of their own containment and restriction.[138] It was under pressure from the CARC and the Council of Ministers that the AUCECB issued the two fateful documents, the *New Statutes* and the *Letter of Instructions*, documents that can be found in the archive files of AUCECB under the title 'The Error of the AUCECB'.[139] By means of the *Statutes,* the AUCECB re-asserted its authority over ECB churches, while the idea of the Congress of ECB churches as a body with any authority was correspondingly diminished. The *Letter* was sent to senior presbyters to guide them in the implementation of the statutes. The

---

[136] *NARM*, F. 3305, Inv. 1, D. 5, pp. 37-38.
[137] Ibid.
[138] Beeson, *Discretion and Valour*, p. 98.
[139] Nelli Klimenko, 'Doklad: Sovet Tserkvey I Dvizhenie Nezavisimykh Tserkvey'; retrieved from the Electronic Christian Library 'History of the Euro-Asian Evangelical Movement: Primary Sources' (EAAA: 2001).

Letter of Instructions, which was issued by the presidium of the AUCECB,[140] changed some of the existing principles in the local ECB churches and added some new ones, which were seen by many churches in Moldavia and elsewhere as very negative.

The Division in the Kishinev ECB Church at Vokzal'naya Street

If the local churches' views had been taken into account more seriously, then perhaps the reform movement among ECB churches—a movement resistant to the AUCECB—would not have gained the momentum it did in the 1960s. The most controversial parts of the *Letter of Instructions*, from the point of view of the local churches, were the following: children were to be excluded from acts of public worship, baptism of people between the ages of eighteen and thirty was to be discouraged and reduced to a minimum and evangelistic activities were curtailed.[141] Though these prohibitions had appeared earlier in the circular letters to senior presbyters, the *Letter of Instructions* was the last spark that ignited the fire. The AUCECB proclaimed a new purpose for religious services, as Beeson notes, which was 'not the attraction of new members but the satisfaction of the necessary spiritual needs of the believers'.[142] This was a major challenge to traditional Baptist views. The decisions of the AUCECB were, of course, made under state pressure and were seen by many Baptist leaders as a necessary adjustment of Baptist life. Those who disagreed, however, formed *Initsiativniki* (the *Initiative Group*) a leading body representing those known also as Reform Baptists. This group was formed at the beginning of the 1960s. It is important to note, however, that in Moldavia, for example in the Kishinev ECB church, some reform ideas were present even before the wider Initiative Group was formed.

When the above mentioned AUCECB documents appeared in Moldavia, the senior presbyter, Dmitry Ponomarciuk, warned believers not to bring children to worship services, 'for they understand nothing and only disturb, make noise, and run outside. Later, when they mature, then they will attend services.'[143] Many of the church members did not agree with these rules. 'How could they leave the children to the mercy of fate'[144] until they were 18 years old, they asked? Artur Mitskevich, a member of the AUCECB, arrived in Kishinev for the purpose of introducing the new documents. Mitskevich explained that all these restrictions were added because the practice of the churches contradicted

---

[140] The content of those documents was probably prepared by the CARC.

[141] Beeson, *Discretion and Valour*, pp. 98-99.

[142] Beeson, *Discretion and Valour*, pp. 98-99.

[143] 'Interview with Vasiliy Perebykovskiy', Project of Oral History 'Protestantism in former Soviet Union'; retrieved from the Electronic Christian Library 'History of the Euro-Asian Evangelical Movement: primary sources' (EAAA: 2001).

[144] Ibid.

Soviet laws. 'But what about the Bible?' local Baptists asked. They were following their practice of testing everything with the Bible, and they could not harmonise the restrictions with the biblical message. The next morning, Perebykovskiy remembers, 'the militia took away the discontented church members and sentenced them to fifteen days imprisonment'. Among them were: Rudenko, Davniy, Dubchak, Astakhov,[145] Madan and others. Then Ponomarchuk, together with Mitskevich, excommunicated the group from the Kishenev church.[146] In this way the two AUCECB documents were introduced to Kishinev's central church.

The summer of 1960 brought another problem to the Kishinev ECB church at Vokzal'naya Street and this was the demolition of their church building. According to the new residential construction project in the area, the prayer house of the ECB church was to be torn down. Instead of a prayer house a kindergarten had been planned to stand on the site.[147] However, after the church building was demolished, the building project was changed. The new main street now lay far from the former location of the church. Brothers and sisters were left without a prayer house and began to gather in homes. The authorities saw that the situation might become even worse in terms of their ability to control what happened and advised Ivan Slobodchikov, the presbyter of the church, to find a building in which church members could gather. Members of the church reconstructed an old Jewish synagogue on Il'inskaya Street and they gathered there until the beginning of the 1980s.

These events influenced the movement for reform, and later the division and separation that took place in the Kishinev church. Believers were imprisoned, effectively for questioning the AUCECB line. Also, the local authorities promised, at first, to provide a new place for the church building, but later the church was left without any place to gather for meetings. It was again evident through these events that it was impossible to cooperate with the atheist authorities and this deepened the mistrust among church members towards the docile line of the AUCECB regarding church-state relationships.

Grigoriy Rudenko's Separatist Group

Another factor that gave momentum to the separatist reform movement in the Kishinev church was the return in 1958 of Grigoriy Rudenko, the former pastor of the church, from imprisonment. Though he had been the pastor of this church he was now not allowed to actively participate in church life; he was even prohibited from preaching. As a result of these restrictions, in 1960 Grigoriy Rudenko became the leader of a group of believers who were critical

---

[145] This was not the senior presbyter, but Kusima Fedorovich Astakhov.
[146] 'Interview with Vasiliy Perebykovskiy'.
[147] *NARM*, F. 3305, Inv. 1, D. 83, p. 30.

of the AUCECB. They were seeking support for their positions from the Bible, and were convinced that the concessions that had been made by the AUCECB to the authorities in the sphere of mission and church life were 'not the evangelical way...'[148] This group consisted of fifty church members.[149]

Thus the reform[150] movement among Baptist churches in the MSSR, especially in Kishinev, began approximately a year before the formation of the wider Initiative Group, which came out of the Baptist Congress of 13 August 1961. However, in Kishinev, the reform movement was not strongly separatist at the beginning. Rudenko's group gathered on Tuesdays and Fridays separately, but on Sundays, Thursdays and Saturdays they continued to attend meetings at the central registered ECB church. By 1965 this reform group numbered 170 members, and at Vokzal'naya Street the registered ECB church had 350 members. Grigoriy Rudenko died in 1966, and, at least during his lifetime, the members of this 'underground group' were never urged to stop attending the registered church in Kishinev. Nevertheless, later, separatist views became widespread among unregistered churches.

In Rudenko's period of leadership, however, the reform church took a more formal shape: a Sunday school[151] began to function, a choir and a 'brothers' council' were formed. This church did not have a building for meeting and the members gathered in homes, and as a result the authorities began to persecute and to fine the owners of the houses. The believers who came together for worship were often fined as well. However, these gatherings brought together many people and the windows of the house were kept open so that people standing outside could hear the songs and sermons. 'When we had guests,' Perebykovsky remembers, 'it was around two-hundred people. Outsiders visited and repented.'[152] In this way, at the beginning of the 1960s, there emerged a new ECB church in Kishinev, though without any legal status or official permission.

The Council of Churches of the ECB and the Movement of Independent ECB Churches in Moldavia

The reform movement among Baptists in the Soviet Union began to spread after August 1961. Under the leadership of three determined men, Alexey Prokof'ev, Gennadiy Kryuchkov and later Georgiy Vins, this opposition

---

[148] *NARM*, F. 3305, Inv. 1, D. 83, p. 30.

[149] Pavel Belev, 'History of the Baptist Church "Spring of Life" in Chisinau' (unpubl. paper, Chisinau: Chisinau College of Theology and Education, 2000).

[150] This was a 'reform' movement as its initial goals were to awaken the ECB churches and to seek to show that it was wrong to follow the way that was chosen by the leaders of AUCECB. Later, separatist tendencies began to dominate this movement.

[151] In registered churches Sunday schools were prohibited.

[152] 'Interview with Vasiliy Perebykovskiy'.

crystallised into the *Initsiativniky*, which challenged the AUCECB to recant its decisions. At the same time the Initiative Group sought to win as many congregations as possible over to its side and organised a number of activities, such as unauthorised meetings and illegal publications. The Initiative Group sent letters to local church communities all over the Soviet Union. These letters reached both registered and unregistered churches. The impact was felt in Moldavia. While in 1953 there were twelve unregistered groups in Moldavia,[153] by 1961 there were twenty-six unregistered groups.[154] Throughout 1962 the number of members in registered ECB churches declined considerably. Four ECB churches with a total of four-hundred members were closed. The documents mention that at least 182 members of ECB churches began to support the claims of the Initiative Group.[155] Thus, the activity of the Initiative Group in the MSSR was spreading among the Moldavian brotherhood at the beginning of the 1960s. At least thirty-seven churches, probably even more, joined the Council of Churches of the ECB (CCECB), which was formed by the Initiative Group in 1965 as an opposition organisation to the AUCECB. In 1961, there were at least twenty-seven ECB churches in Moldavia that were affected by controversies and difficulties. In some cases more 'radical' groups left the church; in some cases the church was deprived of registration.

Many ECB churches that supported the Initiative Group at the All-Union Congress of the AUCECB later experienced arrests, trials, and imprisonments. In the Moldavian SSR, probably the first person who was arrested after the emergence of the Initiative Group was Boris Gladkevich, one of the leaders of a dissident church in Kishinev. According to the decision made by the People's Court of the October district in Kishinev on 11 June 1964, Boris Gladkevich was condemned to four years imprisonment.[156] Many members of the unregistered church in Kishinev were fined or lost their jobs.[157] Accusations were directed towards the AUCECB leadership for ignoring the principles related to local church autonomy. The Baptist movement in the MSSR was brought to the point of schism. The authorities, at least partly, provoked the schism, a strategy that had been employed earlier in the 1920s to destroy rival political parties and groupings in the Soviet Union. Now the same method was used on Evangelical churches. The authorities could hardly have been unaware of the discontent the *New Statutes* and *Letter of Instructions* would create, especially in the unregistered churches that were, by that time, already strongly opposed to the AUCECB.[158]

---

[153] *NARM*, F. 3305, Inv. 1, D. 65, p. 21.
[154] *NARM*, F. 3305, Inv. 1, D. 82, p. 52. 'List of the leaders of the religious groups of ECB (unregistered).'
[155] *NARM*, F. 3305, Inv. 1, D. 90, p. 273.
[156] *NARM*, F. 3305, Inv. 1, D. 88, pp. 22-24.
[157] 'Interview with Vasiliy Perebykovskiy'.
[158] Sannikov, *Dvadtsat' Vekov Khristianstva*, pp. 522-527.

Broken Fellowship

In the early stages the split did not destroy long-standing relationships among the ordinary members of the registered and unregistered churches. As Vasiliy Perebekovskiy commented: 'We did not quarrel with registered [believers] but communicated with them. Mainly the leadership quarrelled with each other.'[159] But some difficulties occurred. The life of the registered churches was slightly easier. Unregistered churches began to see themselves as more holy. However, the major question that divided ordinary members was: 'Should we submit to the authorities in religious questions?' Many of those I interviewed stated that the appearance of the Initiative Group and its policy of reform were caused first of all by the AUCECB's policy of close co-operation with the government. Later, the actions of the Council of Churches of the ECB were influenced by the tendency of this movement towards separation. In addition, Gennadiy Kryuchkov's authoritarian leadership methods aggravated the situation. In both cases the leadership of these two bodies broke the Baptist principle of the autonomy of every local church community as the leadership bodies wielded authoritarian power over local communities through their representatives and authorised persons.[160]

Thus, the tendency towards authoritarian leadership and mutual excommunications caused serious problems in the whole ECB body. The unity of the church was destroyed. The AUCECB later made some attempts to reunite ECB churches, but it was too late. At the 1963 and 1966 Congresses, the AUCECB admitted that the controversial documents of 1960 had gone too far. Unfortunately, only a few leaders of the *Orgkomitet* (the Initiative Group had by then been renamed *Orgkomitet*) were permitted to participate in the 1963 Congress of the AUCECB. They had no chance to speak. Consequently, the leaders of *Orgkomitet* regarded the attempts at repentance on the part of the Presidium of the AUCECB as insincere.

As noted above, in 1965 the Council of the Churches of the ECB (CCECB) was formed. According to Nelli Klimenko it was a decision taken first and foremost by Gennady Krychkov personally. Klimenko pointed out that Kryuchkov had an authoritarian and at times even dictatorial nature.[161] Kryuchkov had criticised the AUCECB for the liquidation of two Baptist principles: separation of the church from the state and the autonomy of each local church. Kryuchkov said: 'Every church is autonomous, independent and does not have a spiritual centre, which could dictate or press the church.'[162] The

---

[159] 'Interview with Vasiliy Perebykovskiy'.

[160] Both the AUCECB and the CCECB had authorized persons who represented leadership policy at places. See Klimenko, 'Doklad: Sovet Tserkvey' and Synichkin, 'Istoriya EKHB v SSSR s 1959 po 1966 god'.

[161] Klimenko, 'Doklad: Sovet Tserkvey'.

[162] Nelli Klimenko, 'Interview with Grigoriy Fedorovich Rotar' (Project of Oral History, *Protestantism in Former Soviet Union*; Donetsk Christian University, 1999).

Council of Churches was supposed to be the body 'which could help the church, give advice, but could not insist on a church accepting this advice'.[163] However, some years later, Kryuchkov seems to have forgotten his own words.

'Was it possible to avoid the division of the church in the 1960s?' This question was voiced immediately after the formation of the CCECB and continues to be voiced today. Most of the witnesses from the 1960s unanimously conclude that in the first stages the schism probably could have been avoided. The former senior presbyter Ivan Slobodchikov believed that even after 1963 a reunification was still possible.[164] However, the AUCECB was reluctant to admit its mistakes with regards to its forcing the controversial documents of 1960 on the churches. Likewise, the Council of Churches (CCECB) developed rigid attitudes. In addition, it should be noted that the AUCECB was under strong state pressure. The leadership of the AUCECB must have been aware of the consequences the *New Statutes* and *The Letter of Instructions* would bring for the churches. During the AUCECB Plenum of 1961 Karev said, 'The soil for the activity of the *Initiative Group* is favourable enough.'[165] In spite of this awareness, at the Plenum two years earlier, according to the record, 'Karev by the power of his authority insisted on acceptance of these documents.'[166] The question remains: what if the AUCECB had opposed State pressure? The authorities probably could not have destroyed the entire Union in the 1960s, taking into account the growing dissident movement in the society and the world-wide political situation.[167]

It may be that the leaders of the Union, by signing these documents, hoped that local churches would make adjustments according to their situation.[168] In some places in Moldavia this worked, for example in the village of Krasnoarmeysk the whole church decided to let children attend services.[169] In Asnasanii-Noi[170] and in Biruinta in the Belti area,[171] the churches did not follow these documents very strictly, though all of these churches remained registered. In the village of Mihailovca the situation was even more remarkable. The members of the church, after discussing together, entirely refused to follow these documents. As the result, the church was added to the list of dissident

---

[163] Klimenko, 'Interview with Grigoriy Fedorovich Rotar'.
[164] 'Interview with Ivan Slobodchikov'.
[165] Ibid.
[166] Ibid.
[167] Klimenko, 'Doklad: Sovet Tserkvey'.
[168] Reschetnikov and Sannikov, *Obzor Istorii*, p. 194.
[169] 'Interview with Vasiliy Perebykovskiy'.
[170] Grischuk Andrey, 'The Historic Sketch of Asnasanii-Noi Church' (unpubl. paper, Chisinau: College of Theology and Education, 2001).
[171] Marco Sergiu, 'History of the Baptist Church in Biruinta Town' (unpubl. paper, Chisinau: College of Theology and Education, 2001).

churches but never lost its registration status!¹⁷² Certainly, much depended on the attitude of the local authorities.

This division in the AUCECB and among Moldavian Baptists weakened the believers' communities in Moldavia. Several Moldavian Baptist churches or groups chose to operate illegally. As a result, there was much suffering in the lives of ordinary church members. Most young people from unregistered churches could not get a University education or a good job. Many of them were persecuted in the workplace or fined. Misunderstandings grew between registered and unregistered churches. Both parties were rather weak in the area of conflict resolution. Even today some village churches of the ECB do not communicate with formerly separated churches and vice versa. For example, the church in the village of Antonesti in Stefan Voda district, or the schismatic Kishinev church at Vadu lui Voda Street, do not have any relationships with other churches that used to belong to the 'other camp'. The restoration of relationships that were broken in the 1960s remains a challenge for contemporary Baptists in Moldova.

Attempts to Foster Unity

From 1944 onwards, the leaders of the AUCECB paid a lot of attention to developing new ways and new methods to maintain and foster the unity of Evangelical Christian and Baptist believers, not only in theory but in practice. They visited churches, issued circular letters, prepared ECB Statutes, and spread the Bratskiy Vestnik magazine in every registered church. All this was no doubt done with an aim to strengthen the 'Union'. Unity was an important keyword during those years, though it sometimes sounded like a cliché, especially when painful problems shattered this unity. Nevertheless, the AUCECB continued to declare its support for unity, and tried to keep as many evangelical bodies under its organisational umbrella as possible. It tried to work for restoration of unity in the 1960s, though it could be asked today if there was any real attempt made to listen carefully to opponents and critics.

Attempts to Restore Unity by Congresses

It would be wrong to say that the AUCECB was not interested in unity. Unity was an important goal at the All-Union level, though it was often interpreted as uniformity rather than as a respect towards different traditions. In 1962, the AUCECB leaders appealed to the CARC three times to have a congress, which would draw together representatives from local unions. Only in 1963 did they

---

[172] Kobivnic Serghey, 'History of the Baptist church in Mihailovca village' (unpubl. paper, Chisinau: College of Theology and Education, 2002).

finally get permission from the authorities and the congress took place on 15–17 October of the same year. The CCECB churches were represented by G.P. Vins, A.A. Schalaschov, M.T. Schaptala, and G.I. Maiboroda. To begin with, the AUCECB cancelled the two fateful documents—the *New Statutes* and *The Letter of Instructions*. These statutes were replaced by new versions of the statutes, with the approval of the congress. The new statutes gave relatively more freedom to local unions, thus offering them a feeling of belonging to the AUCECB on a partnership basis.

The matter of unity was taken into consideration during the broadened assembly of the AUCECB on 2–3 September 1964. Later, the AUCECB made a series of attempts to meet with CCECB representatives for discussions. However, as time passed it became more and more difficult to find a common language for dialogue. Either the AUCECB was taking the position of an 'older brother' and demanding concessions which the CCECB viewed as impossible to make or the CCECB made severe accusations against the AUCECB and refused to continue the negotiations. Though some representatives of the CCECB attended the AUCECB congresses, they felt that they were not given enough voice to express their positions. However, on a local level, some separated groups of believers, for example in Kishinev, returned to the registered church, especially after 1963.

In an additional attempt to restore unity, at the beginning of 1965 the AUCECB welcomed ten thousand Mennonites from sixty-one churches and offered them registration, which considerably increased the numbers of AUCECB members.[173] This was an attempt to embrace a movement that was spiritually close to the AUCECB tradition. Unfortunately, about the same number of members left the union. Two hundred and eighty three churches and groups with a total number of 8,686 members had separated from the AUCECB by 1 January 1965 and joined the Reform or 'underground' Baptists.[174] In 1965 another twenty groups with 1,329 members separated from the AUCECB. For its part, the AUCECB was looking for new ways to strengthen unity, or at this stage, to stop fragmentation and splintering. After 1965, the 'Moscow brotherhood' worked on getting registration for evangelical groups that for years had gathered together, but were still unregistered. In the Moldavian Republic, for example, a community in Ungheni[175] was registered in 1966, though it had gathered since 1955, and in Agronomovcha[176] a congregation received registration until 1967, though it had been meeting since 1927.

---

[173] *Istoriya Evangel'skikh*, p. 245.

[174] Ibid.

[175] Voronov Sergey, 'History of the Baptist Church in Ungheni City' (Chisinau: College of Theology and Education, 2002).

[176] Voronova Olga, 'History of the Baptist Church in Agronomovca' (Chisinau: College of Theology and Education, 2002).

In 1966, the AUCECB formed a Committee for Unification under the leadership of V.M. Kovalkov.[177] The Committee achieved some positive results in its negotiations with the underground Baptist communities. As a result, some of these churches and individuals returned to the AUCECB. Nevertheless, more than ten thousand Reform Baptists remained with the CCECB. A. Mitskevich and I. Ivanov from Moscow visited Moldavia on several occasions in the 1960s. In 1963, the Moldavian brotherhood gathered together for its fourteenth conference.[178] There they discussed the issue of the separatist movement and some possible perspectives for reunification. The separation issue, which had divided Baptists in Moldavia, was not neglected by local pastors. Attempts were made to solve the problem. Unfortunately, in many cases, it was already too late.

On 5 March 1965 the fifteenth conference of representatives from the Moldavian ECB churches took place in Kishinev. The meeting was presided over by the representative of the AUCECB, A.I. Mitskevich. The positive outcome of this conference was the election of Sergei Malanchuk as senior presbyter. Sergei Malanchuk, one of the well-known presbyters of the Moldavian brotherhood, was significant in his attempts to restore lost unity. Even if many separatist churches did not return to the Union, Malanchuk, coming from Moldavia (unlike the previous senior presbyters), was able to give a sense of 'belonging together' to the registered churches. It was a time when the state granted more freedom to registered churches, probably hoping to soften the consequences of the split for the registered churches. However, the broken unity was never fully restored, and up to the present time in Moldovia a number of former CCECB churches refuse to talk about any kind of unification.

Attempts to Find Unity in Fellowship and Worship

It is widely known that according to Soviet laws church activities were allowed only inside church buildings. Special church ministries were forbidden. The Commissioner of CARC, Sergey Desyatnikov, said in 1945 that Evangelical Christians–Baptists had a wide system of Sunday schools, as well as special missionary, youth and women's societies, and that their propaganda was conducted outside of prayer houses. The Commissioner added: 'Presently, these kinds of activities do not take place, though the tendencies towards them and individual occurrences continue to happen…'[179] However, the state authorities effectively restricted Christian work and cut it off from any public dimension. For Moldavian Baptists this condition was especially hard, as they were used to having open-air baptisms and worship services. In 1949, the Commissioner of

---

[177] *Istoriya Evangel'skikh*, p. 246.
[178] Ibid., p. 328.
[179] Pasat, ed., *Trudnye Stranitsy*, p. 602.

the AUCECB instructed presbyters that 'the mass processions and gatherings' during baptismal services outside church buildings 'have to be put to an end'.[180] Most of the presbyters who did not submit to this demand received a reprimand or were removed from service. Panteleiy Mikhailov, under whose leadership in 1946-1948 the Vulcanesti church membership increased from forty to 116, was often reprimanded because of his inclination to 'organise meetings in apartments, out of the prayer house'.[181] However, many church leaders tried to find ways to maintain the continuity of church life and practices that linked the Moldavian Baptists in the Soviet years with their previous experience.

Keeping the local worship traditions and supporting fellowship between believers was more important for local leaders than formal unity on the AUCECB level. Though senior presbyters and representatives from Moscow sometimes visited local churches, for the most part this did not increase the sense of wider unity. Relationships with the 'Moscow brotherhood' were also controversial. Instead of spiritual support, it was often regulations and instructive letters that the local churches received from Moscow. An immediate sense of fellowship was crucial for local Baptist communities and Moldavian Baptists nevertheless tried to strengthen unity in their churches. Worship became an important means for this: not only participating in worship, but also meeting brothers and sisters and having a sense of visible community. Several meetings during the week and two services on Sunday conveyed a sense of belonging to one Christian family. Often these services, as older people remember, continued for several hours. Small groups of believers also visited each other's homes and had meals and fellowship together, often on Sundays between the morning and evening services. This tradition is still alive in Moldova. As not every church building had a baptistery, it was often necessary to go to neighbouring churches to administer baptism. The state authorities probably did not recognise that while baptism lost its meaning as public witness, these visits strengthened spiritual links between Baptist churches.

Another element that helped to achieve deeper unity in the local church, and on the wider scale in the Moldavian Baptist Union, was the common celebration of holidays: Christmas, New Year, Annunciation, Easter, Ascension Day, Pentecost Day, The Transfiguration, Harvest Day, and Unification Day. The last-named was introduced by the AUCECB to commemorate the unification meeting in Moscow in 1944. During these holidays believers knew that all churches celebrated, prayed and worshipped God together. Special programmes were prepared for services and church members worked together to make these days as meaningful as possible. Often relatives and neighbours were invited to these services, though evangelism was severely restricted by the government authorities. During Harvest Day some of the communities continued to have feasts outside church buildings, though the authorities from

---

[180] *NARM*, F. 3305, Inv. 1, D. 5, p. 14.
[181] *NARM*, F. 3305, Inv. 1, D. 5, p. 69.

Kishinev categorically forbade it. It was a time when unbelievers could join church members and hear the word of God. As Astakhov reported to the CARC in 1949: 'In some communities of Evangelical Christians–Baptists during Easter services there was repentance—conversions, i.e. some individuals from the visiting attendees prayed at these services.' In ten communities, according to his report, twenty-eight people repented.[182]

Besides the festivals already mentioned, every church usually celebrated its anniversary, despite the fact that state officials discouraged these events. Often, a love feast that bound the whole church together in prayer and thankfulness for God's help accompanied these celebrations. In addition, practical help offered to fellow believers built community relationships. Often church members helped each other with larger projects, such as building houses. Shared food and prayer times were a part of working together. Wedding ceremonies were another source for congregational meeting and even for evangelistic ministry. A Baptist wedding was not just fun and music, it included several sermons, the reading of poems, songs by the choir and good wishes to the young family; however, the main message was addressed to unbelievers who attended the wedding. An invitation to repent and follow Jesus was inseparable from these sermons and speeches.

Other important aspects of unity and at the same time of separation were pastoral care and church discipline. After World War II, many church members who had been excommunicated or who had left for the Orthodox Church in the time of the Romanian persecutions (1941-1944) returned to Baptist churches. Other members who were excommunicated were those who had made ethical mistakes, for example those who had stolen food during the years of starvation (1947-1949) in Moldavia. The AUCECB suggested that presbyters and senior brothers use strict testing and a probation period for these categories of people. However, pastoral considerations put the issue into proper balance. Sergei Malanchuk, a senior presbyter from 1965, as well as Silvester Tsurkan, often visited local churches and offered pastoral care, which was desperately needed in churches struggling to fulfil their mission in an atheistic setting. For church members, a sense of belonging was deepened by their support for the church's ministry. Voluntary donations were collected at church meetings,[183] and usually, five times a year an 'offering' was collected for the AUCECB.

Baptism as a Theological-ecclesiological Centre for Moldavian Baptists

One Lord, one faith, one baptism! Certainly, this credal saying, referring back to the biblical text, was known to Moldavian Baptists. Baptism as a witness to a person's faith and a door to church fellowship was an important theological and

---

[182] *NARM*, F. 3305, Inv. 1, D. 40, pp. 48-49.
[183] *NARM*, F. 3305, Inv. 1, D. 5, pp. 37-38.

ecclesial anchor for Baptists in Moldavia. However, in practical terms the churches had to affirm this view in the midst of government restrictions. According to the AUCECB Statutes of 1948, which were no doubt prepared under state pressure, the members of Evangelical Christian–Baptist churches could be persons 'no younger than eighteen years old'. With the approval of the CARC the age requirement was increased several times. For example, in 1951 the Senior Presbyter Frol Astakhov[184] advised the AUCECB on this, saying that it would be better to abstain from baptising persons under twenty-five years old.[185] After receiving a positive answer from Karev and Zhidkov, in 1953, Astakhov emphasised this self-made rule in almost every letter to the presbyters.[186]

The local churches, however, could not so easily deny their mission. Evangelism oriented toward conversions and baptisms was an integral part of Moldavian Baptist identity. This is why restrictions in this field, coming from the Union's leader, were profoundly problematic. In a 1952 report Astakhov wrote that from the seventy-five Baptist communities of the Moldavian SSR, only forty-eight applied to have baptisms. Astakhov only gave permission to forty-six of them, as two others were late with applications, according to the data given by Astakhov. The number of baptismal candidates in these forty-six communities was 730 persons, but the executive councils of local churches asked for only 451 of them to be baptised, and in the end 'the communities got permission to baptise 271 persons'.[187] Actually, the number of new members who were baptised and joined the churches in 1952 was even smaller—245 persons.[188] At the beginning of the 1950s, Astakhov demanded that only those who had at least a year of probation after conversion could be baptised. In addition, these persons had to be local inhabitants and not students.[189]

Application for baptism was a complicated process. Ivan Slobodchikov described this:

> Authorities interfered very much in the church's affairs. For example, the church tested the souls for baptism; these lists were given to the senior presbyter and he in turn gave them to the Commissioner of CARC. The Commissioner looked at them, crossed out all the young men and gave it back to the senior presbyter, who said those crossed out cannot be baptized.[190]

---

[184] Frol Astakhov held this position of senior presbyter over MSSR from 1949 until 1957.

[185] *NARM*, F. 3305, Inv. 1, D. 55, p. 32.

[186] *NARM*, F. 3305, Inv. 1, D. 60, p. 21. The Commissioner underlined this part of the document; he probably found it especially important.

[187] Ibid., p. 3.

[188] Ibid.

[189] *NARM*, F. 3305, Inv. 1, D. 59, p. 23.

[190] 'Interview with Ivan Slobodchikov'.

'The period of probation no less than a year after the conversion...'[191] was one stipulation that prolonged the process. In addition, baptisms could take place only in special baptisteries or in quiet and remote places outside. Under no circumstances were preaching or large crowds allowed. 'The baptismal service has to be conducted in the quietest surroundings so as not to attract the attention of outsiders.'[192] (This document reveals that at least sometimes baptisms were administered in rivers or lakes.) In earlier times, the Bessarabian Baptists used every baptismal service to evangelise. Now this was impossible. However, baptismal services encouraged local churches.

In the 1940s, statistics of baptisms show a clear tendency towards decline. In 1948 there were 697 baptisms in Moldavian Baptist churches; in 1949 the number was 411; in 1950 it dropped to 261. The local churches, however, tried to continue their mission and to receive new members into their fellowship through baptism. The statistical records show that in the 1940s and 1950s the number of new converts was typically two–three times higher than the permission given for baptisms. In the 1950s, in spite of some fluctuation, total membership numbers began to grow gradually. In 1949 there were 4,702 members, in 1953 there were 4,895 members, and in 1964 there were 6,145 members in Moldavian ECB churches.[193] On the whole, the local churches managed to increase their membership and conduct baptisms. The role of baptismal services, as well as the theological understanding of baptism as a witness to a person's faith and a door to church fellowship, cannot be underestimated—this was a spiritually meaningful and theologically binding element of Baptist faith.

Attempts to Unify the Theology of Moldavian Baptist Believers

Representatives from the AUCECB periodically visited regional churches and checked the ministry of senior presbyters and local presbyters. During these visits not only organisational but also theological issues were discussed. The Moldavian ECB churches, particularly the central Kishinev church, when seeking to resolve problems with Astakhov's ministry in Moldova in 1957, immediately got a visit from Mitskevich and Ivanov who appeared as peacemakers and tried to calm the church. Nevertheless, at this stage, the AUCECB did not take into consideration the desire of the Moldavian churches to appoint a senior presbyter from within their own ranks. Instead, the AUCECB took a decision and, as we have seen, Dmitriy Ponomarchuk, the

---

[191] *NARM*, F. 3305, Inv. 1, D. 50, 46-50, pp. 48-49.
[192] *NARM*, F. 3305, Inv. 1, D. 40, p. 142a.
[193] See *NARM*, F. 3305, Inv. 1, D. 40, p. 71, 79-81; *NARM*, F. 3305, Inv. 1, D. 50, pp. 27-28; *NARM*, F. 3305, Inv. 1, D. 65, pp. 18-19, 22-23; *NARM*, F. 3305, Inv. 1, D. 90, p. 4-5, 23-25, 32-33, 273.

leader of the Pentecostals in Ukraine, became the senior presbyter of Moldavian Evangelical Christians–Baptists. Later on in 1960 the AUCECB played the same role, trying to keep the church in Kishinev 'in order', while introducing the documents issued by the AUCECB at the beginning of the 1960s.[194] After the split happened in the 1960s, the AUCECB paid more attention to the needs and expectations of the local churches.

It would be wrong to say that the AUCECB did not work for unity. But, because the AUCECB used mostly administrative measures, and spoke often from the upper ranks of their centralised hierarchical leadership structures, actual unity was difficult to achieve. *Bratskiy Vestnik*, the only periodical of the AUCECB, was also intended to support the 'official' and 'Moscow oriented' line. Nevertheless, in a situation where Christian literature was lacking, the publication offered some spiritual nourishment and functioned as a means of consolidating theological unity within the All-Union Council of ECB churches. It re-emphasised the Evangelical Christians and Baptists' core doctrinal elements, and published some choral songs with music. Besides the information received from *Bratskiy Vestnik*, the local communities had to follow the Statutes that played a major role in defining church life and worship. The 'holy obligation', as it might be termed, for every Baptist community appeared in terms of obedience to every point of Section IV of the *Statutes* that 'related to the structure and function of our communities'.[195] Every local community received rules and regulations[196] concerning how to organise church life and worship. Even today we see the fruits of that unification 'campaign'. For the older generation it is very hard to develop and adopt new forms[197] and styles in church worship or service.

During the period studied here, one of the main principles of Baptist ecclesiology was not followed. This is the principle of the autonomy of every local community. The role of local church meetings was lost. Instead, according the *Statutes* of the AUCECB, the 'All-Union Council of Evangelical Christians–Baptists is the central and directive body of Evangelical Christians–Baptists'.[198] Such accountability to the regulations of AUCECB diminished the principle of local church autonomy. From 1946, in Moldavia, business meetings of church members became a rare event. Instead, for resolving problems or discussing pressing matters, the executive committee or council was chosen by each local community. In this way, ordinary members were deprived of the opportunity to influence the life of their community. If the community continued to organise business meetings with participation by all

---

[194] 'Interview with Vasiliy Perebykovskiy'.

[195] *NARM*, F. 3305, Inv. 1, D. 50, p. 45.

[196] See previous sections on Baptism and Registrations.

[197] Often these 'older' forms are related to more traditional patterns of worship or sermon style.

[198] Ibid., p. 46.

church members, it was described in the official documents as a 'shortcoming'.[199] However, the attempts of local churches, as in Kishinev Baptist Church, to maintain church meetings and to involve all church members in the decision-making process was a sign that Moldavian Baptists tried to keep continuity with the past and retain the principle of communal decision-making that was so central to Baptist communities before the Soviet years. Theological unity and the co-operation of church members were undermined by both the external pressure and by the inner conflicts which characterised the post-war period in Moldavian Baptist life.

Conclusion

After World War II, the life of the formerly well organized and spiritually active Baptist churches of Bessarabia was, to a large extent, destroyed, with the churches being deprived of any possibility to function publicly. The Moldavian Evangelical Christian and Baptist churches existed in a semi-legal state by the end of the 1940s. The Soviet authorities initiated a registration process for the churches, which was accompanied by church closures and mergers. Along with this, anti-religious work was led by the local authorities, often by administrative means. The situation became even more difficult with Khrushchev's anti-religious campaign, which began at the end of the 1950s. Unfortunately, the mergers of local churches did not always lead to greater unity and co-operation, but instead created inner tensions.

Political repression was a major cause of the fragmentation and separation among Baptists in Moldavia. Deportations and arrests of believers in the 1940s not only diminished church membership and deprived many churches of their leaders, but also scattered Baptist believers all over Moldavia, and even to distant locations in the Soviet Union. In addition, under this regime Baptist churches could not exercise their faith as they had been used to before. Weakness and fragmentation, not only in the area of the individual life of the believer and his or her human relationships, but also in theology and church practice, became a harsh reality. Religious laws blatantly denied the exercise of religious freedom; members' meetings in churches became a rare event. Decisions which were previously made by church members meeting together at local church level came to be made by the Union leadership or even by the ECB Moscow headquarters.

Many churches discontinued the bulk of their ministries. The distribution of Christian literature, the running of nursing homes, the organising of youth work—all this was forbidden. For many local churches, the steps taken by the All-Union Council of Evangelical Christians–Baptists were a symbol of the close co-operation of the Baptist leadership with the state. This situation

---

[199] *NARM*, F. 3305, Inv. 1, D. 5, pp. 37-38.

sparked opposition in the form of a movement that spoke against the AUCECB, and that, in turn, led to a painful division and the emergence of two separate bodies of authority among Evangelical Christians–Baptists. All this affected the Moldavian Baptists. The AUCECB represented hierarchical and highly centralised leadership patterns, which did not assist the course of co-operation. Opportunities for Moldavian Baptists to have closer co-operation with the AUCECB were also undermined by the fact that the first senior presbyters in Moldavia tended to speak the language of the state authorities rather than that of the local Moldavian churches. The situation changed in 1965, when Sergeiy Malanchuk, a presbyter from Moldavia, became senior presbyter. He made serious efforts to strengthen the unity within the body of Moldavian Baptists, or at least among registered churches.

The division among the Evangelical Christians–Baptists in the USSR created a new structure, which had to exist illegally—the Council of Churches of Evangelical Christians–Baptists. Starting in 1962, the AUCECB made a number of attempts to restore the former unity through congresses, circular letters, visitations and the publication *Bratskiy Vestnik*. In 1966 the Committee for Unification was formed by the AUCECB, in order to soften the consequences of the painful split among Baptists in the Soviet Union. Representatives of the Committee also visited Moldavia. In some cases their work did bring positive results; some of the earlier separated groups returned to the registered churches and registered churches were joined more closely together. However, in most cases there was little success: even today many former 'underground' Baptist churches refuse to co-operate with the formerly 'registered' churches.

Separation and co-operation was also an issue on the local church level. Baptist leaders in Moldavia tried to enhance the sense of believers belonging together. Celebrations of local church anniversaries, love feasts, fellowship, baptismal services, as well as wedding ceremonies that were often turned into evangelistic meetings—all these events helped the 'Baptist flock' to stay together in face of government pressure. In addition, the attempts of the AUCECB to keep contact with Moldavian Baptists should not be played down. However, it seems that only after the 1960s did the Moldavian registered churches begin to be better integrated into the All-Union work, though the other—opposite—trend was that the 'underground' churches drifted away from the official Union.

At present, the Moldovan Baptist body is represented by three main structures. The oldest one is the Union of the Churches of Evangelical Christians–Baptists of Moldova (UCECBM), with its bishop Valeriu Giletchi and general secretary Victor Popovich. The second Union appeared as a result of the schism among Baptists in 1961; this is the Council of the Churches of Evangelical Christians–Baptists in Moldova. The third Baptist body is the product of an attempt by some leaders of unregistered churches toward reconciliation between the CCECB and the registered churches of the

UCECBM, one that finally brought about another division among the CCECB. This ultimately gave birth, in 1986, to the Independent Churches. In 2000, the Association of Independent Churches in Moldova was formed with its present leader Vladimir Scherbina. Together all three bodies include about 25,000 Baptist church members. The challenge of how to co-operate as Baptists still remains.

Bibliography

Archives

National Archives of the Republic of Moldova (*NARM*), Files of the Commissioner of the Affairs of Religious Cults (F. No. 3305).

Unpublished Sources

Agaev, Emil, 'History of the Baptist Church 'Bethel' in Chisinau in Period 1945-1972' (Chisinau: College of Theology and Education, 2000).
Alimatov, Anvar, 'History of the Baptist Church in Ceadir-Lunga Village in Period 1945-1992' (Chisinau: College of Theology and Education, 2000).
Andriuta, Anatol, 'History of the Baptist Church in Singerenii Noi Village' (Chisinau: College of Theology and Education, 2001).
Arabadji, Mikhail, 'History of the Baptist Church in Sofievca' (Chisinau: College of Theology and Education, 2000).
Arnaut, Dmitriy, 'History of the Baptist Church in Taraclia Village' (Chisinau: College of Theology and Education, 2000).
Belev, Pavel, 'History of the Baptist Church 'Spring of Life' in Chisinau' (Chisinau: College of Theology and Education, 2000).
Botnari, Alexeiy, 'History of the Baptist Church in Tintareni Village' (Chisinau: College of Theology and Education, 2000).
Cornei, Andreiy, 'History of the Baptist Church in Pirlita Village' (Chisinau: College of Theology and Education, 2001).
Cucer, Ion, 'History of the Baptist Church in Carpineni Village' (Chisinau: College of Theology and Education, 2002).
Davnyy, Vasiliy, 'Grigoriy Antonovich Rudenko' (Chisinau, 2000).
_____, 'History of the Appearance and Development of the Evangelical Christian –Baptist Movement in Moldova' (Chisinau, 2000).
Diduc, Alexander, 'History of Origin and Development of the Baptist Movement in Balti City' (Chisinau: College of Theology and Education, 2002).
Donchev, Ivan, 'The Brief Historic Sketch of the Church in Congaz Village' (Chisinau: College of Theology and Education, 2001).
Gheata, Vadim, 'History of the Baptist Church in Baltata' (Chisinau: College of Theology and Education, 2001).
Grischuk, Andrey, 'The Historic Sketch of Asnasanii-Noi Church' (Chisinau: College of Theology and Education, 2001).
'History of the Church in Iscalau' (Chisinau: College of Theology and Education, 2001).
Khmelev, Valeriy, 'History of the Church in Dollinoe Village' (Chisinau: College of Theology and Education, 2002).
Kobivnic, Serghey, 'History of the Baptist Church in Mihailovca Village' (Chisinau: College of Theology and Education, 2002).

Malancea, Viorel, 'History of the Baptist Church in Slobozia Village, Stefan Voda' (Chisinau: College of Theology and Education, 2002).
Marco, Sergiu, 'History of the Baptist Church in Biruinta Town', (Chisinau College of Theology and Education, 2001).
Nikolov, Andreiy, 'History of the Baptist Church in Iscalau Village' (Chisinau: College of Theology and Education, 2002).
Pascan, Alexandru, 'History of the Baptist Church in Pohrebeni Village' (Chisinau: College of Theology and Education, 2002).
Patrascu, Petru, 'History of Baptist Church 'Betania' in Bascalia' (Chisinau: College of Theology and Education, 2002).
Plamadeala, Ion, 'History of Baptist Church in Singerei City' (Chisinau: College of Theology and Education, 2001).
Popesku, Andrey, 'History of the Development of the Local Church in the Village Buzduganii, de Sus' (Chisinau: College of Theology and Education, 2001).
Roman, Carp, 'History of the Baptist Church in Crasnoarmeisc Village' (Chisinau: College of Theology and Education, 2001).
Rotaru, Eduard, 'History of the Baptist Church in Orhei' (Chisinau: College of Theology and Education, 2001).
Saharnean, Victor, 'History of the Baptist Church in Olanesti, Tighina' (Chisinau: College of Theology and Education, 2002).
Schablenco, Evgheniy, 'History of the Baptist Church in Grigoriopol' (Chisinau: College of Theology and Education, 2001).
Schuparskiy, Denis, 'History of the ECB Church in Zozuleni Noi village' (Chisinau: College of Theology and Education, 2001).
Sinogaci, M., 'History of the Baptist Church in Bascalia Village' (Chisinau: College of Theology and Education, 2001).
Taranu, Andreiy, 'History of the Baptist Church in Causeni City' (Chisinau: College of Theology and Education, 2002).
Tutelea, Sergiu, 'History of the Baptist Church in Calmatui Village' (Chisinau: College of Theology and Education, 2002).
Voronov, Sergey, 'History of the Baptist Church in Ungheni City' (Chisinau: College of Theology and Education, 2002).
Voronova, Olga, 'History of the Baptist Church in Agronomovca' (Chisinau: College of Theology and Education, 2002).
Vrancean, Ion, 'History of the Baptist Church in Vadu- lui- Isaak' (Chisinau: College of Theology and Education, 2001).
_____, 'History of the Baptist Church in Vulcanesti Town' (Chisinau: College of Theology and Education, 2001).

Electronic Sources

Ubeivolk, V.I. 'Interview with Rymskoy' in 'Protestantism in the Former Soviet Union', The History of the Evangelical Movement in Eurasia (Electronic Christian Library; Euro-Asian Accrediting Association of Evangelical Schools, 2001).

'Interview with Vasiliy Perebykovskiy', Project of Oral History, 'Protestantism in the Former Soviet Union', in History of Euro-Asian Evangelical Movement, Primary Sources, Electronic Christian Library (EAAA, 2001).
'Interview with Anatoliy Zakhartsev', Project of Oral History, 'Protestantism in the Former Soviet Union', in History of Euro-Asian Evangelical Movement, Primary Sources, Electronic Christian Library (EAAA, 2001).
'Interview with Ivan Slobodchikov', Project of Oral History 'Protestantism in the Former Soviet Union', in History of Euro-Asian Evangelical Movement, Primary Sources, Electronic Christian Library (EAAA, 2001).
'Interview with Mitskevich', taken by Kornilov N. A., Project of Oral History 'Protestantism in the Former Soviet Union', in History of Euro-Asian Evangelical Movement, Primary Sources, Electronic Christian Library (EAAA, 2001).
Klimenko, Nelli, 'Doklad: Sovet Tserkvey I Dvizhenie Nezavisimykh Tserkvey', from Electronic Christian Library 'History Of Euro-Asian Evangelical Movement: Primary Sources' (EAAA: 2001).
Lubaschenko V.I., Istoriya Protestantizmu v Ukraine: Kurs Lektsiy., 2nd ed., added and revised. (Kiev: Polys, 1995), from Electronic Christian Library 'History of Euro-Asian Evangelical Movement: Primary Sources', (EAAA: 2001).
Nikol'skaya, Tat'yana, 'Kto Takie 'Otdelennye'?'(Who Is 'Separated'?), Мирт (Mirt) 5:30 (September-October 2001), online at www.gazeta.mirt.ru.
Rushbrooke, J.H., 'About the Attitude to the Government', P.V. Ivanov-Klyschnikov (trans.), Baptist, 1 (1927) 18, in History of Euro-Asian Evangelical Movement, Primary Sources, Electronic Christian Library (EAAA, 2001).
State Archive of Lviv Region (SALR), F. No. 1332, Inv. No. 1, D. No. 37, 32, 50, 55, 57-58, from Electronic Christian Library 'History Of Euro-Asian Evangelical Movement: primary sources' (EAAA: 2001).

Published Sources in English

Beeson, Trevor, *Discretion and Valour, Religious Conditions in Russia and Eastern Europe* (Glasgow: Fontana-Collins, 1974).
'Bessarabia', Link 24 (1940), p. 3.
Bondareva, Irina, 'Baptist Origins and Early Development in Moldova', *Journal of European Baptist Studies* 2:3 (2002), p. 31-44.
Brooks, Charles A. and J.H. Rushbrooke, 'Report of Commissioners of the Baptist World Alliance, Presented at the Conference in London, 19 July 1920', *Baptist Work in Europe* (London: Baptist Union Publication Department, 1920).
Cocutz, J., 'Baptists of Bessarabia', *The Watchman–Examiner* (15 August 1940), pp. 886-887.
Craighead, W.E., 'The Gospel in Bessarabia', *Home and Foreign Fields* (April 1935), pp. 10-11.

_____, 'Bessarabian Russians Pressing Toward The Mark', *Home and Foreign Fields* (May 1937), p. 19.
_____, 'Redeeming the Time', *The Commission* (September 1940), p. 249.
_____, 'The Soviet Invasion', *The Commission* 3:9 (1940), p. 275.
_____, 'Watchman, What of the Night? The Morning Cometh', *The Commission* 2:9 (1939), pp. 299, 316.
King, Charles, *The Moldovans: Romania, Russia and the Politics of Culture* (Stanford, Calif.: Hoover Institution Press, 1999).
McBeth, H. Leon, *The Baptist Heritage* (Nashville: Broadman Press, 1987).
Russell, D.S., 'Church-State Relations in the Soviet Union: Recollections and Reflections on the 'Cold War' Years', *The Baptist Quarterly* 36 (1995-1996), pp. 21-28.
'Soviet Local Authorities Combat Religion', *Documents in Religion in Communist Land* 7:3 (1979).
Trutza, Peter, Mrs., 'A Short History of Roumanian Baptists', *The Chronicle* 5:1 (1942), pp. 12-13.
Wardin, W. Albert, ed., *Baptists Around the World* (Nashville: Broadman and Holman Publishers, 1995).

Published Sources in Russian and Romanian

Alexeeva, Alla, 'Special Blessing', *Svet Jizni* 2-3 (1998), pp. 22-28.
Vestnik Istiny (The Messenger of Truth) 1-2 (2002); 1-3 (2001); 3 (2000); 4 (1999).
Davnyy, V., 'It was so...' *Svet Zhizni* (The Light of Life) 2-3 (1999), pp. 36-41.
Istoriya Evangel'skikh Khristian-Baptistov v SSSR (A History of Evangelical Christians-Baptists in the USSR) (Moscow: All-Union Council of Evangelical Christians-Baptists, 1989).
Loginov, Victor, 'The Brotherhood of EChB in Moldova', *Khristianskoe Slovo* (Christian Word), (September-October 1993), p. 2.
Meaun, Alexander, 'Tempered by Fire', *Svet Zhizni* 5-6 (1998), pp. 36-37.
Mitskevich, A.I., 'Vospominaniya o Vozniknovenii Dela Gospodnego v Moldavii' (Remembering the Origins of God's Work in Moldavia), *Bratskiy Vestnik* 2 (1955), pp. 53-57.
Mocan, Olga, 'Lydia', *Svet Zhizni,* 1 (1995), pp. 7-8; 2 (1995), p. 14.
_____, 'Many Knew Him', *Svet Zhizni* 1 (1999), pp. 18-21.
'Novo-Asnashanskaya Tserkov' (The Church in Novo-Asnasani Village), *Svet Zhizni* 8-9 (2000), pp. 2-7.
Popovici, Alexa, *Istoria Baptiștilor din România Vol. 2, 1919-1944* (A History of Baptists in Romania) (Chicago: Editura Bisericii Baptiste Romāne, 1989).
Tentuyk, Grigoriy, 'Tropoyu Muzhestva' (The Path of Courage), *Svet Zhizni* 4 (1998), pp. 6-14.
Pasat, Valeriy (ed.), *Trudnye Stranitsy Istorii Moldavii 1940-1950-e gody* (Hard Pages in the History of Moldavia) (Moscow: Terra, 1994).
Placinta, S., 'Revival', *Svet Zhizni* 3-4 (1996), pp. 6-7; 5 (1996), pp. 4-5.

Reschetnikov, Y. and S. Sannikov, *Obzor Istorii Evangel'sko-Baptistskogo Bratstva na Ukraine* (A Review of the History of Evangelical Baptist Brotherhood in Ukraine) (Bogomyslie: Odessa, 2000).

Sannikov, S.V., *Dvadtsat' Vekov Khristianstva, Vtoroe Tysyacheletie* (Twenty Centuries of Christianity) (Odessa: Bogomyslie, 2001).

Savinsky, S.N., *Istoriya Russko-Ykrainskogo Baptizma* (A History of the Russian-Ukrainian Baptist Movement) (Odessa: Odessa Theological Seminary, Bogomyslie, 1995).

Sawatsky, Walter, *Evangelicheskoe Dvizhenie v SSSR Posle Vtoroy Mirovoy Voyny* (Soviet Evangelicals Since World War II), N.A. Kornylov (trans.) (Moscow, 1995).

Schemchishin, V.P., 'Zarozhdenie I Razvitie Evangel'sko-Baptistskogo Dvizheniya v Bessarsbii (Opyt Opisaniya Istochnikov)' ('The Origins and Development of Evangelical-Baptist Movement in Bessarabia'), unpub. thesis (Kiev: Kiev Theological Seminary, 1998).

Sorochan, G., 'Northern Lights', *Svet Zhizni* 2 (1997), pp. 4-5.

'Southern Legacy', *Svet Zhizni,* 3 (1997), pp. 4-5.

'The Congress of the Union of EChB of Moldova', *Khristianskoe Slovo* (Christian Word) (April 1992), p. 8.

Vartichan, I.K., ed., *Moldavskaya Sovetskaya Encyclopediya* (Moldavian Soviet Encyclopedia) (Chisinau: Redactia Principala A Enciclopediei Sovetice Moldovenesti, 1979).

CHAPTER 3

August Jauhiainen and the Pentecostal Dilemma in the Finnish Baptist Union (1930-1953)

Anneli Lohikko

Baptist history in Finland began in 1856 in Ahvenanmaa (Åland)[1] Island, which is situated between Finland and Sweden. Ahvenanmaa, though part of Finland, is Swedish-speaking, and its connections with Sweden have always been important. It was natural, then, that Baptist ideas, which had come to Sweden in 1839 through a seaman, Fredrik Olaus Nilsson,[2] first reached that part of the country. A Lutheran priest from Ahvenanmaa had written a letter to some of his friends in Stockholm asking them to send an evangelist.[3] In response, the Evangelical Alliance sent Karl Justus Mathias Möllersvärd, a Baptist. Möllersvärd had been converted in the First Baptist Mariners' Church in New York.[4] On mainland Finland, Baptist beliefs 'came ashore' in 1869, also spreading first of all among Swedish-speaking Finns.[5] The Lutheran Cathedral Chapter in Turku (Åbo) arranged two hearings to discuss the activities of some Ahvenanmaa Baptists, and at the second of these, the clergyman Henrik Heikel,

---

[1] Many place names in Finland have both a Finnish and a Swedish name. In this study, when a place is mentioned for the first time its Finnish form is given first and the Swedish name follows it in brackets; otherwise only the Finnish form is used.

[2] George Fridén (ed.), *Svensk Baptism Genom 100 år, En Krönika i Ord och Bild* (The Swedish Baptist Movement through 100 Years, A Chronicle with Words and Pictures) (Stockholm: Ernst Westerbergs Boktryckeri AB, 1948), pp. 4-5.

[3] David Edén, *Svenska Baptisternas i Finland Historia 1856-1931* (The History of the Swedish-speaking Baptists in Finland 1856-1931) (Wasa: 1931), p. 29.

[4] Ibid., p. 29.

[5] Finland has two official languages, Swedish and Finnish. Although the Finnish-speaking population has always been the absolute majority, equality of languages was declared in 1902, but it was not until the 1930s that Finnish really gained equality alongside Swedish. (J. Ekonen, V. Kulju, T. Mantsinen and J. Tarkka, *Ihmisen Tiet*, 3-4 painos (The Ways of Man, 3rd-4th edition) (Helsinki-Keuruu: Otava, 1995), p. 7.) New ideas used to gain a footing first among the Swedish-speaking population, and thus also the first Free Church congregations were usually Swedish-speaking.

who was the head of the Chapter, attended. He became interested while listening to these Baptists.[6] His family was also drawn to Baptist beliefs. It was his son, Viktor Heikel, who was the first of the Heikel family to be baptized as a believer. His baptiser was a well-known Swedish Baptist leader, Anders Wiberg. This happened in Sweden on 5 June, 1868, and Viktor's sister, Anna Heikel, was baptized three weeks later in Örebro, Sweden.[7]

The first Finnish-speaking Baptist groups in Finland were formed in 1871; one in Luvia, on the west coast of the country, the other far away from it, in Parikkala, Karelia, in the eastern part of Finland.[8] In the 1870s Baptist work was started in Jurva and Laihia (Laihela).[9] The Kuopio Baptist congregation[10] was established in 1886, and Turku in 1887. In the 1890s Baptist congregations came into being in Tampere, in Viipuri (Viborg), in Ylistaro, in Oulu, and in Pori (Björneborg). The congregations were small, with about three-hundred members altogether.[11] At first Finnish and Swedish speaking Baptist congregations worked together. Towards the end of the nineteenth century the language problem became evident. Finnish-speaking Baptists founded their own publication, *Totuuden Kaiku*, in 1896. This was not enough, though. In the July issue of *Totuuden Kaiku* in 1897 we read that Finnish-speaking Baptists felt frustrated in the Annual Meetings of the Union because very few of them spoke Swedish. Only occasionally were some of the items translated into Finnish, which was not enough for the Finnish-speaking delegates to understand properly the issues being discussed in the meeting.[12] The inevitable

---

[6] Nils Näsman, *Baptismen i Svenska Österbotten 1868-1905, Finska Kyrkohistoriska Samfundets Handlingar 63*. (The Baptist Movement in Swedish East Bothnia 1868-1905, The Publications of the Finnish Church Historical Society 63) (Helsingfors: Finska Kyrkohistoriska Samfundet, 1962), p. 62.
[7] Ibid., pp. 67-68.
[8] J. D. Hughey, M. Kolomainen, V. Toivola, *Baptistit, Oppi–Käytäntö–Historia* (Baptists, Doctrine–Practice–History) (Jyväskylä: 1970), p. 111. In Parikkala Baptist work was started by a former Lutheran priest, John Hymander. He was baptized in Stockholm in 1872. After returning home, Hymander baptized his wife and a couple of others who had been converted through his preaching. He was already sixty-nine, and did not live long after his baptism. Ibid., p. 112.
[9] Hughey, et al, *Baptistit*, p. 112.
[10] The Finnish Free Churches use the word *congregation* (*seurakunta* in Finnish) instead of *church* (*kirkko* in Finnish) of their individual churches. In some cases both words are used, as in *Tampereen Vapaakirkkoseurakunta*, Tampere Free Church Congregation. Methodists, Free Evangelicals, and Pentecostals use the word *Church* about the denomination as a whole, whereas Baptists stick to the term *Union*. The distinction between *congregation* and *church* was not made in earlier dissertations written in English about the Finnish Baptists, but I find it important to make because this is still the praxis.
[11] Hughey, et al, *Baptisti*, pp. 115-116.
[12] Hughey, et al, *Baptistit*, gives more insight into this matter. Kolomainen notes that important Swedish speeches and comments in Annual Meetings were translated into Finnish but those in Finnish were not translated into Swedish at all, p. 122.

happened, and the Finnish-speaking congregations decided on 15 June 1902 to form a body separate from the Swedish-speaking Baptists, and a board was elected to lead its work.[13]

When studying the history of the Finnish-speaking Baptists I have used various sources. There are no history books that specifically address the subject. Mikko Kolomainen, the rector of the Finnish Baptist Union's Bible School (1949-1971), wrote a short account of developments (about five thousand words) in the book by Hughey, Kolomainen and Toivola, *Baptistit, Oppi—Käytäntö—Historia (Baptists, Doctrine—Practice—History)*.[14] Teuvo Aaltio, who studied at the International Baptist Theological Seminary in Rüschlikon, wrote his dissertation about the history of the Union, but it is also very limited in scope.[15] Markku Niskanen studied in his treatise the history of the Finnish-speaking Baptists 1896-1922.[16] The lack of a more comprehensive study has both complicated my work and made it challenging.

The unpublished sources available for this dissertation are Minutes of the Baptist Union's Executive Committee, Minutes of the Official Meetings of delegates, Annual Reports of the Union to Annual Meetings, Minutes of the Preachers' Union, together with an extensive correspondence of August Jauhiainen, both official and private.[17] I have also studied the Minutes of the Congregational Meetings of the two biggest Finnish Baptist congregations: Tampere, and Vaajakoski. These together with the Union's magazine, *Totuuden Kaiku*, have been my guides to the history of the Finnish Baptist Union (FBU). The first observation while reading through these sources was that *Totuuden Kaiku* gives a one-sided picture of the history. Difficult things are never discussed on its pages during the time that I am focusing on. However it is almost the only source for Finnish Baptist theology. It is important to recognise when studying the life of the Finnish Baptist Union, or any other Free Church Movement in Finland, that they are all marginal groups in a predominantly Lutheran country.[18] There are almost no surveys available about Free Church theology, dogmatics or doctrinal issues. It is necessary to read the publications and documents of each denomination to learn what they think.

In the history of the Finnish Baptist Union there are three men and three periods that are prominent: John Gustaf Kokki's period (1902-1931); August

---

[13] J.G. Kokki, 'Kotoa ja Muualta' (From Home and Elsewhere), *Totuuden Kaiku* 7 (The Echo of Truth, the Finnish Baptist Union's monthly publication) (1902), p. 3.

[14] Hughey, et al, *Baptistit*, pp. 107-134.

[15] Teuvo Aaltio, *The History of the National Baptists in Finland*, unpub. thesis (Rüschlikon-Zürich, Switzerland: Baptist Theological Seminary, 1958).

[16] Markku Niskanen, *The Finnish-speaking Baptists 1896-1922*, unpub. thesis (Rüschlikon-Zürich, Switzerland: Baptist Theological Seminary, 1984).

[17] This correspondence takes up 110 cms of a storage unit. The Finnish Baptist Unions Archives.

[18] About 1.2% of the population belong to different Free Churches, 83.2% are Lutherans (national church), and 1.1% are Orthodox Christians (national church).

Jauhiainen's period (1931-1953); and Jouko Neulanen's period (1970-1991). All these men were powerful leaders of the Union: they were the Union Presidents, the chief editors of the Union's magazine, even the treasurers of the Union. In this study I will concentrate on the time period from 1930 to 1953. There are two reasons for that. First, Markku Niskanen has studied in his dissertation the earliest period of FBU history, i.e. John Gustaf Kokki's period. Second, the period of 1930-1953 is of personal interest to me, because August Jauhiainen, who was the President through that period, is my grandfather. This has made my work both fascinating and difficult. Studying the life of such a close relative demands special caution in order not to be partial or guilty of favouritism.

The decade of the 1930s was a time both to disentangle and to build. The former President J.G. Kokki had led the Union since 1904. He seems to have run short of new ideas in his work and there were, as we will see, serious problems. The enthusiasm had gone. After the end of his presidency it took time to put everything in order again, and to create and re-establish trust. Jauhiainen, who became President in 1931, was a firm leader, and he worked very hard. His strategy is dealt with in detail in this study because that forms the foundation of his work during the decades he worked for the Union. The task was not easy for the new leader. For most of the Union members, Jauhiainen was quite an unknown person since he had returned to Finland from Inkeri, in Russia, only two years before he was elected President. He was straightforward, even strict, which, although quite typical of the leaders of that time, did not make his task easier. From a theological point of view especially, his view of the Holy Spirit is of interest because questions about the Holy Spirit were in his time (and still are) a much-discussed topic in the Union. These questions were mostly discussed with emotion, and generally were not studied thoroughly and seriously within the Union. This must be one of the main reasons why they were, and still are, something of a problem for many Finnish Baptists.

During the early 1940s war was raging all over Europe. Finland was having a very difficult time with its neighbour, the Soviet Union. The Winter War in 1939-1940 was hard, but Finland was able to maintain its independence, which was a miracle. Then there was a short period of peace, which ended in 1941. Finland, in order to secure its independence, entered into alliance with Germany, and by so doing was again drawn into war against the Soviet Union when Germany attacked it in 1941. The Continuation War began, and lasted until 2 September 1944.[19] This was not the end of war, however. According to the peace pact, Finns had to disarm German troops that still were on Finnish soil. Now Finland was at war with its former ally Germany. By the end of April

---

[19] Arvi Korhonen, ed., *Suomen Historian Käsikirja, Jälkimmäinen Osa* (The Handbook of Finnish History, Latter Part) (Helsinki: WSOY, 1949), p. 656.

1945 the last German troops had gone.[20] During the war years, life in Baptist congregations was quiet, but the end of war meant many new opportunities for the Union. Towards the end of the 1940s financial help from abroad increased considerably. The Union was able to start a three-year course in a newly established Bible School. Mikko Kolomainen, who had just graduated from Bristol Baptist College, England, became its first rector. What had been a dream for decades had finally come true. A new enthusiasm swept across Finnish Baptist congregations. New books were published by *Totuuden Kaiku*, and a committee was started to increase publishing.[21]

In the late 1940s the majority of the preachers and leaders of the FBU were Pentecostally-minded. For Jauhiainen the sphere of the Holy Spirit was important, but he did not understand it in the Pentecostal way. He supported the Baptist principle of freedom of thought, and as Union leader he gave space for opinions that differed from his own on the question of the so-called 'baptism in the Holy Spirit'. But he belonged to the minority with his view, and was put in a difficult situation.[22] The first really serious conflict happened at the beginning of 1948. The Executive Committee (EC) would not give him permission to publish his *Raamatuntutkisteluopas* (*A Guide to the Study of the Bible*), before three other preachers had read it, paying special attention to his teaching about the Holy Spirit.[23] Jauhiainen's work in the 1950s as Union President turned out to be short. His official and personal correspondence at that time do not indicate difficulties between him and other preachers and leaders of the FBU. But in 1953 he was dismissed. The reason, according to the official decision, was his universalist doctrine—that all would ultimately be saved.[24] Jauhiainen himself did not agree that this was the reason, because, although having come to believe this doctrine, he never preached about it and had even promised the Executive Committee that he would never do so. He considered that the real reason for his dismissal was that he was not a Pentecostally-minded preacher.[25]

The topic of this dissertation is important within Finland, because different views about the work of the Holy Spirit are still alive and are still causing problems in the Finnish Baptist Union. Many people even think that the Union has remained small over the years because it has not paid enough attention to the issue of the work of the Holy Spirit. My own conclusion, after studying the history of FBU, is different. I will seek to argue that the main reason the Union has remained so small has been the constant quarrels that from time to time

---

[20] Korhonen, ed., *Suomen Historian Käsikirja,* pp. 656-660.
[21] *The Minutes of the Meeting of Delegates* [hereafter *MOMD*] (24 June 1948), § [article] 14.
[22] A. Jauhiainen, Letter to four members of the Executive Committee living in Turku, *Official Correspondence* [hereafter *OC*] (12 May 1949).
[23] *Minutes of the Executive Committee* [hereafter *MEC*] (3 January 1948) § 6.
[24] This question was dealt with in the *MEC* (2 July 1953), § 12.
[25] A. Jauhiainen, Letter to Dr Edwin A. Bell (the representative of the American Baptist Foreign Mission Society in Europe), *OC* (6 July 1953).

have torn the Union from inside. When these quarrels and the issues behind them were not properly dealt with, the problems remained. The issues from the first part of the twentieth century were not forgotten but kept on influencing the life of this small Union even after several decades had passed.

Having given this introduction, which alludes to topics which I will examine in more detail, I now turn in the next chapter to the wider picture of Free Church life in Finland during the time being studied here. I will briefly introduce the two other Free Church denominations which are closest to Baptists, namely *Suomen Vapaakirkko*, the Finnish Free Evangelical Church, and *Helluntaiherätys*, the Pentecostal Movement or more exactly the Pentecostal Revival.

Baptists and Other Free Churches in Finland

Baptists were the oldest but were by no means the only Free Church movement coming on to Finnish soil in the nineteenth century. To sharpen the picture of the special Baptist emphases in the history of broader Finnish Free Church life, I will give a short account in this chapter of two other Finnish Free Churches, namely the Free Evangelical Church, and the Pentecostal Movement,[26] looking especially at aspects of their experience during an important period of their life in the first half of the twentieth century. These two Free churches are quite close doctrinally to the FBU in a number of important respects and I will examine their relationships with Baptists.[27]

The Free Evangelical Church started its activities only a few years later than the Baptists. Constantine Boije, who was born in 1854 to a noble family, started arranging free religious meetings in Southern Finland, in Sipoo[28] and its surroundings, during 1873-1874, with his friend Jakob Forsberg.[29] This work was carried out in Swedish, and the Free Finnish Home Mission (*Den Fria Inre*

---

[26] The Finnish Pentecostal Movement did not form itself into an official church until 2002 when a small minority of Pentecostal congregations expressed their willingness to become part of the Finnish Pentecostal Church. Their congregations were, and most of them still are, independent, without any kind of official umbrella organization.

[27] For an analysis of Baptist Free Churchmanship see N.G. Wright, *Free Church, Free State* (Carlisle: Paternoster, 2005).

[28] S.S. Salmensaari writes in *Suomen Vapaakirkko, Piirteitä Sen Synnystä ja Kehityksestä* (The Finnish Free Evangelical Church, Traits of its Beginning and Development) (Tampere: Päivä, 1957), p. 39, that it is evidently Boije who first taught and put into practice the communion of baptised believers in Finland in Sipoo, in 1880. This was not, however, the first time. In 1856, in Ahvenanmaa, five people had communion after the baptism of three believers. Alwar Sundell, *De började—Vi Fortsätter, Baptismen i Finland 100 år, 1856-1956* (They Began—We Continue, Baptists in Finland 100 Years, 1856-1956) (Vasa: AB Frams Tryckeri, 1956), p. 14.

[29] Salmensaari, *Suomen Vapaakirkko*, p. 38.

Missionen i Finland) was established, but because of lack of financial resources this work did not have any further success. Boije started to work for the British and Foreign Bible Society. From 1879 he received support for a couple of years for his work in Finland from Sweden.[30] A revival broke out in 1877. The first church building was built in Vehkakoski, near Sipoo in southern Finland the same year. In Oulu, which is in the northern part of Finland, there had been a revival as early as 1860 among the Swedish-speaking population, and in 1877 again, this time especially among young people.[31] Another influence was Lord Radstock, from England, who visited Finland for the first time during the autumn of 1879. He was part of the Plymouth Brethren, and encouraged free evangelistic work without any church structures led by clergy, an approach which certainly affected Free Evangelicals. His visits to Finland were significant for the spread of the Free Evangelical Mission.[32]

The Free Evangelical Church first functioned as a Home Mission Movement inside the national Lutheran Church in a way that had parallels in other Lutheran Churches.[33] Quite soon it became evident that this was not a viable solution: the Lutherans started to demand separation because the evangelicals were seen as 'enemies of faith'. This was due to their active efforts to bring about what, from their point of view, was the 'real Christian faith, and biblical changes among the Lutherans'.[34] On the other hand, there was pressure to enlarge the Free Church constituency from both Baptists and Methodists, both of which had formed themselves into independent church movements.[35] It was not until 1921 that the Swedish-speaking Free Church people formed their own church, *Fria Missionsförbundet* and the Finnish-speaking followed their example in 1923, forming the Finnish Free Evangelical Church, *Suomen Vapaakirkko*.[36]

The Finnish-speaking Free Evangelical Church, started to grow significantly during the 1920s. Membership doubled from 1,202 in 1921 to 2,427 in 1930.[37] From then on it grew and has continued to grow steadily, being now the second biggest Free Church movement in Finland with a membership of 8,669.[38] One of the main ideas of the Free Evangelical Church was that the visible church should be as much as possible like the invisible unity of all believers, to which

---

[30] Ibid., pp. 38-39.
[31] Ibid., p. 40.
[32] Ibid., p. 42.
[33] For background see N. Hope, *German and Scandinavian Protestantism 1700-1918* (Oxford: Oxford University Press, 1999).
[34] Salmensaari, *Suomen Vapaakirkko,* pp. 141-142.
[35] Ibid., p. 142.
[36] Ibid., pp. 255, 258.
[37] Ibid., p. 455.
[38] *Vapaakirkon Vuosikirja 2002*. (The Annual Report of the Free Evangelical Church, 2002) At the end of 2002 there were 8,669 baptized members, 3,313 children, and 2,082 associate members, which makes more than 14,000 members in all.

all God's children belonged, and every believer should have freedom to live according to the light that was given to him/her by God.[39] Baptists and Free Evangelicals did not get along well together. In *Totuuden Kaiku* there were articles and warnings against Free Evangelicals. Perhaps the most striking reasons for that were that the Free Evangelicals then practised both infant baptism and believers' baptism and had open communion, which Baptists interpreted as a mixing together of believers and non-believers.[40] They had also started their work inside the Lutheran Church hoping to be able to remain there,[41] which Baptists, whom the Lutheran Church had persecuted for their faith, considered as fraternizing with the church which besides persecuting 'true believers' had 'kept the mark of the beast, infant baptism...'[42] Strong feelings were in evidence.

S.S. Salmensaari, the author of the latest available history of the Free Evangelical Church, gives an account and an analysis of the relationships between Baptists and Free Evangelicals. In East Botnia, the upper western coast of Finland, many people from Baptist congregations[43] moved to local Free Evangelical congregations, and many of those Baptists who did not move still had a Free Evangelical ideology. This was especially the case regarding the issue of baptism. Salmensaari sees that Baptists had a difficult choice to make: either to stick to their opinion of believer's baptism only as the prerequisite for church membership or to open the membership of the churches to those who were baptized as infants. Salmensaari draws the conclusion that when the more 'tolerant' people left the Baptists, the Baptist movement became more and more intolerant, and from then on they did not attract Free Evangelicals, who saw themselves as 'the champions of the unity of all believers', into their congregations.[44] During the period examined in this dissertation both Unions seemed to concentrate on their own work without much connection with each other except on a personal level.

When the Pentecostal Movement came to Finland in the early years of the twentieth century, it affected all the Free Churches which were already working in the country. The Pentecostal movements in Norway and Sweden were

---

[39] Salmensaari, *Suomen Vapaakirkko*, p. 456.

[40] J. Nostaja, 'Upotus ja Ehtoollinen' ('Baptism and Eucharist'), *Totuuden Kaiku* 4, (1897), pp. 5-7.

[41] See more about the subject in Salmensaari, 'Allianssikokous Tampereella' ('Alliance Meeting in Tampere'), *Suomen Vapaakirkko*, pp. 84-88,

[42] V. Palomaa, 'Uskottomia Kristityitä' ('Unfaithful Believers'), *Totuuden Kaiku* 2, (1896), pp. 1-4.

[43] Anna Heikel, a pioneer of Sunday School work in Finland, was one of them. She came into contact with P.P. Waldenström's books *Smärtornas Man* (The Man of Agony), and *Försoningen* (Redemption), and found Baptists too radical, while she herself was moderate. More about relations between Baptists and Free Evangelicals is to be found in Nils Näsman, *Baptismen i Svenska Österbotten 1868-1905*, pp. 280-286.

[44] Salmensaari, *Suomen Vapaakirkko*, p. 90.

indebted to Baptist life.⁴⁵ In Finland many people from Free Evangelical churches left these congregations for Pentecostal churches, and the Pentecostal teaching about baptism in the Holy Spirit gained many followers among them. Salmensaari sees in both an insistence on Spirit-baptism—which is central to Pentecostal teaching—and on believers' baptism—which is central to Baptist teaching—a narrow-mindedness which he finds very regrettable. This, according to him, alienated many Free Evangelicals from the idea of a really free church, and displaced the diversity of which the New Testament speaks so much.⁴⁶ He was definitely not positive about Baptist or Pentecostal ideas among the Free Evangelicals. On the contrary, he saw Pentecostalism as in many ways a disturbing influence, especially through some Pentecostal prophets who were listened to and respected by Free Evangelicals.⁴⁷

From the beginning of the Pentecostal revivals in Finland the activity of the Holy Spirit was a known phenomenon in the Finnish Baptist Union. A Methodist pastor from Kristiania (nowadays Oslo), Thomas Ball Barratt (1862-1940),⁴⁸ who has been called the Pentecostal Apostle of Europe,⁴⁹ visited Finland for the first time in 1911.⁵⁰ Also another Norwegian, G.O. Smidt, a former Salvation Army officer in the USA, came to visit Finland. He had been dismissed from Salvation Army when he was filled with the Holy Spirit and he had joined the Pentecostals. When Smidt met with Barratt in Norway, Barratt told him about Finland, and Smidt felt called to work there,⁵¹ which he did for a couple of years. Many Finns did not like his way of preaching—they felt he was too American—nevertheless, many people were converted in his meetings in different parts of Finland.⁵² A Baptist businessman, Albin Kervinen, visited Pentecostal meetings in Helsinki in 1912. He described them in these terms:

---

⁴⁵ N. Bloch-Hoell, *The Pentecostal Movement* (London: Allen & Unwin, 1964), pp. 66-72, 75-77. For the Evangelical roots of Pentecostalism see W.J. Hollenweger, *Pentecostalism: Origins and Development Worldwide* (Peabody, Mass.: Hendrickson, 1997), chapters 14 and 15.

⁴⁶ Salmensaari, *Suomen Vapaakirkko*, p. 373.

⁴⁷ Ibid., pp. 373-377.

⁴⁸ D. Bundy, 'Thomas Ball Barratt: From Methodist to Pentecostal', *Journal of the European Pentecostal Theological Association* XII (1994), pp. 19-49; Salmensaari, *Suomen Vapaakirkko*, p. 168.

⁴⁹ Juhani Kuosmanen, *Herätyksen Historia* (History of Revival) (Tikkurila: Ristin Voitto, 1979), p. 272.

⁵⁰ Lauri K. Ahonen, *Suomen Helluntaiherätyksen Historia* (The History of the Finnish Pentecostal Movement) (Jyväskylä: Päivä Oy, 1994), p. 32.

⁵¹ Gunnar Westin, *Den Kristna Friförsamlingen i Norden, Frikyrklighetens Uppkomst och Utveckling, 4:e Upplagan* (The Christian Free Congregations in the North, The Origin and the Development of Free Churches, 4th edition) (Stockholm: Westerbergs, 1956), pp. 362-363.

⁵² Ahonen, *Suomen Helluntaiherätyksen Historia*, pp. 62-68.

Right from the beginning I noticed in preachers and other persons near to them, something extraordinary, which I had never seen before. From their faces and their eyes there shone a blissful joy. In the room there seemed to be a power unknown and mysterious to me... In great doubt I was sitting at the back row wondering at this new phenomenon. I continued to attend the meetings... I started to feel dirty, although for many years I had been a believer, I had even preached. The same was felt by others who were touched by the power.[53]

It was Kervinen who established the first Pentecostal congregation in Helsinki. This happened in 1915. He had to leave the Baptist congregation along with forty other members because of his espousal of the baptism in the Holy Spirit.[54] This congregation is significant because it was held to be a Pentecostal-Baptist congregation, which was at first avoided by other Pentecostals.[55] The congregation was called *Siloam*.[56] Kervinen affected the young Pentecostal movement by publishing a booklet about the local church concept (congregationalism), which was to influence greatly the formation of other Pentecostal congregations.[57] Later on, in 1928, many more people from the Helsinki Baptist congregation joined the Pentecostal congregation,[58] among them a gifted preacher, and a former schoolteacher, Antti Ammunet (who later changed his family name later to Ruishalme).[59] Other Baptist pastors who experienced the baptism in the Spirit in the 1910s were Pekka Mikkonen,[60] Antti Lajunen[61] and Juho Antikainen.[62] Their departure to Pentecostalism was a hard blow for Baptists, some of whom had themselves experienced or were personally interested in the so-called baptism of the Holy Spirit.

In the 1920s the number of new active workers among the Pentecostals in Finland grew steadily, as was also the case in Britain, where leaders such as George Jeffreys had widespread influence.[63] In 1923 they had thirty workers,

---

[53] Ahonen, *Suomen Helluntaiherätyksen Historia*, p. 68. Many kinds of empowering of the Holy Spirit were felt in Helsinki Baptist Church. Kervinen describes how 'even strong men fell to the floor'.

[54] Ibid., p. 107. The Pentecostal preacher Eino Heinonen mentions that Kervinen had been one of the best Baptist preachers.

[55] Kuosmanen, *Herätyksen Historia*, p. 342.

[56] Ibid.

[57] Lauri Ahonen, *Missions Growth:A Case Study On Finnish Free Foreign Mission*. (Pasadena: William Carey Library, 1984), p. 39.

[58] Gunnar Engelberg, 'Helsingin Seurakunta' (Helsinki Congregation), *Totuuden Kaiku* 11 (1928), p. 3.

[59] *Ristin Voitto* (The Victory of the Cross) 16 (1949).

[60] Mikkonen was dismissed from the Baptists because of his doctrine of feet washing, and he joined the Pentecostals in 1915. Westin, *Den Kristna Ffriförsamlingen*, p. 364.

[61] Ahonen, *Suomen Helluntaiherätyksen Historia*, p. 83.

[62] Ibid., p. 79.

[63] I.M. Randall, *Evangelical Experiences: A Study in the Spirituality of English Evangelicalism, 1918-1939* (Carlisle: Paternoster, 1999), chapter 8.

sixteen of whom were women evangelists, but two years later the number was forty-nine. More and more of these workers started to appear from within their own circles, not from other denominations. Eino Heinonen (1887-1977), the 'grand old man' of the movement, established, during his fifty-seven years of service, many new churches in the southwest part of Finland.[64] The decade of the 1930s was also a very good time for Pentecostals in Finland. The number of congregations doubled by the end of the decade to ninety.[65] Congregations started to pay more and more attention to work among children and young people. The children's magazine, *Hyvä Paimen* (Good Shepherd), increased its circulation from 6,415 to 18,300, which shows real interest.[66] For the main Pentecostal magazine, *Ristin Voitto* ('The Victory of the Cross', established in 1922), the corresponding numbers are 5,876 in 1930 and 14,470 in 1939.[67] Yet another focus was mission work abroad. By the end of the decade Pentecostal congregations had sent twenty-one missionaries abroad [68], and this missionary zeal seems to have been one of the reasons why they were so successful. Pentecostals also had a two-year Bible School, which was not so much for strengthening theological knowledge as for helping people to grow towards a more mature Christian life.[69]

During the 1930s Pentecostals also started to ponder seriously some of the problems in their ranks. There were 'fleshly' phenomena, as they were termed, and 'ecstasy'. There were 'fleshly' rather than 'spiritual' workers, revivals, Spirit baptisms and prophets. Because of this, Pentecostals were given a bad name in some places, and 'Pentecostal truth' fell into disrepute.[70] To solve this and other problems that emerged in the 1930s seven men were elected in 1944 as so-called advisory brothers, available to congregations to help solve problems.[71] The Pentecostal movement grew steadily, the membership being about 15,300 in 1950.[72] During this time relations between Baptists and Pentecostals were somewhat stiff. For example, it was suggested that Baptists and Pentecostals might share a common song book and that the Pentecostals would convene the first meeting about it. When nothing happened the Baptists came to a decision about their hymnbook on 25 June 1945.[73] Four years later Dr Suomela from the Pentecostal Movement wrote to the Baptists that the leader of the songbook committee, brother Heinonen, 'had forgotten to invite Baptist

---

[64] Ahonen, *Suomen Helluntaiherätyksen Historia*, pp. 135-136.
[65] Ibid., p. 186.
[66] Ibid., p. 203.
[67] Ibid., p. 206.
[68] Ibid., p. 230.
[69] Ibid., p. 179.
[70] Ahonen, *Suomen Helluntaiherätyksen Historia*, pp. 210-211.
[71] Ibid., p. 262.
[72] Ibid., p. 296. Today Pentecostals count about 50,000 members in their Finnish-speaking congregations.
[73] *MOMD* (25 June 1945), § 11.

delegates to the committee meeting'.[74] In 1949 a common songbook was printed, but with two different titles: the Pentecostals wanted to keep the name of their former songbook, *Herramme Tulee* (*Our Lord is Coming*).[75] So did the Baptists; their hymnbook was called *Kaikuja Kotimaasta* (*Echoes from the Homeland*), which in turn matched the title of their magazine, *Totuuden Kaiku* (*The Echo of the Truth*).

The Baptists gave Finnish Pentecostal theology many of its basic beliefs.[76] Among these were believer's baptism and the believers' church. Juhani Kuosmanen, a known Pentecostal preacher, writes that 'Baptists gave a tighter note to Pentecostalism'.[77] Kervinen, a former Baptist pastor, was, as we have noted, a key person in convincing the Finnish Pentecostals about the congregational understanding of the church. He wrote a booklet on the subject which was spread widely in Pentecostal circles, and it was accepted as the biblical view.[78] The strong emphasis that was given to baptism in the Holy Spirit was the main issue that separated Pentecostal Christians from Baptists. This led some Baptist preachers and ordinary congregational members to think that the reason for the lack of revival in their congregations was that teaching on the Holy Spirit was not given the prominence it had in Pentecostal circles.[79] Year by year the number of those convinced about this idea increased. A thorough discussion about the subject never took place, however. This is perhaps why baptism in the Holy Spirit remained like an unsolved problem, a question not properly dealt with, thus causing uncertainty among Baptist members. This is part of the dilemma even today. The Pentecostals through the years learned from their mistakes, and corrected misuse and misunderstandings about charismatic gifts, but the Baptists did not develop very much in their understanding of these gifts. There seems to have been a fear that teaching about the subject and correcting misuse would extinguish the gifts of the Holy Spirit.

Baptists and Free Evangelicals alike accused Pentecostals of 'sheep-stealing'—attracting people away from their congregations. While this is true in part, in thinking about the state of Baptist work in Finland, it was not a decisive factor in the problems Baptists faced. A more important question for Baptists to

---

[74] *MEC* (15 March 1949), § 5.

[75] Ahonen, *Suomen Helluntaiherätyksen Historia*, p. 175. The Pentecostal songbook was published in 1927.

[76] For the wider interaction of Baptist and Pentecostals, see I.M. Randall, 'Days of Pentecostal Overflowing: Baptists and the Shaping of Pentecostalism', in D.W. Beddington, ed., *The Gospel in the World: Studies in Baptist History and Thought* 1 (Carlisle: Paternoster, 2002), pp. 80-104.

[77] Kuosmanen, *Herätyksen Historia*, p. 340.

[78] Ibid., p. 343.

[79] This claim is found both in Tauno Kivelä, 'Kevätsade' (Spring Rain), *Totuuden Kaiku* 6-7 (1935), p.11 and in Jaakko Kalliomäki, 'Turusta' (From Turku), *Totuuden Kaiku* 6 (1936), pp. 5-6.

have asked themselves would have been why so many of their members were ready to leave for Pentecostal congregations. And instead of accepting the simple answer given by some, that the Holy Spirit was the only reason for this, they should have examined more critically their own situation. A close reading of *Totuuden Kaiku*, the minutes of the Executive Committee, the minutes of the meetings of delegates, and the official as well as the personal correspondence of August Jauhiainen, shows that many quarrels and disagreements were commonplace in Baptist Union life. Thus in *Totuuden Kaiku* in 1933, A. Hiljanen, a Baptist pastor, wrote: 'On my travels [to Baptist churches] I have heard much evil gossip. It is so cruelly mean that it is impossible to repeat these stories here if you want to spare the readers from depraved thoughts.'[80] These difficulties came from inside Baptist ranks, and surely hindered growth. For the same reason, I consider, even the times of revivals in some Baptist congregations during the 1930s mostly remained short-lived.

Jauhiainen himself was a man who would have liked Baptists, Free Evangelicals and Pentecostals to work peacefully together. His views can be seen in an article he wrote in 1933 in *Totuuden Kaiku*[81] in which he commented on another article, which had been published in *Suomen Viikkolehti (Finnish Weekly)*, the paper of the Free Evangelicals. This article spoke about a Baptist and a Free Evangelical. The latter wanted to suggest that the two denominations, both small groups, should start working together. The Baptist answer was: 'No. Free Evangelicals are our hereditary enemies.' A Pentecostal would have used exactly the same expression about Free Evangelicals. Jauhiainen wondered how this kind of article, which was not an official opinion but was private by its nature, was even published in *Viikkolehti*. He ended his article by saying:

> I think it would be practical for movements so closely kindred with each other to elect one to two brothers among themselves, who would then form a council of brothers, the purpose of which would be to deal with things like this, in order that we could keep walking on the path, not beside it.

By suggesting this he actually said something which became true over three decades later—in 1967. In that year a Council of Free Evangelical Christians was formed representing Baptists, Free Evangelicals, Methodists and Pentecostals. Jauhiainen's vision for Baptist and wider Free Church life, as was often the case, was broader than that of many of his contemporaries.

---

[80] A. Hiljanen, 'Huonoja Pöytäpuheita' (Bad talks), *Totuuden Kaiku* 5 (1933), p. 8. The article continues: 'On the one hand they may be so sadly amusing in their naive inconsequence, on the other hand they are false slanders, by which the honour and reputation of some are dragged through the mire, if possible.'

[81] Kristitty, 'Polulta ja "Polun Varrelta"' (On the Path and Beside It), *Totuuden Kaiku* 5 (1933), p. 6. (Kristitty [Christian] is one of the pseudonyms Jauhiainen used.)

A New Leader for the Union

Towards the end of the 1920s the situation in Baptist congregations weakened in several ways. The official statistics of the FBU show, however, that the Union was growing steadily until the year 1927 and that there was a drastic dropping-off in membership only in 1930. But the official meetings of delegates tell a somewhat different story. A number of Baptist members left their congregations and joined the Pentecostals in the late 1920s. [82] Also the work of the FBU was at a standstill, and people became irritated. Baptist preachers and members of the Executive Committee started to criticize the Union's President, J.G. Kokki, quite severely. Kokki, who was also the treasurer of all the Union's funds, had not taken care of money matters accurately. Misuse of funds was a constant topic. Kokki had taken at least some of the Union's money for his own personal use. In 1931 there was a reminder from the Baptist World Alliance (BWA) that the Union had not paid its membership fees for three years. In the account books there were, however, receipts showing that Kokki had taken the money to send it to the BWA.[83] He was also accused of putting pressure on other preachers and of being a dictatorial type of leader.[84] Also, he signed a letter of recommendation regarding a certain Kalle Mäkelä, who had moved to America, which stated that Mäkelä was authorized by the FBU to gather money for an orphanage. The orphanage was said to be owned by the Finnish Baptist Union, but the Union did not have any orphanage. Kokki had pressed an elderly church member to lend money to Mäkelä for his tickets to America and had even forged the signature of another member of the EC, the Union secretary, Walfred Karala.[85]

Not surprisingly, Kokki was dismissed as Union President. It is revealing that later on Kokki wrote to the secretary of the Executive Committee, Karala, suggesting that all official Union papers should be burned in order that 'the things would not be remembered anymore'.[86] In that same letter Kokki wrote his own estimation of the situation of the FBU:

---

[82] In Hammaslahti there was a schism because of the Pentecostals; in Kuopio the congregation worked together with the Pentecostals; and in Oulu a 'Pentecostal preacher Lahtinen preached the congregation into pieces'. *MOMD* (7 January 1921), § 3. In Impilahti Pekka Mikkonen caused division in a Baptist congregation; he is called 'a Pentecostal'. *MOMD* (23-26 June 1922), § 8. In Räisälä there was division because of Pentecostal work. *MOMD* (27-29 June 1925), § 9. There were difficulties in Keuruu, and in Vaajakoski, where some members joined the Pentecostals. *MOMD* (23-25 June 1927), § 8. A Baptist preacher, Väinö Saukkonen, defamed the EC, and moved to the Pentecostals. *MEC* (8 January 1928), § 8.

[83] *MEC* (25 June 1931), § 2.

[84] *MEC* (3 January 1931), § 1.

[85] Jauhiainen, Letter to Walfred Karala, Private Correspondence [hereafter PC] (12 December 1930).

[86] Kokki, Letter to Walfred Karala, OC (4 April 1932).

Everything is now a mess in the Union, but I am happy not to be part of that. It is yet to be seen where this leads. Previously we had the spirit of peace and love, respect and esteem among brothers, but this is gone now... A cold frost is damaging the vineyard of our Lord... That precious field, where we have worked together for decades hand in hand and side by side, is now ruined. O God, help us to be faithful to our Lord.[87]

The Union urgently needed a new leader. August Jauhiainen, who was already an experienced leader when he moved back to Finland from Russia in 1929, was chosen for this task. The involvement of Jauhiainen in the Finnish Baptist Union leadership began when he was elected vice-president of the FBU. This happened in the Executive Committee meeting on 3 January 1931. In the summer of the same year his vice-presidency was changed to presidency.[88] Kokki himself was treated very discreetly. He was named Honorary President of the FBU, and the real state of affairs—as outlined above—was not passed on to Union members. It was simply said that Kokki resigned 'because of his advancing age'.[89]

August Jauhiainen[90] was born on 29 March 1888 in Suonenjoki. He learned to read early, but the only books that his parents had were the Bible, a History of the Bible, the Lutheran Catechism, and the hymnbook used in Lutheran churches. He started with what they had. At the age of six he read the Old Testament stories, because, he said later, he found them exciting. When the family moved house, August learned that there was a small library in the local Lutheran parsonage, which he started to visit often. But when his parents learned about it, they refused to let him go there, thinking that such books were dangerous for a small boy. At the age of eight he saw his first Christmas magazine with many interesting stories and also beautiful pictures. It was an extraordinary experience for him to read through it.[91]

At the young age of twelve, August left his family home and moved from Finland to St. Petersburg, Russia, to help his aunt and her husband to take care of their baby. They were Baptists, and very soon after he went to live with them August himself came to a personal evangelical experience.[92] In 1903 he was baptized by immersion, and he became a member of the Swedish-Finnish

---

[87] Ibid.
[88] *MEC* (28 June 1931).
[89] *MOMD* (5 January 1931), § 7.
[90] Veikko Toivola, 'August Jauhiaista Haastattelemassa' (Interviewing August Jauhiainen), cassettes 1-2. This is an interview with A. Jauhiainen that was recorded on two C-60 cassettes in Vaasa by V. Toivola in the 1960s. The interview has been transcribed from the cassettes; thus when referring to it page numbers are given.
[91] August Jauhiainen, 'Elämäni Vaiheita' ('Vicissitudes of My Life'), p. 12. Jauhiainen started to write his memoirs, and this work is now collected together with some additional notes.
[92] Toivola, 'August Jauhiaista Haastattelemassa', p. 3.

Baptist congregation in St Petersburg. Jauhiainen mentions that this Baptist Church was at first a German-language church, led by Adam Reinhold Schiewe. Soon the church reached many Swedish-speaking people, who established a Swedish Baptist Church. When Schiewe was banished in 1895, the churches united, but later on the Germans again established their own church, and the Swedish congregation later became a Swedish-Finnish Baptist Church, with Swedish mostly used in the meetings.[93] At that time Jauhiainen was already learning to become a shoemaker, but right from the beginning of his Christian life he felt a strong desire to tell other people about his faith. A major change took place when his aunt's family decided to move to America. August was left alone in a big city. At that time he joined one of the ten Christian Endeavour (CE) groups in the area,[94] where he met his wife, Miina, and they were married in 1909. Neither of them understood Swedish, and they decided to join the Russian Baptist congregation in St. Petersburg in 1912, where William Fetler (also known as Basil Malov) had started a thriving work.[95] In this period of time Jauhiainen preached both in this congregation (he spoke fluent Russian) and also in the countryside. The Jauhiainens had five children, three of whom died of smallpox.

Jauhiainen had started preaching the same year as he was married, but he was also a good shoemaker, and he was granted the title of Master Shoemaker in 1913. That same year he established his own cobbler's shop. His future direction at that point was not clear. In 1915, however, Jauhiainen became a board member of his congregation; his leadership gifts within the church setting were being increasingly recognised. During the years 1918-1921 he was the Baptist representative in a joint committee of Russian Baptists and Evangelical Christians, which was charting the differences in these two denominations in order to prepare them to join together.[96] In 1920 in Moscow he was elected to

---

[93] August Jauhiainen, 'Pastori Oskar E. Signuel 28.10.1858—23.7.1936' ('Pastor Oskar E. Signuel 28.10.1858—23.7.1936), *Totuuden Kaiku* No. 9 (1936), p. 9.

[94] Heikki Piiparinen writes in 'Muistikuvia Inkeristä' (Recollections from Inkeri), *Totuuden Kaiku* No. 2, 1932, pp. 4-5: 'Before the bloom of the Bolshevist Revolution we had more than ten Christian Endeavour (CE) associations for young people. In many of them the work was very lively... In 1922 we managed to register our CE work as part of the work of our Mission organization, and we proceeded in full sail. But that happy time lasted only for a couple of years. Then the government gave orders to stop all youth work... We went underground... The work continued.'

[95] For Fetler see J.A. Stewart, *A Man in a Hurry: The Story of the Life and Work of Pastor Basil A. Malof* (Asheville, N.C.; Orebro, Sweden: Russian Bible Society, 1968); J. Wood, *Born in the Fire: The Story of William Fetler alias Basil Malof (1883-1957): Church Planting Evangelist in Russia and Latvia* (Stanway: self-published, 1998).

[96] Toivola, 'August Jauhiaista Haastattelemassa', p. 5. For more about Russian Baptists and Evangelical Christians in this period see S. Savinskii, *Istorija Evangelskih Hristian-baptistov Ukrainy, Rossii, Belorussii, 1917-1967* (History of Evangelical Christians-Baptists in Ukraine, Russia and Byelorussia, 1917-1967) 2 (Saint Petersburg: Biblija dlja Vseh, 2001), the first volume of Savinskii's book, covering the years 1867-

the Executive Committee of the Russian Baptists. One year later he asked and was permitted to resign from the Committee, because by that time he had moved from St. Petersburg to the countryside, to Inkeri (Ingermanland), and his new work there was taking up all his time and energy.[97]

The year 1917 was a turning point in Russia. The Bolshevik Revolution changed everything, the lives of Evangelical Christians included.[98] At that time August Jauhiainen had ten apprentices working for him in his business, but he lost the business to the Bolshevik State. He was, however, asked to continue as its manager. It was a year after this, in 1918, that he made the decision to become a Baptist preacher. He moved from St. Petersburg to Inkeri, where many Finnish people lived. The family lived there until they returned to Finland. After the Revolution the situation was initially promising for Christians. Jauhiainen preached throughout the whole Inkeri area, where Baptists and the Free Evangelicals worked together.[99] A revival broke out. Many people were converted, were baptized and joined the revival movement, the leaders of which were Heikki Piiparinen, a Free Evangelical pastor, and August Jauhiainen. Wherever meetings were arranged, people came to listen to the preaching. The following story as later told by August Jauhiainen is typical:

> It was wintertime. The roads were blocked by snow. I cannot remember where I was coming from with a brother. When we reached his home, I decided to stay there overnight, because I was still far away from home. According to the custom of the country there is a samovar on the table. The water is hot, and we sit with the rest of the family at the table. The farmer says: 'Should not we arrange a meeting now that you are here?' I reply: 'But it is already night.' The farmer says: 'I will go and wake them up. So he did. It was almost midnight, when I started to preach.'[100]

August Jauhiainen worked in Inkeri about eleven years, and he himself thought these years, when he was in his thirties, were his best. He writes: 'There was a real brotherly love and mutual understanding both between

---

1917, was published in 1999. For later developments see Walter Sawatsky, *Soviet Evangelicals Since World War II* (Kitchener, Ontario: Herald Press, 1981).

[97] Toivola, 'August Jauhiaista Haastattelemassa', p. 5.

[98] For more see Heather J. Coleman, *Russian Baptists and Spiritual Revolution, 1905-1929* (Bloomington, In.: Indiana Unversity Press, 2005).

[99] Baptists and Free Evangelicals joined together in July 1920 under the name Inkerin Evankeelisten Kristittyjen Liitto, IEKL. August Jauhiainen, 'Inkerin Evankeelisten Kristittyjen Tie, (The Evangelical Christians in Inkeri)in J. Lehto, K. Salmensaari, (eds.), Tehkää Tie Erämaahan (Prepare the Way in the Desert) (Tampere: Hämeen Kirjapaino, 1954), p. 111. See also, Mikko Kolomainen, Inkerin 'Toisinajattelijat': Muistelmia Inkerin Vapaiden Herätysliikkeiden Syntyvaiheista (The 'Dissidents' in Inkeri: Recollections from the Birth of Free Revival Movements in Inkeri) (Helsinki: Ristin Voitto, 1989), pp. 34-37.

[100] Toivola, 'August Jauhiaista Haastattelemassa', p. 8.

pastors and congregations. God was blessing our ministry. The membership in the congregations increased from 250 to about 2000.' The number of congregations rose from six in 1921 to forty-one in 1929.[101] He continues: 'These congregations formed an independent mission. We did not receive any help from abroad. We were hardly known outside of our own circles. My responsibility was to organize the congregations. I also worked as the pastor in the main congregation.' [102] In spring 1929, however, the Russian government published new laws that restricted spiritual work considerably. The Jauhiainen family returned to Finland in 1929, and two weeks after they left, their village in Inkeri was emptied. Men were shot, put into prison or taken to work camps. Women and children were taken in cattle wagons to Siberia.[103]

What can be said about Jauhiainen's theological and spiritual development during this period? He can be called a theologian, although he did not have the chance to go to seminary or Bible school. Since his childhood he had been a keen reader. Books were his most valued property. He acquired a wide knowledge of theology, and he knew his Bible well. In many ways he was well equipped to give wider spiritual leadership. But when he was asked, after his return to Finland, to become the President of the Finnish Baptist Union, he was very reluctant.[104] This is understandable, because learning about the situation in the Finnish Baptist Union was a shock for Jauhiainen. He wrote to his wife from the Finnish Baptist Union conference in 1930, in Vaasa,

> It was interesting to attend the conference after a long time of absence. The first day I was only astonished, because everything was so different compared to Inkeri. Next day it was my turn to speak. In a confused state of mind I entered the pulpit... I did not meet the Baptist Mission in a state I had expected and some must have thought the same about me. An indescribable pain filled my heart... Baptist Mission is not what it ought to be! It is with sorrow I have seen it now. [105]

He was not alone in these thoughts. In Vaasa he had met some who shared the same worries about the situation. In a personal letter to the Union secretary, Walfred Karala, he wrote about how depressed he was: 'Baptists are behindhand, and their mutual bickering is hindering them from rising from that point.'[106] Some months later he wrote again to him: 'It is very sad that things

---

[101] Pauli Hyppönen, 'Inkerin Herätys ja Herätysliikkeet 1890-1929' (Revival in Inkeri and the Revival Movements 1890-1929'), p. 47. Päättötyö, *Suomen Baptistiyhdyskunnan Raamattuopisto*, unpub. paper (Tampere: The Bible College of the Finnish Baptist Union, 1998).

[102] Jauhiainen, 'Elämäni Vaiheita', pp. 23-25.

[103] Ibid.

[104] Jauhiainen, Letter to Heikki Piiparinen, PC (2 January 1931).

[105] Jauhiainen, Letter to Miina Jauhiainen, PC (8 January 1930).

[106] Jauhiainen, Letter to Walfred Karala, the Secretary of the FBU, PC (22 July 1930).

are the way they are... If I was not a BAPTIST, I would not stay under such a Baptist Board. But because I have absorbed the Baptist way of thinking already in my childhood, I cannot help but be what I am, although I have to weep because of this low state of affairs here.'[107] At least part of his strong negative feelings arose from his having to leave a flourishing work in Russia and move to Finland to serve congregations he did not know. His letter to the other leader of the work in Inkeri, Heikki Piiparinen, shows this: 'I am afraid that a deep longing to Inkeri may come soon, because I still have the feeling of being a stranger [in Finland]... It is as if nobody understands me like the people in Inkeri did.' [108]

Jauhiainen longed for the kind of spiritual atmosphere he was used to in Inkeri.[109] In accepting the leadership of the Finnish Baptist Union he wanted to stop the quarrels and root out all misuses; he also felt that preachers and church members needed basic teaching. 'Even ordinary church members in Inkeri had better knowledge in spiritual matters than the preachers in the Finnish Baptist Union,' he wrote to a friend. When he started his work as Union leader, the membership was 641; the Union had lost more than half of its members during the last years of the 1920s. In his letter to the European and world Baptist leader, Dr J.H. Rushbrooke, in December 1931, he mentioned three things concerning the poor condition in Baptist congregations: a) The neglect of schooling and educating young preachers; b) the neglect of teaching in the congregations; c) the lack of the mind of Christ.[110] Typically, Jauhiainen started to work very hard to improve the situation. He travelled, preached in the congregations and arranged Bible study weeks. He always devoted his summer vacation to visiting Baptist congregations and prayer groups, and even individual members who were living in areas where there was no regular Baptist work. He made another round of the congregations each year in December. Along with this he was the full-time pastor and chairman of the Tampere Baptist congregation (this was his paid work), the chief-editor of *Totuuden Kaiku* and treasurer as well as president of the Union.

Jauhiainen brought to the leadership of the FBU a burning vision. From his experience as a pastor he wanted to see healthy congregations. Starting his career as Union leader by dealing with misuses and quarrels was not a rewarding task, however, and he soon encountered opponents. He had a strong desire to train new leaders, but the poor economic situation at the time hindered

---

[107] Jauhiainen, Letter to Walfred Karala, PC (25 September 1930).

[108] Jauhiainen, Letter to Piiparinen, PC (15 December 1930). Four months later Jauhiainen wrote about his longing to see Inkeri again. Piiparinen shared the same feelings with him. Jauhiainen, Letter to Piiparinen, PC (24 April 1931); and Piiparinen's reply (28 April 1931).

[109] Jauhiainen, Letter to Piiparinen, PC (15 December 1930).

[110] Jauhiainen, Letter to J.H. Rushbrooke, PC (December 1931). For Rushbrooke see B. Green, *Tomorrow's Man: A Biography of James Henry Rushbrooke* (Didcot: Baptist Historical Society, 1997).

him from establishing any systematic teaching for them. He encouraged all the preachers and evangelists to attend his Bible study weeks in different congregations, but very often the attendance was poor, which affirms the weak state of affairs in the Union. Coming from outside of the Union to lead the Union's work had both advantages and disadvantages. Jauhiainen undoubtedly made mistakes, but he attempted to deal with all the issues he faced in a way that had integrity. Over the years, from the early 1930s on, appreciation for his work on behalf of the Union increased. Although difficulties lay further in the future, he became a respected leader. Teuvo Aaltio, in his study, comments on the influence of his leadership: 'Jauhiainen had a good self-education in the biblical field, and his Bible courses and sermons were "solid food"... He travelled much and had a great influence in Finland.'[111]

Jauhiainen's Theology of the Holy Spirit and Pentecostal Teaching

In Inkeri, Baptists, Free Evangelicals and Pentecostals had worked together. They formed 'The Alliance of Christian Evangelicals in Inkeri' in 1920, deliberately choosing to be an 'alliance' because any kind of official united church or a union of churches was held to be too binding.[112] In 1927, however, the Pentecostals in Inkeri separated from the cooperative body.[113] In Finland the Pentecostals were already the biggest Free Church group in the 1920s. In 1925 the number of Pentecostal preachers and evangelists was almost one hundred, which shows the vitality of the movement.[114] When returning to Finland, Jauhiainen had to learn to live in a totally new situation compared with that in Inkeri. Here the Free Church denominations were separate bodies, and the Pentecostals were felt by others to be aggressive in drawing believers from other congregations.[115] Pentecostal teaching about the Holy Spirit was discussed in all church circles, including the Baptists. Jauhiainen of course wanted Baptists to stay in Baptist congregations. He had a clear theology of the Holy Spirit: in Christ every believer already had the Holy Spirit and the spiritual gifts. The challenge for the believer was to give space to the work of the Spirit—then his fullness would fill the believer. Two things had led

---

[111] Teuvo Aaltio, 'A History of the National Baptists in Finland', p. 62.

[112] Jauhiainen, 'Inkerin Evankeelisten Kristittyjen Tie', in *Tehkää Tie Erämaahan*, pp. 110-111.

[113] Jauhiainen, 'Venäjältä' ('From Russia'), *Totuuden Kaiku* 11 (1927), pp. 3-4.

[114] Ahonen, *Suomen Helluntaiherätyksen Historia*, pp. 422-423.

[115] This was not only a Finnish phenomenon. Everett A. Wilson states in his article 'They Crossed the Red Sea, Didn't They? Critical History and Pentecostal Beginnings', in M.W. Dempster, B.D. Klaus, and D. Petersen, eds., *The Globalization of Pentecostalism, A Religion Made To Travel*, p. 86: '...members...were recruited for the most part from other conservative Christian traditions with similar values and theology'.

Jauhiainen to that conclusion. The first was his meeting with a Baptist preacher from Finland. He writes about this:

> My good friend, a Baptist preacher from Finland, Johannes Jalkanen, visited us in St. Petersburg. He had received Spirit baptism; he spoke in tongues, and prophesied. But, strangely enough, he had a feeling that there was something wrong, something erroneous to genuine Christianity in the seeking of Spirit baptism. And because he knew I was longing for that experience myself, he seriously warned me not to join the Pentecostals.[116]

This visit made Jauhiainen ponder the subject very thoroughly. The other incident that affected him strongly was a meeting in the 1920s with Aleksandra Kruzen, a member of the Russian aristocracy who had been converted to evangelical Christianity through Lord Radstock. She spoke many languages and studied different Bible translations. According to Jauhiainen she was 'a capable and faithful teacher' and he felt that he owed her a great deal. When discussing with her, Jauhiainen started to understand that in Christ he already had everything he needed, even the fullness of the Holy Spirit. This became the basis of his theology of the Holy Spirit.[117]

When discussing the issue of the Holy Spirit as it affected Finnish Baptists I will concentrate on Spirit baptism and the fullness of the Spirit. Jauhiainen made a clear distinction between Spirit baptism and fullness of the Spirit;[118] for him Spirit baptism happens only once, like water baptism, and it coincides with conversion,[119] while fullness of the Spirit is a repeated experience. All

---

[116] Jauhiainen, 'Elämäni Vaiheita', pp. 117-118.

[117] Aleksandra Kruzen had contact with people who had a Baptist background such as Ivan Kargel. August Jauhiainen 'Elämäni Vaiheita', pp. 121-123.

[118] See also, Siegfried Grossmann, *Der Geist ist Leben* (The Spirit is Life) (Clausthall-Zellerfeld: Papierflieger, 2001), pp. 45-52, 58-60.

[119] This is the teaching also in other Baptist denominations. See e.g. Grossmann, *Der Geist ist Leben*. He writes: 'Wer Christus angenommen har, der hat auch den Heiligen Geist aufgenommen. So ist der Geist Gottes nicht nur der Unfassbare, der "weht, wo er will,, sondern auch der konkret Anwesende, der „in mir wohnt"... Wenn ich Christus angenommen habe, wohnt der Geist Gottes auch dann in mir, wenn ich nichts davon spüre.' (He who has received Christ has also received the Holy Spirit. Thus the Spirit of God is not only incomprehensible, the one who 'blows where it wishes' but also a concrete presence, who 'lives in me'... After receiving Christ, the Spirit of God lives in me even when I do not speak about it.) Grossmann also points out that the Holy Spirit is not the originator of power; he is only the one who mediates it. More about the subject is in Grossmann, pp. 41-44. Pentecostal teaching about baptism in the Spirit met opposition also among British Baptists. Randall, 'Days of Pentecostal Overflowing: Baptists and the Shaping of Pentecostalism', pp. 80-104. Graham Scroggie, whom Randall mentions as the foremost British Baptist opponent of Pentecostal theology, argued against the doctrine that multitudes of Christians had never received the baptism of the Spirit, and that all such should seek it. For Scroggie Spirit baptism was the same as regeneration.

Christians have experienced Spirit baptism, but not all are full of the Spirit. He writes,

> The words 'we were all baptized by one Spirit into one body' (1 Corinthians 12:13), testify that this verse speaks about regeneration as baptism, because it firmly says that only through baptism in the Holy Spirit does one enter into the membership of the body of Christ. If baptism in the Spirit was a deeper experience than regeneration, then the regenerated were not members of the Body of Christ but were outside of it and thus not even saved. But this, being totally out of the question, and the Word as well as experience testifying that for the regenerated there is also a deeper share of the experience of the Spirit than most of them had in rebirth, it is clear that that is exactly what is called being filled with the Spirit. This is why it is both biblical and based on facts to use the expression being full of the Spirit when speaking about it.[120]

In one of his articles, Jauhiainen explains more fully this 'deeper share of the experience of the Spirit', which he connects with dying to oneself and abiding in Christ—which are also the evidences of the fullness of the Spirit:

> When God encourages us to be filled with the Spirit, He has also taken care that this is possible for us. We have to come back to the starting point, to CHRIST: 'For in him dwells all the fullness of the Godhead bodily; and you are filled [Finnish translation] in Him' (Col. 2:9-10a). The only thing needed is that we give ourselves more thoroughly to Him, which means that we participate in the death of Christ, i.e. we have to die to ourselves... The carnal mind is enmity against God, and as long as one lives under the control of the flesh, he cannot be filled with the Spirit nor walk in the Spirit, even if he speaks in the tongues of angels.[121]

Jauhiainen taught that experiencing Pentecost changed the first disciples. Only after the day of Pentecost did they understand what Jesus had taught them, why he had to suffer and die, and what their own calling was: to take the message of Christ to unbelievers. Jauhiainen argued that the Holy Spirit means an end to 'I', to carnal Christianity, and to selfish plans, and when that change takes place a Christian thereafter lives in the experience of Pentecost; the Spirit rules and reveals Christ.[122]

In order to understand 'the Pentecostal dilemma' in Baptist churches we have to study what Pentecostals taught about the Holy Spirit because their teaching influenced many Baptist preachers. In his study of the emergence of the Pentecostal Movement in Finland, Lauri Ahonen, the son of a long-standing Pentecostal preacher, Eino O. Ahonen, states that first a person is converted,

---

[120] Jauhiainen, *Raamatuntutkisteluopas* (How to study the Bible) (Tampere: Totuuden Kaiku, 1948), p. 146.

[121] Jauhiainen, 'Hengentäyteys' (Fullness of Spirit), *Tot. Kaiku* 9 (1936), pp. 6-7.

[122] Ibid.

and after that both the baptism of the Holy Spirit and water baptism should closely follow. The Holy Spirit is a gift from God, but 'apostolic laying on of hands may have a part in it'.[123] He also mentions that the tongues are considered as the outward sign of the baptism of the Spirit.[124] The purpose of Spirit baptism is to equip the believer with power for service; without this the evangelisation of the world cannot be accomplished. The gifts of the Spirit are given to individual believers for the benefit of the whole church.[125] Thus for Pentecostals, baptism in the Holy Spirit is a second experience of God's grace.[126] They understand that the Holy Spirit is acting differently in regeneration and in the work of Spirit baptism, the latter having more the nature of empowerment for ministry.[127] Actually, the whole Pentecostal movement came into being because Spirit baptism was understood anew again, and this new experience was seen as an expression of primitive Christianity.[128]

Although Jauhiainen's view differed from that of the Pentecostals he was careful not to attack their position. Later on, looking back to the time of his presidency of the FBU, he wrote to Baptist congregations: 'During my presidency the Pentecostal attitudes in preaching were met with sympathy, and those who supported it were dealt with in a brotherly way.'[129] Many quarrels, including the negative attitude of the Executive Committee of the FBU towards Pentecostals in the 1920s, had had a negative impact on Baptist congregations. Jauhiainen saw these quarrels as one of the reasons why Baptists had decreased so much during the late 1920s, and he wanted to bring about a different climate in the union by strengthening unity and discouraging unfruitful disputes about doctrinal matters. But quarrels were happening. The first confrontation occurred during Jauhiainen's first year as FBU President. He was accused of 'not tolerating those filled with the Spirit'. A Baptist evangelist, Eva Korpela, claimed that Jauhiainen had dismissed from his Inkeri congregations members who spoke in tongues, and she further claimed that in the light of that 'he himself has not experienced the filling with the Holy Spirit'.[130] There is no evidence that such dismissals had happened. On the contrary, Jauhiainen had been a warm supporter of the Pentecostal message. He wrote in his biographical

---

[123] Ahonen, *Missions Growth*, p. 37.
[124] Ibid.
[125] Ibid., p. 38.
[126] For a thorough study of Spirit baptism in the Finnish Pentecostal context, see Veli-Matti Kärkkäinen, *Spiritus ubi Vult Spirat, Pneumatology in Roman Catholic-Pentecostal Dialogue (1972-1989)* (Gummerus, Saarijärvi: Luther-Agricola-Society, 1998), especially chapter 4.3.1.: 'Pentecostal Ordo Salutis and Different Interpretations of Spirit-Baptism'.
[127] Ibid., pp. 182, 427.
[128] Wilson, 'Red Sea', p. 110.
[129] Jauhiainen, 'Suomen baptistiyhdyskunnan seurakunnille ja jäsenille' (To congregations and members of the Finnish Baptist Union), OC (September 1953), p. 4.
[130] Eva Korpela, Letter to Jauhiainen, PC (2 December 1931).

notes: 'I was the first one in St. Petersburg, and in Inkeri to distribute Pentecostal papers and literature.'[131]

It is more likely that Eva Korpela, who was one of a remarkable group of Free Church (not just Baptist) women evangelists who helped in farmhouses and in return received food and lodging and permission to hold meetings, did not understand or accept the way in which Jauhiainen taught about the subject of the Holy Spirit. In 1931 alone Jauhiainen wrote in three of his articles in *Totuuden Kaiku* about the importance of the Holy Spirit. I take only one example:

> The redemptive work of Christ guarantees also the fullness of the Holy Spirit... 'For it pleased the Father that in Him all the fullness should dwell' (Col. 1:19) ... If anyone is in Christ, he is a new creation (2 Cor. 5:17), and because 'all the fullness of the Godhead' bodily dwells in Him, then 'you are filled [Finnish translation] in Him'... Thus this important filling with the Holy Spirit is in close connection with the redeemed being and remaining in Christ. Those who are in Christ are filled with the Spirit, and outside of Christ there is no filling with the Holy Spirit.[132]

To obtain a more comprehensive understanding of the conversation about the Holy Spirit in Baptist circles during Jauhiainen's time, we will study the articles about this subject in *Totuuden Kaiku*, the Baptist magazine he was editing. At first there were only a few articles about the subject, but towards the latter part of the 1940s the articles increased considerably. The articles are not quoted in their chronological order, but rather with a view to letting the two different positions, that of Jauhiainen and that of the Pentecostally-minded, or Pentecostals, be heard.

Jaakko Kalliomäki, a young Baptist preacher and evangelist, did not accept Jauhiainen's view about Spirit baptism. For him, regeneration and Spirit baptism were two separate experiences, but he did not make a distinction between Spirit baptism and fullness of the Spirit. In the editorial of *Totuuden Kaiku* in 1938 he attacked Jauhiainen's view, stating that many Baptists 'have longed for the experience of Pentecost, but they have been robbed of the hope of ever experiencing it. We have been taught...that we should just own that for ourselves by believing that we have it.' He went on to explain that Peter and John (in Acts chapter 8) did not teach the Samaritans that they had received that blessing and the fullness of the Holy Spirit when they were converted. They lacked those, and the apostles prayed for them. 'They did not say: "When your faith gets stronger, and you learn to know Christ, you will also learn that you

---

[131] Jauhiainen, 'Elämäni Vaiheita', p. 117.

[132] Muukalainen, 'Kristus on Noussut Kuolleista' (Christ has risen), *Totuuden Kaiku* 4 (1931), pp. 1-3. Jauhiainen wrote under the pseudonym of *Muukalainen* (A Stranger). It must have been evident to readers that *Muukalainen* was Jauhiainen, because he often used this name in his editorials.

already have the Holy Spirit."'[133] His article shows that he had not understood what Jauhiainen taught about the need for the fullness of the Spirit.

A Pentecostal preacher, Aarne Ylppö,[134] also writing in 1938, stressed the change that Spirit baptism makes in a person's life. For him, too, Spirit baptism and fullness of the Spirit were one and the same experience.

> Christians living now are powerless. Why? Because God's Word has not become true in their lives as in the lives of Jesus' disciples. Jesus said before his ascension: 'But you shall receive power when the Holy Spirit has come upon you' (Acts 1:8a), and 'tarry in the city of Jerusalem until you are endued with power from on high' (Luke 24:49b). The disciples waited 10 days to be filled with the Spirit. When the day of Pentecost came, they all received Spirit baptism... Those who had been shy and cowards were now full of the Spirit and full of life.[135]

Toivo Wacklin, writing a decade later, shared this view. When writing the article cited here, he was still a Baptist preacher. Later on he moved to the Pentecostals.

> ...they [the disciples] had to be provided with the *fullness*, in order to be able to get through the battles ahead... They could not have endured hardships without being filled with the Holy Spirit... The Lord baptizes...his regenerated children with the Holy Spirit even today... In new tongues they thank the Lamb of God, and charismatic gifts are at work, where people believe the way it is written.[136]

Jauhiainen also wrote about powerless Christians: the same power that raised Christ from the dead is theirs if only they remain in Christ and let him live in them through faith. In him gracious riches are theirs, too. They do not need to feel powerless, nor do they need to live by small portions of food when abundant life is offered to them in Christ.[137]

Ylppö, the Pentecostal preacher, even seemed to suggest that baptism in the Holy Spirit was necessary for salvation. He spoke about the 'upper room blessing', 'the fire baptism in the Holy Spirit'. He wrote that neither nominal Christianity nor outward formal piety help, if a person is not born again through

---

[133] Jaakko Kalliomäki, 'Helluntaituli' (The Fire of Pentecostal), *Totuuden Kaiku* 6, (1938), pp. 1-3.

[134] Aarne Ylppö was studying law when he was converted in 1919 in a Pentecostal meeting. He became a prominent Pentecostal prison worker through whose activities many prisoners found personal faith. Lauri K. Ahonen, *Suomen Helluntaiherätyksen Historia*, pp. 141-145. At the end of the 1940s, during Kalliomäki's time as editor, his articles started to be published regularly.

[135] Aarne Ylppö, 'Sanan ja Pyhän Hengen Voima' (The Power of the Word and the Holy Spirit), *Totuuden Kaiku* 10 (1949), p. 1.

[136] Toivo Wacklin, 'Uudestisyntyminen ja Pyhän Hengen Kaste' ('Regeneration and baptism in the Holy Spirit'), *Totuuden Kaiku* 1 (1949), pp. 2-3.

[137] Jauhiainen, 'Voiman Puute' (Lack of Power), *Totuuden Kaiku* 5 (1931), pp. 1-3.

the Word and the Spirit and has not received the oil of the Holy Spirit. 'There is now a fierce battle going on in the world concerning the holy oil... Without oil, i.e. the Holy Spirit, we have to surrender in the battle. But if we are full of the word of faith and the Holy Spirit, we will conquer in the blood of the Lamb, and we are allowed to be witnesses of His Word to the ends of the world.'[138] For Ylppö, the sign of Spirit baptism was that 'you may speak here on earth the language of Canaan, and you will experience the holy fire in your soul, even in your whole being'.[139] Jauhiainen did not believe that speaking in tongues was the ultimate sign of this. In a personal letter to his cousin Lilyan he writes,

> I do believe that God's Holy Spirit causes people even now to speak in tongues. But I cannot believe that that it is the only sign of Spirit baptism, as is emphasised among Pentecostal people. It is said that the Spirit gives gifts as He pleases. Unfortunately it is true that often by emphasizing tongues people have gone further than the Bible teaches. History tells us about great men of the Spirit, and even nowadays there are many men of the Spirit who have not spoken in tongues. I know such. And my personal experience is the same; I have never spoken in tongues other than those that I have learned, and yet I am convinced of having the fullness of the Holy Spirit.[140]

In the 1930s, most probably because of Jauhiainen's sympathetic and tactful behaviour towards Pentecostally-minded people in the Union, there seem to have been no actual quarrels about Spirit baptism. The first years of the 1940s were also the war years. Towards the end of the decade Spirit baptism became a hot issue. The Pentecostally-minded preachers such as Toivo Wacklin, Eva and August Korpela, Paavo Ketonen, and Jaakko Kalliomäki, had a strong position in the Union. Ketonen led the FBU's Inner Mission and Kalliomäki was elected editor-in-chief of *Totuuden Kaiku* in 1949 and he used the magazine to give special emphasis to Pentecostal teaching about the Holy Spirit, which he himself held, while not giving space to Jauhiainen. From then on articles about the Holy Spirit started to appear regularly: in 1949 there were seven articles; in 1950 there were thirteen articles and three short stories about baptism in the Holy Spirit; and in 1951 there were nine articles and two stories about being born again and being filled with the Holy Spirit. Baptist preachers wrote most of the articles. Aarne Ylppö also wrote regularly. The two different views were discussed in the FBU Executive Committee in the 1940s. Jauhiainen wondered why his articles were not published in the magazine, although he considered them to be biblical. No unity was found, only a hope for a kind of middle course was expressed. The situation was exacerbated. Jauhiainen even feared

---

[138] Aarne Ylppö, 'Pyhän Hengen Kaste' (Baptism in the Holy Spirit), *Totuuden Kaiku* 6 (1950), pp. 6-7.
[139] Ibid.
[140] Jauhiainen, Letter to Lilyan, PC (22 November 1931).

that the Union would break apart. He expressed this in an official letter[141] to members of the Executive Committee and now started to use stronger language. He explaine,

> There was a time in the Union—which many of you hardly even remember—when the majority, sticking to the old Baptist view, terrorized the Pentecostal-minded minority [he must have meant here the end of the 1920s]. Because of that this minority had to leave, and there was a gaping hole in the Union. Now the situation has changed, and the Pentecostal-minded are in the majority... I am an advocate of the old Baptist view, and I am not ashamed to confess that I belong to the minority. Even though...Kalliomäki especially wanted to stress that I am alone, I can assure you, that I am not alone. I have the whole Bible on my side!

Jauhiainen considered that the Pentecostally-minded had tyrannized him. Among other things they had accused him of lacking 'the anointing', and this was the reason for 'dryness'. The magazine 'was taken away' from him. Jauhiainen had then decided not to write any articles about the Holy Spirit so that there would not be too many articles stressing 'the old policy'. But many people wanted him to write. According to him, he had made 'every effort to explain things the best way in order not to give [these people] the possibility in any way to guess the tension which was to be found among them [the EC members]'. Jauhiainen reminded the Executive Committee members about freedom of thought, which ought to be evident in the Baptist Union.[142]

This letter did not improve the situation. The atmosphere among the Executive Committee (EC) members remained tense. People on both sides used strong words to uphold their views. Poor relationships during the first years of the 1950s were leading Jauhiainen towards an inevitable conflict with other Baptist leaders. Pentecostal expressions became the norm; they were accepted as the only biblical ones by the EC. This was, in a way, natural. The successful ones, i.e. the Pentecostals, are always looked upon favourably. They become trailblazers. Unfortunately, with this dilemma about different teachings of how a Christian receives Spirit baptism and the fullness of the Spirit, there remained a deeper, unsolved issue. People thought the real question was whether one accepted the Holy Spirit as a reality or not, but this was not the problem. Finnish Baptists, unlike many other Baptists, have always been very open to the

---

[141] Jauhiainen , Letter to Jaakko Kalliomäki, Einar Sévon, Benjam Lehtonen, and Olavi Nieminen, OC (12 May 1949). These men, with the exception of Kalliomäki, were businessmen, and as such very influential in the Union. From a theological standpoint, they were laypersons.

[142] Jauhiainen, Letter to Jaakko Kalliomäki, Einar Sévon, Benjam Lehtonen, and Olavi Nieminen, OC (12 May 1949).

Holy Spirit. In Dr Hughey's[143] words, 'The Pentecostal influence among Finnish Baptists has been considerable. When Baptists see the growth of Pentecostal churches, they are tempted to imitate their methods.'[144] When reading the issues of the Union magazine produced after the 1920s, and all the documents that exist, I cannot find any Baptist preacher or evangelist who had opposed the Holy Spirit. The question has always been: What is your understanding about the way the Holy Spirit comes into one's life?

There are still many people, however, who think that the Finnish Baptist Union has remained small because some of its preachers opposed the Holy Spirit. These people are not even ready to hear any other explanation.[145] When this is what they think, they want—sometimes unconsciously, at other times consciously—to imitate the Pentecostal congregations, to be free from the mistakes of the past. This has led to a weaker and weaker Baptist identity, which means that Baptist congregations are not offering a real alternative among the Free Churches in Finland. This, together with the fact that people tend to go to congregations that have more to offer (i.e. big congregations), makes it difficult for small Unions with small congregations, as is the case with Baptists, to grow. Along with this there is lack of real interest in theological questions. This is why a thorough and fact-based discussion about the Holy Spirit theology among Finnish Baptists has never taken place. When we add to this that Baptists have only one book written about their theology, August Jauhiainen's *Raamatuntutkisteluopas*, we understand that the problem is not easily solved. Even the history of the Union remains to be written. In order to understand the theological issues today, a deeper understanding of past debates is necessary, particularly the debates in which Jauhiainen was involved.

Trying to Re-build Baptist Identity (1930s)

Jauhiainen's involvement in Finnish Baptist Union leadership began, as we have seen, when he was elected Union Vice-president on 3 January 1931. On 5 January, in the meeting of Union delegates, he was also appointed editor-in-

---

[143] Dr Hughey was well acquainted with European Baptists. In 1964 he was named secretary for Europe, the Middle East and South Asia for the Foreign Mission Board, the Southern Baptist Mission organization. Dr Hughey's interest in European Baptists is evident in his publications, like *Die Baptisten* (J.G. Oncken Verlag, Kassel, 1959), and *Baptist Partnership in Europe, The HOW of Christian Missions in Europe Today* (Tennessee: Broadman Press, 1982).

[144] J.D. Hughey, *Baptist Partnership in Europe*, p. 74.

[145] When speaking to Baptist women in summer 2003, I mentioned that in studying our Union's history I had not found any Baptist preachers who had opposed the Holy Spirit. Afterwards I got both angry remarks and 'motherly' corrections. I was plainly told that I was wrong, and did not know the real state of affairs.

chief of *Totuuden Kaiku*.[146] He wrote to 'Baptist brothers and sisters': 'I have but one goal: to serve fully the Lord of the harvest. This is my programme! ... We need whole-hearted Christians, total surrender and self-sacrifice; otherwise we will not fulfil our task... Let our money, time, gifts and abilities be totally and undividedly consecrated to the Lord Jesus Christ!'[147] In the summer of 1931 Jauhiainen's vice-presidency was changed to presidency and as president he did himself what he encouraged others to do. He worked hard on all levels of church work. Baptists needed to be Baptists, 'people of the Book', as they were called. He wanted to equip them to the best of his abilities. From the beginning he also wanted to pay attention to work done among children and young people. His speech to the delegates of the Baptist congregations at the 1931 Annual Meeting was reported as follows:

> The President spoke about Bible study weeks, and the teaching and nurture of young people...including Sunday school work... He based this on the fact so obvious in normal life: the poorer the upbringing, the poorer the adults. This is true also in Christian life. This is why we ought to pay serious attention to nurturing them. We have to encourage more teachers for Sunday schools, who are able to teach small groups. The abilities of teachers should not be judged too severely, even though knowledge is not a burden either. Every now and then we ought to arrange special meetings where all children would gather together to celebrate. ...The main thing is that teachers love children. Then even modest teaching will give fruit in due time. According to the same principles the congregations were encouraged to arrange yearly Bible study weeks for young people.[148]

There were only two Youth Societies, in two Baptist congregations: one in Turku, another in Tampere.[149] Jauhiainen encouraged other congregations to establish similar societies in order that they might reach more young people. Young people were also given a special place in *Totuuden Kaiku*. From 1931 onwards '*Nuorison Nurkka*' (Young People's Corner) was published regularly in its pages.

Jauhiainen started to visit Baptist congregations regularly. He attended the Annual celebrations of congregations, too. It is amazing how energetically he devoted himself to this work, although leading the Union was only a secondary post. Jauhiainen received his salary not from the Union but from being full-time pastor in the Tampere Baptist congregation (1930-1937). He wrote about his

---

[146] *MEC* (3 January 1931) and (5 January 1931).

[147] Jauhiainen, 'Suomen Baptistiveljille ja Sisarille, Rauhaa!' (To Finnish Baptist Brothers and Sisters, Peace!), *Totuuden Kaiku* 3 (1931), p. 3.

[148] T. K., 'Piirteitä Vuosikokouksestamme' (Traits from our Annual Meeting), *Totuuden Kaiku* 7 (1931), pp. 6-7.

[149] John [Kokki], 'Nuoristyöstä' (About Youth Work), *Totuuden Kaiku* 4 (1928), pp. 3-4.

first visits as the Union President to the General Secretary of the Baptist World Alliance, Dr Rushbrooke:

> I made a long trip to our congregations, and to my sorrow I had to note that our work is in decline. Our members are for the most part old; there are far too few young people. The only encouraging thing is that our small group is probably now a convinced elite. Economically our congregations are poor, and they work in very scanty conditions.[150]

He then moved on to write about a Bible school. Dr Rushbrooke had asked him what it would cost to start one in Finland.[151] Jauhiainen made financial calculations. Money was not the only problem, however. He mentioned to Dr Rushbrooke that there were few young men in the FBU whom he could think of as future pastors. He knew three brothers from Inkeri who would 'gladly attend the school, and it would be important for them if they could one day return to their homeland'. He suggested Tampere as the most suitable place for the school. About three months later he received Rushbrooke's answer, which was negative: establishing the school would cost too much. He suggested instead that older preachers ought to take young men beside them, and educate them to pastor congregations.[152] For Jauhiainen this reply was a great disappointment. He knew how insufficient the theological knowledge of the preachers was; in no way could they properly teach the younger generation.

The lack of a Bible School had its consequences. It hindered the Baptist Union from developing into a more mature Baptist movement. How could a movement build a strong identity, if even its preachers were unable to understand the most elementary theological issues? On top of this, there was a general tendency among the Free Churches, Baptists included, to stress not education but revival. A constant waiting for revival was over-emphasised: people were taught that the main thing was that the gospel was preached, and new people were converted. Gunnar Westin takes up this question in his article in *Sanningsvittnet*:[153]

> ...in Free Churches revival work has been overestimated at the expense of education... There were revival preachers and colporteurs in great numbers, and

---

[150] Jauhiainen, Letter to Dr Rushbrooke, OC (14 August 1931).

[151] As early as 1908 the Baptist World Alliance (BWA) had made a decision to help to establish seminaries in Europe. (See more: B. Green, *Crossing the Boundaries: A History of the European Baptist Federation* (Didcot: Baptist Historical Society, 1999), p. 2). After World War II it was again listed as one of the goals of the BWA. Ibid., p. 8.

[152] Rushbrooke, Letter to Jauhiainen, OC (9 October 1931).

[153] Gunnar Westin, *Sanningsvittnet* (Witness to Truth) 27 (1933), as cited in Salmensaari, pp. 189-191. The article is actually about counselling, but it also deals with church life in a broader sense.

congregations were established, but...it was easier to bring about revival than to lead it the right way.

The Baptist Union did not appreciate the education of its pastors, nor did it pay attention to the teaching ministry in congregations. Thus, the Union remained a lay movement.[154] Pastors might have clarified theological concepts; they might have built and strengthened the identity of the movement. But, as Jauhiainen claimed, preachers did not have a proper education; they were more lay people than professionals, which seriously affected the Union.

Shortly after Jauhiainen had been elected to lead the Union there arose a crisis; one which also affected Baptist identity. The leader of the Helsinki Baptist congregation, Mr Engelberg, who had been the leader and preacher of this congregation since 1923,[155] came to the conclusion that the FBU was non-biblical, and non-brotherly, and it had to be dissolved. On 5 July 1928 the Finnish Baptist Union had been formed as an official independent religious union according to the Law of Religious Freedom that came into effect in Finland from the beginning of 1923. Engelberg, who had been a member of the Committee that wrote the bylaws for the Finnish Baptist Union,[156] now wanted the Union to become a registered organization in the same way as Pentecostal congregations. The Union structure ought to be what it had been before it was officially accepted as an independent denomination.[157] When Engelberg's suggestion was not accepted, he and the majority of the Helsinki congregation left the Union, and formed an independent Baptist congregation, which was then organized as a registered association, Rukoushuoneyhdistys Elim r.y. (Elim Prayer House, registered association).[158] Jauhiainen tried to discuss these disagreements with the congregation, and many members agreed with him. The majority, however, accepted Engelberg's view, and the congregation was no longer a member of the Union. Jauhiainen saw this dispute as being a consequence of Engelberg's personal disappointment when he was not elected as Union President, which may have been the case.[159] Because Engelberg had

---

[154] The Bible school was started in 1949. In the 1950s it started to offer two and three-year courses. When the rector changed in 1971, the curriculum was changed, and it became more a Bible school to deepen one's Christian life, not so much a place for theological studies. From 1992 on it has again concentrated on giving theological training for those becoming pastors.

[155] Veikko Toivola, *Suomalaisen Baptismin Teinraivaajia* (Trailblazers of Finnish Baptists) (Tampere: KY-paino, 1983), p. 7. Engelberg (later Enkovaara) owned a confectionery, and his work in the Baptist congregation was a side-line. Ibid.

[156] Veikko Toivola, *Suomalaisen Baptismin Tienraivaajia*, p. 8.

[157] G. Engelberg, Letter to Petäjävesi Baptist congregation, OC (14 December 1931).

[158] Jauhiainen, Letter to the EC members, OC (16 March 1932).

[159] Ibid. In the years 1929-1930 Engelberg wrote regularly in *Totuuden Kaiku*, which may have been a sign of his willingness to lead the FBU.

worked long term in the Executive Committee, his action caused confusion in the FBU.

However, positive things happened, too. The year 1932 was a year of revival in the Vaajakoski, Petäjävesi, and Turku Baptist congregations. When the Union gathered for its biannual meeting in January 1933 this was reported. The Vaajakoski congregation had built a church building, and had baptized forty-four people. Turku had baptized fifty-nine, and Petäjävesi fifteen.[160] The number of baptized believers in the Union rose from 730 in 1931 to 841 in 1932. When speaking about that time people use the expression 'Tervonen's revivals', which is a rather simplified remark. Toivo Tervonen was important, but there were many other field-workers and evangelists who visited the congregations regularly. No single name can be mentioned, for instance in connection with the revival in Vaajakoski. In *Totuuden Kaiku* we read that during that year A. Hiljanen, W. Karala, T. Vainonen, and A. Jauhiainen visited Vaajakoski and people were converted in their meetings. Matti Lehtonen was then taking care of the Vaajakoski congregation. In Turku, on the other hand, it seems that we may speak about one person. On 31 December, 1931, a Swedish pastor, Eric R. Lundin, visited the congregation, and a revival began. He stayed there for some months, and dozens of people were converted. Toivo Tervonen was then called to become pastor of the Turku congregation.[161] He stayed there less than a year. The year 1933 was a good one in Tampere, with twenty-one people baptized during the three first months. In Tampere, Toivo Tervonen was the main speaker at the revival meetings. The Petäjävesi congregation grew during the years 1932-1934, adding thirty-eight new members—this in a small rural village. It was mostly the field-workers and evangelists of the FBU who were active there.

Why did the growth in these congregations, with the exception of Turku, stop? In Jauhiainen's own Tampere Baptist congregation the reason is obvious: quarrels arose between those for and against Jauhiainen after Jauhiainen had admonished Toivo Tervonen about something.[162] The board of elders of the Tampere congregation sided with Tervonen, and asked Jauhiainen to quit in their meeting of 16 February 1934. When members of the congregation heard about this, they were astonished; they did not want that to happen. According to Union bylaws it was only the congregation that could dismiss the pastor. Appealing to this, Jauhiainen did not quit. Jauhiainen wrote to the Union secretary Karala: 'I have had great troubles. Tervonen has openly started to act against me. It has caused great restlessness in the congregation. Remember me

---

[160] 'Piirteitä S.B. Yhdyskunnan Toiminnasta v:na 1932' (Traits about the work of the Finnish Baptist Union in 1932'), *Totuuden Kaiku* 8 (1933), pp. 4-5.

[161] Toivo Tervonen, 'Vuosikertomus Turun Baptistiseurakunnan 45-Vuotisjuhlassa, 12-13 p:nä Marraskuuta 1932', (Annual report of Turku Baptist congregation in its 45th anniversary, 12-13 of November 1932) *Totuuden Kaiku* 12 (1932), pp. 3-5.

[162] Minutes of the Meeting of Elders in Tampere (16 February 1934).

and the congregation in your prayers.'[163] It may be that Toivo Tervonen wanted to become pastor of the Tampere congregation. Some of the elders wanted this: the revival in 1933 when Tervonen[164] was conducting revival meetings in Tampere was fresh in their minds. Jauhiainen was not an evangelist, he was a teacher. In congregations there were always those people who saw revival meetings as the most important part of the work. The teaching of new members was in the background; many people did not even understand the importance of it. This is why Tervonen, a gifted evangelist, had many supporters. The disagreements in Tampere did not quiet down and the elders asked the Executive Committee to help them. The EC and the elders gathered in Tampere on 14 September 1934. After discussions, the EC decided that Jauhiainen had done nothing wrong, but that those who opposed him had to repent. Jauhiainen continued pastoring the congregation until 1937.

Things were not going smoothly in the Vaajakoski congregation either. Kustaa V. Siiriäinen had to leave in 1934, and a young man, Toivo Wacklin, was elected in his place.[165] Wacklin had become a Christian in that congregation only seven months earlier. He had also experienced Spirit baptism shortly after his conversion.[166] This is indicative: an experienced pastor, 'to whom the Lord had given the gift of teaching',[167] was dismissed, and a very young Christian was elected to pastor the congregation. The deciding factor may have been that he was baptized with the Holy Spirit. This shows that two different views were fighting with each other in the Union, but it would still take almost two decades for the newer one, that which emphasised Holy Spirit baptism as Pentecostals taught it, to gain a fully dominant position.

In Turku the beginning of the revival was mostly connected to Pastor Lundin from Sweden. The revival continued there for some years even after he left. The congregation gained 155 new members, the membership being about 200 in 1937. Jaakko Kalliomäki, a promising young preacher, was then pastoring the congregation. Even bigger premises had to be rented.[168] In 1939 Turku sent

---

[163] Jauhiainen, Letter to Karala, OC (13 March 1934).

[164] Tervonen lived then in Tampere and had the full support of Jauhiainen. The Tampere congregation provided free housing for him in one of its apartments, and Tervonen himself was travelling around Baptist congregations as an evangelist. Minutes of the Meeting of the Elders, (Tampere: 9 August 1933). Jauhiainen wrote a letter to Baptist congregations asking them to send money for Tervonen's support. He says in that letter that 130 people had been converted and were baptized due to Tervonen's evangelistic meetings in one year in Baptist congregations. Jauhiainen, A Circular Letter to Baptist Congregations, OC (29 August 1933).

[165] Minutes of Vaajakoski Congregation Meeting (29 April 1934), § 2 and § 6.

[166] Toivo Wacklin, 'Henkikastekokemukseni' (My Baptism in the Spirit), *Totuuden Kaiku* 8 (1940), pp. 2-3.

[167] Toivola, *Suomalaisen Baptismin Tienraivaajia*, p. 62.

[168] Heimo Himanen, *Turun Baptistiseurakunta 1887-1987* (Turku Baptist Congregation 1887-1987) (Tampere: Kodin Ystävä, 1987), pp. 10, 46.

out four women evangelists: Martta Mörsky to Pohjanmaa in the neighbourhood of Vaasa, Anja Henelä to Ahvenanmaa, and Selma Pohjasmäki with Irma Koskinen to Satakunta in the surroundings of Pori.[169] There were many signs of spiritual vitality in this congregation.

The economic situation of the congregations and the FBU grew worse with the recession of the 1930s. Political changes also had an effect. At the same time, to use Jauhiainen's words, 'there was a lot of work, if only we had workers we would not be losing the battle in this struggle between religious movements'. This is what Jauhiainen wrote to Karala. His own work was focussed on building up the churches. He mentioned also that he had recently travelled 1,750 kilometres in twenty-four days, and had had twenty-eight meetings during that trip.[170] According to the information that is available, the year 1933 was one of his most active years concerning visits to congregations. No Union leader before or after him has been so diligent in his contacts with congregations. This may have affected negatively his work in the Tampere congregation, however. His many tasks as Union leader would have required that to be his full-time post. Toivo Tervonen, who as we have seen had been a valuable person in the outreach of the FBU, received a call from Canada in 1939 to become a pastor of the Finnish Baptist Congregation of Toronto.[171] Later in the same year Finland found itself at war with the Soviet Union, and a totally new era of the Finnish life began.

On 8 January 1935 a Preachers' Union was established.[172] This took place to help preachers to get to know each other better, and to stay in the Union, unlike many others who had left for other denominations, mainly the Pentecostals. Jauhiainen told the preachers why he supported the establishing of this organization:

> 1. It is important that the Holy Spirit may totally fill preachers that they may be able to help each other.
> 2. Preachers ought to be able to penetrate into God's perfect Word in order to fulfil His plans and purposes.

The attempt to foster FBU work was successful as twelve preachers joined the Preachers' Union immediately.[173] In the second Preachers' Union Meeting J.G. Kokki was elected President. Other members of the board were: Jauhiainen (vice-president), W. Karala (secretary), E. Kuusisto (treasurer), A. Hiljanen,

---

[169] Jauhiainen, 'Työstä ja Työntekomahdollisuuksista' (About Work and Working Possibilities), *Totuuden Kaiku* 2 (1939), pp. 7-8.

[170] Jauhiainen, Letter to Karala, OC (3 April 1933).

[171] 'Uutisia' (News'), *Totuuden Kaiku* 2 (1939), p. 8.

[172] *Minutes of the Meetings of the Preacher Union* [hereafter *MMPU*] (8 January 1935), §2.

[173] *MMPU* (8 January 1935), § 5.

and M. Nurmela (deputy).[174] Two years later women were accepted as members of the Preachers' Union.[175] It was also suggested that every member of the FBU should pay five marks per year for the Preachers' Union, and the money gathered would be used to pay pensions for retired preachers.[176] Later on it was decided that the Preachers' Union could have two different types of members: actual members and supportive members. The Union suggested that every congregation would take one offering a year for the Preachers' Union in order to increase its funds.[177] The role of the Preachers' Union seems to have been relatively minor. It was important that it paid attention to the financial situation of those preachers who had already retired. They were living in poor conditions and it was necessary to help them. Study courses and Bible study weeks were also held for preachers. The last available record of the Preachers' Union is dated 26 June 1950. When the state secured a national pension for every citizen, the Preachers' Union did not have to take care of retired preachers anymore. The tradition of arranging Bible weeks or days for pastors and evangelists continued.

Did Jauhiainen succeed in his efforts to help the Union to become more mature? Yes and no is probably the answer. In the Sunday schools the number of children started to grow at first but then declined again: in 1931 there were 221 Sunday school children, in 1933 the number had increased to 659, but in 1939 it was again low, only 261.[178] Concerning young people the situation was better. Many congregations had started special youth work, and new Youth Societies were established. This brought many young people into Baptist congregations, and they were actively taking part in congregational life. Some young men were interested in becoming preachers and evangelists, but their schooling continued to be a problem. In spite of some efforts that were made, the Union was not able to start the Bible School, which surely would have strengthened Baptist identity. On the whole, the Union had a much healthier basis by the end of the 1930s than it had had a decade before. Questions about the Holy Spirit were not so much to the fore. They would, however, cause real trouble during the coming decades.

---

[174] *MMPU* (25 June 1935), § 4.
[175] *MMPU* (26 June 1937), § 4.
[176] *MMPU* (26 June 1937), § 6.
[177] *MMPU* (3 January 1949), § 3.
[178] Jorma Parviainen, 'Suomenkielisen Baptistikirkon Toiminta Synnystä Nykyaikaan: Poikkileikkaustutkimus Suomenkielisen Baptistikirkon Toimintamuodoista ja Niiden Kehityksestä' (The Activities of the Finnish-speaking Baptist Union from its Birth to Present: A Cross Section of Baptist Union's Activities and Development), unpub. diss, (Helsinki: Helsinki University Theological Faculty, 1974), pp. 132-133.

The 1940s: A New Wave of Pentecostalism

The war years affected the life of the Baptist congregations in several ways. Most men were at the front. But even during wartime the FBU held its Annual Meetings regularly, the only exception being June 1941.[179] Some work was done in new places with good results, but generally life in the FBU was quiet. Jauhiainen wrote, however, that in many country villages where he had arranged meetings, people came in great numbers, and many were converted. Also Jaakko Kalliomäki wrote to Jauhiainen that when he had preached in a village in Northern Finland, more than 20 people had made a decision to follow Jesus.[180] Encouraged by this, Jauhiainen asked other evangelists and all Union members to try to go to new places where work could be started.[181] During the war there were no significant overall changes in the FBU membership. In 1939 the number of members in the Union was 931, and in 1945 the Union was able to publish statistics showing twenty more members. Those preachers and evangelists who were not at the front held meetings regularly, but many of the older preachers started to be in poor health. When delegates spoke about the work in their congregations in 1943, many reported only that they 'had tried to gather together'.[182]

During the war, in 1943 one new congregation was started, that in Vihtavuori[183], and the Kuopio congregation was dissolved in 1940.[184] Vihtavuori is a village about twenty kilometres away from Vaajakoski village. Although the Baptist group here was functioning as a congregation, it was not independent, but worked as a branch congregation of Vaajakoski. From the very beginning the work of the Holy Spirit was emphasized in Vihtavuori. This congregation was also very eager to arrange Bible study weeks. It is significant that August Jauhiainen was a warmly welcomed speaker. Perhaps more clearly than in any other Baptist congregation, his teaching was valued there, and no difficulties arose concerning his views of the Holy Spirit. A short report in *Totuuden Kaiku* gives some insight:

---

[179] Because Finland was an ally of Germany, the Soviet Union attacked it. This in spite of the fact that Finland had declared its neutrality, and many nations, Germany and Great Britain included, had affirmed it. Korhonen, *Suomen Historian Käsikirja*, p. 598.

[180] Jaakko Kalliomäki, Letter to A. Jauhiainen, OC (18 May 1941).

[181] *MOMD* (5 January 1941), § 8.

[182] *MOMD* (13 June 1943), § 12.

[183] Teuvo Aaltio mentions in his dissertation, 'The History of the National Baptists in Finland', that the congregation was founded only in 1948, which is not correct. The congregation dedicated its first church building that year, but it was established on 17 October 1943. Aino Lindeman, *Vihtavuoren Baptistiseurakunta 1943-1993* (Vihtavuori Baptist Congregation 1943-1993) (Tampere: Kharis Oy, 1993), p. 6.

[184] *MEC* (22 June 1940), § 3.

Worth specially mentioning is the Bible week in May where our greatly beloved teacher, and President of our Union spoke... Our teacher himself was fervent in Spirit, and the teaching penetrated deep in the truths of the Bible... It is grace that we have ministers of the Word, who themselves live in continuous fullness, in living connection with the Father, and who, knowing the Word, are able to take their listeners to see the riches of the Word, and not only to see, but first of all to own them.[185]

The life in this new congregation was active, and soon members wanted to obtain a permanent place for their gatherings. This happened in 1948.[186]

The war affected the Union magazine; it became quite one-sided. Jauhiainen himself wrote many articles, and almost all of them were educational in nature. There seem to have been no other writers who sent articles for publishing. The year 1942 was exceptionally difficult. *Totuuden Kaiku* ran into economic difficulties, because printing costs had risen enormously, and the number of subscribers was only about 800. The Executive Committee asked 'evangelist sisters and preacher brothers and other Union members to work to get new subscribers for the paper'.[187] People were also encouraged to 'sell diligently' the special Christmas issue of *Totuuden Kaiku*, which was called *Jouluaamu* (*Christmas Morning*). Its circulation was more than four times that of regular issues. With the income from selling *Jouluaamu* the publishing of *Totuuden Kaiku* could continue. To make the magazine more attractive, the Official Meeting of delegates, at their meeting on 25 June 1942, chose a board of editors to enrich the content. One lady was asked to assist the paper by translating articles from Swedish Baptist magazines. It may be that she never accepted the task; at least there were no translated articles in *Totuuden Kaiku*. The same passivity can be seen in the work of the board of editors. The paper remained the same, to the dissatisfaction of its readers.

After the war congregational life was slowly restored. In 1946 four new workers started their service: a woman evangelist and three men.[188] One of the men was Vesa Jauhiainen, the son of August Jauhiainen. He started to work among children and young people, which had been one of the main emphases of his father throughout his presidency. Half a year later Vesa Jauhiainen spoke in the Meeting of delegates 'warm-hearted about raising children in a Christian spirit'. He also mentioned that 'only about half of Finnish school children attend Sunday schools, and therefore something had to be done'.[189] From then on there was a more thorough preparation of Sunday school texts in every issue of *Totuuden Kaiku*.

---

[185] Emmi Anttila, 'Tervehdys Vihtavuoren Seurakunnasta' (Greetings From the Vihtavuori Congregation), *Totuuden Kaiku* 7-8 (1951), p. 10.
[186] Aino Lindeman, *Vihtavuoren Baptistiseurakunta 1943-1993*, p. 11.
[187] *MOMD* (5 January 1943), § 5.
[188] *MEC* (24 June 1946), § 4.
[189] *MOMD* (5 January 1947), § 9

There were big changes in the Executive Committee in 1946. Older men, who had served there for decades, were withdrawing, and younger men were elected. Jauhiainen's sixteen-year-long editorship of *Totuuden Kaiku* ended and Toivo Kylliäinen, who had been sub-editor during the years 1931-1934, was elected Editor-in-Chief in June 1946.[190] Jauhiainen then became a member of the board of editors. Readers wanted a change in the content of the magazine. It seems evident that they had grown tired of a publication with almost nothing other than educational articles. The finances of the magazine were good: when Jauhiainen handed it to Kylliäinen there were fifty thousand FIM on its account.[191] During Kylliäinen's time articles became shorter, and news from different congregations started to appear regularly, which made the paper more a real organ of the Union. Preachers and evangelists started writing articles. This shows that there was a new willingness among them to get involved. Why did it not happen earlier? One of the reasons was certainly that the general atmosphere in the whole country was more enthusiastic now that the war had ended. People were looking to the future with new hope. Another reason may have been that Jauhiainen had been too busy and slow to encourage others to send articles for publishing. He was also known to be a sharp and accurate man, a man who was respected and even feared to a certain extent, and this may explain the reluctance of other preachers to offer their articles. Jauhiainen's character becomes evident in a humorous way in a short poem. A woman evangelist, who had worked with him in Inkeri, wrote about him:

After him comes Jauhiainen,
a man like arctic bramble.
But if something bad he sees,
that he surely handles.

Kylliäinen's editorship was a short one—only two and a half years. During his time *Totuuden Kaiku's* circulation increased from 800 to 1,100, which shows that he succeeded well. Jaakko Kalliomäki[192] was elected to the position after him in 1949.[193] By that time Jauhiainen had already resigned from the board of editors.[194] With Kalliomäki, the editing moved from Tampere to

---

[190] *MOMD* (9 June 1946), § 17.

[191] To give an idea about the value of the money, I will note that Kylliäinen's wages for editing the paper was FIM 30,000 a year. This was not, however, his main job, only a secondary occupation.

[192] After being informed by Kylliäinen that he would not continue editing *Totuuden Kaiku*, Jauhiainen wrote to Kalliomäki that he would want him to succeed Kylliäinen. OC (23 November 1948). This shows that Jauhiainen fully supported him, although their views differed from each other concerning the Holy Spirit.

[193] *MOMD* (4 January 1949), § 12.

[194] *MOMD* (3 January 1948), § 18.

Turku, and the new board members, Aini Holmberg and Olavi Nieminen, were also elected from there.[195]

During the latter part of the 1940s a new wave of Pentecostalism swept over the Union. In the FBU the Pentecostally-minded pastors and evangelists were now in the majority, and they started to emphasize the power of the Holy Spirit as an answer to the need for new growth among Baptists. This is openly stated in an article 'Pysähtymisen Vaara' (The Danger of Stagnation) in 1946 by Paavo Ketonen, then a thirty-six-year-old Baptist preacher, who had pastored Baptist congregations in Turku and in Helsinki. He had read Frank Mang's article about Spirit baptism, and inspired by that he wrote this article.

> There was a time in our Union, too, when we had stagnated... We were satisfied with the power of Good Friday and Easter. But, thanks be to God, we are now finally afloat, we are going forward, to wider and deeper waters. This has not happened without struggles. And there is still a danger of stagnation, especially if we stick to the view that has been presented sometimes also on the pages of this paper. The question is about the misleading teaching about the Holy Spirit... According to that, regeneration and the Pentecostal experience would be one and the same thing... Let us not go astray. Let us keep to the prophetic word.[196]

These were heavy accusations, with a clear reference to August Jauhiainen's teaching about the Holy Spirit, teaching which Ketonen found not only misleading but unbiblical. According to him, the Union had stagnated during Jauhiainen's time. When the majority of the Executive Committee members adopted Pentecostal teaching about the Holy Spirit, they also started to treat those not using the Pentecostal language with suspicion. Naturally August Jauhiainen was one of them.

Towards the end of the decade there was an upswing of publishing activities, and a special FBU committee was elected to promote it.[197] In 1948 a children's magazine, *Lasten Kaiku* (The Echo of Children), started to be published.[198] Vesa Jauhiainen edited it. At first it came out twice a year; later on four times a year. In 1947 the FBU obtained permission from the Finnish Ministry of Supply[199] to publish the second edition of a Finnish Baptist pioneer's book *Lähteitä Kyynelten Laaksosta*[200] (Springs in the Valley of Tears). The book was

---

[195] *MOMD* (4 January 1949), § 12.

[196] Paavo Ketonen, 'Pysähtymisen Vaara' (The Danger of Stagnation), *Totuuden Kaiku* 10 (1946), p. 3.

[197] *MOMD* (24 June 1948), § 14.

[198] *MOMD* (3 January 1948), § 15.

[199] After the war there was a lack of paper. This is why the Executive Committee had to ask permission for printing books, papers etc., and they had to inform the Ministry of Supply how much paper was needed for printing.

[200] Erik Jansson, *Lähteitä Kyynelten Laaksosta*, 2. painos (Springs in the Valley of T Tears, 2nd ed.) (Tampere: Totuuden Kaiku, 1949.) The first edition dated from 1901.

originally written in Swedish but was translated into Finnish. The book gives an account of difficulties, even persecution, during the early years of Baptist work in Finland, and was thus an important book for Finnish Baptists. Jauhiainen's systematic study guide to the Bible, *Raamatuntutkisteluopas*, was published in 1948. A preacher and an author, Vilho Rantanen, from the Free Evangelical Movement, reviewed the book in their youth magazine, *Nuorten Todistus:*

> We have to give credit to those ministers of the Word who take pains to share the Word both by proclaiming and by writing. To these untiring workers belongs Aug. Jauhiainen, who after many years' toil has published a manual for those who study the Word. The value of the book is even enhanced by the fact that Kaarlo Vaismaa, who is well acquainted with the Scriptures, has checked it before publication. All who want to dig deep into the gold mines of the Word should buy this book... It handles the integrated whole, not some fragments here and there.[201]

In the FBU Executive Committee the book did not receive such unreserved approval. This becomes evident in the following episode. Jauhiainen had asked the EC if either the FBU or *Totuuden Kaiku* had money to publish his book. This started a lively conversation. It became evident that there had already been some talk in the Union to the effect that Jauhiainen's forthcoming book was unbiblical, which Jauhiainen denied. The EC came to the conclusion that the book could be published only if certain preachers, namely Kalliomäki, Korpela, and Lehtonen, all of whom belonged to the Pentecostally-minded, would accept it after reading it through and paying special attention to Jauhiainen's teachings about Christology and the Holy Spirit.[202] They read the manuscript but did not have any remarks or corrections to make. However they would have liked to publish a dissenting opinion concerning baptism in the Holy Spirit in *Totuuden Kaiku* before the book was published. In his letter to Kalliomäki, Jauhiainen suggested that they abstain from that, mentioning that he had presented his case 'biblically', and that 'a kingdom fighting against itself will not last'.[203] Although Kalliomäki decided not to publish this conflicting opinion, Jauhiainen could no longer work in peace; from then on he was on the defensive.

When Kalliomäki became the editor of *Totuuden Kaiku* in 1949, the conflict between him and Jauhiainen really broke out. Jauhiainen accused him of turning the policy of the magazine towards Pentecostalism. According to him, the preachers and other brothers in prominent positions should stay faithful both to their calling and to Baptist doctrines. Even if they themselves wanted to turn away from these, they should not prevent those representing Baptist views from speaking and writing about them. Jauhiainen continued: 'This is the right thing to do, thinking of those members who share a different view, and on top

---

[201] *Nuorten Todistus* (Young Testimony) as cited in *Totuuden Kaiku* 10 (1948).
[202] *MEC* (3 January 1948), § 6.
[203] Jauhiainen, Letter to Jaakko Kalliomäki, OC (24 January 1948).

of this, Baptists have always stressed freedom of thinking without anybody forcing them to believe otherwise.'[204] These claims were just. Jauhiainen asked that he be treated in the same way as he had treated the Pentecostally-minded earlier: in a brotherly spirit. When his claims were not listened to, Jauhiainen also lost this brotherly spirit. He asked if he could start publishing another paper, if agreement could not be reached. This is the first time we really see him fighting for his rights. The conflict was solved in the EC meeting on 23 June 1949. The committee agreed that everybody had freedom to indicate his thoughts, and that teaching should not be one-sided. Members of the EC stated that Jauhiainen, being an experienced preacher, would not write anything to harm the Union. Kalliomäki promised to publish his articles, and the thing was settled. The truth is, however, that, under the surface, agitation was going on. A change in publication policy was a fact. *Totuuden Kaiku* published more and more articles about the Holy Spirit representing the Pentecostal view. Also testimonies from people who had received this gift were constantly published. This further strengthened the position of this new generation of leaders.

Wider Finnish Baptist life carried on in the difficult period after the war. As a result of a local revival, a new congregation was established in Kauhajoki with thirty-six members.[205] This strengthened the Baptist witness in the surroundings of Vaasa on the North Sea coast. After the war the FBU received material and financial help from other Baptists. This was truly needed, because life in post-war Finland was a great struggle. The state was paying heavy reparations to Russia.[206] The enormous reparations, territorial losses (about 12.5% of the original territories were lost to Russia), and, due to this, the resettling of the displaced population (almost half a million people), were the biggest challenges. The BWA offered both support and friendship.[207] Foreign help was a reminder that fellow Christians had not forgotten them. Besides the BWA, both the Swedish Baptist Union and British Baptists sent money, most of which was used for the work in Helsinki.[208] Often money was distributed to Baptist preachers and evangelists, who did not have a regular salary but got twice a year what the Union succeeded in gathering from congregations.[209] Finland received CARE-packages through American Baptist Relief, which had joined CARE.[210] The Relief Committee of the Foreign Mission Board of the

---

[204] *MEC* (4 June 1949), § 2.
[205] Kauhajoki congregation, Letter to A. Jauhiainen, OC (24 July 1949).
[206] Over six years Finland had to pay $300 million to the Soviet Union. On top of this, the national debt after the war had risen to 67.3 million. Korhonen, *Suomen Historian Käsikirja*, pp. 660-661.
[207] Green, *Crossing the Boundaries*, p. 8.
[208] *MEC* (28 March 1946), § 7.
[209] *MEC* (3 July 1946), § 2.
[210] A. T. Ohrn, ed., *Eighth Baptist World Congress, Cleveland, Ohio, 1950, Official Report* (Philadelphia: Judson Press, 1950), p. 329.

Southern Baptist Convention also sent goods to Finland.[211] In 1947 a smaller amount of money was sent for the FBU's youth work, and the money was used to buy a tent for evangelistic meetings.[212] Through the Salvation Army the FBU twice received clothes and shoes from America.[213]

In 1949 Jauhiainen saw perhaps the dearest of his dreams come true. The Finnish Baptist Union had established a Bible School on 5 January 1947, but it was not fully opened at first. From 1947 to 1949 money was gathered, and the Bible School was a much-discussed topic in the Union. In October 1949 the time came to start the first one-year course. Mikko Kolomainen had just returned from England after studying there for three years at Bristol Baptist College.[214] He was elected rector of the Bible School, and six students were accepted to study there, four women and two men.[215] At the opening lecture of the school, Jauhiainen spoke about God's work, which often starts with small things. It is faith that makes small beginnings grow in a way that nobody can imagine. Perhaps wanting to ease the tension in the FBU because of different opinions about the necessity of theological studies, and also because of the tension he himself was going through in matters concerning the Holy Spirit, he dealt with both these subjects in his speech.

> We often hear in our midst people speaking disparagingly about knowledge. Those who do that forget that the Holy Spirit is also the Spirit of wisdom and understanding. Both of these are needed. As Christians and preachers we badly need to know the Bible... It is only this knowledge that without any restrictions is based on the Bible together with faith that conquers the world.[216]

---

[211] Ohrn, *Eighth Baptist World Congress*, p. 335.

[212] *MEC* (21 June 1947), § 15.

[213] Pelastusarmeijan Miesyhteiskunnallinen Toimisto (The Salvation Army Social Office of Men), Letter to August Jauhiainen, OC (15 February 1947).

[214] Kolomainen was also born in Inkeri, and he came to Finland in 1931. He then lived for a while with the Jauhiainens. After he finished his studies in Bristol, the Union almost lost him, because Toivo Tervonen, who had moved to America earlier, transmitted an invitation letter from American Baptists to Kolomainen to work there. Kolomainen had given a positive answer because life in post-war Finland was very difficult. In a letter to Jauhiainen Kolomainen mentioned that he was still open to return to Finland, if he was needed. He had but one wish: that he would get a regular salary when serving the FBU. (Kolomainen, Letter to Jauhiainen, OC (28 November 1948).) Jauhiainen wrote a forthright letter to Kolomainen, telling him that his duty was to return to work for the FBU, which had helped him in getting a three-year scholarship from the BWA to study in Bristol. (Jauhiainen, Letter to Kolomainen, OC (10 December 1948).)

[215] Anneli Lohikko, *Suomen Baptistiyhdyskunnan Raamattuopisto 1949-1999* (The Finnish Baptist Union's Bible School 1949-1999) (Tampere: Kharis Oy, 1999), p. 11.

[216] Ibid., p. 13.

The subjects taught in the school were: New Testament Exegesis, Old Testament Introduction, Homiletics, Church History, History of Philosophy, Psychology, Finnish, English, and Music. Later the Swedish language, the History of Mission, and Isagogics were added.[217] For the first time in its history the FBU now had a good basic teaching for those becoming preachers. During weekends and summer vacations the students worked in Baptist congregations, where they could put into practice what they learned during the lessons. In the coming years the School attracted many young people, and the Union got many new preachers through it. This was really needed because the Union had lost nine preachers and evangelists during the 1940s.[218] Unfortunately disagreements about the policy of the school rose between Jauhiainen and Kolomainen. Jauhiainen strongly supported a conservative Bible-centred teaching, whereas Kolomainen wanted to introduce his students more widely to the theological field of his time, which was understandable and necessary, thinking of the pastoral work with which many of his students would be occupied. The students appreciated Kolomainen highly, and the FBU benefited from many good preachers from 'his' School.

Statistics show that membership in the FBU remained about the same during the war years, but after the war it began to decline, the worst year being 1948. There was almost a similar downward trend in the membership to that which the FBU had experienced twenty years before. The membership had been 1,000 in 1939; in 1948 it was only 711. I do not consider this to have happened by coincidence. The Union was at a turning point and in a time of crisis. Two different teachings about the Holy Spirit were fighting against each other, which affected the atmosphere in the Union. The Pentecostally-minded preachers were again strong, and they wanted to further strengthen their position. As a matter of fact the result was already sealed, because the majority of preachers and the majority of the EC agreed that the Pentecostal way of understanding the work of the Holy Spirit was right. When we add to this the fact that the Christian literature published at that time came almost solely from the Pentecostal Movement's publishing house, we can very easily understand that the literature all Finnish Free Church people read was to a great extent dealing with questions about the Holy Spirit. No wonder this affected all Free Church movements, Baptists included.

The Beginning of the 1950s and the Final Conflict

In 1948, after serving the Union as president for almost twenty years, Jauhiainen had turned sixty. He was not satisfied with what he had achieved so

---

[217] Ibid., p. 14.
[218] Veikko Toivola, 'Miespolvet Vaipuvat Unholaan' (Generations Falling into Oblivion), *Kodin Ystävä* 12 (1971), pp. 8-10.

far, and wanted to continue serving the Union. He was a strong leader, even stubborn at times, and these personal characteristics must have been among the reasons why, over time, other preachers wanted to depose him from his leadership position in the Union. Another reason was that the younger generation wanted power. In 1950 talks about Jauhiainen's 'heresies' increased.[219] These 'heresies' must have included both his teaching about the Holy Spirit, and, more controversially, his universalism—the belief that all will ultimately be saved. He had spoken about the latter belief only in private conversations with some Baptist preachers, which shows that he trusted them as his friends and he thought he could be open with them. He had not preached about the subject at all, but those who knew about it had surely spoken about it at least in their private conversations.

There were a few other specific issues, some more significant than others. In 1949 a special women's organization, the Finnish Baptist Women (FBW), had been formed, and August Jauhiainen, who understood the meaning of women's work, warmly supported it from the beginning. There were different opinions about it, though, and Jauhiainen became more of an oddity because of his positive attitude to the FBW. In the FBW's annual report of the year 1951 we read: 'Here in Finland this work is new and strange; it is perhaps the Finnish rigidity that hinders an unprejudiced acceptance of it.'[220] More broadly within the FBU, the Turku Baptist congregation was in the 1950s the biggest Baptist congregation in the Union, and it was becoming more and more influential Union-wide. The records show that this congregation had not invited Jauhiainen to hold Bible study weeks there at all since 1948, and even before that Jauhiainen had visited the congregation very rarely.[221] Kalliomäki was then their preacher and leader, and it seems evident that for personal reasons he did not want Jauhiainen to visit Turku. Some of the congregation members had even asked Jauhiainen why he did not visit them anymore. Jauhiainen had given them diplomatic answers, not wanting any difficulties to arise.[222]

One serious conflict affected the FBU in 1950. Toivo Wacklin, a member of the Executive Committee, moved over to the Pentecostals. He made the decision after a dispute in the Kauhajoki Baptist congregation. Wacklin joined the Pentecostal congregation, Saalem, in Tampere.[223] When he left, some members of the Tampere Baptist congregation left with him.[224] Wacklin had wanted the Kauhajoki Baptist congregation[225] to unite with the Pentecostals

---

[219] A. Jauhiainen, Letter to Vesa Jauhiainen, OC (3 March 1950).

[220] Aino Lindeman, *Suomen Baptistinaiset 1949-1999* (Finnish Baptist Women 1949-1999) (Tampere: Kharis Oy, 1999), p. 7.

[221] Jauhiainen, Letter to EC members, PC (10 July 1953).

[222] Jauhiainen, Letter to Helmi Sihvonen, PC (5 September 1953).

[223] Jauhiainen, Letter to Senja Kujala, OC (15 February1950).

[224] Jauhiainen, Letter to Senja Kujala, OC (5 April 1950).

[225] The Kauhajoki congregation was not an independent congregation, but worked under the Jurva Baptist congregation.

there,[226] but this attempt had failed. He had served as a chairman in an official meeting that he hoped would make this decision but the meeting was convened before Baptists were even asked to take part in it.[227] The name of the new congregation had been already talked about; it would be either *Smyrna* or *Siion*.[228] According to Senja Kujala, an elder and the treasurer of the Kauhajoki Baptist congregation, Wacklin had said that if the meeting was not successful from his point of view (that is, if Baptists did not decide to join with the Pentecostals), he would move to the Pentecostals.[229] But instead of acknowledging this as the reason for his resignation, he accused Jauhiainen of forcing him to resign. The Kauhajoki Baptist congregation lost some of its members to the Pentecostals during this episode. When Wacklin, as a former Baptist, later visited the Pentecostals in Kauhajoki, he asked local Baptists if he could preach in their congregation, too. The elders of the church welcomed him.[230] When discussing with them, Wacklin defamed Jauhiainen and another Baptist preacher.[231] He visited many ordinary Baptist members in Kauhajoki, too, accusing Jauhiainen of dismissing him, which was not true.[232]

In a letter to Benjam Lehtonen, an EC member and the secretary of the Union, Jauhiainen wrote that in the light of what was happening the EC should seriously discuss the Baptist work. 'As far as I understand, it is not wise that we train up members for Pentecostal congregations, and that we have even preachers who encourage our members to move to the Pentecostals. Such talk, that there are no differences between Pentecostals and Baptists, ought to come to an end, because this shows us where they lead to.' This was Jauhiainen's view about close work with Pentecostals and the Pentecostally-minded.[233] He goes on to write that the EC, in contrast with the policy during Kokki's time,

---

[226] Wacklin had asked one of the elders in the Kauhajoki Baptist congregation to write about this meeting to Ketonen. In this letter, which Ketonen then sent to Jauhiainen, the elder writes that young people, who had recently learned to know Christ, wanted to work together with Pentecostals. And because Pentecostals and Baptists 'had no doctrinal differences' they should unite into one congregation. At the end of the meeting the Pentecostal preacher, K. Rissanen, commented that it was not an easy thing to make two congregations into one. Pentecostals and Baptists closed the meeting in harmony, praying that God would be in charge of the possible unification. A copy of Eero Lehtikevari's letter to Paavo Ketonen, 29 January 1950 in A. Jauhiainen's official correspondence from the year 1950.

[227] A copy of Senja Kujala's letter to Jaakko Kalliomäki, OC (30 Januay 1950).

[228] Senja Kujala, Letter to A. Jauhiainen, OC (2 March 1950).

[229] Senja Kujala, Letter to A. Jauhiainen, OC (19 March 1950).

[230] Senja Kujala, Letter to A. Jauhiainen, OC (19 February 1950).

[231] Ibid. It is difficult to understand this defamation because Wacklin himself had sent A. Jauhiainen a polite farewell letter in a spirit of reconciliation wishing God's blessings on all Baptist work, and ending his letter by sending greetings of peace to him. Toivo Wacklin, Letter to A. Jauhiainen, OC (13 February 1950).

[232] Jauhiainen, Letter to Benjam Lehtonen, OC (7 March 1950).

[233] Ibid.

had been too gentle. Then, admitting that he was foolish to write this, he said that if 'his gospel' was accepted, things would improve.[234] By this expression he must have been pointing to his teaching about the Holy Spirit. How deep the marks were that this left on the Kauhajoki congregation was shown by the fact that not much more than a year later the congregation voted on whether it wanted to remain in the FBU. The result was clear: only four members voted for separation from the FBU, and sixteen were against it. When writing about this to his son, August Jauhiainen mentions especially Senja Kujala and two other women as very devoted members, who did not hesitate to express their thoughts to the congregation.[235]

There were similar difficulties in Kivesjärvi in Northern Finland. Baptists and some Pentecostals in the village visited each other's meetings and there was an attempt to work officially together, but this failed. People did not come to Baptist meetings, nor did they attend Pentecostal meetings. The Pentecostals then suggested that they would once more try to work together. Jauhiainen, who had regularly visited the small Baptist group, was not willing to do that.[236] At the end of the year 1950, Mikko Kolomainen, the seminary rector, warned Jauhiainen not to exacerbate the problems. He wrote: 'What is needed now, is flexibility and diplomacy. With this I do not mean lack of principle.'[237] According to Kolomainen, the questions and disputes concerning the Holy Spirit could mean the break-up of the Union. This was a real threat. Kolomainen must have been aware of what had happened to the Baptist Union of Sweden. In the late 1930s it split into two; many congregations and parts of congregations left the Union to join the Örebro Mission, which 'some people regarded as semi-Pentecostal'.[238] Kolomainen was not the only one to have warned Jauhiainen. Kalliomäki had done the same thing, but what Kalliomäki had in mind was power politics. Jauhiainen related the conversation with him concerning this in a letter to Helmi Sihvonen:

> Kalliomäki: 'Move to our side. It is not so important that you think as we do as long as you are on the same side, and pretend to agree with us.'

> Jauhiainen comments thus to Sihvonen: 'By this he meant that I would have pretended to be Pentecostal-minded.' I answered him: 'Is it of such great importance, on what side I stand, and what would you profit from me being on your side?'

---

[234] Ibid.
[235] Jauhiainen, Letter to Vesa Jauhiainen, OC (23 May 1951).
[236] Jauhiainen, Letter to J. Kalliomäki, OC (2 February 1953).
[237] Mikko Kolomainen, Letter to A. Jauhiainen, OC (28 December 1950). Over time Jauhiainen's view about the Pentecostals had turned quite negative.
[238] Hughey, *Baptist Partnership in Europe*, p. 73.

Kalliomäki answered: 'You have such a great authority.' Jauhiainen comments to Sihvonen that he had always found pretence very disgusting.[239]

Jauhiainen knew by 1951 that his position was no longer tenable. This becomes evident in his letter to E. Kuusisto, an EC member:

> People have tried to depose me, but have not succeeded so far. I myself would not be offended even if they did that, because 'a fool always rushes to the fore'. My conviction has been, and still is, that I work as hard as I can as long as I am still in charge. Others may do what they want to after I have stepped aside.[240]

Among the areas of tension was dissatisfaction with the Bible school. Students wanted more time for studying the Bible, and considered that subjects like English and the history of philosophy should be left out. Jauhiainen told Kolomainen this, mentioning that it would be good if he would pay attention to these wishes.[241] In a later letter to him, Jauhiainen mentioned *Totuuden Kaiku*, too. Many people, some even outside the Union, had contacted him during the first part of the year (1951) wondering if there was not a more competent editor-in-chief than Kalliomäki among Baptists. He asked if Kolomainen could take up *Totuuden Kaiku*'s condition in the next EC meeting, which shows that he was beginning to get tired of speaking up about difficult issues. Whether Kolomainen did this or not is not known, because the minutes of that meeting are missing from the archives. Kalliomäki continued editing the paper until 1958. In 1953 all publication activities were transferred to Kalliomäki, who had moved from Turku to pastor the Vaajakoski congregation.[242]

The mistrust of Jauhiainen was growing. In the EC meeting on 24 June 1953, Jauhiainen made a proposal that there should be an obligatory Bible course for Baptist teenagers. This course, corresponding to Lutheran confirmation classes, would provide them with a basic knowledge of the Bible as well as Baptist beliefs. The proposal was not accepted. Members of the EC came to the conclusion that—according to Baptist principles—such obligatory courses could not be arranged. Instead they stated that all congregations should be encouraged to arrange voluntary Bible courses for young people attending their meetings. Mikko Kolomainen and Vesa Jauhiainen were asked to write a booklet about Baptist beliefs.[243] So, in a way they themselves understood the importance of such a course, otherwise they would not have asked for this booklet to be written. It is clear that in fact it was a question of the person, not of the matter itself. August Jauhiainen had lost the confidence of the EC; indeed the EC wanted to depose him. Mistrust did not come as a surprise to

---

[239] Jauhiainen, Letter to Helmi Sihvonen, PC (5 September 1953).
[240] Jauhiainen, Letter to E. Kuusisto, OC (12 February 1951).
[241] Jauhiainen, Letter to Mikko Kolomainen, OC (22 May 1951).
[242] *MMOD* (5 January 1953), § 7.
[243] *MEC* (24 June 1953), § 2. There is no evidence that this booklet was ever written.

Jauhiainen. In a letter written to his son after his dismissal, he wrote that for a long time he had already expected such a catastrophe to happen.[244] For his dismissal from the Union, and also the prohibition to preach in its congregations, however, he was not prepared. This painful episode is the subject of the last part of this study.

Jauhiainen's Dismissal

The first very stormy EC meeting concerning Jauhiainen's position was held in Turku at the end of June 1953, but the Union membership did not know about any serious conflicts as yet. All that they knew was that Jauhiainen's suggestion of obligatory Bible courses for young people had not been accepted in the meeting of delegates earlier in June. After that meeting Jauhiainen suggested in a letter to Kalliomäki that he would like either to continue one more year as Union President if possible, or else to resign immediately. He wrote: 'I am ready to withdraw… Yesterday I was collecting all bond papers…in order to be able to hand them over.'[245] On the request of two EC members another EC meeting was arranged very quickly. It took place in Tampere, on 2 July 1953. Jauhiainen was not given the option of resigning; he was dismissed. His long period of service to the Union had come to an abrupt end.

The official records of the 2 July meeting state that Jauhiainen was told that either he should repent of his alleged belief in universal salvation or he could not continue as President of the Union. The minutes of the EC meeting read,

> Because Jauhiainen has adopted the doctrine of universal salvation alien to Baptists, we have to fear that through him this doctrine, and this wrong teaching, is spreading to our congregations, and thus the fear of God will disappear from the hearts of many friends. The EC meeting considered that Aug. Jauhiainen had given up Baptist doctrine and the biblical standpoint despite the EC's advice and warnings, and was sticking to his own views. This being the situation the EC considers that Aug. Jauhiainen can no more officiate as a preacher in our Union. A written document will be sent to the leaders of the congregations informing them about this.[246]

The strongly worded dismissal letter sent to Baptist congregations reads as follows:

> Authorized by the Executive Committee of the Finnish Baptist Union we the undersigned make known the following:

---

[244] Jauhiainen, Letter to Vesa Jauhiainen, PC (3 July 1953).
[245] Jauhiainen, Letter to J. Kalliomäki, OC (28 June 1953).
[246] *MEC* (2 July 1953), § 12.

1. In Tampere, in the EC meeting, 2 July 1953, preacher Aug. Jauhiainen was relieved of his presidency, and the same meeting chose preacher Paavo Ketonen[247] from Helsinki to take over this post.

2. Because Aug. Jauhiainen has embraced the doctrine that all will be saved, even Satan one day, and because preacher Jauhiainen in spite of the EC's serious warnings has not abandoned this dangerous and unbiblical view, the EC cannot accept him any longer to serve as our worker, and thus it is not recommended to welcome him to our congregations.

Turku, 16 July 1953

Paavo Ketonen, President; Benjam Lehtonen, Secretary

Jauhiainen wrote a letter to the EC members reminding them that he had promised not to speak publicly about the doctrine of universal salvation at all, but this commitment had not been enough for them. Concerning his doctrine he wrote:

You, brothers, found me to be a heretic. However, you cannot mention one single occasion when in a public meeting I would have presented this doctrine, of which you have accused me. Only in private, confidential conversations with my fellow workers did I speak about it.[248]

Later on Jauhiainen wrote to two EC members, Ketonen and Kalliomäki, about another very serious matter concerning his dismissal. These two preachers had gone so far in the EC meeting of 2 July as to reveal what can be termed a 'confessional secret' of Jauhiainen.[249] There had been indiscretions in Jauhiainen's life, and he had confessed it. This was now used as a weapon against him. The episode shows that the EC was not doing its work properly. Other EC members should have stopped these preachers from disclosing what Jauhiainen had confessed them. That they did not do so shows that they had already made a decision to get rid of Jauhiainen. What they wanted was as

---

[247] This was A. Jauhiainen's suggestion, which other EC members accepted. Paavo Ketonen's letter to Baptist congregations 4 August 1953, the copy of which is in Jauhiainen's personal archives.

[248] Jauhiainen, Letter to EC members, PC (15 July 1953). For more on this topic as discussed by evangelicals see *The Nature of Hell: A Report by the Evangelical Alliance Commission on Unity and Truth among Evangelicals* (Carlisle: ACUTE, 2000); R.A. Parry and C.H. Partridge, eds., *Universal Salvation? The Current Debate* (Carlisle: Paternoster, 2003).

[249] Jauhiainen, Letter to Paavo Ketonen and Jaakko Kalliomäki, PC (1 August 1953). Jauhiainen points out that Kalliomäki had presented 'two awful lies' when telling his confessional secret. Jauhiainen had learned from his son, Vesa, what Kalliomäki had said in the EC meeting. He regretted in his letter that he was not even allowed to defend himself.

much evidence as possible that this was the right thing to do. All possible accusations were gathered against Jauhiainen, the meanest of them being this disclosure of a confessional secret.

Jauhiainen had been a respected authority among Finnish Baptists. His Bible studies had been highly valued. Many people were completely shocked by his dismissal. His opponents must have understood beforehand that accusing Jauhiainen about wrong teaching concerning the Holy Spirit would not have convinced these people. They needed much stronger claims. This inevitably was the reason why in the official dismissal letter to congregations they did not mention his teaching about the Holy Spirit at all, but instead informed congregations about his 'heretical doctrine of universal salvation', which was a misleading statement to say the least. Why should they have been so afraid of this? Jauhiainen had promised not to preach about it at all, and they must have known him to be an honest man, who stood behind his promises.

Once more, in September 1953, Jauhiainen sat over his typewriter, wrote a long letter, and sent it to all Baptist congregations.[250] The letter gives a more thorough insight into the July EC meeting in Tampere. Jauhiainen wonders why the question of the Holy Spirit was never even mentioned in the official minutes of that meeting, although it was the most serious accusation that was directed against him in that meeting. Those who accused him had argued that first of all Jauhiainen had opposed the Holy Spirit, and this had led him to heresy, i.e. universal salvation. Jauhiainen had then been asked to repent of both these heresies. On the basis of the many discussions about the Holy Spirit in the EC over the years, and on the basis of Jauhiainen's letter to the congregations, it seems evident that the main reason for his dismissal was his teaching about the Holy Spirit. The EC in its July meeting had accused Jauhiainen of opposing the Holy Spirit, and Spirit baptism, and of belittling prophetic messages. Jauhiainen commented on this in his letter to Baptist congregations in September 1953,[251] saying that he had always confessed the necessity of the fullness of the Spirit, and of spiritual gifts. He also mentioned that he had always treated the Pentecostal-minded brothers with understanding. But his brotherly spirit had now been repaid by them 'in opposite currency'.[252]

---

[250] Jauhiainen, Suomen Baptistiyhdyskunnan Seurakunnille ja Niiden Jäsenille, Syyskuu 1953 (A. Jauhiainen to the Congregations of the Finnish Baptist Union, September 1953), PC (September 1953). In this long letter (eighteen pages) Jauhiainen also explains his doctrine of universal salvation. Now that he had been removed from the Union he no longer felt obliged to keep quiet about this doctrine. Later on he wrote a book about it: *Ihminen ja Pahan Ongelma Raamatun Valokeilassa (Man and the Problem of Evil in the Light of the Bible)* (Tampere: Hermes Oy, 1963).

[251] Ibid.

[252] In the EC meeting Ketonen had spoken about prophecies against Jauhiainen, but he did not mention them in his letter to the congregations. Jauhiainen mentions these prophecies in his letter noting: 'There is a valid reason why he [Ketonen] was silent

His opponents wanted to change the Baptist Union. 'This change they started by firing a man who had been a Baptist for fifty years, and had served as a Baptist preacher for forty-four years.' [253]

Jauhiainen continued his letter by noting that his message had always been Christ-centred. He had always stressed that in Christ a Christian already has everything. 'This is one of the precious truths of the Bible. This is what Baptists believe.' The policy of his opponents had been to stress Spirit baptism as an emotional experience. Jauhiainen also wanted to correct the mistakes that Ketonen had made in his letter to the Baptist congregations of 4 August 1953 concerning his dismissal.[254] He pointed out that he had never said that even Satan would be saved; instead he had said that there are those who say so. Ketonen had mentioned 'Pilate, that false judge', 'Hitler, that beast', and 'Mussolini, that robber' in his letter, and asked if heaven would be heaven if these men were to be there. Concerning this, Jauhiainen explained that he did not believe that they would get to heaven without first repenting. He then pointed out that Baptists all over the world emphasised freedom of thought, which was not practised by the leaders of the FBU. On the contrary, they wanted to limit this freedom by force.[255] There was yet another mistake in Ketonen's letter which Jauhiainen wanted to correct. The letter read: 'Jauhiainen does not admit that eternal punishment exists; against the Word of God he denies it.'[256] Jauhiainen confirmed in his own letter that the Bible speaks a lot about punishment in this world and the world to come. What he believed was that the word 'eternal' is not synonymous to 'unending'. He also denied that his doctrine would paralyse the zeal for Christian work. Ketonen had written that evangelism would stop if the FBU adopted Jauhiainen's doctrine. Jauhiainen commented on this by reminding the congregations how much he had worked for it while serving the Union, 'more than any other Baptist preacher', thus nullifying this claim that Ketonen had made.[257]

Examining the reasons for Jauhiainen's dismissal is important for a full understanding of Finnish Baptist history. Only a few people in Finnish Baptist congregations have known the real reason for his dismissal. The EC policy of not saying a word about the theology concerning the Holy Spirit must have

---

about them...there are others, too, in this Union, who would not consider all these messages to be sent from heaven.'

[253] A. Jauhiainen to the Congregations of the Finnish Baptist Union (September 1953).

[254] Ketonen's Letter to Baptist Congregations (4 August 1953).

[255] A. Jauhiainen to the Congregations of the Finnish Baptist Union (September 1953).

[256] Ketonen's Letter to Baptist Congregations (4 August 1953).

[257] After studying the history of the FBU, I agree with him. Had Ketonen only thought about the untiring work Jauhiainen did during his presidency, and his many requests to congregations to evangelise people, especially children and youth, he would have realized how untenable this claim was.

been a deliberate decision. Instead, universal salvation was misleadingly mentioned as the only reason. Jauhiainen's dismissal was not the only serious thing that happened in the FBU in 1953. Another, perhaps even more serious thing that still affects the whole Baptist community happened. People were given an expectation that the problems of the FBU would be solved once Jauhiainen and his teachings were removed. Yet the Pentecostal dilemma, which was in fact at the heart of the dispute, has never left the life of the FBU. Accepting the Pentecostal teaching of the Holy Spirit has not resulted in the growth of the Baptist movement among the Finnish-speaking population—as was thought in the 1950s. On the contrary, since then the number of Baptists has decreased.

Conclusion

The work of the Holy Spirit continues to be a much-discussed topic in the Finnish Baptist Union. The idea that the FBU has remained small because it has not accepted the work of the Holy Spirit is especially prevalent among members of the older generation, but in some congregations the younger members have adopted this view as well. I personally became interested in the subject after I realised how widespread and influential this particular interpretation of our Union's past had become, and I wanted to study whether the claim being made had any merit. In the light of the hitherto unused material I have examined, I have to conclude that there is little evidence to back up the claim. During the years 1930-1953 there was not one preacher within the Union who opposed the Holy Spirit. The FBU has in fact been very open to the Holy Spirit since the 1930s. This is despite the fact that the Pentecostal movement has taken members away from the FBU ever since its arrival in Finland.

How did the older generation come to this opinion about the past experience of the Union? When the Pentecostally-minded preachers became the majority in the Union towards the end of 1940s, they started to stress the Holy Spirit. It was important for them that the Baptist teaching about the Holy Spirit was in harmony with that of the Pentecostals. Their teaching became the norm, the only 'biblical' view. Those who did not share this view were treated with suspicion, or even as opponents of the Holy Spirit, as was the case with Jauhiainen. But Jauhiainen deeply appreciated the Holy Spirit, and spiritual gifts. He was a Christ-centred preacher, though, who rooted all his teaching, including his teaching about the Holy Spirit, in Christ. In Christ, he argued, a Christian had everything, even the Holy Spirit, who entered at the moment of new birth. Along with this, Jauhiainen spoke about the fullness of the Spirit as an important factor in a Christian's everyday life. According to him, for himself and for other preachers of the Word this fullness was a necessity, but it did not happen automatically; a person had to become conscious of the Spirit and be open to experience his power.

The 'Pentecostal dilemma' arose and has continued mainly because instead of openly discussing the different understandings of how Spirit baptism and fullness of the Spirit are perceived, many Baptists have simply adopted Pentecostal teaching. Jauhiainen, by contrast, stressed the Baptist principle of freedom of thought. He gave space to Pentecostal-minded preachers in the Union magazine. Had that principle of openness to differing views been accepted by the FBU, it would have strengthened its Baptist identity. But Finnish Baptists chose to limit this freedom, to their own loss. It is ironic that it was over the issue of the Holy Spirit, an area where Jauhiainen was so tolerant towards others, that he himself was not tolerated. His doctrine of universalism was brought up as the only reason for dismissing him, which was not actually the case. He had not preached about the subject, knowing it would cause confusion. He was branded as a heretic, his reputation was blackened, and he was even forbidden to preach in Baptist congregations.

Jauhiainen's accusers were wise. By accusing him of heresy they achieved two things. First, the accusation was strong enough to convince people that the EC had made the right decision to dismiss him; that would not have been the case had the EC only spoken about Jauhiainen's theology concerning the Holy Spirit. Jauhiainen had been a respected and a greatly beloved preacher in the FBU, and it must have been clear to most people that he understood the importance of Spirit baptism and fullness of the Spirit. But of course when he was labelled a heretic most Baptist believers would understandably be wary of him. His opponents used emotive language when describing his universalism, and this had an effect. Secondly, Pentecostally-minded preachers could now continue their own work in peace, without having to be afraid of criticisms; on the contrary, they would be seen as having protected the Union from heresies. For the Union life, all this seemed to be healthy; the Union was not divided into two camps. For almost a decade things went well, but then came a standstill—the enthusiasm was gone. Spirit baptism did not prove to be the decisive element in church growth after all.

It is clear that one more conclusion can be drawn here: dismissing Jauhiainen was justified on theological grounds, but it was also a question of power politics. The younger generation wanted the power, and they obtained it. Unfortunately they obtained it in a way which was dubious at best. This power play was clearly seen by some of those outside the Union, too. Vilho Rantanen, a pastor, and a long-time editor of the Free Evangelicals' magazine, wrote to Jauhiainen suggesting the mistake he considered Jauhiainen had made and also pointing to the reality of what had happened:

> Already for a long time I have thought that when the young generation get enough air under their wings, a revolution will happen. This I wanted to say to you many times, because I had the impression that you were too autocratic in an old

patriarchal way. This will not do in these Free Church circles... All that talk about heresy is but throwing dust to mislead people. The fact is that younger generation wanted power, and you were in the way... [258]

Rantanen saw the real issue about the accusation of heresy. He was also right in mentioning the problem of Jauhiainen's autocracy. The only thing that could have prevented the tragedy would have been if Jauhiainen himself had left his position as Union President when tensions were not yet acute. For two decades he had given his best to the FBU, at a time of great challenge and debate, especially about the Pentecostal dilemma. But the FBU unfortunately chose to turn its back on him. Thus Jauhiainen ended his days outside Baptist life. He remained, however, a Baptist at heart, as he had been all his life. This study has sought to understand his significance as a leader of the Finnish Baptist Union.

---

[258] Vilho Rantanen, Letter to A. Jauhiainen, PC (21 July 1953).

Bibliography

Unpublished Material

Aaltio, Teuvo, 'The History of the National Baptists in Finland', unpub. thesis, (Rüschlikon-Zürich: Baptist Theological Seminary, 1958).
Hyppönen, Pauli, 'Inkerin Herätys ja Herätysliikkeet 1890-1929' (Revival and the Revival Movements in Inkeri 1890-1929), unpub. paper (Tampere: Bible College of the Finnish Baptist Union).
Niskanen, Markku, 'The Finnish-speaking Baptists 1896-1922', unpub. thesis (Rüschlikon: Baptist Theological Seminary, 1984).
Parviainen, Jorma, 'Suomenkielisen Baptistikirkon Toiminta Synnystä Nykyaikaan: Poikkileikkaustutkimus Suomenkielisen Baptistikirkon Toimintamuodoista ja Niiden Kehityksestä', Kirkkososiologian Laudaturtutkimus (The Activities of the Finnish-speaking Baptist Union from its Birth to Present: A Cross Section of Baptist Union's Activities and Development, MTh thesis) (Helsingin Yliopisto, 1974).

Books

Ahonen, Lauri, *Missions Growth: A Case Study On Finnish Free Foreign Mission* (Pasadena: William Carey Library, 1984).
_____, *Suomen Helluntaiherätyksen Historia* (The History of the Finnish Pentecostal Movement) (Jyväskylä: Päivä Oy, 1994).
Bloch-Hoell, N., *The Pentecostal Movement* (London: Allen & Unwin, 1964).
Coleman, Heather J., *Russian Baptists and Spiritual Revolution, 1905-1929* (Bloomington, IN : Indiana University Press, 2005).
Dempster, Murray W., Byron D. Klaus, and D. Petersen (eds.), *The Globalization of Pentecostalism, A Religion Made To Travel* (Oxfordshire: Regnum Books International, R. R. Donnelley & Sons, 1999).
Edén, David, *Svenska Baptisternas i Finland Historia 1856-1931* (The History of the Swedish-speaking Baptists in Finland 1856-1931) (Wasa: 1931).
Eighth Baptist World Congress, Cleveland, Ohio, 1950, Official Report, Arnold T. Ohrn (ed.) (Philadelphia: The Judson Press, 1950).
Ekonen, J., V. Kulju, T. Mantsinen, and J. Tarkka, *Ihmisen Tiet, 3-4 Painos* (The Ways of Man, 3rd-4th edition) (Helsinki-Keuruu: Otava, 1995).
Fridén, George (ed.), *Svensk Baptism Genom 100 år: En Krönika i Ord Och Bild* (The Swedish Baptist Movement Through 100 Years: A Chronicle with Words and Pictures) (Stockholm: Ernst Westerbergs Boktryckeri AB, 1948).
Green, Bernard, *Crossing the Boundaries: A History of the European Baptist Federation* (The Baptist Historical Society on Behalf of the European Baptist Federation, 1999).
_____, *Tomorrow's Man: A Biography of James Henry Rushbrooke* (Didcot: Baptist Historical Society, 1997).

Grossmann, Siegfried, *Haushalter der Gnade Gottes: Von der Charismatischen Bewegung zur Charismatischen Erneuerung der Gemeinde* (Stewards of God's Grace: From the Charismatic Movement to Charismatic Renewal of Congregation) (Wuppertal und Kassel: Oncken Verlag, 1977).

_____, *Der Geist ist Leben* (The Spirit is Life) (Clausthall-Zellerfeld: Papierflieger, 2001).

Hollenweger, W.J., *Pentecostalism: Origins and Development Worldwide* (Peabody, Mass.: Hendrickson, 1997).

Hope, N., *German and Scandinavian Protestantism 1700-1918* (Oxford: Oxford University Press, 1999).

Hughey, J.D., *Baptist Partnership in Europe: The HOW of Christian Missions in Europe Today* (Tennessee: Broadman Press, 1982).

_____, *Die Baptisten* (Kassel: J.G. Oncken Verlag, 1959).

Hughey, J.D., M. Kolomainen, and V. Toivola, *Baptistit, Oppi – Käytäntö - Historia* (Baptists, Doctrine – Practice – History) (Jyväskylä: Raamattuopisto, 1970).

Jansson, Erik, *Lähteitä Kyynelten Laaksosta, 2. painos* (Springs in the Valley of Tears, 2nd ed.) (Tampere: Totuuden Kaiku, 1949).

Jauhiainen, August, 'Inkerin Evankeelisten Kristittyjen Tie' in *Tehkää Tie Erämaahan* ('The Evangelical Christians in Inkeri' in Prepare the Way in the Desert) (Tampere: Hämeen Kirjapaino, 1954).

_____, *Raamatuntutkisteluopas* (How to Study the Bible) (Tampere: Totuuden Kaiku, 1948).

_____, *Ihminen ja Pahan Ongelma Raamatun Valokeilassa* (Man and the Problem of Evil in the Light of the Bible) (Tampere: Hermes Oy, 1963).

Kolomainen, Mikko, *Inkerin 'Toisinajattelijat', Muistelmia Inkerin Vapaiden Herätysliikkeiden Syntyvaiheista* (The 'Dissidents' in Inkeri, Recollections from the Birth of Free Revival Movements in Inkeri) (Helsinki: Ristin Voitto, 1989).

Korhonen, Arvi (ed.), *Suomen Historian Käsikirja, Jälkimmäinen Osa* (The Handbook of the Finnish History, Latter Part) (Helsinki: WSOY, 1949).

Kuosmanen, Juhani, *Herätyksen Historia* (History of Revival) (Tikkurila: Ristin Voitto, 1979).

Kärkkäinen, Veli-Matti, *Spiritus ubi Vult Spirat: Pneumatology in Roman Catholic-Pentecostal Dialogue (1972-1989)* (Saarijärvi: Luther-Agricola-Society, Gummerus, 1998).

The Nature of Hell: A Report by the Evangelical Alliance Commission on Unity and Truth among Evangelicals (Carlisle: ACUTE, 2000).

Näsman, Nils, *Baptismen i Svenska Österbotten 1868-1905: Finska Kyrkohistoriska Samfundets Handlingar 63.* (The Baptist Movement in Swedish East Bothnia 1868-1905: Publication of the Finnish Church Historical Society 63) (Helsingfors: Finska Kyrkohistoriska Samfundet, 1962).

Ohrn, Arnold T. (ed.), *Eighth Baptist World Congress, Cleveland, Ohio, 1950, Official Report* (Philadelphia: Judson Press, 1950).

Parry, R.A. and C.H. Partridge, (eds.), *Universal Salvation? The Current Debate* (Carlisle: Paternoster, 2003).

Randall, Ian M., 'Days of Pentecostal Overflowing': Baptists and the Shaping of Pentecostalism', in D.W. Beddington (ed.), *The Gospel in the World: Studies in Baptist History and Thought, Vol. 1* (Carlisle: Paternoster, 2002).
Salmensaari, S.S., *Suomen Vapaakirkko, Piirteitä sen Synnystä ja Kehityksestä* (The Finnish Free Evangelical Church: Traits of its Beginning and Development) (Tampere: Päivä, 1957).
Sawatsky, Walter, *Soviet Evangelicals Since World War II* (Kitchener, Ontario: Herald Press, 1981).
Savinskii, S., *Istorija Evangelskih Hristian-baptistov Ukrainy, Rossii, Belorussii, 1917-1967, Vol. 2* (History of Evangelical Christians-Baptists in Ukraine, Russia and Byelorussia, 1917-1967) (Saint Petersburg: Biblija dlja vseh, 2001).
Stewart, J.A., *A Man in a Hurry: The Story of the Life and Work of Pastor Basil A. Malof* (Asheville, N.C.; Russian Bible Society, 1968).
Sundell, Alwar, *De Började—Vi Fortsätter: Baptismen i Finland 100 år, 1856-1956* (They Began—We Continue: Baptists in Finland 100 Years, 1856-1956) (Vasa: Ab Frams Tryckeri, 1956).
Toivola, Veikko, *Suomalaisen Baptismin Tienraivaajia* (Trailblazers of Finnish Baptists) (Tampere: KY-paino, 1983).
Westin, Gunnar, *Den Kristna Friförsamlingen i Norden: Frikyrklighetens Uppkomst och Utveckling, 4:e upplagan* (The Christian Free Congregations in the North: The Origin and the Development of Free Churches, 4th edition) (Stockholm: Westerbergs, 1956).
Wood, J., *Born in the Fire: The Story of William Fetler alias Basil Malof (1883-1957): Church Planting Evangelist in Russia and Latvia* (Stanway: The Author, 1998).
Wright, N.G., *Free Church, Free State* (Carlisle: Paternoster, 2005).

Journal Articles

Bundy, D., 'Thomas Ball Barratt: From Methodist to Pentecostal', *Journal of the European Pentecostal Theological Association* XII (1994).
Totuuden Kaiku (The Echo of Truth), The FBU's monthly magazine, 1896-1953.
Kodin Ystävä (The Friend of Homes, formerly *Totuuden Kaiku*), The FBU's monthly magazine, 1961-1971.
Westin, Gunnar, *Sanningsvittnet* (Witness to Truth) 27 (1933).
Ristin Voitto (The Victory of the Cross), the Pentecostal Magazine, 16 (1949).
Nuorten Todistus (Young Testimony), A youth paper of the Free Evangelical Church (1948).

Pamphlets

Himanen, Heimo, *Turun Baptistiseurakunta 1887-1987* (Turku Baptist Congregation) (Tampere: Kodin Ystävä, 1987).
Lindeman, Aino, *Suomen Baptistinaiset 1949-1999* (Finnish Baptist Women) (Tampere: Kharis Oy, 1999).

_____, Lindeman, Aino (ed.), *Vihtavuoren baptistiseurakunta 1943-1993* (Vihtavuori Baptist Congregation) (Tampere: Kharis Oy, 1993).
Lohikko, Anneli, *Suomen Baptistiyhdyskunnan Raamattuopisto* (The Finnish Baptist Union's Bible School) (Tampere: Kharis Oy, 1999).
Vapaakirkon Vuosikirja 2002 (The Annual Report of the Free Evangelical Church 2002) (Hämeenlinna: Päivä Oy, 2002).

Reports and Minutes

Minutes of the Executive Committee Meetings (MEC), 1920-1953
Minutes of the Official Meetings of Delegates (MOMD), 1920-1953
Minutes of the Meetings of the Preacher Union (MMPU), 1935-1950.
Annual Reports of the Finnish Baptist Union, 1920-1953
Minutes of the Official Meetings of Tampere Baptist Congregation, 1934, 1937
Minutes of the Official Meetings of Vaajakoski Baptist Congregation, 1934.
Official Correspondence (OC) of August Jauhiainen, 1929-1953.
Private Correspondence (PC) of August Jauhiainen, 1929-1953.

August Jauhiainen's Biographical Data

Jauhiainen, August, 'Elämäni Vaiheita' ('Vicissitudes of My Life'). (This is a collection of personal memoirs that Jauhiainen started to write, and it is now collected together with some additional notes.) Baptist archives, Tampere.
Toivola, Veikko, 'August Jauhiaista Haastattelemassa' ('Interviewing August Jauhiainen'), C-60 kasetit 1-2. (Toivola's interview of August Jauhiainen. Two audiocassettes recorded in Vaasa in the 1960s.) Baptist archives, Tampere.

CHAPTER 4

The Theology of Baptist Believers in Bulgaria as Reflected in the Publication *Evangelist* (1920-1939)

Teodor B. Oprenov

Very little has been written on Bulgarian Baptist history and theology, either by Bulgarian or Western authors. In recent times, Baptists in this Southern European country have faced identity challenges, presented by the major religious entities within Bulgaria and by a flood of outside theological influences through various Protestant missions. In the light of this, a study of the theological roots and development of Bulgarian Baptist faith and practice is of great importance to the Bulgarian Baptist community today. In addition, it may yield some fresh insights within the wider field of research into the history of Bulgarian evangelicals.

The primary difficulty in attempting such a study is the limited number of sources available. Investigation into the first forty years of Baptist life in Bulgaria is constrained by the limited number of letters and documents. These are kept in various archives, mainly in the USA and Germany.[1] For almost the entire period of Communist rule in Bulgaria (1945-1989) there are no records or publications which clearly express theological convictions. The only period that is better covered with documentary evidence is 1920 to 1939. This is the period when the Baptist periodical *Evangelist* was published. It is the only comprehensive source of information for Bulgarian Baptist history and theology for the first 110 years of the Baptist movement in Bulgaria. This is why *Evangelist* represents the starting point for research on the issue.

The lack of sources and archive materials is due to historical circumstances. Prior to World War II no one ever attempted to make a systematic study of the Baptist movement in Bulgaria. Then, after the Communist regime established itself in the period 1945-1950, most of the archives of Baptist organizations—

---

[1] Such as American Baptist Historical Society (ABHS), Valley Forge, Phillladelphia, USA; Archives of the North American Baptist Conference (NABC), Oakbrook Terrace, Illinois, USA; Archives of the German Baptist Seminary (AGBS), Berlin (Estal), Germany.

church records, personal correspondence and publications—were confiscated by the Communist secret police. The systematic 'erasing of religion', which was at the heart of 'aggressive atheism',[2] brought the early imprisonment of ten Baptist pastors after a fake political trial in 1949 and began forty-five years of severe persecution of Baptists. As early as 1949, some church leaders came to the decision to destroy all of the historical records and information.[3] They wanted to be sure these documents did not fall into the hands of the security police. However, some Christians took the personal risk of keeping some documents, old photographs and issues of old magazines published between World War I and World War II.[4] These 'miraculously' preserved documents provide invaluable source material for present day historians. Some materials were also published from a Marxist perspective during the communist period,[5] but they were entirely focused on discrediting the Protestants and are, for the most part, of little use in determining the beliefs of the Baptists.

After Communism collapsed in Eastern Europe, Albert Wardin published in 1991 an article 'Baptists in Bulgaria',[6] based on primary sources found in Baptist periodicals published in the West. Using German archives for his sources, Dobrinka Dadder wrote an article on Baptist beginnings in 1994.[7] Neither of these pieces, nor more recent articles,[8] have examined in depth any

---

[2] The term 'aggressive atheism' or 'militant atheism' was first introduced in Russia after the 1917 Revolution and was invented to prompt fighting against religion in general. See J. Thrower, *Marxist-Leninist Scientific Atheism and the Study of Religion and Atheism in the USSR* (New York: Mounton Publishers, 1983); R. Pipes, *Communism: A History* (Modern Library Paperback ed.; New York: Random House, 2003); S. Courtois, et al, *The Black Book of Communism: Crimes, Terror, Repression* (Paris: Edditions Robert Laffont, S.A., 1997).

[3] For example, the story is told that the leaders of Sofia Baptist Church during the political trials of Protestant pastors in Bulgaria (1949) gathered all the documents of the Baptist Union and Sofia Baptist Church that were hidden in the church building's attic and burned them, so that the secret police could not get their hands on the information.

[4] Pastor Bojidar Igoff took the risk, for example, of keeping a copy of the oldest protocol of the founding of the first Baptist Church in Bulgaria—Kazanluck. He even translated the document into English in 1971 and managed to send it to the West for safekeeping.

[5] Such as: K. Krustev, *Protestantstkite Secti v Bulgaria* (The Protestant Sects in Bulgaria) (Sofia: Prtizdat, 1972); M. Stoiyanov, 'Nachalo na Protestantstkata Propaganda v Bulgaria' (The Beginning of Protestant Propaganda in Bulgaria), *Izvestia na Instituta za Istroia* 14-15, pp. 45-67; P. Shopov, 'Propagandnata I Prosvetna Deinost na Americanskite Bibleiski Obshtestva v Bulgarskite Zemi prez XIX Vek' (The Propaganda and Enlightening Activity of the American Bible Societies in the Bulgarian Lands during XIXc.), *Izvestia na Instituta za Istroia* 23, pp. 149-184.

[6] A. Wardin, 'The Baptists in Bulgaria', *The Baptist Quarterly* 34:4 (1991), p. 4.

[7] D. Dadder, 'History of Baptism in Bulgaria', *Vitania* (Sofia: Artgraph, 1997).

[8] Such as: T. Angelov, 'The Baptist Movement in Bulgaria', *Journal of European Baptist Studies* 1 (2001), pp. 8-18; T. Oprenov, 'Baptists and the Orthodox Church: The

aspect of the theological convictions of the Baptist believers. One of the vital sources of information regarding Bulgarian Baptist theological convictions that is now available is the full set of the issues of *Evangelist* (1920-1939), the only Bulgarian Baptist periodical published before the democratic changes of 1989. *Evangelist* captures the general development of the Baptist churches between WWI and WWII and contains memories of believers who recalled the very beginnings of the Baptist movement. It also published a number of theological articles, sermons and doctrinally based accounts of events. The present study attempts to find the main characteristics of Bulgarian Baptist theology as reflected by *Evangelist*. It will account for the wider context of theological influences from sources outside Bulgaria, such as influences through mission agencies and translated articles. Political and religious realities in Bulgaria also form the background for this research.

The first section of this study briefly traces the history of the Baptist movement in Bulgaria, investigates the different sources of theological influence and then looks at the key leaders that played a role in the formation of Baptist beliefs. It seeks to account for some of the particularities of the historical, religious and psychological background which helped to shape Baptist theological thinking of the first fifty years of the movement. The second section looks at the motives behind the periodical *Evangelist*, together with its goals, and accounts for some of the key points in the Baptist struggle for historical identity and theological uniformity. This section discusses the crucial doctrines of God, salvation, sanctification, baptism, communion, Holy Spirit, suffering, prayer and marriage, as expressed in *Evangelist*. The third section discusses Baptist theology of the Church, ministry, mission and evangelism. Here the relations of the Baptists to their partners outside Bulgaria, as well as relations with the Orthodox Church, are analysed from a theological perspective. Baptist pre-war social involvement and the Baptist attitude toward the state and the authorities are also explored in this chapter. Finally, the fourth section evaluates the significance of *Evangelist* in shaping theological convictions in Bulgaria and its influence on the Baptist churches in the 1920s and 1930s, and later, during the time of Communism and its aftermath. The question is posed as to whether or not the theology expressed in *Evangelist* was a complete set of theological convictions or a developing theology in-the-making, centered on the missionary calling of the church and shaped by the circumstances of ministry in Bulgaria. The Conclusion offers some thoughts for further research.

'Kostenets' Disputes of 1920' in Bulgaria', *Journal of European Baptist Studies* 4 (Prague: IBTS, 2004), pp. 33-47.

The Foundation of Early Baptist Theology and Practice in Bulgaria

The first Protestants to work in an organized way in the territory of present day Bulgaria were the Methodists and the Congregationalists, who arrived in the 1850s.[9] The first missionary station of the American Board of Commissioners for Foreign Missions (ABCFM, also referred to as The 'American Board')[10] was established in July 1858 at Adrianopol.[11] That work, with its strong Protestant theological emphasis, preceded by a quarter of a century the appearance of the first Baptist communities in what was then Muslim dominated Bulgarian territory.[12] There are two major issues that have to be addressed in approaching the question of Baptist theology in Bulgaria. The first is the fact that Baptist evangelical convictions were introduced into Bulgaria entirely from external sources and represented theological beliefs alien to the Bulgarian Orthodox religion and culture.[13] Secondly, to understand the development of theological convictions, some of the particularities of the religious and political context of the Baptist movement must be taken into account.

Studying the history of Baptist beginnings in Bulgaria,[14] it is possible to distinguish three major sources influencing the theology of the early Baptist communities. First, there was the evangelistic Protestant theology of the Methodist and Congregationalist missionaries working in Bulgaria. Second, there was the settlement in Northern Bulgaria of Baptist refugees of German origin from Southern Russia who were fleeing religious persecution. Some of them became colporteurs of the British and Foreign Bible Society (BFBS). As well as distributing Bibles and evangelistic literature in the territories under Ottoman control during the later part of the nineteenth century, the colporteurs spoke about their theological beliefs with the people they met. Third, there

---

[9] Stoiyanov, 'Nachalo na Protestantstkata Propaganda', p. 66.

[10] ABCFM—this mission was Congregational in its composition. It was established in America in 1819.

[11] T. Nestorova, *American Missionaries Among the Bulgarians: (1858-1912)* (New York: Columbia University Press, 1987), p. 8.

[12] Wardin, 'The Baptists in Bulgaria', p. 148.

[13] For a general understanding of the Orthodox religion and culture, please refer to *Nashata Viara* (Our Faith) (Sofia: Plovdiv Bishopric, 1996); Prot. I. Stefanov, *Pravila na Svetata Pravoslavna Tsurkva* (Rules of the Holy Orthodox Church) (Steva Gora: Monastery St. Georgi Zograph, 1936); Prot. S. Sloboskoi, *Zakon Bojii* (The Law of God) (Assenovgrad: Holy Synod, 2001); Prez. A. Shleman, *Liturgia i Jivot* (Liturgy and Life) (Sofia: Practis, 2002); J.M. Hussey, *The Orthodox Church in the Byzantine Empire* (Oxford: Oxford University Press 1983); V. Lossky, *The Mystical Theology of the Eastern Church* (Cambridge: James Clark & Co., 1991); Bish. K. Ware, *The Orthodox Way* (Crestwood, N.Y.: St. Vladimir Seminary Press, 1993).

[14] T. Oprenov, 'The origins and Early Development of Baptists in Bulgaria' in *Baptist History & Heritage*, (Baptist Historical Society, Nashville, TN) n.1, vol. XLII, Winter 2007, pp. 8-23.

were Bulgarians who came into contact with Baptists outside of Bulgaria and became convinced of Baptist principles, or were trained in Western theological schools and later returned to Bulgaria having become aware of Baptists.

Many of the first Baptists were 'converted' to Baptist beliefs from Methodism or Congregationalism.[15] A good example of this process is found in the history of the first Baptist church in Kazanluck, established in 1880. The first evangelical in the town, Stefan Kurdov, was a tradesman. During one of his trips to Tsarigrad, the capital of the Ottoman Empire, in 1867, he experienced an evangelical conversion through a group of Armenian Congregationalists.[16] Upon his return home a Congregational community was formed[17] and he was later appointed a colporteur by the BFBS. Nine years later, in 1876, the European Turkey Mission (Congregationalist) reported: 'At Kazanluck much apparent injury has been done by discussion and division on the subject of baptism.'[18] Apparently, a year earlier another BFBS colporteur, M. Herbold, had visited the Congregationalist group in Kazanluck and had suggested a different understanding of baptism, sowing the seeds of Baptist views in that town.[19] Apart from a good number of Congregationalists who embraced Baptist principles, a significant number of Baptist pastors and leaders received their initial exposure to and training in evangelical principles in the Congregational high school and seminary in Samokov, Bulgaria, run by the ABCFM.

A second influence in the area of theology was, as noted, the view put forward by colporteurs of the British and Foreign Bible Society, who worked in the territory of Bulgaria from the 1860s. The BFBS, together with the American Board, published in 1871 the 'complete edition of the Bible in the vernacular',[20] and played a key role in distributing it to every part of the land. In 1867 the BFBS appointed two Polish Baptists, Kutsichewsky and Krzossa, as their distributors for Northwest Bulgaria. Later, two refugees, Martin Herringer and Jacob Klundt, were also appointed. Herringer had influence on the church in Lompalanka and later in Ruschuk. Despite the strict rules given

---

[15] H. Kulichev, *Vestiteli na Istinata* (The Heralds of Truth) (Sofia: Bulgarian Bible Society, 1994), pp. 228-229.

[16] P. Kirkilanov, 'Kratka Istoriya na Evangelskata Baptistska Tsurkva v Grad Kazanluck' (A Short History of the Evangelical Baptist church in the Town of Kazanluck), *Evangelist* 9-10 (1924), p. 5.

[17] Wardin, 'The Baptists in Bulgaria', p. 148.

[18] 'European Turkey Mission', *Report of the Board of Commissioners for Foreign Missions* (Boston: Board of Commissioners of Foreign Missions, 1876), p. 11.

[19] Kirkilanov, 'Kratka Istoriya na Evangelskata Baptistska Tsurkva', p. 6.

[20] Although the work on translation was mostly organised under the supervision of the American Board and the European Turkey Mission, particularly by Dr Elias Riggs in Tzsarigrad, the financial cost of this endeavour was covered by the British and Foreign Bible Society. See T. Nestorova, *American Missionaries among the Bulgarians: (1858-1912)* (New York: Columbia University Press, 1987), p. 89.

by the BFBS to those workers about 'not sharing their own Evangelical convictions'[21] and 'not organizing any public meetings',[22] they did not always stick to these limitations. They were not content simply to sell books; they also took opportunities to speak about aspects of their faith.

For some, this included Baptist beliefs. Herringer, Klundt and Herbold were part of a group of Baptist settlers who played a crucial role in laying the foundations for the theological convictions that shaped the Baptist churches in Bulgaria. Believers' church ideas in the wider region can be traced as far back as the sixteenth-century Anabaptists, with the initial emigration of Anabaptists to Russia in the 1540s, under the leadership of Menno Simons' co-worker Dirk Philips.[23] Two centuries later, when in 1773 Russia conquered the Crimea Khanate from Turkey and added that territory within its borders under the name Tavricheska Gubernia (Tavrian Province), two manifestos were issued by Catherine II[24] and a stream of foreigners entered Russia, drawn by the privileges that the manifestos guaranteed for immigrants. Most of those who came were German-speaking Mennonites. The German colonies of Rorbach and Neu Danzig were probably formed at that time.

A statement written by the bishop of the Elisavetskiy Uezd is evidence of the involvement in that part of Russia of J.G. Oncken, who pioneered Baptist beliefs in German-speaking territories in Europe in the nineteenth century.[25] Uezd wrote: 'Oncken was indeed preaching and was baptizing the Germans...but he did not turn any of the Orthodox believers away from the right faith...'[26] Most probably it was at this point that some people in Rorbach and Neu Danzig accepted the Baptist faith. The Orthodox Church in the area was deeply disturbed by this and was swift to react with violence. In 1866, this caused thirty-seven families to emigrate from Russia to the village of Katalui, fourteen kilometers from Tulcha in the northeast corner of Bulgaria.[27] These German-speaking Baptists began regular meetings for Bible study and prayer,

---

[21] H. Kulitchev, *Vestiteli na Istinata,* p. 330.

[22] D. Dadder, 'History of Baptism in Bulgaria', *Vitania* 4, (1997), p. 4.

[23] See P. Friesen, *The Mennonite Brotherhood in Russia 1789-1910* (Fresno, Calif.: Board of Christian Literature, General Conference of Mennonite Brethren Churches, 1978).

[24] One on 4 December 1762 and the other on 22 July 1783.

[25] For Oncken's work see I.M. Randall, 'Every Apostolic Church a Mission Society: European Baptist Origins and Identity', in A.R. Cross, ed., *Ecumenism and History: Studies in Honour of John H.Y. Briggs* (Carlisle: Paternoster, 2002), pp. 281-301.

[26] Episcop Alexey (Doroditsin), *Materialy dlia Istoriiy Religiozno-Ratsionalisticheskovo Dvijeniya na uge Rossii vo Vtoroi Polovine XIX Stoletiya* (Kazan, 1908), p. 80.

[27] A very important article entitled 'Brother Jacob Klundt' was published in 1921 in *Evangelist* 2 (1921), pp. 1-4. It contains the memories of Jacob Klundt about the settlement of the refugees in 1866. It was published as a commemoration of this great Baptist who died on 28 March 1921 in Kazanluck.

and in 1869, after a visit by Oncken, a Baptist church was founded.[28] Some of their members were soon involved in the work of the BFBS and began to travel around Bulgaria spreading distinctly Baptist convictions.[29]

This is the background to the beginning of the first German-speaking Baptist Church in today's territory of Bulgaria. It was established in the town of Ruschuk,[30] where a depot of the BFBS was established in 1868. A further important development, which brought in ethnic Bulgarians, was the arrival in the area in 1880 of Ivan (Johann) Kargel, a leader in the German-Russian Baptist movement. At this point the stage was set for a further penetration of Baptist convictions in the country. It was partly in response to 'The Macedonian Cry Re-Echoed from Macedonia Itself', an article in the German Baptist Paper *Der Wahrheitszeuge* and the *Quarterly Reporter of the German Baptist Mission*,[31] which embodied a plea coming from a group of people in Kazanluck already convinced about 'true baptism' and begging for someone to 'come and baptize the true believers',[32] that Kargel travelled to the town. On 7 September 1880 he baptized members of this group in the river Tundja, thus starting the first Bulgarian Baptist Church.

From these humble beginnings the movement evolved over the years, giving birth to independent Bulgarian Baptist communities in the towns of Lompalanka[33] (1884), through the work of Jacob Klundt, and in Ruschuk[34] (from 1884), through the ministry of Kargel and then later through consolidation by Krzossa, after Kargel left in 1884.[35] It was in 1887 that the German-speaking congregation in Ruschuk became a fully constituted Bulgarian-speaking church, with a native Bulgarian, Vassil Marchov, as pastor. An entire group of churches was started through people moving from Kazanluck, Lompalanka and Ruschuk to places such as Sofia (1888), Ferdinand[36] (1898), Berkovitsa (1898) and Golintsi[37] (1908). The connections between the churches were, from the outset, expressed in a shared theological outlook nurtured by preachers and others in church leadership. Prior to WWI this mainly took place through various people working on the ground, notably

---

[28] Wardin, 'The Baptists in Bulgaria', p. 149.

[29] D. Dadder, 'Istoria na Baptisma v Bulgaria' (History of Baptists In Bulgaria), *Vitania* 5, (1997), p. 14.

[30] Today's Russe.

[31] *Der Wahrheitszeuge*, 15 September 1880, pp. 142-143; *Quarterly Reporter of the German Baptist Mission* (Oct. 1880), pp. 1-2.

[32] P. Kirkilanov, 'Kratka Istoriya...', *Evangelist* 9-10 (1924), p. 8.

[33] Renamed 'Lom' shortly after the liberation from the Ottoman rule in 1878.

[34] Renamed 'Russe' shortly after the liberation from the Ottoman rule in 1878.

[35] Vassil Marchov was installed as a pastor after being previously sent to the Hamburg Seminary (commenced by J.G. Oncken) for training.

[36] Later, this was renamed 'Ferdinand', and is today's town of Montana.

[37] Today this is Mladenovo, and it has a Gypsy church.

indigenous missionaries supported by the BFBS and the German Baptist Union, including both German-Russians and Bulgarians.

A dramatic change ensued after a decision was made at the European Baptist Conference in London, in 1920, which assigned the mission in Bulgaria to the care of the General Missionary Society of the German Baptist General Conference (GBGC) of the USA.[38] The representatives of the GBGC, first C.E. Petrick (1858-1930) and then from 1924 to 1940, Karl Fullbrandt, took their responsibilities seriously. They understood the needs—the heavy financial burden of the ministry, the organizational needs of the Bulgarian Evangelical Baptist Union (formed in 1908, and usually known as the Bulgarian Baptist Union), the training of leaders, and the Baptist struggle for recognition in an Orthodox country—and they organized welcome assistance. During that period, before WWII, the Baptists tripled in size and gained an identity and level of theological maturity only comparable to post-Communist times. *Evangelist*, which was published in that period, presents us with an informative account of the historical events and the theological clarification of Baptist beliefs.

The theological understanding of the Bulgarian Baptists has always been shaped by leaders and pastors who were educated outside Bulgaria and thus exposed to theological influences outside the country, and who then returned home.[39] We have already mentioned Vasil K. Marchev, who started his ministry as a colporteur of the congregation in Ruschuk at the time when Kargel was the pastor there. After four years at the Baptist Seminary in Hamburg (1883-1887), which was a product of Oncken's work, Marchev became the pastor of the Ruschuk church, doubling its membership in a short period and opening several preaching stations.[40] Vasil Kiyosev (1867-1942), a Bulgarian who graduated from the Methodist Cliff College, near Sheffield, England, returned to Lompalanka, and was supported for a few years by the American Baptist Missionary Union (ABMU). He had a fruitful ministry in north-west Bulgaria, and then in Sofia, where he settled in 1899.[41]

One of the most influential Bulgarian pastor-missionaries in the first years of the twentieth century was Peter Doychev (1856-1913). He was trained in America, graduating from Princeton Theological Seminary, and later studied at the Theological Seminary in Chicago. He returned from America with Baptist

---

[38] Today's North American Baptist Conference.

[39] For details of these people and their influence, I am indebted to papers in the private archive of Peter II. Furtunov, secretary of Sofia Baptist Church Board in the period 1925-1950, who collected some vital biographical data in his files. This material is still under investigation, as it has not yet been completely released for study by the family. Parts of it were made available in May 2005, and will have to be further examined.

[40] Wardin, 'The Baptists in Bulgaria', p. 150.

[41] *Kratka Istoriya na Evangelskata Baptistka Tsurkva v gr. Lompalanka*, (Short History of the Evangelical Baptist Church in the Town of Lompalanka) (Ferdinant, 1930), pp. 4-5.

convictions and despite fearful opposition, had a remarkable pioneering work in Chirpan in central Bulgaria. It was under his leadership that the Bulgarian Baptist Union was formed. Zaprian Vidolov (1882-1965) studied at the Samokov Congregationalist School in Bulgaria and later graduated from a Baptist Seminary in the USA. He was the first editor of *Evangelist*, and was an influential thinker and an excellent pastor. He ministered in Sofia until 1921 when he was commissioned by the Bulgarian government to go to Washington, DC, as a Secretary and later Vice-Consul of the Bulgarian Legation in the USA. Later, he established the Bulgarian Baptist Mission in Chicago. One more name that must be included in this line of leaders is Trifon Dimitrov (1899-1964), one of the descendants of the German settlers in Tulcha, who came of a long family line of pastors, missionaries and colporteurs. He graduated from the Baptist Seminary in Hamburg and was the editor of *Evangelist* for fifteen years. His influential leadership, evangelistic gifts and his twenty year ministry as Secretary of the Baptist Union in Bulgaria were 'rewarded' with five years imprisonment by the Communists after 1950.

It is also important to note several key people of non-Bulgarian origin, without whose ministry the Bulgarian Baptists would have had a differently shaped theology. Karl Grabein (1878-1945?) was a German-Russian who had been a missionary for many years in Ukraine, Belarus and Russia. He settled in Bulgaria in 1911 and pastored churches in Lom, Chirpan, Varna and Kazanluck. He was an inspiring preacher and a systematic theologian, and he was invited to read papers on different subjects at almost every pastor's conference in Bulgaria. He translated numerous articles from German Baptist periodicals, as well as materials from Russian, Polish and Czech, some of which were published in *Evangelist*. Evgeniy Gerassimenko (1859-1943) was a native Russian who was trained first at Spurgeon's College, London and then at the Baptist Seminary in Hamburg. He served with the Romanian-Bulgarian Association, formed to assist the German speaking Baptist work in the area. He had ministries in Tulcha Baptist Church, Ruschuk and later in Kazanluck. Finally, C.E. Petrick was a German missionary who served in Assam, India, for twenty-five years with the American Baptist Foreign Mission Society. In 1914 he moved to Sofia. His sermons and his benevolent work were widely known in the capital well beyond the walls of the small Baptist building—which he helped the congregation to build in 1923. He served as a missionary inspector for the GBGC until his retirement in 1926.

Before attention is given to *Evangelist* and its theology, it is necessary to mention some characteristics of the religious, social and political background, such as the Orthodox religious environment and the socio-political realities, including the advance of socialist ideology in the period 1917-1944. The Baptists, unlike the Methodists and the Congregationalists, were well aware that the Bulgarian national church, the Orthodox Church, would never tolerate an evangelical revival within its doors. James F. Clark, an American

Missionary to the Bulgarians, wrote in 1864: 'We do not come to ask you [the Bulgarians] to leave your church, but to receive the Bible and live by it in the church.'[42] However, a decade later he expressed a different opinion and according to his later writings, any spiritual reform achieved prior to 1881 'was not in the [Orthodox] Church, but rather despite it...' Thus, he concluded: 'our hope for the renovation of the Bulgarian people is rather in the [forming] of Evangelical communities...'[43] This mirrored Baptist beliefs.

The Orthodox Church was not idle in the face of the growth of the new evangelical movements, but brought pressure to bear on them. It played on the nationalistic feelings of the Bulgarians and was often backed up by the State officials, with anti-Protestant propaganda and physical force being used to stop the evangelicals. One can see that Orthodoxy felt threatened for several reasons. The Protestant movement in Bulgaria in the middle of the nineteenth century was seen as a foreign religion destroying the 'faith homogeneity of the Bulgarian nation'.[44] In those times, 'Christian' Bulgaria was fighting for liberation from five hundred years of Ottoman rule and there was a strong tendency to 'equate belonging to the Bulgarian nation with belonging to Orthodoxy'.[45] The evangelicals were considered carriers of Western political and ideological thinking, and were seen as a threat to national identity. That was evident not only during the first ten to twenty years after the liberation of the Bulgarian nation (1878), but also during the years following the Balkan, the All-European and the Inter-allied wars (1912-1918). Even much later, in 1930, newspapers wrote of Baptists that 'they change religion, they destroy tradition, they up-root us from the past and make people lack any love toward their native country'.[46]

Furthermore, the Orthodox claim for canonical (Orthodox) territories, their theology of infant baptism which incorporated everyone in the Church and their emphasis on the power and importance of ecclesiastical rituals, immediately placed the 'newcomers' in the position of proselytizing communities. The Protestant (and Baptist) principle of 'faith alone' was very different from the 'mystical power' of the Orthodox sacraments that conveyed 'secret grace' to the participant. The claim of the Baptist that a person should be sure about his or her salvation was seen as a monstrous blasphemy by the Orthodox, who were convinced that by doing good and keeping rituals they would have a better chance of entering heaven. Speaking about the religious state of the Bulgarians,

---

[42] F. Shashko, B. Greenberg, R. Genov, *American Travel Notes for Bulgaria during the XIX Century* (Sofia: Planeta 3, 2001), p. 79.

[43] W. William, quoted by T. Nestorova, *American Missionaries Among the Bulgarians (1858-1912)* (New York, Columbia University Press, 1987), pp. 9, 15.

[44] N. Krastev, *Protestantskite Secti v Bulgaria,* (The Protestant Sects in Bulgaria), (Sofia: Partizdat, 1972), p. 94.

[45] Ibid.

[46] *Razgradski Novini* (Razgrad News) 187 (1930), pp. 7-8.

we can agree with K. Krustev who wrote that despite the 'particular place that the Orthodox Church had taken during the Ottoman Yoke...only the very basic religious needs of people were met, and above else, through rituals'.[47] The average Bulgarian was basically ignorant about the Bible, was not committed to Christian values and had a paradoxical understanding of being Orthodox because he or she was Bulgarian. Not only Orthodox priests, but also 'a large percentage of the ordinary population viewed the Baptists as proselytizers, breakers of people's traditions, cosmopolitans, and carriers of ideas and interests foreign to the people'.[48]

The poor state of the Bulgarian nation in the years after liberation from the Ottoman Rule (1878), and the disastrous effects of the Balkan Wars and WWI, resulted in many social needs. The state of orphanages and prisons, the needs of a 'work force' living in appalling conditions, the problems of depression and alcoholism—these all presented a strong challenge to Baptist congregations. On the one hand, the churches struggled financially and had to rely on foreign help. But on the other hand, social involvement was possible in several ways: benevolent ministries, opposition to alcohol abuse by forming Abstention Societies or taking a firm stand for world peace. This period coincided with the growth of socialist and atheistic ideology from Bolshevik Russia. The pro-German Bulgarian governments opposed these ideas only to find out that the general population, and especially the poorer social classes, were very sympathetic toward them. The Bulgarian Baptists were open to the communist ideals of fighting for justice and equality, but had to come to terms with the atheistic background of Bolshevik thinking. The church had to deal with issues of brotherhood, equality, social justice, and later, as things developed negatively for Baptists, with suffering and persecution.

Evangelist's Role in Shaping the Theological Identity of Early Bulgarian Baptists

The Birth of Evangelist

Evangelical publications in Bulgaria started in 1840 with the re-translation of the New Testament into the vernacular by Neoffit Rilski.[49] The whole Bible was then translated and published in 1871. In 1864, the first evangelical periodical, called *Zornitsa*, started being published by the American Board.[50] In printed literature the evangelicals saw a way to spread their faith, argue their

---

[47] Krastev, *Protestantskite Secti v Bulgaria*, p. 95.
[48] Ibid., p. 96.
[49] R. Angelova, Periodicals of the Protestant Churches in Bulgaria (1844-1944), (Sofia: BHSU, 2003), p. 7.
[50] Kulichev, *Vestiteli na Istinata*, pp. 108-113.

convictions and 'popularise ideas, views and knowledge, much wider than simply religious issues'.[51] The Baptist churches saw a particular need for evangelistic literature in reaching 'the lost'. This work began remarkably early with the first Baptist booklet being published in Kazanluck in 1876. During his visit there in 1875, Herbolt argued from scripture against infant baptism. His arguments, fully accepted by the group, were put together in a booklet. One hundred copies were printed and distributed.[52] In 1886, Drumnikov, who was an educated tradesman, started a local literature mission which published evangelistic sermons by the famous English Baptist preacher, C.H. Spurgeon.[53] By 1921 there were 107 different evangelistic sermons published in Kazanluck, sponsored entirely by Drumnikov, running to over 200,000 copies.[54] This number doubled by 1931, the year Drumnikov died. Three years before his death he established a fund of 100,000 levs for publishing tracts. Publishing in Kazanluck was continued until WWII.

Another clear example of how important the publication and delivery of Bibles and tracts were to Baptists is seen in the activities of Sofia Baptists during the Balkan, All-European and First World wars. The leaders of one thirty-five member congregation, which had sent eight people to fight in the wars, formed and supported a Bulgarian Baptist Brochure Society.[55] Between 1912 and 1918 the Society printed and distributed twenty-nine different brochures among the soldiers (a total of 253,000 copies) and 42,200 New Testaments in Bulgarian, Serbian, German, Turkish and Hebrew.[56] Bulgarian Baptists firmly believed in the power of the Scriptures and evangelistic sermons in printed form. I have identified nine out of the twenty Baptist leaders during the first thirty years of the movement in Bulgaria as colporteurs of the BFBS. They were convinced, as they put it, that 'while one person in a church hall or auditorium will be heard by 20, 100, or 200 people, a printed booklet in 1,000 copies would reach...ten, twenty, a hundred thousand people'.[57]

Until 1920 the Baptists had no regular periodical of their own. Then, on 31 August 1919, at the Congress of the Baptist Union of Bulgaria, a decision was made to start a Union magazine. The first issue of *Evangelist*, in March 1920, clarified why a publication of that kind was necessary. First of all, it was to

---

[51] Angelova, Periodicals of the Protestant Churches, p. 5.
[52] P. Kirkilanov, 'Kratka Istoriya...', *Evangelist* 9-10 (1924), p. 6.
[53] H. Michailov, 'Edna Tri-godishnina' (A Three-year Anniversary) *Evangelist* 2 (1931), p. 6.
[54] P. Kirkilanov, 'Kratka Istoriya...', *Evangelist* 8-9 (1924), p. 4.
[55] It was in operation for the period 1912-1918, see 'Baptistkata Literatura', *Evangelist* 2 (1920), p. 13.
[56] V. Marchev, 'Deiatelnostta na Even. Bapt. Tsurkva v Sofia prez Balkanskata i Obshtoevropeiskite Voini (1912-1918)' (The Activity of the Evangelical Baptist Church in Sofia during the Balkan and the All-European Wars, 1912-1918), *Evangelist* 3 (1920), pp. 13,14; *Evangelist* 1, (1921), pp. 3-8.
[57] Kulichev, *Vestiteli na Istinata*, p. 94.

provide a platform for early Baptists who were still alive to tell the history of their churches and the movement. Secondly, it was to become an 'organ' of the united Baptist churches.[58] The first editor, Zaprian Vidolov, named it *Evangelist*, referring to the third major goal that was to be achieved by it. He wrote: '*Evangelist* should be a weapon for opening the eyes of people for the truth of Christ. It should make the secret of the good news widely known to people, and it should shine upon people's souls with heavenly grace.'[59] This idea was restated every time *Evangelist* outlined its goals. Baptists were convinced that the publication was a way to build a path for Christian beliefs and principles in society and in the lives of individuals.[60]

The phrase 'organ of the Union' implied several ideas. It was summed up rather dramatically when an appeal for funds to keep the magazine in circulation was made in 1933 by Vasil Chomonev, one of the oldest Baptists still living at that time.

> *Evangelist* is our flag, the most desired preacher, the cheapest missionary-evangelist, the easiest way to approach a pastor, a constantly opened and free pulpit, our indestructible public tribune...our advancement, our history, the guarantee of our stability, the secret of our union and unity in spiritual power...[61]

It seems that three main issues were at stake and *Evangelist* was seen as relevant to each of these issues. First, there was a desire for Baptist identity. Although the Baptists had by now been in Bulgaria for forty years they were still, in 1919, a tiny minority of barely two hundred people in the entire country. The question of identity was crucial. Baptists wanted to 'defend the principles of Christ's teachings which they preached',[62] especially as they were constantly under attack from the Orthodox Church. Secondly, it is clear that there was a perceived need for strong unity among the Baptist churches, particularly as Baptist beliefs spread slowly but surely over a wider territory among different ethnic groups.[63] Thirdly, Baptists needed a printed tool for reaching the people of Bulgaria with the Good News of Jesus Christ.

Evangelist was published for twenty years. Publication was halted for eighteen months between July 1935 and January 1937. Then there was a further

---

[58] Editor, 'Godishna Pastirska Conferentsia v Stara Zagora' (The Annual Pastoral Conference in Stara Zagora), *Evangelist* 1 (1920), p. 7.

[59] Z. Vidolov, 'Chada na Boga Jivago: Razprostraniavaite *Evangelist*' (Children of the Living God: Spread the News about *Evangelist*), *Evangelist* 3 (1921), p. 12.

[60] See *Evangelist* 1 (1924), p. 1; 11 (1925), p. 88; 6-7 (1928), pp. 1, 17, 18; 1 (1931), p. 12; 1-2 (1933), p. 1; 7 (1934), pp. 10-11.

[61] V. Chomonev, 'Evangelist da Stabilizira Rabotata Ni' (*Evangelist* Should Stabilise Our Work), *Evangelist* 4 (1933), p. 12.

[62] Editors, 'Okrujno N54, 23 Nov. 1921' (Circular Letter N54, 23 Nov. 1921), *Evangelist* 1 (1922), p. 15.

[63] Gypsies, Muslims, Jews and Russian refugees.

period of publication, which was brought to a standstill with the outbreak of WWII. It was supported by the Baptist Union, but had a small monthly subscription fee, paid annually by or for the subscribers. Many subscriptions of the poor were paid by the Union or other committed individuals. It had subscribers in the USA, Russia, England, Germany and Romania. The circulation was between 900 and 1,500 copies per issue. It had five editors over the period of its publication[64] and was published from six different locations.[65] Over the years, it included a total of more than 1,400 articles and comprised 2,300 pages. Approximately fifty-five percent of the articles were written by Bulgarians, twenty percent were written by missionaries and pastors of non-Bulgarian origin working in Bulgaria, and twenty-five percent were translations. The percentage written by Bulgarians is noteworthy. A major theme in *Evangelist* was the search for a true and meaningful Baptist identity. The following pressing questions were asked: 'Who are we?' (the quest for historical identity); 'What do we believe?' (the quest for theological uniformity); 'How do we worship and practise?' (the question of the church); 'How do we multiply?' (mission); and finally, 'How do we fit and relate to others?' (relationships to other religious groups, the society and the State).

Historical Identity: Search for Spiritual Roots

In an article in *Evangelist* in 1937 entitled 'The True Protestants', the author stated that, among other reasons, the Baptists were a despised minority because there was a deep ignorance among people in Bulgaria as to the historical roots of the Baptists.[66] Baptists themselves had to deal with this question. In their quest for historical belonging, there was a desire among Bulgarian Baptists to show a connection with the Anabaptist movement of the sixteenth century. Also helpful for their historical identity was knowledge of the Baptist movement in Amsterdam, England and America, and information about historical events leading to the early years of Baptist work in Bulgaria. In 1928 a series of articles covered the celebrations of the four-hundredth anniversary of Balthasar Hubmaier's martyrdom at the stake in Vienna. This Anabaptist leader was seen as the first 'true fighter for free Baptist expression of faith'.[67] His death sealed (with blood) two important principles; that of the 'spiritual

---

[64] Z.Vidolov (1920-1921); V. Tachtadjiev (1921-1922); P. Minkov (1922-1925; 1929-1933); T. Dimitrov (1925-1929; 1934-1939); V.Chakalov (1933-1934).

[65] Sofia (1920, 1931-1934, 1938-1939); Chirpan (1921-1924); Lom (1925-1928), Russe (1928-1931); Kazanluck (1935); Ferdinand (1924-1925).

[66] M.P., 'Istinskite Protestanti' (The True Protestants), *Evangelist* 6-7 (1937), pp. 13-15.

[67] V. Chakalov, 'Dve Skupi Imena' (Two Precious Names), *Evangelist* 4 (1928), p. 6.

freedom of the soul to believe and the separation of church and state'.[68] Hubmaier's famous words, 'Truth is immortal', were seen as an inspiration in times when the truth of the Gospel was 'restrained, beaten, crowned with thorns, crucified and buried, but was to rise from the ashes, and rule, and rejoice'.[69] In 1937, those words were proclaimed as a motto for the Bulgarian Baptist Union.[70] However simplistic the description of Hubmaier might seem to us today, it was significant that his life and work was known, and the adoption of his motto was an expression of a search for identity through building a bridge between the Anabaptist times and the 1920s and 1930s in Bulgaria.

Two other articles by George Vasov, one in 1934 and one in 1935, retold the story of the Anabaptist movement and of Baptist beginnings in England and later in America. The articles give little evidence of attention to historical accuracy. Bulgarian Baptists often relied on the theory of Baptist successionism and argued for an unbroken line of Baptists through the centuries. Vasov concluded: 'Luther and his helpers opened the door of the temple of freedom in Christ, but remained in the foyer, while we, *the Baptists*, went in, and without fear entered the Holy of Holiest, and were ridiculed, mocked, dishonoured, murdered.'[71] He then stated that 'those [earlier Baptists] were the ones' that entrusted to us 'the faith in Chirst'.[72] Baptistic views were often sought from the times of John the Baptist, Jesus Christ and the Early Church.[73]

Evangelist launched its first issue in 1920 with the story of the way the Baptist movement appeared in Bulgaria.[74] The stories of the existing churches, and of Baptist leaders, were also told by *Evangelist* in almost every issue. Inspiring stories were featured, including accounts of early missionaries and colporteurs such as Jacob Klundt[75] and Ivan Kargel;[76] of key Bulgarian leaders such as Peter Doychev,[77] one of the most influential pastors; of Peter Punchov[78], the first Gypsy pastor; of Spass Raichev[79], the first Bulgarian

---

[68] Ibid. p. 7.

[69] D. Stoichev, 'Baltazar Hubmaier', *Evangelist* 4-5 (1928), pp. 5.

[70] T. Dimitrov, 'Putia na Lujata' (The Way of Truth), *Evangelist* 1-2 (1937), p. 4.

[71] G. Vasov, 'Duhut na Krusteniat s Kruv' (The Spirit of the Baptized in Blood), *Evangelist* 2 (1935), p. 4.

[72] Ibid. p. 4.

[73] See 'Kakvo Dulji Christianstvoto na Baptistkata Tsurkva' (What does Christianity own to the Baptist Church), *Evangelist* 5 (1935), pp. 2-6, a translation of an article probably printed in 1934 by Zion Herald, USA.

[74] G. Chomonev, 'Poiaviavaneto na Baptisma v Bulgaria' (The Appearance of Baptism in Bulgaria), *Evangelist* 2 (1920), pp. 1-5.

[75] *Evangelist* 2 (1921), pp. 1-4.

[76] *Evangelist* 1 (1924), pp. 3,4.

[77] *Evangelist* 2 (1920), pp. 3-8.

[78] *Evangelist* 12 (1924), p. 4.

[79] *Evangelist* 11 (1926), pp. 83-84.

missionary; of Avram Barba,[80] the missionary among the Romanians south of the Danube river; and of international Baptist leaders such as C.H. Spurgeon.[81] Three of the Baptist World Alliance (BWA) congresses were extensively reported in *Evangelist*, thus identifying with the Baptist family worldwide. For example, in 1923, a declaration of the BWA Congress directed at the worldwide brotherhood of Baptists was translated. It contained the key distinctives of Baptist theology, which were fully accepted by Baptists in Bulgaria, such as: freedom of religion, Christian unity based not on belonging to a given church but on basic convictions of faith (Christ's divinity and redemptive work, his resurrection, ascension and second coming), the priesthood of all believers, the necessity of spiritual birth for salvation and believer's baptism by immersion.[82]

The quest for clearer identity and the search for common theological convictions were regarded as highly important for the Baptist Christians in Bulgaria. As Baptists were considered a newly formed sect, without firm roots in history or theology, Baptists were also forced to clarify their identity in relation to the established Orthodox Church, and also in relation to Congregationalists and Methodists, who had a longer history of work in Bulgaria.

Theological Identity: Defining the Basics of Christian Life and Belief

As already stated, in 1871 the Bulgarians were presented with the Protestant edition of the Bible. In 1925 a new Orthodox translation was launched with an accusation against the Protestant Bible that it was 'foreign' (translated by missionaries), was 'not full' (it lacked the apocryphal books), was 'not spiritual' (did not use Old Slavonic), and was not to be used as it was 'not the Bible' at all.[83] Furthermore, the Bible in the Orthodox understanding, although considered the Word of God, was placed second to Holy Tradition, since the latter was viewed as the 'last revelation'. In 1931, *Evangelist* wrote openly against what they saw as the Orthodox understanding that 'no one should have the Gospel [meaning the New Testament] in their hands, people should not read it, because it is a holy book. Only priests should have it.'[84] In effect, even when ordinary people had the New Testament available, it was 'rolled in fabric, and

---

[80] *Evangelist* 2 (1939), p. 14.

[81] *Evangelist* 1 (1926), pp. 7, 8; 2 (1926), p. 12.

[82] Editor, 'Declaratsia na Vsesvetskia Baptistki Sauz Kum Baptistkoto Bratstvo' (Declaration of the Baptist World Alliance to the Baptist Brotherhood), *Evangelist* 7 (1923), pp. 1-7.

[83] S. Tomov, 'Synodalniat Prevod of the Bible' (The Orthodox Translation of the Bible), *Evangelist* 5-6 (1925), p. 39.

[84] Editor, 'Izpitvaite Piasniata' (Examine the Scriptures), *Evangelist* 5 (1931), p. 2.

hidden behind the candle at the iconostases, only to be "used", when someone got sick, to place it under their pillow until they recovered'.[85]

Against this background, Baptist theology held that the Bible was the Word of God and the sole source for revelation, faith, salvation and practical living. Scripture was not dependent on Holy Tradition for its interpretation; everyone was urged to read it and thus to allow God to speak to them directly. Baptists stated: 'Whenever and wherever a person was born, and to whatever church he might belong, if he was not born "from above", he could not see the Kingdom of God, and that was only achieved by reading and experiencing the message of the Bible.'[86] The Bible was seen as supernatural in its revelation about God the Father and about Christ as the sole Saviour of humanity. A key sermon affirming the whole Bible as the inspired Word of God by a great American preacher of the time, R.A. Torrey, was translated. Torrey stressed that the Bible had a clear harmony among its books, had survived numerous attacks against itself and revealed the way people's lives could be changed. Most importantly, 'a person could receive an inner peace and a proof by the Holy Spirit that the Bible was the Word of God by experiencing the new birth through faith in its message'.[87]

The Baptists, therefore, saw in the Bible not only the inspired Word of God, but the only source for life and conduct,[88] as the 'Christian could not be a real Christian in life, without diligent and assiduous reading, studying and applying the Word of God'.[89] The primary interest of the Baptists to preach the Good News of Jesus Christ as revealed in scripture dominated *Evangelist*, and indeed God the Father and his attributes were rarely mentioned in it. Nevertheless, at times God was presented as the Creator, all-powerful and sovereign, the God of justice and holiness, but primarily as the all-loving Father who sent his Son to die for us. The person of the Holy Spirit was discussed, but mainly when stating his equality with the Father and the Son and in connection with the issue of being filled with the Holy Spirit, which was of concern to Baptists at the time. The belief in Jesus' virgin conception, his deity and true humanity and the fact of his resurrection from the dead, were included in sermons every Christmas and Easter. People were declared dead by the law of God in the Old Testament, but could now be declared righteous by the blood of Jesus in the new covenant. That was why 'without faith in His substitutionary death on the

---

[85] Ibid.

[86] Translation, 'Isusovoto Stanovishte varhu Staria Zavet' (Jesus' Standpoint Regarding the Old Testament), *Evangelist* 18-19 (1924), p. 1.

[87] R. Torrey, 'Zashto Viarvam Che Bibliata e Bojie Slovo?' (Why I Believe that the Bible is the Word of God), *Evangelist* 3-7 (1935), p. 10.

[88] See: *Evangelist* 10 (1931), pp. 2-3; 2 (1921), pp. 9-10; 5-6 (1932), pp. 9-10, and many others.

[89] Editor, 'Izpitvaite Piasniata', p. 2.

cross and his resurrection on the third day, there was no true Christianity, there was no Church, there was no life'.[90]

The style of ninety-five percent of the articles dealing with theological issues was homiletically loaded and shows the sincere desire of Baptists to proclaim the elements of the Gospel story. This emphasis found expression in every issue of *Evangelist* and was the key message. It is obvious that this approach underlined not only missionary proclamation, but was a strong critique of the lack or the very limited understanding of preaching in the Orthodox Liturgy. In Baptist preaching, sin was seen as the ultimate source of everything evil. It was defined as 'living without God, and willfully acting wrong and doing evil'.[91] It was seen as a universal sickness, as a plague, as a rotting from within, as a death that had spread to all.[92] This death was already working in the life of the sinner now, on earth, and was bringing eternal death in the future.[93] Salvation from sin was therefore urgent. This theology was not only following mainstream Baptist teaching, but it also defended Baptist preaching and mission in the Bulgarian context. Accusations of proselytizing from other churches lost their sharpness in Baptist eyes; regardless of church affiliation, people needed personal salvation.

Salvation was believed to have three steps: repentance, turning to God in faith and being born again.[94] In repentance, a person realised that he or she had sinned against God. So, such a person repented before God and confessed his/her sins in prayer directly to God (not to a priest or in front of an icon). True repentance was seen as bringing about a desire to change. Turning to God in faith was the moment of decision to make a u-turn from sin to God. So, at the moment of turning to God, there were three issues person had to deal with: first, to admit sin against God; second, to be ready to break with all known sin; third, to be prepared to do everything that was in line the scriptures and according to the will of God.[95] Baptists were by no means unique in their emphasis on repentance, but, in an Orthodox context they were significant in stressing personal repentance without the help of a mediator (priest), and the absolute necessity of turning away from sin and living a radically new life.

---

[90] Editor, 'Dva Puti Rajdane' (Twice-Born), *Evangelist* 1 (1931), p. 7.

[91] Editor, 'Iskash li da Ozdraveesh?' (Do You Want to be Healed?), *Evangelist* 2 (1928), pp. 11, 12.

[92] H. Marchev, 'Prokazata na Greha' (The Leprosy of Sin), *Evangelist* 2 (1927), pp. 5-6.

[93] T. Dimitrov, 'Grehut shte te Nameri' (Sin Will Find You), *Evangelist* 2 (1930), p. 6.

[94] See Editor, 'Shto e Pokaianie?' (What is Repentance?), *Evangelist* 3 (1929), pp. 2-4; A. Georgiev, 'Vreme e Da Se Sabudim' (It is Time to Wake Up), *Evangelist* 8-9 (1924), p. 3; and D. Hristova, 'Proletta na Duhovniat mi Jivot' (The Spring of My Spiritual Life), *Evangelist* 4 (1927), pp. 9, 10.

[95] Editor, 'Shto e Pokaianie?' (What is Repentance?), *Evangelist* 3 (1929), pp. 2, 3.

Repentance and turning to God brought about the experience of the new birth. 'If a man through true repentance and conversion has turned to God, God in his turn performs the new birth in the forgiven sinner's heart.'[96] Salvation was by grace and had nothing to do with the effort of the sinner in trying to refine himself and change his life. Neither was salvation related to his belonging to a certain church or community. One can see clearly that such theological conviction was emphasized in the context of an Orthodox theology of 'purgatory' and ideas held by many that good deeds contributed to salvation. In a translated article in *Evangelist*, C.H. Spurgeon stated: 'Do not place anything upon Christ. We can add nothing to the blood! Not even the honouring of the blood saves, but the blood of Christ itself. Even faith is not the basis of your salvation, it is the blood! Not your experience, but the blood!'[97] Being 'born again' was also crucial to church membership.[98] In an article entitled 'The New Birth', which is typical of a dozen of that kind, it is stated that being 'born again' was different from water baptism (in opposition to the Orthodox view that one is 'saved at the moment of baptism') and different from going to church. It was not the same as striving 'to do deeds of kindness' (against the Seventh-Day Adventists' view of keeping the law). It was by nothing, other than faith in Christ crucified.[99]

One had to be sure about one's new birth; but how could one know that salvation had taken place? 'There is no place for feelings, it's all about faith',[100] Baptists were convinced. The issue of 'being sure' seemed to have been answered from two points of view—that of scripture and that of experience. Salvation by faith was a promise of the Father and he was going to keep it. Additional indications were seen in freedom, inner peace and victory over sin in the life of the believer, and inner conviction, which only the Holy Spirit could give.[101] Reading the numerous stories in *Evangelist* of people being 'born again', one can see the experiences that repeat themselves in ninety percent of the stories: first, deep sorrow about being a sinner; second, prayer to God about the sin; third, tears and distress; fourth, an overwhelming feeling of joy when the reality of salvation is realized and there is assurance; and finally, a burning desire to witness to others.[102] An example is found in the memories of Pastor

---

[96] Ibid., p. 4.

[97] C. Spurgeon, 'Kogato vidia Kruvta, Shte Otmina' (When I See the Blood, I Will Pass By), *Evangelist* 3 (1923), p. 2.

[98] T. Dimitrov, 'Novoto Suzdanie' (The New Creation), *Evangelist* 8-9 (1928), p. 5.

[99] Translation of an article published in *Christian Thought*, entitled: 'The New Birth', *Evangelist* 1 (1922), p. 1.

[100] G. Vasov, 'Kushta na Piasuk' (House on Sand), *Evangelist* 8-10 (1937), p. 7.

[101] Translation: 'Tsurkvata na Hristos i Uverenie za Oproshtenie' (The Church of Christ and the Assurance of Salvation), *Evangelist* 6 (1930), pp. 4-5.

[102] See: *Evangelist* 4 (1927), pp. 9-10; 3 (1929), p. 2; 5 (1933), pp. 4-10; 3 (1937), pp. 5-7; 8-10 (1937), pp. 7-9 and many others.

Trifon Dimitrov, who telling the story of one of his preaching weeks in the town of Stanimaka in central Bulgaria, recalled:

> Early in the morning they brought to me a woman called Vassa. They told me: 'She listened to your sermon last night. She has repented this morning and has found salvation.' And I saw that this dear sister was deeply in emotion and tenderness, overwhelmed by uncontrollable weeping. With difficulty she told us about her sorrow for her sins, her prayer with tears, and the feeling of joy when she realised she was saved by Christ. While she was telling us that, suddenly...her brother-in-law threw himself on the ground and started crying out for forgiveness for his sins, and God heard his prayer, because he voiced out his joy about it... And in the other corner, little Pavel, the mischievous teenager, cried in heartbrokenness for his condition...[103]

Although the salvation experience was seen as finalised by God, the repentance and turning to God for salvation were viewed as something initiated by man, an act of free will. Questions about predestination did not seem to bother Bulgarian Baptists very much as there was only one reference in *Evangelist* that answered the question: 'Who are the people that God has chosen to be saved?' The answer was the following: First, 'those that feel sinful (1 Tim. 1:15; Rom. 5:8,10; 1 Cor. 1:26-29) and if you are one of them, how could you even think that you might not be chosen?' Second, 'the ones that are ready to go to him, because he has promised not to turn them away (Jn. 6:37)'. The article continued, 'so go to Him now, this is how you will know your destiny!'[104] Thus, the free will of man was crucial in one's approach to salvation. That was why the primary emphasis was placed on preaching the good news and motivating people to respond to it.

Against the background of known immorality on the part of Orthodox priests and the lack of a visible connection between Orthodox Liturgy and everyday life, the Baptists saw the new spiritual life as a life of holiness. This was the doctrine of sanctification. The motivation for holiness was love towards God.[105] Sanctification was seen as a process that lasted throughout a lifetime and involved every area of life—thoughts, desires, actions, speech and relationships were to be pure.[106] Believers were seen as Christ's letter to the world, the 'living Bible' (2 Cor. 3:3). Real sanctification could only be

---

[103] T. Dimitrov, 'Edna Neinteresna Obikolka s Interesni Sluchki' (One Uninteresting Journey, with Interesting Events), *Evangelist* 4 (1933), p. 5.

[104] K. Grabein, 'Niama da go Izpudia!' (I will not Chase Him Out!), *Evangelist* 4-5 (1937), p. 10.

[105] K. Grabein, 'Chistota I Sviatost' (Purity and Holiness), *Evangelist* 1-2 (1925), p. 11.

[106] T. Dimitrov, 'Novoto Suzdanie' (The New Creation), *Evangelist* 8-9 (1928), pp. 5-8.

achieved by faith, in the way forgiveness and justification were obtained.[107] One can see points of tension with the Orthodox Church. Saved people who had a personal experience with God and emphasized a life of holiness were very different from those 'considered part of the parish'—people who rarely went to church and essentially lived pagan lives.

For a newborn Christian, there was a clear command to be baptized as a believer. Bulgarian Baptists were very sensitive about this issue for several reasons. First, this was a major point of controversy with the Orthodox Church who saw in baptism a sacrament that could not be repeated. For Orthodoxy, baptism was the means of salvation for the individual and was the person's incorporation into the only true Church of Christ. Second, there were Protestants who baptised infants and who were viewed by Baptists as untrue to the Word of God and 'bathing children into ignorance'. Third, Baptists 're-baptised' people—Orthodox and Protestants—who had already been baptised as infants. Baptists were often accused of being a proselytising community. For Baptists, baptism as a believer was a command of Christ and was clearly the practice of the Early Church.[108] Also, in the ordinance of baptism, some biblical facts were clearly represented: an image of being washed in the blood of Christ; the death and the resurrection of Christ; and death to sin and new life in the light of the resurrection. Finally, only the converted were called to baptism:

> We, the Baptists, do not believe in 'baptismal redemption' or in 'baptismal rebirth' as others wrongly do. We believe that salvation is a purely spiritual connection with God in Christ Jesus and that baptism is an outside physically-religious ordinance, which represents the death of Christ and resurrection, and a Symbol of death of the believer toward sin and resurrection into new spiritual life. (Rom. 6:3-5; Col. 2:12; Gal. 3:26, 27).[109]

Infant baptism was totally rejected, on the grounds that babies could not have personal faith. Furthermore, Baptists could not find any proof of children being baptised in the New Testament. Baptisms previously performed on individuals at an infant stage were totally rejected as 'untrue'. The 'true baptism' was administered only by full immersion, because, according to Bulgarian Baptist understanding, this was the way the early church baptised people in the New Testament.[110] One should point out the connection the Baptists saw between church membership and baptism. Candidates for Baptism were strictly examined by church leaders and the members of the church voted

---

[107] K. Grabein, 'Hristovoto Pismo' (Christ's Letter), *Evangelist* 9 (1925), p. 66.

[108] See A. Karev, 'Krushtenie po Viara—Propoved Jum Krushtavashtite se' (Baptism by Faith—A Sermon to the Ones Being Baptized), *Evangelist* 5-6 (1927), pp. 11-13.

[109] I. Kendall, 'Evangelskite Osnovania za Vervashtoto Krushtenie' (The Evangelical Foundations of Believer's Baptism), *Evangelist* 1 (1922), p. 9.

[110] Ibid., p. 11.

on the question of whether they should be baptised. A prominent Baptist leader, V. Chomonev, wrote in 1926: 'Before we hear them confess voluntarily, clearly and categorically, that they believe in the saving blood of the Lord Jesus Christ and in the forgiveness of their own sins, we do not allow anyone to 'cross the Jordan' [to be baptized].'[111] Baptism was not seen as a way into church membership; it was seen as an outward sign of salvation and commitment to the church, a sign that had already been recognised by the community in their 'hearing' from the baptismal candidate the testimony of his/her faith.

Although baptism as a means of salvation was rejected by Baptists, there was a strong feeling that baptism, with its clear statement of commitment to the Christian life, was a source of strength and a realisation of the assurance of salvation. This idea, although not fully defended or developed, was nevertheless expressed in several articles. For example: 'Today thousands of Christians do not know joy after baptism. They cannot rejoice, since they are not sure in their salvation. This is because they reject the clear command of Christ [baptism].'[112] It is difficult to say whether this view was developed because of people who thought baptism was not important for salvation and therefore never wanted to be baptised, or in relation to those who were afraid to identify with the Baptist Churches (especially people from Muslim and Gypsy communities or people from an Orthodox background) for fear of rejection by the rest of their peers.

The first time a person was allowed to take part in the Lord's Supper was usually on the day of their baptism, after they came out of the water. The Lord's Supper was seen as a holy ordinance given by the Saviour and it was administered in the church by the pastor and the deacons once a month, and usually followed by sharing an ordinary meal—a 'love evening' or 'love feast'.[113] The Baptist understanding of Orthodox belief about the Eucharist ('Prichastie') was that it offered mystical cleansing of sins. The Baptists were convinced that the Lord's Supper brought no forgiveness. Neither did they believe that the elements were transformed into the real flesh and blood of Christ. For them, it was an ordinance of remembrance, a memorial, as they understood the Scriptures to teach (Mk. 14). The understanding was that drinking of one cup symbolised their common participation in the blood of Christ and the sharing the bread among many symbolised their unity, expectation of Christ's second coming and yearning for sanctification. Their intention was not to 're-create Christ. He was real enough! Their intention was to commemorate him'.[114] Questions about participation in the Supper by

---

[111] V. Chomonev, 'Malko Za Krustenieto' (A Little about Baptism), *Evangelist* 5 (1926), p. 37.

[112] V. Chomonev, 'Oshte Neshto za Krushtenieto' (One More Thing about Baptism), *Evangelist* 10 (1925), p. 75.

[113] Editor, 'Gospodnata Vecheria' (The Lord's Supper), *Evangelist* 6 (1931), p. 2.

[114] Ibid.

Christians from other churches, or about members of Baptist churches taking part in the Lord's Supper in other evangelical churches were not discussed in *Evangelist*.

There was an eschatological dimension to Bulgarian Baptist beliefs. Baptists believed they were in the 'last days'. It was enough to remind oneself of the consequences of WWI, or to think about natural disasters,[115] or to consider the strong opposition to Baptists in Bulgaria by religious and secular forces, to get a sense of the 'end times'. In addition, there was the growth of atheistic Bolshevism in Russia. The Second Coming was the only hope as the future was concerned. It was promised by Jesus, and would happen soon.[116] The millennium was not discussed by Bulgarian Baptists as a theological issue, but one is left with the impression that the commonly agreed belief was in a thousand year reign of Christ following the rapture of the church, which was to happen at the moment of Jesus' Second Advent. The Christian should be pure and ready to meet Christ.[117]

A new challenge to Baptists developed through the entrance of Pentecostal teaching into Bulgaria in the 1920s. Reading through *Evangelist*, one can see that although no particular attention was given to the person of the Holy Spirit within the Trinity, his ministry was always seen as the spiritual power of God in the lives of Christians, bringing about conviction, salvation and sanctification, and empowering the Church with spiritual gifts.[118] An article in 1929, by Dr William Kuhn, then the Foreign Mission secretary of the GBGC, had as its theme the Day of Pentecost in Acts (2:14-21). It stated that three different words used to describe the ministry of the Holy Spirit—namely the *pouring out* of the Spirit, being *filled* with the Spirit and being *baptized* in the Spirit—described the same thing: a continued, unreserved and always deepening submission to the presence and leading of the Spirit.[119] To be filled with the Spirit did not mean 'more of the Spirit', or 'a second, third, fourth new filling after the first new birth experience, it simply meant a continuous surrender of oneself after conversion'.[120] This interpretation was generally accepted by Bulgarian Baptists. As far as the gifts of the Spirit were concerned, they were recognised as distributed by God to all church members. Some gifts, however, such as speaking in tongues, prophesy and healing, were seen as

---

[115] A massive earthquake happened in Chirpan, central Bulgaria, in 1928.

[116] Editor, 'V Kakvo Se Sustoi Nadejdata na Tsurkvata' (What Constitutes the Hope of the Church), *Evangelist* 3 (1921), p. 10.

[117] H. Krustev, 'Isus Pak Shte Doide' (Jesus will Come Again), *Evangelist* 3 (1927), p. 8.

[118] W. Kuhn, 'Zapechatan Sus Sviatiat Duh' (Being Sealed with the Spirit), *Evangelist* 5 (1930), pp. 3,4.

[119] W. Kuhn, 'Kak Se Obiasniava Chudoto na Petdesiatnitsata?' (How Do We Explain the Miracle of Pentecost?), *Evangelist* 9 (1929), p. 10.

[120] Editor, 'Shto e Pokaianie' (What is Repentance?), *Evangelist* 3 (1929), p. 2.

being only for the time of the apostles, and had now ceased to exist.[121] In a sermon, 'Pentecost', K. Grabein, pastor of Kazanluck Baptist Church, disturbed by the growing influence of Pentecostal teaching in Bulgaria, stated that Pentecostal doctrines were not of God. He wrote: 'What we see in their meetings has the character of a religious ecstasy, of being drunk, they all shout and fall on their backs in convulsions...that cannot be of God, can it!?!'[122] This critical approach to Pentecostalism was held for almost the entire later history of Bulgarian Baptists.

In reaction to the accusations of Pentecostals about Baptists not having the complete blessing of God, deeper attention was given by Baptists to the Fruit of the Spirit (Gal. 5:22-23), as the real sign of the presence, seal and filling of the Spirit. A thousand copies of Ivan (Johann) Kargel's book on the subject were printed in 1929, and a selection of the text was published in *Evangelist* the same year. Kargel firmly stated that because 'the Holy Spirit could not be fruitless';[123] it was in the Christian character of the believer that the Spirit's presence was clearly visible. He wrote: 'Before God, not what we do has meaning, but who we are in our character.'[124] Prayer for specific gifts was never mentioned and we have no indication that healing, prophesy and speaking in tongues were practised by the Baptists at the time in Bulgaria.

Whereas Pentecostals often emphasized victory over adverse circumstances, among Baptists there was more the theology of suffering. In cases of persecution for the faith, suffering was considered an attack of the Evil one against the Gospel. Jesus was killed at the hands of the ungodly, the first church suffered, and one was called to witness for God and share in Jesus' suffering until the Kingdom of peace and righteousness came. Wars were seen as being a direct result of sin and could only be avoided if the Gospel of Christ could penetrate the hearts of people and governments.[125] Natural disasters were allowed by God not as punishment for sins, but as warnings. Asking what might have been the reason in God's mind behind the earthquake in Chirpan, Bulgaria, in 1928, which killed hundreds of people and destroyed thousands of buildings, the answer in *Evangelist* was that God wanted to 'shake the people into their senses', to remind them about 'how temporary they were', to 'allow them to feel His power', to 'bring them to repentance', and finally, to 'prompt them to sympathy, selflessness, and true compassion to each other'.[126] At an individual level, when Christians were sick, lost a loved one or suffered

---

[121] Editor, 'Tsurkvata na Hristos' (Church of Christ), *Evangelist* 5 (1929), p. 7.

[122] K. Grabein, 'Petdesiatnitsa' (Pentecost), *Evangelist* 6 (1926), p. 45.

[123] I. Kargel, 'Ploda na Duha' (The Fruit of the Spirit), *Evangelist* 6 (1929), pp. 4-6.

[124] Ibid., p. 5.

[125] P. Mishkov, 'Kakvo e Evangelism?' (What is Evangelism?), *Evangelist* 6 (1935), p. 2.

[126] T. Dimitrov, 'Bog I Zemetreseniata' (God and the Earthquakes), *Evangelist* 5 (1928), pp. 3, 4.

personal afflictions, this was not a punishment from God. Rather, it was allowed by the loving God for perfecting the believer.[127]

It was in moments like those, moments of suffering and depression, that Bulgarians often went not only to the Orthodox Church but also to 'seers' or to places with supposed miraculous healing powers.[128] Baptists totally rejected the seers as being of the devil. The true believer turned to Christ. No healing waters, fortune telling or magic rituals were part of the Kingdom of God.[129] Personal prayer was directed to God, not mediated. Like the seers, Orthodox icons, saints or the mediation of a priest were rejected by Baptists. In the exercise of believing prayer, the life of Jesus and the holy characters of the Bible were the examples to follow. Prayer had to be sincere, clear and short when pronounced in public, always with faith, according to the will of God as found in the scriptures.[130] People were encouraged to unite in prayer at all times, in trouble and need, in joy and fellowship, because 'the prayer of those agreeing to ask in the name of God would surely receive an answer from Him'.[131] Prayer meetings were held in local churches once or twice a week.[132]

Bulgarian Baptists theology regarding the relationship of a believer with God and of the personal spiritual journey developed in the Orthodox setting. Baptist views about new birth and personal conversion, a turning around that must be reflected in changes in the everyday life of a Christian, were alien in the Bulgarian context of the nineteenth century and the beginning of the twentieth century. Bulgarian Baptists emphasised the need for personal sanctification and spiritual fruit in a Christian's life. In addition, the Baptist understandings of baptism of believers as witness and of the Lord's Supper as a memorial event, not conveying grace to believers, were criticised by Orthodox clergy. However, Baptists engaged in little constructive dialogue with Orthodoxy. Rather, Baptist theology developed in a situation of confrontation.

---

[127] M. Popov, 'Tselta na Stradaniata' (The Purpose of Suffering), *Evangelist* 11 (1925), p. 85.

[128] For example, in 1926, a man in the village of Dulgodeshevo supposedly had a vision about a muddy stream on the outskirts of his village. He was 'told' the water there had miraculous healing powers. For the next ten years, hundreds of thousands of people went to drink and bathe in the water. Many became sick by drinking the water and had skin infections by rubbing it on their bodies, but nevertheless there were countless (unverified) stories of people being healed. The local man was revered as a holy man and became very rich. *Evangelist* had eight articles by medical doctors, pastors and ordinary people, all warning about what was happening. See *Evangelist* 9 (1926), pp. 73, 74; 11 (1926), pp. 85, 87; 1 (1927), p. 10; 2 (1927), pp. 9-11.

[129] M. Kazandjieva, 'I Slovoto Stana Plut i se Vseli Mejdu Nas' (And the Word Became Flesh and Came to Dwell Among Us), *Evangelist* 1 (1935), p. 4.

[130] H. Marchev, 'Za Molitvata' (About Prayer), *Evangelist* 3 (1926), p. 19.

[131] W. Kuhn, 'Ako Dvama ot Vas se Suglasiat za Neshto' (If Two of You Agree on Something), *Evangelist* 2 (1930), p. 7.

[132] T. Dimitrov, 'Nadmennost v Molitvite Ni' (Haughtiness in Prayer), *Evangelist* 12 (1924), p. 4.

However, the tensions which shaped Bulgarian Baptist theological identity were not only with Orthodoxy. The emergence of the Pentecostal movement in Bulgaria, especially in the 1920s, forced Baptists to verbalise their position regarding the work of the Holy Spirit. In this process, Bulgarian Baptists, probably partly influenced by some American Baptist positions, tended to reject the theology of the baptism of the Holy Spirit as a second blessing. Instead, they emphasised the need for believers to surrender to God and his Spirit and to live a life of trust and prayer.

The Church and its Mission as Reflected by *Evangelist*

Church

It is important to underline the theological dependence that the Bulgarian Baptists had on the beliefs of Germans and German-speaking Russians, residing and ministering in the country, in relation to ecclesiology, church membership, church leadership and even the particularities of church structure and mission activities. The minutes of the Lom Baptist Church from 1898-1930 indicate how much of what the Bulgarian church was doing was a reflection of what Jacob Klundt, the BFMS colporteur, gave them as advice.[133] It is clear that Baptist beliefs regarding ecclesiology and mission could find no parallel in the Orthodox Church. They also differed from those of the Congregationalists and Methodists, although the main evangelical points were similar. Bulgarian Baptist ecclesiology, one could say, was not influenced as much by the circumstances of life and ministry in Bulgaria, as by German Baptist and, later, German-speaking American Baptist understandings of the church. The Church was seen as instituted by Christ and it was the means by which God called people to salvation. Its head was Christ who had acquired it by his own blood (Acts 20:28).[134] For Baptists, the church was the sum of all the redeemed. The Church was the body of Christ, the universal Bride of Christ for whom he gave his life. The local community of Christians was a manifestation of this church in a given locality.[135]

A faithful Baptist church was described as having the following characteristics: first, belief that the scriptures were the only source of direction for Christian faith and living; second, belief that Jesus Christ was the Son of God, the only and sufficient Saviour; third, a commitment to lifting up the cross of Jesus; fourth, upholding Sunday as a holy day, a day dedicated to the Lord

---

[133] *Kratka Istoriya na Evangelskata Baptistka Tsurkva v gr. Lompalanka.*

[134] A. Georgiev, 'Tsurkvata na Hrista' (The Church of Christ), *Evangelist* 8-9 (1931), pp. 5-6.

[135] P. Minkov, 'Primernata Evangelska Tsurkva Dnes' (The Exemplary Baptist Church Today), *Evangelist* 7 (1927), pp. 4-6.

for rest and a day for the church to gather around the Lord's table and the Word of God; and finally, seeing the church as a missionary church, seeking to reach the lost.[136] Members of the church could only be people who had repented of their sins and believed in Jesus Christ as their personal Saviour. Their account of that experience ('testimony') was shared with the church. After a time of testing as to whether a real change had occurred in their lives, and after voting by the church members, a person was welcomed into church membership. The visible moment of that happening was the moment of water baptism. Voting took place after the person's testimony was heard and confirmed, and before baptism and participation in the Lord's Supper had taken place.[137] Thus 'being saved by faith', and being baptized, were conditions of membership, and in their rejection of the baptism of infants Baptists differed from the rest of the Christians in Bulgaria.

The organization of the church was seen following instructions found in Philippians 1:1. The church had two major offices: overseers (pastor-preachers) and deacons. The pastor-preacher was to lead the church spiritually, care for its growth and faithfully preach the Word of God. He was ordained after a church had called him to the ministry, being convinced that he could fulfill the requirements for this office, as found in 1 Timothy 3 and Titus 1. Similarly, the deacon was to minister to the needy and to oversee the administrative needs of the church. His election and ordination followed the same pattern as that of the preacher-pastor. Pastors and deacons were ordained for life.[138] The church also had two elected boards of leadership: a Board of Elders and a Church Council. The former provided spiritual guidance, exercised discipline and organised spiritual life. The latter was responsible for everyday issues concerning property and administration. The church had a treasurer, a member of the Church Council responsible for accounting the finances.[139]

Tithing was never compulsory, but teaching on giving and supporting the church and mission was very clear. Given the number of poor people and middle-class people who struggled with financial pressures in most of the churches at the time, and the number of Gypsy communities with high levels of unemployment, compassion was the natural way of reacting in the spirit of Christ. Old Testament tithing was seen as giving way to a total 'belonging of everything to Christ in the New Testament'.[140] Two ways of raising support are

---

[136] M. Popov, 'Sushtnostta na Tsurkovnata Rabota' (The Essence of Church Work), *Evangelist* 12 (1927), pp. 2, 11, 12.

[137] Editor, 'Organizatsia na Mestnata Tsurkva' (Organization in the Local Church), *Evangelist* 2 (1931), pp. 7-9.

[138] Ibid., p. 8. For an example of a service of ordination see P. Fortunov, 'Skromno ala Surdechno' (Humble, but Wholehearted), *Evangelist* 3 (1938), pp. 8-13.

[139] E. Raichev, 'Tsurkovniat Kasier' (The Church Treasurer), *Evangelist* 4-5 (1937), pp. 11-13.

[140] K. Grabein, 'Vzemi!' (Take!), *Evangelist* 5 (1926), p. 35.

indicated in *Evangelist*—one by committing to regular giving for the ministry of the local church,[141] and the other by separate collections for mission and specific needs.[142] However, the poor background of most of the people prevented all but one of the churches from becoming financially stable enough to do mission and ministry without outside support.

A number of articles in *Evangelist* were dedicated to requirements for successful pastoral ministry[143] and effective preaching.[144] Their major concern was the personal conduct of the preacher. A clear difference from the main religion of the country was apparent. The lives of Orthodox priests did not differ significantly from the lives of their parishioners. But in Baptist churches, exemplary lifestyle was expected from leaders. Some articles in *Evangelist* dealt with the relations between the church and preacher.[145] Often problems were discussed. One dealt with the remuneration of pastors; churches were unable to support their own pastors so funds had to come from outside. Another touched on unrealistic expectations of the workload of pastors. Sometimes there was too much control over the pastor by the church council and the board of elders; sometimes there was a dictatorial style of leadership by pastor. *Evangelist* 'discussed' all of these issues, but without clear answers being offered. This was an indication of a lack of guidelines on the part of the Baptist Union leadership.

A clear case of Bulgarians following the practice of the German Baptist 'founding fathers' was the degree of discipline (the church 'ban') exercised in the church. People were voted out of membership or communion for a period of time or permanently. That was done when serious sins were committed or people declared a change in their basic convictions. Reasons for banning people from membership or communion were often unclear, apart from cases of unfaithfulness to one's spouse. There were obviously a significant number of people affected, because on two occasions pastors wrote that 'churches should show more grace and have more people accepted into membership, than voted out of it!'[146]

Bulgarian Baptists believed that the role of women in the church was focused on three areas: First, women teaching and preaching to other women; second, women's missionary efforts; third, social and benevolent ministry. One kind of group, at a local church level, was the women's group led by a 'lady-

---

[141] G. Vasov, 'Shest Vida Davane' (Six Kinds of Giving), *Evangelist* 8 (1932), p. 4.

[142] I. Igov, 'Nashata Radost v Sofia' (Our Joy in Sofia), *Evangelist* 8 (1932), p. 8.

[143] See: *Evangelist* 3 (1923); 9-10 (1923); 5 (1924).

[144] See: *Evangelist* 6 (1923); 6 (1926); 5-6 (1927); 4-5 (1938); 6 (1939). C. Spurgeon, 'Dobri Suveti Kum Propovednika' (Useful Advice for the Preacher), Translation, *Evangelist,* 5-6 (1927), pp. 7-8.

[145] E. Kutuktchiev, 'Kakvo se Ochakva ot Mirianite?' (What is to be Expected from the Lay People?), *Evangelist* 6 (1926), pp. 46-48; 7 (1926), pp. 54-55.

[146] G. Negev, 'Disciplina v Tsurkvata' (Church Discipline), *Evangelist* 4 (1925), pp. 26-29.

pastor', usually the wife of the pastor.[147] The purpose of those groups was to encourage each other in the Word (the Bible), to be faithful to the role the women had at home, and to take part in prayer and in benevolent ministries. Women usually led the Children's hour and often had freedom to teach and preach to congregations. There were even women who were asked to lead teaching sessions at the national congresses of the Baptist Union.[148] There were also articles in *Evangelist* penned by women, consisting of sermons and teaching materials.[149] In 1928, an article by Komitski, a deacon in one of the central churches, even stated,

> I wish there were as many women preachers as we have men preaching; then humanity would have been further ahead in the knowledge of the truth. My advice to you dear sisters and mothers in Christ would be: preach Christ boldly at home, in the church and before the society...with power and authority by God, not men.[150]

The freedom that Baptist women found in their involvement in the church was unique to Baptists in that period. The Orthodox Church, the Congregationalists and Methodists never saw women as called to undertake ministry. I am convinced that two factors contributed to this situation. First, most of the ministering women were related (married) to pastors and deacons, and their husbands were open to some form of a team ministry. Second, all of them were well educated and, judging by some of their teaching they were as eloquent and gifted as the best male preachers of the time. One finds no indication, though, that women were ever ordained as pastors or deacons, or that they ever administered the Lord's Supper in official church services. Nonetheless, their freedom to exercise ministry in the church was significant.

The churches placed particular value on Adult Sunday schools and the Children's hour—Sunday school for Children.[151] The Adult school was always before the main service, was led by the pastor and had a form of systematic teaching through the books of the Bible. The children's hour was primarily during the service, in another room, where Sunday school teachers offered specially prepared lessons for children. Youth activities were three-fold. First, there were Christian Youth Societies (youth groups in the church). Second, there was participation in choirs. Third, there was missionary activity via Youth

---

[147] *Evangelist* 3 (1935), pp. 1, 17.

[148] For example, M. Kazanjieva in 1924, *Evangelist* 16-17 (1924), pp. 5-8; R. Mihailova in 1932, *Evangelist* 5-6 (1932), pp. 4-5.

[149] M. Kazanjieva in 1932, *Evangelist* 1 (1932), p. 13; *Evangelist* 5-6, pp. 4-5; R. Mihailova in 1927, *Evangelist* 2 (1927), p. 8.

[150] G. Komitski, 'Pismo Do Viarvasthite Jeni' (A Letter to Christian Women), *Evangelist* 5 (1928), pp. 8-9.

[151] I. Kazanjiev, 'Znachenieto na Nedelnoto Uchilishte' (The Purpose of the Sunday School), *Evangelist* 11 (1927), p. 7.

Christian Abstention Societies (dedicated to abstention from alcohol and dependencies). The first consisted of regular youth meetings for Bible study and also involved organising open-air evangelistic meetings for young people, youth and sport activities, and a practical service ministry to church members and outsiders.[152] Although the primary worship was communal singing accompanied by organ, additional choral singing, poetry recitation, and simple art plays were frequently part of services organised by young people.[153]

Mission and Evangelism

The theological belief that the human soul was eternally lost in sin and needed salvation, meant that fulfillment of Jesus' Great Commission (Mt. 28) was seen as the ultimate task for the people of God. They were to 'go and teach every nation, and every man, through the preaching of the Gospel, and to make them disciples of the Kingdom'.[154] 'Making disciples' was to bring them to the 'saving assurance' of new life in Jesus.[155] Preaching the Gospel of Christ was the primary way of evangelism. This was done through verbal preaching from the pulpit, at evangelistic meetings and secular gatherings, and through printed literature including the pages of *Evangelist*. There was also the 'voices' of believers' lives—Christ-like lives. Bulgarian Baptists emphasised that such 'preaching' 'could not be ignored, it always opened hearts and souls, and could never be forgotten'.[156] A study of the over one-hundred evangelistic sermons in *Evangelist* led me to conclude that there was a distinctive pattern for preaching an evangelistic sermon. The sermons covered sin and its consequences; the fallen, helpless state of the sinner; God's love in Christ; full assurance of salvation by trusting in Jesus' redemptive work; and finally, the testimony of the Holy Spirit in one's heart. An invitation to make a step of faith at the point of hearing the sermon was always implied.[157] In his advice to the 'faithful pastors who preached the true Gospel', Vasil Chomonev, one of the founders of Lom Baptist Church, wrote,

> This is what evangelism is: it is a sermon, a story, a song, a discussion, or a conversation that clearly sets before the individual that man is sinful by nature,

---

[152] Editor, 'Za mladeji', (For the Young People), *Evangelist* 8, (1925), p. 61.

[153] R. Kovatcheva, 'Vuzpitatelnoto Deistvie na Religioznata Musica' (The Nurturing Effect of Religious Music), *Evangelist* 6 (1939), pp. 14-15.

[154] Editor, 'Zadachata na Bojiite Chada' (The Task before the Children of God), *Evangelist* 2 (1931), p. 4.

[155] Ibid.

[156] P. Mishkov, 'Kakvo e Evangelism?' (What is Evangelism?), *Evangelist* 6 (1935), p. 1.

[157] For an example of a typical sermon, see: A. Georgiev, 'Spassen Li Si?' (Are You Saved?), *Evangelist* 2 (1938), pp. 5-6.

that he is a slave of his own sin, for which he will face the anger of God and receive his judgment, that he cannot by his own strength deliver himself, that forgiveness of sin is only possible by the blood of Christ, so that by faith the sinner may be proclaimed righteous and be at peace with God. Then he will fully know by the testimony of the Spirit of God that he has gone from death to life.[158]

Pastors often took part in evangelistic revival meetings—evening services in private homes or rented public halls. These meetings often lasted for a whole week. One can see in this a continuation of pattern of the colporteurs' visits which made such an impact in the first stages of the Baptist movement. Also, there was inspiration from similar strategies in the USA and Germany. 'We should not stop, until the last town, village, house and heart are reached! One-to-one, or one-to-many, through the spoken word and print, Christ should be preached!'[159] exclaimed Pavel Mishkov, a full time Baptist evangelist during the period from 1920-1932. 'Just imagine what the world would look like if the Gospel had been preached to the man in Serbia, who in 1914 killed the Prince, or if Stalin today is turned to Christ...'[160] As an example of the extent of missionary zeal, Trifon Dimitrov, in 1937, when a secretary of the Baptist Union, wrote that a national revival could come if only Baptists could improve the quality of preaching and the preparation of leaders, develop better choirs and music, introduce an evangelistic presence in every public school and win teachers, politicians and sociologists for Christ.[161]

The Baptist Union had impressive results in reaching ethnic minority groups in the country, namely Gypsies, Muslims and other smaller minorities. The first Gypsy Baptist Church was established in 1915 in the village of Golintsi, near Lom.[162] The first Gypsy pastor in Bulgaria, Peter Punchov, was ordained in 1924.[163] Another Gypsy, Petar Minkov, started a Baptist Gypsy Mission in 1926, originally working only in the Lom area, but later extending his work to Sofia. By 1931, the mission managed to publish in the Gypsy language the Gospels of Matthew and Luke, two songbooks and a number of evangelistic brochures.[164] In 1932, the Baptist Union reported five Gypsy congregations with four Gypsy preachers.[165] As a response to the poor conditions of the

---

[158] V. Chomonev, 'Shto e Blagovestie?' (What is Sharing Good News?), *Evangelist* 1-2 (1933), p. 6.

[159] Mishkov, 'Kakvo e Evangelism?', p. 2.

[160] Ibid.

[161] T. Dimitrov, 'Duhovno Probujdane' (Spiritual Awakening), *Evangelist* 6-7 (1937), pp. 3-5.

[162] Wardin, 'The Baptists in Bulgaria', p. 151.

[163] T. Dimitrov, 'Kradenoto Evangelie' (The Stolen New Testament), *Evangelist* 6 (1924), p. 2.

[164] H. Kulitchev, *Vestiteli na Istinata,* pp. 324-325.

[165] V. Chakalov, 'Iz Jivota na Tsurkvite' (Church Reports), *Evangelist* 9-10 (1932), pp. 13, 14.

Gypsies, who were often without adequate water supply and had a high level of unemployment, a Diakonia (medical) ministry was developed between 1928-1934 with help from the German Baptist Union. With additional support from the German Baptist General Conference (GBGC), a Diakonia building was obtained in 1939, in Lom.[166] Apparently, the Baptists were the only people to offer teaching for illiterate children, and arguably the only ones to provide organised medical and humanitarian help between the wars in Bulgaria. Thus they clearly believed in social ministry and care as being part and parcel of their Christian identity and ministry.

By 1920, the American Board[167] had two missionaries among Muslims in Bulgaria.[168] A young man of Turkish origin, M. Naziffov, was converted through their efforts in Plovdiv in 1914. In 1921, the Danish Baptist Mission, encouraged by the German Baptist Union, sent a missionary, Gotfrid Pederson, to work with Muslims and Jews in Bulgaria. He settled in Plovdiv and got to know Naziffov, who soon became his translator and co-worker. The two were able to develop a fruitful ministry among the Muslims in Plovdiv and the surrounding area. In 1922, with the help of Pedersen, a Gypsy-Muslim 'school' was opened in Plovdiv for teaching illiterate children to read and write. The work progressed well until Pedersen was called back by his mission board in 1923,[169] and despite the efforts of Naziffov to keep the ministry going, the work gradually died out. We are not sure about the fate of Naziffov, but in 1932 *Evangelist* noted that 'these wretched Muslim people, fanatically "guarded" by their religious leaders, are "dying" in their enclosed villages for now there is no one to bring them the light of Christ'.[170]

Some work was done among Russian refugees in Sofia, where we hear about a Russian group meeting in 1938.[171] A successful ministry among Romanian-speaking settlers in the villages of Murtvitsa and Guliantsy started in 1915, led by Avram Barba, a Hungarian-Romanian pastor. Further attempts to preach to Jews and Armenians are evident, but there is very little data.[172] The churches organised evangelistic visits in the prisons, where the Gospel was preached and practical help was given in terms of clothes, food, medicine and presents. The vision was simple: it was not the prison sentence, hard labour or long lonely

---

[166] Editor, 'Purviat Diakoniiski Dom V Bulgaria' (The First Diakonia Home in Bulgaria), *Evangelist* 1 (1939), p. 11.

[167] American Congregationalists.

[168] Ursulla Marsh in Plovdiv and Johaness Avetarian in Shoumen, see: Kulitchev, *Vestiteli na Istinata,* p. 319.

[169] The Danish Mission Board had made a decision to stop the work in Bulgaria in favour of work in the Congo for financial reasons. See: G. Pedersen, 'Otvoreno Pismo' (An Open Letter), *Evangelist* 4 (1927), p. 2.

[170] M. Kazanjieva, 'Rabotata Mejdu Mohamedanite' (Work Among the Bulgarian Muslims), *Evangelist* 5-6 (1932), p. 4.

[171] Editor, 'Chronika' (Chronicles), *Evangelist* 1-2 (1937), p. 2.

[172] Pedersen, 'Otvoreno Pismo', p. 2.

nights that would change someone's soul, 'but only the Word of God in Christ, a sincere love and genuine concern could melt these hardened sinners' hearts'.[173] The ministry reached its peak 1925-1926, when dozens of prisoners were converted and baptised in the prisons, but later the ministry died out due to lack of funds.[174]

Analysing the mission activities of the Bulgarian Baptists, one has to admit that they were mostly inspired by foreign mission programmes and supported by foreign mission funding. All of them suffered as the funding was cut off with the beginning of WWII, or in the case of the Muslim work, with the withdrawal of Danish support. Despite the Bulgarian Baptist theological emphasis on mission, it seems that there was little practical and financial support forthcoming from the native Bulgarians to see that vision realised. That weakness continues in the present time, after the democratic changes of 1989. Theology and its outworking in practice do not always go hand in hand.

Baptists and Others

The founding of the Bulgarian Evangelical Baptist Union (the full title) on 14 September 1908, in Chirpan, had at its foundation the need for organised work in evangelism and building Baptist unity in the country. In its constitution of 1923, the goal of the Union was stated as being: to unite the Baptist Churches for proclaiming the Gospel of Jesus Christ, to represent them officially, to aid the discipleship process and help weaker churches grow.[175] That same year, Karl Grabein wrote: 'In a sense the union is primarily a Missionary Society.'[176] Besides evangelistic activities, there was a great deal of social action and practical Christian involvement planned. Some was already underway. The constitution spoke of how the union, for example, 'organised and supported a Baptist orphanage, an elderly people's home, a Diakonia home, and did every kind of benevolent work'.[177]

As we have seen, however, most of the activity depended on foreign support. Of great importance for Baptist work and arguably one of the main reasons behind Baptists in Bulgaria tripling in number between 1918 and 1939, was the partnership with the American GBGC. This partnership provided a much needed identity within the world body of Baptists. It brought financial support for ministries and churches. The mission among the Gypsies and the

---

[173] M. Kazanjieva, 'Pismo ot Plovdiv' (Letter from Plovdiv), *Evangelist* 7 (1926), p. 56.

[174] T. Dimitrov, 'V Zatvora' (In the Prison), *Evangelist* 5 (1926), pp. 38-39.

[175] *Constitution of the Union of Baptist Churches in Bulgaria* (Sofia, 1934), p. 2.

[176] K. Grabein, 'Naznachenieto Na Evangelskiat Baptistki Sauz I negovite Nujdi' (The Purpose of the Evangelical Baptist Union and Its Goals), *Evangelist* 1 (1923), p. 3.

[177] *Constitution of the Union of Baptist Churches*, p. 3.

social work of the Union were to benefit from it most. It also centralised efforts in evangelism and mission under a GBGC mission inspector who oversaw the ministry in Bulgaria. Much help was offered in building new church buildings and helping repair old ones. It also encouraged systematic Baptist teaching at conferences, congresses and in pastoral training.[178]

A 1922 GBGC report, translated by *Evangelist*, stated that the GBGC supported sixty-eight 'missionary workers' in nine countries—fifteen of them in Bulgaria.[179] At the conference of the Bulgarian Baptist Union in 1920, in Stara Zagora, the Baptists reported twenty-one churches with seven pastors and preachers, and a total membership of 280.[180] In 1922, apart from C.E. Petrick, the GBGC inspector ministering in Sofia, and the three other foreign individuals pastoring churches in Bulgaria, namely Grebein, Gerassimenko and Barba, the mission supported at least eleven other people, most probably Bulgarian nationals (Bulgarians and possible one or two Gypsies). Therefore, one can safely conclude that the GBGC was taking financial care of the entire Baptist pastoral leadership by the time. This substantial support was ensured for many years to come, reaching its peak in 1935, when twenty-two people were supported in Bulgaria alone.[181] Frequent visits of representatives of the GBGC were accompanied with preaching in churches, teaching at conferences, organising pastors' seminars. The connection was always close, and the theological influence undisputed.[182] The GBGC Secretary, William Kuhn, based in Chicago, visited Bulgaria on three occasions—in 1925, 1929 and 1938.[183] During his first visit, a Bulgarian Missionary Committee was set up in Bulgaria, with a view to strengthening the work of the churches.

As we have seen, the GBGC took an interest in the Gypsy work, which resulted in frequent visits to their villages—something considered a great sign of brotherly acceptance and love by the Gypsies themselves. The GBGC ensured support for four Gypsy pastors in the 1930s and developed social programmes.[184] The depth of that involvement is indicated by the words of Kuhn himself, spoken in 1940, when he described World War II as having created a desperate need in all of the 'Danubian Mission' fields:

---

[178] Editor, '15 Redoven Kongress na Evangelskiat Baptistki Sauiz' (Fifteenth Regular Congress of the Evangelical Baptist Union), *Evangelist* 9 (1927), pp. 3-5.

[179] A reprint of an article in *Sendbote*, a German Baptist periodical, under the title: 'Missiata v Evropa' (The Mission in Europe), *Evangelist* 3 (1923), p. 24.

[180] Z. Vidolov, 'Godishnata Baptistka Conferentsia v Stara Zagora' (The Annual Baptist Conference in Stara Zagora), *Evangelist* 1 (1920), pp. 5-8.

[181] F. Woyke, *Heritage and Ministry of the North American Baptist Conference*, (Oak Brook Terrace, Ill.: NABC, 1990), p. 309.

[182] P. Minkov, 'Karl Fulbrandt, Koi e toi?' (Karl Fulbrandt, Who is He?), *Evangelist* 7 (1925), p. 51.

[183] Wardin, 'The Baptists in Bulgaria', p. 152.

[184] Editor, '15 Redoven Kongress na Evangelskiat Baptistki Sauiz', p. 5.

From the Gypsy village, Golintzi, (Bulgaria), there will rise up one of the poorest of the poor, clothed in tattered garments and with a breaking heart, with his face turned toward us and thinking of us, their benefactors of earlier years, he will cry day and night in agony of spirit: 'Come over and help us!' He will not only speak for the Gypsies, but also for our brethren in all the Danubian countries. We shall not shirk this difficult task, because the Lord himself has committed it to us.[185]

Although social involvement was 'secondary to the preaching of the Gospel and the concern for personal salvation of the individual',[186] social work was nonetheless encouraged in *Evangelist* and here the leading edge belonged to the Women's Benevolent Societies, which were the local church women's groups. They organised fundraising 'sales' of handmade crafts and had special offerings.[187] Examples of their mission were evident in a support of a particular orphanage in Sofia over several years,[188] in helping Russian refugees and old people,[189] and the Diakonia ministry in Lom and Sofia, where 'hundreds of orphan children, widows, helpless old men and stooped old ladies were finding nutritious food, sisters' care and Christian love'.[190] *Evangelist* explained the theological convictions behind the social involvement of the Baptists:

Every real Christian will have to not only pray and preach for the Kingdom of God to come, but to commit himself in ministry of this Kingdom. For Christ, this ministry is so important, that according to His words, in the Judgment day he will check whether we have fed the hungry, gave water to the thirsty, cared for the sick and visited the prisoner...we should remember, that feeding the hungry is not simply giving them a piece of bread, but fighting for better economic conditions, so that they do not fall into hunger and misery.[191]

A major effort is visible on the pages of *Evangelist* in the fight against alcoholism and some other negative tendencies among 'others' in society. Influenced by American and Western European emphasis on abstention from

---

[185] As quoted in Woyke, *Heritage and Ministry of the North American Baptist Conference*, p. 311.

[186] P. Mishkov, 'Sotsialno Evangelie' (Social Gospel), *Evangelist* 5 (1935), p. 1.

[187] M. Kazanjieva, 'Kakvo Mogat da Storiat Jenite ot Edna Tsurkva?' (What Could the Women in One Church Do?), *Evangelist* 1 (1939), p. 13.

[188] Z. Furnadjeva, 'Daite im Vie da Iadat' (You Give Them to Eat), *Evangelist* 8 (1923), p. 5, and Editor, 'Svobodna Tribuna' (Free Tribune), *Evangelist* 1 (1926), p. 8.

[189] Editor, 'Vesti I Belejki' (News and Notes), *Evangelist* 13-15 (1924), p. 8.

[190] Editor, 'Dobre Doshla Sestra Ioanna v Bulgaria' (Welcome Sister Ioanna to Bulgaria), *Evangelist* 6 (1931), pp. 3-4. see also, T. Dimitrov, 'Diakonissenheim "Tabea", Milosurdbiat Dom "Tavita' (The Diakonia Home "Tabea"), *Evangelist* 10 (1927), p. 7.

[191] K. Grabein, 'Bojieto Tsarstvo I Sotsialnite Vuprosi' (God's Kingdom and the Social Issues), *Evangelist* 3 (1935), pp. 5-6.

alcohol, many Bulgarian churches organized their Abstention Societies, which in most cases comprised the youth groups in the churches. Youth abstention gatherings and mass demonstrations in front of pubs and restaurants were organised, often resulting in clashes with the pub owners.[192] Books and leaflets against alcohol and tobacco were printed and distributed. Over fifty articles in *Evangelist* were dedicated to anti-alcohol propaganda. Serious warnings were directed against Christians drinking alcohol, and those who produced brandy; both were considered 'sinners' in the eyes of God.[193] Baptists emphasised the personal example of purity and abstention from alcohol,[194] smoking,[195] dancing,[196] going to the theatre[197] and wearing 'liberated' dresses.[198] There was also a fight for anti-alcohol awareness in schools, and in favour of State laws against selling alcohol, or importing and exporting alcoholic drinks.[199] The Baptist believer of 1910-1940 was a teetotal campaigner. As a result of that, and of the pietism in Communist times, the Bulgarian Baptist community today is one-hundred percent anti-smoking and mostly teetotal.

Their missionary efforts and their rejection of the beliefs of the main religious 'other'—the Orthodox Church—brought Bulgarian Baptists into stormy relations with the Orthodox majority in the country. The entire history of the Baptist movement was marked by struggles with Orthodoxy: in *Evangelist*, over forty different conflicts are noted.[200] There were two disputations between Orthodox priests and Baptist leaders, the first of which ended with pastors being beaten in the village of Kostenets, central Bulgaria, in 1920.[201] Baptist understanding of the Bible as their sole authority was in a

---

[192] See for example, G. Pantev, 'Otvoreno Pismo do Vidinskiat "Democrat", "Sgovor" I "Svet"' (An Open Letter to *the editors of newspapers* "Vidinski Demokrat", "Sgovor" and "Svet"), *Evangelist* 7 (1926), p. 56.

[193] Editor, 'Moje li Evangelista da Proizvejda, Upotrebiava ili Prodava Spirtni Pitieta?' (Is the Evangelical allowed to Produce, Use and Sell Alcoholic Beverages?), *Evangelist* 11 (1924), p. 2. see also G.M. Chomonev 'Varenie Rakia' (Distilling Brandy), *Evangelist* 2 (1926), p. 15.

[194] T. Dinitrov, 'Kogato e Trezven' (When He Is Sober), *Evangelist* 5-6 (1932), p. 8.

[195] J. Popov, 'Vuzdurjanie' (Abstention), *Evangelist* 8 (1938), pp. 3-4.

[196] Editor, 'Nova Voina' (New War), *Evangelist* 8 (1925), p. 63.

[197] V. Chakalov, 'Kude e Gniloto?' (Where Is The Rotten Part?), *Evangelist* 8-9 (1931), p. 2.

[198] Editor, 'Borba s Diculetata' (Battle With the Low Neck-line), *Evangelist* 9 (1925), p. 72.

[199] T. Popov, 'Resolutsia na Drujestvata za Borba s Alkohola v Bulgaria' (Resolution of the Societies for the Fight Against Alcohol in Bulgaria), *Evangelist* 4 (1922), pp. 5-7.

[200] See for example: *Evangelist* 12 (1926), pp. 94-97; 1 (1928), pp. 2, 11; 1-2 (1933), p. 19.

[201] See T. Oprenov, 'Baptists and the Orthodox Church: The "Kostenets" Disputes of 1920 in Bulgaria', *Journal of European Baptist Studies* 4:3 (2004), pp. 33-47.

conflict with the emphasis by the Orthodox on Holy Tradition.[202] Baptists challenged the 'gate-keeping' responsibilities given to Orthodox priests, some of whom admitted: 'We call ourselves Christians, but we do not know much about Christian teaching, we are totally passive and far away from it. We just do our job for the money. We do not even pray...'[203] Evangelical worship was in the mother tongue of the listeners, while the Orthodox liturgy was in old Slavonic, was mystical and lacked verbal address to the people. The many rituals the Orthodox priest performed for money, such as prayers for the dead or sanctifying buildings and animals, were all rejected by Baptists. A major point of conflict was Orthodox prayers for the dead. Baptists were convinced that there was no second chance of salvation after death, 'otherwise, what need would anyone have to repent now, if he had a chance of that after death?'[204] The Orthodox response was to refuse burial places for Baptists in 'Orthodox ground' cemeteries.[205]

Pastor Trifon Dimitrov, one of the most outspoken Baptist pastors on Orthodox-Baptist relations, stated,

> The Orthodox Church is totally lost in endless liturgies, Byzantine deception and needless rituals, which all rob the pockets of the poor followers. The priesthood is only concerned with rites: holy water sprinkling, reading 'mystical' words on the tummies of pregnant women, marriages of dead virgins... prayers for the souls in purgatory, levelling graves for blessings and pointless (to the participant) baptism of infants. The priests have lost their primary objective in preaching the message of salvation...[206]

From the Orthodox side, Baptists were often referred to as 'secret gravediggers of Bulgaria and our native church',[207] 'creeping grasshoppers and spitting flies'[208] or simply 'dangerous sectarians'.[209] One of the main

---

[202] Z. Vldolov, 'Gonenieto na Evangelistite v Kostenets' (The Persecution of the Evangelicals in Kostenets), *Evangelist* 4 (1920), p. 7.

[203] F. Shashko, B. Greenberg, R. Genov, *American Travel Notes for Bulgaria During the XIX Century*, p. 47.

[204] T. Dimitrov, 'Otvoreno Pismo do Redaktsiata na Tsurkoven Vestnik', (An Open Letter to the Editor of the Orthodox Newspaper), *Evangelist* 8-9 (1928), pp. 13, 14.

[205] For example in Kazanluck, in 1871, when Kurdov's wife's died, her body stayed for three days 'waiting for permission' to be buried and ending up outside of the graveyards. See P. Kirkilanov, 'Kratka Istoriya na Evangelskata Baptistska Tsurkva v Grad Kazanluck' (A Short History of the Evangelical Baptist church in the Town of Kazanluck), *Evangelist* 5 (1924), p. 2, and T. Dimitrov, 'Is Dnevnika na Edin Koito ne Pishe Dnevnik' (The Diary of a Person that has no Diary), *Evangelist* 7 (1934), pp. 4-8.

[206] T. Dimitrov, 'Istinata' (The Truth), *Evangelist* 10 (1926), pp. 75-77.

[207] P. Angelov, 'Svobodna Tribuna' (Free Tribune), *Evangelist* 3 (1926), p. 23.

[208] Editor, 'Sectants in Russe' (Sectants in Russe), *Evangelist* 5 (1926), p. 38.

[209] T. Dimitrov, 'Baptistite ne sa Secta' (The Baptists are not a Sect), *Evangelist* 2 (1938), p. 2.

accusations against the Baptists was that of being 'bought by American dollars', referring to the support that the pastors were receiving from abroad.[210] It is interesting that this accusation against the pastors, of being 'Western spies', was to be the main political point of incrimination in the Pastoral trials arranged by the Communists to discredit the churches and imprison leaders in 1949.

The Baptist view of the State was two-fold. First, Baptists claimed that the State was God's provision for a nation and the government was allowed and installed by God. The State, however, was of 'this world' and the Church belonged to the 'coming Kingdom of God'.[211] They refused to take an 'oath' before the State.[212] Being faithful to one's nation and State, however, was of important for Baptists. Although a desire for world peace is clear in *Evangelist*,[213] Baptist believers were willing to take part in the wars for national independence, and in WWI.[214] However, membership of political parties and being politically active were viewed negatively. They believed that the Church had different means through which to bring the Kingdom of Christ about, 'not like those lying politicians in the Bulgarian parliament, or the members of the communist party, who saw freedom in term of killing the opposition'.[215]

Second, they called for separation of church and state. This was in accordance with the wider Baptist movement in England and America. More importantly, the reality in Bulgaria was always that of a State-Orthodox Church connection which elevated the national church almost to the level of a 'State Church'. The priests' salaries were paid by the state, and laws placing the Orthodox in a privileged position were easily passed. In ninety percent of the instances of confrontation with the Orthodox Church, the state would defend Orthodoxy and restrain Baptists. A clear example, among many told in *Evangelist,* is the story of the youth group in Sofia, in 1926, when they visited a city hospital to deliver tracts and help the sick:

---

[210] See *Evangelist* 2 (1926), pp. 13-14; 10 (1926), p. 82.

[211] Editor, 'Durjava I Narod' (State and Nation), *Evangelist* 6 (1931), p. 11.

[212] Two cases are mentioned. One in terms of taking an oath in a court situation, when the Baptist was dismissed as a member of the jury after refusing to take an oath. (*Evangelist* 1 (1926), p. 8) The other, in terms of a Gypsy boy, who was forced to take an oath in the Kings Army after being threatened with imprisonment. (*Evangelist* 7 (1931), p. 12). In both cases, there was an argument about being faithful to Jesus' words in the Gospel—Matthew 5:34.

[213] See *Evangelist* 1 (1923), p. 1; 5-6 (1925), p. 37; and 8-9 (1931), pp. 4, 15.

[214] V. Marchev, 'Deiatelnostta na Even. Bapt. Tsurkva v Sofia prez Balkanskata i Obshtoevropeiskite Voini, 1912-1918', (The Activity of the Evangelical Baptist Church during the Balkan and All-European Wars, 1912-1918), *Evangelist* 3 (1920), pp. 13, 14; 1 (1921), pp. 3-8.

[215] Editor, 'Predi Vsichko i Nad Vsichko e Evangelieto' (Before Anything and Above All is the Gospel), *Evangelist* 11 (1927), p. 1.

When the priest saw us giving brochures to sick patients, he lifted up his walking stick, ran toward us and shouted: 'Schismatics! You have come to steal the fruit of my garden!' Then immediately he called the hospital guard, who brought two policemen and a detective with him and we were promptly arrested and brought to the local police station. There, we were beaten...with the literature being confiscated from us. Finally, we were reluctantly released, without our books, and with a clear warning: 'The hospital is Orthodox! You have no right to preach there!'[216]

The Constitution of Bulgaria of 1879 guaranteed religious freedom by its statement that 'people who hold non-Orthodox convictions...and other faiths...have complete freedom in their beliefs and practices as long as the latter are not in breach of the existing laws of the Kingdom'.[217] However, the common understanding was that every religious teaching which 'opposed the ruling religion' in the country was dangerous for the state, because it was 'killing the national identity', and 'preparing the soil for spreading unrest'.[218] The answer of the Baptists could be seen in their stating that they:

protest and will continue to protest against the exploitation of the superstition of the people by Orthodoxy, and will fight for waking up the spiritually sleeping souls to eternal life in Christ. This is unifying, not dividing, because this is what real Christianity is all about.[219]

Against this background of Orthodoxy backed up by the state, many theological beliefs of Baptists crystallised: the fight for religious freedom; separation of Church and State; true and meaningful Baptist identity; 'faith alone' as the basis for salvation, and 'Scripture alone' as the basis for instructions for life.

Bulgarian Baptist Theology in the Making: Internal Convictions, External Influences

Evangelist gave a 'face' to the Baptist community in Bulgaria. During the period 1920-1939, it represented the Baptist presence in the country by presenting a platform for evangelical theological views, stating the case against

---

[216] T. Dimitrov, 'Edno pricluchenie na Christianskata Spasitelna Drujina v Sofia' (An Adventure of the Evangelistic Christian Group in Sofia), *Evangelist* 11 (1926), pp. 82, 83.

[217] *Constitution of the Bulgarian Kingdom* (Turnovo, 1879), chs. 40, 41.

[218] As a leading newspaper *Razgradski Novini* (Razgrad News), once described it; quoted by *Evangelist* 8 (1930), pp. 11-12.

[219] P. Minkov, 'Zadachi na Bulgarskiat Evangelism' (Tasks of Bulgarian Evangelism), *Evangelist* 1-2 (1925), pp. 3, 4.

limitations of religious freedom, giving historical data that helped to shape Baptist identity and offering evangelistic teaching. Through its pages Baptists could 'speak', but could also 'hear' one another. They could share what they believed in and discuss Baptist teaching. They could encourage each other and also proclaim to outsiders what they held dear. The number of copies of *Evangelist* was always higher than the number of Baptist believers in the country. For example, in 1920, *Evangelist* started with nine-hundred copies whereas in the country there were only roughly 280 Baptists. Similarly, in 1939, the fifteen-hundred copies produced were distributed far beyond the seven-hundred homes of Baptist believers.[220] Thus, the theology and history expressed in it informed people beyond Baptist circles about who the Baptists were.

There are, however, several pressing questions. For example: how much was the theology expressed in *Evangelist* actually the theology of all Bulgarian Baptist churches? This question is difficult to answer since besides *Evangelist* one can find only very few Baptist sources—mainly translations of sermons written by foreign preachers and teachers. Looking at *Evangelist*, however, we can see that key Baptist leaders were the main Bulgarian authors of articles: Trifon Dimitrov, editor of most of the issues, Vasil Chakalov, another editor and president of the Baptist Union for a few years, Karl Grabein, one of the most influential pastors and teachers in central Bulgaria, and Vassil Marchev, probably the first trained Bulgarian pastor in the history of Baptists in the country. These, together with Peter Kirlkilanov in Kazanluck, were also the main translators of outside sources. Those people, under whose leadership the Union developed during one of the most crucial periods of its history, obviously had very good access to outside periodicals in German and English, sermons of prominent international preachers and theological institutions and key leaders of influential Baptist communities outside Bulgaria. Together with a few other leaders of the Baptist Union, all pastors and leaders of individual churches, they played a decisive role in shaping the theology of the publication, and since this was the only centralised theological source of information, they determined theological thinking for the entire Union. Through the means of the publication, these views were widely circulated, and, given the number of copies of *Evangelist* printed, they were widely accepted and treated as theological and practical guidelines by most, if not all the churches and individual believers.

A second issue is that of the extent of development of theological beliefs. One cannot help but notice through the 'window' of *Evangelist* that Bulgarian Baptist theology was never developed to the extent that there was a determined set of convictions. Bulgarian Baptists never believed in set confessions of faith

---

[220] Angelova, *Periodicals of the Protestant Churches*, p. 8.

that were agreed upon by all the members.[221] There was, however, a desire to be united by common Baptist beliefs for the sake of identity and unity, leading to some lists of Baptist convictions being expressed.[222] At the same time, there was the recognition of freedom of interpretation of the Scriptures under the leadership of the Holy Spirit as a privilege given to both the individual believer and the local church. There is little indication of a quest for a systematic approach to theology. For instance, we have no clear picture of what Baptists believed about God, apart from the general conviction of his existence, his being the Creator and his redemptive work in his Son. Similarly, the whole eschatological dimension was limited to a warning to the Christian to be prepared for Christ's return; there was no serious treatment of the book of Revelation for example. None of the Baptist Union constitutions or organisational guides ever had a section with Baptist convictions listed.

Many theological issues and doctrines we see treated in *Evangelist* were prompted by tensions, practical needs and real questions in the lives of believers and churches. This was the case with the treatment of subjects such as 'prayers for the dead', prompted by the clash with Orthodox teaching on the subject, and the 'gifts of the Spirit', prompted by the appearance of the Pentecostal teaching and experience. It is interesting to note the influence of the area of experience in a theology of the Christian life. An expectation of 'how one might go through the experience' of being born again was predetermined. This was so much the case that people who did not have the experience 'in the same way' were considered as 'people who never truly had it'. This tradition dominated the years of Communism, and was strong until the first years of democratic changes after 1989.[223] Baptist theology, springing out of its roots, was always a theology-in-the-making. The lack of a full set of Baptist convictions was a disadvantage in seeking to portray the full theological identity of Baptist believers, and there could be rigidity in practice, but to some extent at least Baptists were open and free to deal with the practical issues in their lives.

Yet there were strong outside influences. Bulgarian Baptist convictions reflected the theological convictions of the founding organisations, the theological systematic thinking of some of the leading Baptist colleges and seminaries in Europe and America, and the particularities of church life and

---

[221] G. Vassov, 'Bibleiskata Osnova na Nasheto Viarvane i Izpoviadvane' (The Biblical Foundation of Our Faith and Confession), *Evangelist* 9 (1938), p. 9.

[222] Ibid., p. 8.

[223] In one of my research interviews in 1999, I heard an 'all too familiar' story of a man who went to a Baptist deacon to share his excitement of being sure about Jesus' saving work on the cross for him. He was coldly met with the words: 'Tell me how it happened, and I will tell you whether it was a genuine conversion.' After hearing his story, the deacon declared him 'not saved' since he had missed two of the 'official' steps. I personally had a similar experience in 1986.

organisation of the Baptist communities abroad. That subjected them to a strong theological influence, but built their Baptist identity. Throughout the period of the production of *Evangelist*, the majority of articles containing teaching on biblical doctrines and theological practices were by non-Bulgarian teachers, preachers and spiritual leaders.[224] Bulgarian authors were mainly writing evangelistic sermons, criticising the religious stance of other religious groups, or reporting on special events. In the few cases when Bulgarians were discussing theological doctrines, they were usually quoting and explaining the theological views of foreign authors. The fact that there was no organised (seminary) theological training in Bulgaria for leaders, and (disappointingly) no vision about that, shows that at the time the Baptists in Bulgaria were very much dependent on outside theological thinking. *Evangelist* did very little to encourage independent Bulgarian Baptist theological research. The publication failed to address some of the pressing theological challenges of the times, such as the Communistic ideology which was undermining the foundations of Christianity.

There is no doubt that the Baptist movement in Bulgaria owed much to the wholehearted support of foreign missions, such as the German Baptist General Conference in the USA, the British and Foreign Bible Society and the German Baptist Union, to mention the most influential ones. One cannot miss the very positive role these partnerships played in the theological formation of Bulgarian beliefs and mission expansion. Their role in the growth of the churches is undisputed. However, it should also be noted that some of the unavoidable results that the many years of support brought were: a weak (under-developed) theology of giving and personal sacrifices for mission; the lack of a key theological strategy for building up self-supporting churches; and the lack of financial commitment to their national movement through the Baptist Union. Most of the committees and union initiatives were formed and undertaken only after 'funds were available' or 'missionaries had been sent', rather than through the vision being developed and then backed up with financial support. This was definitely the case with the Bulgarian Missionary Committee, which was apparently not formed as a result of a vision, but to supervise and to report about mission to an outside mission agency.[225] A similar situation could be noted with the development of the Diakonia ministry, which was entirely established and operated through foreign support and guidance.[226]

Another key area of practical expression of the Christian faith, again dominated by the Western Baptist tradition, was that of church worship and

---

[224] Editor, 'Organizatsia na Mestnata Tsurkva' (Organisation of the Local Church), *Evangelist* 2 (1931), pp. 7-9.

[225] See Editor, '15 Redoven Kongress na Evangelskiat Baptistki Sauz' (Fifteenth Regular Congress of the Evangelical Baptist Union), *Evangelist* 9 (1927), pp. 3-5.

[226] T. Dimitrov, 'Diakonissenheim "Tabea", Milosurdbiat Dom "Tavita"' (Diakonia Home 'Tabea'), *Evangelist* 10 (1927), p. 7.

patterns of music and singing in the church. So strong was the early dependence on Western worship music, that even today, 120 years later, ninety-five percent of our songs in the churches are translations of the evangelical songs of Western churches. The general characteristics of the Bulgarian sociological particularities of character were never employed to work for the shaping of church life and the cause of the Gospel. The naturally hospitable, friendly and socialising Bulgarians were taught to separate in enclosed communities, to dislike their national traditions such as national Bulgarian dancing and some family social events, and they were told to stand up, often quite unnecessarily against their own culture and background. The 'purity' of the Gospel of faith in Christ was clothed in an unsuitable way for Bulgarians.

Related to this challenge of how to be Bulgarian was the Baptist relationship to the Orthodox Church and its theology. One can understand the natural reaction to the sharp antagonism of Orthodoxy against the new Baptist movement that undermined its power, authority and even income. However, to what extent was the Baptist view justified that the Orthodox Church was dead, nominal, and untrue to the Gospel, reason and history?[227] Was this the only possible theological conclusion that Bulgarian Baptists could reach? Was it not to a degree an unhelpful projection of the historical Baptist struggles with national and state churches in the countries where the Baptist movement came from, before the beginnings in Bulgaria? One cannot see much evidence in Baptist theological thinking of a sincere desire for cooperation or any kind of a dialogue with Orthodoxy. In Baptist rejection of Orthodox practices, there was no research into Orthodox theology through reading Orthodox theological books. That was how a vast area of spirituality and symbolism, which was by no means in opposition to the message of the New Testament, was completely missed by Baptists. This is true for the entire history of the Baptist movement in Bulgaria up until today.

And finally, there are questions about the influence of the theological convictions of *Evangelist* upon the theology and practice of the Baptist churches in Bulgaria during the communist years, 1945-1989, and after the democratic changes from 1990 onwards. This is not the focus of this study, but some lines of thought are important. With the Communist system fully in place by 1948, the Baptist churches were cut off from the rest of the world. Their leadership was arrested in 1949 and the most influential pastors and union leaders were sent to prison and concentration camps for a good part of the next decade. Deprived of even a Bible, forbidden to take their children to church, often experiencing fear and a lack of trust of each other, and with a real danger of losing jobs, freedom and even life—this was the everyday life of the Baptist believer, especially in the 1950-1960s.[228] Very little, if any, written material can

---

[227] *Evangelist* 4 (1920), p. 7.
[228] Wardin, 'The Baptists in Bulgaria', pp. 153-155.

be discovered about that period, and there are very few people left who remember the times. The impression is of a very legalistic but basically unchanged theology, much as described in *Evangelist*. The freedom of expressing one's convictions was lost, but the basic Baptist principles of salvation by faith and experiencing a personal conversion were kept intact. Believers were not afraid to stand up for their faith and be baptised, although baptisms were performed secretly. The Word of God was possessed at great risk and diligently memorised.[229] In this situation the churches addressed such issues as: Jesus' second coming (believing it was close); suffering for Christ (as an inevitable part of Christian life); and the total impossibility of changing anything (as far as politics and social life were concerned). In terms of changes in internal practice, there was a softening in the style of addressing problems in the church, financial giving was not encouraged as the finances of the church were in effect under the atheistic state, and there was a concern to ensure that the State had as little access as possible to church affairs—affairs that it always wished to control.[230]

The sudden changes of 1989, which put an end to Communist rule, allowed the churches to regain much of their 'political' freedom. This new period in the religious history of the nation saw some renewed clashes between Baptists and Orthodoxy. It also allowed the Baptists for the first time in their history to experience full freedom of theological expression, development and research. The theology of the Bulgarian Baptist churches today owes its entire foundation to the convictions shaped before the Communist time. Among them are: a strong emphasis on the Word of God; a high Christology and a theology of salvation by faith in the redemptive work of God in Christ; a commitment to believer's baptism by immersion; an ecclesiology based on voluntary membership; and a vigorous evangelism. A continuation of the mission that was undertaken before WWII still includes people of all nationalities and is now strengthened by the opportunity to stand openly for freedom of conscience and belief, human rights, and the total separation of Church and State—all of which are deeply rooted in Baptist theology and were lived out from the time of the beginning of the Baptist movement.

---

[229] T. Angelov, 'The Baptist Movement in Bulgaria', p. 16.

[230] That law required official registration, but many groups preferred to remain underground communities for security reasons. Sofia Baptist Church, for example, one of the biggest churches in the country, became an underground community when the secret police installed a communist agent as pastor of the church in 1985. The people left the building and started meeting in secret places at great personal, family and community cost. (As witnessed by the author of this study).

Conclusion

It is important to be able to look through windows such as *Evangelist* to see, over a period of years, the development and life of Christian communities. Contemporary Baptists are very much indebted to those that published it, and to those that kept copies at home at great personal risk over the years of persecution. The sacrifice of the latter believers is probably the greatest sign of how important they viewed this window to be. For them, *Evangelist* was also a mirror, by which one could check one's true identity, shape one's theology and encourage oneself by looking at priorities in life and ministry.

Undoubtedly Bulgarian Baptist theology as portrayed in *Evangelist* was strongly dependent on outside sources, principally the German-speaking founders of the Baptist movement in the country and the assisting agencies of the BFBS and the GBGC. It was also a theology that was shaped and often provoked by a dominant Bulgarian Orthodox reality, with its challenge to Baptist identity and theological convictions. Bulgarian Baptist thinking reflected the common Baptist emphasis on personal experience of Christ and the foundational character of the Scriptures as the only guidelines for faith and life. The practices in Bulgaria, springing out of Baptist beliefs, followed Western Baptist emphases to a large extent, but were nevertheless developed in the context of contact with other religious groups in Bulgaria. The faith issues were tested and clarified against a background of open persecution and religious and political intolerance toward the Baptist movement.

Yet the picture is not complete. The present attempt to trace the roots of the theological convictions of Bulgarian Baptists can be expanded. Further research should investigate to what extent the Baptist movement in Bulgaria was a planned mission by Western agencies and to what extent it appeared without being strategically started. Further research is also in order now to investigate the theological relationships between the colporteurs of the BFBS, the German-speaking missionaries and the Bulgarian nationals in their effort to spread the Gospel in Bulgaria. One could ask whether the interests of the powerful foreign agencies, the missionary organizations and the Bulgarian leaders really matched each other, or were there points of contention, and what did that imply for the theology of mission, evangelism and church-planting?

The years of Communism, which followed the time of *Evangelist* in 1920-1939, when the Church went into survival mode, present a challenge for research in the years to come. As already stated, almost no church records are available and very little is known about the period as far as theology is concerned. Looking at the Baptist churches today, we cannot overestimate the continuing influence of the doctrines and practices affirmed in the period before WWII. Although the very existence of the churches was threatened during

Communism, very few of the early convictions were seriously challenged and even fewer were altered to accommodate the survival mode of the Church. What the dynamics of that process really were is still to be uncovered.

Finally, the weaker points of Baptist theology and practice in relation to issues like unhelpful dependency on outside sources, a strong anti-Orthodox understanding, some limitation of freedom of expression and experience, and the lack of a systematic approach to theology, will all have to be re-visited in thinking about contemporary theology and practice in the Baptist churches today.

Bibliography

Primary Sources

Angelov, P., 'Svobodna Tribuna' (Free Tribune), *Evangelist* 3 (1926), pp. 23-24.
Chakalov, V., 'Dve Skupi Imena' (Two Precious Names), *Evangelist* 4, (1928), pp. 6-7.
_____, 'Iz Jivota na Tsurkvite', (Reports From the Churches), *Evangelist* 9-10, (1932), pp. 13,14.
_____, 'Kude e Gniloto?', (Where is the Rotten Part?), *Evangelist* 8-9, (1931), p. 2.
Chomonev G. M., 'Varenie Rakia', (Distilling Brandy), *Evangelist* 2, (1926), p. 15.
_____, 'Poiaviavaneto na Baptisma v Bulgaria', (The Appearance of Baptists in Bulgaria), *Evangelist* 2, (1920), pp. 1-5.
Chomonev, V., 'Evangelist da Stabilizira Rabotata Ni', (*Evangelist* Should Stabilise Our Work), *Evangelist* 4, (1933), p. 12.
_____, 'Shto e Blagovestie?', (What is Sharing the Good News?), *Evangelist* 1-2, (1933), p. 6.
_____, 'Oshte Neshto za Krushtenieto', (More About Water Baptism), *Evangelist*, 10, (1925), pp. 75-76.
Dimitrov, T., 'Baptistite Ne Sa Secta', (The Baptists are not a Sect), *Evangelist* 2, (1938), pp. 1, 2, 15.
_____, 'Bog i Zemetreseniata', (God and the Earthquakes), *Evangelist* 5, (1928), pp. 3,4.
_____, 'Diakonissenheim 'Tabea', Milosurdbiat Dom 'Tavita'', (The Mission House 'Tabea'), *Evangelist* 10, (1927), p. 7.
_____, 'Duhovno Probujdane', (Spiritual Awakening), *Evangelist* 6-7, (1937), pp. 3-5.
_____, 'Edna Neinteresna Obikolka s Interesni Sluchki', (One Uninteresting Journey, with Interesting Events), *Evangelist* 4, (1933), pp. 4-10; 5, (1933), pp. 4-10.
_____, 'Edno Pricluchenie na Christianskata Spasitelna Drujina v Sofia', (An Adventure of the Evangelistic Christian Group in Sofia), *Evangelist* 11, (1926), pp. 82-83.
_____, 'Is Dnevnika na Edin Koito ne Pishe Dnevnik', (The Diary of a Person that has no Diary), *Evangelist* 7, (1934), pp. 4-8.
_____, 'Istinata', (Truth), *Evangelist* 10, (1926), pp. 75-77.
_____, 'Kogato e Trezven', (When He is Sober), *Evangelist* 5-6, (1932), p. 8.
_____, 'Kradenoto Evangelie', (The Stolen Gospel), *Evangelist* 6, (1924), pp. 2-3.
_____, 'Nadmennost v Molitvite Ni', (Haughtiness in Prayer), *Evangelist* 12, (1924), pp. 4,5.

_____, 'Novoto Suzdanie', (The New Creation), *Evangelist* 8-9, (1928), pp. 5-8.

_____, 'Otvoreno Pismo do Redaktsiata na Tsurkoven Vestnik', (Open Letter to the Editor of 'Church Newspaper'), *Evangelist* 8-9, (1928), pp. 13-14.

_____, 'Putia na Lujata', (The Way of the Lie), *Evangelist* 1-2, (1937), p. 4-5.

_____, 'V Zatvora', (In Prison), *Evangelist* 5, (1926), pp. 38-39.

Editor, '15 Redoven Kongress na Evangelskiat Baptistki Sauiz', (Fifteenth Regular Congress of the Evangelical Baptist Union), *Evangelist* 9, (1927), pp. 3-5.

_____, 'Borba s Dicultetata', (Battle with the Low Neck-line), *Evangelist* 9, (1925), p. 72.

_____, 'Tsurkvata na Hristos', (Church of Christ), *Evangelist* 5, (1929), pp. 6-8.

_____, 'Declaratsia na Vsesvetskia Baptistki Sauz Kum Baptistkoto Bratstvo', (Declaration of the Baptist World Alliance to the Worldwide Brotherhood), *Evangelist* 7, (1923), pp. 1-7.

_____, 'Dobre Doshla Sestra Ioanna v Bulgaria', (Welcome Sister Ioanna to Bulgaria), *Evangelist* 6, (1931), pp. 3-4.

_____, 'Durjava I Narod', (State and Nation), *Evangelist* 6, (1931), p. 11.

_____, 'Dva Puti Rajdane', (Twice-Born), *Evangelist* 1, (1931), p. 7.

_____, 'Godishna Pastirska Conferentsia v Stara Zagora', (Annual Pastoral Conference in Stara Zagora), *Evangelist* 1, (1920), p. 7.

_____, 'Gospodnata Vecheria', (The Lord's Supper), *Evangelist* 6, (1931), p. 2.

_____, 'Iskash li da ozdraveesh?', (Do You Want to be Healed?), *Evangelist* 2, (1928), pp. 11,12.

_____, 'Izpitvaite Pisaniata', (Examine the Scriptures), *Evangelist* 5, (1931), p. 2.

_____, 'Missiata v Evropa', (The Mission in Europe), *Evangelist* 3, (1923), p. 24.

_____, 'Moje li Evangelista da Proizvejda, Upotrebiava ili Prodava Spirtni Pitieta?', (Is the Evangelical Allowed to Produce, Use and Sell Alcoholic Beverages?), *Evangelist* 11, (1924), p. 2.

_____, 'Nova Voina', (New War), *Evangelist* 8, (1925), p. 63.

_____, 'Okrujno N54, 23 Nov, (1921)', (Circular N54, 23 Nov, 1921), *Evangelist* 1, (1922), p. 15.

_____, 'Organizatsia na Mestnata Tsurkva', (Organisation of the Local Church), *Evangelist* 2, (1931), pp.7-9.

_____, 'Predi Vsichko i Nad Vsichko e Evangelieto', (Before Anything and Above Everything is the Gospel), *Evangelist* 11, (1927), pp. 1,11.

_____, 'Purviat Diakoniiski Dom V Bulgaria', (The First Diakonia Home in Bulgaria), *Evangelist* 1, (1939), pp. 11-12.

_____, 'Sectants in Russe', (Sectants in Russe), *Evangelist* 5, (1926), pp. 38-39.

_____, 'Shto e Pokaianie?', (What is Repentance?), *Evangelist* 3, (1929), pp. 2-4.

_____, 'Svobodna Tribuna', (Free Tribune), *Evangelist* 1, (1926), p. 8.

_____, 'V Kakvo Se Sustoi Nadejdata na Tsurkvata', (What Constitutes the Hope of the Church?), *Evangelist* 3, (1921), p. 10.
_____, 'Vesti I Belejki', (News and Notes), *Evangelist* 13-15, (1924), p. 8.
_____, 'Za mladeji', (For Young People), *Evagelist*, 8, (1925), p. 61.
_____, 'Zadachata na Bojiite Chada', (The Task Before the Children of God), *Evangelist* 2, (1931), p. 4.
Fortunov, P., 'Skromno ala Surdechno', (Humble, but Wholehearted), *Evangelist* 3, (1938), pp. 8-13.
Furnadjeva, Z., 'Daite im Vie da Iadat', (You Give Them to Eat), *Evangelist* 8, (1923), p. 5.
Georgiev, A., 'Spassen Li Si?', (Are You Saved?), *Evangelist* 2, (1938), pp. 5-6.
_____, 'Tsurkvata na Hrista', (The Church of Christ), *Evangelist* 8-9, (1931), pp. 5-6.
_____, 'Vreme e Da Se Sabudim', (It is Time to Wake Up), *Evangelist* 8-9, (1924), p. 3.
Grabein, K., 'Bojieto Tsarstvo i Sotsialnite Vuprosi', (The Kingdom of God and the Social Issues), *Evangelist* 3, (1935), pp. 5-6.
_____, 'Chistota i Sviatost', (Purity and Holiness), *Evangelist* 1-2, (1925), pp. 9-14.
_____, 'Hristovoto Pismo', (Christ's Letter), *Evangelist* 9, (1925), pp. 66-67.
_____, 'Naznachenieto Na Evangelskiat Baptistki Sauz I Negovite Nujdi', (The Goals of the Evangelical Baptist Union and its Needs), *Evangelist* 1, (1923), pp. 3-4.
_____, 'Niama da go Izpudia!', (I Will Not Drive Him Out), *Evangelist* 4-5, (1937), pp. 10-11.
_____, 'Petdesiatnitsa', (Pentecost), *Evangelist* 6, (1926), p. 45.
_____, 'Vzemi!', (Take!), *Evangelist* 5, (1926), p. 35.
Hardy, E., 'Shtastieto v Braka', (Happiness in Marriage), *Evangelist* 3, (1930), pp. 6-7.
Hristova, D., 'Proletta na Duhovniat mi Jivot', (The Spring of My Spiritual Life), *Evangelist* 4, (1927), pp. 9,10.
Igov, I., 'Nashata Radost v Sofia', (Our Joy in Sofia), *Evangelist* 8, (1932), p. 8.
Karev, A., 'Krushtenie po Viara—Propoved Jum Krushtavashtite Se', (A Baptism By Faith—A Sermon to the Ones Being Baptised), *Evangelist* 5-6, (1927), pp. 11-13.
Kargel, I., 'Ploda na Duha', (The Fruit of the Spirit), *Evangelist* 6, (1929), pp. 4-6.
Kazanjiev, I., 'Znachenieto na Nedelnoto Uchilishte', (The Purpose of the Sunday School), *Evangelist* 11, (1927), p. 7.
Kazanjieva, M., 'Edna Obikolka', (One Missionary Trip), *Evangelist* 8-9, (1928), pp. 9-13.
_____, 'I Slovoto Stana Plut i Se Vseli Mejdu Nas', (And the Word Became Flesh and Came to Dwell Among us), *Evangelist* 1, (1935), p. 4.
_____, 'Kakvo Mogat da Storiat Jenite ot Edna Tsurkva?', (What Could the Women in a Church Do?), *Evangelist* 1, (1939), p. 13.

_____, 'Rabotata Mejdu Mohamedanite', (Work Among the Muslims), *Evangelist* 5-6, (1932), pp. 4-5.
Kendall, I.M., 'Evangelskite Osnovania za Vervashtoto Krushtenie', (The Evangelical Foundations of Believer's Baptism), *Evangelist* 1, (1922), pp. 9-11.
Kirkilanov, P.T. 'Kratka Istoriya na Evangelskata Baptistska Tsurkva v Grad Kazanluck, (A Short History of the Evangelical Church in Kazanluck), *Evangelist* 9-10, (1923), pp. 5-8.; 1, (1924), pp. 2-5.; 5, (1924), pp. 2-4.; 6, (1924), pp. 2-3.; 8-9, (1924), pp. 4-6.
Komitski, G., 'Pismo Do Viarvasthite Jeni'. (A Letter to Believing Women), *Evangelist* 5, (1928), pp. 8-9.
Kovatcheva, R., 'Vuzpitatelnoto Deistvie na Religioznata Musica', (The Nurturing Effect of the Religious Music), *Evangelist* 6, (1939), pp. 14-15.
Krustev, H., 'Isus Pak Shte Doide', (Jesus Will Come Again), *Evangelist* 3, (1927), p. 8.
Kuhn, W., 'Ako Dvama ot Vas se Suglasiat za Neshto', (If Two of You Agree on Something), *Evangelist* 2, (1930), p. 7.
_____, 'Being Sealed with the Spirit', translated by K. Grabein, *Evangelist* 5, (1930), pp. 3-4.
_____, 'Kak Se Obiasniava Chudoto na Petdesiatnitsata?', (How Do We Explain the Miracle of Pentecost?), *Evangelist* 9, (1929), p. 10.
Kutuktchiev, E., 'Kakvo se Ochakva ot Mirianite?', (What Do We Expect From the Lay People?), *Evangelist* 6, (1926), pp. 46-48; 7, (1926), pp. 54-55.
Lechov, S., 'Brat Jacob Klundt', (Brother Jacob Klundt), *Evangelist* 2, (1921), pp. 1-4.
Marchev H., 'Prokazata na Greha', (The Leprosy of Sin), *Evangelist* 2, (1927), pp. 5-6.
_____, 'Za Molitvata', (About Prayer), *Evangelist* 3, (1926), p. 19.
Marchev, V., 'Deiatelnostta na Even. Bapt. Tsurkva v Sofia prez Balkanskata I Obshtoevropeiskite Voini (1912-1918)', (The Activity of the Evangelical Baptist Church during the Balkan and All-European Wars, 1912-1918), *Evangelist* 3, (1920), pp. 13,14; 1, (1921), pp. 3-8.
Michailov, H., 'Edna Tri-godishnina', (A Three Year Anniversary), *Evangelist* 2, (1931), p. 6.
Minkov, P., 'Karl Fullbrandt, Koi e Toi?', (Karl Fullbrandt, Who is He?), *Evangelist* 7, (1925), p. 51.
_____, 'Primernata Evangelska Tsurkva Dnes', (The Exemplary Baptist Church Today), *Evangelist* 7, (1927), pp. 4-6.
_____, 'Zadachi na Bulgarskiat Evangelism', (Tasks of Bulgarian Evangelism), *Evangelist* 1-2, (1925), pp. 3-4.
Mishkov, P., 'Kakvo e Evangelism?', (What is Evangelism?), *Evangelist* 6, (1935), pp. 1,2.
P., H., 'Istinskite Protestanti', (The Real Protestants), *Evangelist* 6-7, (1937), pp. 13-15.
Pantev, G., 'Otvoreno Pismo do 'Vidinskiat Democrat', 'Sgovor' I 'Svet'', (An Open Letter to the Editors of Newspapers 'Vidinski Demokrat', 'Sgovor' and 'Svet'), *Evangelist* 7, (1926) p. 56.

Pedersen, G., 'Otvoreno Pismo', (Open Letter), *Evangelist* 4, (1927), p. 2.
Popov, J., 'Vuzdurjanie', (Abstention), *Evangelist* 8, (1938), pp. 3-4.
Popov, M., 'Sushtnostta na Tsurkovnata Rabota', (The Essence of Church Work), *Evangelist* 12, (1927), pp. 2,11,12.
_____, 'Tselta na Stradaniata', (The Purpose of Suffering), *Evangelist* 11, (1925), p. 85.
Popov, T., 'Resolutsia na Drujestvata za Borba s Alkohola v Bulgaria', (Resolution of the Societies for the Fight Against Alcohol in Bulgaria), *Evangelist* 4, (1922), pp. 5-7.
Raichev, E., 'Tsurkovniat Kasier', (The Church Treasurer), *Evangelist* 4-5, (1937), pp. 11-13.
Spurgeon, C., 'Dobri Suveti Kum Propovednika', (Good Advice for the Preacher), *Evangelist* 5-6, (1927), pp. 7-8.
_____, 'Kogato Vidia Kruvta, Shte Otmina', (When I see the blood, I will pass by), *Evangelist* 3, (1923), pp. 2-4.
Stoichev D., 'Baltazar Hubmaier', *Evangelist* 4-5, (1928), pp. 4-5.
Tomov, S., 'Synodalniat Prevod', (The Orthodox Translation of the Bible) *Evangelist* 5-6, (1925), pp. 39-41.
Torrey, R.A., 'Zashto Viarvam v Bibliata Kato Bojie Slovo?', (Why I believe that the Bible is the Word of God), *Evangelist* 3-7, (1935), p. 10.
Translation, 'Isusovoto Stanovishte varhu Staria Zavet', (Jesus' Standpoint Regarding the Old Testament), *Evangelist* 18-19, (1924), p. 1.
Translation, 'Novoto Rajdane', (The New Birth), reprinted from *Christian Thought, Evangelist* 1, (1922), p. 1.
Translation, 'Tsurkvata na Hristos and Uverenie za Oproshtenie', (The Church of Christ and the Assurance of Forgiveness), *Evangelist* 6, (1930), pp. 4-5; no. 7, (1930), pp. 4-6.
Vasov, G., 'Duhut na Krusteniat s Kruv', (The Spirit of the Baptised in Blood), *Evangelist* 2, (1935), pp. 4-5.
_____, 'Kushta na Piasuk', (House on Sand), *Evangelist* 8-10, (1937), pp. 7-10.
_____, 'Shest Vida Davane', (Six Kinds of Giving), *Evangelist* 8, (1932), p. 4.
_____, 'Bibleiskata Osnova na Nasheto Viarvane i Izpoviadvane', (The Biblical Foundation of Our Belief and Confession), *Evangelist* 9, (1938), pp. 8,9.
Vidolov, Z, 'Chada na Boga Jivago, razprostraniavaite Evangelist', (Children of the Living God, Spread the News About *Evangelist*), *Evangelist* 3, (1921), p. 12.
_____, 'Gonenieto na Evangelistite v Kostenets', (The Persecution in Kostenets), *Evangelist* 4, (1920), p. 7.
_____, 'Godishnata Baptistka Conferentsia v Stara Zagora', (The Annual Baptist Conference in Stara Zagora), *Evangelist* 1, (1920), pp. 5-8.

Secondary Sources

Angelov, T., 'The Baptist Movement in Bulgaria', *Journal of European Baptist Studies,* Vol. 1, no 3 (2001), pp. 8-18.

Angelova, R., *Periodicals of the protestant churches in Bulgaria (1844-1944)*, Sofia, BHSU, 2003.
Bankov, S., *Dossieto*, Varna, EOS Printing House, 2001.
Constant, S., *Foxy Ferdinant—Tsar of Bulgaria*, London, Sidgwick & Jackson, 1979.
Constitution of the Bulgarian Kingdom, Turnovo, 1879.
Constitution of the Union of Baptist Churches in Bulgaria, Sofia, 1934, p. 2.
Dadder, D., 'History of Baptism in Bulgaria', *Vitania*, 1 (1996)—4 (1997), Sofia, Artgraph.
Edditor, 'Against the Evangelicals', *Razgrad News*, Vol. 187, (1930), pp. 7,8.
Furtunov, P., Private archive. This material is under investigation, as it is not completely disclosed by the family yet, but parts of it were made available in May 2005.
Groueff, S., *Crown of Thorns*, New York, Madison Books, 1987.
Halcomb, M., *Imprisoned for Christ: a true story*, Wheaton, IL, Tyndale, 2001.
Ignatov, P., *The bloodless perseqution of the Church*, Sofia, Lik, 2004.
Kratka Istoriya na Evangelskata Baptistka Tsurkva v gr. Lompalanka, (Short History of the Evangelical Baptist Church in the Town of Lompalanka), Ferdinant, 1930.
Krustev, K., *Protestantstkite secti v Bulgaria*, (The Protestant Sects in Bulgaria), Sofia, Partizdat, 1972.
Kulichev, H., *Vestiteli na Istinata*, (Heralds of Truth), Sofia, Bulgarian Bible Society, 1994.
McBeth, H., *A Sourcebook for Baptist Heritage*, Nashville TN, Broadman Press, 1990.
Nestorova, T., *American Missionaries Among the Bulgarians: (1858-1912)*, New York, Columbia University Press, 1987.
Oprenov, T., 'Baptists and the Orthodox Church: The 'Kostenets' Disputes of 1920 in Bulgaria', *Journal of European Baptist Studies*, Vol. 4 no. 3 (2004), pp. 33-47.
_____, 'Investigate and Give a Critical Account of Baptist Origins and Early Development in Bulgaria, Using Primary Sources', unpublished paper, submitted as part of module 'Baptist Origin and Development in Continental Europe', part of MTh studies at IBTS, Prague, May, 2002.
Raichevski, S., *America and the Bulgarians*, Sofia, National Museum of Bulgarian Books and Polygraphy, 2003.
Sechanov, I., 'History of the Bulgarian Bible', *Domashen Priatel*, Bulgarian Evangelical Society, Vol. 4-5, (1900-XII), pp. 88-90.
Shopov, P., 'Propagandnata I prosvetna deinost na Americanskite Bibleiski Obshtestva v Bulgarskite Zemi prez XIX vek', (The Propaganda and Enlightening Activity of the American Bible Societies in the Bulgarian Lands during XIXc.), *Izvestia na Instituta za Istoria* 23 (Sofia), pp. 149-184.
Stoiyanov, M., 'Nachalo na Protestantstkata Propaganda v Bulgaria', (The Beginning of the Protestant Propaganda in Bulgaria), *Izvestia na Instituta za Istroia*, N14-15, pp. 45-67.
Wardin A.,'The Baptists in Bulgaria', *The Baptist Quarterly*, Vol. 34, 4, (1991), pp. 148-158.

Woyke, F., *Heritage and Ministry of the North American Baptist Conference*, NABC, Oakbrook Terrace, IL, 1990.

CHAPTER 5

Baptist Mission Efforts in Bosnia-Herzegovina: 150 Years of Discontinuity and Struggle

Oksana Raychynets

There have been numerous attempts to write a history of the Baptist church of Yugoslavia. Among these are: J.D. Hopper, *History of Baptists in Yugoslavia: 1862-1962*;[1] W.A. Wardin, *Baptists Around the World: A Comprehensive Handbook*;[2] Leon McBeth, *The Baptist Heritage: Four Centuries of Baptist Witness*,[3] and T.F. Adams, *Baptists Around the World*.[4] The Baptist mission work in Bosnia-Herzegovina is briefly mentioned in these studies as a part of the whole Baptist movement in Yugoslavia, but in-depth attention has not been paid to the history of Baptist mission work in Bosnia-Herzegovina. This study is the first historical investigation of the history of Baptists in Bosnia-Herzegovina, presenting a chronological development of Baptist missionary efforts in Bosnia-Herzegovina, from their beginnings to the present, and offering analysis.

The historical research consists of three parts. Each chapter considers Baptist Mission endeavours during a certain period—Austro-Hungarian rule, the Kingdom of Yugoslavia, and the Socialist Federal Republic of Yugoslavia—and indicates how political, religious and socio-economic circumstances influenced the mission work. The main questions addressed are why the Baptist movement in Bosnia-Herzegovina is the smallest in Europe, what obstacles prevented the success of mission, and why the Baptist community sometimes stagnated and, at other times, nearly ceased to exist.

---

[1] John David Hopper, 'A History of Baptists in Yugoslavia: 1862-1962', unpub. paper (Fort Worth, Tex.: Southwestern Baptist Theological Seminary, 1977).

[2] W.A. Wardin, *Baptists Around the World: A Comprehensive Handbook* (Nashville: Broadman & Holman Publishers, 1995), p. 258.

[3] H. Leon McBeth, *The Baptist Heritage* (Nashville: Broadman, 1987), pp. 489-493.

[4] Theodore F. Adams, *Baptists Around the World* (Nashville: Broadman Press, 1967), pp. 59-64.

While writing the dissertation, I had access to some primary materials. I came across certain difficulties in collecting some of the materials related to the Baptist mission activities. Many valuable archive documents are missing. Some were lost during the two World Wars and the last Yugoslav war (1992-1995). It has not been easy, therefore, to reconstruct the whole picture of Baptist mission. During each historic period Bosnia-Herzegovina was a part of a bigger country with new political, religious and socio-economic circumstances. The primary sources which were available and were used in this study include documents from the archives of the Sarajevo and Tuzla Baptist churches and the private archive of the former leader of the Sarajevo church, Luka Šumic. Several Baptist leaders and members of Baptist churches in Bosnia-Herzegovina were interviewed. I have also used Yugoslavian Baptist magazines such as *Glas Evandjelja* (The Voice of the Gospel) and *Glasnik* (The Herald).

The Beginnings: The Baptist Church under Austro-Hungarian Rule (1878-1918)

The First Baptist Group in Sarajevo: Under Turkish Occupation

The first Baptist mission activity in Bosnia-Herzegovina occurred in the 1860s when Franz and Maria Tabory came to Sarajevo. This Hungarian couple from Novi Sad, Serbia and Montenegro, went to Bucharest, Rumania, probably, like many others, to find work. They were from a Nazarene congregation. During their stay in Bucharest, Franz and Maria looked for fellowship with people who held similar views. In 1862 they met Carl Johann Scharschmidt and a pastor, Heinrich Koch, at a German Baptist church.[5] They were impressed by the Christian zeal and love of these brothers, who showed the Taborys another way to be Christian. Franz and Maria soon became convinced of the truth of the message they heard, publicly confessed their faith, and were baptised by Koch on 26 October 1862.[6] In their Christian zeal they were open to mission work and in 1863, under the influence of Koch, they decided to go to Sarajevo, Bosnia-Herzegovina, as missionaries to the German settlement. The same year Franz was appointed to work in Bosnia-Herzegovina as a 'colporteur' of the British and Foreign Bible Society.

---

[5] Mile Imerovski, *Baptist Origins: The Nineteenth Century in Present Day Yugoslavia*, unpub. paper (Rüschlikon: Seminary, 1986), p. 51, and Hopper, pp. 13-14.

[6] Adolf Lehotsky, 'Baptizam u Jugoslaviji' (Baptists in Yugoslavia), unpub. document (Novi Sad: Baptist Seminary Library Archives) and Ruben Knežević, *Pregled Povijesti Baptizma na Hrvatskom Prostoru* (A Historical Overview of Baptist in Croatia) (Zagreb: Savez Baptističkih Crkava u Republici Hrvatskoj, Baptistički Institut, 2001), p. 34.

The British and Foreign Bible Society (BFBS) was an interdenominational, evangelical organisation and was one of the most important channels through which Baptist life flowed into Bosnia-Herzegovina. The BFBS was a voluntary society, one among many that sprung up in the wake of the Evangelical Revival of the eighteenth century. It was founded on 7 March 1804 with the declared aim 'to encourage a wider circulation of the Holy Scriptures at home and abroad'.[7] The Society was a publisher and distributor only. According to Roger Steer, in its first fifty years the Bible Society had issued nearly twenty-eight million copies of the Scriptures in 152 languages and dialects. Of these: fifty-four were complete Bibles, sixty-four were New Testaments and thirty-four consisted of single Bible books published as individual portions. The majority of these versions were in the languages of Europe and Asia.[8] The BFBS always relied on individual supporters, such as clergymen, travellers, merchants, soldiers and sailors to distribute Bibles—for sale or as gifts. The BFBS founded a system of agencies at home and abroad, subordinate to the central office in London. From about 1830, a pattern of territorial 'agencies' began to emerge, with the establishment of permanent depots and the employment of travelling salesman—'colporteurs'.[9] The responsibility of colporteurs was to sell and distribute Bibles, but evangelism was prohibited. At the time, Tabory was asked to work for this organisation in Sarajevo, Bosnia-Herzegovina was under Turkish occupation. In the BFBS, responsibility for the Turkish controlled, European countries lay with the Constantinople agency, which was under the leadership of Alexander Thomson from 1860 till 1896.[10] In the sixtieth annual report of the BFBS, he wrote about a new colporteur: 'With the sanction of the Committee, Mr Tabory has been appointed to superintend the work in this province and has taken up his abode at Sarajevo.'[11]

Thus, shortly after his baptism, Tabory obtained employment as a colporteur of the BFBS and, together with his wife, Maria, moved to the predominantly Muslim city of Sarajevo, the capital of Bosnia-Herzegovina. Tabory started his job and was very successful. In 1863, during his trip through Albania and Bosnia-Herzegovina, Thompson visited the Sarajevo depot[12] and was very satisfied with

---

[7] 'British and Foreign Bible Society, Identity Statement', *British and Foreign Bible Society's Library*, Cambridge University Library, 'Janus' database, http://www.janus.lib.com.ac.uk, accessed 7 June 2005.

[8] Roger Steer, *Good News for the World: The Story of Bible Society* (Oxford: Monarch, 2004), p. 222.

[9] 'British and Foreign Bible Society, Identity Statement', 'Janus' database, http://www.janus.lib.com.ac.uk, accessed 7 June 2005.

[10] Peter Kuzmič, *Vuk-Daničićevo Sveto Pismo I Biblijska Društva* (Vuk-Danichichevo Holy Scripture and Bible Societies) (Zagreb: Kršćanska Sadašnjost, 1983), p. 198.

[11] Quoted in Imerovski, *Baptist Origins*, p. 46.

[12] Kuzmič, *Vuk- Daničićevo*, p. 206.

the work of the new colporteur, Tabory. In the sixty-first report of the BFBS, Dr A. Thomson wrote about Tabory's work: 'His sales during the year amount to 704 copies, of which 574 were in Serbian, the common language of the people, and the rest in Turkish, German, French, etc'.[13] Tabory spent much time travelling through Bosnia-Herzegovina, meeting people and selling Bibles and other Christian literature. In the sixty-first report his journeys were described:

Mr Tabory, who holds your Depot at Sarajevo, spends much time in travelling. During the last year he visited Mostar, the Capital of Herzegovina, and the famous fortress town of Stolatz and sold a considerable number of Scriptures but there was not the same readiness in the province to receive the Word of God as in Bosnia.

Another tour was undertaken by Mr Tabory in the course of which he visited Travnik, Zvornik, Bijelina and passed along the Sava to Brod, Berber, Banja Luka and other towns on the Austrian frontier, realising almost everywhere encouraging sales and a strong desire for the Scriptures among the Romanists.[14]

In 1863, in spite of all his business and the prohibition of BFBS against evangelising people, Tabory formed a small group of believers for fellowship and reading of the Bible. This group contained mainly German-speaking foreigners, many of whom had a Lutheran background. This small congregation was the first Baptist church in the whole of what was later called Yugoslavia. By 1866, several other Christian believers had joined this Baptist church. These included three teachers who worked in the Christian school and in the orphanage run by Miss Adeline Irby.[15] This school played an important role in the mission activity of the Baptist church in Sarajevo.

Miss Adeline Pavlia Irby, an English lady, with her friend, Miss Georgina Muir Mackenzie, had gone on a trip through continental Europe in 1859. The two women were especially interested in the people of the South Slavic countries of the Turkish Empire, who were largely unknown to the people of the West. In a few short years, these brave ladies visited Germany, Poland, Czechoslovakia, Hungary, Austria, Italy, Montenegro, Greece, Turkey, Bulgaria and Serbia. The most important experience Miss Irby and Miss Mackenzie had on their trip was in Bosnia-Herzegovina, one of the poorest European countries at that time.[16] They saw a special need for Christian mission in this country, especially to work with Slavic children. In 1865 in England, they founded the 'Association for the Promotion of Education among the South

---

[13] Quoted in Imerovski, *Baptist Origins*, p. 52.
[14] Ibid., p. 52.
[15] Hopper, 'A History of Baptists in Yugoslavia', pp. 13-14.
[16] Julijan Jelenić, *Kultura i Bosanski Franjevci* (Culture and Bosnian Franciscans) (Sarajevo: Svjetlost, 1915), p. 340

Slavic Christians in Bosnia-Herzegovina'.[17] The aim of this organisation was to collect money to establish schools.

According to Todor Kriševac, Miss Irby and Miss Mackenzie came to Sarajevo in 1866, and shortly after, with the help of the Prussian Consul, Dr Oton Blau, established a school for the education of girls.[18] This was the first Protestant education organisation of this kind in Bosnia-Herzegovina. It was very important to Miss Irby whom she chose as teachers and which language they would use. Eventually suitable teachers, who spoke the Bosnian language, were found in Prussia. 'They were deaconesses who had learned the language from the Vuk Stefanović Karadžić's translation of the Bible and his collection of Serbian folk songs.'[19] They were probably Frideri Nibel and Maria Hirsch, who were referred to by J.D. Hopper as teachers at Miss Irby's school.[20] In the beginning the school was under the supervision of the Serbian bishop, Vujičić, and mainly poor Serbian girls were educated there. Because of their excellent teaching skills, these deaconesses soon acquired the support of prominent people in Sarajevo, both Orthodox and Catholic. They started to send their daughters to the school, but with the one condition: that nothing was said about faith.[21] During lessons the teachers used translations of the New Testament and Psalms as textbooks.[22] These were translations of Vuk Stefanović Karadžić and Đuro Daničić from Luther's German New Testament and from John Termellius' Latin Old Testament, written in the Serbian language. The complete Bible was published in 1868. This was the first complete Bible ever published in the Slavic languages.[23] New Testament books had been supplied to Miss Irby's school by colporteurs of the BFBS. Besides educating children, Miss Irby led an adult literacy programme and other social activities among the poor.

Very soon, Miss Irby and her school were accused by Bishop Vujičić, on the Orthodox side, and Friar Miju Gujić, on the Catholic side, of spreading

---

[17] Imerovski, *Baptist Origins*, p. 47.

[18] There are different dates of the establishing of the school of Miss Irby given by different authors: 1966 by Todor Kruševac, *Sarajevo pod Austro-Ugarskom Upravom 1878-1918* (Sarajevo in the Time of Austro-Hungarian Reign 1878-1918) (Sarajevo: Svjetlost, 1960), p. 395; November, 1869 by Imerovski, *Baptist Origins*, p. 47; in 1870 by Noel Malcolm, *Bosnia: A Short History* (London: Macmillan, 1996), p. 131.

[19] Vuk Karadjić's New Testament was first published in 1847. Kuzmič, *Vuk-Daničićevo*, p. 107; 'At that time the New Testament in Serb was published in 1862, a version of the Psalms appeared in 1864.' W. Canton, *A History of the British and Foreign Bible Society, Vol. III* (London: John Murray, 1904-1910), p. 202; Imerovski, *Baptist Origins*, p. 47.

[20] Hopper, 'A History of Baptists in Yugoslavia', pp. 13-14.

[21] Jelenić, *Kultura i Bosanski Franjevci*, p. 340.

[22] Imerovski, *Baptist Origins*, p.47.

[23] Canton, *Vol. III*, p. 202.

Protestantism among the Slavic people.[24] As a result of these accusations, in 1870 the teacher-deaconesses left Sarajevo and Orthodox and Catholic girls were withdrawn from the school. Only a few of the girls stayed with Miss Irby. The problem of finding suitable teachers appeared again. Miss Irby asked Maria Tabory to be a teacher. Maria and another Englishwoman, Miss Priscilla Johnson, became the new teachers at the Christian school. In 1872 the report to the Committee of the BFBS in London[25] stated,

> The Committees are already aware that on the withdrawal of the deaconesses, Mrs. Tabory, the wife of the Society's Depositary, was invited to become the matron of the institution. It is highly gratifying to learn that in this capacity she has won the confidence and esteem of Miss Irby, who has herself taught the pupils for about a year past.[26]

After these events, Dr A. Thomson, leader of the Constantinople BFBS station, became more interested in the work of the school and recommended 'the hearty support of all friends of Scriptural Female Education for the Seminary and Orphanage under the care of Miss Irby'.[27] With this co-operation of Baptist missionaries, BFBS colporteurs and Protestant teachers, the message of the Bible spread among the population of Bosnia-Herzegovina.

In the meantime, mission activity by the German Baptist movement, founded by Johann Gerhard Oncken, with his strong evangelistic convictions, led to the spread of Baptists throughout eastern and south-eastern Europe. It was Oncken who suggested that August Liebig, a locksmith and an active member of the Hamburg congregation since 1859, 'take up the missionary call in south-east Europe among the various nationalities and the German settlers'.[28] So, in 1863, Liebig moved to Bucharest and, shortly after, Oncken sent Liebig on a mission trip to South Russia and the Balkans by way of Serbia and Bosnia.[29] During this trip Liebig proclaimed the riches of Christ, as he put it, among his countrymen in Bosnia-Herzegovina and he went on to baptise several converts. On 20 June 1868 in Lukovac, near Tuzla, he baptised two brothers, Josip and Georg Lichtenegger.[30] In the history of Baptists in this region, this was the first baptismal service in Bosnia-Herzegovina. Shortly after their baptism, the brothers moved to Sarajevo and joined the small Baptist

---

[24] Jelenić, *Kultura i Bosanski Franjevci*, p. 332.
[25] Knežević, *Pregled Povijesti*, p. 34.
[26] Imerovski, *Baptist Origins*, p.57.
[27] Quoted in Imerovski, *Baptist Origins*, p.57.
[28] Hopper, 'A History of Baptists in Yugoslavia', pp. 10-11.
[29] G. Keith Parker, *Baptist in Europe: History & Confessions of Faith* (Nashville: Broadman Press, 1982), p. 202.
[30] Adolf Lehotsky, 'Baptizam u Jugoslaviji', p. 106.

group under the leadership of Tabory. The Sarajevo Baptist church was growing and was a centre of mission activity.

In the autumn of 1875 the great rebellion of the Christian population of Herzegovina against Muslim landlords and tax-gatherers took place.[31] The long-suffering Christian peasants had been driven to despair by the bad harvest and their poor living conditions. By the end of the year at least 100,000 refugees from Bosnia-Herzegovina had fled to the Austrian frontier. By mid-1876 this large but local crisis had become an international one. In July 1876, Serbia and Montenegro declared war on the Ottoman Empire.[32] This was a hard time for the church but believers did everything they could. The Society received rights to organise their work among soldiers when the Serbian War Office gave them permission to visit military hospitals.[33] In these hospitals, colporteurs of the BFBS distributed thousands of copies of the Scriptures among soldiers and officers. Baptist missionaries helped many refugees who had left their homes and come to Sarajevo. They bought food, blankets and shoes for them, read them verses of hope and gave portions of the Word of God to those who could read. Private friends gave the Baptist missionaries much help. All schools in Bosnia-Herzegovina were closed. Miss Irby returned to England and started to collect money for the support of orphans from Bosnia-Herzegovina.[34] Tabory's activity was stopped by a serious illness and the rebellion.

The great powers of Europe met at the Congress of Berlin in July 1878 to try and stop the war. The Congress announced that 'Bosnia-Herzegovina, while still in theory under Ottoman suzerainty, would be occupied and administered by Austria-Hungary'.[35] On 18 August the Austrians reached the outskirts of Sarajevo and by 20 October the entire occupation of Bosnia-Herzegovina was complete.[36] The Austro-Hungarian occupation of 1878 saw the end of four-hundred years of Ottoman rule.

Baptist Mission under Austro-Hungarian Rule: Possibilities and Difficulties

Tabory passed safely through the Bosnian conflict and held his ground till the Austrian troops forced entry into Sarajevo. At that time, the Sarajevo Baptist

---

[31] Matjaž Klemenčić and Mitja Žagar, *The Former Yugoslavia's Diverse Peoples: A Reference Sourcebook* (Santa Barbara: ABC-CLIO, 2004), p. 77.
[32] Malcolm, *Bosnia*, p. 132.
[33] Canton, *Vol. III*, p. 204.
[34] Imerovski, *Baptist Origins*, p. 48.
[35] Enver Halilović, *Bošnjaci i Vrijeme* (Bosniacs and Time) (Tuzla: Filozofski fakultet, 1995), p. 38; Malcolm, *Bosnia*, p. 134.
[36] Malcolm, *Bosnia*, pp. 134-35.

church become a BFBS depot of the Vienna agency[37] and new BFBS colporteurs arrived with a fresh stock of scriptures. One of these colporteurs was Baptist missionary, Adolf Hempt (1845-c.1927),[38] who was from Novi Sad, Serbia and Montenegro, where he attended a Nazarene church. During his stay in Budapest, Hempt had come into contact with Baptists and met a Baptist missionary, Heinrich Meyer. Under Meyer's influence, Hempt accepted Baptist beliefs and invited Meyer to visit his Nazarene church in Novi Sad. It was here that Hempt publicly professed his faith and was baptised along with others by Meyer on 16 June 1875.[39] As a new believer, Hempt had great zeal to be a missionary. Like many other Baptists in south-eastern Europe, Hempt became a colporteur of the BFBS and started to travel throughout Serbia and Bosnia-Herzegovina. He soon moved to Sarajevo and joined the Sarajevo Baptist church. In Sarajevo, Hempt become an active member of the church that had been under the leadership of Tabory since 1863. In Bosnia-Herzegovina, Hempt actively bore witness to his newly found faith, preached and distributed the Scriptures all over the country, mostly among the German-speaking population. Hempt took over the leadership of the Baptist congregation because of the illness of Tabory.

When Bosnia-Herzegovina came under the administration of the Austro-Hungarian Empire, German people were encouraged to settle in the new province.[40] Families from Silesia and the Rhineland arrived, bought land near the Croatian border and built a settlement. Altogether, fifty-four such colonies were established. One such settlement was a colony of German Protestants from Hungary named *Franzjosefsfeld*, which later became a Baptist mission station in Bosnia-Herzegovina. The government looked favourably on these farmers and, in 1890, passed a special law on 'agrarian colonies' giving them tax concessions.[41] These German settlements were often visited by Baptist missionary-colporteurs and became mission stations. Colporteurs of the BFBS also visited soldiers in hospitals and shared their beliefs and distributed Bibles and other Christian literature. Hempt was also actively engaged in this evangelistic work. He opened his apartment for meetings of the Sarajevo Baptist congregation. A group of Baptist soldiers from the Austro-Hungarian forces joined the worship. By the time the occupation was a year old, many existing Christians and new converts came to Sarajevo and joined the church. Among them was Terezija Megerle, who moved from Belgrade to Sarajevo in June 1879.[42] In the same year, Miss Irby re-opened her Christian school and, in

---

[37] Kuzmič, *Vuk-Daničićevo*, p. 206.

[38] Knežević, *Pregled Povijesti*, p. 35.

[39] J.H. Rushbrooke, *The Baptist Movement in the Continent of Europe*, (London: Kingsgate Press, 1923), pp. 164-165; Imerovski, *Baptist Origins*, p.54.

[40] Parker, *Baptists in Europe*, p. 202.

[41] Malcolm, *Bosnia*, p. 143.

[42] Imerovski, *Baptist Origins*, p.52.

November, some girls and their teacher, Miss Walker, come back to Sarajevo.[43] The church had grown so quickly that Hempt's apartment become too small for the growing church and he had to rent a larger room on Ferhanji Street. Later, an even larger apartment, where the congregation could worship and sing freely, was found on Terazija Street.[44] At that time the congregation consisted of about thirty-five members and friends, mainly from Austro-Hungarian, German speaking settlements.[45] At the beginning of the 1880s, Edward Millard (1822-1906),[46] director of the BFBS' Vienna agency and one of the greatest Baptist workers in the Balkans in the nineteenth century, arrived in Sarajevo.

Baptist work in Bosnia-Herzegovina and indeed the whole of Yugoslavia owes a great debt to Millard. He devoted his life to the BFBS and evangelism. In 1839, the BFBS had sent Millard as their representative to the continent where 'he propagated the Scriptures in Holland from 1839 and worked also as a teacher there until 1845'.[47] In 1851, they appointed him as an agent in Vienna covering the Austrian empire. Unfortunately, he was forced to leave the country in 1852 and came back just twelve years later. During this period, Millard paid great attention to the South Slavic countries. He was a BFBS colporteur in Zagreb in 1863. R. Knežević commented that his was 'the earliest sojourn of Baptist workers in Croatia'.[48] That same year, on 24 June 1863, Millard proposed that the Committee of the BFBS publish a Bible in the languages of south-Slavic ethnic groups.[49] In June 1868, the first Bible in Latin and Cyrillic was published.[50] According to Imerovski, it was Millard who encouraged Tabory to become a BFBS colporteur. In the sixtieth annual report of the BFBS Thomson wrote,

> In the early part of last year, when at Bucharest, he [E. Millard] met with a suitable agent, and he proposed that the work of Colporteur in Bosnia should be entrusted to him; with the sanction of your Committee, Mr Tabory has been appointed to superintend the work in this province, and has taken up his abode at Sarajevo.[51]

---

[43] Hamdija Kresevljaković, *Sarajevo za Vrijeme Austrougarske Uprave* (1878-1918) (Sarajevo Under the Austro-Hungarian Empire) (Sarajevo: Svjetlost, 1969), p. 46.
[44] Hopper, 'A History of Baptists in Yugoslavia', pp. 15-16.
[45] Branco Bjelajac, *Protestants and Evangelicals in Serbia Until 1945* (Belgrade, Novi Sad: Color System, 2001), p. 56.
[46] Knežević, *Pregled Povijesti*, p. 35.
[47] Imerovski, *Baptist Origins*, p.54.
[48] Knežević, *Pregled Povijesti*, p. 39.
[49] Kuzmič, *Vuk-Daničićevo*, p. 123.
[50] Hopper, 'A History of Baptists in Yugoslavia', p. 60.
[51] Imerovski, *Baptist Origins*, p.46.

On 14 November 1864, Millard returned to Vienna and re-opened the Vienna Bible depository.[52] The colporteurs travelled on foot throughout the Yugoslavian countries, distributing Bibles and biblical literature. In 1870 he was the Society's senior agent abroad[53] and in 1871, Millard appointed Meyer as colporteur in Zagreb. Later this man became an influential missionary in Bosnia-Herzegovina. Millard was accused by some colporteurs from Austro-Hungary, Slavonia and Croatia of breaking the instructions of the BFBS only to sell Bibles. After an examination of the situation, Thomson wrote in a letter to the Committee:

> There is no proof that there has been any undue leaning toward Baptist Selection. At the same time it must be recollected and as the Baptists are perhaps more active than any other body in labouring in Austria for the real conversion of souls it follows that many of that persuasion offer themselves for Colportage, offers which Mr Millard does not seem it his duty to dismiss when he can assign no other reason than that come from the Baptists.[54]

Alongside his activity for the BFBS, Millard was also involved in pastoral work. Even though full religious liberty did not come to Austria until early in the twentieth century, Millard had organised and lead a small Baptist group in Vienna, which was legally registered as a Baptist church in 1869. At the beginning of 1880s, Millard decided to go to Bosnia-Herzegovina to help with the Baptist mission, becoming a pastor of the Baptist church in Sarajevo in 1884 and working there until 1887.[55] In 1885, the government, after a long delay, granted a licence for the Society to sell Bibles in Bosnia and some time later in Herzegovina. Millard, with the help of other members of the church who were also BFBS colporteurs, started to work with even more enthusiasm. In 1891, at the base of the Sarajevo church, a small depot of the Vienna BFBS agency was opened. 'The Word of God found its way into schools, prisons, hospitals, and was readily bought by the soldiers, poor as they were.'[56] The Roman Catholic Church was against the work of the BFBS and did everything to stop their activity. As a result, BFBS colporteurs did not obtain official permission to continue the distribution of Scripture legally in Sarajevo until 1907.[57] During Millard's pastorate the church contained around twenty five

---

[52] Hopper, 'A History of Baptists in Yugoslavia', p. 62.
[53] Canton, *Vol. IV*, p. 335.
[54] Imerovski, *Baptist Origins*, p.58-59.
[55] Hopper, 'A History of Baptists in Yugoslavia', p. 16; Knežević, p. 35; Imerovski, *Baptist Origins*, p.56.
[56] Canton, Vol. IV, p. 341.
[57] James Moulton Roe, *British and Foreign Bible Society: 1805-1854* (London: British and Foreign Bible Society, 1865), p. 75.

members. On 31 January 1887, Millard resigned his charge of the great agency and left Sarajevo.[58]

A German Baptist missionary, Heinrich Meyer (1842-1919), played one of the most influential roles in the early history of Baptist work and life in Bosnia-Herzegovina.[59] This Baptist pioneer was born in Hungary. The Baptist church in Hamburg planned to send Meyer to be a missionary in Ukraine in 1869.[60] Meyer, however, had a different vision. Perhaps because he saw more opportunity to use his native languages—Hungarian and German—Meyer wanted to work in the Balkan countries where people of many nationalities such as Hungarians, Germans and Austrians lived. The work of the BFBS in Europe was well known in Christian circles. Through his friends, Meyer came into contact with Millard and asked for a job. Millard offered him the position of colporteur in Zagreb, where he moved in 1871. Even though he had received instructions not to do anything except sell Bibles, Meyer started a Bible study group in 1872.[61] Those meetings seemed unusual to local people who had not previously experienced prayer and Bible study led by someone who was not a priest. Meyer's meetings became a place for conversation and sharing Christian literature. Millard, as a Baptist, never stopped this activity and even gave Meyer help with Christian books and tracts.[62] This work of Meyer's was not liked by other colporteurs in Zagreb. Some doctrinal conflict also appeared between Meyer and other Protestant colporteurs. As a result, Meyer was forced to leave Zagreb and moved to Budapest on 5 March 1873.[63] Meyer resigned from his job as a BFBS colporteur, devoting himself to establishing Baptist work and organising new mission stations among the Germans in Hungary and other countries.[64]

Scholars have noted the key role Meyer played in spreading the Baptist movement. J.H. Rushbrooke writes: 'The Baptist advance was furthered by the missionary zeal of Heinrich Meyer, of Budapest, who extended his evangelistic journeys over all parts of the former Hungary, Serbia and Bosnia Herzegovina.'[65] According to Hopper, 'between 1875 and 1891, Heinrich Meyer laid the foundation of ethnic German Baptist work in Yugoslavia'.[66] Meyer's main role in Bosnia-Herzegovina was to prepare others to be missionaries. Under his influence there were many new converts, especially people who originally came from Southern Slavic countries. After their

---

[58] Canton, Vol. IV, p. 335.
[59] Knežević, *Pregled Povijesti*, p. 35.
[60] Bjelajac, 'Protestantism in Serbia', *Religion, State and Society* 30:3 (2002), p. 185.
[61] J.D. Hopper, 'Baptist Beginnings in Yugoslavia', *Baptist History and Heritage* 17:4 (1982), p. 29.
[62] Knežević, *Pregled Povijesti*, pp. 43-44.
[63] Hopper, 'Baptist Beginnings in Yugoslavia', p. 12.
[64] Knežević, *Pregled Povijesti*, p. 45.
[65] Rushbrooke, *Baptist Movement*, pp. 164-165.
[66] Hopper, 'Baptist Beginnings in Yugoslavia', p. 21.

baptism, these converts returned to their home villages, witnessed to their faith and established Baptist groups. One of the greatest examples of such a missionary was Hempt. Hopper suggests that Hempt 're-awoke Heinrich Meyer's interest in the possibilities of mission work among the German-speaking population among the Southern Slavic population'.[67]

Meyer baptized many people during his missionary trips. On 17 March 1878 Meyer baptised David and Anna Solti, a Hungarian couple converted in the Baptist congregation in Budapest. Under Meyer's influence and with his encouragement, they moved to a small Bosnian village called Brezovo Polje and started a small Baptist group, which later developed into a congregation. In 1881 they were joined by Peter and Elizabeth Pfaff and Peter's brother, Jacob. The three of them were baptised by Meyer in Serbia. This small group of believers formed the nucleus of the developing Baptist work in Brezovo Polje.[68] During a missionary trip to Feketić, Serbia on 17 May 1883 Meyer also baptised Jakob Brausch. In 1884 Brausch, together with Frederich and Wilhemina Kinkel, who had been baptised earlier, moved to Bosnia-Herzegovina as Baptist missionaries. They lived in Franzjosefsfeld, the settlement of Protestant Germans from Hungary, and began to develop Baptist mission work there.[69] On 26 June 1887, during a missionary trip to Romania, Meyer baptised Katherina Pokorny and her daughter. These two ladies returned to Bosnia-Herzegovina to the small town of Bijelina and started Baptist work among relatives and friends.[70]

In November 1887, during a missionary trip to Novi Sad, Meyer baptised five converts, some of whom moved to Bosnia-Herzegovina as Baptist missionaries. Samuel Senne went to Brezovo Polje and joined an already existing Baptist group. Martin Klein returned to Bijelina and became a leader of the Baptist group there. In a few years, two others from that baptismal service moved to Brezovo Polje to help with evangelisation.[71] This was a new place for Baptist work in Bosnia-Herzegovina. Meyer later visited these converts and baptised some of them. Bible study groups sprang up around these centres.[72] Thus, in the period from 1875 to 1891 Meyer laid the foundation for German Baptist work in Bosnia-Herzegovina.

After Millard left Bosnia-Herzegovina the Sarajevo Baptist church had no pastor. However, the congregation was not left on its own. The Baptist church in Novi Sad and its pastor, Julious Peter, took responsibility for the Sarajevo Baptist church and other Baptist churches in Bosnia-Herzegovina. Rushbrooke

---

[67] Ibid., p. 29.
[68] Hopper, 'A History of Baptists in Yugoslavia', p. 19; Bjelajac, 'Protestantism in Serbia', p. 186.
[69] Hopper, 'A History of Baptists in Yugoslavia', pp. 19-20.
[70] Ibid., p. 20.
[71] Ibid.
[72] Ibid., p. 21.

called Peter 'the doyen of German Baptists in what is now Jugo-Slavia'.[73] On 21 December 1891, in Brezovo Polje, Peter conducted a baptismal service.[74] The Sarajevo Baptist church organised a Sunday school for children. The Megerle children, Panhartel and Ana, along with Stazi and Sali Horak, the daughters of a Croatian Baptist missionary, attended this school.[75] Baptist churches in Brezovo Polje, Bijelina and Franzjosefsfeld become small stations of the Sarajevo depot that had been working since 1878 but legally opened only in 1891. Its work continued until 1902.[76] In 1902, the Sarajevo Depot of the BFBS was closed by the London Committee for Foreign Depots.[77]

In such co-operation, Baptists missionaries and colporteurs worked until the First World War broke out. Hopper summarises the early period of Baptist missionary work under the Austro-Hungarian Empire: '[T]he first forty-eight years indicate steady progress in the development of the Baptist movement among ethnic Germans in Yugoslavia.'[78] Unfortunately, local rebellions against the Austro-Hungarian authorities and the First World War forced many Baptists, who were mainly Germans or Austrians, to leave the country and the churches barely survived.

Political, Economic, Social and Religious Circumstances

The development of Baptist mission in Bosnia-Herzegovina during 1863-1918 cannot be understood without an understanding of the political, religious, economic and social circumstance in which missionary activity took place. Between 1863 and 1918, the circumstances in Bosnia-Herzegovina were not amendable for Baptist mission and Christian churches were not destined to enjoy a peaceful development. In the last years of Ottoman occupation, Bosnia-Herzegovina was the poorest European country, with a weak economy and political instability. The terrible harvest of 1875 led to the breakdown of Ottoman rule and the intervention of the Austrian army paralysed Baptist mission work for a few years. Immediately after the occupation, Austro-Hungary showed that its aim was to organise the country as a colonial territory. Although in the first years of Austrian-Hungarian occupation many things had changed, political and religious circumstances were not stable. The Austrian authorities made the mistake of thinking that the people of Bosnia-Herzegovina would welcome them as rulers. The first reaction among the people, especially among Bosnian Muslims, was general depression, lack of confidence, disdain,

---

[73] Rushbrooke, *Baptist Movement*, pp. 164-165.
[74] Hopper, 'A History of Baptists in Yugoslavia', pp. 22-23.
[75] Knežević, *Pregled Povijesti*, p. 41.
[76] Canton, *Vol. IV*, p. 345; Wardin, *Baptists Around the World*, p. 258.
[77] Kuzmič, *Vuk- Daničićevo*, p. 207.
[78] Hopper, 'A History of Baptists in Yugoslavia', p. 37.

and hatred of the 'Swabs'. In the villages, Muslim women were so afraid and confused that they did not want to go outside their homes.[79] The more sympathetic attitude of the Austro-Hungarian administration toward Catholics led to suspicion and a lack of trust between different ethnic groups. Even though the Austro-Hungarian authorities brought a large number of troops which should have been sufficient to keep the peace, revolts occurred in 1882, 1883, 1899 and 1908.[80] In 1908 Bosnia's status as an occupied Ottoman territory changed. On 5 October 1908 the Austro-Hungarian Emperor, Francis Joseph, declared the full annexation of Bosnia-Herzegovina into Austria-Hungary,[81] provoking a new revolt against Austria-Hungary authority. A peasant movement revolted in 1910.[82] In the autumn of 1912 the Balkan wars started and in 1914 the situation developed into the First World War.

Under the Austro-Hungarian occupation, socio-economic circumstances were poor, despite the influence of the new administration. At first the Austro-Hungarian administrators were energetic in their efforts to develop the Bosnian economy. They thought that railways were necessary for the economy to grow: in Ottoman Bosnia-Herzegovina only a few roads existed and these were not able to cope with bad weather. A railway was built from the Croatian border to Sarajevo. By the end of the nineteenth century more than nine-hundred kilometres of broad-gauge railway and more than one thousand kilometres of main and local roads had been built.[83] No doubt some roads and railways had military purposes, but they were also part of a huge drive for economic improvement.[84] The newly built roads helped to speed up the missionaries' trips. After 1878, the ethnic German population moved easily from Vienna and Budapest into the outlying provinces of Bosnia-Herzegovina and German Baptist missionaries could visit their brothers and sisters without difficulties. Prior to 1878, Bosnia's economy was in decline. Only a small part of the country was good farmland. There was almost no industry. As a result, there was rural overpopulation and underemployment. Many people had no money to

---

[79] Enver Halilović, *Bošnjaci i Vrijeme*, pp. 40-41; Mustafa Imamović, *Historija Bošnjaka* (History of Bosniacs) (Sarajevo: Bosanski Kulturni Centar, 1998), p. 362.

[80] Malcolm, *Bosnia*, p. 138; Imamović, *Historija Bošnjaka*, pp. 362, 389, 454; I. Hadzibegović and M. Imamović, 'BiH u Vrijeme Austrougarske Vladavine (1878-1918)' (Bosnia and Herzegovina in the Time of the Austro-Hungarian Empire 1878-1918) in Safet Halilović, ed., *Bosna i Hercegovina od Najstarijih Vremena do Kraja Drugog Svijetskog Rata* (Bosnia and Herzegovina from Ancient Times till the End of the Second World War) (Sarajevo: Bosanski Kulturni Centar, 1998), p. 278.

[81] Klemenčić, *Diverse Peoples*, p. 78; S. Ramić and F. Veladžić, eds., *Kratak Pregled Historije Bosne i Hercegovine i Historija Islama* (Brief Overview of the History of Bosnia-Herzegovina and the History of Islam) (Tuzla: Kulturno i Naučno Društvo Muslimana Preporod, 1994), p. 55; Imamović, *Historija Bošnjaka*, p. 422.

[82] Imamović, *Historija Bošnjaka*, p. 449.

[83] Ramić and Veladžić, *Kratak Pregled,* pp. 52-53.

[84] Malcolm, *Bosnia*, p. 141.

buy what they needed. The Bible, offered by BFBS's colporteurs, was accessible only to some people. Under the Austro-Hungarian occupation, forestry, and coal mining were developed, iron and steel works were built, and many factories were opened.[85] The next stage was mass education. At the turn of the century, literacy in Bosnia-Herzegovina was much lower than in other countries. In 1878-1879 over eighty-five percent of the population could not read and write and just five percent of children could go to elementary school.[86] Muslim Bosnians who knew how to read usually read only Arabic. The Austro-Hungarians built many primary schools and three high schools and educational reform developed slowly, but in 1906 just twenty percent of children attended school.[87] In 1907 'Serbo-Croatian' was pronounced the official language.[88] In 1910 still only twelve percent of the population could read and write.[89] According to Malcolm, 'peasants were unlikely to rush to send their children to acquire an education, which they themselves had never received'.[90]

During Austro-Hungarian rule the ethnic composition of Bosnia-Herzegovina changed. When the Austrian-Hungarian troops and administrators arrived in 1878, the population of Bosnia and Herzegovina was around 1.1 million people: thirty-eight percent of them were Muslim, forty-two percent Orthodox and eighteen percent Catholic.[91] Soon after this, the migration of people started. Being very unhappy with their new rulers, the majority of the Muslim Bosnian population started their emigration to Turkey. According to Mustafa Imamović there was no single year that thousands of them migrated to Turkey.[92] The great majority of these emigrants were peasants. The Austro-Hungarian authorities issued official figures stating that around 56,625 people left Bosnia and Herzegovina between 1883 and 1918.[93] Some people left the country for economic reasons. Among them were Baptists, such as the Horak sisters and Baptist colporteur, Alois Sixta, who went to the USA. At the same time, in North Bosnia around fifty-thousand colonists from all over the monarchy came to live in Bosnia-Herzegovina.[94] According to the last official census of the Austro-Hungarian authorities, in 1910, the population at that time

---

[85] Ibid.
[86] Ramić and Veladžić, *Kratak Pregled*, p. 53; Hadzibegović and Imamović, p. 256.
[87] Ramić and Veladžić, *Kratak Pregled*, p. 55.
[88] Imamović, *Historija Bošnjaka*, p. 382.
[89] Hadzibegović and Imamović, 'BiH', p. 257.
[90] Malcolm, *Bosnia*, p. 144.
[91] Steven W. Sowards, 'Bosnia-Herzegovina and the Failure of Reform in Austria-Hungry', *Twenty-Five Lectures on Modern Balkan History* (The Balkans in the Age of Nationalism) 12, http://www.lib.msu.edu/sowards/balkan/lect12.htm, accessed 8 January 2007.
[92] Imamović, *Historija Bošnjaka*, p. 367.
[93] Malcolm, *Bosnia*, p. 139.
[94] Ramić and Veladžić, *Kratak Pregled*, p. 53.

consisted of: forty-three percent Orthodox; thirty-two percent Muslim; twenty-three percent Catholic; 0.6% Jewish and 0.8% others.[95]

Under the Austro-Hungarians the religious situation in Bosnia-Herzegovina was intricate and difficult. Although migration had changed the ethnic mix, no group had a majority. The Austro-Hungarian administration guaranteed religious freedom for all the population of Bosnia-Herzegovina;[96] however, the reality was different: 'The administration has been doing everything to put the Catholic, Orthodox and Muslim communities under its influence.'[97] With the establishment of Austro-Hungarian authority, the Orthodox Church lost its favoured position in the country. Serbian books, teachers, and priests were regarded as anti-Austrian and were excluded. The Muslim community lost the status it enjoyed during the Ottoman Empire. According to Noel Malcolm, 'of the three religious organisations, the Catholic Church was the one most visibly growing and changing'.[98] The influx of people from Austria-Hungary swelled the Catholic population. They became socially, economically, and politically privileged. The Catholic Church had the support of the new administration. They activated mission work and provoked many problems among people of other confessions. The most disruptive issue was conversions: the Muslim community accused the Catholic Church of converting Muslim girls to Catholicism either by marriage or through nuns who stole girls from their families.[99] The Bosnian historian, Mustafa Imamović, wrote about the attitude of Muslims toward Christian mission activity, both Catholic and otherwise, saying that with the occupation many missionaries sneaked in to the country and immediately started to spread Christianity.[100] The Catholic Church often held the whole power of local authorities in their hands and frequently used it to create barriers to the activity of other Christian communities.

According to Ruben Knežević, the religious situation under the Austro-Hungarian administration contained many obstacles for the new Protestant confessions until the beginning of the twentieth century. Even though 'liberty of conscience had been guaranteed by the Treaty, the usual Austrian restrictions were imposed on society, and at the close of the period a solitary colporteur was patiently labouring in Bosnia in the hope of better days'.[101] Licences in provinces of Austro-Hungary Empire did not enable the colporteurs to sell Bibles freely; they were allowed merely to show books and take orders for them.[102] Baptist churches were free to have their meetings but did not receive

---

[95] Hadzibegović and Imamović, 'BiH', p. 224.
[96] Ibid., p. 230.
[97] Ramić, Veladžić, *Kratak Pregled*, p. 52.
[98] Malcolm, *Bosnia*, pp. 144-145.
[99] Ibid., p. 145.
[100] Imamović, *Historija Bošnjaka*, p. 389.
[101] Canton, *Vol. III*, pp. 207-208.
[102] Ibid., p. 189.

legal status until 1918.[103] The Catholic Church often used its power to stop the activities of other Christian communities which they considered heretical. The Catholic Church was also against the activities of other Christians, such as Baptist missionaries and colporteurs of the BFBS. Many of these circumstances—political, social, economic and religious—made Baptist Mission activity very difficult, although there were some factors which aided growth.

The 'Golden Age': Between Two World Wars (1919-1945)

The Revitalisation of Baptist Mission

After the First World War (hereafter WWI), Bosnia-Herzegovina was under the rule of the Serbian King Petar. The National Council of Bosnia-Herzegovina wrote a letter to the Regent Aleksandra Karadjordjevic in which he was asked to take control of Bosnia-Herzegovina. On 1 December 1918 he announced 'the unification of the Kingdom of Serbia with the independent countries of Slovenia, Croatia and Serbia into a Kingdom of Serbs, Croats and Slovenes (Kingdom SCS)'.[104] Later, in 1929, it was announced that Kingdom SCS would be known as the Kingdom of Yugoslavia. For more than seventy years, Baptist mission work in Bosnia-Herzegovina had been firmly tied with that of the countries that would make up the new kingdom.[105]

Baptist congregations in Bosnia-Herzegovina barely survived WWI. The majority of Baptist churches in the country ceased to exist. Many German-speaking members left the country. Others members left Bosnia-Herzegovina for economic reasons and moved to the USA or other Western countries. Miss Adelina Pavlia Irbi died in 1911 and, soon after, the training school for girls closed its doors.[106] Adolf Hempt and his wife moved from Sarajevo to Lukavac, a small town near Tuzla, where they later died.[107] The Sarajevo Baptist church remained without a pastor. Only the Magerle and Černy families remained, with a few other individual members. Baptist churches in Brezovo Polje, Bijelina, and Franzjosefsfeld almost ceased to exist. However, the Baptist group in Sarajevo survived with the support of German-speaking Baptists from Novi Sad, Budapest, and evangelists from Germany and Switzerland.[108]

---

[103] Knežević, *Pregled Povijesti*, p. 28.
[104] Hadzibegović and Imamović, 'BiH', p. 293; Klementić and Žadar, *Diverse Peoples*, p. 90.
[105] Imamović, *Historija Bošnjaka*, pp. 505-506.
[106] Kruševac, *Sarajevo*, p. 395.
[107] Hopper, 'A History of Baptists in Yugoslavia', pp. 15-16.
[108] Ibid., pp. 86-87.

The revitalising of Baptist work in the newly formed Kingdom SCS started when a significant group of converts returned to their hometowns where they were willing to witness to their new beliefs among relatives and friends. The newly established country prompted the Baptists of various language groups—Serbian, Croatian, German, Hungarian, Slovakian, Slovenian, and others—to work together. The most significant of these were the Serbo-Croatian and German Baptist groups. German Baptists worked mainly among the German-speaking population. Some of them were former prisoners of war who had become Baptists in Russian captivity. These included Carl Sepper, Josip Baluban, Adalbert Beregszaszi, Stevan Scheinow, Adolf Lehotsky, and Đuro Vezmar. Many members of the Serbo-Croatian group were returnees from America, who came back with new beliefs and new hope for the country. 'Among them were Jovo Jekić, Dušan Tatić, Milan Brkić, N. Paunović family and Steve Nedućin.'[109] According to Bjelajac, a Serbian historian, 'after the First World War the Baptist work in Yugoslavia became a more lively movement'.[110] However, as we will see, mission work in Bosnia-Herzegovina was only 'an echo' of the mission activity in Serbia, Croatia and Slovenia.

Baptist mission work among the population of the Kingdom SCS was organised only with the appearance of two Mission Organisations from the USA: the Southern Baptist Convention (hereafter SBC) and the North American Baptist General Conference of German Baptists. WWI had impoverished Europe; many churches were left without preachers, and Baptist literature had almost disappeared. The Baptist World Alliance (hereafter BWA) which was created in 1905, at the World Congress in London,[111] decided, 'to request the stronger Baptist groups in conjunction with their Mission Boards, to make special study of fields allocated to them'.[112] A BWA Committee, held in London from 19 to 23 July 1920, organised an International Baptist conference on Post-War Needs, which J.H. Rushbrooke, European Commissioner of BWA, called 'the most significant missionary meeting that Baptist have held in modern times'.[113] At that meeting, a co-ordinated Baptist programme for Europe was adopted and SBC from the USA agreed to give missionary support to Baptists in several European countries. 'Southern Baptists accepted the assignment of Spain, Yugoslavia, Hungary, Rumania, the Ukraine, and

---

[109] Hopper, 'Baptist Beginnings in Yugoslavia' p. 34.

[110] Bjelajac, 'Protestantism in Serbia', p. 188.

[111] Carl W. Tiller, 'Baptists Hold First World Congress in London, Create Permanent Global Alliance' in *The Twentieth Century Baptist: Chronicles of the Baptist World Alliance* (Valley Forge, Pennsylvania: Judson Press, 1980), p. 1.

[112] F. Townley Lord, *Baptist World Fellowship* (London: Carey Kingsgate Press,1955), p. 40.

[113] J.H. Rushbrooke, 'Baptist Belief and Mission Work in Europe' in *Baptist World Alliance Record of Proceedings* (Stockholm, 21-27 July 1923), p. 46.

southern USSR.'[114] They sent their missionaries, mainly immigrants who had been converted in the USA, to their homelands and supported them financially and with Christian literature.

A few years later, in September 1924, a special conference of German-speaking Baptists was held in Budapest. Their main questions were:

> Are the German-speaking groups in south-eastern Europe sufficiently numerous to justify a special work? Does the Baptist World Alliance have enough sympathy and interest to carry out work among ethnic Germans? Is it practical for the German Baptists in America and later the German Baptists from Germany to undertake this missionary responsibility in south-eastern Europe? Should the German work in south-eastern Europe be totally integrated into the Baptist movement in Germany?[115]

The North American Baptist General Conference of German Baptists (hereafter NABGC of GB), from Illinois, USA, who gave financial support to the German mission in Europe, suggested the development of the South-eastern European German Mission Committee (hereafter SEGMC), in order to strengthen the mission work in the South-Eastern Slavic countries.[116] Carl Fullbrandt was appointed its Mission Inspector in South-eastern Europe. The office of SEGMC was in Vienna, from which Fullbrandt regularly visited the mission churches and provided preachers and leadership among Germans in the South-eastern Slavic countries, including Bosnia-Herzegovina in the Kingdom SCS. The German Mission Committee also provided financial support. Thus, prior to 1925 Baptist mission work in Kingdom SCS was shared between these two American groups.

MISSION OF THE SOUTHERN BAPTIST CONVENTION, USA

The most prominent missionary of the SBC in the Kingdom SCS was Vinko Vacek. He was born in 1882, near Daruvar, into a Catholic family with a Czech background. In 1910 Vacek moved with his family to Detroit, USA, to find work. There he started to attend a Baptist church where services were held in different Slavic languages, including Serbo-Croatian. He was baptised and become a member of the church in December 1913. In 1920, Vacek was ordained lay Pastor of the First Yugoslavian Baptist church in Detroit.[117] Under his leadership, many immigrants from Yugoslavia become members of that church. When the new country of the Kingdom SCS was created, they had new hope for their country and decided to return. Some returnees became active

---

[114] Tiller, 'Significant Conference Called by BWA at London', in Tiller, p. 1.
[115] Hopper, 'A History of Baptists in Yugoslavia', p. 87.
[116] Ibid., pp. 86-87.
[117] Knežević, *Pregled Povijesti*, p. 62.

missionaries- one of them was Jovo Jekić. He immediately began to share his new faith with relatives and neighbours. Soon Jekić founded a small Baptist church in Bačuga which met in his home. Jekić also visited many places in the Kingdom SCS, including the Bosnian village, Brezovo Polje, where he shared the Gospel.[118] He also visited and evangelised relatives of some immigrants who were still in America. In his missionary work, Jekić used Bibles, hymnbooks, and other Christian literature, which he had brought with him from America.[119] He kept up a good relationship with his pastor in Detroit, Vinko Vacek. Through correspondence, Jekić informed his pastor about his work and the many opportunities for mission. Vacek energetically supported all of those who returned to the Kingdom of SCS with Christian literature and encouragement.

In 1921, a general mission foundation for mutual co-ordination of the Serbo-Croatian Baptist movement was established with the help of the Detroit Baptist Church.[120] This foundation organised evangelism groups to visit mission stations throughout the country. Bjelajac gives an example one of these groups:

> They go in groups to villages where there are no Baptists and hold a service in some home, whose head is well disposed toward Baptists. Almost everyone can play some instrument, be it trombone, guitar or hand organ. And they use instruments to attract people to the services. There is also a circulating library.[121]

Vacek's desire to support mission work in the Kingdom SCS overlapped with the decision of the SBC to start their missionary activities in South-eastern European countries. Vacek was proposed as a missionary of the SBC in the Kingdom SCS. On 22 September 1922, Vacek, with his family, arrived in the Kingdom SCS and engaged in mission work.[122]

At the time of his arrival separate Baptist ethnic movements existed. They assisted and served each other. The German preachers helped Hungarian and Serbian churches and led Baptist mission work in Bosnia-Herzegovina, mostly among the German-speaking settlements. Vacek started to work mainly 'among the churches of Croatian, Serbian, Slovak, Czech, Slovenian and Romanian language groups'.[123] He and his co-workers travelled regularly to the Slavic Churches with words of encouragement and Christian literature.[124] From time to time, leaders of Baptist churches held meetings to share successes, solve

---

[118] *Glas Evandjelja* (Voice of the Gospel) 5 (1928), p. 79.
[119] Bjelajac, *Protestants and Evangelicals*, p. 63.
[120] Rushbrooke, *Baptist Movement*, p. 164.
[121] Bjelajac, *Protestants and Evangelicals*, p. 67.
[122] Vacek, Vinko, 'Baptisticki Pokret u Kraljevini SHS' (Baptist Movement in the Kingdom of SCS), *Glas Evandjelja* 11 (1927), p. 134; *Glas Evandjelja* 9 (1939), p. 46.
[123] Franjo Klem, 'Yugoslavia,' in J.D. Franks, ed., *European Baptists Today* (Zürich-Rüschlikon: Baublatt AG., 1950), p. 88
[124] *Glas Evandjelja* 7 (1930), pp.109-111; 9 (1930), pp. 138-142

current problems, and plan strategies for future activities. The many differences in nationality, language and views created many obstacles. The Southern Baptist European representative, Everett Gill, encouraged Vacek to establish a union that would unite the various Baptist groups of the Kingdom SCS.[125] The Baptist Union of Regional Associations of the Kingdom SCS (hereafter Baptist Union of KSCS) was founded somewhere between 1922 and 1924. In 1929, this was changed to the Baptist Union of Regional Associations of the Kingdom of Yugoslavia (hereafter Baptist Union of Kingdom of Yugoslavia). According to Hopper, there is no official record of a date for the formal founding of the Baptist Union of KSCS; various church leaders and historians offer different dates.[126] Adolf Lehotsky suggested 1924,[127] while Knežević, a Croatian historian, offers March 1922.[128] Under the auspices of the Union, different ethnic-based regional associations were organised. Each regional association had the right to organise their activity.[129] The first President of Baptist Union of Regional Associations was Vinko Vacek. The main purpose of the Union was 'the maintenance of general mission work'.[130] The SBC assisted the new Union. The Union held annual conferences which discussed various issues: mission work, publications, rules of Christian life, Christian education, women's work and youth work, etc.[131]

Vacek and Nikola Dulić, organised the publication of a Baptist magazine, *Glas Evandjelja* (Voice of the Gospel), the first edition of which appeared in July 1923. Articles in the magazine covered such things as Christian ethics, history, reports from mission field, Baptist news from all over the world, sermons, evangelistic messages, and materials for leaders of Bible groups and Sunday schools. It was published a few times each year until WWII. A Book of Songs in the Croatian language and many tracts were also published and distributed all over the country.[132] The Baptist Union of KSCS also organised Bible classes for Baptist church leaders of all the regional associations. Nikola Dulić held the first classes. Later, Carl Sepper, a member of the German-speaking Association and non-residential student of the Hamburg Baptist Seminary, took this responsibility. The Baptist Union of KSCS also planned some social projects. In 1924, a Baptist home for retired believers was opened in Novi Sad where old Baptist believers 'would spend the last days of their

---

[125] *Glas Evandjelja* 9 (1923), pp. 24-25
[126] Hopper, 'A History of Baptists in Yugoslavia', pp. 82-83
[127] Knežević, *Pregled Povijesti*, p. 74
[128] Lehosky, 'Baptizam u Jugoslaviji', p. 4
[129] Knežević, *Pregled Povijesti*, p. 113
[130] Rushbrooke, *Baptist Movement*, p. 164.
[131] Gilbert Laws, 'Sto se Ocekuje od Clanova Crkve' (What is Expected from the Members of the Church), *Glas Evandjelja* 7 (1931), pp. 98-103.
[132] *Glas Evandjelja* 11 (1927), p. 134.

lives in peace and prayer'.[133] All Regional Associations and the SBC supported this project.[134]

In 1925, the State Authority of the Kingdom SCS recognised the Baptist Union of Regional Associations of the Kingdom SCS and legalised the existence of the Baptist confession.[135] The Ministry of Justice published in the official newspaper a list of recognised religions: 'Orthodox, Roman Catholic and Greek Catholic Churches, Evangelical Calvinist and Lutheran Churches, Old Catholic Church, Jewish...Muslim and Baptist'.[136] According to article 11 of the law it guarantees freedom of faith and conscience. Recognised religions are equal before the Law and can confess their beliefs in public.[137]

Baptist churches were free to have meetings in their Prayer houses and even public places, and to maintain baptismal, funeral, and wedding services.[138] From that time, the Union actively started to build church buildings. Previously, congregations held their services in private houses. Between 1923 and 1940, at least eight churches were built in Croatia, Serbia, and Slovenia.[139] Significant assistance was received from American brethren.[140] In Bosnia-Herzegovina, Baptist congregations still met in the houses of church members. They were not persecuted with the same intensity as before.[141] The authorities, however, did pursue a discriminatory policy towards Baptists in comparison to the Catholic and Orthodox Churches. There were no problems with the Muslims, presumably because they lived so separately from other groups. For them, Baptists were just some foreign religion. On the other hand, Baptists primarily concentrated on the evangelism of people from their own ethnic group.

In 1927, the Slavic Baptist Regional Association (hereafter SBRA) reorganised its work. The scattered fellowship of the SBRA was now organised

---

[133] '...sprovode dane svojega života u miru I molitvama', *Glas Evandjelja* 11 (1926), p. 130.

[134] Hopper, 'A History of Baptists in Yugoslavia', pp. 80-82.

[135] *Glas Evandjelja* 11 (1935), p. 103; Emir Kovačević, 'Legal Position of Churches and Religious Communities in B&H', unpub. paper (Sarajevo: World Conference on Religion and Peace, Bosnia-Herzegovina, 2001), pp. 1-2.

[136] 'Pravoslavna, katolička, rimskog I grčkog obreda, evangelička, kalvinskog I luteranskog obreda, starokatolička, jevrejska, sva tri obreda, muslimanska I baptistička'. *Narodne Novine* (People's News) 150 (Zagreb, 2 June 1930) quoted in *Glas Evandjelja* 7 (1930), p. 109.

[137] *Glas Evandjelja* 2 (1935), p. 19.

[138] Klem, p. 88; Vacek, 'Baptistički Pokret u Kraljevini SHS' (Baptist Movement in the Kingdom of SCS), *Glas Evandjelja* 11 (1927), p. 133; *Glas Evandjelja* 7-8 (1932), pp. 83-84.

[139] *Glas Evandjelja* 10 (1926), p. 118; 11 (1927), p. 134; 12 (1927), p. 148; 9-10 (1935), p. 94; 3-4 (1936), p. 43; 8-10 (1938), pp. 53, 54, 56.

[140] *Glas Evandjelja* 7 (1930), p. 111.

[141] *Glas Evandjelja* 2 (1931), p. 30; 6 (1931), pp. 85-87; 4 (1932), pp. 45-46; 10-11 (1933), p. 94; 2 (1935), p. 23; 3 (1935), p. 31; 7-8 (1935), p. 80.

into five church councils, each of them responsible for certain churches. Two of them were responsible for mission work and church planting in Bosnia-Herzegovina: Daruvar Baptist church became responsible for Derventa and Sarajevo, and Bačuga Baptist church became responsible for Brezovo Polje.[142] As we have seen, Baptist churches in Bosnia-Herzegovina had small numbers of believers and were without pastors. Every Church Council of SBRA organised groups, which went to churches with Bibles, tracts, and other Christian literature and shared their beliefs with people. Members of each church were taught that the most effective evangelism was personal evangelism.[143] The Daruvar Baptist church maintained close contact with believers in Derventa and Sarajevo. Vacek, and later Fritz Lotz, the new pastor of the Daruvar church, or other preachers or groups of believers visited these Baptist groups with sermons and songs. In Derventa the Baptist meetings were held at the house of Vaclav Horak until 1930, when the Horak family moved to Beograd.[144] The Sarajevo Baptist group was led by Josip Černy. Originally from Daruvar, Černy moved to Bosnia-Herzegovina before the First World War. During the war, Černy stayed in Sarajevo and supported those who remained in the city. Later he opened his house for meetings of the Sarajevo Baptist group.

Many leaders of the Baptist Union of KSCS, such as Vacek, Erlih, Lotz, Drobny visited the Sarajevo church.[145] Černy also sometimes visited different churches and shared from the Word of God.[146] The Daruvar Baptist church oversaw the Baptist group in Sarajevo until it became a station of the German Baptist Regional Association.[147] The Bačuga Baptist church was the centre of the mission work of pastor Jekić. Alone or with a group of believers, he travelled throughout the country and visited mission stations.[148] He revitalised Baptist work in Brezovo Polje. Before the First World War, a German-speaking Baptist church and station of the BFBS had existed in Brezovo Polje, but during the war the majority of German-speaking members left Bosnia-Herzegovina and the church died. In 1924, Jekić founded a new Baptist group in Brezovo Polje at house of the Petrovič' family and visited it regularly to lead services.[149]

The Baptist Union of Kingdom SCS gave great attention to the development of Sunday schools and youth ministry. Sunday schools for children and teenagers were developed in every church. From 1926, local Baptist Youth

---

[142] *Glas Evandjelja* 6 (1927), p. 71.
[143] *Glas Evandjelja* 12 (1927), p. 146.
[144] *Glas Evandjelja* 11 (1928), p. 174.
[145] *Glas Evandjelja* 11 (1932), p. 117; 3-4 (1936), p. 41; 11-12 (1939), p. 73.
[146] *Glas Evandjelja* 11-12 (1939), pp. 73-75; 1-2 (1940), p. 10.
[147] *Glas Evandjelja* 6-7 (1933), p. 63.
[148] *Glas Evandjelja* 11 (1926), p. 130.
[149] *Glas Evandjelja* 6-7 (1933), p. 64.

Societies were organised in many churches.[150] Their aim was to bring up young people in Jesus' teaching, in morality and purity, and to spread Christian literature among people.[151] The Baptist Union of KSCS held annual conferences for young people where they discussed various themes in their life, held teaching classes, and received encouragement from older leaders. Sometimes there were baptismal services.[152] In 1931, at a Youth Conference in Daruvar, it was decided to publish a press release *Mladi Krščanin* (Youth Christian) in cooperation with *Glas Evandelja* (Voice of the Gospel).[153]

In 1930, the Baptist Union of the Kingdom of Yugoslavia started to think seriously about Christian education for Baptist leaders. In 1931, Everet Gill, together with co-workers, organised Bible courses in B. Petrovac, Mošćenica, Beograd and other places.[154] In 1938, John Allen Moore, the representative of the Foreign Mission Board of the SBC, came to the Kingdom of Yugoslavia with his wife, Pauline Willingham Moore.[155] He was the first full-time missionary of the SBC to the Kingdom of Yugoslavia. Moore came with a goal to establish a Christian education institution for Baptist churches. In 1939, he was elected President of the Missions Committee of the SBRA.[156] He began a Baptist seminary in the Beograd church in 1940. Many conservative members of the churches criticised the work of the seminary. Bjelajac reports, 'Among the Yugoslavs themselves there [was] dissension also over an educated ministry, the majority opposed the new seminary at Belgrade on the grounds that educated leaders might influence government officials and cause trouble.'[157] Bjelajac also suggests the criticism possibly came from members with a Nazarene background. They considered that it was not permissible for 'people of the Bible to read any books besides the Bible'.[158] As a result, trained and educated preachers were considered as worldly and not worthy to preach the Gospel. Nevertheless, many young believers had a great desire for education. Moore purchased a building where a small group of Baptist students lived and had their classes.[159]

---

[150] *Glas Evandjelja* 11 (1926), p. 130; 7 (1930), p.104; 3-4 (1940), p. 8.

[151] See more in *Glas Evandjelja* 7 (1930), p. 105, and Knežević, p. 78.

[152] See more in *Glas Evandjelja* 7 (1930), pp. 102-107; 10 (1930), pp. 157-159; 6 (1931), pp. 83-85.

[153] *Glas Evandjelja* 6 (1931), pp. 84-85.

[154] *Glas Evandjelja* 2 (1931), p. 30; *Glas Evandjelja* 11 (1932); Teofil Lehotsky, 'Prilog Istoriji Baptistickog Teoloskog Obrazovanja u Nas' (A Contribution to the History of Theological Education in Serbia), *Teoloski Casopis* (Theological Journal) 4 (2004), p. 23.

[155] Hopper, 'A History of Baptists in Yugoslavia', p. 151.

[156] *Glas Evandjelja* 11-12 (1939), p. 73.

[157] Bjelajac, *Protestants and Evangelicals*, p. 70.

[158] Ibid., p. 69.

[159] *Glas Evandjelja* 3-4 (1940), p. 30.

The Baptist Union saw a great need for a women's ministry. On 10 October 1937, the First Baptist Women's Society met in Zagreb. In a few years, women's societies were organised in almost all the Baptist churches in the Union.[160] In 1939, the Union of Baptist Women's Societies of the Kingdom Yugoslavia was organised. A Russian lady, Lydia Kalmikov, became the President of this Union. The goal of the organisation was to consider the issues related to women and how they could become more involved in the life and work of the church and Union, spiritual growth, and prayer.[161] The Women's Missionary Union of the SBC was a great partner in the first steps of the young Baptist Women's Organisation of Yugoslavia. One of them was Mrs. Moore, who supported the work and helped to found the Christian magazine *Sestrinski List* (The Sisters' Newspaper).[162]

MISSION OF THE SOUTH-EASTERN EUROPEAN GERMAN MISSION COMMITTEE

The South-eastern European German Mission Committee (hereafter SEGMC) began its work in the Kingdom SCS in 1924. By that time, the German Baptist work had already been making progress among the German-speaking settlements for almost fifty years. German Baptist colporteurs walked from place to place, mostly German villages, and distributed Bibles and other Christian literature. The Gospel had a good response and the largest growth took place in and around the German villages. According to the statistics of 1921, German-speaking churches had 212 members in the Kingdom.[163] There were 'twenty-four fellowships with 241 children enrolled in Sunday School, 126 in the Youth Movement, and 89 Women Societies regularly studying the Bible together'[164] among the German-speaking population. All German-speaking Baptist groups that had been founded before the First World War were mission stations of the Baptist church in Novi Sad. This church played an important role in mission work in Bosnia-Herzegovina during the time between the two wars, as it had done before the First World War. Peter Julious, the pastor, actively visited the Baptist groups in Sarajevo, Brezovo Polje, and Franzjosefsfeld before the First World War and continued to do so until his retirement in 1921. He encouraged other Baptist leaders to do mission work in Bosnia-Herzegovina. Because of the number of members who left the country, the only Baptist church that still existed was the Sarajevo Baptist church under the leadership of Josip Černy.

---

[160] *Glas Evandjelja* 8-10 (1938), p. 58.

[161] *Glas Evandjelja* 8-10 (1938), p. 57; 11-12 (1938), p. 68.

[162] Hopper, 'A History of Baptists in Yugoslavia', pp. 95-96, 151; *Glas Evandjelja* 1-2 (1940), p. 9, 12.

[163] T. Lehotsky, 'Prilog Istoriji' p. 17.

[164] Hopper, 'A History of Baptists in Yugoslavia', p. 37.

Another active worker among the German-speaking settlements at that time was Carl Sepper. He served in Serbia and Bosnia-Herzegovina as colporteur of the Baptist Publishing House in Kassel, Germany, distributing Christian literature among the German congregations. In 1923, Sepper became editor and active writer of the Baptist magazine *Evangeliumsbote* that was started by the German-speaking churches. In this magazine, members of German-speaking Baptist churches could find information about mission work, articles with words of encouragement and practical help, and reports from churches all over the country and from Baptist movements in other countries. In addition, Sepper held regular evangelistic services in churches and in public places. At these services, preachers often preached in different languages depending on who was gathered.[165] The Baptist magazine *Evangeliumsbote* gave an account of one of these services in Derventa:

> We had guests from Backa, the preacher Sepper with his wife. On Sunday, 28 February at 10 a.m. in a richly visited service, we praised our Almighty, Heavenly Father and thanked our Lord for his unchangeable love, and proclaimed the Holy message about our Creator and Saviour. From 2 to 3 in the afternoon, we had Sunday school. At 3 p.m. we had another richly visited service. Brother Sepper spoke on the theme 'Jesus and the Samaritan woman'...listeners came from near and far, and from the surrounding German colonies: Kosince, Kalendrovci, Susberg, Korace, Bosanski Brod...[166]

Sepper actively co-operated with Baptist workers of other nationalities and especially with the Slavic Baptist Regional Association. He was the one who helped in the founding of a Baptist home for retired people in Novi Sad in 1924 and was involved in the educational ministry. In 1926, *Evangeliumsbote* was incorporated into the *Friedensbote* which was published in Vienna and later in Bucharest. The former editor, Sepper, was asked by the German Conference to be evangelist-at-large with special attention to the scattered German groups throughout Bosnia-Herzegovina and Slovenia.[167] Sepper accepted this position, and from 1927 he actively visited Baptists in Sarajevo, Derventa, Brezovo Polje, and Petrovo Polje. Although, in December of 1928, he moved to Sajkaš-

---

[165] *Evangeliumsbote* 4:3 (1926), pp. 6-7, translated from German by Ruta Lehotsky (2005).

[166] 'Imali smo drage goste iz Bačke, propovednika Seppera sa suprugom. U nedelju, 28. februara u 10 sati pre podne smo na bogato posećenom bogosluženju slavili našeg svemočnog, nebeskog Oca i zahvalili našem Gospodu na njegovoj neizmernoj ljubavi, te navestili svetu poruku o našem Stvoritelju i Spasitelju. Posle podne od 2-3 sati imali smo nedeljnu školu. Od 3 sata smo ponovo imali bogato posećeno bogosluženje. Brat je govorio na temu 'Isus i Samarjanka'... Dragi slusaoci su došli iz bliza i daleka i iz okolnih nemačkih kolonija: Kosince, Kalendrovci, Susberg, Korace i Bosanski Brod...' in *Evangeliumsbote* 4:3 (1926), pp. 6-7.

[167] Hopper, 'A History of Baptists in Yugoslavia', pp. 91-92.

Sveti Ivan to help with the Baptist church, Sepper continued to carry out his evangelistic and colportage work all over the country.

With the organising of SEGMC, the Baptist work among the German-speaking population gained impetus. The SEGMC existed to provide support to existing missionary workers. In practical terms, they organised a German Baptist Regional Association that included all the German-speaking churches of the Kingdom SCS. Before that, leaders of German-speaking churches were actively involved in the work of Baptist Union of Regional Associations of Kingdom SCS, but they saw a need for a committee that would deal with the issues of German-speaking Baptist churches. On 17 to 18 February 1925, an organising conference was held in Novi Sad.[168] Some guests from other countries attended the conference: from Hungary: Georg Gerwich, Michael Berleth and pastors, Welker and Klees, and from the USA: Mission Inspector Carl Fullbrandt, who represented the American German Baptists. At this conference, the German Baptist Regional Association (hereafter GBRA) of German-speaking Baptist churches of Kingdom SCS was established.[169] The Novi Sad church became the centre of the Association of German-speaking Baptist churches. The goal of the GBRA was to validate Baptist mission work among the German population. Annual conferences were organised to co-ordinate the work.[170]

Carl Fullbrandt lived in Yugoslavia and helped to develop the work of the Association. In 1925, he was ordained and became pastor of the German-speaking church in Sajkaš-Sveti Ivan, Serbia. Fullbrandt also served as Recording Secretary of the Association from 1926 till 1928. His most significant contribution to the work of Association was its statute. The government of Kingdom SCS required that all faith communities who wanted to be registered had to have their own statute. The Association asked Fullbrandt to prepare this statute. With the help of others Baptist leaders, he formulated the statutes and presented them at the annual conference in January 1928.[171] The same year, Fullbrandt left the country and returned to Germany, from where he continued to co-ordinate Baptist work in the Kingdom SCS. In February 1929, in order to strengthen the mission work of GBRA, Fullbrandt ordained Josef Unterwiener, Johann Wahl, Robert Schlosser, Carl Sepper and Adolf Lehotsky as leaders of Baptist mission work.[172]

GBRA took responsibility for the colportage ministry. It financially supported and supervised the work of such colporteurs as Carl Sepper, Georg Bechtler, and Stevan Scheinov. The GBRA also presented and recommended Adalbert Beregszaszi and K. Haug to the Scottish Bible Society for Bible

---

[168] Ibid., pp. 95-96.
[169] Ibid., pp. 88-89.
[170] *Glas Evandjelja* 2 (1936), p. 23.
[171] Hopper, 'A History of Baptists in Yugoslavia', p. 98.
[172] Ibid., p. 93.

distribution.¹⁷³ GBRA continued to develop Sunday schools and the youth ministry. Until 1925, Jakob Berleth had been actively engaged into the work of Sunday schools and youth work. For many years the youth ministry was led in close co-operation with the Baptist Union. In May 1931, the GBRA organised a conference for the young people of the German-speaking churches in Petrovo Polje.¹⁷⁴ In 1932, Heinz Herman was supplied to promote the Sunday schools and youth ministry in the GBRA.¹⁷⁵

SEGMC also gave special assistance in the theological education of Baptist leaders. Under their influence many leaders studied in European theological institutions. Adolf Lehotsky, Johann Wahl, Johann Sepper, and Phillip Scherer finished Baptist Theological Seminary in Hamburg. Károly Tary received theological education in Saint Andrea's Bible school in Austria.¹⁷⁶ During their vacations, students always helped their local churches and missionaries.¹⁷⁷ Adolf Lehotsky wrote in a letter to a friend about one of the mission trips to Bosnia-Herzegovina: 'After the visit to Bačka, Banat and Srem (provinces in Vojvodina, Serbia) we travelled to Bosnia. In Derventa and Sarajevo, we held evening sermons… We obtained a slight insight into the core of Islam'.¹⁷⁸ After their studies, former students again entered into the work of the GBRA and the Baptist Union. In the winter of 1929, Lehotsky became pastor of the Baptist church in Novi Sad. He was the first to intercede for mission work among the Slavic population. From 1931, Lehotski served as Secretary of the GBRA till he was drafted into the German army in 1944.¹⁷⁹ Another former student, Johann Sepper, moved to Bosnia-Herzegovina after his studies in Hamburg to be a missionary among the German-speaking population.

From 1928, the GBRA developed the work in the Bosnian village of Franzjosefsfeld. In the new Kingdom of SCS, Franzjosefsfeld was renamed in Petrovo Polje in honour of Tsar Petar I. Karadjordjevic.¹⁸⁰ Phillip Scherer moved there with his family, becoming the first full-time worker in Bosnia-Herzegovina and establishing Baptist work in this village. GBRA saw great potential in him and decided to send him to study. In 1930, Scherer left Bosnia-Herzegovina to attend the Baptist Seminary at Hamburg.¹⁸¹ Károly Tary, a

---

[173] Ibid., p. 101.
[174] *Glas Evandjelja* 7 (1931), p. 92.
[175] Hopper, 'A History of Baptists in Yugoslavia', pp. 91-92, 97-98.
[176] Knežević, *Pregled Povijestii*, pp. 47- 48.
[177] *Glas Evandjelja* 10 (1926), p. 118.
[178] 'Posle našeg rada u Bačkoj, Banatu i Sremu (pokrajine u Vojvodini, Srbija), otputovali smo jos u Bosnu. U Derventi i Sarajevu smo održali vecernja bogosluženja... Ujedno smo dobili mali uvid u bit Islama.' *Evangeliumsbote* 3:11 (1925), pp. 6-7.
[179] Hopper, 'A History of Baptists in Yugoslavia', pp. 91-92.
[180] Alija Muratbegović, 'Saga o Kafi na Bosanski Način' (Saga about Bosnian Coffee), *Bosanskohercegovacki Dani* 270 (16 August 2002), http://www.bhdani.com/arhiva/270/t27012.shtml, accessed 4 January 2007.
[181] Hopper, 'A History of Baptists in Yugoslavia', pp. 97-98.

Hungarian Baptist from Žabanj, asked the leaders of the GBRA to let him to take responsibility for Petrovo Polje, replacing Scherer. The GBRA agreed to give him this duty, but only temporarily. They felt strongly that Tary should also go to the Bible school to study to prepare for work among the Hungarian churches. After a short stay in Petrovo Polje, Tary left to go to the Bible school in Sankt Andrea, Austria.[182]

In 1932, after completing his studies, Johann Sepper returned from Germany. The GBRA sent him to Petrovo Polje as pastor of the local Baptist church. Like his father, Carl Sepper, Johann visited the scattered German congregations throughout Bosnia-Herzegovina. Under his leadership, the German-speaking congregation in Petrovo Polje become an independent church and in 1932 it became a member of GBRA.[183] Johann Sepper was also actively engaged in the life and work of the Sarajevo church.[184] As we have seen, after the First World War the Sarajevo Baptist church was a mission station of SBRA. Its leader, Josip Černy, closely co-operated with the leaders of SBRA and visited their meetings and conferences. Under the influence of Sepper, the members of the Sarajevo church decided to join the GBRA and it became a member in 1935. That same year, Sepper left Bosnia-Herzegovina and moved to Kikinda and served there as pastor of the Baptist church until the Second World War.

In 1935, the GBRA accepted Peter Blatt as a full-time worker and sent him to Petrovo Polje as pastor. He also actively served Baptist churches throughout Bosnia until the Second World War.[185]

In the years between the two World Wars, the churches of the Baptist Union of the Kingdom of Yugoslavia demonstrated stable growth. In 1937, the Baptist Union recorded twenty-nine churches with 2,041 members, and 844 pupils of Sunday schools that were located mainly in Croatia, Serbia, Vojvodina, and Slovenia.[186] In Bosnia-Herzegovina the growth was not so evident. There were only small Baptist churches in Sarajevo and Petrovo Polje, and Baptist groups in Derventa and Brezovo Polje. Two different Mission organizations—SBC and SEGMC—worked there.[187] Each of them had their own mission philosophy: while the SBC sent missionaries and workers, the German Mission Committee supported native workers and educated them for future work.

The occupation of the Kingdom of Yugoslavia in April 1941 by German and Italian troops divided the Baptist Union into several small groups that were separated from one another.[188] The GBRA was dissolved at the end of the

---

[182] Ibid., pp. 98-99.
[183] Knežević, *Pregled Povijesti*, p. 46.
[184] *Glas Evandjelja* 9-10 (1935), pp. 91-92; 3-4 (1936), p. 41; 7-8 (1936), pp. 70-71.
[185] Hopper, 'A History of Baptists in Yugoslavia', pp. 99-100.
[186] *Glas Evandjelja* 5-6 (1937), p. 38.
[187] H. Leon McBeth, *Baptist Heritage* (Nashville: Broadman, 1987), p. 489.
[188] Klementić and Žadar, *Diverse Peoples*, p. 184.

war.[189] Many members of German-speaking churches left the country because of the threat to their lives. Some of them, such as Lehostky, were drafted into the German army. Some members of the Baptist churches, such as Andrew Dercher, were killed by members of Nationalist military organizations. Franjo Klem explained that time:

> Then the occupation came. The body of the Federation was torn into pieces. Part of the Baptist churches in Slovenia came under German occupation, and soon some of our members were taken to concentration camps in Germany. Others had to flee to the guerrillas in the Alps, to save their lives. Another part of the Churches in this area came under Italian administration... The North of our country came under Hungarian occupation but Baptists there were soon able to link up with Hungarian Baptists who had many large and lively churches... The Eastern part of our country, Serbia, was under German occupation, but our Mission was able to continue there without being disturbed.[190]

The Baptist Christian magazines *Glas Evandjelja* and *Sestrinski List* stopped being published. The Baptist seminary that had been working for only a few years was closed. Moore and his family were forced to leave the country. War was a deterrent to Baptist work in Yugoslavia and all development work ceased.

Political, Religious, Economic and Social Circumstances

The end of the First World War and the breakdown of Austro-Hungarian rule brought about great changes in the whole Balkan area.[191] The unification of the Kingdom of Serbia with the independent countries of Slovenia, Croatia, and Bosnia-Herzegovina into the Kingdom of SCS brought socio-economic and political instability. According to Imamovic, between the two World Wars in Europe, the political situation in Bosnia-Herzegovina was difficult. In 1918, when the Kingdom of Serbia was joined by Croatia, Slovenia, and Bosnia-Herzegovina, democratic government with a parliament was announced. The intention was that each ethnic group would have representation in the government. Many political parties appeared at that time, usually on a religious basis. However, in 1929, Tsar Aleksandar pronounced himself Regent of the new country—the Kingdom of Yugoslavia. This resulted in the dismissal of parliament. The country was divided into areas called *Banovinas*. Bosnia-Herzegovina was divided into four *banovinas*. Each *banovina* had its own rules concerning religious freedom and that made Baptist work difficult. Churches

---

[189] Hopper, 'A History of Baptists in Yugoslavia', pp. 91-92.
[190] Klem, 'Yugoslavia', p. 89.
[191] Imamović, *Historija Bošnjaka*, p. 492.

had to reorganise their activities in accordance with the new geographical divisions and political situation.

During all the time of the Kingdom SCS/Yugoslavia, Tsar Alexandar tried to unite the nation under the one name—Yugoslavia. Each nation, however, wanted to keep its own ethnic identity. This was a crucial issue for them. Even Baptist churches were organised on ethnic lines, likely believing that this was the best way to reach new converts. This may explain why Baptists in Bosnia-Herzegovina did not wish to evangelise Muslims. Muslims lived very separately from others and considered Baptists as another foreign institution. When Hungary, Rumania, and Bulgaria approached the Tripartite Pact (Germany-Italy-Japan), the Kingdom of Yugoslavia found itself surrounded by Fascists. In March 1941, the administration of the Kingdom of Yugoslavia signed an agreement to join the Tripartite Pact. However, on 6 April 1941, Hitler's army attacked Belgrade.[192] That was the end of Baptist mission work in Bosnia-Herzegovina until to the end of the Second World War.

The religious situation in Bosnia-Herzegovina during the Kingdom of SCS/Yugoslavia was complex. In 1921, the population of Bosnia-Herzegovina was 1,890,460 including: 829,360 Orthodox; 588,173 Muslims; 444,309 Catholics; 12,051 Jews and, 16,567 of other religious affiliation.[193] Each ethnic group identified itself according to its religion. The attitude of the new administration to all religions was important for the population. In 1920, the new administration guaranteed 'the freedom of religion and conscience'. The St Vitus' Day Constitution states: 'Adopted religious beliefs are equal before the law and people may publicly profess their religious doctrine.'[194] The administration was, in theory, obliged to give the Bosnian people and their religious institutions full protection. In reality, the situation did not change and very often local administrations did not implement the law. Baptist believers were persecuted. Many mosques were also destroyed or reorganised into schools.[195] Later, the administration of the Kingdom of Yugoslavia decreed that all churches and religious congregations had to be put under the supervision of the law. They cancelled the Ministry of Religions and empowered the Ministry of Justice to supervise all religious activities. In a short time, this ministry applied the law to the Orthodox Church, the Jewish Religious community, and the Protestant congregations.[196] It gave Baptist congregations freedom to express their beliefs and legalised their existence. From that time, Baptist missionaries could travel freely throughout the country.

The social-economic situation in Bosnia-Herzegovina at that time was also difficult. The economy was in crisis. Bosnia-Herzegovina was agrarian—

---

[192] Ibid., p. 529.
[193] Ibid, p. 492.
[194] Kovačević, 'Legal Position', p. 2.
[195] Imamović, *Historija Bošnjaka*, p. 491.
[196] Imamović, *Historija Bošnjaka*, p. 508.

86.37% of population lived in villages and worked on the land.[197] The majority were poor. Industrial units were in bad condition. The railways were narrow-gauge and also in bad condition. Many people in the cities were unemployed. Around eighty percent of the population was illiterate.[198] In these conditions, emigration increased. Many people moved to the USA, Argentina, and Turkey, hoping to find a better life. During the First World War, many Muslims left the country because of fear, in the Kingdom SCS the majority of emigrants left the country because of the poor economic situation. The Muslim population had many difficulties not only from the authorities but also from their Slavic neighbours. The Slavic population was unfriendly and, at times, aggressive. They told them to 'Go back to Asia!'. Muslim farmers often lost all their property and land. Hatred arose between the nationalities. All these conditions made mission work in Bosnia-Herzegovina extremely complicated.

Stagnation: Baptist Mission in Bosnia-Herzegovina in Communist Times (1946-1994)

The Baptist Union: Emerging Hope

Right after WWII came to an end, Bosnia-Herzegovina found itself in a new political situation and as part of a new country—The Socialist Federal Republic of Yugoslavia. Franjo Klem, one of the Baptist leaders, described the feelings of believers at that time: 'When in 1945 our country was set free by Partisan units assisted by the Big Three Allies (Churchill, Roosevelt and Stalin), a new period in the history of Baptist Mission in Yugoslavia began.'[199] On 29 September 1945, it was declared that in 'accordance with the freely expressed will of all nations', there would be a new country named 'The Socialist Federal Republic of Yugoslavia' (hereafter SFRY).[200] Josip Broz Tito, the leader of the Communist Party of Yugoslavia, was elected as a President of the SFRY and the territory was divided into six constituent Republics. Bosnia-Herzegovina became 'The Socialist Republic of Bosnia-Herzegovina' with its own interior administration and territory as a part of SFRY.[201] The Constitution of 1974 said that the Socialist Republic of Bosnia-Herzegovina was 'a socialist democratic

---

[197] Tomislav Išek, 'Bosna i Hercegovina od Stvaranja do Propasti Prve Zajedničke Države (1918-1941)' (Bosnia and Herzegovina from its Creation to the Fall of the First Common State) in Safet Halilović, ed., *Bosna i Hercegovina od Najstarijih Vremena do Kraja Drugog Svijetskog Rata* (Bosnia and Herzegovina from Ancient Times till the End of the Second World War) (Sarajevo: Bosanski Kulturni Centar, 1998), p. 306.

[198] Išek, 'Bosna i Hercegovina' p. 310.

[199] Klem, 'Yugoslavia', p. 89.

[200] Klementić and Žadar, *Diverse Peoples*, p. 197.

[201] Imamović, *Historija Bošnjaka*, p. 556.

country and a self-managing socialist democratic community of workers and citizens, the people of Bosnia-Herzegovina—Muslims, Serbs and Croats'.[202] The other republics of SFRY were defined as national countries.

As with WWI, the Baptist churches in Bosnia-Herzegovina barely survived WWII. All faith communities in Yugoslavia had suffered. The death of many people, deportation, migration, evacuation, and refugees affected Baptists as well as other Protestant churches. In 1944, German troops withdrew from Yugoslavia to their homeland. Many ethnic Germans left Yugoslavia with them. According to Hopper, around five-hundred members of GBRA left the Kingdom of Yugoslavia.[203] German colonies were evacuated.[204] Petrovo Polje in Bosnia-Herzegovina was one of them. All the German churches and their mission stations lost members and closed. Mission stations, such as Brezovo Polje and Petrovo Polje, became small Baptist groups. The only Baptist church left in Bosnia-Herzegovina was in Sarajevo. Despite all these problems, Baptist churches started to renovate their work. In October 1945, Baptist leaders met in Novi Sad 'to evaluate the situation in the churches and constitute a Union'.[205]

In 1946, all faith communities that were registered in pre-war Yugoslavia were recognised as legal religious communities.[206] Paul Mojzes, a Yugoslavian scholar, suggests 'the Yugoslav Marxists hastened to declare the separation of church and state and to enact laws of religious liberties'.[207] They were not actually prepared to tolerate different thinking and could not stand the Church as a holder of privileges. The Communist government was rigorous and atheistic towards religion and faith communities. They sought to crush the churches and eradicate religious sentiments and they condemned religious leaders for collaboration with ethnic wartime regimes and foreign invaders. Many religious leaders were executed, jailed, or exiled. The Baptist church was considered a sect. Baptist leaders were under suspicion, persecuted and even imprisoned because of their connections with Germans or other foreigners. Communist leaders especially examined Baptists with German roots. For example, after Lehotsky returned from Russian captivity, he was imprisoned because of his participation in the German Army.[208] V. Korovec was sentenced to eleven years of hard labour.[209] S. Pinter and F. Klem were imprisoned for a

---

[202] Enver Halilović, *Bošnjaci i Vrijeme*, pp. 125-126.

[203] Hopper, 'A History of Baptists in Yugoslavia', p. 3.

[204] J Boisset, *Kratka Povijest Protestantizma* (Brief History of Protestantism) (Zagreb: Kršćanska Sadašnjost, 1985), p. 193.

[205] Hopper, 'A History of Baptists in Yugoslavia', p. 161.

[206] Knežević, *Pregled Povijesti*, p. 92.

[207] Paul Mojzes, 'Christian-Marxist Encounter in the Context of Socialist Society', *Journal of Ecumenical Studies* 9:1 (Winter, 1972), p. 5.

[208] Hilda Lehotsky, 'Personalna Opazanja o Njenom Ocu Adofu Lehotskom' (Personal Notes about Her Father Adolf Lehotsky), personal notes, original is owned by Teofil Lehotsky, January 2001.

[209] Knežević, *Pregled Povijesti*, p. 92.

short period without concrete accusations.[210] Things were worse for political dissidents such as Angela Baumann: she and others were executed.[211]

Despite the State attitude, Baptist leaders continued to re-organise a new Baptist Union. The Pre-war Union had been a Union of many regional associations. The post-war Baptist leaders recognised that this type of organisation was weak. The Union had not been a homogeneous and strong organisation because it had consisted of ethnic based associations: German, Serb-Croatian, Slovenian, and others. In the new political situation, they decided to jointly reorganise. From 1946 to 1948, several organisational conferences were held. At the conferences the Union was reorganised and divided into districts, Republic Unions and the Baptist Union of Yugoslavia (hereafter BUY).[212] In 1963, the BUY was renamed the 'Union of Baptist Churches in the Socialist Federation of Republics of Yugoslavia' (UBC SFRY).[213] The BUY received financial support from SBC for preachers' salaries, for renovating church buildings and the purchase of a new building for publishing Christian literature and theological education.[214] Unfortunately, the small number of Baptists in Bosnia-Herzegovina made it impossible to organise the Republic Union. So Baptist work in Bosnia-Herzegovina was put under the supervision of BUY. During these conferences, 'The Statute of the Baptist Church of SFRY' was issued, corrected, and supplemented. Also drawn up was the 'Fundamentals of the Baptist Faith'.[215] From that point on, BUY was determined to promote its work in a new, progressive way.

From 1953, the State policy towards religions and faith communities changed. The Law of Legal State of Faith Communities (*Zakon o pravnom položaju vjerskih zajednica*) was ratified, formally and legally equalising all faith communities. Article 154 states,

> Citizens are equal in rights and duties without regard to nationality, race, sex, language, religious profession or social position. All are equal in eyes of the law.[216]

The law annulled the pre-war classification of faith communities. The new law recognised all faith communities. This status gave them certain religious

---

[210] Theodore F. Adams, *Baptists Around the Word* (Nashville: Broadman Press, 1967), p. 61.
[211] See more in Knežević, *Pregled Povijesti*, p. 92.
[212] Ibid., p. 89.
[213] Parker, *Baptists in Europe*, p. 204.
[214] Teofil Lehotsky, 'Prilog Istoriji', p. 20; 'Tenth Baptist World Congress', *Baptist World Alliance* (Rio de Janeiro: Baptist World Alliance, 26 June-3 July 1960), p. 188.
[214] *Glasnik* 7:9 (1965), p. 135.
[215] Klem, 'Yugoslavia', p. 90.
[216] Josip Horak, 'Church, State, and Religious Freedom in Yugoslavia: An Ideological and Constitutional Study', *Journal of Church and State* 19 (1977), p. 293.

freedoms not available in other socialist countries in Eastern Europe.[217] 'Priests and members of the hierarchy were allowed to travel freely abroad and foreign ecclesiastical dignitaries allowed to visit the churches.'[218] Many of the remaining imprisoned clergy were released. Baptist leaders received permission to go abroad. In 1953, Josip Horak, one of the new Baptist leaders in Yugoslavia, participated in a European Baptist Youth Leadership Conference that was held in Rüschlikon, Switzerland.[219] In 1960, Klem participated in the Tenth Baptist World Congress in Brazil.[220] In 1965, a group of Yugoslav leaders participated in the World Congress of Baptists in Miami, USA.[221]

The Communist administration now allowed the activity of churches under the principle of separation of Church and state, liberty of conscience and religion.[222] From that time, the government dropped much of its anti-religious propaganda. Believers could ask the government to respect its own laws. The new law gave permission for religious press, after which BUY started to publish their own magazine. In 1959, Klem published the first edition of a Christian magazine *Glasnik* (The Herald) in Rijeka.[223] This magazine was a replacement for *Glas Evandjelja* (Voice of the Gospel) that had stopped right before WWII broke out. *Glasnik* was published until the late 1980s. At that time, BUY was given the opportunity to spread the word of God through mass media. Josip Horak became a permanent speaker on Trans World Radio whose programmes were transmitted in Croatian and other languages of South-east Europe.[224] These evangelistic programmes were transmitted twice each week from TWR Monte Carlo.[225] These new socio-political realities of SFRY assisted the gradual restoration of Protestant churches. J. Boisset noted that, in the 1950s, many communities such as the Baptists began to bloom.[226] According to Klem, in 1950 the BUY had 'more than 30 average-sized churches and many more small ones, with about 3,500 adult members'.[227] In Bosnia-Herzegovina there was only one small congregation.

---

[217] Knežević, *Pregled Povijesti*, p. 93.
[218] Mojzes, 'Christian-Marxist Encounter', p. 10.
[219] Knežević, *Pregled Povijesti*, p. 94.
[220] 'Tenth Baptist World Congress', p. 188.
[221] *Glasnik* 7:9 (1965), p. 135.
[222] Imamović, *Historija Bošnjaka*, p. 562; Branko Petranović and Čedomir Strbac, *Istorija Socijalisticke Jugoslavije* (History of Socialistic Yugoslavia) (Beograd: Radnicka Stampa, 1977), p. 69.
[223] Hopper, 'A History of Baptists in Yugoslavia', p. 155.
[224] Teofil Lehotsky, 'Prilog Istoriji', p. 28.
[225] *Glasnik* 7:10 (1965), pp. 156-157.
[226] Boisset, *Kratka Povijest*, p. 193.
[227] Klem, 'Yugoslavia', p. 91.

MISSION

After the war, the number of church members was reduced and several mission stations transformed into small Baptist groups. So the first goal of the leadership of BUY was to connect all the churches that were left and revitalise mission work. According to Knežević, at that time there were fourteen Baptist preachers,[228] such as Vacek, Jekić, Carl Sepper, and Johann Sepper. They travelled throughout the country, often visiting churches and providing help not only with baptismal, wedding, and funeral services, but also leading worship and preaching. The number of such missionaries was reduced to six. At that point, Franjo Klem, Josip Horak, Adolf Lehotsky, Károly Tary, and others took over mission responsibilities in full or part-time service.[229] The churches were visited rarely, usually only on special occasions. Very often pastors combined a few services. Klem was pastor of six churches and served in ten mission stations in addition.[230] Another reason for that was that each missionary had a larger and wider mission field. Klem wrote,

> Some preachers have to care for whole provinces. One has to travel 14,000 km (8,750 miles) every years by railway, bicycle or on foot. More than half the year he spends in the mission field. They sacrificed themselves and often even their families on the altar of the Mission.[231]

In these new circumstances, the leaders of BUY recognised a need to change their methods of missionary work. Before WWII, Baptists had usually worked among relatives, friends, and acquaintances in their own ethnic groups. After the war, they turned to a wider circle of the population. To implement this goal, BUY organised 'courses for preachers, prospective preachers, Sunday school teachers, and young leaders'.[232] However, BUY did not devise other constructive mission methods that would work in the new political system. This resulted in few individual projects being implemented. In June 1948, the Yugoslav Communist Party was thrown out of Cominform and the USSR. Tito turned to the West, asking for financial and other assistance. Despite the fact that SFRY remained a communist authoritarian country, it received considerable humanitarian and financial help from abroad. The Baptist churches also received humanitarian help, mainly from SBF. With that help, the Yugoslav Baptists could reach a wider circle of people and their mission work was successful.[233]

---

[228] Knežević, *Pregled Povijesti*, p. 89.
[229] Hopper, 'A History of Baptists in Yugoslavia', p. 156.
[230] Adams, *Baptists Around the World*, p. 62.
[231] Klem, 'Yugoslavia', p. 90.
[232] Ibid.
[233] Knežević, *Pregled Povijesti*, p. 90.

The socio-economic situation of the 1950s and rapid urbanisation was a challenge to the BUY policy of church planting. During the Kingdom of Yugoslavia, Baptist fellowships had been founded primarily in the villages, after WWII churches in cities were given primary attention. One of the reasons for that change was the significant movement of young people from the villages to the growing industrial centres for schooling and employment in the 1950s. As a result, the Baptist leadership shifted their attention from villages and concentrated on establishing new mission stations in the cities.[234] A large number of provincial churches lost their members. Unfortunately, many churches in villages died.[235] In 1961, another reorganisation of BUY mission work took place. That year in Novi Sad, leaders of BUY founded 'Home Mission', whose goals were to co-ordinate the mission activities of BUY and to care for preachers and other mission workers.[236] The work of Home Mission concentrated mainly on financial support for preachers.

In the middle of the 1960s, BUY had opportunities linked to the mission activities of some Baptist leaders from abroad. In 1967, Horak organised a visit of the famous American evangelist, Billy Graham, to SFRY.[237] On 8 to 9 July, he held two evangelistic rallies in Zagreb, a conference for Yugoslavian journalists, and preached in the Evangelical church. Many thousands of people heard him. On 28 to 29 March 1968, Cliff Richard held a concert. In 1970, Graham preached at 'Euro 70' in Dortmund, this was televised in most European countries and the BUY organised its transmission to Yugoslavia,[238] where many people watched it. In 1976, the Communist administration gave permission to Dr James Archie Williams and his wife Nela (Nada) Horak-Williams to work permanently in SFRY, developing Christian theological education.[239] They were the first Southern Baptist missionaries to Communist Yugoslavia.

Not all these mission activities were successful. Theirs was not a coherent mission strategy. While Klem and Lehotsky proposed some mission projects, virtually nobody else was interested. There was still great ethnic separation within the BUY. This separation was vivid in cultural, religious, and mission aspects. Even though they were united in one Union, each ethnic group cared mostly for their believers and areas. No one was interested in evangelising the Muslims. In *Glasnik* (1965) a believer from Bosnia-Herzegovina even asked: 'Do we have to evangelise Muslims? Could Muslims believe in Christ as the Saviour and be saved?'[240] There was no motivation for mission in the local

---

[234] Hopper, 'A History of Baptists in Yugoslavia', pp. 156-157.
[235] Knežević, *Pregled Povijesti*, p. 95.
[236] Ibid., p. 107.
[237] Teofil Lehotsky, 'Prilog Istoriji', p. 28.
[238] Knežević, *Pregled Povijesti*, pp. 109-110.
[239] Teofil Lehotsky, 'Prilog Istoriji', p. 29.
[240] *Glasnik* 7:10, (1965), p. 157.

churches. Many believers neither wanted to support missionaries financially nor had any willingness to evangelise people themselves.

SUNDAY SCHOOL AND YOUTH MINISTRY

After WWII, the BUY again started Sunday schools and youth ministry. In the first years after the war, each association began youth work within its own ranks. Because the law did not allow churches to organise youth movements, some churches organised mountain climbing clubs.[241] Others organised summer meetings for young Baptists. Congregations usually had some activities for children and young people, but there were no BUY youth meetings or conferences until the middle of the 1950s. The first BUY youth conference was held in Novi Sad in 1955. According to Knežević, there were another ten, the last in 1988.[242] Klem was an active promoter of Sunday schools. He worked on the development of handbooks for Sunday school teachers and a guide for daily worship for the BUY.[243] Twice, in 1956 and in 1960, Klem was sent to the US to attend courses on seminary and church organisation and Sunday school work. After his return, Klem organised an 'all-age' Sunday school.[244] This was something new for Yugoslavian Baptists. This innovation had a good reception and 'in a short time the church had over forty members'.[245]

THEOLOGICAL EDUCATION

Another issue that became urgent at this time was the education of Baptist leaders. The previous educational programme was in ruins. The Baptist Seminary in Belgrade that had started its work in 1940 was closed immediately after the beginning of the German attacks on Yugoslavia in 1941. Unfortunately, most of its students did not finish their education. Only a few students had opportunities to finish their theological education in other countries. For instance, Klem completed his education at the Baptist Seminary in Budapest.[246] Immediately after the war, BUY had no chance to restart the school. The Communist administration did not give John Allen Moore, the pre-war director of the Bible school in Beograd, a permit for permanent stay and work in SFRY. He continued to visit churches and to collaborate in mission and develop theological education for BUY.[247] From 1946 to 1950, short seminars

---

[241] Hopper, 'A History of Baptists in Yugoslavia', p. 163.
[242] Knežević, *Pregled Povijesti*, p. 104.
[243] Adams, *Baptists Around the World*, p. 63.
[244] Davorin Peterlin, 'Theological Education Among Croatian Baptists: A Sociohistorical Survey', *Baptist Quarterly* 5 (2000), p. 243.
[245] Adams, *Baptists Around the World*, p. 62.
[246] Peterlin, 'Theological Education', p. 242.
[247] Teofil Lehotsky, 'Prilog Istoriji', p. 25.

were organised for church leaders twice a year. In 1952 it was proposed to re-open the school. Horak, Klem, and Lehotsky took the initiative and re-opened the school in 1954 in Zagreb. Horak was elected President and Klem General Secretary of the School. Sandor Pintér, Ludovik Drobný, Lehotsky, and M. Lovrec constituted the first faculty.[248] The school began with a two-year secondary level programme and was actually a pastoral training centre.[249] Ten students enrolled in the programme. The conditions of the school were poor: it did not have its own building and lectures were held in the church building. Students slept at the home of Tomo Vincetić, a member of the church. In addition to the residential programme, the school also ran 'theological weeks'.[250]

In was obvious that the school needed a new location. After a few years of looking, it moved to newly built premises in Novi Sad in June 1967.[251] The Baptist School was 'subsidised by the Foreign Mission Board of the Southern Baptist Convention (SBC), who paid for the building in Novi Sad and provided lecturers' salaries'.[252] New and better conditions brought new possibilities for the school and needed reforms took place. The programme was extended to four years. From that time it became a Baptist Theological School (hereafter BTS). Although most lecturers of BTS were Yugoslavian citizens, foreign teachers were also invited. According to Hopper, these included John Watts and John Allen Moor from the seminary at Rüschlikon, Switzerland.[253] Ten men and five women were enrolled in BTS. Each year student enrolment soared and in autumn 1976 forty-three students enrolled for study.

Another important aspect of BTS' work was 'theological education by extension' (TEE). In 1977, Dr James A. Williams, a Rüschlikon graduate and one of the Southern Baptist missionaries to Communist Yugoslavia, proposed and drew up a plan for this programme. The programme was intended for active pastors and workers who could not afford a full-time study. The school prepared and produced appropriate theological textbooks. In 1979 the programme was launched.[254] Due to the sudden death of Williams (who was killed in car accident), Ruth Lehotsky, a lecturer at BTS, became the director of the programme.[255] In late 1980s, FMB finances were scaled down and

---

[248] Hopper, 'A History of Baptists in Yugoslavia', pp. 161-162.
[249] Peterlin, 'Theological Education', p. 244.
[250] In Novi Sad: 22-25 August 1961, in Daruvar: 4-11 February 1964, and in Sisak: 19-25 January 1965. Peterlin, p. 244.
[251] Knežević, *Pregled Povijesti*, p. 103; Hopper, 'A History of Baptists in Yugoslavia', p. 162.
[252] Peterlin, 'Theological Education', p. 244.
[253] Hopper, 'A History of Baptists in Yugoslavia', p. 162.
[254] Teofil Lehotsky, 'Prilog Istoriji', p. 32.
[255] Knežević, *Pregled Povijesti*, p. 103; Peterlin, p. 244.

eventually cut off.[256] From that time until the Yugoslav war the BTS had serious financial problems.

Mission Work in Bosnia-Herzegovina: Stagnation

After WWII, Baptist Mission work in Bosnia-Herzegovina stagnated. The whole Republic had only a small number of believers. Small Baptist groups in Derventa and Brezovo Polje that in pre-war time were under the supervision of the Slavic Regional Association lost many members. Those who left found themselves in a situation where they had to join Baptist churches in other places. The Baptist church in Petrovo Polje, which in pre-war Yugoslavia was under the supervision of the German Regional Association, almost disappeared. At the end of WWII, this village was evacuated by German troops, leaving just a few families. In Communist Yugoslavia, the village was renamed Novo Selo.[257] There is no evidence of any Baptist presence there after this time. The only Baptist church left was in Sarajevo with a small number of members. According to Šumić, a small Baptist church was later founded in Mostar, but this church integrated with the Mostar Pentecostal church in the 1980s.[258] So we can say that during the period of Communist Yugoslavia, Baptist mission work was concentrated mostly in Sarajevo.

During the SFRY, Baptist mission work in Bosnia-Herzegovina was weak and inconsistent. There were only a small number of missionaries, especially those who wanted to stay in Bosnia-Herzegovina. These missionaries rarely visited the Sarajevo church. In the first post-war years only a few faithful Baptists, such as Lehotsky and Klem, still visited and worked in Bosnia-Herzegovina. They supervised and encouraged the Sarajevo Baptist church, the only church left in the whole of Bosnia-Herzegovina. During those trips they evangelised through conversation and the distribution of Christian tracts. This was the only way that they could tell people about Christ. The biggest problem at that time was the lack of mission strategy for the evangelisation of Bosnia-Herzegovina under the new Communist system. The Communist authorities did not allow believers to testify to their beliefs in public.[259] So they could only practice personal evangelism to tell people about God. Many believers were not even sure whether they should evangelise Muslims.[260] This situation did not change much in future years.

---

[256] Peterlin, 'Theological Education', p. 244.

[257] Muratbegović, 'Saga o Kafi na Bosanski Način' (Saga about Bosnian Coffee), *Bosanskohercegovacki Dani* 270 (16 August 2002), http://www.bhdani.com/arhiva/270/t27012.shtml, accessed 4 January 2007.

[258] Luka Šumić, personal interview (Sarajevo, Bosnia-Herzegovina: 19 May 2005).

[259] *Glasnik* 7:3 (1965), pp. 39, 48.

[260] *Glasnik* 7:10 (1965), p. 157.

SARAJEVO BAPTIST CHURCH

The Sarajevo Baptist church lived through WWII with great loss. In the pre-war Kingdom of Yugoslavia, the majority of members were German. During WWII, the church lost all the German-speaking members. That left only around fifteen believers with their leader, Josip Černy (1881-1968). For many years, Černy was the leader of the Sarajevo Baptist church. He came to Sarajevo during the Austro-Hungarian rule, serving the church during WWI and remaining during WWII. He was not ordained, but he was dedicated to the congregation and he encouraged believers during the worst time of the church's life. The Sarajevo Baptist church did not have its own church building, so Černy opened his own house for church meetings. From time to time, some preachers visited the church to lead the service and conduct the Lord's Supper. In 1955, the Sarajevo Baptist church had a service where several believers were baptised. Among them was Luka Šumić who later was the leader of Sarajevo congregation for many years.

In the 1960s, the Sarajevo church received a new pastor, Jaroš Varga. Even though Varga served in Sarajevo for only a short time, he played an important role. Under his leadership and for the first time in its history, the church obtained a church building. In 1961, the Sarajevo Baptist church signed a contract to purchase half of a building from Josip and Maria Černy.[261] Even though it was only a small ground floor room, it was very important for the church because it now had its own legal place for worship. There was also a small apartment for a pastor. In 1967, Varga moved to Karlovac, and, in 1969, he moved to Germany for the rest of his life.[262] After Varga left Sarajevo, the church was again left without a pastor. In 1968, Josip Černy died and Luka Šumić took responsibility for the church. Šumic's first contact with a Baptist believer had been with Zigmund Fedatov, a Baptist and employee of the Agriculture Faculty in Sarajevo. This meeting changed Šumic's life. In 1955, he was baptised and became a member of the Sarajevo church. By the time he took responsibility for the Sarajevo church, he had been a Baptist for fifteen years. He could not become pastor because the BUY policy was that only theologically-educated believers could take up that position. So, for several years the church had no pastor only occasional visits from BUY preachers. The Baptist work again stagnated.

In 1970, BUY sent Otto Bayer to Sarajevo. Bayer was a German from Vukovar. At the time when he first came to Sarajevo, Bayer was a student of BTS in Novi Sad. At first he only made occasional visits to the Sarajevo church

---

[261] 'Kupoprodajni Ugovor izmedu Sarajevske Baptisticke Crkve I Josipom I Marijom Černi' (Sales Contract between Sarajevo Baptist Church, and Josip and Maria Černy), unpub. document, private archive of Luka Šumić (2 December 1961).

[262] Knežević, *Pregled Povijesti*, p. 99.

to lead a service and preach. After he finished at BTS, Bayer moved to Sarajevo with his wife Ruženka.[263] The Bayer family stayed in Sarajevo only for a short time, but played a significant role. In 1972, a Muslim woman, Jasmina Karamehmedović, came to confess Christ as her Saviour. She was, to the best of my knowledge, the first Muslim convert in the history of the Baptist church of Bosnia-Herzegovina and is still a member of the Sarajevo Baptist church. In 1973, the Bayer family moved from Sarajevo to Germany.[264] According to Šumic, this was because of the conflict which arose in the church over the question of the Trinity.[265] After Bayer moved, the church was again without a pastor for a long time. The BUY ordained Ivan Vlašić to be leader of the church but he did not live in Sarajevo and was only a visiting preacher.[266] So we see that during the 1970s the church was mainly without a pastor and did not grow or develop.

More missionary work started after the Winter Olympics Games of 1984, held in Sarajevo. At that time, many foreigners came to the SFRY, among them many Baptists. The Communist authorities could not do anything against them, so these Baptists were able to organise church meetings. At that time, the church building was being renovated.[267] After the Olympics Games, Bosnia-Herzegovina became more interesting to others as a mission field. There were some attempts at Baptist work in Bijelina and Bosanski Brod, but without substantial results. From 1986 to 1992, Milan Tavarloza from Mošćenica was doing mission work for the Croatian Baptist Union in Banja Luka,[268] but he had to leave Bosnia-Herzegovina when the Yugoslav war started, at which point there was only the church in Sarajevo and a few individual believers in the country.

In the 1980s, Home Mission tried to help those churches which did not have a pastor. They made a schedule of those who would visit these churches. According to the schedule from 1985, all Baptist leaders, often with a family, had to visit the Sarajevo church at least once a year;[269] however, this did not work in practice. On 22 March 1986, the Home Mission discussed how to improve mission work in Sarajevo. At that time the church contained eight members. The Board proposed that the church in Zagreb consider overseeing

---

[263] Jasmina Karamehmedović, personal interview (Sarajevo, Bosnia-Herzegovina: 19 May 2005).
[264] Ibid.
[265] Luka Šumić, personal interview; Ljubica and Luka Šumić, 'Letter to the Board of Zagreb Baptist Church', unpub. letter, private archive of Luka Šumić (10 November 1998).
[266] Šumić and Šumić, 'Letter to Board of Zagreb Baptist Church from Ljubica i Luka Šumić'.
[267] Ruben Knežević, interview by correspondence (8 December 2003).
[268] Mark Vanderwerf, interview by correspondence (9 December 2003).
[269] 'Raspored posjeta Sarajevo 1985' (Schedule of Visit to Sarajevo, 1985), unpub. document, private archive of Luka Šumić (5 January 1985).

the Sarajevo church.[270] Unfortunately, there was some misunderstanding and the work was very inconsistent. A few months later, a letter complaining 'nobody has come from Zagreb for three months' was mailed on 17 June 1986 to the Board of Home Mission.[271] On 20 to 21 September 1986, the board of Home Mission held a meeting with members of the Sarajevo church about the possibility that the Zagreb Baptist church would be responsible for the church. At that meeting it was announced that the Zagreb church was willing to work in Bosnia-Herzegovina. The Sarajevo church accepted the proposition. The Zagreb church put the responsibility on two members, Josip Mikulić and Josip Čeh.[272] After half a year of such co-operation, the Committee of the Zagreb Baptist church wrote to the Home Mission Board. They explained that the Sarajevo Baptist church had to have some leader in the congregation constantly. They proposed that Luka Šumic be ordained a deacon.[273] There is no evidence of a response. Instead, on 26 June 1988, the Zagreb Baptist Church, with the blessing of Home Mission, sent Dragan Vojnica to Sarajevo for a month to help the church.[274] Vojnica was a student at BTS and he had to have a summer placement in a local church. Soon, Home Mission founded another solution for the Sarajevo church, sending Boris Kačarević (Boris Kacharevich) to be pastor.

Kačarević was a Serb from Valjevo. His wife, Senka, was a Muslim, who had become a Christian. They both had a desire to work in Bosnia-Herzegovina with Muslim people. Kačarević had studied at the Evangelical Bible Institute in Vienna for two years and then in the Bible School in Osijek.[275] After he finished his education, he came to Sarajevo and immediately started to look at the possibility of work with Muslims. At that time, Sarajevo had a mixed population of Serbs, Croats and Muslims. The centre of the Muslim community was the old part of town that called 'Barščašja' (Barshchashya). Kačarević decided that if he wanted to work with Muslims, he had to be as close to them as possible. He started to look for a building in Barščašja that he could buy for a church. Jim Smith, who was responsible for the finances of International Mission Board (IMB, US) for Europe at that time, came up with the finance

---

[270] 'Letter to Sarajevo Baptist Church from Board Secretary', unpub. letter, private archive of Luka Šumić (23 April 1986).

[271] 'Letter to the Board of Home Mission', unpub. letter, private archive of Luka Šumić (17 June 1986).

[272] 'Prepis Odluke Donesene Između Zajednica Sarajevo I Zagreba' (Transcript of the Decision that was made between the Sarajevo and Zagreb Congregations), unpub. document, private archive of Luka Šumić (20-21 September 1986).

[273] 'Letter to Home Mission from Zagreb Baptist Church', unpub. letter, private archive of Luka Šumić (11 March 1987).

[274] 'Potsetnik sa Dogovora u Zagrebu, o Dolazku brata Vojnica Dragana na Ferijalnu Praksu' (Reminder of the Zagreb Agreement about Brother Vojnica Dragana coming for Vocational Practice), unpub. document, private archive of Luka Šumić (26 June 1988).

[275] Vanderwerf, interview by correspondence.

and Kačarević bought a building in Baršćašja on Potok Street.[276] There he organised church meetings and fellowship. However, after that, the church split into two parts. Some of members stayed with Šumić in the old building on Ljubljanska Street and others left and joined Kačarević on Baršćašja. The division could have been caused by statements from the Home Mission Board and the Zagreb church, or by disagreements over the vision and mission of the church. Kačarević excluded Šumić from the church but the problem was not solved.[277] Šumić, with some members, started to gather at his house on Iljidja— as a church of eight members. After the separation, Kačarević started a new Baptist church working among Muslims. The church was visited by some Baptist leaders, Žarko Djordjović from Novi Sad, and Branko Lovrac from Zagreb. There was some success and a few Muslims started to attend services. Among them, Teufik and Vojka Cerović, who are members of the current Baptist church in Sarajevo.[278] Unfortunately, Kačarević did not stay for long.

On 9 February 1991 the BUY held a special conference in Belgrade where it was decided that, because of the new post-communist situation, the Union had to disband. On 2 March of 1991, after almost seventy years of work, the Baptist Union of Yugoslavia ceased to exist.[279] The Baptist church in Sarajevo was left without any support. In 1992, the Yugoslav war began and all mission work stopped. Kačarević stayed with his family in Sarajevo until 1994. During the blockade of Sarajevo, he organised some humanitarian help for the city.[280] Eventually they left Sarajevo and went as refugees to Germany.[281] The Sarajevo Baptist church ceased to exist.

Political, Religious, Social and Economic Circumstances

During the post-war decades of development, SFRY experienced an economic, social and political transformation that had a great influence on Baptist mission work in the country as a whole and in Bosnia-Herzegovina in particular. Many of these changes prevented mission work to a great extent. After WWII, Bosnia-Herzegovina became a part of SFRY and a people's republic within historic boundaries.[282] The Bosniacs did not receive the same national and political rights as other the other nationalities who lived in Bosnia-

---

[276] Tomislav and Lidija Dobutović, personal interview (Sarajevo, Bosnia-Herzegovina: 19 July 2005).
[277] Ibid.
[278] Ibid.
[279] Knežević, *Pregled Povijesti*, pp. 116-117.
[280] Vanderwerf, interview by correspondence.
[281] Wardin, *Baptists Around the World*, p. 258.
[282] Smail Cekić, 'Fašizam i Antifašizam u Bosni' (Fascism and Antifascism in Bosnia) (Sarajevo: Tribina Viječa Kongresa Bosnjačkjih Intelektualaca, 2001), p. 2.

Herzegovina. The Communists did not recognise the political state of the Bosniacs as a nation until the 1970s. Bosniacs did not have the opportunity for authentic expression of their nationality. The Communists tried to 'nationalise' the Bosniacs and force them to identify themselves as Serbs, Croats, or Montenegrins. It was not until the 1960s that it was understood in political and academic circles that Bosniacs were a particular ethic and national group. On 17 February 1968 a conference of CK SK Bosnia-Herzegovina proclaimed, 'Muslims are a special nation.'[283] From that time on, Bosnia-Herzegovina became the only country in which the name 'Muslim' indicated both the nationality and the confession of the person.

The post WWII system tolerated the existence of various religious groups, religious organisations, and communities. Among them was the Baptist community. The Catholic and Orthodox churches lost their pre-war positions as state churches. The new political and social structures did not give the church any privileges. In the new political system, the new Marxist theory proclaimed the separation of church and state.[284] The 'Basic Law on the Legal Position of Religious Communities' (1953) elaborated legal guarantees and provided the basis for greater legality in church-state relations. The Constitution guaranteed freedom of conscience and religion and prescribed punishment for anybody who encroached on that freedom and spread hatred and discord. The Communist administration established a whole series of legal mechanisms for the limitation of their activities with the goal of social marginalisation of religious organisations. For instance, they limited the freedom of religious activity only to the freedom of liturgical activity within church buildings.[285] Christians were not allowed public evangelism. They could share the Gospel only through private conversation.

In 1974, the Constitution was rewritten and, from that time, religious communities had limited freedom. In Article 174 of the Law entitled 'On the Legal Position of Religious Communities' it said,

> Religious communities may establish *only* religious schools for the training of clergy. It is forbidden to misuse religion and religious activities for political purposes. Socio-political communities may give material assistance to religious communities. Religious communities may have, within the limits defined by law, the right to own real estate.[286]

---

[283] Imamović, *Historija Bošnjaka*, pp. 564-565.

[284] Petranović and Strbac, *Istorija Socijalističke Jugoslavije*, p. 69.

[285] Zdenko Roter, 'The Position of Believers as Second-Class Citizens in Socialist Countries: The Case of Yugoslavia', *Occasional Papers on Religion in Eastern Europe* (Succeeded by: *Religion in Eastern Europe*) 9:3 (1989), p. 5.

[286] Horak, pp. 286, 292-294.

Despite Communist proclamations of religious freedom, the secret police still initiated occasional periods of terror.[287] These kept believers permanently intimidated. These were not outright persecutions, but surveillance, administrative nuances, restrictions upon religious press and abnormally heavy taxation.[288] For example, the Communists required that teachers could not be religious because 'schools had to be free from all religious shackles and had to be atheistic'.[289] Students of theology were not treated equally with other students.[290] Believers were not allowed to join the Communist Party. They were absent from the organs of government and other centres of political and social power. Religion was limited to the private sphere. 'The believer can function only as an abstract citizen and must leave her or his religious convictions "at home".'[291] As Zdenko Roter noted, 'believers were regarded as second-class citizens'.[292]

In SFRY, crude anti-religious, atheist propaganda had flooded society through the mass media. A general negative atmosphere in regard to religion was created in society. Many critical and derisive articles about religion were published in the press where it was identified with superstition, trickery, and fallacy. The Communist party of Yugoslavia stated that religion was 'the opium of the people', 'a reminder of an exploitative past', and 'a brake on progress'.[293] The church was a scapegoat that was blamed for failures in the 'building of socialism'.[294] The State's efforts were to influence people's way of thinking so that 'the working class is in principle against religion and against every other form of idealist thinking',[295] but according to Paul Moizes, '87 per cent of the population have declared religious preferences'.[296]

These socio-economic circumstances influenced the development of Baptist mission work. After WWII, the country was in ruins. Much of it was completely destroyed, including 150 firms and mines and more than 1,100 schools. 'The material damage was assessed to be 47 billion U.S. dollars.'[297] There was also a great loss of human life. According to Imamović, during WWII, between 1.027 and 1.14 million people were killed in the whole of

---

[287] Oleg Mandić, *Religija, Država, Nauka* (Religion, State, and Science) (Zagreb: Seljačka Sloga, 1956), pp. 31-32.
[288] Mojzes, 'Christian-Marxist Encounter', p. 8.
[289] Miloš B Jankovič, *Škola i Religija* (School and Religion) (Beograd: Narodna Knjiga, 1952), p. 50.
[290] Roter, 'Position of Believers', pp. 14-15.
[291] Ibid., p. 7.
[292] Ibid.
[293] Mandić, *Religija, Država, Nauka*, pp. 31-32.
[294] Roter, 'Position of Believers', pp. 6, 14-15.
[295] Mojzes, 'Christian-Marxist Encounter', p. 7.
[296] Ibid., p. 3.
[297] Klementić and Žadar, *Diverse Peoples*, p. 194.

Yugoslavia.[298] Of those, 500,000 were from Bosnia-Herzegovina. Bosnia-Herzegovina contained the most damage and the biggest number of destroyed villages and cities. So, restoring the destroyed country became the major task of the new Communist government. During the post-war years, SFRY made progress in economic and cultural development. Industrialisation and electrification of the country were the central economic goals. This was a time of great urbanisation. Many people moved from villages to the cities and the ethnic structure changed in several areas. 'Around 1.2 million people migrated from the countryside to the industrial centres.'[299] Many people emigrated to other countries such as Australia, the USA, Argentina, and Denmark. These migrations had a great influence on the life and mission of the Baptist church.

From 1986, political events were characterised by the appearance of stronger nationalism and fascism. It brought the country to an internal crisis that shook the foundation of Socialist Yugoslavia and divided the country. On 29 February 1992, the citizens of Bosnia-Herzegovina chose to become an independent and sovereign country. This decision brought Bosnia-Herzegovina to the brink of civil war which eventually broke out in April 1992.

The Revitalisation of the Baptist Mission in Independent Bosnia-Herzegovina

In the referendum of 29 February 1992, the majority of the population of Bosnia-Herzegovina voted for an independent and sovereign Bosnia-Herzegovina.[300] In 1992, on 6 April, the European Union recognised the independence of Bosnia-Herzegovina.[301] The same month, one of the bloodiest wars in the history of Europe began and the life of the country somehow stopped. The work of all Baptist local churches in Bosnia-Herzegovina was terminated. The Yugoslavian war ended in 1995. In accordance with the Dayton Peace Accord (December of 1995), post-war Bosnia-Herzegovina was re-organised into two entities: the Federation of Bosnia-Herzegovina and the Republic of Serbia.[302] By the time the war ended there were less than a dozen Baptist believers in the whole country, mainly in Sarajevo.[303] Thus, we can say

---

[298] Imamović, *Historija Bošnjaka*, p. 549.
[299] Klementić and Žadar, *Diverse Peoples*, p. 197.
[300] Klementić and Žadar, *Diverse Peoples*, p. 313.
[301] Imamović, *Historija Bošnjaka*, p. 568.
[302] 'The General Framework Agreement for Peace in Bosnia and Herzegovina (Initialled in Dayton on 21 November 1995 and signed in Paris on 14 December 1995)', *Organization for Security and Peace in Europe: Mission to Bosnia and Herzegovina*, http://www.oscebih.org/overview/gfap/eng/home.asp, accessed 9 January 2007.
[303] *The Baptist Church in Bosnia-Herzegovina: The Baptist Union in Bosnia-Herzegovina–A Short History and Vision*, unpub. document, archives of Sarajevo Baptist Church (2003).

that the Baptist Mission work in new independent Bosnia-Herzegovina went through a 'new start'.

After the Yugoslavian war, Baptist Mission work had to start from the beginning. Many Christian Mission organisations, such as the SBC International Mission Board, Pioneers, and others, came to Bosnia to help people with humanitarian aid. The eventual aim of some humanitarian activities was 'to plant churches among the unreached'.[304] In a short time, small Baptist groups were organised in Sarajevo, Zenica, Tuzla, Novi Travnik and Goražde. About the same time, the European Baptist Federation appealed to the Union of Baptist Churches in the Republic of Croatia (hereafter UBC RC) to take the Federation of Bosnia-Herzegovina as their mission field. The same proposition was put to the Baptist Union of Serbia in relation to the Republic of Serbia.[305] The Serbian Baptist Union sent their missionary worker, Dragan Kocič, to Banja Luka. Kocić soon organised a small Baptist church. At the same time, the Baptist Union of Serbia had undergone some internal turmoil, which resulted in a split into two Unions. This split, in turn, influenced mission endeavour in the Republic of Serbia.[306] Kocić left the country in 2004 and the church in Banja Luka dispersed.

The UBC RC took the proposition seriously. The Board of the Union organised the work so that each big church took responsibility over one town or church in Bosnia-Herzegovina. The Rijeka Baptist church, the biggest Baptist church in Croatia at that time, and its pastor, Giorgio Grlj, took responsibility for the Sarajevo church.[307] Actually, there was no church, only four or five pre-war members lived in Sarajevo. The others had either left the country or moved to other towns. The old church building on Ljubljanska had been severely damaged. Refugees occupied the building that had been bought by Kačarević just before the Yugoslavian war. There was a group of about forty people who visited services of the Pioneers team.[308] Such attendance was related to the distribution of the humanitarian aid. The UBC RC made an agreement with Pioneers to co-operate with work at the Sarajevo Baptist church.[309] The Rijeka Baptist church organised humanitarian help from the Croatian organisation *Moj Bližnji* (My Neighbour) for Sarajevo. Ted Esler, Pioneers' Bosnia/Croatia Team

---

[304] J. Ted Esler, 'Letter to Tomislav and Lidia Dobutović', unpub. letter, archives of Sarajevo Baptist Church (13 December 1996).
[305] Tomislav and Lidija Dobutović, personal interview.
[306] Ibid.
[307] 'Izvjesće o Posjeti Baptističkoj Crkvi u Sarajevu' (Report on Visit to Baptist Church in Sarajevo), archive of Sarajevo church (10-12 July 1996).
[308] Ibid.
[309] 'Ugovor o Misijskom Djelovanju u Sarajevu, Republika BiH' (Agreement on Missionary Activities in Sarajevo, Republic of Bosnia and Herzegovina), archives of Sarajevo Baptist Church (1 March 1997).

Leader from Sarajevo, was involved in *Moj Bližnij*.[310] The leadership of the Rijeka Baptist church felt that the Sarajevo church would need workers who would stay there. Thus, in the summer of 1996, a group of UBC RC leaders, volunteers from the Rijeka Baptist church and potential missionaries, Tomislav and Lidija Dobutović, visited Sarajevo several times in order to understand the situation.[311] Tomislav and Lidija Dobutović had both been educated at the International Theological Seminary in Osijek, Croatia. Their period of study had overlapped with the war in Bosnia-Herzegovina and, during that time, they had been working with refugees from Bosnia-Herzegovina: in refugee camps in Osijek, Đakovo, Gašinci; in 'Life Centre' Crkvenica, Croatia; and in refugee camps in Austria as a part of an international team.[312] So when the leadership of the Rijeka Baptist church suggested that they work in Bosnia-Herzegovina, their decision was positive. On 1 March 1997, an agreement on mission activity was signed between UBC RC and the Dobutovićs.[313] Only one week later, Tomislav and Lidija moved to Sarajevo.

When the Dobutovićs came to Sarajevo, the city was devastated; buildings were in ruins, and the city was under curfew in the evenings the city. They lived in the apartment of the Sarajevo church on Barščašja that was empty, without furniture and household appliances, and with no electricity or heating. Tomislav and Lidija started their mission work in co-operation with Pioneers under the leadership of Esler. They were involved in many activities such as discipleship, teaching, preaching, help with humanitarian aid, work with students, and leading of home groups with young people. Pioneers organised different seminars on reconciliation, confidence, and other topics.[314] As a result of these activities, several Baptist home groups were founded. People of all ethnic nationalities visited these groups and the leaders avoided organizing groups based on ethnicity. In a few months, the Dobutovićs re-opened Sunday services, to which they invited all interested. Along with that, a branch of *Moj Bližnji* was established in Sarajevo under the leadership of Dobutović. In a short period of time, *Moj Bližnji* organised its humanitarian activity in the whole territory of Bosnia-Herzegovina.

From the beginning, Tomislav and Lidija worked on the papers of the church. The Sarajevo Baptist church had used half of the building of the Černy family. Dobutović established contact with a daughter of Josip Černy, Lidija Glavina, who lived in Germany, and bought the other part of the house. The building was in ruins. In 1997 Pioneers, UBC RC, and other Christian mission

---

[310] Tomislav and Lidija Dobutović, personal interview.

[311] Giorgio Grlj, 'Pismo do brata Teufika i sestre Vojke od Giorgio Grlj' (Letter to Teufic and Vojka Cerović), archives of Sarajevo Baptist Church (20 July 1996).

[312] Tomislav and Lidija Dobutović, personal interview.

[313] 'Ugovor o Misijkom Djelovanju u Sarajevu, Republica BiH' (Agreement on Missionary Activities in Sarajevo, Republic of B&H).

[314] Tomislav and Lidija Dobutović, personal interview.

organisations started to renovate the church building on Ljubljanska Street.[315] The vision for the building was to serve as a new church meeting facility, guest house, ESL School and as a strategic point of outreach to the community. In spring 1998, after the building was renovated, 'Kairos Centre' was founded. On 1 May that same year, the first conference of the post-war Sarajevo Baptist church was organised and Tomislav Dobutović was ordained pastor. This was a new beginning for the church.

Meanwhile Baptist churches were planted in other towns in Bosnia-Herzegovina. In Novi Travnik, a church was planted under the supervision of the Zagreb Baptist church which, in 1996, ordained Tim Horvat to be a deacon of that church.[316] In Tuzla, Troy and Mary Donahou, missionaries of the IMB, planted a church in 1996.[317] In Zenica, a missionary group from Pioneers, led by Jeff Warner, also organised a church.[318] There were also small Baptist congregations in Goražde, Konjic, and Živinice. Tomislav and Lidia Dobutović, together with the leaders of all these congregations, started to think about establishing an organisation that would unite all their undertakings. At a conference held on 15 July 2000, the Union of Baptist churches of Bosnia and Herzegovina was established.[319] This union was named *The Baptist Church in Bosnia-Herzegovina* (hereafter BC of B&H). The same year the BC of B&H made applications for full membership in the Baptist World Alliance (BWA) and the European Baptist Federation (EBF).[320] The BC of B&H was accepted into the EBF as fifty-first member[321] and shortly after to the BWA.

The leadership of the Union recognised a need for theological education of indigenous leaders. Different seminars and training for all the believers who were interested was organised. In 2001, Tomislav Dobutović, co-ordinator of the Baptist Church of Bosnia-Herzegovina at that time, invited Fyodor Raychynets, a theologian who had just finished his postgraduate studies at the International Baptist Theological Seminary (Prague, Czech Republic), to assist the BC of B&H in organising a Bible Institute. In the autumn of that same year,

---

[315] Ibid.

[316] Knežević, *Pregled Povijesti*, p. 140.

[317] Oksana Raychynets, 'The Origin, Formation and Development of Baptist Church in Tuzla, Bosnia-Herzegovina', unpub. paper, 2004; 'Pregled Istorije Baptističke Crkve 'Novi Život' u Tuzli' (Survey of the History of the Baptist Church 'New Life'), unpub. handwritten manuscript, archives of Tuzla Baptist Church (no date).

[318] Hiba Mehić, personal interview (Zenica, Bosnia-Herzegovina, August 2005).

[319] 'Spisak Osnivača Saveza Baptističkih Crkava u Bosni i Hercegovini' (List of the Founders of the Union of Baptist Churches in Bosnia and Herzegovina), archives of Sarajevo Baptist Church (15 July 2000).

[320] 'Application for Full Membership in BWA', unpub. letter, archives of Sarajevo Baptist Church, no date; 'Application for Full Membership in EBF', unpub. letter, archives of Sarajevo Baptist Church (no date).

[321] *The Baptist Church in Bosnia-Herzegovina: The Baptist Union in Bosnia-Herzegovina–A Short History and Vision*.

Fyodor Raychynets moved with his family from Prague to Sarajevo. In October of 2001, the Bible Institute of the Baptist Church in Bosnia-Herzegovina was established and ten students were enrolled.[322]

Conclusion

The results of this investigation indicate that this period of about 150 years of Baptist Mission endeavour in Bosnia-Herzegovina was a period that was marked by struggle and discontinuity. Political turmoil in the country, obstacles from traditional faith communities, a permanent struggle for ethnic identity, disagreement and lack of clear vision in mission activities and strategies in different periods of its history caused stagnation in the development of Baptist work and life in the country. During the history of the Baptist church in Bosnia-Herzegovina, the country found itself three times at the centre of bloody wars that brought Baptist mission efforts to an end. The aftermaths of all the wars were marked by a complete devastation of the political, economical, social, and religious life of the country. Churches were closed and members were forced to leave the country or were simply dispersed throughout the nation. In terms of Baptist mission and church life, it meant a new beginning—beginning from the scratch after each war.

Mission activities by German Baptists missionaries, and colporteurs of BFBS, marked a promising beginning of Baptist mission in Bosnia and Herzegovina. Thus, in 1863 the first Baptist group in Sarajevo was established. Soon, due to the great rebellion of 1875 and the war of 1876 between the Kingdom of Serbia and the Ottoman Empire, all mission activities were stopped. The Austro-Hungarian occupation in 1878, however, opened a new window of opportunities for Baptist mission activity. It resulted in the founding of new Baptist groups in other places, besides Sarajevo. The beginning of WWI brought to an end all Baptist mission efforts. Baptist groups of Bosnia-Herzegovina lost almost all their members. The only group that survived this war was a small Baptist congregation in Sarajevo.

The period between WWI and WWII was a period of new Baptist missionary attempts. The Baptist mission activities started once again from the beginning. This time, two new Mission Organizations, SBC and SEGMC, emerged on Yugoslavian soil. The mission endeavour of these organizations was mainly focused on the German and Slavic population of Yugoslavia and was marked by relative success. In Bosnia-Herzegovina, however, the results were rather small and insignificant. The apogee of this period was the establishment of the Baptist Union of Yugoslavia, in the 1920s, which united

---

[322] Oksana Raychynets, 'Baptist History in Bosnia and Herzegovina', unpub. paper, (2004).

several regional associations. The spirit of unity and cooperation, however, did not characterise the Union; each association worked on its own. The beginning of WWII forced all German missionaries and members of the Baptist churches to leave the country. Eventually all Baptist activities in Bosnia-Herzegovina came to end as the result of the war.

In the post-WWII Republic, only a small number of Baptist believers remained in Bosnia-Herzegovina. Baptist Mission activities were stagnant during this period in Bosnia-Herzegovina. There were two main hindrances to development: external and internal. The external had to do with the new Communist authority with its atheistic ideology and anti-religious propaganda. The new political authorities reduced religion to the private sphere and created all possible subversive obstacles for development of Baptist mission activity. On the other hand, there was also an internal problem, which had to do with the lack of a good mission strategy for the evangelisation and church growth in Bosnia-Herzegovina under the Communist system. At the end of the 1980s, there were some good signs and attempts that had some positive results in the development of Baptist mission, but the beginning of the Yugoslav war in 1992 again stopped all Baptist activities is Bosnia-Herzegovina.

After the recent Yugoslav war (1992-1995), Baptist mission work in the new independent Bosnia-Herzegovina was revitalised from the ruins. The new beginning is promising and holds hope for the future. New Baptist churches and groups have emerged in different cities, the Union of Baptist churches of Bosnia-Herzegovina has been established and an educational institution for education and equipment of native leadership has been set up. The story continues...

Bibliography

Primary Sources

'Application for Full Membership in EBF'. Unpublished document. Archives of Sarajevo Baptist Church (no date).
'Application for Full Membership in BWA'. Unpublished document. Archives of Sarajevo Baptist Church (no date).
Esler, J. 'Letter to Tomislav and Lidia Dobutović'. Unpublished document. Archives of Sarajevo Baptist Church (13 December 1996).
'Izvjesće o Posjeti Baptističkoj Crkvi u Sarajevu' (Report on Visit to Baptist Church in Sarajevo). Archive of Sarajevo church (10-12 July 1996).
Grlj, Giorgio, 'Pismo do brata Teufika i sestre Vojke od Giorgio Grlj' (Letter to Teufic and Vojka Cerović). Archives of Sarajevo Baptist Church (20 July 1996).
'Kupoprodajni Ugovor između Sarajevske Baptističke Crkve i Josipom and Marijom Černi' (Sales Contract between Sarajevo Baptist Church and Josip and Maria Černy). Unpublished document. Private archive of Luka Šumić (2 December 1961).
Lehotsky, Adolf, 'Baptizam u Jugoslaviji' (Baptist Life in Yugoslavia). Unpublished document. (Novi Sad, Yugoslavia: Baptist Seminary Library Archives, no date).
'Letter to Home Mission from Zagreb Baptist Church'. Unpublished letter. Private archive of Luka Šumić (11 March 1987).
'Letter to Sarajevo Baptist Church from Board Secretary'. Unpublished letter. Private archive of Luka Šumić (23 April 1986).
'Letter to the Board of Home Mission'. Unpublished letter. Private archive of Luka Šumić (17 June 1986).
'Potsetnik sa Dogovora u Zagrebu, o Dolazku brata Vojnica Dragana na Ferijalnu Praksu' (Reminder of the Zagreb Agreement about the Coming of Brother Vojnica Dragana for Vocational Practice). Unpublished document. Private archive of Luka Šumić (26 June 1988).
'Pregled Istorije Baptističke Crkve 'Novi Život' u Tuzli' (Survey of the History of the Baptist Church—'New Life'). Unpublished handwritten manuscript. Archives of Tuzla Baptist Church (no date).
'Prepis Odluke Donesene Između Zajednica Sarajevo I Zagreba' (Transcript of the Decision that was made between the Sarajevo and Zagreb Congregations). Unpublished document. Private archive of Luka Šumić (20-21 September 1986).
'Prva Skupština Članstva' (First Conference on Membership). Unpublished document. Archives of Sarajevo Baptist Church (5 August 1998).
'Promemorija Razgovora s Taufikom Cerovićem' (Aide-memoir of Conversation with Taufik Cerović). Archives of Sarajevo Baptist Church (no date).

'Raspored Posjeta Sarajevo, 1985' (Schedule of Visiting of Sarajevo, 1985). Unpublished document. Private archive of Luka Šumić (5 January 1985).

'Spisak Osnivača Saveza Baptističkih Crkava u Bosni i Hercegovini' (List of the Founders of the Union of Baptist Churches in Bosnia and Herzegovina). Archives of Sarajevo Baptist Church (15 July 2000).

Šumić, Ljubica and Luka, 'Letter to the Board of Zagreb Baptist Church'. Unpublished letter. Private archive of Luka Šumić (10 November 1998).

The Baptist Church in Bosnia-Herzegovina: The Baptist Union in Bosnia-Herzegovina—A Short History and Vision. Unpublished document. Archives of Sarajevo Baptist Church (2003).

'Ugovor o Misijskom Djelovanju u Sarajevu, Republika BiH' (Agreement on Missionary Activities in Sarajevo, Republic of Bosnia and Herzegovina). Archives of Sarajevo Baptist Church (1 March 1997).

'Ugovor o Volonterskom Radu u Kršćanskoj Baptističkoj Crkvi' (Agreement on Volunteer's Activity in Christian Baptist Church). Archives of Sarajevo Baptist Church 26/2003 (23 August 2003).

'Ugovor o Volonterskom Radu u Kršćanskoj Baptističkoj Crkvi' (Agreement on Volunteer's Activity in the Christian Baptist Church). Archives of Sarajevo Baptist Church 22/2005 (1 September 2005).

Interviews (all interviews were conducted by the author)

Dobutović, Tomislav and Lidija, Sarajevo, Bosnia-Herzegovina (19 July 2005).
Karamehmedović, Jasmina, Sarajevo, Bosnia-Herzegovina (19 May 2005).
Knežević, Ruben, interview by correspondence (8 December 2003).
Mehić, Hiba, Zenica, Bosnia-Herzegovina (2005).
Šumić, Luka, Sarajevo, Bosnia-Herzegovina (19 May 2005).
Vanderwerf, Mark, interview by correspondence (9 December 2003).

Secondary Sources

ENGLISH

Adams, Theodore F., *Baptists Around the World* (Nashville: Broadman Press, 1967).

'Tenth Baptist World Congress', (Rio de Janeiro: Baptist World Alliance, 26 June - 3 July 1960).

Bjelajac, Branko, *Protestants and Evangelicals in Serbia Until 1945* (Belgrade, Novi Sad: Color System, 2001).

_____, 'Protestantism in Serbia', *Religion, State and Society* 30:3 (2002), pp. 169-218.

'British and Foreign Bible Society, Identity Statement', British and Foreign Bible Society's Library, Cambridge University Library, 'Janus' database, http://www.janus.lib.com.ac.uk, accessed 7 June 2005.

Canton, W., *A History of the British and Foreign Bible Society* (5 volumes; London: John Murray, 1904-1910).

Franks, J.D., ed., *European Baptists Today* (Zürich-Rüschlikon: Baublatt AG, 1950).
'The General Framework Agreement for Peace in Bosnia and Herzegovina (Initialled in Dayton on 21 November 1995 and signed in Paris on 14 December 1995)'. *Organization for Security and Peace in Europe: Mission to Bosnia and Herzegovina.* http://www.oscebih.org/overview/gfap/eng/home.asp, accessed 9 January 2007.
Hopper, John D., 'A History of Baptists in Yugoslavia: 1862-1962'. Unpub. diss (Forth Worth, Tex.: Southwestern Baptist Theological Seminary, 1977).
_____, 'Baptist Beginnings in Yugoslavia'. *Baptist History and Heritage*, 17:4 (October 1982), pp. 28-37.
Horak, Josip, 'Church, State, and Religious Freedom in Yugoslavia: An Ideological and Constitutional Study'. *Journal of Church and State* 19 (1977), pp. 278-300.
Imerovski, Milo, 'Baptist Origins: The Nineteenth Century in Present Day Yugoslavia', unpub. thesis (Rüschlikon: Baptist Theological Seminary, 1986).
Klem, Franjo, 'Yugoslavia' in *European Baptists Today,* J.D. Franks, (ed.) (Zürich-Rüschlikon: Baublatt AG, 1950), pp. 86-93.
Klemenčić, Matjaž and Mitja Žagar, *The Former Yugoslavia's Diverse Peoples: A Reference Sourcebook* (Santa Barbara, Calif.: ABC-CLIO, 2004).
Kovačević, Emir, 'Legal Position of Church and Religious Communities in B&H', unpub. paper (Sarajevo: World Conference on Religion and Peace, 2001).
Lord, F. Townley, *Baptist World Fellowship* (London: Carey Kingsgate Press, 1955).
Malcolm, Noel, *Bosnia: A Short History* (London: Macmillan, 1996).
McBeth, H. Leon, *The Baptist Heritage* (Nashville: Broadman, 1987).
Mojzes, Paul, 'Christian-Marxist Encounter in the Context of Socialist Society', *Journal of Ecumenical Studies* 9:1 (Winter 1972), pp. 1-28.
Parker, G. Keith, *Baptists in Europe: History &Confessions of Faith* (Nashville: Broadman Press, 1982).
Peterlin, Davorin, 'Theological Education Among Croatian Baptists: A Socio-historical Survey', *Baptist Quarterly* 5 (2000), pp. 239-259.
Raychynets, Oksana, 'Baptist History in Bosnia and Herzegovina', unpub. paper (2004).
_____, 'The Origin, Formation and Development of Baptist Church in Tuzla, Bosnia-Herzegovina', unpub. paper (2004).
Roe, James Moulton, *British and Foreign Bible Society: 1905-1954* (London: British and Foreign Bible Society, 1965).
Roter, Zdenko, 'The Position of Believers as Second-Class citizens in Socialist Countries: The Case of Yugoslavia', *Occasional Papers on Religion in Eastern Europe (*Succeeded by *Religion in Eastern Europe*) 9:3 (June 1989), pp. 1-17.
Rushbrooke, J.H., 'Baptist Belief and Mission Work in Europe' in *Baptist World Alliance Record of Proceedings* (Stockholm: Baptist World Alliace, 21-27 July 1923), pp. 46-51.

_____, *The Baptist Movement in the Continent of Europe* (London: Kingsgate Press, 1923).
Sowards, Steven W., 'Bosnia-Herzegovina and the Failure of Reform in Austria-Hungry', *Twenty-Five Lectures on Modern Balkan History (The Balkans in the Age of Nationalism)* 12, http://www.lib.msu.edu/sowards/balkan/lect12.htm, accessed 8 January 2007.
Steer, Roger, (ed.), *Good News for the World: The Story of Bible Society*, (Oxford: Monarch, 2004).
Tiller, Carl W., *The Twentieth Century Baptist: Chronicles of the Baptist World Alliance* (Valley Forge, Pennsylvania: Judson Press, 1980).
Vincent, Henri, 'Panorama: Europe' in *Baptist World Alliance*, 'The Truth That Makes Men Free', Official Report of the Eleventh Congress (Miami Beach, Florida, 25-30 June 1965), pp. 156-160.
Wardin, W.A., *Baptists Around the World: A Comprehensive Handbook*. (Nashville: Broadman & Holman Publishers, 1995).

OTHER LANGUAGES

Boisset, J., *Kratka Povijest Protestantizma* (Brief History of Protestantism) (Zagreb: Kršćanska Sadašnjost, 1985).
Cekić, Smail, 'Fašizam i Antifašizam u Bosni' (Fascism and Antifascism in Bosnia) (Sarajevo: Tribina Viječa Kongresa Bosnjačkjih Intelektualaca, 2001).
Imamović, Mustafa, *Historija Bošnjaka* (History of Bosniacs) (Sarajevo: Bosanski Kulturni Centar, 1998).
Išek, Tomislav, 'Bosna i Hercegovina od Stvaranja do Propasti Prve Zajedničke Države (1918-1941)' (Bosnia and Herzegovina from Creation to the Fall of the First Common State) in Safet Halilović, (ed.), *Bosna i Hercegovina od Najstarijih Vremena do Kraja Drugog Svijetskog Rata* (Bosnia and Herzegovina from the Ancient Times till the End of the Second World War). (Sarajevo: Bosanski Kulturni Centar, 1998), pp. 299-337.
Janković, Miloš B, *Škola i Religija* (School and Religion) (Beograd: Narodna Knjiga, 1952).
Jelenić, Julijan, *Kultira i Bosanski Franjevci* (Culture and Bosnian Franciscans) (Sarajevo: Svjetlost, 1915).
Hadzibegovic, I, and M Imamovic, 'BiH u Vrijeme Austrougarske Vladavine (1878-1918)' (Bosnia and Herzegovina in the Time of Austro-Hungarian Empire 1878-1918) in Safet Halilović, ed., *Bosna i Hercegovina od Najstarijih Vremena do Kraja Drugog Svijetskog Rata* (Bosnia and Herzegovina from the Ancient Times till the End of the Second World War). (Sarajevo: Bosanski Kulturni Centar, 1998), pp. 223-293.
Halilović, Enver, *Bošnjaci i vrijeme* (Bosniacs and Time) (Tuzla: Filozofski Fakultet, 1995).
Halilović, Safet, *Bosna i Hercegovina of Najstarijih Vremena do Kraja Drugog Svjetskog Rata* (Bosnia and Herzegovina from the Ancient Times till the End of the Second World War) (Sarajevo: Bosanski Kulturni Centar, 1998).

Horak, Josip, 'Utisci s Puta na Svjetski Kongres Baptista' (An impression of the attendance of World Baptist Congress). *Glasnik* (Herald) 7:9 (Rijeka, 1965), pp. 135-138.
Knežević, Ruben, *Pregled Povijesti Baptizma na Hrvatskom Prostoru* (A Historical Overview of Baptism in Croatia) (Zagreb: Savez Baptistističkih Crkava u Republici Hrvatskoj Baptistički Institut, 2001).
Kresevljaković, Hamdija, *Sarajevo za Vrijeme Austrougarske Uprave* (1878-1918) (Sarajevo in the Time of the Austro-Hungarian Empire) (Sarajevo: Svjetlost, 1969).
Kruševac, Todor, *Sarajevo pod Austro-Ugarskom Upravom 1878-1918* (Sarajevo in the Time of the Austro-Hungarian Reign 1878-1918) (Sarajevo: Svjetlost, 1960).
Kuzmič, Peter, *Vuk-Daničićevo Sveto Pismo I Biblijska Društva* (Vuk-Danichichevo Holy Scripture and Bible Societies) (Zagreb: Kršćanska Sadašnjost, 1983).
Laws, Gilbert, 'Što se Ocekuje od Clanova Crkve' (What is Expected from the Members of the Church). *Glas Evandjelja* (Voice of the Gospel) 7 (1931), pp. 98-103.
Lehotsky, Adolf, 'Baptizam u Jugoslaviji' (Baptists in Yugoslavia), unpub. doc. (Novi Sad, Yugoslavia: Baptist Seminary Library Archives).
Lehotsky, Hilda, 'Personalna Opazanja o Njenom Ocu Adofu Lehotskom' (Personal Notes about Her Father Adolf Lehotsky), unpub. notes. Original is owned by Teofil Lehotsky (January 2001).
Lehotsky, Teofil, 'Prilog Istoriji Baptistickog Teoloskog Obrazovanja u Nas' (A Contribution to the History of Theological Education in Serbia), *Teoloski Casopis* (Theological Journal) 4 (2004), pp. 13-49.
Mandić, Oleg, *Religija, Država, Nauka* (Religion, State, and Science) (Zagreb: Seljačka Sloga, 1956).
Muratbegović, Alija, 'Saga o Kafi na Bosanski Način' (Saga about Bosnian Coffee) *Bosanskohercegovacki Dani* 270 (16 August 2002), http://www.bhdani.com/arhiva/270/t27012.shtml, accessed 4 January 2007.
Petranović, Branko and Čedomir Strbac, *Istorija Socijalističke Jugoslavije* (History of Socialist Yugoslavia) (Beograd: Radnička Štampa, 1977).
Ramić, Sulejman and Fehim Veladžić, eds., *Kratak Pregled Historije Bosne i Hercegovine i Historija Islama* (Brief Overview of the History of Bosnia and Herzegovina and the History of Islam) (Tuzla: Kulturno i Naučno Društvo Muslimana Preporod, 1994).
Tepić, Ibrahim, 'Bosna i Hercegovina od Kraja XVIII Stoljeća do Austrougarske Okupacije 1878 godine' (Bosnia and Herzegovina from the End of XVIII Century until the Austro-Hungarian Occupation in 1878) in Safet Halilović, (ed.), *Bosna i Hercegovina od Najstarijih Vremena do Kraja Drugog Svijetskog Rata* (Bosnia and Herzegovina from the Ancient Times till the End of the Second World War) (Sarajevo: Bosanski Kulturni Centar, 1998), pp. 175-222.
Vacek, Vinko, 'Baptistički Pokret u Kraljevini SHS' (Baptist Movement in the Kingdom of SCS), *Glas Evandjelja* 11 (1927), pp. 133-134.

Vacek, Vinko, 'Baptistički Pokret u Kraljevini SHS' (Baptist Movement in the Kingdom of SHS), *Glas Evandjelja* 12 (1927), pp. 146-147.

CHAPTER 6

'The Practical, Visible Witness of Discipleship': The Life and Convictions of Hans Meier (1902-1992)

Dejan Adam

It was in June 1920 that Eberhard Arnold, his wife Emmy and her sister Else Von Hollander founded the first Bruderhof settlement at Sannerz in Germany.[1] Ever since then, the Bruderhof has been a gathering place for individuals interested in communal living.[2] The Bruderhof communities identify with the early Anabaptist tradition. However, unlike the Amish communities (for example), the members of the Bruderhof emphasise 'the ministry of presence' in relation to the society around them rather than adopting a lifestyle that rejects the wider society.[3] Members of the Bruderhof community have been actively involved in many important political and social movements for justice and peace, including their opposition to Hitler's national socialism and the Third Reich. They were not afraid to express their convictions clearly and openly. In the 1930s in Germany they opposed the prevailing popular attitude that put the State and its precepts above God and his Word. Additionally during the 1930s-1940s, the Bruderhof was actively involved in helping victims of oppression and war refugees, and during the 1960s and 1970s, they protested against US foreign policy (especially regarding the wars being waged overseas) and against racial discrimination.[4]

Hans Meier, who was from Switzerland, was one of the key people within the Bruderhof who was actively involved in most of these events. For several decades, his life was dedicated to the search for and building up of true

---

[1] For more about the Bruderhof see Markus Baum, *Against the Wind: Eberhard Arnold and the Bruderhof* (Farmington, Penn.: Plough, 1998); see Peter Mommsen, *Homage to a Broken Man* (Rifton, N.Y.: Plough, 2004).

[2] Baum, *Against the Wind*, p. 126.

[3] Arnold C. Snyder, *Anabaptist History and Theology: An Introduction* (Kitchener, Ontario: Pandora Press, 2002), pp. 177-184.

[4] Peter Mommsen to Dejan Adam, 21 November 2005. In the possession of Dejan Adam.

community. Given his personality and his involvement with many political and social events of importance, his story offers valuable insights into the history and character of the Bruderhof community.[5] Nevertheless, very little (if any) constructive historical and theological work has been done to provide an in-depth analysis of the relationship between the religious experience of the Bruderhof and its theological significance. In order to contribute to this task, this study investigates Hans Meier's life and his theological views. My framework is suggested by James Wm. McClendon in his book *Biography as Theology* that in thinking about the formation of Christian beliefs it is crucial to start by paying attention to specific lives as they are lived.[6] Life stories illuminate the nature and theology of the Christian community, and in this sense, as McClendon puts it, 'theology must be at least biography'.[7] Meier's life revolved around three major theological images—a common table, Christian communities as 'embassies' of the Kingdom of God, and authentic discipleship focused on Christ. These images helped Meier to understand himself better, face critical life situations, and work out his own path through life. Moreover, his encounter with these images formed Meier's character and convictions.[8]

Meier's biography centres on his membership in the Bruderhof community. Both the community he belonged to and the way he understood the world around him shaped his character. Indeed Meier was formed by the necessity to concur with or to dissent from Bruderhof convictions. At the same time however, he also had a significant impact on the story of the Bruderhof. Meier's personal narrative will also be evaluated through the prism of leading early sixteenth century Anabaptists, including Michael Sattler and Peter Rideman.[9] Furthermore, in terms of shaping Meier's convictions, some of his contemporary theologians will be included in the discussion, including Eberhard Arnold and Leonhard Ragaz.[10]

---

[5] 'Introduction', in Heini Gut and Raymond Pittet, eds., 'As Long as there is Light: The Life of Hans Meier (1902-1992)' (Deer Spring Bruderhof, USA, 1991). An unpublished document in Bruderhof Archives, Woodcrest, Rifton, New York.

[6] James Wm. McClendon, Jr., *Biography as Theology* (Nashvile: Abingdon Press, 1974), p. 38.

[7] James Wm. McClendon, Jr., *Ethics: Systematic Theology, Volume I* (Nashville: Abingdon Press, 2002), p. 30; McClendon, *Biography*, p. 38.

[8] Hans Meier, '*Why we Live in Full Community*' (Deer Spring, USA, December 24, 1992), pp. 1-3 (my pagination). Personal notes. An unpublished document in Bruderhof Archives, Woodcrest, Rifton, New York.

[9] Some authors use the alternative spellings Riedeman or Riedemann.

[10] Meier read also Martin Buber, Martin Niemoeller, Dietrich Bonhoeffer, the Blumhardts and many others, but the author could find no documentation about their influence upon Meier. Therefore, the persons mentioned will be excluded from further discussions; see Klaus Meier (Beech Grove Bruderhof, UK) to Dejan Adam, 7 March 2006. In the possession of Dejan Adam.

While collecting bibliographical references, the author has relied primarily on assistance provided by several people who were involved in Hans Meier's life. Details related by Klaus and Andreas Meier (Meier's sons) and Chris Meier (Meier's grandson) were the starting point in terms of clarifying sources. They sometimes held differing viewpoints but worked together to confirm significant events and dates related to Meier's life. I am also especially indebted to them because they made some missing elements and moments from Meier's narrative come alive again, including events which have never been recorded before. Secondly, I owe a great deal to Emmy Barth and Miriam Potts who work in the Bruderhof Archives located at the Woodcrest community in Rifton, New York. They provided me with numerous primary and secondary documents from the Bruderhof Archives, to which I could not have otherwise had access. These documents included personal correspondence, testimonies, personal diaries of Bruderhof members, and interviews with people connected with Meier. Additionally, numerous stories told by Meier and later recorded as short biographical portraits were made available as well. Some of the primary sources are English translations owned by the Bruderhof Archives. Finally, this study would never have been conceived without the help of Peter Mommsen, who connected me with the people mentioned above. His book *Homage to a Broken Man*[11] describes living in community—both how bad it can be, and how good it can and should be. His suggestions, clarifications, and explanations were crucial.

The Bruderhof Archives do not have any documents relating to Hans Meier from the period before 1933, which was when Meier joined the Bruderhof. Therefore, available sources regarding that part of Meier's life came exclusively from autobiographical accounts and were supplemented by correspondence with Klaus, Andreas and Chris Meier. The period between 1931 and 1940 can be described as the most formative for Meier, and is well covered with a variety of resources. Consequently, this period can be extensively evaluated. The same cannot be said for the period 1941-1960, which covers Meier's journey from England to Paraguay as well as his time in Paraguay. The Bruderhof Archives were able to provide only a dozen or so documents and letters written by Meier during that time. There are also significant gaps after 1959, when Meier, as we will see, left the Bruderhof. Meier was reconciled with the Bruderhof in 1972, and the period between the 1970s and 1992 is supported with a fair number of documents. There is much correspondence, particularly from the 1980s, and the author also had access to videotapes and transcripts from this period provided by the video department of the Bruderhof Archives. Video materials show footage of Meier speaking to college classes and television reports, as well as videos about the Bruderhof history.

---

[11] Peter Mommsen, *Homage to a Broken Man* (Rifton, New York: Plough, 2004).

This study deals with questions of peace, justice, and community, questions that remain relevant today. It explores attempts made to pursue counter-cultural convictions in concrete situations. The study also has a strong trans-national dimension, since Meier's work was carried out in Europe, across the Atlantic in Paraguay, and in the United States. Finally, what is examined here is not a story of a sequence of successes in seeking to live out a commitment to communal discipleship. The reality of struggle is at the heart of Meier's life and work.

'The Way of Discipleship'

Hans Meier (9 March 1902 - 24 December 1992)[12] was born into a family in which both parents belonged to the Reformed Church of the Canton of Zurich in Switzerland. There he was baptised as an infant. In 1912, as a member of the Social Democratic Party, Meier's father attended the International Socialist Congress at Basle as a delegate. He returned believing that a new time of peace, justice and community was ahead for humanity. Meier's father was idealistically convinced there would be no more wars in the future because the internationally united workers had agreed to protest and not to participate if the capitalistic governments of the world ever initiated another armed conflict. This enthusiasm of his father for peace, and his subsequent disillusionment when World War I broke out within a few years, made a big impression on Hans Meier as a boy.[13]

Hans Meier's father had been born into a poor peasant family and worked as a locomotive driver. However, he saved money through great self–sacrifice and was able to pay for Hans to study electrical engineering. Because the family lacked social status, his father wanted Hans to achieve a more advanced position in society. To achieve this goal, Hans attended the Industrial School in Zurich during the early years of World War I, followed by matriculation at the Polytechnic School.[14] At the same time, as war was being waged, Hans Meier started to search for the true meaning of life. During the war he witnessed thousands of severely wounded young men who had been sent by their governments into a meaningless war against each other (as he saw it), returning in special trains arranged by the Red Cross. Meier could not understand how even socialists on both sides who were committed to peace had subordinated themselves to the interests of their governments and fought for their countries.

---

[12] Klaus Meier to Dejan Adam, 16 March 2006. In the possession of Dejan Adam.

[13] 'Hans Meier tells his Life Story' (Deer Spring, USA, 9 March to 26 March 1990). The minutes of a meeting presided over by Hans Meier. An unpublished document in the Bruderhof Archives, Woodcrest, Rifton, New York, pp. 1-2.

[14] Hans Meier, 'Early Inquiries into the Meaning of Social Justice and of Life', in Heini Gut and Raymond Pittet (eds.), *As Long as there is Light: The Life of Hans Meier (1902-1992)*, p. 2.

Yet the fact that struck him most was that people on both sides of the conflict prayed for victory to the same Christ, and were encouraged by their state churches to go and fight each other for the sake of their national interests.[15]

Feeling let down by both the Socialist International Solidarity Movement, and by Switzerland (which though supposedly neutral was involved in supporting the war machine on both sides), Meier was above all disappointed by the attitudes of the official churches in not standing against the war. He came to see the Christ of the churches as questionable and lacking spiritual power, and Meier, along with many young men and women of that time, began to seek the truth by turning to human and political ideals. As a result of this search, he became a member of the organisation called the Swiss *Freischar* in 1923. The *Freischar* (the Fellowship of Freedom) was comprised of young people committed to a radical search for a life of true peace, unity, and social justice lived by all humankind.[16]

Membership in the *Freischar* included attendance at educational evenings organised by the leading Swiss religious socialist and theologian Leonhard Ragaz,[17] as well as discussions about issues such as Gandhi's non–violent revolution in India. They also read and discussed the writings of Tolstoy, Kropotkin, Landauer, Rolland, Dostoyevsky, and Marx. These activities resulted in Meier's involvement in the International Voluntary Service for Peace (I.V.C.P.) and eventually in his decision not to do military service. His decision for pacifism, in a country where military service was required of all males, shattered any possibility for advanced social status as an electrical engineer, which made Meier's father very unhappy. As a compromise, and through the help of a friend of his father who was an army chief, Meier accepted service in a military medical unit where he would not be asked to use weapons. After four year of this service, his questioning of serving in the military in any capacity was becoming stronger and stronger, and in 1927

---

[15] 'Hans Meier talking with Amos Hoover and other Mennonites' (n.p., 15 October 1990). Personal notes. An unpublished document in Bruderhof Archives, Woodcrest, Rifton, New York, p. 1; see Baum, *Against the Wind*, pp. 83-85.

[16] 'Hans Meier tells his Story to a Friend' (Deer Spring, USA, December, 1978). The minutes of a meeting presided over by Hans Meier. An unpublished document in Bruderhof Archives, Woodcrest, Rifton, New York, pp. 2-3.

[17] Leonhard Ragaz (1868-1965) was a leading figure in early twentieth century Swiss religious socialism, a movement that paralleled the social gospel movement in America and helped to arouse Protestantism to its social responsibility: see Paul Bock, ed., *Signs of the Kingdom: A Ragaz Reader* (Grand Rapids, Mich.: Eerdmans, 1984), pp. xi-xxi. Regarding Swiss religious socialism see Claude Welch, *Protestant Thought in the Nineteenth Century Vol. 2, 1870-1914* (New Haven, Conn.: Yale University Press, 1985), pp. 245-51; see Chris Meier to Dejan Adam, 17 March 17 2006. In the possession of Dejan Adam.

Meier decided to reject service in the Army Medical Corps as well.[18] This refusal stamped him as a criminal according to Switzerland's civil law and the right to any employment in his profession was denied. Moreover, a military jury sentenced Meier to three months imprisonment instead of the regular two for rejecting military service, due to the fact that as an academic he gave an especially bad example to the rest of the recruits. At Meier's sentencing, the judge also strongly criticised Leonhard Ragaz, who was present in the audience, for persuading others to refuse military service.[19]

After completing his sentence in 1928, Meier travelled by bicycle through Germany, intending to travel to Russia to work as an engineer and to get a first-hand impression of the Socialist revolution that had taken place there. However, he was refused a visa to Russia because of his pacifism, so he refocused his search for work in Germany. While looking for employment, he used the opportunity to visit different communities in order to learn about how they practised social justice and peace. The first to grasp his attention was the Rhön Bruderhof, which had been in existence since 1920. Meier spent several weeks there, helping with the Bruderhof Children's House building project. The determination of the Bruderhof to live a life of brotherly justice and communal unity made a deep impression on Meier, but the Bruderhof's basis, which was following Christ, did not fit Meier's worldview after his prior experience of Christianity.[20] He was seeking social justice and understanding in community, but not in the Christian faith. The next important place he visited was Heppenheim by the Bergstraße. A religious socialist conference was held there during the week of Pentecost, and well–known theologians including Leonhard Ragaz and Paul Tillich were invited to reflect on religious socialism. The participants however, failed to reach a consensus in terms of defining an appropriate lifestyle lined with this concept. Workers who were present felt the discussions were too theoretical and above their comprehension.[21]

Meier eventually found employment as a fitting engineer at the Siemens Schuckert Works in Cologne, Germany. His job was to change the process of production and to improve productivity in neighbouring companies including coal and lead mines, chemical and cement factories, and spinning and weaving mills. The extra profit he generated for the companies through increased

---

[18] Meier, 'Early Inquiries', pp. 4-5; see Klaus Meier to Dejan Adam, 9 March 2006. In the possession of Dejan Adam.

[19] Meier, 'Early Inquiries', p. 5.

[20] Klaus Meier to Dejan Adam, 20 March 2006. In the possession of Dejan Adam. Although the community had men and women within it, the language 'brotherly' was used. I will also refer to the members, as they did, as 'brothers' and 'sisters'.

[21] Hans Meier, 'A Bicycle Trip with Consequences', in Heini Gut and Raymond Pittet (eds.), *As Long as there is Light: The Life of Hans Meier* (1902-1992) (Deer Spring Bruderhof, USA, 1991). An unpublished document in Bruderhof Archives, Woodcrest, Rifton, New York, pp. 5-6; see 'Hans Meier tells his Story' p. 3; see Klaus Meier to Dejan Adam, 17 March 2006. In the possession of Dejan Adam.

productivity however was not used for the betterment of the workers. Instead, Meier's innovations put many of the workers out of work because they were no longer needed, which worsened the economic and social conditions of their families.[22] By becoming a little cog in the capitalistic mechanism Meier unintentionally 'contributed to the rising numbers of unemployed, through which Hitler later came to power in a totally democratic way' (as Meier later came to see it.)[23] His encounters with those who were harmed by his inventions made Meier increasingly aware of the injustice of the capitalist economic system. It also posed him an ethical dilemma.

The increasing social problems of the 1930s gradually led to the belief among those who were fighting for peace and social justice that the words spoken at conferences and at protest marches had little value, and that what was needed was action. Meier also believed that peace and justice for all humankind had to begin with action at the local level. As he saw it, such a life should be lived out within intentional communities of like–minded people.[24] Meier recalled that period saying, 'We knew from our own experience that words of challenge are believable and effective only if they are backed up by corresponding action, even if only as an example.'[25] Issues of justice such as a just wage cannot be calculated in numbers and figures. True justice, according to Meier, reigns if 'everyone gives everything he has and is able to do in service for the whole, and, on the other hand, receives from what is available all he is in need of for life and work'.[26] Therefore, a holistic understanding of life and work must lead toward an actual life of peace and social justice. At this point in his life, Meier's vision undoubtedly came from a socialist perspective.

The image of a common table where all work for the whole and are invited to eat and satisfy their needs together later became a motivation for Meier and this drew inspiration from the experience of the Jewish people after their liberation from Egyptian slavery—the 'Exodus reiterated'.[27] In addition, this image recalled the narrative of the early Christians living in Jerusalem who, through the Spirit of Christ, gathered in a peaceful, just, and united community, sharing all their possessions. Meier was inspired by this image. During the late 1920s and early 1930s, he observed the lack of this spirit in the Christian

---

[22] Hinkey, 'Hans Meier Talking with Amos Hoover', p. 2.

[23] Meier, 'A Bicycle Trip', p. 7.

[24] 'Hans Meier tells his Story', p. 3.

[25] Hans Meier, 'In Quest of a Communal Life of Peace and Justice', in Heini Gut and Raymond Pittet (eds.), *As Long as there is Light: The Life of Hans Meier (1902-1992)* (Deer Spring Bruderhof, USA, 1991). An unpublished document in Bruderhof Archives, Woodcrest, Rifton, New York, p. 9.

[26] Meier, 'In Quest of a Communal Life', p. 8.

[27] Meier, *'Why we Live in Full Community'*, pp. 1-3 (my pagination); Regarding the metaphor of the 'Exodus reiterated' I owe an insight to Parush R. Parushev. For the nature of the metaphor see Michael Walzer, *Thick and Thin: Moral Argument at Home and Abroad* (Notre Dame, Indiana: University of Notre Dame Press, 1994), pp. 1-19.

churches, and noted that this lack kept many from truly following Christ. Instead, influenced predominantly by economic and social systems, so-called 'Christians' were showing 'the worst possible example to the whole world'[28] by limiting their helping of others only to the sphere of their free time, and not extending it to the whole of life as described in the book of Acts 2:44-45 and Acts 4:32. This critical opinion of the traditional church was an important part of Meier's thinking at that time.

While he was pursuing this quest for a communal life of peace and justice, Meier married. On 11 May 1929 he and Margrit Fischli were married; Margrit was someone Meier had met and worked with in the *Freischar*. Together with others from the *Freischar*, they now began to think seriously about beginning to live a life of full community.[29] Through their connection with Leonhard Ragaz, they heard how inner disunity in a religious–socialist community in Herrliberg on the Zurich Lake had eventually brought about its dissolution. Ragaz, who was involved in giving advice to the Herrliberg community, had urged its members to work for a communal–minded spirit.[30] In his personal memories Ragaz wrote about the paradox encountered there:

> At the very moment when these people should have unfolded all the devotion, ability to make sacrifices, and all the communal–mindedness that was in them, it was just the other way round. All the egoism, desire to assert themselves, thirst for domineering and jealousy which had accumulated in them, broke out. I spent whole evenings in this circle fighting for another spirit to rule.[31]

Though Ragaz referred to the necessity of being united by a true communal spirit, he never fully joined the Herrliberg settlement. It was easier for him to give theoretical advice as an outsider than to work together with other members on a daily basis to achieve a spirit of unity.[32] After failing to preserve the Herrliberger settlement, Ragaz deliberately avoided advising and influencing other group of enthusiasts, including the one Hans and Margrit Meier belonged to, in their search for the true spirit of communal unity.

Undeterred by what they heard about the Herrliberg settlement, Hans and Margrit Meier joined another attempt to find a way of living in community in November 1930. They, together with two other young couples, began a new

---

[28] Meier, 'In Quest of a Communal Life', p. 9.

[29] Klaus Meier to Dejan Adam (Beech Grove Bruderhof, UK, March 17, 2006); see 'Hans Meier Tells His Story', p. 3.

[30] Hans Meier, 'The Werkhof', in Heini Gut and Raymond Pittet (eds.), *As Long as there is Light: The Life of Hans Meier (1902-1992)* (Deer Spring Bruderhof, USA, 1991). An unpublished document in Bruderhof Archives, Woodcrest, Rifton, New York, pp. 9-10.

[31] Ibid., p. 10; see Chris Meier to Dejan Adam (Woodcrest, USA, March 17, 2006).

[32] Klaus Meier to Dejan Adam (Beech Grove Bruderhof, UK, March 07, 2006). Personal correspondence. In the possession of Dejan Adam.

communal settlement on a farm in Längimoos in Switzerland. The plan was to build a community on an altruistic basis. They named the settlement the Werkhof (Work Farm), in the sense of a community of people working together in house, farm and field. The other founders of the Werkhof were two young couples that they knew from the *Freischar*. The first couple, Max and Eva Lezzi, decided to spend several weeks at the Rhön Bruderhof before the Werkhof started with the aim of gaining experience of how to live in community. The second couple, Peter and Anni Mathis, were motivated to join the Werkhof by Ragaz's communal–orientated thinking.[33]

Soon after the three couples started to live together, a fourth family, Hans and Else Boller with their four children, requested to join the Werkhof. Boller had studied theology with Ragaz, and felt that as a person in Christian ministry he was failing to live out what he preached.[34] At the Werkhof he believed a life as lived by the early Christians would be possible. However, the Lezzi family suggested that he and his wife visit the Rhön Bruderhof before coming to the Werkhof to experience life in a community based on 'following after Christ'— *Nachfolge Christi*.[35] Although hesitant to do so, the Bollers accepted this advice, went to the Rhön, and felt so at home that they decided to stay at the Bruderhof and not join the Werkhof. Hans Boller reported his impression of the Bruderhof to his friend and teacher Leonhard Ragaz:

> It is our clear feeling that we must decide for Bruderhof instead of the Werkhof. Bruderhof is based much more clearly on faith in the creative power of the Spirit of Christ... For I am indebted to the 'voice of the One who calls in the wilderness' that it has now come to a break through in my and my dear wife's lives. This voice has again and again shaken me up and kept me restless until the time came when the way of discipleship was revealed to me.[36]

Meanwhile, Meier was summoned to take a military refresher course in Switzerland. Because he refused to do so, he was sentenced by the court to spend an additional five months in prison, and his civil rights were also restricted. The court based its decision on Meier's refusal to assist injured people while serving as a soldier in the medical corps. Meier in defending his case explained that 'he would help anybody in need at anytime, including

---

[33] Meier, 'The Werkhof', pp. 10-11. see 'Hans Meier tells his Story', pp. 3-4.

[34] Hans Boller was a pastor in a Reformed Church in Zurich.

[35] Meier, 'The Werkhof', pp. 10-11; see Hinkey, 'Hans Meier talking with Amos Hoover', p. 2. For *Nachfolge Christi* in Anabaptist tradition, see Arnold C. Snyder, *Following in the Footsteps of Christ* (London: Darton, Longman and Todd, 2004), pp. 138-158.

[36] Meier, 'The Werkhof', p. 11. For some reason Hans Meier in his writings hardly ever referred to the sources where the quotations used by him came from. See Chris Meier to Dejan Adam (Woodcrest, USA, March 17, 2006).

anybody wearing a uniform',[37] yet as a pacifist he could not agree to being subject to military authority. Meier ended his argument before the court by pointing to the witness of Jesus whose crucifix hung on the wall above the judges, and whose example they were supposed to follow.

While a prisoner, Meier was visited by the founder of the Bruderhof, Eberhard Arnold, who had recently returned from visiting the Hutterian Brethren in the USA.[38] During the visit, Arnold asked Hans to transcribe *The Hutterian Ordnung*,[39] the 'orders' or 'discipline' of this Anabaptist community, into a typed document. Upon completion of the transcription, Arnold asked Meier his opinion of the communal regulations set forth in *The Hutterian Ordnung*. Meier told Arnold he did not think that it was necessary to write down such a set of rules, which surely must be taken for granted by all living in an intentional community. Arnold replied that Meier was unrealistic and 'had no inkling of true human nature.'[40] Arnold understood fallen human nature and reminded Meier how people easily give up their ideals and resolutions. Meier, like his father, certainly had an idealistic aspect to his views, an idealism that was to be tested during the course of his life.

After his release from the prison, Meier was challenged by another problem. According to Swiss civil law, rejection of military service and serving the accompanying prison sentence did not exempt a person from paying the annual military tax, which was compulsory until the age of sixty. As Meier refused to do so, his mother paid the tax on his behalf to protect him from further complications and imprisonment.[41]

Since the Werkhof had been founded, it had become increasingly evident that there were almost as many different ideas on how to organise the community as there were members. The variety of attitudes toward the development of the community, particularly the schooling of the children, the approaches to political as well as to affairs connected to church and religion gradually resulted in disagreements and conflicts within the Werkhof.

---

[37] Hans Meier, 'Confrontation with the State', in Heini Gut and Raymond Pittet (eds.), *As Long as there is Light: The Life of Hans Meier (1902-1992)* (Deer Spring Bruderhof, USA, 1991). An unpublished document in Bruderhof Archives, Woodcrest, Rifton, New York, p. 11.

[38] Baum, *Against the Wind*, pp. 193-204; see Merrill Mow, 'Torches Rekindled: The Bruderhof's Struggle for Renewal' (Pasadena, Calif., July, 2005). Personal notes. An unpublished document in Bruderhof Archives, Woodcrest, Rifton, New York, p. 14. There is also a book, which I got after finishing the dissertation. Pagination in the book is different from the one which I used while writing the dissertation.

[39] *Ordnung* (pl. *Ordnungen*), retained in the present translation, often rendered as *orders* or *discipline*, is a charter of rule, both spiritual and practical, of the communal life among the Hutterian Brethren. See The Hutterian Brethren (eds.), *The Chronicle of the Hutterian Brethren* (Rifton, New York: Plough, 1987), pp. 77-79.

[40] Meier, 'Confrontation', p. 12.

[41] Ibid.

Meanwhile, it was proposed by some of the members that they consider joining the Bruderhof. The decision was made by the community that Max Lezzi and Hans Meier should travel to the Rhön Bruderhof to explore such a possibility. However, this attempt to unite the two communities failed. According to Meier, the biggest disagreement arose regarding unconditional commitment to *Nachfolge Christi*. Members of the Werkhof were reluctant to accept the life of radical discipleship of Jesus as lived by those at the Bruderhof.[42]

Nevertheless, at the beginning of 1933, Hans Boller once more visited the Werkhof in order to bring a reconciling message from the Bruderhof. Arnold on behalf of the Bruderhof urged those living at the Werkhof 'to fight for unity as a witness to the power of the Spirit of Jesus in the present world situation'.[43] At the same time, an inclination toward separation and division had continually troubled the Werkhof, with little possibility of finding a way to compromise. In the face of unpromising circumstances, Meier's wife Margrit was the first to respond to Arnold's call and she decided to go to the Rhön Bruderhof, believing it was inevitable that the two communities would unite.[44] Reflecting later on Margrit's reaction, Meier spoke of experiencing the power of prayer for the first time in his life.

> Because I had some doubts about Margrit's decision, I went into the woods and there, for the first time in my life, consciously called to God and asked Him for His advice. When I had received certainty about this, I accompanied Margrit and our little son to the Bruderhof in order to find out which spirit could unite men.[45]

Thus Hans and Margrit Meier arrived at the Rhön Bruderhof at the beginning of February 1933, just a few days after Hitler became chancellor of Germany.[46] Shortly thereafter, they were baptised upon their confession of faith, together with nineteen others, on Easter Monday 1933.[47] It was the unity he found in the Bruderhof, as expressed in the mutual commitment of those belonging to this community, that made Hans Meier decide to join them. He found his ideals for peace and social justice realized in community under Jesus Christ, and from that point on he would become a seeker eager to discern the mind of Christ.

---

[42] Hans Meier, 'Difficulties on the Werkhof', in Heini Gut and Raymond Pittet (eds.), *As Long as there is Light: The Life of Hans Meier (1902-1992)* (Deer Spring Bruderhof, USA, 1991). An unpublished document in Bruderhof Archives, Woodcrest, Rifton, New York, pp. 12-13.
[43] Meier, 'Difficulties', p. 13.
[44] 'Hans Meier Tells His Story', p. 4; see Baum, *Against the Wind*, pp. 223-225.
[45] Meier, 'Difficulties', p. 14.
[46] Gordon A. Craig, *Germany, 1866-1945* (Oxford: Oxford University Press, 1981), pp. 565-578.
[47] Chris Meier to Dejan Adam (Woodcrest, USA, March 29, 2006). Personal correspondence. In the possession of Dejan Adam.

'To Follow the Holy Spirit's Promptings'

In taking the step of joining the Bruderhof and through his baptism as an adult believer, Meier experienced a deep personal change. He would later describe this experience as follows:

> Such a conversion cannot be described in words. I wonder if Nicodemus grasped intellectually what Jesus tried to make clear to him for his new birth by using the symbol of the blowing wind?[48]

In Matthew 7:15-20 Jesus says that one can recognise a tree by its fruit and goes on to apply this in the area of discernment of spirits. It was this kind of picture that Meier had in mind when he tried to describe the spirit that was able to bind the Rhön Bruderhof together. He said,

> It would be possible to study...communities in psychological, anthropological, and theological ways, but the Bruderhof was something which one could only get to know by experience... This can be compared to the relationship between a living organism and a human organisation.[49]

This statement suggests that, as Meier saw it, the members of the Bruderhof, due to their faith, acted as different parts of the same body. In spite of all the individual differences in the members of the body, they lived in balanced cooperation. Conversely, the Werkhof could be compared with a human organisation where many opposing ideas and ideals of leadership fail to achieve the expected results. The members of the Werkhof had tried to achieve agreement and unity in an 'idealistic democratic way'.[50] Yet, their democracy manifested itself as disunity and repression by the majority who were convinced they represented something better. The Bruderhof on the other hand tried to live by the rule of God, who, in his love, requires free and willing submission. With this attitude, the Bruderhof challenged the Werkhof to accept the way of Christ.[51]

However, the Bruderhof was not considered by its members to be *the* Church, but rather an 'embassy' of the Kingdom of God within the kingdom of

---

[48] Meier, 'Difficulties', p. 14.

[49] Hans Meier, 'The Bruderhof', in Heini Gut and Raymond Pittet (eds.), *As Long as there is Light: The Life of Hans Meier (1902-1992)* (Deer Spring Bruderhof, USA, 1991). An unpublished document in Bruderhof Archives, Woodcrest, Rifton, New York, p. 14. I owe this insight to Dr Parush R. Parushev. This statement presents a Wittgensteinean shift in the understanding of the functioning of language. See e.g. Fergus Kerr, *Theology after Wittgenstein*, 2nd edition (London: SPCK, 1997, 1986).

[50] Meier, 'The Bruderhof', p. 14.

[51] Baum, *Against the Wind*, pp. 223-225.

this world, a world to which political powers such as the emerging Third Reich also belonged. According to Meier,

> Only the Spirit of Christ was allowed to rule on its land; a spirit which recognises no nationalism for instance. Every witness of this kind is always attacked, inwardly as well as outwardly, by the enemy of Christ. For that reason the Bruderhof and its members wage a constant battle of the Spirit, especially in places where the enemy has already made some inroads.[52]

Therefore, seeing itself as an embassy, the Bruderhof opened its doors to all those willing to be transformed into servants of God. The most challenging part of such a transformation was to learn to live a life of full community and sharing—a convincing, observable witness to the coming Kingdom of God's peace and justice.[53]

Two previously mentioned individuals were crucial in terms of influencing Meier's decision to live a life of full community. Both of them viewed communal life as vital to the spiritual struggle for freedom, unity, peace, and social justice. One was Eberhard Arnold, a founder of the Bruderhof with his wife Emmy and her sister Else Von Hollander, and its spiritual leader until his death in 1935. Arnold emphasised that *Nachfolge Christi* (following Christ) must be the foundation of communal life as lived on the Bruderhof.[54] The second person was Leonhard Ragaz, who had abandoned his professorship at the University of Zurich in order to reach out to workers in Zurich for the sake of the Kingdom of God.[55]

Arnold and Ragaz had an ongoing dialogue over the years that was fruitful but was also often contentious. After World War I, the first religious–socialist conference on the theme *The Christian in Church, State, and Society* took place in Tambach (Thuringia), in September 1919. Arnold was scheduled to present an essay that would complement Ragaz's keynote address on *The Christian in Society*. Ragaz ended up not attending the conference due to poor health, and a then unknown Swiss pastor, Karl Barth (who later became the leading Protestant theologian of the twentieth century), replaced him. Barth's presentation on how the Kingdom of God is *totalier aliter* or 'totally other' had such an impact on the conference that it ended up depriving the religious socialist movement of power from within. Barth's *Tambach* speech came to be recognised as one of his masterpieces, while Arnold's call to engage with the

---

[52] Meier, 'The Bruderhof', p. 15.

[53] Hans Meier, 'The Fight for the Kingdom Goes On', in Heini Gut and Raymond Pittet (eds.), *As Long as there is Light: The Life of Hans Meier (1902-1992)* (Deer Spring Bruderhof, USA, 1991). An unpublished document in Bruderhof Archives, Woodcrest, Rifton, New York, p. 57; see Mommsen, *Homage*, pp. 89-95.

[54] Eberhard Arnold, *Why We Live in Community* (Farmington, Penn.: Plough Publishing, 2002), pp. 9-29.

[55] Bock, *Signs of the Kingdom*, p. viii.

radical discipleship of Jesus by living out the Sermon on the Mount here and now was largely ignored.[56]

Both Ragaz and Arnold fought constantly for a deeper commitment to practical discipleship—following the way of Christ—in contrast to a 'dogmatising and theologising of the cause of Christ, which is one of the many tragedies of the kingdom of God'.[57] However, they held different positions in terms of formulating the way of discipleship and fitting that into their contemporary social context. Meier wrote, in what is in places a rather difficult passage to understand:

> Ragaz recognized Arnold's way and his Christian communistic Bruderhof idea totally, which he valued highly. At the same time though, he raised the question (which he had decided for himself already), as to whether there is also a way of discipleship of Jesus beside 'the separated from the political life atmosphere of the Bruderhof,' in other words, fully integrated into public life in which only relative, not absolute, decisions are made. Ragaz himself hoped for a synthesis of both these ways, although this was never given by him.[58]

In addition, the fact that two of the Werkhof's founding families decided to join the Bruderhof[59] generated further discussions between Ragaz and Arnold. According to Meier, the purpose of these discussions was to answer Ragaz's question whether or not the Bruderhof was to be considered *the* Church of Christ, which eventually all determined followers of Jesus would have to join.[60] In answer to this question, Arnold explained,

> When we are asked whether we...are God's church, the *Gemeinde*, we have to say 'No, we are not. We are an object of God's love just like all other people, and we are unworthy, powerless, and unfit to follow the Holy Spirit's promptings, to

---

[56] Baum, *Against the Wind*, pp. 106-108; Regarding Arnold's essay see 'Present Experience, Future Kingdom' in Arnold, *Salt and Light*, pp. 133-146; Regarding Barth's 'Tambah speech', see 'The Christian's Place in Society', in Karl Barth, *The Word of God and the Word of Man* (Boston: Pilgrim Press, 1928), pp. 272-327.

[57] Leonhard Ragaz to Eberhard Arnold (n.p., October 28, 1922). Personal correspondence. In the possession of Bruderhof Archives, Woodcrest, Rifton, New York.

[58] Hans Meier, 'Community as seen by Eberhard Arnold and as seen by Leonhard Ragaz', in Heini Gut and Raymond Pittet (eds.), *As Long as there is Light: The Life of Hans Meier (1902-1992)* (Deer Spring Bruderhof, USA, 1991). An unpublished document in Bruderhof Archives, Woodcrest, Rifton, New York, p. 16.

[59] Peter and Anni Mathis in the late summer of 1932 and Hans and Margrit Meier in February, 1933; See Baum, *Against the Wind*, p. 224.

[60] Hans Meier, 'The Rhön Bruderhof', in Heini Gut and Raymond Pittet (eds.), *As Long as there is Light: The Life of Hans Meier (1902-1992)* (Deer Spring Bruderhof, USA, 1991). An unpublished document in Bruderhof Archives, Woodcrest, Rifton, New York, pp. 18-20.

build up the *Gemeinde*, or to go on mission into all the world.' But when we are asked, 'Is the church of God among you?...' Then we have to answer, 'Yes, that is so. Wherever believing people are gathered and have no other will than the one, single will that the kingdom of God may come and that the church of Christ may be revealed as the perfect unity of his spirit—then the church is in every such place because the Holy Spirit is there.'[61]

On 11 March 1935 Ragaz and Arnold met for the last time in Zurich. On that occasion Arnold made it unambiguously clear that 'the witness of the communal life is one decisive witness in our day; this does not mean, however, that no other witness exists.'[62] In reply, Ragaz said: 'To me the contradiction in these attitudes has not been a disturbance, since it is also present within myself... We might be able to talk together about this in friendship and brotherliness.'[63] Unfortunately, such further discussion never occurred because Arnold died that same year. However, Arnold's words and actions continued to challenge those wanting to live a life of radical discipleship of Jesus. On the one hand, Arnold believed that the life in common lived by the early Christians in Jerusalem and based upon Jesus' Sermon on the Mount could answer all the questions of life. On the other hand, he carefully avoided both trying to imitate exactly the life of the early Christians and adopting the teaching of the Sermon on the Mount as a set of regulations. The communal life of the early Christians, as Arnold viewed it, was not a sociological concept but the outcome of the work of the Spirit of Jesus Christ. Through that spirit alone was it possible to create and maintain a socially just and peaceful community.[64] Therefore, led by Arnold, the Bruderhof sought to establish a relationship between power and property in which property belonged to the whole community. They rejected what they saw as the state church's perversion of power.[65]

In order to practise full discipleship and commitment to Jesus, Meier looked to the way of faith in action modelled by Arnold. Meier rejected the idea of Ragaz that it was possible to follow Christ in a relative rather than an absolute way. According to Meier,

---

[61] Eberhard Arnold to Leonhard Ragaz (n.p., March 11, 1933). Personal correspondence. In the Bruderhof Archives, Woodcrest, Rifton, New York.

[62] Eberhard Arnold, 'A Talk given to Leonhard Ragaz and Members of the Werkhof' (Zurich, Switzerland, 11 March 1935). The minutes of a meeting presided over by Eberhard Arnold. Unpublished document in Bruderhof Archives, Woodcrest, Rifton, New York.

[63] Meier, 'Community', pp. 16-17; see Baum, *Against the Wind*, pp. 242-243.

[64] Arnold, *Why We Live in Community*, pp. 5-18; see Eberhard Arnold, *God's Revolution: Justice, Community, and the Coming Kingdom* (Farmington, Penn.: Plough Publishing, 2004), pp. 54-65.

[65] Meier, 'The Rhön Bruderhof', p. 20.

Jesus rejected the relative way, 'the for the time being way,' for in His kingdom of true peace and genuine justice, He only wants to have completely voluntary, personally responsible citizens. He made it clear to Pilate that He had no interest in the political power of the kingdoms of the world and that He had come only to give a witness for truth. The decisive thing then is the practical, visible witness of discipleship. Therefore 'theological–dogmatic lip–confessions' are not sufficient. Only a realistic life gives power to the witness of the disciples of Jesus![66]

Though Ragaz wrote that his sociological ideal had always been the communism—the sharing together—of the 'apostolic community of Christ'[67] which originated at Pentecost, belonging to such an intentional community of Christ was his unfulfilled dream. The full discipleship of Jesus in community of goods as put into action by the Bruderhof confronted Ragaz in a way that caused him inner turmoil. As Ragaz admitted,

> A twofold hindrance stood in the way of absolute discipleship. On the one hand, I did not quite dare to take my family on this way of poverty, and this all the more so because my wife had hesitations on my account. But there was still another stumbling block, just as big. The paralysis which came from my theological profession also held me back, for it prevented the hard decision demanded by the other way.[68]

Both as a Bruderhof member and a sympathiser with religious socialists, Hans Meier had many things in common with Leonhard Ragaz, particularly his doubts about an uncertain future lived in poverty. Yet Arnold's stand, on the witness of communal life built upon Jesus' Sermon on the Mount, was decisive in influencing Meier to accept life on the social margins for the cause of Christ.[69] Meier often recalled Arnold's words when he said that 'if we fully grasp the Sermon on the Mount and believe it, then nothing can frighten us— neither our self-recognition, nor financial threats nor our personal weakness.'[70] Therefore, one can argue that Arnold had the final word in terms of helping Meier to make up his mind to join the Bruderhof and remain a member until the end of his life. However, living in a community—even in a Christian community—is never an easy commitment, and soon Meier experienced the inner struggle to maintain integrity in fellowship.

---

[66] Meier, 'Community', p. 17.

[67] Bock, *Signs of the Kingdom*, p. 105.

[68] Meier, 'Community', p. 17.

[69] Eberhard Arnold (ed.), *The Early Christians in Their Own Words* (Farmington, Penn.: Plough Publishing, 2003), pp. 2-4.

[70] Eberhard Arnold, *Salt and Light: Living the Sermon on the Mount* (Farmington, Penn.: Plough Publishing, 2004), p. 1.

On 22 November 1935, Eberhard Arnold unexpectedly died. His death was a great challenge for the community.[71] Outwardly the Bruderhof had endured the accusations and hostility of National Socialists while within the community 'there was a struggle for God's rulership against an incipient rule of men and false human love'.[72] Recalling those days, Arnold's widow Emmy wrote,

> How many guests had told us that very summer that a life like ours would last only as long as Eberhard and our enthusiastic and convinced beginning members were still living. After their death, people said, the whole thing would crumble. In answer to this Eberhard had always said that it would be that way with human establishment, but that true community could be founded and supported by the Holy Spirit alone. This would have to be proven here again.[73]

Until that point the main threat to the Bruderhof had seemed to come from the Third Reich. Due to Hitler's tightening grip on Germany, the Bruderhof had been forced to live in two separate settlements. Yet, in the wake of Arnold's death, the more dangerous threat to the communal way of life emerged internally through inter-personal dynamics within the community. The Bruderhof now had to struggle to overcome the arrogance of individuals exercising important functions within the community who were convinced that their ministry put them on a pedestal. Because of their misguided understanding of responsibility, these individuals held back the free movement of the Spirit among the other members of the Bruderhof. Another problem revolved around an inclination toward personal moralism, where certain individuals positioned themselves and their moral norms above others. Consequently, they spoke and thought with disrespect of those they saw as below their highly self-estimated spiritual level. The third internal problem encountered within the Bruderhof was manifested as a spirit of financial efficiency, which focused communal attention on earning money at the expense of the inner life of the community. The source of all these problems lay in personal pride, with individuals considering themselves as the most competent and perceptive community members while seeing others as valueless. These problems within the movement led to depression and disillusionment as the communal ideals were no longer being achieved. For those earnestly seeking the *Nachfolge Christi*, these issues were seen as a matter of spiritual life and death. Everything that did not come out of agape love led toward spiritual death.[74]

---

[71] Baum, *Against the Wind*, p. 252; see Mommsen, *Homage*, pp. 126-129.

[72] Hans Meier, 'The Alm Bruderhof', in Heini Gut and Raymond Pittet (eds.), *As Long as there is Light: The Life of Hans Meier (1902-1992)* (Deer Spring Bruderhof, USA, 1991). An unpublished document in Bruderhof Archives, Woodcrest, Rifton, New York, p. 29.

[73] Emmy Arnold, *Torches Together: The Beginning and Early Years of the Bruderhof Communities* (Farmington, Penn.: Plough Publishing, 1971), p. 203.

[74] Ibid., pp. 166-167; see Mommsen, *Homage*, pp. 130-135.

This period in Meier's life was one of inner turmoil and repeated self-examination. Though Arnold had died his words, and in particular his direction to follow Jesus above all, still had a formative influence on Meier's convictions. In looking at the life and death of Jesus, who was sacrificed to establish peace between God and humankind, Meier felt it to be of the utmost importance that the brotherhood, including himself, become refocused on the importance of laying down one's life for others. Meier believed that whoever was not prepared to die in the struggle for truth and justice was not worthy to live for peace.[75]

In his thinking at this time Meier was in line with the Anabaptist tradition that took shape in the sixteenth century, as represented in *The Schleitheim Confession*.[76] In reply to the challenging question of how a disciple of Christ is to relate to the community, including in the area of obedience to its authorities, Michael Sattler (ca. 1490-1527), the principal author of the confession, pointed to a simple yet central command to 'be like Christ'[77] in whose footsteps his followers, including communal leaders, ought to walk. Similarly Meier saw the leaders of the Bruderhof as people who accompanied him in *Nachfolge Christi*.[78] Also, according to *Schleitheim*, a leader who sinned should be publicly reprimanded, so that others might fear.[79] Meier believed that just as he might need both admonition and support upon doing wrong, it was his obligation to use the same approach to others without considering their status within the Bruderhof. In other words, those causing inner disorder at that point within the Bruderhof were also vulnerable people who needed help to bear their burdens and to grow in Christlikeness.[80]

Eventually, through the painful experience of Arnold's death, which was accompanied by problems pressing the Bruderhof from both within and without, the membership found a way to be reconciled and to work together again. They were prepared in this way for another challenging task—the relocation of the settlements to England, a move forced by the growing power of National Socialism in Germany and the resulting hostility of the German authorities towards the Bruderhof community, hostility which gathered strength

---

[75] Meier, '*Why we Live in Full Community*'; see Meier, 'The Fight for the Kingdom Goes On', pp. 58-59; see Eberhard Arnold, *Innerland: A Guide into the Heart of the Gospel* (Farmington, Penn.: Plough Publishing, 2003), p. 197; see Brinkman, 'Between God and Fatherland', p. 174.

[76] Regarding the Schleitheim Confession see John H. Yoder (ed.), *The Schleitheim Confession* (Scottdale, Penn.: Herald Press, 1977); see Arnold C. Snyder, 'The Influence of the Schleitheim Articles on the Anabaptist Movement: An Historical Evaluation', *The Mennonite Quarterly Review* LXIII (October, 1989), pp. 323-345.

[77] Arnold C. Snyder, *The Life and Thought of Michael Sattler* (Scottdale, Penn.: Herald Press, 1984), p. 145.

[78] Meier, '*Why we Live in Full Community*', pp. 1-2 (my pagination).

[79] Yoder, *The Schleitheim Confession*, p. 13.

[80] Meier, '*Why we Live in Full Community*', pp. 1-2 (my pagination).

through the 1930s. These moves were their way of responding to the Holy Spirit.

'A State which Claims Absolute Power'

Eberhard Arnold's response to the changing political circumstances of German society continued to influence Meier. Arnold had emphasised the approaching hardships the Bruderhof was facing, which he believed could end up requiring the sacrifice of one's whole life. Those who were not ready to live lives of radical discipleship were warned to leave the Bruderhof. However, in response to this call, the majority of the members found themselves bound more tightly than ever before to each other and only a few people left the community.[81] The National Socialists came to power in Germany on 31 January 1933, the day after Hitler became chancellor of Germany. From that point on, life at the Rhön Bruderhof was increasingly threatened by external forces. The Bruderhof was affected by the aggressive, exclusive politics of the Third Reich, especially after community members expressed their concerns in the plebiscite which took place on 12 November 1933.[82] This is how Meier described the circumstances of the Bruderhof at that time:

> We closed ranks in the faith that the kingdom of God would in the end be victorious over the Third Reich. Since we did not expect salvation to come from Hitler, we could not use the greeting 'Heil Hitler' [salvation from Hitler], which everyone was expected to say. We were often attacked because of this. Our community of goods and life was compared to Bolshevist communism. Our known refusal to do military service, which from 1935 on was illegal and punishable, marked us straightaway as enemies of the National Socialists.[83]

With the intention of defending the Bruderhof's stance on the separation between church and state, Arnold wrote letters to the highest state authorities including Hindenburg, Hitler, the president of the government of Hessen, the Reichs–Bishop, and the State Secret police (the Gestapo). These letters were read out in full members' meetings and were sent only when there was obviously unanimous community backing for the contents—a demonstration of unity that was a powerful witness for the Kingdom of God. By acting in such a manner, the Bruderhof protested in a public way against the unjust and discriminatory politics of the Third Reich. They also urged the German

---

[81] Brinkman, 'Between God and Fatherland', pp. 225-227.
[82] Baum, *Against the Wind*, pp. 229-232; see Mommsen, *Homage*, p. 96.
[83] Hans Meier, 'Face to Face with National Socialism', in Heini Gut and Raymond Pittet (eds.), *As Long as there is Light: The Life of Hans Meier (1902-1992)* (Deer Spring Bruderhof, USA, 1991). An unpublished document in Bruderhof Archives, Woodcrest, Rifton, New York, p. 21.

authorities to pay attention to their responsibilities and restrictions from a biblical viewpoint.[84] According to Meier's account, the Bruderhof objected in the following very detailed terms,

> First, against a state which claims absolute power, as does the present government with its philosophy of life that dominates the whole nation, and does this in contrast to obedience to God and the will of the kingdom of God, which stands above everything else. Second, against the prevailing popular attitude that puts man and his place in life, the State and its precepts, above God and his Word, above Christ and his Spirit whereas all those called to be Christians should honour and listen to God more than to men. Third, against the restrictions placed upon the freedom of speech and education in relation to the apostolic mission of Jesus Christ, which makes all convinced Christians obey the call of God, without looking to the right or the left. Fourth, against the prevailing movement of the people, by which man and his prevailing authority, the state and its demands, take a place above God and his Word, above Christ and his Spirit, whereas all called Christian shall give the honour to God above everything else and obey him more than men. Fifth, against total belief in Aryan blood, which offends God's measure of justice and equality given to people of different blood. We wished for Adolf Hitler that he would change from being a tool of the wrath of God to becoming a tool of the love of God, and we warned him not to shed innocent blood.[85]

In evaluating Meier's stand on political ethics, one can argue that his views were formed in part by the writings of two prominent sixteenth-century Anabaptist leaders whose influence was intermingled with that of Arnold. The first was Peter Rideman (1506-1556), whose *Confession of Faith*[86] clearly shaped the Bruderhof's attitude toward government, and the second was Michael Sattler and the Schleitheim Confession.[87] The common characteristic of both Rideman and Sattler was that their writings highlighted a

---

[84] Baum, *Against the Wind*, pp. 219-221; see Brinkman, 'Between God and Fatherland', pp. 23-24; see Klaus Meier to Dejan Adam (Beech Grove Bruderhof, UK, 28 March 2006). Personal correspondence. In the possession of Dejan Adam.

[85] Meier, 'Face to Face', pp. 22-23.

[86] Regarding the Confession of Faith see Peter Rideman, *Account of Our Religion, Doctrine and Faith* (Rifton, N.Y.: Plough Publishing, 1970); see Franz Heimann, 'The Hutterite Doctrines of Church and Common Life: A Study of Peter Riedemann's Confession of Faith of 1540', *The Mennonite Quarterly Review* XXVI (January 1952), pp. 22-47; see Franz Heimann, 'The Hutterite Doctrines of Church and Common Life: A Study of Peter Riedemann's Confession of Faith of 1540, II', *The Mennonite Quarterly Review* XXVI (April 1952), pp. 142-160.

[87] Klaus Meier wrote: 'I also know that my dad read and re-read Peter Rideman, who is very basic to our whole communal life, attitude to the State, the Churches, marriage, baptism, confession, remorse and all the principal Christian tenets. The same is true for Michael Sattler.' See Klaus Meier to Dejan Adam (Beech Grove Bruderhof, UK, May 16, 2006). Personal correspondence. In the possession of Dejan Adam.

Christocentric, New Testament standard of behaviour.[88] In describing his approach to the Old and the New Testaments, Rideman argued that 'the light of divine truth hath appeared more brightly in Christ, who hath revealed to us the real will of the Father...the law was given by Moses, but truth came by Christ'.[89] Rideman proposed that God's demand for His people was found in the words spoken by Jesus and not in the 'shadows'[90] of the Old Testament. Continuing this line of argument, Rideman wrote,

> God in Christ, alone is king and commander of his people, as it is written, 'God hath set a ruler over every people, but over Israel he alone is Lord.' Even as he is a spiritual king, he also has spiritual servants and wields a spiritual sword—both he and all his servants—that pierces soul and spirit... Thus is Christ King of all kings, and at the same time the opposite of all the rulers of this world... Thus, he sets up quite a different kingdom and rule and desires that his servants submit themselves to it and become like him.[91]

Rideman's Christocentric understanding required that only Christ is the king of his committed followers and that the call is to follow in his ways. A particular application of this principle, which influenced Meier to oppose the Third Reich, was that as Christ had demonstrated non-violence, so the subjects of his Kingdom must do likewise. In the words of John Howard Yoder, the argument against supporting Hitler's dictatorship revolved around the paradigm of *revolutionary subordination*.[92] Meier was revolutionarily subordinated to the National Socialist regime through his membership in the Bruderhof. The outcome of such subordination was hoped to be a spiritually based corrective to the Third Reich. Such a desired transformation to the increasingly oppressive German government never occurred however, and Meier had to struggle to overcome a growing feeling of hatred against Hitler by urging himself 'to recognise that the way of Jesus leads to hate of sin, yet to love of the sinner'.[93]

One can argue that the Christocentric hermeneutic revolving around 'the perfection of Christ'[94] was the key concept in Sattler's approach to the Scriptures. According to this approach, authentic followers of Jesus comply

---

[88] Snyder, *Anabaptist History and Theology*, p. 185. Regarding the Christocentrism of the Anabaptists' approach to hermeneutics see Stuart Murray, *Biblical Interpretation in the Anabaptist Tradition* (Kitchener, Ontario: Pandora Press, 2000), pp. 70-92.

[89] Rideman, *Account of Our Religion*, p. 196.

[90] This word is used to refer to the Old Testament in Rideman, *Account*, p. 195; see Murray, *Biblical Interpretation*, p. 93, n. 14.

[91] Rideman, *Account of Our Religion*, pp. 106-107.

[92] Regarding 'revolutionary subordination' see John H. Yoder, *The Politics of Jesus* (Carlisle, UK: Paternoster Press, 2003), pp. 162-187.

[93] Meier, 'Face to Face', p. 23.

[94] Arnold C. Snyder, *The Life and Thought of Michael Sattler* (Scottdale, Penn.: Herald Press, 1984), p. 119.

with the commands of the Bible, above all the commands of Christ. The Sermon on the Mount seems to have become for many sixteenth-century Anabaptists 'a further canon within an already Christocentric canon.'[95] Driven by 'the perfection of Christ', Sattler's Schleitheim articles number six and seven regulating the use of the sword and the oath were seen by his opponents as the most controversial, reflecting on the separation between the church and state. Meier concurred with Sattler on these two articles. He had already experienced the fact that Hitler's Third Reich found the Bruderhof's position counter to the state, which claimed absolute domination over the life of the entire nation, as exceptionally threatening and subversive. Additionally, the Third Reich had, through the absolute imposition of its dictatorship, marginalised those who sought to put the kingdom of God in the first place in their lives.

Meier also followed Sattler's thinking in *The Schleitheim Confession* regarding the use of the sword and the swearing of an oath. The confession states:

> Thereby shall also fall away from us the diabolical weapons of violence—such as sword, armour, and the like, and their use to protect friends or against enemies—by virtue of the word of Christ: 'you shall not resist evil.'[96]

Although this brief passage in its original context alluded to the impending Turkish threat upon Europe, Meier's refusal to support the expansionistic and aggressive politics of Hitler might be connected with this statement. However, Meier seemed to have been more interested in the article in the confession which explicitly evaluated 'the sword of government',[97] while putting aside the evaluation of 'the sword of war'.[98] The reason for his interest in this article (article number six) was that at that time Hitler had not yet started World War II. The opening statement in article number six is undeniably direct:

> The sword is an ordering of God outside the perfection of Christ. It punishes and kills the wicked, and guards and protects the good. In the law the sword is established over the wicked for punishment and for death, and the secular rulers are established to wield the same.[99]

Influenced by this thinking, Meier raised his voice against the self-confidence in the Aryan race of the Third Reich, while also hoping for a transformation of Hitler that would change him into a messenger of God's love.

---

[95] Murray, *Biblical Interpretation*, p. 79; see Snyder, *The Life and Thought*, pp. 135-145.
[96] Yoder, *The Schleitheim Confession*, p. 13; see Matt 5:39.
[97] Snyder, *The Life and Thought*, p. 119.
[98] Ibid.
[99] Yoder, *The Schleitheim Confession*, p. 14.

His hope was that such a transformation would mean that Hitler stopped the shedding of innocent blood.[100] The last article of *The Schleithem Confession* addresses the swearing of oaths. The confession insists that the words of Christ, 'do not swear at all', cannot be interpreted ambiguously. Nothing else but complete obedience is needed.[101] Influenced by this argument, Meier accepted the social consequences of refusing to swear an oath to Hitler. It is not surprising that the Bruderhof was accused by German officials of perpetuating subversive and anarchistic ideas and of threatening state politics.

In evaluating the influence of both Rideman and Sattler on Meier's stand on political ethics, one more critical observation must be spelled out. While remaining faithful to the Anabaptist Christocentric interpretation of the Scriptures, Meier at the same time was interested in knowing to what extent the Old Testament might be incorporated in the practice of *Nachfolge Christi*. Generally speaking, Meier had a more positive view of the Old Testament than Rideman and Sattler. In order to illuminate clearly his position on non-participation in politics, Meier often used two stories from the Old Testament. The first was the story of the Exodus, which Meier used to demonstrate how God led the Israelites out of Egypt without them using any military or human force. The second was the story about the prophet Daniel who remained faithful to his convictions even at the risk of a horrifying execution. Putting aside Daniel's involvement in governmental matters, Meier's interest centred on Daniel's persistence in 'giving thanks to his God'[102] in spite of King Darius' edict against praying. According to Meier, the lesson of these two stories was that the nations needed to follow the example of the Jewish people in these two stories from the Old Testament. They needed to lay down their arms, turn away from the power of human governments, and turn to God to lead them in everything.[103]

The intention of both Rideman and Sattler to build their scriptural interpretation on the centrality of Christ failed to consider the methodological suitability of such an approach for later generations of interpreters who would develop their hermeneutical theories in different contexts.[104] Yet, it was an issue that Meier as an interpreter of the Scriptures would raise. Whilst bearing in mind that Christ himself was theocentric, Meier didn't think that Christocentrism should be reduced to a 'Christo–monism'.[105] Meier saw Christ as the centre of God's self–revelation

---

[100] Snyder, *The Life and Thought*, p. 120; see Meier, 'Face to Face', pp. 22-23.

[101] Snyder, *The Life and Thought*, p. 121.

[102] NIV, Daniel 6:10.

[103] Andreas Meier to Dejan Adam (Woodcrest, USA, 13 March 2006). Personal correspondence. In the possession of Dejan Adam; see Klaus Meier to Dejan Adam (Beech Grove Bruderhof, UK, 17 March 2006). Personal correspondence. In the possession of Dejan Adam.

[104] Murray, *Biblical Interpretation*, p. 91.

[105] Stanley Samartha, 'The Lordship of Christ and Religious Pluralism', in Gerald H. Anderson and Thomas F. Stransky (eds.), *Christ's Lordship and Religious Pluralism* (Maryknoll, N.Y.: Orbis Books, 1981), p. 27.

without renouncing the authenticity of such revelation in the rest of the Bible. Thus, Meier approached Christ in a more holistic way than Rideman and Sattler did in the sixteenth century. He saw the incarnated Christ 'as the revelation of God in Christ rather than a revelation of Christ alone'.[106]

All these events and theological reflections led Meier, as well as the wider Bruderhof community, now numbering 120, into a growing confrontation with the Third Reich. It was increasingly difficult to practise their convictions and spiritual practices in peace. They hoped to find partners among other Christian groups in Germany and the surrounding countries, but they felt increasingly isolated. The consequence of the community's stance was that on 16 November 1933 about 150 heavily armed storm troopers led by a Gestapo official surrounded the Rhön Bruderhof in an act of intimidation.[107] Surprisingly, some of the storm troopers were ready to talk to Meier and others in the community. The troopers argued that the National Socialists also insisted on community in which mutual well being was more important than self–interest. The point on which they disagreed with Meier and the Bruderhof was that the community they envisioned 'could not be brought about voluntarily and had to be enforced by laws'.[108] This visit by the Gestapo demonstrated the attitudes of the German authorities toward those who refused to put Hitler above God in their lives. The storm troopers also searched through the houses, and took many papers, letters, books and other 'evidence'.

There is evidence that already in 1933 the Gestapo were planning to close the Rhön Bruderhof. The foremost reason for this was that the Gestapo, during the raid of 16 November 1933, discovered several reports from Bruderhof communal meetings saying that Hitler's Germany demonstrated clearly the quality of a state portrayed in Revelation 13:1 as 'a beast coming out of the sea'.[109] However, some of the highest state authorities had refused the Gestapo's prompting to dissolve the Bruderhof on the grounds that such an action would trigger 'atrocity propaganda',[110] as it was termed, in the USA and Canada, where the Bruderhof had many friends. Potential accusations of persecuting Christians would be at odds with the German propaganda

---

[106] Murray, *Biblical Interpretation*, p. 91; see Charles Scriven, *The Transformation of Culture: Christian Social Ethics after H. Richard Niebuhr* (Scottdale, Penn.: Herald Press, 1988), pp. 162-163.

[107] Brinkman, 'Between God and Fatherland', pp. 68-72; See Hans Meier, 'Article Written for Johannes Halkenhauser' (Deer Spring, USA, March, 1982). Personal notes. An unpublished document in Bruderhof
Archives, Woodcrest, Rifton, New York, p. 5; see Mommsen, *Homage*, pp. 98-102.

[108] Meier, 'Face to Face', p. 24.

[109] NIV; see Brinkman, 'Between God and Fatherland', p. 84.

[110] Meier, 'Face to Face', p. 26.

portraying the Third Reich as standing for 'positive Christianity'.[111] As an attempted solution to this objection, those wanting to close the Bruderhof agreed to accuse its members of drug–addiction.[112]

In the event another approach was taken. The local authorities decided to close the Rhön Bruderhof's school, alleging that it did not provide an education for its students consistent with German National Socialism. On 5 December 1933, the school was inspected by the local Inspector of Schools who reported to his superiors that the pupils did not know any National Socialist songs. Later that month, on 29 December, a letter was received from the chief government official in Kasel, specifying that the private elementary and middle school of the Bruderhof was no longer authorised and should be closed.[113] Upon hearing this news, Meier was sent by the community to visit Switzerland in order to find an appropriate location for a new school outside of Germany for the Bruderhof children. In addition, he took all the records from the Bruderhof, which the Gestapo had failed to discover, into safety, and wrote to the Hutterian brothers in North America from Switzerland about the hardships they were experiencing. Meier also checked whether any of the old Moravian Brethren settlements from the sixteenth century[114] were affordable and available for purchase in Moravia in case the Bruderhof was expelled from Germany. Ragaz wrote a letter recommending Meier to his friend Thomas Masaryk, the President of Czechoslovakia.[115] Unfortunately, Masaryk was ill and was not able to help, but his personal secretary offered Meier all the assistance he could. However, all the remaining Brethren buildings from the sixteenth century were preserved by the state as historical monuments and consequently were not available. In Switzerland the officials said that the children belonging to the Bruderhof were not welcome to continue their schooling there. Therefore, another place had to be found.[116]

As the next step, Eberhard and Emmy Arnold tried to find a place for the school in the Principality of Liechtenstein. During the sixteenth century the Princes of Liechtenstein, who were the Lords of Nikolsburg (nowadays Mikulov), in Moravia, had provided shelter to thousands of Anabaptist refugees

---

[111] Regarding Hitler's Positive Christianity see Doug Krieger, 'Hitler's Positive Christianity…Unleashing the Patriotic Church', http://www.buzzle.com/editorials/6-30-2005-72402.asp, accessed 22 April 2006.

[112] Hinkey, 'Hans Meier Talking with Amos Hoover', p. 6.

[113] Baum, *Against the Wind*, pp. 232-234; see Mommsen, *Homage*, pp. 103-104.

[114] Jerold Knox Zeman, *The Anabaptists and the Czech Brethren in Moravia 1526-1628: A Study of Origins and Contacts* (The Hague: Mouton, 1969).

[115] Antonie Van Den Beld, Humanity: *The Political and Social Philosophy of Thomas G. Masaryk* (The Hague: Mouton, 1975), pp. 9-13.

[116] Hans Meier, 'A Report on the Journey to Switzerland and Czechoslovakia in November, 1933' (n.p., n.d.). Personal notes. An unpublished document in Bruderhof Archives, Woodcrest, Rifton, New York.

escaping from different parts of Europe because of religious persecution.[117] The small country of Liechtenstein, governed by the ancestors of the same family, now welcomed again in the twentieth century a group of threatened children. The Rhön Bruderhof found a new home for the children in the simple summer hotel, *Silum*, situated two thousand meters above Triesenberg.[118] The children arrived there on 19 March 1934, and on 27 April 1934 they were issued a permit of residency. The Rhön Bruderhof bore the responsibility of supplying the new settlement with all it needed. Both the rent of *Silum* and the initial expenses (6,500 francs) were paid for by a Swiss woman named Julia Lerchy, who later joined the Bruderhof and gave her property to the community. The newly established settlement was named the Alm Bruderhof.[119] One year after its opening the Alm Bruderhof again became a place of refuge for young brothers affected by the compulsory military service reinstituted by Hitler in Germany in March 1935. Having considered their position, the brotherhood agreed that the lives of these young brothers would be better used in developing the Alm Bruderhof than in the service of the Third Reich or even worse in concentration camps where they were sure to end up if they stayed in Germany.[120] Through this action, the Bruderhof remained faithful to the early Anabaptist beliefs as described in *The Schleitheim Confession*, in particular through the refusal to accept obligatory military service in accordance with the confession's statement that 'the rule of the government is according to the flesh, that of the Christians according to the Spirit'.[121] This was an important collective decision to make in order to maintain the pacifist integrity of the community.

In order to discuss the possibility of wider working together 'in the spiritual battle against the approaching darkness',[122] Meier, on behalf of the Bruderhof, met with Martin Niemöller in Dahlem, Germany, in December 1933. Niemöller was a Lutheran pastor who had previously initiated the *Pfarrernotbund* [123] as well as the *Bekennende Kirche*.[124] At this meeting, Meier 'discussed the very same question with Niemöller'[125] as *The Confessional Synod of the German Evangelical Church* would talk about a few months later in Barmen on 29-31 May 1934. The purpose of the Confessional Synod was to gather the

---

[117] Snyder, *Anabaptist History and Theology*, pp. 118-121.
[118] Meier, 'The Alm Bruderhof', pp. 27-28.
[119] Klaus Meier to Dejan Adam (Beech Grove Bruderhof, UK, 3 April 2006). Personal correspondence. In the possession of Dejan Adam; see Chris Meier to Dejan Adam (Woodcrest, USA, 3 April 2006). Personal correspondence. In the possession of Dejan Adam.
[120] Meier, 'The Alm Bruderhof', p. 28.
[121] Yoder, *The Schleitheim Confession*, p. 15.
[122] Meier, 'Face to Face', p. 26.
[123] The Pastors' Emergency League.
[124] The Confessing Church.
[125] Meier, 'Face to Face', p. 26.

Evangelical Christian (Lutheran) Congregations in Germany together to seek a common message for the needs and challenges of the Church in contemporary society. The confession of faith that this group, to be known as the Confessing Church, arrived at became known as *The Confession of Barmen*.[126] Niemöller however refused to work with the Bruderhof because he said they were disobedient to the God-given government in their refusal to do military service.[127]

Meier also met Benjamin Unruh, who was at that time the leader of the German Mennonites, in an attempt to find a way of mutual co-operation between the Bruderhof and the Mennonites in the spirit of the early sixteenth-century Anabaptists. Unruh, however, was also not interested in cooperating with the Bruderhof.[128] According to Meier, Unruh said that 'the German Mennonites had changed their attitude toward the state. Now they were ready to obey the government even to the extent of military service.'[129] By interpreting Romans 13:1-7 in such a way as to stress 'obedience to the authorities', the German Mennonites were neglecting important aspects of their Anabaptist roots and the peace tradition to which they belonged. Half a year later, in new statutes adopted by the *Federation of German Mennonite Churches* on 11 June 1934, the principle of non-resistance was officially abandoned.[130]

Over the four years starting in 1933, the Gestapo put a great deal of effort into trying to close the Rhön Bruderhof and disperse its members. Meier recalled his conversation with the Mayor of Veitsteinbach who had a letter showing that the Rhön Bruderhof was observed by the Gestapo from the beginning of 1933. According to Meier, the Mayor claimed that a Gestapo official had placed this letter before him and demanded his signature. This letter accused the Bruderhof of reaching out actively for new members, in spite of the order issued at the end of 1933 stipulating that their radical witness to the public must be halted. The witness of the Bruderhof was considered to involve propaganda hostile to the state.[131] Thus the convictions held by the Bruderhof confronted the philosophy of the Third Reich, built as it was upon the unquestionable prerogative of the National Socialist state in human affairs as well as on its basic law of blood and race which assumed the exclusion and persecution of the Jews.[132] They refused to give the state absolute power.

---

[126] Regarding the Confession of Barmen see 'Theological Declaration of Barmen', http://www.creeds.net/reformed/barmen.htm, accessed April 20, 2006.
[127] Meier, 'Face to Face', p. 26.
[128] Brinkman, 'Between God and Fatherland', pp. 86-87.
[129] Meier, 'Face to Face', p. 27.
[130] Brinkman, 'Between God and Fatherland', p. 86.
[131] Meier, 'The Alm Bruderhof', pp. 28-29.
[132] Brinkman, 'Between God and Fatherland', pp. 169-170.

'Seriously Seeking People'

Through the witness of Arnold's oldest son Hardy, who had been training as a teacher in England in 1934, a number of English people had come to visit the Bruderhofs in Germany and Liechtenstein—the Rhön Bruderholf and the Alm Bruderholf. Eventually, five of these English guests decided to join the Bruderhof. The contacts Hardy made in England turned out to be crucial in finding a new place of refuge when on 15 February 1936 the Liechtenstein authorities warned Meier that Hitler's government was expecting them to hand over all German men of military age living in their principality. The local officers were reluctant to arrest the men of draft age at the Alm Bruderhof, yet they felt themselves too insignificant as a tiny country bordering Germany to oppose the German orders. Thus those affected needed to flee out of Liechtenstein quickly, and several Bruderholf members were sent to England to look for a place of refuge for the young German men.[133]

After some time, they found the Ashton Fields Farm in Wiltshire, in the Cotswolds area of England, which became the Cotswold Bruderhof. Once the property was located and purchased, a founders' meeting was held on 15 March 1936, and eleven people began living at the Cotswold Bruderhof, soon to be joined by many others.[134] This period in England just before World War II began was a time when many people were seeking for true peace and social justice. Out of this search came the founding of a number of settlements trying to live in peace and justice in intentional community. The Bruderhof had established relationships with some of these settlements, and eventually a number of them abandoned their own projects and joined the Cotswold Bruderhof.[135] As a result of this, as well as a continuing influx of brothers and sisters from the communities in Germany, the Cotswold Bruderhof quickly grew in size. By 15 March 1938, there were 248 people living in the community, including those who had arrived from the Alm and Rhön Bruderhofs. Soon it became necessary to start and build up a second English Bruderhof to accommodate the growth. Property was purchased in December of

---

[133] Hans Meier, 'Our Next Goal: England', in Heini Gut and Raymond Pittet (eds.), *As Long as there is Light: The Life of Hans Meier (1902-1992)* (Deer Spring Bruderhof, USA, 1991). An unpublished document in Bruderhof Archives, Woodcrest, Rifton, New York, p. 30; see Brinkman, 'Between God and Fatherland', pp. 185-187.

[134] Klaus Meier to Dejan Adam (Beech Grove Bruderhof, UK, 5 April 2006). Personal correspondence. In the possession of Dejan Adam; see Chris Meier to Dejan Adam (Woodcrest, USA, 4 April 2006). Personal correspondence. In the possession of Dejan Adam.

[135] Hans Meier, 'Five Years in the Cotswold', in Heini Gut and Raymond Pittet (eds.), *As long as there is Light: The Life of Hans Meier* (1902-1992) (Deer Spring Bruderhof, USA, 1991). Unpub. doc. in Bruderhof Archives, Woodcrest, Rifton, New York, p. 42.

1938 and the Oaksey Bruderhof (also in the Cotswolds) was begun, with the first people moving there in March 1939.[136]

Meanwhile, the community welcomed several Jewish families who were trying to reach either Israel or some other destination. The Cotswold Bruderhof also took in a number of Jewish children from the continent of Europe whose parents had been deported to concentration camps.[137] Describing the varied forms of communal life at these two newly-founded Bruderhofs, Meier said,

> Agriculture and gardening, stock farming and dairy farming, a publishing house with printing shop, and a turning shop with handcraft workshop were the work departments of the two Bruderhofs in England. In addition there was a private school and a maternity house. We sold our own products such as milk, bread, cake, cream, etc. in the neighbouring town of Swindon. At weekends, buses often came full of curious people and also people who were interested in our community. Among them there were seriously seeking people who stayed a longer time and worked with us. We were also invited to various meetings and events up and down the country to tell and report about our experiences.[138]

After spending almost a year at the Cotswold Bruderhof, Meier was sent back to Rhön to serve as its steward, responsible for financial matters. He arrived there just a few days before the final dissolution of the Rhön Bruderhof, which took place on 14 April 1937. As Meier remembered,

> With a force of about fifty armed men, the Gestapo appeared in the early morning and declared the dissolution of the Bruderhof, based on paragraphs 1 and 4 of the decree of the Reich President for the protection of the nation and the state against acts of Communist violence.[139]

Meier was approached by a Gestapo official who declared the Rhön Bruderhof dissolved and insisted that everybody living in the community must return to the places they had come from before joining the Bruderhof. Later, the Gestapo official repeated the same demand in front of the full brotherhood, and added that all German subjects were to report immediately for military service. The brotherhood unanimously decided that nobody would leave as they had left their homes for the sake of joining the Bruderhof. Moreover, the brothers again

---

[136] Chris Meier to Dejan Adam (Woodcrest, USA, April 10, 2006). Personal correspondence. In the possession of Dejan Adam.

[137] 'Hans Meier tells his Story', p. 14.

[138] Meier, 'Five Years', p. 42.

[139] Hans Meier, 'The Dissolution of the Rhön Bruderhof', in Heini Gut and Raymond Pittet (eds.), *As Long as there is Light: The Life of Hans Meier (1902-1992)* (Deer Spring Bruderhof, USA, 1991). An unpublished document in Bruderhof Archives, Woodcrest, Rifton, New York, pp. 33-34.

rejected enrolment in the military (although by then most of the German nationals of military age had already left the country).[140]

Remarkably, a few days before the Gestapo appeared, two brothers from the Hutterian Brethren in North America had arrived—David Hofer from the James Valley community in Manitoba, Canada, and Michael Waldner from the Bon Homme community in South Dakota in the USA. The Gestapo discovered them unexpectedly, while rummaging around the houses for suspected 'prohibited materials', when the two brothers refused to have their suitcases searched. The presence of the two North Americans on the Rhön Bruderhof caused serious problems for the Gestapo. They were afraid that after returning to North America, the brothers might complain to their governments about how the German National Socialists mistreated pacifist Christians, even up to the point of blaming them for being violent communists.[141] Therefore, to protect themselves against such anticipated accusations, the Gestapo summoned the Executive Committee of the Rhön Bruderhof [142] to Fulda the next day in order to discuss the future of the community in Germany. Conscious of the political issues, the Gestapo allowed all those dwelling at the Rhön Bruderhof to leave Germany and go to either to Liechtenstein or England. They were given a period of two days to pack up and get out of the country. The two brothers from the Hutterian Brethren were expected to cover their own travel expenses. The Gestapo imprisoned and indicted Meier and two other brothers However, in an attempt to pre-empt any additional 'atrocity propaganda'[143] overseas against Germany, the three—as members of the Rhön Bruderhof's financial committee—were accused of 'criminal doctoring of the accounts'.[144] Meier recorded,

> At the dissolution all the capital was confiscated. After that we were told to pay all our debts, including the mortgages. But we told them we were not able to do that as long as they kept our assets, which they refused to release. The Gestapo accused us of criminal bankruptcy to the criminal judge. The criminal court, however, only accepted this accusation later, under pressure by the Gestapo. When we protested at their taking photos and fingerprints for the Gestapo's album of criminals, it was smilingly pointed out that in any case, as enemies of the

---

[140] Brinkman, 'Between God and Fatherland', pp. 224-225; see Mommsen, *Homage*, p. 143.

[141] Meier, 'The Dissolution', p. 34.

[142] Hans Meier, Hans Boller, and Karl Keiderling.

[143] Meier, 'The Dissolution', p. 35.

[144] Hans Meier, 'In the Prison at Fulda', in Heini Gut and Raymond Pittet (eds.), *As Long as there is Light: The Life of Hans Meier (1902-1992)* (Deer Spring Bruderhof, USA, 1991). An unpublished document in Bruderhof Archives, Woodcrest, Rifton, New York, p. 37.

people, we would be fetched from the prison and taken to the concentration camp in the event that the judge would free us.[145]

The three brothers were put together with six other prisoners in a large cell. The rest of the prisoners were mainly homeless men already acquainted with the Bruderhof's social work. In the past, the Rhön Bruderhof had frequently provided them with food and temporary accommodation. Eventually, though, the brothers were put in single cells so as to keep them from influencing the other prisoners. During the day, they were allowed to stay together in the same room and read the Bible, which was the only book they had. While in prison a number of investigations took place, including a court hearing concerning hereditary farm rights.[146] But although the Rhön Bruderhof had struggled financially and rarely had enough money, neither the Gestapo nor the court could produce any evidence that they had cheated their creditors through mismanagement. In an attempt to explain the impoverishment of the Rhön Bruderhof, Meier told the judges to consider two important facts. First, the community had been subjected to severe restrictions by the National Socialists. Second, because of this persecution, the Bruderhof had needed to build and support two additional settlements in foreign countries, which had been financially a difficult task to fulfil.[147]

At the same time, reports of these events, published in Holland and Switzerland, strained not only the relationship between the German Mennonites on the one hand, and the Bruderhof on the other, but also German-Dutch Mennonite relationships. Reports of the Rhön Bruderhof's dissolution appeared in a secular Dutch daily, *Het Volk*, on 20 April 1937, as well as in a Swiss Catholic paper *Basler Nachrichten*, on 22 April. Both reports were basically correct, but mistakenly identified the Rhön Bruderhof as Mennonites. In order to refute these two newspaper accounts, the German Mennonites tried to clarify the inaccuracy by identifying as 'Hutterites' those banished from Germany. The German foreign office reacted immediately by demanding an official explanation of the matter from the side of the Federation of German Mennonite Churches. In order to distance themselves from the Bruderhof, the German Mennonites emphasised in this official explanation their dedication to the Fatherland, their willing sacrifice in World War I, their inclination to do military service, and the complete incorporation of Mennonite youth into Hitler's youth associations.[148] According to Meier,

> They went on to say that the Mennonites enjoyed the protection of the National Socialist State and would not refuse military service. Moreover, although

---

[145] Meier, 'The Dissolution', p. 35.
[146] 'Hans Meier Tells His Story', p. 10; see Meier, 'In the Prison', p. 37.
[147] Meier, 'The Dissolution', pp. 36-37.
[148] Brinkman, 'Between God and Fatherland', p. 239.

Mennonites for religious reasons refused the oath, they were ready to vow unconditional obedience to Adolf Hitler, the leader of the German Reich and people and supreme commander of the armed forces, and as courageous soldiers they were ready to lay down their lives for this vow at any time.[149]

Being in support of the Third Reich, the German Mennonites prevented any positive discussion about peace at the Mennonite World Conference, which took place in Amsterdam between 29 June and 3 July 1936. Therefore, a separate assembly was held on 4 July 1936 at the Friesian Mennonite Brotherhood House for participants who still emphasised their Anabaptist roots and specifically the peace tradition. At this assembly, two Bruderhof members were in attendance, Hans Zumpe and Emmy Arnold, and they met Harold Bender and Orie O. Miller who were both important leaders of the Mennonite Central Committee (MCC). It is important to note that Bender, who became one of the most influential Mennonites of his generation, had already visited the Rhön Bruderhof in 1930 and had been impressed with the communal life he saw there. Bender was also interested in receiving accurate reports about the conditions of the Bruderhof under the Third Reich, and put considerable effort into providing practical assistance for the community. Orie O. Miller, the Secretary of the MCC, was inspired by the Bruderhof's stand on peace. On behalf of the MCC, he promised to support the Bruderhof financially or in any other way needed.[150]

MCC interest in the Bruderhof continued in the later 1930s. John Horsch of Scottsdale, Pennsylvania, sent a letter to his brother Michael Horsh in Hellmannsberg, Germany, requesting that he visit the Rhön Bruderhof in order to assess the assistance the brotherhood needed, and Michael arrived at the Rhön Bruderhof in early 1937. He sent a report of his impressions of the situation to his brother. Stirred by his words, John Horsch sent him money to help the Bruderhof. However, this money was never handed over to the community's management because Michael arrived with it on the day after the Rhön Bruderhof's dissolution. He met Meier and several other brothers and sisters being watched over by policemen.[151] According to Meier (who was about to be imprisoned),

> He greeted those police by raising his hand and saying 'Heil Hitler'. This is a sign of the heavy atmosphere which at that time lay on all Germans, whether they were conscious of it or not. He returned the money which was meant for us back to North America. But the Gestapo must have put pressure on him too, for later with a Gestapo officer, he visited us in prison in order to convince us that we had

---

[149] Meier, 'The Dissolution', p. 35.
[150] Brinkman, 'Between God and Fatherland', pp. 195-196.
[151] Hinkey, 'Hans Meier Talking with Amos Hoover', p. 8.

set the capital value of the Rhön Bruderhof much too high and by so doing we had committed criminal doctoring of the accounts.[152]

Finally, after three months of imprisonment and investigation, Meier and the two other brothers that comprised the Executive Committee of the Rhön Bruderhof were released from prison on 26 June 1937. The court had failed to find any support for their sentence and incarceration. However, knowing that the Gestapo would refuse to allow their release, the three brothers decided to escape to England as quickly as possible. After a very eventful, dangerous and dramatic trip, they arrived at the Cotswold Bruderhof on 2 July 1937.[153]

At both the Cotswold and the Oaksey Bruderhofs, community life continued, with much inner and outer building up taking place, until 3 September 1939, when the British Prime Minister Neville Chamberlain declared war against Germany. When the first German air strikes on Britain began on 6 September 1939,[154] the Bruderhof was seen as a foreign element in England because it brought together German aliens along with English conscientious objectors.[155] Even some of the members of the Peace Pledge Union—a British organization that pledged renunciation of war—began to think that 'the evil German spirit could only be fought with guns and bombs'.[156] On the day that England entered World War II, a mob of about fifty furious men showed up at the Cotswold community, wanting to set the 'German Bruderhof' on fire, and were only prevented from doing this at the last moment by the local police.

Because of the increasing suspicion of the Bruderhof on the part of their neighbours, on account of the large number of Germans living there, those belonging to the community who were not British citizens were categorised as 'neutral aliens', and were not allowed to go beyond five miles from the Bruderhof.[157] As the war gathered strength and the situation further devolved, conservative neighbours around the Cotswold Bruderhof raised the question of whether the community was perhaps a Fifth Column conducting espionage on behalf of Germany. This charge was even brought up in the British

---

[152] Meier, 'The Dissolution', p. 36.

[153] Brinkman, 'Between God and Fatherland', pp. 248-251; see Hans Meier, 'Freedom!', in Heini Gut and Raymond Pittet (eds.), *As Long as there is Light: The Life of Hans Meier (1902-1992)* (Deer Spring Bruderhof, USA, 1991). An unpublished document in Bruderhof Archives, Woodcrest, Rifton, New York, pp. 40-41; see Chris Meier to Dejan Adam (Woodcrest, USA, 10 April 2006). Personal correspondence. In the possession of Dejan Adam.

[154] Robin W. Winks and R.J.Q. Adams, *Europe, 1890-1945: Crisis and Conflict* (New York: Oxford University Press, 2003), p. 222.

[155] Arnold A. Mason, 'Early Memories, 7: Tensions and War' (n.p., n.d.). Personal notes. An unpublished document in Bruderhof Archives, Woodcrest, Rifton, New York, pp. 1-4.

[156] Meier, 'Five Years', p. 43.

[157] Ibid.

Parliament.[158] However, according to Meier, certain Members of Parliament defended the Bruderhof, claiming that,

> they knew us and that we would never do such a thing, and that we should be left alone because we contributed a great deal to the production of food in this time. In the end, however, the government became more and more occupied with the prosecution of the war, and the danger arose that aliens would nevertheless be interned and separated from the English members of the Bruderhof.[159]

Therefore, some of the English citizens belonging to the Cotswold Bruderhof who had been in contact with the Home Office over the previous four years suggested that for the sake of peace the Bruderhof should leave England. In response to their request to leave as a group, the Home Office, on behalf of the government, guaranteed to issue the emigrating authorisation, including authorisation for the English brothers who were liable to be called up for military service.[160] Enquiries were made in various countries, and as the next step, Meier and another brother, Guy Johnson, who was an English national, were instructed by the community to try and find a place in the United States where the Bruderhof could move to.[161]

During this dangerous time in Germany and during the transition to England, Meier carried out a significant ministry within the Bruderhof community. He offered courageous leadership which enabled others to remain faithful to their calling. His wider witness was manifested through the numerous attempts he made to develop personal as well as institutional contacts and relationships, mainly with German officials. Meier's character remained unwavering throughout, and he was never open to any kind of influence from the side of the Third Reich or any other party acting which he saw as against the Kingdom God. It was for this Kingdom that he wanted to work. Meier remained engaged in seeking peace and social justice, while living in a world that was about to be thrown into a state of hopelessness and catastrophe. He did not see the lack of access to political power as a drawback; indeed he saw marginality in a positive way. Due to his faith in Christ, he considered human power to be irrelevant.[162] Those who were serious about discipleship formed a counter-cultural community.

---

[158] Mason, 'Early Memories, 7', pp. 8-11.

[159] Meier, 'Five Years', pp. 43-44.

[160] Mason, 'Early Memories, 7', pp. 8-11; see Mommsen, *Homage*, pp. 157-160.

[161] Klaus Meier to Dejan Adam (Beech Grove Bruderhof, UK, 11 April 2006). Personal correspondence. In the possession of Dejan Adam.

[162] I am indebted to Dr Wilbert R. Shenk for the notion of Anabaptist mission and marginality.

'We, Like They, Wanted to Live in Community'

In considering the establishment a new settlement outside of Europe, Meier first thought of finding an appropriate place somewhere in the area of the Hutterian Brethren colonies in South Dakota, Manitoba, or Alberta. For the purpose of visiting these areas to look into the possibilities, the American Consul in Bristol agreed to issue a three-month visitor's visa for Meier and Guy Johnson.[163] According to Meier,

> As a sign of sincerity he required an oath taken on the Bible. When we showed him the place in the New Testament which forbids swearing, he was rather at a loss, but after a phone call to the Embassy in London he was satisfied with a simple promise to tell the truth, although he warned us of the punishment for perjury.[164]

Meier and Johnson departed from Liverpool on 1 August 1940 and arrived in New York after sailing for twelve days. After travelling several more days, they reached the communities of the Hutterian Brethren in South Dakota who were willing to welcome the Bruderhof and to offer the necessary guarantees for their coming. To further explore how to accomplish this purpose they made many other contacts. One of their appointments was with the wife of the President of the United States, Eleanor Roosevelt. Meier and Johnson met with her in her apartment in New York City on 24 September 1940.[165] Following their meeting, Eleanor Roosevelt reported in her syndicated weekly newspaper column,

> I think my most unusual visitors were Mr Hans Meier and Mr Guy Johnson. They come from a group who believe in living, here and now, in real brotherhood. For the moment, while the Government of England understands their position, the people about them are making their community life somewhat difficult, for they have every nationality in the community in order to show that there really is a brotherhood of man... It is evident that they would be model citizens and their conception of democracy is certainly a pure and practical one. But even these two men with fine, calm faces, agreed that community living was not without its

---

[163] Hans Meier, 'Our Search for a new Home', in Heini Gut and Raymond Pittet (eds.), *As Long as there is Light: The Life of Hans Meier (1902-1992)* (Deer Spring Bruderhof, USA, 1991). An unpublished document in Bruderhof Archives, Woodcrest, Rifton, New York, p. 44.

[164] Ibid.

[165] Arnold A. Mason, 'Early Memories, 8: Seeking Refuge' (n.p., n.d.). Personal notes. An unpublished document in Bruderhof Archives, Woodcrest, Rifton, New York, pp. 10-12.

problems. I wonder if it will be easier in South Dakota than in England. I hope so, for they could not fail to be a good influence.[166]

Eleanor Roosevelt understood the Bruderhof to be a community of followers of Jesus with underlying shared communal practices. In particular, she expressed her appreciation that the community welcomed outsiders and was interested in Jesus' social agenda of non-violent action and its accompanying transformation of behaviour and action.

However, neither the willingness of Hutterian Brethren to vouch for them, nor the contacts with prominent people in the US government, were successful in obtaining permission for the Bruderhofs to emigrate from Britain to the United States. Though many of those they met with had a positive attitude toward the two brothers, the concept of accommodating a community of conscientious objectors who would also refuse to swear an oath to the American flag was not very palatable to the US authorities. Those in political positions responsible for issues of immigration decided to delay giving the Bruderhof immigration approval until after the expected presidential inauguration of Franklin D. Roosevelt on 20 January 1941.[167] Unfortunately for the Bruderhof, the need to move was pressing, and waiting until January was not an option.

Meanwhile, the communities in England were becoming increasingly endangered by the socio-political circumstances around them, and the need to move out of the country to somewhere else where they would be accepted was becoming urgent. South America seemed to offer the best possibilities, and Meier and Guy Johnson started to search for a Latin American country that would allow the Bruderhof to immigrate. In an effort to help them out, Orie Miller of the MCC sent a telegram to the Paraguayan Ambassador in Washington on 15 August 1940 enquiring whether immigration to Paraguay would be possible.[168] In response to Miller's request, according to Meier,

> This gentleman invited us to visit him and told us that by tomorrow he could have permission to immigrate by phoning his father in law, the President of Paraguay. The next day he phoned to tell us of the agreement of the President.[169]

---

[166] Eleanor Roosevelt, 'My Day' (New York City, 25 September 1940). The minutes of a meeting with Hans Meier and Guy Johnson. An unpublished document in Bruderhof Archives, Woodcrest, Rifton, New York.

[167] Meier, 'Our Search for a new Home', p. 45; see Douglas Bukowski, *American History: A Concise Documents Collection, Volume II* (Boston: Bedford, 1999), pp. 213-216.

[168] Chris Meier to Dejan Adam (Woodcrest, USA, 13 April 2006). Personal correspondence. In the possession of Dejan Adam.

[169] Hans Meier, 'To Paraguay', in Heini Gut and Raymond Pittet (eds.), *As Long as there is Light: The Life of Hans Meier (1902-1992)* (Deer Spring Bruderhof, USA,

Hans immediately notified the communities in England, and on 24 August 1940, they sent a telegram in response saying that the Brotherhood accepted God's leading to Paraguay.[170] Meier now needed to travel to Paraguay in order to arrange for the arrival of the first group from England to the Chaco region of Paraguay. Before travelling to South America however, Meier attended a meeting of the MCC in Chicago, held on 5 October 1940. At the meeting, the delegates expressed their support for the move of the Bruderhof to Fernheim in the Chaco region of Paraguay. They told Meier they hoped that the witness of the Bruderhof in this area would help neutralise the impact of certain Mennonite groups from Russia, who had previously emigrated to Fernheim. These groups had passed through Germany en route to Paraguay, and had been influenced by National Socialistic ideas and sympathized with the Nazis—a stance the American MCC adamantly opposed.

While in the USA, Meier heard from some of those that sympathised with the Bruderhof that they could not understand the Bruderhof's decision to emigrate to Paraguay at the very moment when England needed the presence of such an intentional community witnessing to love, peace and justice more than ever before. In response, Meier argued that going to Paraguay did not mean the cutting off of the community from the practical witness of active peace at the international level. Instead, he saw the move to Paraguay as a new possibility to witness to the people in this different part of the world that there is a way of active, constructive peace in the love of Christ.[171]

A few days after the meeting with the MCC, Meier boarded a passenger boat from New York to Rio de Janeiro, where he started to learn Spanish, the official language of Paraguay. Back in England, the communities began rapid preparations to move to Paraguay, and indeed the first group was already travelling from England to Paraguay as Meier began his trip down from the United States. The image of the Exodus of the Israelites in the Old Testament kept occurring to Meier as he preceded the Bruderhof on the crossing over the Atlantic Ocean. Unlike Moses, Meier would enter into the 'promised land' before his people—a promised land that was to give sanctuary, but also years of struggle and turmoil for the Bruderhof. Arriving in the Paraguayan capital of Asuncion, Meier realised that unfortunately there was no government with which to consult about the Bruderhof's plans for resettlement. The President of Paraguay had died a few days before in an aeroplane accident, and his

---

1991). An unpublished document in Bruderhof Archives, Woodcrest, Rifton, New York, p. 45.

[170] Chris Meier to Dejan Adam (Woodcrest, USA, 13 April 2006).

[171] Guy Johnson and Hans Meier, Hans, 'A Report about the Arrival in Paraguay' (n.p., March 1941). Personal notes. An unpublished document in Bruderhof Archives, Woodcrest, Rifton, New York.

successors were locked in a power struggle, and did not have time to deal with everyday matters of state.[172]

In such circumstances, Meier could do nothing else but wait for the first group of his fellow brothers and sisters from England, who eventually arrived in Buenos Aires on 21 December 1940. Among the passengers in this first group were his wife Margrit and their four small sons and two daughters, whom he had not seen for five months. Travelling three more days, the group eventually arrived in Asuncion on Christmas day 1940. The group started to look for an appropriate location right away for developing a new Bruderhof community.[173] According to Meier,

> We deliberately did not only turn to the company, which owned the land, but also to the so-called wild Indians, from whom the land had once been stolen. They were very helpful because we, like they, wanted to live in community. After riding for several hours on small horses...we arrived at a large camp, or tract of land, which the chief indicated was a place for us to settle. As the formal sales price for the area, which contained several hundred hectares, he asked for only one dollar. Instead of a signature on a document, he asked for only a handshake, which was of more value to him than a written statement. We accompanied the chief to the dwelling place of his tribe, consisting of a tree, the lowest branches of which were covered to keep the rain off. All the members sat on the ground in a circle around the tree. They handed in the spoils of hunt or something they had earned to the oldest woman, who gave everyone what she felt he needed.[174]

Two images again came to Meier's mind as they searched for a place in this foreign country to build up a community. The desire to establish an embassy of the Kingdom of God in this remote place was supported by Meier's realization that these so-called 'primitive' Indians already lived in 'primitive' community and had a highly developed sense of the common table where everybody was invited to join and eat. The last thing Meier had expected to find in Paraguay before arriving there was a 'Hutterite'-style community of 'servants and enablers',[175] lacking only Christ in their midst. But here were simple people already living a strong form of community. These two governing images were crucial in assuring Meier that his decision to advise the Bruderhof to settle the

---

[172] Meier, 'To Paraguay', pp. 46-47; see Chris Meier to Dejan Adam (Woodcrest, USA, 13 April 2006).

[173] 'Hans Meier tells his Story', pp. 20-21; see Klaus Meier to Dejan Adam (Beech Grove Bruderhof, UK, 20 April 2006). Personal correspondence. In the possession of Dejan Adam; see Mommsen, *Homage*, pp. 161-170.

[174] Hans Meier, 'Life in the Chaco', in Heini Gut and Raymond Pittet (eds.), *As Long as there is Light: The Life of Hans Meier (1902-1992)* (Deer Spring Bruderhof, USA, 1991). An unpublished document in Bruderhof Archives, Woodcrest, Rifton, New York, p. 50.

[175] Keith G. Jones, 'Rethinking Baptist Ecclesiology', *Journal of European Baptist Studies* 1:1 (January 2000), p. 15.

communities in Paraguay had been right. He also had no doubt that the Paraguayans needed the Gospel as much as people in Europe. Shortly afterward, Meier would be appointed as a servant of the Word[176] by the community—a big responsibility involving him in pastoral work for the first time in his life.

After two months passed—two months since the first group from England was settled in the Chaco—the community became increasingly aware that they could hardly expect guests to come to the Bruderhof in this distant and isolated area. For that reason, Meier, along with Hardy Arnold and Fritz Kleiner, set out to find a location nearer to Asuncion to develop a new community. On 27 January 1941, assisted by Mennonites who lived in the capital, they found a big ranch named Primavera, which fitted their purposes. They purchased the land on 11 February 1941. Arriving in Asuncion four days later, six brothers from the Cotswold Bruderhof went directly to Primavera and began building up the first community named Isla Margarita. Once the initial work was done, in April 1941, the entire community moved from the Chaco and began to live in Isla Margarita. There, children and adults were attacked by different tropical diseases, and seven infants died before the end of the first year there.[177] Meanwhile, there were unexpected developments in England. When the last group left England for Paraguay on 23 April 1941, two brothers and one sister stayed behind to finalize the financial obligations of the Bruderhof and complete the sale of the communities' property. After finishing these matters, they planned to join the others in Paraguay. Due to the bombardment of London however, the sale of the property took more time than was expected, and in the meantime a number of new guests visited and decided to join the Bruderhof. Since these new English members could not obtain permission to leave the country, they had to stay in England. This led to the decision by the Bruderhof in January of 1942 to purchase new property in Shropshire near Ludlow, and start the new Wheathill Bruderhof.[178] Wheathill was to remain there as a community until 1961.

Eventually two more communities named Loma Hoby and Ibate were built up on the Primavera property in Paraguay to accommodate the total Bruderhof population. As an electrical engineer, Meier worked hard to set up an electrical grid for the communities in Paraguay. With Primavera located far from 'civilisation', one can only imagine how difficult it must have been to accomplish this task. It was impossible to purchase normal, standardised,

---

[176] The author could not find the date when this happened.

[177] Chris Meier to Dejan Adam (Woodcrest, USA, 20 April 2006). Personal correspondence. In the possession of Dejan Adam.

[178] Hans Meier, 'Outer and inner Dangers threaten the Community', in Heini Gut and Raymond Pittet (eds.), *As Long as there is Light: The Life of Hans Meier (1902-1992)* (Deer Spring Bruderhof, USA, 1991). An unpublished document in Bruderhof Archives, Woodcrest, Rifton, New York, p. 55.

electrical wires. So Meier used regular fence wire, the only kind of wire available, and installed direct current (DC), which was safer but not as good as alternating current (AC). Meier also purchased a steam tractor and fitted it out to run a dynamo in order to produce electricity. Later the tractor was replaced by an old steam engine repaired (again) by Meier. Meier's goal was to install a wood gas power plant, brought over from England. Helped by many brothers at Primavera he worked hard to get the electrical grid properly established.[179]

Meier was also responsible to keep up correspondence with the MCC and in particular its secretary Orie O. Miller who was a good friend of the Bruderhof.[180] In October of 1940, Meier proposed sending him Bruderhof-related written materials for distribution to different Mennonite publications selected by Miller. Meier hoped to accomplish three goals through this. First, he hoped to update like–minded people living in both Europe and North America about the Bruderhof's experiences in Paraguay. Second, he wished to justify in a public forum, based on the ministry of presence, that coming to Paraguay was God's will for the community. Third, he wished to advertise the Bruderhof in the hope of generating donations for the community, which had very little money.[181] Thus, in the initial stage of the Paraguayan chapter of the history of the Bruderhof, Meier showed himself to be practically inventive and also a responsible servant of the Word who approached his ministry holistically.

Loma Hoby (February 1942-September 1960) was built up with the intention of establishing a hospital, as there were no adequate existing healthcare facilities to service the surrounding area. Helped by donations received from abroad, the hospital was started in a single wing of one house, 'where consultation, treatment, preparation of medicines and laboratory analysis'[182] were done routinely. Explaining his involvement in the work of the hospital during the initial phase, Meier wrote: 'Because I had received a certain medical training in Switzerland, I often had to help with operations by giving the anaesthesia, checking the patient's pulse, and at the same time keeping the flies and midges away from the sores and wounds of the patients.'[183] In Meier's

---

[179] Klaus Meier to Dejan Adam (Beech Grove Bruderhof, UK, 16 March 2006); see Mason, 'Early Memories, 8', p. 71.

[180] Orie Miller to Hans Meier (Washington, D.C., 20 September 1940). Personal correspondence. An unpublished document in Bruderhof Archives, Woodcrest, Rifton, New York.

[181] Hans Meier to Orie Miller (Oaksey Bruderhof, UK, 1 October 1940). Personal correspondence. An unpublished document in Bruderhof Archives, Woodcrest, Rifton, New York.

[182] 'Primavera Hospital (1954)', http://web.archive.org/web/20040624025423/www.bruderhofmuseum.com/bm/PermanentExhibits/080_BruderhofParaguay/hospital.htm?name=hospital, accessed 15 April 2006.

[183] Hans Meier, 'The Founding of Primavera', in Heini Gut and Raymond Pittet (eds.), *As Long as there is Light: The Life of Hans Meier (1902-1992)* (Deer Spring Bruderhof,

work in the hospital, I would argue that the image of *Nachfolge Christi* was crucial. For him this image seems to have been about 'integrity, witness, presence and transformation',[184] in line with Matthew 28:18-20. Meier saw the work in the hospital as a mission field, opening up space for demonstrating the way of Christ to those needing help in the midst of the Paraguayan tropics.[185] The Paraguayan population as a whole was suffering greatly following the 1932-1935 war with Bolivia. This war resulted in the deaths of nearly one million men during the conflict.[186] A later conflict, the Paraguayan civil war of 1947, further affected the life of the Bruderhof. In February 1949, Meier, accompanied by two other brothers, met Paraguayan General Britez who was director of mobilization and recruitment in Asuncion. On that occasion the Bruderhof's exemption from military service which had been promised when they immigrated to Paraguay was confirmed.[187]

Meier bore in mind the imperative of public responsibility as envisioned by the Kingdom of God. This public responsibility was most clearly expressed through the absence of prejudice toward the native Paraguayans. Though most of people who visited the hospital never became Christians, they realised that Meier and the Bruderhof represented a different Christianity—a faith in action that called for forgiveness and reconciliation. Recognising everyone as having equal worth was for the Paraguayans and especially for the Indians, a sign of Meier and the Bruderhof's embrace.[188] This approach was particularly welcome because it was the opposite of the terrible memories of the past when to accept or refuse (Roman Catholic) Christianity meant to chose between life and death.[189]

From the very first days in Paraguay to when the last community there closed twenty years later, both outer and inner difficulties challenged the Bruderhof's unity and communal witness. The 1950s in particular brought a

---

USA, 1991). An unpublished document in Bruderhof Archives, Woodcrest, Rifton, New York, p. 53.

[184] Parush R. Parushev, 'Presence and Witness: Facing the Challenges to Christian Mission Today', *Journal of European Baptist Studies* 4:2 (January 2004), p. 30.

[185] Meier, 'The Founding of Primavera', pp. 53-55.

[186] Herring, Hubert, *A History of Latin America* (New York: Alfred A. Knopf, 1957), pp. 676-679; see Mason, 'Early Memories, 8', p. 52.

[187] 'Report of a Meeting of Hans Meier, Fran Hall, and John Hinde (Bruderhof) with General Britez, Director of Mobilization and Recruitment in Asuncion' (Asuncion, Paraguay, 12 February 1959). The minutes of a meeting regarding military service for Primavera's youth. An unpublished document in Bruderhof Archives, Woodcrest, Rifton, New York.

[188] Regarding the summary of the public responsibility of God's servants see John H. Yoder, *For the Nations* (Grand Rapids, Mich.: Eerdmans, 1997), p. 33; for more see Ibid., pp. 15-37.

[189] Samuel Shapiro, *Integration of Man and Society in Latin America* (London: University of Notre Dame Press, 1987), pp. 27-37.

wind of negative changes. Though the Bruderhof suffered greatly from the demanding living circumstances and subtropical infections, the deeper threat for the community came from internal factors. The Bruderhof suffered one internal upheaval after another caused by a growing difference of viewpoints about the leadership at Primavera. Many of the conflicts revolved around fights for power and domination, and a move from a life based on Jesus toward a strict, legalistically based community.[190] In Meier's view, most of the adult membership was responsible for creating these problems in the Primavera Bruderhofs. Although the communal crises in Primavera were caused by an inclination toward human domination and the associated fear of opponents, the main problem was the absence of the Spirit of God and a focus on human community instead of Christ. Meier later wrote regarding this time:

> The rulership of men would not have been possible on the Bruderhof if all would have fought unanimously and wholeheartedly for the victory of the Spirit of love of Jesus. Because this did not take place, things went downhill, and basically the community became more and more disunited.[191]

The 1950s were characterised for Meier by a shift from reaching out to those outside the community towards focusing on the membership of the Bruderhof. He saw their situation as one of sailing on a damaged boat, which was about to sink yet still had hope for survival. As one of the 'servants of the Word', he was responsible for different communal gatherings such as baptismal meetings, weddings, festivals, and Bible studies. During this period, Meier turned to self-examination while inviting other brothers and sisters to do the same. All were challenged to centre on the Beatitudes from the Sermon on the Mount and (again) on Rideman's *Confession of Faith*. Evidence in reports from that time show how Meier, among others, felt that the Bruderhof needed to return to their roots in early Christian practice as well as that of the early Anabaptists. In the Beatitudes, Meier read of the paradoxes of true religious experience, such as the treasures in God and poverty in oneself; the justice of God's love and the suffering under men's injustice; unity with God and at the same time an unquenchable thirst for him. All Meier could see in himself and in the community around however were people satisfied with their religion and self-justified by their 'virtues'. Above all, Meier found himself in this situation: unqualified along with his brothers and sisters to pray for the coming of the Kingdom in the right way Meier reached the point where he felt he had to face

---

[190] Emmy Arnold, *A Joyful Pilgrimage: My Life in Community* (Farmington, Penn.: Plough Publishing, 2002), pp. 257-258.

[191] Hans Meier, 'Inner Crisis', in Heini Gut and Raymond Pittet (eds.), *As Long as there is Light: The Life of Hans Meier (1902-1992)* (Deer Spring Bruderhof, USA, 1991). An unpublished document in Bruderhof Archives, Woodcrest, Rifton, New York, p. 57.

the darkness and disunity within himself and within the community while trying to find why his governing images had disappeared and how they had lost their power.[192] He realised that he no longer worked for 'the embassy' he had dedicated his life to. About his attitude at that time, Meier wrote,

> After a longer visit in 1954 of five carpenters [brothers] from the old Hutterian Bruderhofs in Manitoba and North Dakota to help us build up Woodcrest, the desire arose to work more closely with us new Hutterites. This came especially from the Forest River Colony in North Dakota, most of whose members felt like this. During the ensuing spiritual fight I behaved very arrogantly, feeling that we 'modern' thinking people were closer to the truth than the 'old fashioned' Hutterites.[193]

The year of 1959 begins a period that is difficult to describe - a period when human failure seemed to dominate everything. The Bruderhof's expression of community had been accompanied by harsh physical conditions and poverty. However, this had not automatically guaranteed absolute trust in God in everything. More than ever before in its history, the Bruderhof came to rely on human strength and the love of Jesus was largely lost. Yet Meier, along with many of the other brothers and sisters, still held to the memory of the 1930s when the entire Bruderhof was engaged in *Nachfolge Christi*. In this spirit, he tried to rediscover repentance and the vision that he and all the members had experienced when they were first called to join the community. Unfortunately, these efforts came to nothing.

---

[192] 'Notes on Baptismal Meetings' (Isla Margarita, Paraguay, 29 November to 6 December 1954). The minutes of meetings presided over by Hans Meier. An unpublished document in Bruderhof Archives, Woodcrest, Rifton, New York; see 'The Beatitudes' (Isla Margarita, Paraguay, 15 September 1954). The minutes of a meeting presided over by Hans Meier. An unpublished document in Bruderhof Archives, Woodcrest, Rifton, New York; see 'Harvest Festival and acceptance of Stan and Hela Ehrlich into the Noviciate' (Isla Margarita, Paraguay, 27 June 1954). The minutes of a meeting presided over by Hans Meier. An unpublished document in Bruderhof Archives, Woodcrest, Rifton, New York; see 'Weddings' (Isla Margarita, Paraguay, 11 May 1958). The minutes of weddings presided over by Hans Meier. An unpublished document in Bruderhof Archives, Woodcrest, Rifton, New York.

[193] Meier, 'Outer and inner Dangers', pp. 56-57. When this conflict happened Meier was residing at the Woodcrest Bruderhof in the US for a short period of time. Two decades later, on 7 January 1974, on behalf of the Bruderhof, Heinrich Arnold, together with several other brothers, reconciled the fellowship with the Hutterian brethren by apologising for their previous offences and arrogance. Evaluating the relationship between the Bruderhof and the Hutterian brethren from the USA and Canada has been out of the scope of this dissertation due to the complexity of the task. However, their attempts to work together ultimately failed in the summer of 1995; see Klaus Meier to Dejan Adam (Beech Grove Bruderhof, UK, 18 April 2006). Personal correspondence. In the possession of Dejan Adam.

In 1961, Meier was on a trip to the two communities in the USA, where the struggles were equally intense. He travelled back to Paraguay, and as the internal struggles there intensified, feelings and sins from the past became revealed. The breakdown was so overwhelming that at one point the whole brotherhood declared themselves bankrupt and dissolved because of the inner divisions and the failure to see things for what they where. A new brotherhood was formed when several couples were asked to start from scratch and begin to build the brotherhood up again. These were trusted to help find clarity. Each committed member of the Bruderhof was given the choice of either following Jesus willingly, giving love and service to God and the other members of the brotherhood, or of taking some time to be clear about what they wanted with their lives. As we will see, Meier himself left the brotherhood. According to Meier's oldest son Klaus,

> My father had also become unclear, or rather was very clear but on the wrong issues, and was asked to think things over, which was best done on one's own. Many talks took place before this between my dad and other brothers and sisters to seek unity, but it was not reached. He was absent from the community for twelve years, while his wife and ten of their children remained faithful—not because they where so good, but because they where ready to give up everything for the love of Jesus.[194]

The general conclusion drawn from the many individual reflections on the history of the Bruderhof's twenty years in Paraguay is that the eventual crisis was caused by a gradually increasing communal over-zealousness, which eventually led to the absence of God's Spirit.[195] For Meier, the time in Paraguay was one in which he experienced two extreme stages in his spiritual life. From the first beginning in South America, with its joyful enthusiasm and sense of the leading of the Spirit, he had come by the end of the twenty years there to a stage of both personal and communal spiritual darkness. From experiencing happiness and fulfilment in the 1940s while creating 'a new heaven' in Paraguay, he came to a point of profound dissatisfaction with himself at the beginning of the 1960s when everything seemed to be separated from the message of Jesus.

'The Forgiveness of the Church'

In 1961, Meier had to completely reconsider his convictions, and he left the Bruderhof to do so. He was confused, yet unwilling to seek the cause for his

---

[194] Klaus Meier to Dejan Adam (Beech Grove Bruderhof, UK, 19 July 2006). Personal correspondence. In the possession of Dejan Adam.

[195] Meier, 'Outer and Inner Dangers', pp. 57-58.

confusion in himself. Rather, he blamed other people for what had gone wrong. At the time he left, most of the community certainly was involved in what had gone wrong. It was a time of uncertainty and change for the entire Bruderhof movement. Meier went to Argentina, where he found employment with an electrical company. He soon earned enough money to buy a piece of land and build a house. Meier stayed true to his calling to a communal way of life, and his intent in buying the house was to have a place where he could invite people to live in community with him, especially others who had left the Bruderhof. However, the community Meier planned to begin was to be based on the socialist ideas of justice, which had dominated his convictions before he came to faith in Christ. In the end however, no one was interested in joining him. Meier resided in Argentina for twelve years while Margrit and the rest of his family moved to the Evergreen[196] community, which had been started in the USA in 1958. Though Meier's family passed through the same personal difficulties as he did, they saw that they needed to change. Only one of his sons gave up the Bruderhof at this time and rejected his baptismal promise to follow Christ. The rest of the family decided, each one of them personally, to try once more to find 'the first love' which had been lost in Paraguay and to find a new unity under God and in the Church.[197]

Throughout this difficult time, Meier's wife Margrit and his sons and daughters were not against him. They only disagreed with the attitudes he held and the outworking of these attitudes. Meier's family as well as others living in the Woodcrest Bruderhof in the USA wrote numerous letters to him, seeking to find unity, forgiveness and peace. Eventually, Heinrich Arnold suggested that the Woodcrest Bruderhof should invite Meier to come and visit and should pay for his air ticket if necessary. Although the Woodcrest community was very poor at that time and could ill-afford the ticket, the desire for unity was more valuable than any amount of money. The main reason that his family and friends wanted to invite Meier to come up to the USA was so that he could see in person the changes that the Bruderhof had gone through since the days in Paraguay, and especially how the community had re-found its basis in Christ. They were aware that at Woodcrest many things had to be seen, which letters could not explain or communicate. Eventually, the Woodcrest community sent several brothers to talk to Meier. Although there were no direct results from this visit, shortly afterward Meier replied to another invitation to visit the Woodcrest by writing: 'I will come but only if you will also pay for the return ticket,'[198] as he wanted to keep all his options open. The Woodcrest community

---

[196] Bruderhof in Norfolk, Connecticut. Begun in 1958, later renamed Deer Spring; see Mow, 'Torches Rekindled', p. 149.

[197] Klaus Meier to Dejan Adam (Beech Grove Bruderhof, UK, 2 May 2006). Personal correspondence. In the possession of Dejan Adam.

[198] Klaus Meier to Dejan Adam (Beech Grove Bruderhof, UK, 2 May 2006). Personal correspondence. In the possession of Dejan Adam.

agreed to accept his conditions, and Meier arrived to visit his family and old friends in 1972 for the first time in over ten years. A number of meetings with the whole community took place in order to find a path to reconciliation. Reconciliation did not happen quickly because Meier continued to condemn other people for the problems of the past while refusing to admit any failure on his own part. Meier seemed to be far from the agape love that he had tried to live before leaving the Bruderhof.[199]

However, among those taking part in the meetings was Hans Herman Arnold, a son of Eberhard and Emmy Arnold and a brother to Heinrich. According to Klaus Meier,

> He [Hans Herman] was dying of lung cancer and was in the last stages of the sickness with a bottle of oxygen tied to the wheel chair he sat in. There came a point when he rolled his wheelchair right across the centre of the gathered brotherhood. He rolled himself up to my father and knocked on his heart saying: 'It is here Hans Meier where things get clear—NOT with the head.' We all sat quiet and then went home. It struck my dad in his heart and a few days later as we sat together again, he could only speak of his guilt, humbling himself and asking for forgiveness. In that meeting were all the members young and old seeking to follow Jesus. In a short time everything was cleared up, my dad received the forgiveness of the church and returned to the Bruderhof.[200]

So after twelve years of absence, Meier renewed his promise to keep fellowship with the members of the community and never to forsake the way of brotherly life at the Bruderhof again. He realised that he had become self-centred and judged other people while hiding behind false excuses for his own shortcomings.[201]

From that moment on Meier once again was led by the spiritual vision that had virtually disappeared from his life for so many years. The early images, the foremost among them being the image of *Nachfolge Christi,* would dominate the struggle for the Kingdom of Heaven until the end of his life. Once again a member of the community, Meier came to realise how this twelve year crisis was actually a wonderful gift. All the hidden things that had separated him from his family and from the community came to the surface and helped him to decide what he truly wanted to live for. According to Meier: 'By taking seriously Jesus' warning to remove the beam out of one's own eye before judging others, the community was able to come together again. I, unfortunately, needed twelve years for that, whereas my family was much sooner ready.'[202]

---

[199] Ibid.; see Mommsen, *Homage*, pp. 297-313.
[200] Klaus Meier to Dejan Adam (Beech Grove Bruderhof, UK, 2 May 2006).
[201] Klaus Meier to Dejan Adam (Beech Grove Bruderhof, UK, 2 May 2006).
[202] Meier, 'Inner Crisis', p. 58.

After coming back to the Bruderhof, the following twenty years until his death in 1992 were some of the most productive of his life. Meier poured his energy into reaching out to others seeking a new society without war and violence by testifying repeatedly that 'truth without love kills and that love without truth lies'.[203] In that spirit, Meier sought co-operation with other individuals as well as religious communities not as a confrontational dispute but as an open-hearted exchange of ideas.[204] Furthermore, as he was struggling to understand the role of the church in society, Meier was aware of the most striking difference between Paul's perception of the church as without spots and wrinkles in reference to Ephesians 5:27 and humans' inclination to a church 'with many spots and wrinkles'.[205] Therefore, alerted by his own life experience he was not so deluded as to consider those believing in God as without shortcomings.

Meier believed that the most important witness of the church in the contemporary world should be a spiritual unity of those believing in and following after Christ, which also supposed pragmatic evaluation of economical matters related to life in community. He wrote:

> Community of goods leads organically to community of work and then to community of the whole life, as a living organism. It must be emphasised that complete community is a fruit of the unifying love of God-agape and not the other way around, as ideological materialism supposes... Disunity is not only an absence of unity, but is a spiritual power, hostile to God, which tears people apart... How can we pray for and seriously expect social transformation unless we experience at least a beginning of it in ourselves and between us? Is it not so that that has to be our inmost and most earnest prayer in order that the prophetic word of the church can be believed?[206]

---

[203] Hans Meier to Hans Haselbarth (Deer Spring, USA, 2 May 1986). Personal correspondence. In the possession of Bruderhof Archives, Woodcrest, Rifton, New York.

[204] Hans Meier to Helmut Gollwitzer (Deer Spring, USA, 24 May 1988). Personal correspondence. In the possession of Bruderhof Archives, Woodcrest, Rifton, New York; see Hans Meier, 'Comments on the above Article by Helmut Gollwitzer' (Deer Spring, USA, May 1988). Personal notes. An unpublished document in Bruderhof Archives, Woodcrest, Rifton, New York; see Hans Meier, 'A Second Letter to the Participants in the Third Consultation in Prague, to be held in 1989 by Representatives of the Movements known as First Radical Reformation' (n.p.,1 December 1988). Personal correspondence. In the possession of Bruderhof Archives, Woodcrest, Rifton, New York.

[205] Meier to Haselbarth.

[206] Hans Meier, 'For the Consultation in Prague 1987 on Eschatology and Social Transformation' (n.p., n.d.). Personal notes. An unpublished document in Bruderhof Archives, Woodcrest, Rifton, New York.

Therefore, Meier viewed social transformation as qualitative conversion taking place in people's relationships with each other. This type of conversion, as Meier believed, also meant living a life of justice inspired by Jesus' narrative of the anticipated kingdom of God.

Christian unity, as viewed by Meier, was a challenging and sensitive issue standing between him and his Jewish friends from the Kibbutz movement in Israel. According to Meier,

> They [Jews] say that Jesus was a good Jew who fulfilled the law and as a prophet he shared a prophet's fate. But they cannot believe that he was the Messiah. He, the Messiah, will come with shalom. The example of Christians shows that shalom is not among them, even if they said it is… The outer form should only be an expression of what is already there; it can never bring about unity as if by magic. Should we not first of all seek the unity Christ offers, the unity which will bring back the salt to our witness? Our words, our decisions, will only be believed when a life stands behind it that demonstrates this possessionlessness, this lack of ownership of anything, be it material goods, intellectual accomplishments or anything else. Such a life can be built up and filled with the brotherly love of the spirit of Christ.[207]

In other words, Meier testified to the Kibbutz movement in Israel that communities such as the Bruderhof could give a strong witness to the fact that it is possible here and now to live Shalom while following the example of Jesus. Apart from that, Meier had a sober view of the political situation in the world, and he realised that both words and deeds were needed for real change to occur. He was thankful for every communal expression of a life of peace and justice—even those that were not based on Jesus. This is why he sought cooperation with other communities including the Kibbutz settlements. His intention was to build a clearer witness through such cooperation, a witness that would be strong enough to support many more people in finding a solution for the present disunity in the world. He believed that disunity was the cause of the madness that threatened the survival of mankind. Thus, it was clear for Meier that all the talk and study about communities only had value if the journeys of individuals and the communities to which they belonged lead to God's Shalom.[208]

---

[207] Hans Meier, 'Thoughts on the 1987 Prague Consultation' (n.p., n.d.). Personal notes. An unpublished document in Bruderhof Archives, Woodcrest, Rifton, New York.

[208] Hans Meier, 'Two Letters to the Kibbutz Movement in Israel' (Deer Spring, USA, November 1985). Personal notes. An unpublished document in Bruderhof Archives, Woodcrest, Rifton, New York; see Yaacov Oved, 'Distant Brothers: A History of Relations between the Bruderhof and the Kibbutz Movements' (n.p., n.d.). Personal notes. An unpublished document in Bruderhof Archives, Woodcrest, Rifton, New York; see Hans Meier, 'Life in Community Today' (Shaker Village, Canterbury, New Hampshire, 9 October 1986). A Speech at the thirteenth annual NHCSA Historical

During these years, Meier read John Howard Yoder's book *The Politics of Jesus* several times, as well as talking a lot about it. This book generally challenged Meier's convictions while he was seeking to talk to other like-minded individuals and communities. On the one hand he was positively influenced by Yoder's arguments as exposed in this book. On the other hand, Meier doubted the authenticity of Yoder's thoughts finding them difficult to accept because of his professorship at the Catholic University of Notre Dame. According to Meier, it was peculiar to find a Mennonite theologian teaching at a Catholic University.[209] Accompanied by his son Andreas, on 22 September 1985 Meier travelled to Goshen, Indiana where they met Yoder. Meier described their meeting in a following way:

> Then we had a talk with John Howard Yoder the day before yesterday. He asked for the talk, and we sat together with him for an hour, and it was very nice. But we didn't touch on any of the difficult points of earlier times. It was interesting that he understood Ragaz and the Religious Socialists. I reported to him that Ragaz himself wrote in his autobiography that he was on the verge of living in community, in the poverty of Christ, but two things hindered him. The first thing was his family. His wife warned him: Will you be able to go through with it, the whole hog? In fact he was fearful that he would not be able to do it and he was also fearful to take his family into this poverty. That was the first reason. The second reason was that he was a theologian, that this hindered him from going the whole way. We told this to John Howard Yoder (who is also a theologian!), and he became pensive and looked a bit sad.[210]

Meier's understanding of Christian unity can be critically evaluated through the dynamics of his encounter with Yoder. This encounter brings into discussion at least two arguments which help in characterizing Meier as an idealist, especially in the area of social justice. Firstly, Meier found it difficult to understand how Yoder, as a Mennonite, could teach at the Catholic University of Notre Dame without questioning how the basis of his faith would and should affect his scholarship at such a prestigious institution. In other words, it seems that Meier found it almost impossible to accept that people belonging to radical Reformation movements, who shared with him pacifistic convictions, might at the same time work with those who held other convictions and ideals mandated by their faith.[211] Secondly, neither the Mennonites in general nor Yoder in particular considered sharing property communally to be a

---

Communal Societies Conference. An unpublished document in Bruderhof Archives, Woodcrest, Rifton, New York.

[209] Klaus Meier to Dejan Adam (Beech Grove Bruderhof, UK, 16 May 2006).

[210] Emmy Barth to Chris Meier (Woodcrest, USA, 18 May 2006). Personal correspondence. In the possession of Bruderhof Archives, Woodcrest, Rifton, New York.

[211] Meier, 'Thoughts on the 1987 Prague Consultation'.

crucial component of following Christ. Contrary to this, both Meier and the Bruderhof saw communal property as an integral part of discipleship, and as a key tenet of the radical Anabaptist witness.[212] In other words, Meier's argument with Yoder revolved around pointing out that Christ's way alone is the only way of achieving Christian unity in community or anywhere esle, and that only through trying to completely follow Christ comes absolute consistency of faith and action. At that point, it seems that Meier had not yet come to a moderate or balanced attitude. It seems that Meier, at least at the beginning, was too much exposed to strict community rules and influenced by relationships that had gone wrong. Furthermore, the practice of the Bruderhof for reaching decisions unanimously impacted Meier deeply, to the extent that he failed to realize that his ideas, or rather his ideals, might not be applicable in other Christian communities. Even though Meier would strongly disagree with discussion of 'his' way, as his whole life was spent trying to follow Christ's way, he failed to realize that the way he had chosen was not the ultimate and unquestionable one in terms of achieving Christian unity.

Meier actively worked until the last moments of his eventful life. The day he died, an article he had been working on entitled *Why We Live in Full Community*[213] in which he summarized years of practical experience in communal living was found in his typewriter. In it he presented an account of the images and convictions that had influenced his life. After working over fifty years in the embassy of the Kingdom, Meier was finally called home to enjoy the citizenship of Heaven. According to his son Andreas Meier:

[My father]...passed out of this world into eternity in the most wonderful way I can imagine. On Christmas Eve, the 24th of December, we (300 men women and children at the Deerspring community) were led as every year by an 'angel' to the manger scene at the cow shed with Mary and Joseph, the crib with a baby, some shepherds, the three kings and some angels, and we all stood there in the cold quietly remembering that night 2000 years ago when Jesus was born. So as not to get too cold, my father at 90 years of age, had put on a poncho and shepherd's hat, and was sitting inside the open barn door on a bale of hay, leaning on the walking stick which he always had with him. After about an hour the community filed past the manger and each received a candle from the angels to carry home for Christmas Eve. Before that happened, my Father asked a brother, Fred, to drive him home so as to get out of the cold. He was leaning on his stick in the vehicle, and pulling up to the front of the house Fred said, 'Hans, wait till I get around to help you out.' On opening the passenger door he saw my father still leaning on his stick, slumped over, and found that he had gone out of this life. He had gone Home on Christmas night directly from the stable, dressed as a shepherd. We could not help but be very thankful for such a going Home, with no pain or fear, and no forewarning. We then buried him just like that with his

---

[212] Klaus Meier to Dejan Adam (Beech Grove Bruderhof, UK, 16 May 2006).
[213] Meier, *'Why we Live in Full Community'*, pp. 1-3 (my pagination).

clothes, shoes and walking stick to signify his constant longing to bring the message of God's kingdom to all people in this world.[214]

Conclusion

Hans Meier was a citizen of the world who joined other like-minded people in seeking to promote and live out the values of the Kingdom of Heaven. Actually, instead of saying that he joined like-minded people, it is more appropriate to say he walked with *companions*. Meier noted that *pan* is the Latin word for *bread*—thus he had joined with a group of people who practised *Nachfolge Christi* and with whom he broke bread regularly while gathering around the common table. Meier and the community he lived in worked for God's embassy while believing and hoping that one day, on this earth, the Kingdom would come to all women and men working for God's justice and galvanized by his love for all creation. Meier's strength was that he stayed open to examining and changing his own convictions, even though this was often difficult. Thus he was led from imperfect human justice to the perfect justice of Christ. His self-acknowledged weakness was a permanent battle between the head and logic on one side, and heart and faith on the other. Though there were periods when head and logic controlled his life, in the end faith and love won through.[215]

Meier's story also contributes to understanding how certain biblical and theological images can have a profound impact on a person's religious experience, and can contribute to the building of a counter-cultural community. Several governing images, notably the embassy of the Kingdom of God, the common table, the Exodus, and above all the *Nachfolge Christi* had a great impact on Meier's life. They influenced Meier in a way that gave heart and soul to the vision by which he lived. While speaking of Meier's primary theology as built upon images, however, it must be emphasized that for him God was the real, living God. In other words, if Meier had approached God merely as an image, symbol, or allegory, then 'his' Christ would have been powerless.

---

[214] Andreas Meier to Dejan Adam (Woodcrest, USA, 1 May 2006).
[215] Andreas Meier to Dejan Adam (Woodcrest, USA, 19 April 2006). Personal correspondence. In the possession of Dejan Adam.

Bibliography

Bruderhof Archives, Woodcrest Community, Rifton, New York

Arnold, Eberhard to Ragaz, Leonhard (n.p., 11 March 1933). Personal correspondence.
Arnold, Eberhard, 'A Talk given to Leonhard Ragaz and Members of the Werkhof' (Zurich, Switzerland, 11 March 1935). Minutes of a meeting presided over by Eberhard Arnold.
Barth, Emmy to Meier, Chris (Woodcrest, USA, 18 May 2006). Personal correspondence.
'The Beatitudes' (Isla Margarita, Paraguay, 15 September 1954). Minutes of a meeting presided over by Hans Meier.
Brinkman, Hugo, 'Between God and Fatherland', Personal notes (n.p., n.d.).
Gut, Heini and Pittet Raymond, 'Introduction', in Heini Gut and Raymond Pittet (eds.), *As Long as there is Light: The Life of Hans Meier (1902-1992)* (Deer Spring Bruderhof, USA, 1991).
'Hans Meier Tells his Life Story' (Deer Spring, USA, 9 March to 26 March 1990). Minutes of a meeting presided over by Hans Meier.
'Hans Meier Tells his Story to a Friend' (Deer Spring, USA, December 1978). Minutes of a meeting presided over by Hans Meier.
'Hans Meier talking with Amos Hoover and other Menonnites' (n.p., 15 October 1990). Personal notes.
'Harvest Festival and Acceptance of Stan and Hela Ehrlich into the Novitiate' (Isla Margarita, Paraguay, 27 June 1954). Minutes of a meeting presided over by Hans Meier.
Johnson, Guy and Meier, Hans, 'A Report about the Arrival in Paraguay' (n.p., March 1941). Personal notes.
Mason, Arnold A., 'Early Memories, 7: Tensions and War' (n.p., n.d.). Personal notes.
_____, 'Early Memories, 8: Seeking Refuge' (n.p., n.d.). Personal notes.
Meier, Hans, 'A Bicycle Trip with Consequences', in Heini Gut and Raymond Pittet (eds.), *As Long as there is Light: The Life of Hans Meier (1902-1992)* (Deer Spring Bruderhof, USA, 1991).
_____, 'A Report on the Journey to Switzerland and Czechoslovakia in November, 1933' (n.p., n.d.). Personal notes.
_____, 'Article Written for Johannes Halkenhauser' (Deer Spring, USA, March, 1982). Personal notes.
_____, 'Community as seen by Eberhard Arnold and as seen by Leonhard Ragaz', in Heini Gut and Raymond Pittet (eds.), *As Long as there is Light: The Life of Hans Meier (1902-1992)* (unpub. doc., Deer Spring Bruderhof, USA, 1991).
_____, 'Confrontation with the State', in Heini Gut and Raymond Pittet (eds.), *As Long as there is Light: The Life of Hans Meier (1902-1992)* (unpub. doc., Deer Spring Bruderhof, USA, 1991).

_____, 'Difficulties on the Werkhof', in Heini Gut and Raymond Pittet (eds.), *As Long as there is Light: The Life of Hans Meier (1902-1992)* (unpub. doc., Deer Spring Bruderhof, USA, 1991).

_____, 'Early Inquiries into the Meaning of Social Justice and of Life', in Heini Gut and Raymond Pittet (eds.), *As Long as there is Light: The Life of Hans Meier (1902-1992)* (unpub. doc., Deer Spring Bruderhof, USA, 1991).

_____, 'Face to Face with National Socialism', in Heini Gut and Raymond Pittet (eds.), *As Long as there is Light: The Life of Hans Meier (1902-1992)* (unpub. doc., Deer Spring Bruderhof, USA, 1991).

_____, 'For the Consultation in Prague 1987 on Eschatology and Social Transformation' (n.p., n.d.). Personal notes.

_____, 'A Second Letter to the Participants in the Third Consultation in Prague, to be held in 1989 by Representatives of the Movements known as First Radical Reformation' (n.p., 1 December 1988).

_____, 'Five Years in the Cotswold', in Heini Gut and Raymond Pittet (eds.), *As Long as there is Light: The Life of Hans Meier (1902-1992)* (unpub. doc., Deer Spring Bruderhof, USA, 1991).

_____, 'Freedom!', in Heini Gut and Raymond Pittet (eds.), *As Long as there is Light: The Life of Hans Meier (1902-1992)* (unpub. doc., Deer Spring Bruderhof, USA, 1991).

_____, 'In Quest of a Communal Life of Peace and Justice', in Heini Gut and Raymond Pittet (eds.), *As Long as there is Light: The Life of Hans Meier (1902-1992)* (unpub. doc., Deer Spring Bruderhof, USA, 1991).

_____, 'In the Prison at Fulda', in Heini Gut and Raymond Pittet (eds.), *As Long as there is Light: The Life of Hans Meier (1902-1992)* (unpub. doc., Deer Spring Bruderhof, USA, 1991).

_____, 'Inner Crisis', in Heini Gut and Raymond Pittet (eds.), *As Long as there is Light: The Life of Hans Meier (1902-1992)* (unpub. doc., Deer Spring Bruderhof, USA, 1991).

_____, 'Life in Community Today' (Shaker Village, Canterbury, New Hampshire, 9 October 1986). A Speech at the Thirteenth Annual NHCSA Historical Communal Societies Conference.

_____, 'Life in the Chaco', in Heini Gut and Raymond Pittet (eds.), *As Long as there is Light: The Life of Hans Meier (1902-1992)* (unpub. doc., Deer Spring Bruderhof, USA, 1991).

_____, 'Our Next Goal: England', in Heini Gut and Raymond Pittet (eds.), *As Long as there is Light: The Life of Hans Meier (1902-1992)* (unpub. doc., Deer Spring Bruderhof, USA, 1991).

_____, 'Our Search for a new Home', in Heini Gut and Raymond Pittet (eds.), *As Long as there is Light: The Life of Hans Meier (1902-1992)* (unpub. doc., Deer Spring Bruderhof, USA, 1991).

_____, 'Outer and inner Dangers threaten the Community', in Heini Gut and Raymond Pittet (eds.), *As Long as there is Light: The Life of Hans Meier (1902-1992)* (unpub. doc., Deer Spring Bruderhof, USA, 1991).

_____, 'The Alm Bruderhof', in Heini Gut and Raymond Pittet (eds.), *As Long as there is Light: The Life of Hans Meier (1902-1992)* (unpub. doc., Deer Spring Bruderhof, USA, 1991).

———, 'The Bruderhof', in Heini Gut and Raymond Pittet (eds.), *As Long as there is Light: The Life of Hans Meier (1902-1992)* (unpub. doc., Deer Spring Bruderhof, USA, 1991).
———, 'The Dissolution of the Rhön Bruderhof', in Heini Gut and Raymond Pittet (eds.), *As Long as there is Light: The Life of Hans Meier (1902-1992)* (unpub. doc., Deer Spring Bruderhof, USA, 1991).
———, 'The Fight for the Kingdom goes on', in Heini Gut and Raymond Pittet (eds.), *As Long as there is Light: The Life of Hans Meier (1902-1992)* (unpub. doc., Deer Spring Bruderhof, USA, 1991).
———, 'The Founding of Primavera', in Heini Gut and Raymond Pittet (eds.), *As Long as there is Light: The Life of Hans Meier (1902-1992)* (unpub. doc., Deer Spring Bruderhof, USA, 1991).
———, 'The Hutterian Communities', in Heini Gut and Raymond Pittet (eds.), *As Long as there is Light: The Life of Hans Meier (1902-1992)* (unpub. doc., Deer Spring Bruderhof, USA, 1991).
———, 'The Rhön Bruderhof', in Heini Gut and Raymond Pittet (eds.), *As Long as there is Light: The Life of Hans Meier (1902-1992)* (unpub. doc., Deer Spring Bruderhof, USA, 1991).
———, 'The Werkhof', in Heini Gut and Raymond Pittet (eds.), *As Long as there is Light: The Life of Hans Meier (1902-1992)* (unpub. doc., Deer Spring Bruderhof, USA, 1991).
———, 'To Paraguay', in Heini Gut and Raymond Pittet (eds.), *As Long as there is Light: The Life of Hans Meier (1902-1992)* (unpub. doc., Deer Spring Bruderhof, USA, 1991).
———, 'Two Letters to the Kibbutz Movement in Israel' (unpub. doc., Deer Spring, USA, November 1985). Personal notes.
———, 'Why we live in Full Community' (Deer Spring, USA, 24 December 1992). Personal notes.
———, 'Comments on the above Article by Helmut Gollwitzer' (Deer Spring, USA, May 1988). Personal notes.
———, 'Thoughts on the 1987 Prague Consultation' (n.p., n.d.). Personal notes.
Meier, Hans to Hans Haselbarth (Deer Spring, USA, 2 May 1986). Personal correspondence.
Meier, Hans to Helmut Gollwitzer (Deer Spring, USA, 24 May 1988). Personal correspondence.
Meier, Hans to Orie Miller (Oaksey Bruderhof, UK, 1 October 1940). Personal correspondence.
Miller, Orie to Hans Meier (Washington, D.C. USA, 20 September 1940). Personal correspondence.
Mow, Merrill, 'Torches Rekindled: The Bruderhof's Struggle for Renewal' (Pasadena, USA, July 2005). Personal notes.
'Notes on Baptismal Meetings' (Isla Margarita, Paraguay, 29 November to 6 December 1954). Minutes of meetings presided over by Hans Meier.
Oved, Yaacov, 'Distant Brothers: A History of Relations between the Bruderhof and the Kibbutz Movements' (n.p., n.d.). Personal notes.
Ragaz, Leonhard to Eberhard Arnold (n.p., 28 October 1922). Personal correspondence.

'Report of a Meeting of Hans Meier, Fran Hall and John Hinde (Bruderhof) with General Britez, Director of Mobilization and Recruitment in Asuncion' (Asuncion, Paraguay, 12 February 1959). Minutes of a meeting regarding military service for Primavera's youth.
Roosevelt, Eleanor, 'My Day' (New York, 25 September 1940). Copy of newspaper column in Bruderhof Archives, Woodcrest, Rifton, New York.
'Weddings' (Isla Margarita, Paraguay, 11 May 1958). Minutes of weddings presided over by Hans Meier.

Personal Correspondence (In the possession of Dejan Adam)

Meier, Andreas to Dejan Adam (Woodcrest, USA, 16 March 2006).
_____ to Dejan Adam (Woodcrest, USA, 19 April 2006).
_____ to Dejan Adam (Woodcrest, USA, 1 May 2006).
Meier, Chris to Dejan Adam (Woodcrest, USA, 3 April 2006).
_____ to Dejan Adam (Woodcrest, USA, 4 April 2006).
_____ to Dejan Adam (Woodcrest, USA, 10 April 2006).
_____ to Dejan Adam (Woodcrest, USA, 13 April 2006).
_____ to Dejan Adam (Woodcrest, USA, 20 April 2006).
_____ to Dejan Adam (Woodcrest, USA, 17 March 2006).
_____ to Dejan Adam (Woodcrest, USA, 29 March 2006).
Meier, Klaus to Dejan Adam (Beech Grove Bruderhof, UK, 3 April 2006).
_____ to Dejan Adam (Beech Grove Bruderhof, UK, 5 April 2006).
_____ to Dejan Adam (Beech Grove Bruderhof, UK, 11 April 2006).
_____ to Dejan Adam (Beech Grove Bruderhof, UK, 18 April 2006).
_____ to Dejan Adam (Beech Grove Bruderhof, UK, 20 April 2006).
_____ to Dejan Adam (Beech Grove Bruderhof, UK, 7 March 2006).
_____ to Dejan Adam (Beech Grove Bruderhof, UK, 7 March 2006).
_____ to Dejan Adam (Beech Grove Bruderhof, UK, 9 March 2006).
_____ to Dejan Adam (Beech Grove Bruderhof, UK, 6 March 2006).
_____ to Dejan Adam (Beech Grove Bruderhof, UK, 17 March 2006).
_____ to Dejan Adam (Beech Grove Bruderhof, UK, 17 March 2006).
_____ to Dejan Adam (Beech Grove Bruderhof, UK, 20 March 2006).
_____ to Dejan Adam (Beech Grove Bruderhof, UK, 28 March 2006).
_____ to Dejan Adam (Beech Grove Bruderhof, UK, 2 May 2006).
_____ to Dejan Adam (Beech Grove Bruderhof, UK, 16 May 2006).
_____ to Dejan Adam (Beech Grove Bruderhof, UK, 22 May 2006).
_____ to Dejan Adam (Beech Grove Bruderhof, UK, 19 July 2006).
Mommsen, Peter to Dejan Adam (Sinntal-Sannerz, Germany, 21 November 2005).

Books and Articles

Arnold, Eberhard, (ed.), *The Early Christians in Their Own Words* (Farmington, Penn.: Plough Publishing House, 2003).
Arnold, Eberhard, *God's Revolution: Justice, Community, and the Coming Kingdom* (Farmington, Penn.: Plough Publishing House, 2004).

_____, *Innerland: A Guide into the Heart of the Gospel* (Farmington, Penn.: Plough Publishing House, 2003).
_____, *Salt and Light: Living the Sermon on the Mount* (Farmington, Penn.: Plough Publishing House, 2004).
_____, *Why We Live in Community* (Farmington, Penn.: Plough Publishing House, 2002).
Arnold, Emmy, *A Joyful Pilgrimage: My Life in Community* (Farmington, Penn.: Plough Publishing House, 2002).
_____, *Torches Together: The Beginning and Early Years of the Bruderhof Communities* (Farmington, Penn.: Plough Publishing House, 1971).
Barth, Karl, *The Word of God and the Word of Man* (Boston, Chicago, USA: The Pilgrim Press, 1928).
Baum, Markus, *Against the Wind: Eberhard Arnold and the Bruderhof* (Farmington, Penn.: Plough Publishing House, 1998).
Beld, Van Den Antonie, *Humanity: The Political and Social Philosophy of Thomas G. Masaryk* (The Hague: Mouton, 1975).
Bock, Paul (ed.), *Signs of the Kingdom: A Ragaz Reader* (Grand Rapids, Mich.: W.B. Eerdmans, 1984).
Bukowski, Douglas, *American History: A Concise Documents Collection, Volume II* (Boston: Bedford, 1999).
Craig, Gordon A., *Germany, 1866-1945* (Oxford: Oxford University Press, 1981).
Heimann, Franz, 'The Hutterite Doctrines of Church and Common Life: A Study of Peter Riedemann's Confession of Faith of 1540', *The Mennonite Quarterly Review* XXVI (January 1952), pp. 22-47.
_____, 'The Hutterite Doctrines of Church and Common Life: A Study of Peter Riedemann's Confession of Faith of 1540, II', *The Mennonite Quarterly Review* XXVI (April 1952), pp. 142-160.
Herring, Hubert, *A History of Latin America* (New York: Alfred A. Knopf, 1957).
Jones, Keith G., 'Rethinking Baptist Ecclesiology', *Journal of European Baptist Studies* 1:1 (January 2000), pp. 4-18.
_____, 'Towards a Model of Mission for Gathering, Intentional, Convictional Koinonia', *Journal of European Baptist Studies* 4:2 (Jan. 2004), pp. 5-13.
Kerr, Fergus, *Theology after Wittgenstein* (London: SPCK, 1997).
McClendon, James Wm., Jr., *Biography as Theology* (Nashvile: Abingdon Press, 1974).
_____, *Ethics: Systematic Theology, Volume I* (Nashvile: Abingdon Press, 2002).
Mommsen, Peter, *Homage to a Broken Man* (Rifton, New York: Plough Publishing House, 2004).
Murray, Stuart, *Biblical Interpretation in the Anabaptist Tradition* (Kitchener, Ontario: Pandora Press, 2000).
Neuman, Lawrence W., *Social Research Methods: Qualitative and Quantitative Approaches* (Boston: Allyn and Bacon, 2000).
NIV Study Bible (Grand Rapids, Michigan: Zondervan, 2002).

Parushev, Parush R., 'Presence and Witness: Facing the Challenges to Christian Mission Today', *Journal of European Baptist Studies* 4:2 (January 2004), pp. 25-33.
Rideman, Peter, *Account of Our Religion, Doctrine and Faith* (Rifton, New York: Plough Publishing House, 1970).
Samartha, Stanley, 'The Lordship of Christ and Religious Pluralism' in Gerald H. Anderson and Thomas F. Stransky (eds.), *Christ's Lordship and Religious Pluralism* (Maryknoll, New York: Orbis Books, 1981).
Scriven, Charles, *The Transformation of Culture: Christian Social Ethics after H. Richard Niebuhr* (Scottdale, Pennsylvania: Herald Press, 1988).
Shapiro, Samuel, *Integration of Man and Society in Latin America* (Notre Dame, Indiana: University of Notre Dame Press, 1987).
Snyder, Arnold C., *Anabaptist History and Theology: An Introduction* (Kitchener, Ontario: Pandora Press, 2002).
_____, *Following in the Footsteps of Christ* (London: Darton, Longman and Todd, 2004).
_____, 'The Influence of the Schleitheim Articles on the Anabaptist Movement: An Historical Evaluation', *The Mennonite Quarterly Review* LXIII (October 1989), pp. 323-345.
_____, *The Life and Thought of Michael Sattler* (Scottdale, Pennsylvania: Herald Press, 1984).
The Hutterian Brethren (eds.), *The Chronicle of the Hutterian Brethren* (Rifton, New York: Plough Publishing House, 1987).
Walzer, Michael, *Thick and Thin: Moral Argument at Home and Abroad* (Notre Dame, Indiana: University of Notre Dame Press, 1994).
Welch, Claude, *Protestant Thought in the Nineteenth Century Vol. 2, 1870-1914* (New Haven, Connecticut: Yale University Press, 1985).
Winks W. Robin and Adams, R.J.Q., *Europe, 1890-1945: Crisis and Conflict* (Oxford: Oxford University Press, 2003).
Yoder, John H., *For the Nations* (Grand Rapids, Michigan: Eerdmans, 1997).
_____, *The Legacy of Michael Sattler* (Scottdale, Pennsylvania: Herald Press, 1973).
_____, *The Politics of Jesus* (Carlisle, UK: The Paternoster Press, 2003).
Yoder, John, H. (ed.), *The Schleitheim Confession* (Scottdale, Pennsylvania: Herald Press, 1977).
Zeman, Jerold Knox, *The Anabaptists and the Czech Brethren in Moravia 1526-1628: A Study of Origins and Contacts* (The Hague: Mouton, 1969).

Internet Sources

'Primavera Hospital (1954)'. Http://web.archive.org/web/20040624025423/ www.bruderhofmuseum.com/bm/PermanentExhibits/080_BruderhofParagua y/hospital.htm?name=hospital. Accessed 15 April 2006.
'Theological Declaration of Barmen'. Http://www.creeds.net/reformed/barmen. htm. Accessed 20 April 2006.

Krieger, Doug, 'Hitler's Positive Christianity... Unleashing the Patriotic Church'. Http://www.buzzle.com/ editorials/6-30-2005-72402.asp. Accessed 22 April 2006.

General Index

Aaltio, Teuvo, dissertation by, 117
ABCFM (American Board of Commissioners for Foreign Missions), 176
ABMU (American Baptist Missionary Union), support of Bulgarian Baptists, 180
About Religious Societies, 73
'About the Reinforcement of Antireligious Propaganda', 73
Abuse of power, church discipline and, 45
Adams, T.F., 227
Ahonen, Eino O., on the Holy Spirit, 136–137
Ahonen, Lauri, 136
Ahvenanmaa, Baptist beginnings in, 115
Alcohol, Bulgarian Baptists on use of, 207–208
Aleshkovsky, Y., *Soviet Easter Song*, 26
All-Romanian Union of the Baptist World Alliance, 67
All-Union Central Soviet of the Trade Unions, Circular Letter 53, 73
All Union Council of Evangelical Christian Baptists (AUCECB), 1
  CARC and, 75–76
  Committee for Unification, 100
  conflict with Initsiativniki, 9–15
  declining in authority of, 8
  forced approval of, 13
  in Moldavia, 84–91
    ECB churches forced to join, 67
    opposition to, 89–91
  rejects 'revolutionary struggle', 12
All-Union Councils, ECB (Russian Evangelical Christians-Baptists) held, 43
Alliance of Christian Evangelicals in Inkeri, 134
Alm Bruderhof
  English visitors join, 312
  Martin Niemöller refuses to work with, 310–311
  members take refuge in England, 312
  replaces Röhn Bruderhof, 310
  see also named Bruderhofs
American Baptist Foreign Mission Society, C.E. Petrick and, 181
American Baptist Missionary Union (ABMU). *See* ABMU (American Baptist Missionary Union)
American Baptist Relief, sends CARE packages to Finland, 155
American Board of Commissioners for Foreign Missions (ABCFM). *See* ABCFM (American Baord of Commissioners for Foreign Missions)
Ammunet, Antti, 124
Among Sectarians, 21
Andropov, Yuri, 52
Anti-religious campaigns, character of, 7–8
Anti-Religious Faculty of Moscow University of Marxism-Leninism, 20
Anti-Religious Sector of the Institute of Philosophy, 20
Antikainen, Juho, baptism of the Spirit of, 124
Apostates, 24–26
Armenian Congregationalists, Stefan Kurdov influenced by, 177
Arnold, Eberhard, 286
  on Bruderhof as church, 298–299
  death of, 299, 301
  emphasis on *Nachfolge Christi*, 297
  first Bruderhof settlement and, 285
  influence of on Hans Meier, 300
  letters of protest to the Third Reich, 303–304
  visits Hans Meier in jail, 294
Arnold, Emmy, 316
  on Bruderhof struggles, 301
  first Bruderhof settlement and, 285
Arnold, Hans Herman, Hans Meier and, 330
Arnold, Hardy
  looks for location near Asuncion, 323

witness of in England, 312
Arnold, Heinrich, 329
Ashton Fields Farm, ALM Brudernhof
  move to, 312
Association for the Promotion of
  Education among the Slavic
  Christians in Bosnia-Herzegovina,
  230–231
Astakhov, Frol
  appointed senior presbyter, 87–88
  on baptising young people, 103
  on discontinuing free will offerings
    for the poor and orphans, 73
  on Moldavian non-compliance to
    AUCECB rules, 90–91
  report on number of Baptist
    churches, 80
Atheistic books, use of by Christians,
  48
Atheistic stereotypes, creating, 20–24
AUCECB (All Union Council of
  Evangelical Christian Baptists), 1
  CARC and, 75–76
  Committee for Unification, 100
  conflict with Initsiativniki, 9–15
  declining in authority of, 8
  forced approval of, 13
  in Moldavia, 84–91
  Moldavian opposition to, 89–91
  rejects 'revolutionary struggle', 12
Austro-Hungarian Empire, Bosnia-
  Herzegovina under, 233–243
Authoritarian leadership, effects of in
  Moldavia, 96
Avvakum, 28–31

Balkan war, beginnings of, 240
Baluban, Josip, 244
Baptism
  Bulgarian Baptists understanding
    of, 193–194
  as a theological-esslesiological
    centre, 102–104
Baptism of the Holy Spirit, as a
  divisive issue in Finland, 123, 126
Baptismal services, 101–104
  strengthened unity through, 101
Baptist and Humanism, 21
*The Baptist Church in Bosnia-
  Herzegovina*. *See* BC of B&H

Baptist churches
  legislation and propaganda against,
    19–20
  see also specific names of countries
Baptist, Doctrine—Practice—History,
  117
*The Baptist Heritage: Four Centuries
  of Baptist Witness*, 227
'Baptist Origins and Early
  Development in Moldavia', 66
Baptist Seminary in Belgrade
  closed, 264
  moves to Novi Sad, 265
  reopened, 265
Baptist Theological School (BTS) in
  Novi Sad, 265
Baptist Union
  crisis in, 8–9
  Finnish. *See* Finnish Baptist Union
Baptist Union of KSCS
  annual youth conferences, 250
  founded, 247
  recognized by the Kingdom SCS,
    248
Baptist Union of Regional
  Associations of the Kingdom SCS.
  See Baptist Union of KSCS
Baptist Union of Serbia, encouraged to
  take Serbia as a mission field, 274
Baptist Union of the Kingdom of
  Yugoslavia, on educating Christian
  leaders, 250
Baptist Union of Yugoslavia (BUY)
  changed methods of, 262–263
  organized, 260
Baptist World Alliance (BWA)
  BC of B&H joins, 276
  begins mission work in Europe,
    244–245
  conferences reported on in the
    Evangelist, 188
  financial aid sent to Finland, 155
Baptistit, Oppi—Käytäntö—Historia,
  117
Baptists
  apostates, 24–26
  in an atheistic context, 41–49
    testimonies of witnesses, 41–42
  demands for emigration by, 41
  extremism among, 31–36

General Index   345

in Finland, 120–127
   relations with Free Evangelicals, 122
   Finnish. *See* Finnish Baptist
as a household church, 45–46
imprisoned, 36
lack of education of, 23, 27–28
local church life, 44–45
loss of local church autonomy, 105–106
mixed attitude of Communist Party toward, 47
Moscow protest demonstration by, 31–32
as shown in propaganda, 20–24
trials of, 36–39
see also specific countries for more on Baptists
Baptists Around the World: A Comprehensive Handbook, 227
'Baptists in Bulgaria', 174
Barba, Avram, missionary to Romanians, 188
Barnaul, protest at, 33
Barratt, Thomas Ball, visit to Finland, 123
Barth, Emmy, 287
Barth, Karl, importance of *Tambach* speech, 297–298
Basic Law on the Legal Position of Religious Communities, 271
Basler Nachrichten, reports the dissolution of Röhn Bruderhof, 315
Baturin, N., fasting as protest by, 32
Baumann, Angela, executed by Communists, 260
Bayer, Otto, work at Sarajevo Baptist church, 267–268
BBC, religious broadcasts, 46
BC of B&H, founded, 276
Bechtler, Georg, supported by the GBRA, 253
Beeson, Trevor, 66
   concern expressed by, 75
   on Moldavian Baptists activities, 86
Bekennende Kirche, 310
Belousov, Mikhail, 85
Bender, Harold, attended meeting at Friesian Mennonite Brotherhood House, 316

Beograd church, Baptist seminary begun in, 250
Beregszaszi, Adalbert, 244
   supported by the GBRA, 253
Berleth, Jakob, 254
Berleth, Michael, 253
Bessarabia. *See* Moldavian
Bessarabian Baptists, evangelism at baptismal services, 104
   see also Moldavian Baptists
BFBS (British and Foreign Bible Society)
   Bosnia-Herzegovina Baptists and, 229
   in Bulgaria, 176–177, 180
   closes Sarajevo Depot, 239
Bible
   Bulgarian Baptists view of, 189–190
   Bulgarian Orthodox Church view of, 188–189
   memorization of, 42
Bible courses, part-time, 44
Bible Institute of the Baptist Church in Bosnia-Herzegovina, founded, 277
Bible School
   consequences of lack of in Finland, 144
   founded by the Finnish Baptist Union, 156–157
Biography as Theology, 286
Birthday, legal right to celebrate, 46
Blatt, Peter, 255
Boije, Constantine, 120–121
Boisset, J., on Baptist growth in Yugoslavia, 261
Boller, Else, Werkhof and, 293
Boller, Hans
   visits Werkof with reconciling message, 295
   Werkhof and, 293
'Bolshevik paradise', twelve commandments of, 6
Bon Homme Hutterite community, 314
Books, atheistic, use of by Christians, 48
Bosnia-Herzegovina, 265–266
   becomes under the rule of Serbian King Petar, 243
   during Communist era, 258–273

mission and evangelism, 262–264
mission work during, 266
political, religious, economic circumstances, 270–273
Sarakevp Baptist Church, 267–270
Sunday school and youth ministry, 264
theological education, 264–266
demographic makeup of under Austro-Hungarian rule, 241–242
division of into Ibanovinas, 256
illiteracy in, 241
lack of infrastructure in, 240–241
revolts in, 240
Bosnia-Herzegovina Baptists
1863-1918 circumstances for, 239–243
beginnings of, 228
legalized, 257
political, religious, economic, social circumstances of, 256–258
revitalisation of Baptist mission in, 243–256
South-Eastern European German Mission Committee, 251–256
Southern Baptist Convention, 245–251
Sarakevp Baptist church during Communist era, 267–270
under Austro-Hungarian rule, 233–239
under Turkish occupation, 228–233
Bratsky Vestnik, 91
doctrinal elements emphasized in, 105
on Lenin's 100th birthday, 9
on Russian takeover of Moldavia, 69
Brausch, Jakob, baptised by Henrich Meyer, 238
Brezhnev, Leonid
description of, 35
religious policies of, 31, 49
on the socialization of Moldavia, 72
British and Foreign Bible Society (BFBS). *See* BFBS (British and Foreign Bible Society)

British Baptists, financial aid sent to Finland, 155
Brkic, Milan, 244
Brodsky, Josef, 37
Bruderhof Children's House, Hans Meier and, 290
Bruderhof settlement
as church, 298–299
considers moving to Hutterian colony, 319
emigration to the U.S. denied, 320
founding of first, 285
Paraguay, 320–328
political and social activities, 285
see also named Bruderhofs
BTS. *See* Baptist Theological School (BTS) in Novi Sad
Bulgaria
church records confiscated/destroyed in, 173–174
Evangelist
birth of, 183–186
on church fund raising, 200
first issue of, 184–185
published in Bulgaria, 173, 180
search for spiritual roots through, 186–188
on successful pastoral ministry, 200
Trifon Dimitrov editor of, 181
Zaprian Vidolov first editor of, 181
German Baptist refugees in, 176, 178–179
lack of church records in, 173
religious freedom in the constitution, 211
Bulgarian Baptist Brochure Society, publishes materials for soldiers, 184
Bulgarian Baptist Mission in Chicago, founded by Zaprian Vidolov, 181
Bulgarian Baptist Union. *See* Bulgarian Evangelical Baptist Union
Peter Dochev and, 181
'truth is immortal' chosen as motto of, 187
Bulgarian Baptists
adult Sunday schools and, 201
alcoholism and, 207–208
beginnings of, 179

Bulgarian Orthodox Church and, 208–210
discipline among, 200
influence of German Christians on, 198, 214
membership requirements, 199
mission in Chicago, founded by Zaprian Vidolov, 181
organization of the church, 199
Pentecostal movement and, 195–196
relations with others, 205–211
social ministries encouraged, 207
theological foundations in, 176–183
theological identify of, 188–198
theology in the making, 211–216
tithing and, 199–200
on tobacco use, 208
view of
   the church, 198–202
   'Holy Tradition', 189
   mission and evangelism, 202–205
   a faithful Baptist Church, 198–199
   the State, 210–211
   women, 200–201
Bulgarian Evangelical Baptist Union, 180
   founded, 205
Bulgarian Missionary Committee, establishment of, 206
Bulgarian Orthodox Church
   Bulgarian Baptists and, 208–210
   opposition to evangelicals work, 182–183
   view 'Holy Tradition', 188
   view of women and ministry, 201
Bushilo, Boris, refuses to leave Romania, 70–71
BUY (Baptist Union of Yugoslavia). *See* Baptist Union of Yugoslavia (BUY)
Buziny, Y., 48
BWA (Baptist World Alliance)
   BC of B&H joins, 276
   begins mission work in Europe, 244–245
   conferences reported on in the *Evangelist*, 188
   financial aid sent to Finland, 155
Bychkov, A., 43

Caesar's kingdom, vs. God's kingdom, 49–52
Caldararu, Lidia, 70
CARC (Council for the Affairs of Religious Cults)
   formation of, 74
   Moldavian Baptist churches and, 64
   resolutions on religious societies liquidation, 77
   use of archives at, 65
CARE packages, received in Finland, 155
Carol II, cedes Moldavia to Russia, 68
CCECB (Council of Churches of the Evangelical Christians—Baptists), 1
   theological innovations of, 51–52
Čeh, Josip, 269
Černy, Josip, 251
   led the Sarajevo Baptist group, 249, 255
   at Sarajevo Baptist church after WW II, 267
   sold building to Sarajevo Baptist church, 267
Černy, Maria, sold building to Sarajevo Baptist church, 267
Chakalov, Vasil, 211
Chamberlain, Neveille, declares war on Germany, 317
Chekhov, A.P., *Malefactor*, 37–38
Chernenko, Konstantin Ustinovich, 52
Children, Christian education of, 46
Children's hour, in Bulgarian Baptist churches, 201
Chislita-Prut, Baptist church in, 72
Chomonev, Vasil
   on baptism, 194
   on evangelism, 202–203
   Evangelist and, 184–185
Christian education, children and, 46
The Christian in Church, State, and Society, conference held in Tamach, 297
The Christian in Society, 297
Christian Youth Societies, Bulgarian Baptists, 201

Christians of the Evangelical Faith. *See* Pentecostals
Christmas Morning, special issue of *Totuuden Kaiku,* 151
Church
  Bulgarian Baptists understanding of, 198–202
  closures in Moldavia, 74–84
  Constantinian relationship with the State, 49–50
  restrictions on workers, 69
  see also specific name or location of church
Clark, James F., Bulgarian ministry of, 181–182
Cliff College, Vasli Kiyosev educated at, 180
Committee for Unification, formed by AUCECB, 100
Common table, Hans Meier's view of, 291–292
Communism, as a goal, 4–8
Communist Party
  mixed attitude of toward Baptists, 47
  religious policies of
    Communism as a goal, 4–8
    historical background, 2–4
  Yugoslavian, thrown out of the Cominform and the USSR, 262
The Confession of Barmen, 311
Confession of Faith, of the ECB, 43
The Confessional Synod of the German Evangelical Church, 310
Confessions of Faith, 326
Congregationalists
  in Bulgaria, 176, 177
  view of women and ministry, 201
Congress of Berlin, 233
Constantinian church/state relationship, 49–50
Continuation War, in Finland, 118
Cotswold Bruderhof ALM Bruderhof move to, 312
  emigration to the U.S. denied, 320
  growth of, 312–313
  under suspicion in England, 317–318
  see also named Bruderhofs

Council for Religious Affairs
  copies of letters required to be sent to, 11
  Episcopalian system spread by, 8
  part-time Bible courses and, 44
Council for Religious Affairs for Religious Cults, approved 'Instructions According to the Application of Legislation of Cults', 74
Council for the Affairs of Religious Cults (CARC). *See* CARC (Council for the Affairs of Religious Cults)
Council of Churches of the Evangelical Christians—Baptists (CCECB). See CCECB (Council of Churches of the Evangelical Christians—Baptists)
  formation of in Moldavia, 96–97
Council of Free Evangelical Christians, formed by AUCECB, 127
Council of Ministers of the Moldavian SSR
  followed Moscow passed religious laws, 74
  registration and closure of churches by, 74–84
Council of Ministers of the Republics, resolutions on religious societies liquidation, 77
Council of Ministries of Moldavian Republic, church registration and, 77
Craighead, Walter, on Moldavian Baptists, 83
Credo, quia absurdum, Baptists and, 48

Dadder, Dobrinka, 174
The Danger of Stagnation, article promoting Pentecostalism as growth tool, 153
Danish Baptist Mission, supports missionaries to Bulgarian Muslims, 204
Danzig, Neu, 178
Daruvar Baptist church, 249
Davny, Vasily, on Russian takeover of Moldavia, 68
A Day in the Life of Ivan Denisovich, 24

'Day of the Prisoner', Novosibirsk community and, 33
Dayton Peace Accord, 272
Den Fria Inre Missionen i Finland. See Free Finnish Home Mission
Denunciation, as church discipline, 45
Department of Scientific Atheism in the Faculty of Philosophy at Moscow University, 20
Der Wahreitszeuge, 'The Macedonian Cry Re-Echoed from Macedonia Itself', 179
Desyatnikov, Sergey
    on Baptist activities outside the church building, 100–101
    CARC duties of, 75–76
    on nationalization of prayer houses, 78
Dimitrov, Trifon, 211
    Bulgarian ministry/imprisonment of, 181
    on evangelism, 203
    on Orthodox-Baptist relations, 209
    salvation story retold by, 192
Discipleship, Ragaz and Arnold disagree on, 298–299
Disciplines
    Bulgarian Baptists and, 200
    Russian Baptist, 44–45
Discretion and Valour, 66
Dobutović, Lidija, missionary work of, 275
Dobutović, Tomislav
    Bible Institute and, 276–277
    missionary work of, 275
Dochev, Peter, Bulgarian ministry of, 180–181
Donahou, Mary, 276
Donahou, Troy, 276
Dostoevsky, Fedor, on atheism, 25
Doychev, Peter, 187
Drecher, Andrew, killed by nationalists, 256
Drobný, Ludovik, Belgrade Baptist seminary faculty member, 265
Drumnikov, Grogor, sponsors religious publications in Bulgaria, 184
Dulic, Nikola
    begins Bible classes for church leaders, 247
    organises the publication *Glas Evandjelja*, 247
Dutch Mennonites, strained relations with German Mennonites, 315–316
Dvadtsatka, 77
Dzhambul, protest at, 33
Dzhetysay Baptist community, incident at, 34

Easter Message, 16
EBF. See European Baptist Federation
ECB (Evangelical Christians-Baptists)
    Moldavian, 63
        weakening of, 80
    Moldavian Council of Churches, independence movement and, 94–96
    Russian
        All-Union Councils of, 43
        Christian youth and, 27
        growth of in 1940's, 2
The Echo of Children, 153
The Echo of the Truth. See *Totuuden Kaiku*
Echoes from the Homeland, 126
Education
    lack of among Baptists, 23
    place of, 7
Elm Prayer House,, withdraws from the Finnish Baptist Union, 145–146
Encroachment on Personality and Rights of Citizens under the Pretence of Discharge of Religious Rites, 19
Engelberg, G., withdrew is church from the Finnish Baptist Union, 145–146
England, ALM Bruderhof move to, 312
Errors in the Realization of Scientific and Atheistic Propaganda Among the Population (On the), 3
Esler, Ted, 274
Euro 70, 263
European Baptist Conference, assigns Bulgarian mission to General Missionary Society of the German Baptist General Conference, 180
European Baptist Federation (EBF)
    BC of B&H joins, 276

encouraged UBC RC to take Bosnia-Herzegovina as a mission field, 274
European Baptist Youth Leadership Conference, 261
Evangelical Christian (Lutheran) Congregations in Germany, Confessional Synod and, 310–311
Evangelical Christians-Baptists. *See* ECB (Evangelical Christians-Baptists)
Evangelicheskoe Dvizhenie v SSSR posle Vtoroy Mirovoy Voyny, 66
Evangelism, Bulgarian Baptists understanding of, 202–205
Evangelist
  birth of, 183–186
  on church fund raising, 200
  first issue of, 184–185
  published in Bulgaria, 173, 180
  search for spiritual roots through, 186–188
  on successful pastoral ministry, 200
  Trifon Dimitrov editor of, 181
  Zaprian Vidolov first editor of, 181
Evangeliumsbote, 252
  incorporated into Friedensbote, 252
Excommunication
  of AUCECB called for, 18
  as church discipline, 45
  effects of in Moldavia, 96

Famine, in Moldavia, 67, 72
Fasting, as protest technique, 32
Father Sergi, *Easter Message* from, 16–17
FBW (Finnish Baptist Women), 158
Fedatov, Zigmund, 267
Federation of German Mennonite Churches, 311
Fellowship, attempt at unity through, 100–102
Fellowship of Freedom. *See Freischar*
Finland
  Baptist in, 115–120
    1940's, 118–120
    early, 115–118
    language division of, 116–117
    women in, 158

Continuation War, 118
Winter War, 118
Finnish Baptist Union
  1930's rebuilding Baptist identity, 142–149
  1940's new wave of Pentecostalism, 150–157
  1950's continued conflict within, 157–162
  August Jauhiainen
    dismissed from, 162–166
    elected head of, 142–143
    see also Jauhiainen, August
  Bible School, 156–157
    begun, 119
  disagreements between leaders of, 127
  historical periods of, 117–118
  over-emphasis of revivals in, 144–145
  reasons for remaining small, 119–120
  receives aid from foreign sources, 155
  sources used in dissertation on, 117
  view of the Holy Spirit within, 119
Finnish Baptist Women (FBW), 158
Finnish Baptists
  accuse Pentecostals of 'sheep-stealing', 126–127
  influence on Pentecostal theology, 126
Finnish Free Evangelical Church
  establishment of, 121
  growth of, 121–122
  relations with Baptists, 122
Finnish Pentecostals. *See* Pentecostal Movement
Finnish Preachers' Union, 148–149
Finnish Weekly, article on unity between believers, 127
First Baptist Women's Society, meets in Zagreb, 251
First Letter to the Whole Church of ECB, 15
Fischli, Margrit, marries Hans Meier, 292
'Fleshly' phenomena', Finnish Pentecostals and, 125–126

General Index 351

Foreign Mission Board of the SBC, aid sent to Finland, 155–156
Franzosefsfeld, German Protestants settle in, 234
Free Churches, in Finland, 120–127
Free Evangelical Church
 accuse Pentecostals of 'sheep-stealing', 126–127
 in Finland, 120–122
Free Finnish Home Mission, 120–121
Free will offerings, discontinued, 73
Freischar, Hans Meier becomes member of, 289
Fria Missionsförbundet, 121
Friedensbote, *Evangeliumsbote* incorporated into, 252
Friesian Mennonite Brotherhood House, Mennonite meeting at, 316
Frosberg, Jakob, 120
Frunze, protest at, 33
Fullbrandt, Carl
 appointed Mission Inspector in South-Eastern Europe, 245
 GBGC representative, 180
 missionary work of, 253
Fullness of the Spirit, Spirit baptism and, 135–136
On the Further Improvement of Ideological and Political-Educational Works, 52

GBGC (German Baptist General Conference)
 American, Bulgarian Baptists and, 205
 Bulgarian mission assigned to, 180
 missionary support by, 206
 supports medical ministry to Bulgarian Gypsies, 204
 supports missionaries to Bulgarian Muslims, 204
Gerassimenko, Evgeniy, Bulgarian ministry of, 181
German Baptist General Conference (GBGC). *See* GBGC (German Baptist General Conference)
German Baptist Regional Association, 253
German Baptist Union, aid to Bulgaria, 180

German Baptists, demands for emigration by, 41
German Mennonites
 abandon principle of non-resistance, 311
 strained relations with Dutch Mennonites, 315–316
 support of the Third Reich, 315–316
German Protestants
 in Kingdom of SCS, 251–256
 left Yugoslavia after WW II, 259
 settle in *Franzosefsfeld*, 234
German Wave, religious broadcasts, 46
Gerwich, Georg, 253
Gestapo
 attempts to close Röhn Bruderhof, 311
 dissolution of Röhn Bruderhof, 313–315
 intimidation visit to Röhn Bruderhof, 308
 results of, 308–309
Giletchi, Valeriu, Moldavian Baptist archives begin by, 64–65
Gill, Everett
 encourages Jovo Jekic, 246
 organised Bible courses, 250
Giurgiulesti, Baptist church in, 72
Gladkevich, Boris, imprisoned, 95
Glas Evangjelja, 228, 250
 begun, 247
 ceased publication, 256
Glasnik, 228
 question about evangelizing Muslims, 263
 replaces *Glas Evandjelja*, 261
Glasnost', 52
Glavina, Lidija, 275
God
 Bulgarian Baptists understanding of, 197
 as remnant of capitalism, 6
God's kingdom
 vs. Caesar's kingdom, 49–52
 see also Church
Goncharenko, E., 48
Good Shepherd magazine, 125
Gorbachev, Mikhail, 52
Grabein, Karl, 211

on the Bulgarian Evangelical
 Baptist Union, 205
Bulgarian ministry of, 181
 sermon on Pentecostals, 196
Graham, Billy, preaches in Zagreb,
 263
*Grave Shortcomings of the Scientific
 and Atheistic Propaganda and
 Mesaures for Its Improvement (On
 the)*, 3
Great Commission, Bulgarian Baptists
 and, 202
Grlj, Giorgio, assumed responsibility
 for Sarajevo Baptist church, 274
A Guide to the Study of the Bible, 119
Gypsies
 Bulgarian Baptists work with, 206–207
 medical ministry to, 204
 Peter Punchov first minister to, 187, 203
Gypsy Baptist Church, in Bulgaria, 203–204

Haug, K., supported by the GBRA, 253
Heikel, Anna, Finnish Baptist and, 116
Heikel, Henrik, Finnish Baptist and, 115–116
Heikel, Viktor, Finnish Baptist and, 116
Heinonen, Eino, Pentecostal
 Movement and, 125
Helluntaiherätys. *See*
 PentecostalMovement
Helsinki Final Act, USSR signs the, 39, 40
Hempt, Adolf
 missionary work of, 234–235
 moves to Lukavac, 243
Henelä, Anja, woman evangelist, 148
Heppenheim by the Bergstraße, Hans
 Meier visits, 290
The Herald, 228
 replaces *Voice of the Gospel*, 261
Herbold, M.
 published beliefs on infant baptism, 184
 visit to Congregationalist group, 177

Herman, Heinz, 254
Herramme Tulee, 126
Herringer, Martin, appointed by BFBS, 177
Herrliberg, religious-socialist
 community in, 292
Herzegovina, rebellion against Muslim
 landlords, 233
Het Volk, reports the dissolution of
 Röhn Bruderhof, 315
Hijniacov, Tikhon, 85
Hiljanen, A., 146
 Preachers' Union and, 148
History of Baptists in Yugoslavia: 1862-1962, 227
*History of the Evangelical
 Christians—Baptists in Russia*, 8
Hofer, David
 imprisoned by the Gestapo, 313–314
 released from prison, 317
 visits Röhn Bruderhof, 314
Holidays, strengthened unity through, 101–102
Holmberg, Aini, 152
Holy Spirit
 August Jauhiainen's theology of, 134–142
 Finnish Baptist Union and, 119
Homage to a Broken Man, 287
Hopper, J.D., 227, 238
 on early Baptist work under Austro-Hungarian Empire, 239
 on the founding of the Baptist
 Union of KSCS, 247
Horak, Josip, 261
 Baptist Seminary in Belgrade and, 265
 Trans World Radio permanent
 speaker, 261
Horak, Sali, 239
Horak, Stazi, 239
Horsch, John, 316
Horsh, Michael, 316
Horvat, Tim, ordained a deacon, 276
House of Scientific Atheism, 20
Household church, Baptist as a, 45–46
Hubmaier, Balthasar, 186

Hughley, J.D., on Pentecostal influence among Finnish Baptists, 142
Hutterian Brethren
  colonies considered as new location, 319
  visit Röhn Bruderhof, 314
The Hutterian Ordnung, Hans Meier and, 294
Hyvä Paimen, 125

Ibate Bruderhof, founded, 323
Illichiov, L., Khrushchev's campaign against believers and, 82–83
Imamovic, Mustafa
  on Muslims immigrating from Bosnia-Herzegovina, 241
  on Muslims view of Christian missions, 242
Industrial School in Zurich, Hans Meier attends, 288
Infant baptism, Bulgarian Baptists understanding of, 193–194
Initiative Group. *See Initsiativniki*
  in Moldavia, 95
Initsiativniki, 1
  Christian youth and, 27
  conflict with the AUCECB, 9–15
  Georgi Vins and, 94–95
  in Moldavia, 95
  growth of, 99
'Instructions According to the Application of Legislation of Cults', 74
Instructions for the Senior Presbyters, 10
International Baptist Theological Seminary, 276
International Socialist Congress at Basle, Hans Meier's father attends, 288
International Voluntary Service (I.V.C.P.), Hans Meier works with, 289
Irby, Adeline
  death of, 243
  reopens Christian school, 234
  work in Bosnia-Herzegovina by, 230–232
Isla Margarita Bruderhof, 323

see also other named Bruderhofs
Issyk Baptist community, protest at, 33
Istoriya Evangel'skikh Khristian-Baptistov v SSSR, 80
Ivancev, Constantin
  banishment of, 71
  imprisoned, 86
Ivanov, Andrey, 70
Ivanov, Ilia
  CARC and, 75
  on Ivan Slobdchikov's dismissal, 87
  on Moldavian Baptists activities, 86
  on Moldavian non-compliance to AUCECB rules, 90–91
  registration of churches and, 79
  sent to organize work in Moldavia, 85
  visits to Moldavia, 100
Izikhovich, Vasiliy, on moving his residence, 71
Izvestiya, on Russian takeover of Moldavia, 68

James Valley Hutterite community, 314
Jauhiainen, August, 117–118, 129–134, 146
  chosen as Finnish Baptist Union president, 129
  conflict with Jaakko Kalliomäki, 154–155
  conversation with Mikko Kolomainen, 160–161
  desire for unity between believers, 127
  dismissed from Finnish Baptist Union, 162–166
  elected head of the Finnish Baptist Union, 142–143
  ended editing *Totuuden Kaiku*, 152
  letter to E. Kuusisto, 161
  Preachers' Union and, 148
  presidency of, 118
  problems between Toivo Tervonen and, 146–147
  proposes Bible course for teens, 161
  theology of, 134–142
  view of the Holy Spirit, 119
  see also Finnish Baptist Union

Jauhiainen, Vesa
  asked to write booklet on Baptist beliefs, 161
  began working with children and young people, 151
Jehovah's Witnesses, accused of activities of anti-state and fanatical character, 74
Jekic, Jovo, 244
  missionary work of, 246–247
Jews, Hans Meier and, 332
Johnson, Guy
  meets with Eleanor Roosevelt, 319–320
  trip to America, 319–320
Joseph, Francis, annexed Bosnia-Herzegovina, 240
Jouluaamu, special issue of Totuuden Kaiku, 151
Journal of European Baptist Studies, 66
Julious, Peter, 251
Justice, Hans Meier view of, 291

Kačarević, Boris, sen as pastor to the Sarajevo Baptist church, 269–270
Kačarević, Selka, 269
Kaikuja Kotimaasts, 126
Kalliomäki, Jaakko, 140, 147
  becomes Editor-in-Chief of *Totuuden Kaiku*, 152
  conflict with August Jauhiainen, 154–155
  criticism of August Jauhiainen by, 138–139
  letter on preaching in Northern Finland, 150
  reveals confidential information about August Jauhiainen, 163
Kalmikov, Lydia, 251
Karadjordejevic, Alexsandra, announces the unification of the Kingdom of Serbia, 243
Karala, W., 146
Karamehmedović, Jasmina, first Mulsim convert, 268
Karev, Alexander
  on church and state, 4
  on separation of Baptists, 17
Kargel, Ivan (Johann), 187
  book on the Holy Spirit, 196
  first Bulgarian Baptist church and, 179
  on government interference, 50
Kauhajoki, Baptist church founded in, 155
Kervinen, Albin
  first Finnish Pentecostal congregation founded by, 124
  influence on Pentecostal theology, 126
  on Pentecostal meetings in Finland, 123–124
Ketonen, Paavo, 140, 153
  reveals confidential information about August Jauhiainen, 163
KGB
  Frol Astakhov and, 88
  goals of in Moldavia, 83
Khmara, N., 36
Khrushchev, Nikita
  campaign against believers, 82–84
  promises of, 5
  religions policies of, 3–5
Kibbutz movement, 332
King, Charles, 66
  on famine in Moldavia, 72
Kingdom of SCS
  becomes Kingdom of Yugoslavia, 243
  German Protestants in, 251–256
Kingdom of Yugoslavia
  all churches put under supervision of law, 257
  effect of Tripartite Pact on, 257
  establishment of, 243
  occupied by German and Italian troops, 255–256
  religious situation in, 257
  see also SFRY
Kingdom SCS
  Baptist work in, 244–256
  recognizes the Baptist Union of KSCS, 248
Kinkel, Frederick, missionary work of, 238
Kinkel, Wilhelmina, missionary work of, 238
Kirlkilanov, Peter, 211
'Kiros Centre', founded, 276

Kishinev ECB Church at Vokzal'naya Street, split within, 92–93
Kiyosev, Vasli, Bulgarian ministry of, 180
Klein, Martin, 238
Kleiner, Fritz, looks for location near Asuncion, 323
Klem, Franjo
  on areas covered by individual pastors, 262
  on Baptist in Yugoslavia, 261
  Baptist Seminary in Belgrade and, 265
  imprisoned, 259–260
  on life undr Tito, 258–261
  missionary work of, 266
  promoted Sunday schools, 264
  studied at the Baptist Seminary in Budapest, 264
  Tenth World Baptist Congress participant, 261
  on years of German/Italian occupation, 256
Klibanov, A., research by, 26–27
Klimenko, A., 43
Klimenko, Nelli, on the formation of the Moldavian CCECB, 96
Klundt, Jacob, 187
  appointed by BFBS, 177
  influence of on Lom Baptist Church, 198
  work of in Lompalanka, 179
Knežević, Ruben
  on Austro-Hungarian religious situation, 243–244
  on BUY youth conferences, 264
  on number of Baptist preachers after WW II, 262
Koch, Henrich, Franz and Maria Tabory influenced by, 228
Kocic, Dragan, missionary work of, 274
Kokki, John Gustaf, 117
  criticisms/dismissal of, 128–129
  first Preachers' Union president, 148
  problems left by, 118
Kolesnikov, N., 44

Kolomainen, Mikko, 117, 160
  asked to write booklet on Baptist beliefs, 161
  conversation with August Jauhiainen, 160–161
  first rector of Finnish Baptist Union Bible School, 119, 156
Korovec, V., sentenced to hard labor, 259
Korpela, August, 140
Korpela, Eva, 140
  criticism of August Jauhiainen by, 137–138
Koskinen, Irma, woman evangelist, 148
Koval'kov, V., 17
Kozubovsky, M., 48
Kreiman, V., 48
Kriševac, Todor, on work of Adeline irby and Georgina muir Mackenzie, 230
Krokodil, 20
Krustev, K., on the Bulgarian Orthodox Church, 183
Kruzen, Aleksandra, August Jauhiainen and, 135
Kryuchkov, Gennadiy, 18
  advice to Georgi Vins, 34–35
  on Baptist demographic situation, 28
  effect of aggressive leadership, 96
  fasting as protest by, 32
  Moldavian independence movement and, 94–95
  personality of, 28–31
Kucherenko, N., 36
Kuhn, William
  article on Day of Pentecost, 195
  visits to Bulgaria by, 206
Kujala, Senja, 160
  on Toivo Wacklin's moving to the Pentecostals, 159
Kuksenko, Yu, on the Baptist Moscow protest demonstration, 31–32
Kuopio, Baptist in, 116
Kuosmanen, Juhani, 126
Kurdov, Stephan, 177
Kuusisto, E.
  letter from August Juhianinen, 161
  Preachers' Union and, 148

Kylliäinen, Toivo, promoted to Editor-in-Chief of *Totuuden Kaiku*, 152

Lähteitä Kyynelten Laaksosta, 153
Lajunen, Antti, baptism of the Spirit of, 124
Längimoos, althruistic based community in, 293
Lasten Kaiku, 153
Law of Legal State of Faith Communities, 260–261
Law on Religious Associations
    re-enforcement of, 3
    redefined, 39
Lefortovo, prisoners fasting protest at, 32
On the Legal Position of Religious Communities, 271
Legislation, against Baptist churches, 19–20
Lehotsky, Adolf, 244
    Baptist Seminary in Belgrade and, 265
    Belgrade Baptist seminary faculty member, 265
    drafted into the German army, 256
    imprisoned, 259
    missionary work of, 254, 266
    ordained, 253
    studied at the Baptist Theological Seminary in Hamburg, 254
Lehotsky, Ruth, theological education by extension and, 265–266
Lehtonen, Benjam, letter on Pentecostalism from August Jauhiainen, 159–160
Lehtonen, Matti, 146
Lenin, Vladimir, Baptist preachers on, 9
Leningrad workers, view of religion held by, 41
Lenin's Socialist Law, 9
Lenten Letter, 16
Lerchy, Julia, pays rent for school at *Silum*, 310
Letter of Instructions, 9–10, 95, 97
    AUCECB cancels the, 99
    AUCECB forced to approve, 137
    effects of in Moldavia, 89–91

Letter of Instructions for the Senior Presbyters, restrictions in, 14–15
Lezzi, Eva, Werkhof and, 293
Lezzi, Max
    visits Röhn Bruderhof, 295
    Werkhof and, 293
Liberty, religious broadcasts, 46
Liechtenstein, allows Röhn Bruderhof school to move to, 309–310
Link, on Moldavian Baptist growth, 67
Logvinenko, V., 44
Lom Baptist Church, influence of Jacob Klundt on, 198
Loma Hoby Bruderhof
    founded, 323
    hospital begn at, 324
Lord Radstock, 135
    visits Finland, 121
Lord's Supper
    Bulgarian Baptists understanding of, 194–195
    church discipline and, 45
Lotz, Fritz, Daruvar Baptist church and, 249
Lovrec, M., Belgrade Baptist seminary faculty member, 265
Luke, published in Gypsy language, 203
Lundin, Eric R., 146, 147
Luvia, Baptist church begun in, 116
Lyalina, G., research by, 26–27

Mackenzie, Georgina Muir, work in Bosnia-Herzegovina by, 230–232
Maiboroda, G.I., 99
Mäkelä, Kalle, 128
Malanchuk, Sergey
    elected Moldavian senior presbyter, 89, 100
    offered pastoral care, 102
Malcolm, Noel, 242
Mang, Frank, 153
Marchov, Vassil K., 179
    Bulgarian ministry of, 180
Masaryk, Thomas, Hans Meier and, 309
Mathis, Anni, Werkhof and, 293
Mathis, Peter, Werkhof and, 293
Matthew, published in Gypsy language, 203

General Index 357

McBeth, T.F., 227
MCC. *See* Mennonite Central Committee (MCC)
McClendon, James William, 286
Medical ministry, to Bulgarian Gypsies, 204
Megerle, Ana, 239
Megerle, Panhartel, 239
Megerle, Terezija, 234
Meier, Andreas, 287
Meier, Chris, 287
Meier, Hans
  baptised, 295
  death of, 334–335
  discussion with the mayor of Veitsteinbach, 311
  documents pertaining to, 287
  early life of, 288–289
  effect of WW I on, 288–289
  finds employment at Siemens Schuckert Works, 290
  on following Christ, 299–300
  on his conversion, 296
  his father, 288
  ignored by history, 285–286
  image of the common table, 291–292
  imprisoned, 290, 293–294
    by the Gestapo, 313–314
  influence of
    Peter Riedman and Michael Sattler on, 304–308
    The Schleitheim Confession on, 304–307
  inner turmoil and self examination by, 302
  on Jews view of Christ and Christians, 332
  leaves the brotherhood, 328
  life/convictions of, 287–288
  looks for location near Asuncion, 323
  gmarries Margrit Fischli, 292
  meeting with John Howard Yoder, 333
  meets with Eleanor Roosevelt, 319–320
  military refresher course and, 293–294
  most important witness of the church, 331
  Paraguay and, 320–328
  rejoins the brotherhood, 330
  released from prison, 317
  on response to pressures from the Third Reich, 303–306
  sends Orie Miller materials for publication, 324
  theological images important to, 286
  trip to America, 319–320
  on unity at Röhn Bruderhof, 296
  view of
    Christ, 307–308
    justice, 291
    on serving in the military, 289–290
  visits and joins Röhn Bruderhof, 295
  years in Argentina, 329
Meier, Klaus, 287
Meier, Margrit
  baptised, 295
  visits and joins Röhn Bruderhof, 295
Menno-Simons, 178
Mennonite Central Committee (MCC)
  attended meeting at Friesian Mennonite Brotherhood House, 316
  Bruderhof settlements and, 316–317
  supports Bruderhof move to Paraguay, 321
Mennonite World Conference, 316
Mennonites
  German
    abandon principle of non-resistance, 311
    immigration to Russia, 178
  offered membership in the AUCECB, 99
Methodists, 285–286
  in Bulgaria, 176
  view of women and ministry, 201
Meyer, Henrich, missionary work of, 237–238
Mikailovich, Sergey. *See* Pimen

Mikhailov, Panteleiy, reprimanded, 101
Mikkonen, Pekka, baptism of the Spirit of, 124
Mikulic, Josip, 269
Military service, Hans Meier's view of, 289–290
Millard, Edward, missionary work of, 235–237
Miller, Orie O.
  attended meeting at Friesian Mennonite Brotherhood House, 316
  Hans Meier sends materials for publication to, 324
  telegram to Paraguayan Ambassador, 320
Mishkov, Pavel, on evangelism, 203
Mission, Bulgarian Baptists understanding of, 202–205
Mitrokhin, L., research by, 26–27
Mitskevich, A.
  on Moldavian church registrations, 77
  part-time Bible courses and, 44
  visits to Moldavia, 100
Mladi Krščanin, 250
Moiseev, I., 36
Moj Bližji, 274, 275
  opened an office in Sarajvo, 275
Mojzes, Paul, 259
Moldavia
  applying Soviet religious laws in, 72–74
  AUCECB (All Union Council of Evangelical Christian Baptists) in, 84–91
  converted to a Soviet Socialist Republic, 68–69
  famine in, 67, 72
  Germans forced from, 71
  KGB goals in, 83
  office of senior presbyter in, 87–89
  restoring God's work in, 85–87
Moldavian Baptist, archives, 64–65
Moldavian Baptist churches
  growth of 1918 to 1940, 67
  post war pressure on, 67–74
Moldavian Baptists
  attempt at unity, 98–106
  by congresses, 98–100
  in fellowship and worship, 100–102
  through theology, 104–106
  baptism as a theological-ecclesiological centre for, 102–104
  broken fellowship among, 96–98
  church closures, 80–82
  church registration and closure of, 74–84
  deportations of, 67–68
  experiences of, 63–64
  loss of local church autonomy, 105–106
  membership decline/fragmentation of, 69–72
  nationalization of property of, 78
  number of churches in 1945, 80
  opposition to AUCECB, 89–91
  registration of churches, 74, 76–79
  split among, 91–98
    Grigoriy Rudenko's separatist group, 93–94
    Kishinev ECB Church at Vokzal'naya Street, 92–93
  underground work, 79–84
  see also Bessarabian Baptists
Moldavian Council of Churches, ECB (Evangelical Christians-Baptists), independence movement and, 94–96
Moldavian Evangelical Christians-Baptist. *See* ECB (Evangelical Christians-Baptists)
Moldavian Soviet Socialist Republic, formation of, 68–69
Moldavian Union of Evangelical Christians—Baptists, records of, 63
The Moldavians, 66
Möllersvärd, Karl Justus Mathias, Finnish Baptist and, 115
Molotov-Ribbentrop pact, 68
Mommsen, Peter, 287
Monte-Carlo, religious broadcasts, 46
Montenegro, declares war on Ottoman Empire, 233
Moore, John Allen
  denied permanent stay in Yugoslavia, 264
  lectures at IBTS, 265

missionary work of, 250
Moore, Pauline Willingham,
  missionary work of, 250
'Moral Code for the Builder of
  Communism', 5
Mörsky, Matta, woman evangelist, 148
Music, as 'sermons in verses', 48–49

Na-vukho-donosor, 25
NABGC of GB, gives support to
  missions in Europe, 245
Nachfolge Christi, 293
  disagreement over, 295
  Eberhart Arnold's emphasis on, 297
  spiritual importance of, 301
National Socialism in Germany
  Hans Meier and, 303–306
  Röhn Bruderhof and, 302–304,
    302–304
  threat of to Bruderhof, 301
Nationalization, of church property, 78
Nauka i Religiya, 20
Naziffov, M., missionary to Bulgarian
  Muslims, 204
Neducin, Steve, 244
Neulanen, Jouko, 118
New Statutes (in the USSR), 9, 95, 97
  AUCECB cancels the, 99
  effects of in Moldavia, 89–91
New Studies, AUCECB forced to
  approve, 13
Nieminen, Olavi, 152
Niemöller, Martin, refuses to work
  with Alm Bruderhof, 310–311
Nilsson, Fredrik Olaus, Finnish Baptist
  and, 115
Niskanen, Markku, treatise on Finnish-
  speaking Baptists, 117–118
North American Baptist General
  Conference of German Baptists. *See*
  NABGC of GB
Novi Sad
  Baptist churches in, 251
  seminary moves to, 265
Novosibirsk community, 'Day of the
  Prisoner' and, 33
Novy Mir, *A Day in the Life of Ivan
  Denisovich* and, 24
Nuorison Nurkka, 143
Nuorten Todistus, 154

Nurmela, M., Preachers' Union and,
  149

Oaksey Bruderhof
  founded, 313
  see also named Bruderhofs
Obscurants Without Masks, 21
*Obzor Istorii Evangel'sko-Bratstva na
  Ukraine*, 66
Odessa Theological Seminary,
  memorization of scripture and, 42
Offerings, discontinued free will, 73
Old Russian Orthodox Church, 28–31
*On the Grace Shortcomings of the
  Scientific and Atheistic Propaganda
  and Measures for Its Improvement*, 3
*On the Measures of the Regulation of
  the Network of Religious
  Communities Consisting of Citizens
  of German Nationality and
  Strengthening of the Control of Its
  Activities*, 40
*On Separation of the Church from the
  State and Schools from the Church*,
  30–40, 73
Oncken, J.G., in Russia, 178–179
'Operation South' deportation, 67
Order for Opening the Churches, 73
Order for Taxation of Ministers of
  Religious Cults, 73
Order for the Opening of Prayer
  Houses of Religious Cults, 73
Örebro Mission, 160
Orgkomitet, 32, 96
  calls for excommunication of
    AUCECB leaders, 18
Orthodox Church
  Bulgarian
    Baptists and, 208–210
    opposition to evangelicals work,
      182–183
    view 'Holy Tradition', 188
    view of women and ministry, 201
  Russian, Baptists compared with,
    15–18
Ottoman Empire
  rule ended, 233
  Serbia/Montenegro declare war on,
    233
Our Lord is Coming, 126

Ozhevskaya, V., 48

Paraguay
  Bruderhof settlement and, 320–328
  effects of wars on, 325
Parikkala, Baptist church begun in, 116
Pasat, Valeriy
  archival documents and, 65
  on reasons for persecutions of Christians, 70
Pastoral care, need for, 102
Pastors, restrictions on, 69
Paunovic, N., 244
Peace Pledge Union, 317
Pederson, Gotfrid, missionary to Bulgarian Muslims/Jews, 204
Penitential testimonies, 24
Pentecostal movement in Finland, 122–127
  accused of 'sheep-stealing', 126–127
  Baptist influence on, 126
  Bulgarian Baptists and, 195–196
  founding of the first Finnish Pentecostal congregation, 124
  growth of, 124–125
Pentecostal teachings, August Jauhiainen's theology of, 134–142
Pentecostals
  accused of activities of anti-state and fanatical character, 74
  join the AUCECB, 84
  in Finland. *See* Pentecostal movement in Finland
  in Norway, 122–123
  in Sweden, 122–123
Perebekovskiy, Vasiliy, on Moldavian broken fellowship, 96–98
Perestroika, 52
Personal spirituality, 41–49
Peter, Julious, 238
Peters, P., fasting as protest by, 32
Petrick, C.E., 206
  Bulgarian ministry of, 181
  GBGC representative, 180
Pfaff, Elizabeth, baptised by Henrich Meyer, 238
Pfaff, Jacob, baptised by Henrich Meyer, 238

Pfaff, Peter, baptised by Henrich Meyer, 238
Pfarrernotbund, 310
Philips, Dirk, 178
Pimen, *Lenten Letter* to, 16
Pintér, Sandor
  Belgrade Baptist seminary faculty member, 265
  imprisoned, 259–260
Plymouth Brethren, 121
Pohjasmäki, Selma, woman evangelist, 148
Pokorny, Katherina, baptised by Henrich Meyer, 238
The Politics of Jesus, 333
Polje, Petrovo, 259
Polyanskiy, Ivan, first CARC chairman, 74
Ponomarchuk, Dmitriy, 88–89, 104–105
  replaces Frol Astakhov as senior presbyter, 88
Pori, Baptist in, 116
Potts, Miriam, 287
Preachers' Union, in Finland, 148–149
Presidium of the Supreme Council, followed Moscow passed religious laws, 74
Primavera
  Cotswold Bruderhof moves to, 323
  internal struggles at, 325–328
Princeton Theological Seminary, Peter Dochev educated at, 180
Principality of Liechtenstein. *See* Liechtenstein
Prokof'ev, Alexy, Moldavian independence movement and, 94–95
Propaganda, against Baptist churches, 19–20
Protest techniques, fasting, 32
Punchov, Peter, first Bulgarian Gypsy pastor, 187, 203
'Pysähtymisen Vaara', article promoting Pentecostalism as growth tool, 153

Quarterly Reporter of the German Baptist Mission, 'The Macedonian Cry Re-Echoed from Macedonia Itself', 179

Raamatuntulkisteluopas, 119, 142
  published, 154
Ragaz, Leonhard, 286
  attends religious socialist
    conference, 290
  criticised by military judge, 290
  Freischar meetings organized by,
    289
  on the Herrliberg religious-socalist
    community, 292
  influence of on Hans Meier, 297
  unfilled dream of an apostolic
    community of Christ, 300
Raichev, Spass, first Bulgarian
  missionary, 187–188
Rantanen, Vilho, 154
Raychynets, Fydor, Bible Institute and,
  276–277
*Reactionary Character of Mysticism in
Contemporary Christian
Sectarianism*, 21
Reform Baptists, 11,
  as a household church, 45–46
  see also, *Initsiativniki*
Registration, of Moldavian churches,
  74
Relief Committee of Foreign Mission
  Board, aid sent to Finland, 155–156
*Religious Illusions on the Threshold of
Life*, 21
Religious policies, Joseph Stalin and, 2
Religious prejudices, warnings against,
  6–7
Religious society, defined/registration
  of, 77
Repentance, Bulgarian Baptists
  understanding of, 191
Reschetnikov, Y., 66
Revivals, over-emphasized in Finland,
  144–145
'Revolutionary struggle', rejected by
  Russian Baptists, 12
Revolutionary subordination, 305
Rhön Bruderhof, Hans Meier and, 290
Richard, Cliff, concert in Zagreb, 263
Rideman, Peter, 286
  influence on Hans Meier, 304–308
  on truth coming from Christ, 305
Rilski, Neoffit, translates the New
  Testament into Bulgarian, 183

Ristin Voitto, 125
Röhn Bruderhof
  conflict with Third Reich grows,
    308
  dissolution of, 313–315
  as 'embassy' of the Kingdom of
    God, 296–297
  English visitors to, 312
  Gestapo
    attempts to close, 311
    makes intimidating visit to, 308
    results of intimidating visit,
      308–309
  Hans and Else Boller join, 293
  Hans and Margrit Meier join, 295
  Hans Meier on unity at, 296
  internal struggles, 301–302
  moves and becomes Alm
    Bruderhof, 310
  pressure on the children's school to
    close or more, 309
  resettles in England, 302
  see also, specific Bruderhof
Roman Catholic Church
  growth of in Bosnia-Herzegovina,
    242
  opposes BFBS work in Bosnia-
    Herzegovina, 236
Romania
  Moldavian ECB churches
    registration and, 76
  persecution of Baptist, 67
Roosevelt, Eleanor, meeting with Hans
  Meier, 319–320
Rostov-on-Don, protest at, 33–34
Roter, Zdenko, on believers under
  Communism, 272
RSFSR criminal code, 19–20
Rudenko, Grigoriy, 85
  imprisoned/exiled, 86, 90
  separatists group led by, 76–79,
    93–94
Ruishalme, Antti, 124
Rukoushuoneyhdistys Elim r.y.,
  withdraws from the Finnish Baptist
  Union, 145–146
Rushbrooke, J.H., 144, 244
  on Henrich Meyer, 237–238
  on Julious Peter, 238–239

Russian Baptists
  apologetic for, 47
  Armenian view held by most, 45
  demands for emigration by, 41
  disciplines, 44–45
  majority reject 'revolutionary struggle', 12
Russian Orthodox Church, Baptists compared with, 15–18
Russian religious broadcasts, 46

Salmensaari, S.S., on relations between Baptists and Finnish Free Evangelicals, 122
Salvation Army, sends clothing and shoes to Finland, 156
Salvation, Bulgarian Baptists understanding of, 190
Samokov Congregationalist School, Zaprian Vidolov educated at, 181
Sanctification, Bulgarian Baptists understanding of, 192–193
Sannikov, S., 66
  on Khrushchev's campaign against believers, 82
Sanningsvittnet, article on over-emphasis of revivals in Finland, 144–145
Sarajevo, first Baptists in, 228
Sarakevp Baptist Church, during Communist era, 267–270
Sattler, Michael, 286
  on Christocentric belief, 305–306
  influence on Hans Meier, 304–308
  The Schleitheim Confession and, 302, 304–305
Savchenko, I., on KGB activities in Moldavia, 83
Savinsky S.
  on CARC in Moldavia, 75
  on 'Joyful news', 76
Sawatsky, Walter, 66
  oral history project begun by, 65
SBC, mission work of, 245–251
SBRA
  loss of membership after WW II, 266
  reorganization of, 248–249
Schalaschov, A.A., 99
Schaptala, M.T., 99

Scharschmidt, Carl Johann, Franz and Maria Tabory influenced by, 228
Scheinov, Stevan, supported by the GBRA, 253
Scheinow, Stevan, 244
Schemchischin, V., thesis by, 65–66
Scherer, Phillip, studied at the Baptist Theological Seminary in Hamburg, 254
The Schleitheim Confession, influence of on Hans Meier, 302, 304–307
Schlosser, Robert, ordained, 253
Scientific Atheistic Editorial Board of the State Publishing House of Political Literature, 20
Scientific Atheistic Section at the Moscow Planetarium, 20
Scientific Atheistic Section attached to the Board of the All-Union *Znanie* Society, 20
Scripture, memorization of, 42
Second Advent
  Bulgarian Baptists understanding of, 195
  stressed, 45
Sectarianism and Family, 21
Sectarians and Their Preaching, 21
Sector of the History of Religion and Atheism of the USSR Academy of Sciences' Institute of History, 20
Sects, Their Beliefs and Deeds, 21
SEGMC, 245
Senne, Samuel, 238
On Separation of the Church from the State and Schools from the Church, 30–40, 73
Sepper, Carl, 244
  editor of *Evangeliumsbote*, 252
  leads Bible classes for church leaders, 247
  missionary work of, 252–253, 255
  ordained, 253
  studied at the Baptist Theological Seminary in Hamburg, 254
Serbia, declares war on Ottoman Empire, 233
Serbo-Croatian Baptist movement, begun, 246
'Sermons in verses', 48–49

Sestrinski List
  ceased publication, 256
  founded, 251
Seventh-Day Adventists, accused of activities of anti-state and fanatical character, 74
SFRY
  establishment of, 258
  Josip Broz Tito elected leader of, 258
  see also Kingdom of Yugoslavia
Sham Brotherhood, 21
Siemens Schuckert Works, Hans Meier finds employment at, 290
Siiriäinen, Kustaa V., 147
Silum, Röhn Bruderhof school located in, 310
Sin, Bulgarian Baptists understanding of, 190
Sinichkin, A., 13
The Sister's Newspaper, founded, 251
Slavic Baptist Regional Association. *See* SBRA
Slobdchikov, Ivan, 85
  on applying for baptism, 103
  dismissed as senior presbyter, 87
  on incident with Frol Astakhov, 88
  on Moldavian broken fellowship, 97
Smidt, G.O., visit to Finland, 123
Smith, Jim, 269
Socialist Federal Republic of Yugoslavia. *See* SFRY
Socialist International Solidarity Movemen, Hans Meier disappointed with, 288–289
Solti, Anna, began Baptist church in Brezovo Polje, 238
Solti, David, began Baptist church in Brezovo Polje, 238
Solzhenitsyn, Alexander
  A Day in the Life of Ivan Denisovich, 24
  Lenten Letter, 16
Songs, as 'sermons in verses', 48–49
South-Eastern European German Mission Committee. *See* SEGMC
Southern Baptist Convention, mission work of, 245–251
Soviet Easter Song, 26

Spirit baptism
  Aarne Ylppö's view of, 139
  fullness of the Spirit and, 135–136
  writings on, 140–141
Spirituality, personal, 42
Springs in the Valley of Tears, 153
Spurgeon, C.H., 188
  on salvation, 191
  sermons published in Bulgarian, 184
St. Vitus' Day Constitution, 257
Stalin, Joseph
  personality cult denounced, 3
  religions policies of, 2
The Statue of the Baptist Church of SFRY, 260
Statues of the Union of the ECB, 13
  disagreeable points of, 13–14
Steer, Roger, on the BFBS, 229
Stereotypes, creating atheistic, 20–24
Šumić, Luka
  baptism of, 267
  becomes leader of Sarajevo Baptist church, 267
  nominated to become a deacon, 269
Sunday school and youth ministry, in Yugoslavia, 264
Sunday school, in Bulgaria, 201
Suomen Vapaakirkko. *See* Vinish Free Evangelical Church
Suomen Vapaakirkko, 121
  article on unity between believers, 127
Swedish Baptist Union, financial aid sent to Finland, 155
Switzerland, refuses to allow Röhn Bruderhof school to move to, 309

Tabory, Franz
  Alexander Thomson writing about, 229–230
  establishes first Baptist church in Sarajevo, 230
  first Baptists in Sarajevo, 228
Tabory, Maria, first Baptists in Sarajevo, 228
Tampere, Baptist in, 116
Tarlev, Mihail, 70
Tary, Károly, studied at Saint Andrea's Bible School, 254–255

Tentiuc, Grigoriy, on persecutions of Moldavian Christians, 70
Tertullian, Quintus Septimius Florente, 48
Tervits, Y., 44
Tervonen, Toivo, 146
   called to Toronto, Canada, 148
   problems between August Jauhiainen and, 146-147
'Tervonen's revivals', 146
'The Macedonian Cry Re-Echoed from Macedonia Itself', 179
'The Victory of the Cross' magazine, 125
Theological education, in Yugoslavia, 264-266
Theology, Moldavian Baptists unity attempts through, 104-106
Third Reich, German Mennonites support of, 315-316
Thomson, Alexander, 229, 235
   on Millard's breaking BFBS rules, 236
Tillich, Paul, attends religious socialist conference, 290
Tithing, Bulgarian Baptists and, 199-200
Tito, Josip Broz, elected leader of the SFRY, 258
Tkachenko, L., 48
Tobacco, Bulgarian Baptists on use of, 208
Torrey, R.A., sermon translated into Bulgarian, 189
Totuuden Kaiku, 116, 119, 122, 126
   article on unity between believers, 127
   August Jauhiainen
      stops editing, 152
      articles on the Holy Spirit in, 138
   on disagreements between Baptist leaders, 127
   dissatisfaction with Mikko Kolomainen's editing of, 161
   economic difficulties at, 151
   increased pentecostal views published in, 155
   Jaakko Kalliomäki becomes editor of, 140, 152
   criticism of August Jauhiainen, 138
   report on church in Vaajakoski, 150-151
   Toivo Kylliäinen become Editor-in-Chief of, 152
   young people emphasized in, 143
Trials, of Baptists, 36-39
Tripartite Pact, effect on the Kingdom of Yugoslavia, 257
The Truth about Sectarianism, 21
'Truth is immortal', as motto of Bulgarian Baptist Union, 187
Trutza, Peter, on Moldavian Baptist deportations, 71
Tsurkan, Silvestr, 85
   offered pastoral care, 102
   criticizes Jakov Zhidkov, 91
Turku, Baptist in, 116

UBC RC
   encouraged to take Bosnia-Herzegovina as a mission field. *See* UBC RC
   missionary work of, 274-275
Uezd, Elisavetskiy, on J.G. Oncken, 178
Ukrainian Baptists, demands for emigration by, 41
Under the Mask of Holiness, 21
Underground congregations, 11
   received official right to exist, 40
   see also, *Initsiativniki*
Union of Baptist Churches in the Republic of Croatia. *See* UBC RC
Union of Baptist Churches in the Socialist Federation of Republics of Yugoslavia, 260
Union of Baptist Women's Societies of the Kingdom of Yugoslavia, 251
Unity
   Moldavian Baptists attempts at, 98-106
      by congresses, 98-100
      in fellowship and worship, 100-102
      through theology, 104-106
Unruh, Benjamin, meeting with Hans Meier, 311
Unterwiener, Josef, ordained, 253

General Index

Vacek, Vinko
  Daruvar Baptist church and, 249
  first president of the Baptist Union of KSCS, 247
  organises the publication *Glas Evandjelja*, 247
Vainonen, T., 146
Varga, Jaroš, Sarajevo Baptist church pastor, 267
Vasenina, L., 48
Vasov, George, on Anabaptist/Baptist beginnings, 187
Vezmar, Đuro, 244
Vidolov, Zaprian
  first editor of *Evangelist*, 181
  reasons for publishing the *Evangelist*, 184–185
Vienna Bible depository, 236
Vincetić, Tomo, 265
Vinko, Vacek, missionary work of, 245–247
Vins, Georgi, 34–35, 99
  attempt at unity and, 99
  on Baptist fasting, 32
  on the brotherhood and the State, 38–39
  on Communist admission about law, 50
  Initsiativniki and, 94–95
  Moldavian independence movement and, 94–95
Violation of the Laws on the Separation of Church from State and School from Church, 19
Vlašic, Ivan, becomes leader of Sarajevo Baptist church, 268
Voice of America, religious broadcasts, 46
Voice of the Andes, religious broadcasts, 46
The Voice of the Gospel, 228
Voice of the Gospel, 228, 250
  begun, 247
Vojnica, Dragan, sent to Sarajevo Baptist church, 269
Von Hollander, Else, first Bruderhof settlement and, 285
Vysotsky, N., 48

Wacklin, Toivo, 140
  elected pastor in Vaajakoski, 147
  on the Holy Spirit, 139
  moves to Pentecostals, 158–159
Wahl, Johann
  ordained, 253
  studied at the Baptist Theological Seminary in Hamburg, 254
Waldegrave, Granville. *See* Lord Radstock
Waldner, Michael
  imprisoned by the Gestapo, 313–314
  released from prison, 317
  visits Röhn Bruderhof, 314
Wardin, Albert
  'Baptists in Bulgaria', 174
  on the persecution of Moldavian Baptists, 67
Wardin, W.A., 227
Warner, Jeff, 276
Watts, John, lectures at BTS, 265
We Were Baptists, 21
Weddings, worship at, 102
Werkhof, 293
  disunity at, 296
  organisational problems within, 294
Westin, Gunnar, article on overemphasis of revivals in Finland, 144–145
Wheathill Bruderhof
  founded, 323
  see also other named Bruderhofs
Why We Live in Full Community, 334
Wiberg, Anders, Finnish Baptist and, 116
Williams, James Archie
  permission given to work at SFRY, 263
  theological education by extension and, 265–266
Williams, Nela (Nada) Horak, permission given to work at SFRY, 263
Winter War, in Finland, 118
Women, Bulgarian Baptists and, 200–201
Women's Benevolent Societies, Bulgarian Baptists and, 207
Woodcrest Bruderhof
  Hans Meier and, 329–330

unity sought from, 329
Work Farm. *See* Werkhof
Worship
　attempt at unity through, 100–102
　at weddings, 102

Ylistaro, Baptist in, 116
Ylppö, Aarne, view of Spirit baptism, 139–140
Yoder, John Howard
　meeting with Hans Meier, 333
　on *revolutionary subordination*, 305
Young People's Corner, 143
Youth Christian Abstention Societies, Bulgarian Baptists, 201–202
Youth, Christian, Baptist communities and, 27
Youth Christian (magazine), 250

Youth Conference in Daruvar, 250
Youth Societies, Finnish, 143
Yugoslavia Communist Party, thrown out of the Cominform and the USSR, 262

Zagreb Baptist church, assumes responsibility for the Sarajevo Baptist church, 269
Zakon o pravnom polož au vjerskih zadednica, 260–261
Zarozhdenie I Razvitie Evangel'sko Baptistskogo Dvizheniya v Bessarabii, 65–66
Zhidkov, Jakov, criticized by Silvestr Tsyrkan, 91
Zornitsa, published by the American Board, 183
Zumpe, Hans, 316

Studies in Baptist History and Thought

(All titles uniform with this volume)
Dates in bold are of projected publication
Volumes in this series are not always published in sequence

David Bebbington and Anthony R. Cross (eds)
Global Baptist History
(SBHT vol. 14)

This book brings together studies from the Second International Conference on Baptist Studies which explore different facets of Baptist life and work especially during the twentieth century.
2006 / 1-84227-214-4 / approx. 350pp

David Bebbington (ed.)
The Gospel in the World
International Baptist Studies
(SBHT vol. 1)

This volume of essays from the First International Conference on Baptist Studies deals with a range of subjects spanning Britain, North America, Europe, Asia and the Antipodes. Topics include studies on religious tolerance, the communion controversy and the development of the international Baptist community, and concludes with two important essays on the future of Baptist life that pay special attention to the United States.
2002 / 1-84227-118-0 / xiv + 362pp

John H.Y. Briggs (ed.)
Pulpit and People
Studies in Eighteenth-Century English Baptist Life and Thought
(SBHT vol. 28)

The eighteenth century was a crucial time in Baptist history. The denomination had its roots in seventeenth-century English Puritanism and Separatism and the persecution of the Stuart kings with only a limited measure of freedom after 1689. Worse, however, was to follow for with toleration came doctrinal conflict, a move away from central Christian understandings and a loss of evangelistic urgency. Both spiritual and numerical decline ensued, to the extent that the denomination was virtually reborn as rather belatedly it came to benefit from the Evangelical Revival which brought new life to both Arminian and Calvinistic Baptists. The papers in this volume study a denomination in transition, and relate to theology, their views of the church and its mission, Baptist spirituality, and engagements with radical politics.
2007 / 1-84227-403-1 / approx. 350pp

July 2005

Damian Brot
Church of the Baptized or Church of Believers?
A Contribution to the Dialogue between the Catholic Church and the Free Churches with Special Reference to Baptists
(SBHT vol. 26)

The dialogue between the Catholic Church and the Free Churches in Europe has hardly taken place. This book pleads for a commencement of such a conversation. It offers, among other things, an introduction to the American and the international dialogues between Baptists and the Catholic Church and strives to allow these conversations to become fruitful in the European context as well.

2006 / 1-84227-334-5 / approx. 364pp

Dennis Bustin
Paradox and Perseverence
Hanserd Knollys, Particular Baptist Pioneer in Seventeenth-Century England
(SBHT vol. 23)

The seventeenth century was a significant period in English history during which the people of England experienced unprecedented change and tumult in all spheres of life. At the same time, the importance of order and the traditional institutions of society were being reinforced. Hanserd Knollys, born during this pivotal period, personified in his life the ambiguity, tension and paradox of it, openly seeking change while at the same time cautiously embracing order. As a founder and leader of the Particular Baptists in London and despite persecution and personal hardship, he played a pivotal role in helping shape their identity externally in society and, internally, as they moved toward becoming more formalised by the end of the century.

2006 / 1-84227-259-4 / approx. 324pp

Anthony R. Cross
Baptism and the Baptists
Theology and Practice in Twentieth-Century Britain
(SBHT vol. 3)

At a time of renewed interest in baptism, *Baptism and the Baptists* is a detailed study of twentieth-century baptismal theology and practice and the factors which have influenced its development.

2000 / 0-85364-959-6 / xx + 530pp

Anthony R. Cross and Philip E. Thompson (eds)
Baptist Sacramentalism
(SBHT vol. 5)

This collection of essays includes biblical, historical and theological studies in the theology of the sacraments from a Baptist perspective. Subjects explored include the physical side of being spiritual, baptism, the Lord's supper, the church, ordination, preaching, worship, religious liberty and the issue of disestablishment.

2003 / 1-84227-119-9 / xvi + 278pp

Anthony R. Cross and Philip E. Thompson (eds)
Baptist Sacramentalism 2
(SBHT vol. 25)

This second collection of essays exploring various dimensions of sacramental theology from a Baptist perspective includes biblical, historical and theological studies from scholars from around the world.

2006 / 1-84227-325-6 / approx. 350pp

Paul S. Fiddes
Tracks and Traces
Baptist Identity in Church and Theology
(SBHT vol. 13)

This is a comprehensive, yet unusual, book on the faith and life of Baptist Christians. It explores the understanding of the church, ministry, sacraments and mission from a thoroughly theological perspective. In a series of interlinked essays, the author relates Baptist identity consistently to a theology of covenant and to participation in the triune communion of God.

2003 / 1-84227-120-2 / xvi + 304pp

Stanley K. Fowler
More Than a Symbol
The British Baptist Recovery of Baptismal Sacramentalism
(SBHT vol. 2)

Fowler surveys the entire scope of British Baptist literature from the seventeenth-century pioneers onwards. He shows that in the twentieth century leading British Baptist pastors and theologians recovered an understanding of baptism that connected experience with soteriology and that in doing so they were recovering what many of their forebears had taught.

2002 / 1-84227-052-4 / xvi + 276pp

Steven R. Harmon
Towards Baptist Catholicity
Essays on Tradition and the Baptist Vision
(SBHT vol. 27)

This series of essays contends that the reconstruction of the Baptist vision in the wake of modernity's dissolution requires a retrieval of the ancient ecumenical tradition that forms Christian identity through rehearsal and practice. Themes explored include catholic identity as an emerging trend in Baptist theology, tradition as a theological category in Baptist perspective, Baptist confessions and the patristic tradition, worship as a principal bearer of tradition, and the role of Baptist higher education in shaping the Christian vision.
2006 / 1-84227-362-0 / approx. 210pp

Michael A.G. Haykin (ed.)
'At the Pure Fountain of Thy Word'
Andrew Fuller as an Apologist
(SBHT vol. 6)

One of the greatest Baptist theologians of the eighteenth and early nineteenth centuries, Andrew Fuller has not had justice done to him. There is little doubt that Fuller's theology lay behind the revitalization of the Baptists in the late eighteenth century and the first few decades of the nineteenth. This collection of essays fills a much needed gap by examining a major area of Fuller's thought, his work as an apologist.
2004 / 1-84227-171-7 / xxii + 276pp

Michael A.G. Haykin
Studies in Calvinistic Baptist Spirituality
(SBHT vol. 15)

In a day when spirituality is in vogue and Christian communities are looking for guidance in this whole area, there is wisdom in looking to the past to find untapped wells. The Calvinistic Baptists, heirs of the rich ecclesial experience in the Puritan era of the seventeenth century, but, by the end of the eighteenth century, also passionately engaged in the catholicity of the Evangelical Revivals, are such a well. This collection of essays, covering such things as the Lord's Supper, friendship and hymnody, seeks to draw out the spiritual riches of this community for reflection and imitation in the present day.
2006 / 1-84227-149-0 / approx. 350pp

Brian Haymes, Anthony R. Cross and Ruth Gouldbourne
On Being the Church
Revisioning Baptist Identity
(SBHT vol. 21)

The aim of the book is to re-examine Baptist theology and practice in the light of the contemporary biblical, theological, ecumenical and missiological context drawing on historical and contemporary writings and issues. It is not a study in denominationalism but rather seeks to revision historical insights from the believers' church tradition for the sake of Baptists and other Christians in the context of the modern–postmodern context.

2006 / 1-84227-121-0 / approx. 350pp

Ken R. Manley
From Woolloomooloo to 'Eternity': A History of Australian Baptists
Volume 1: Growing an Australian Church (1831–1914)
Volume 2: A National Church in a Global Community (1914–2005)
(SBHT vols 16.1 and 16.2)

From their beginnings in Australia in 1831 with the first baptisms in Woolloomoolloo Bay in 1832, this pioneering study describes the quest of Baptists in the different colonies (states) to discover their identity as Australians and Baptists. Although institutional developments are analyzed and the roles of significant individuals traced, the major focus is on the social and theological dimensions of the Baptist movement.

2 vol. set 2006 / 1-84227-405-8 / approx. 900pp

Ken R. Manley
'Redeeming Love Proclaim'
John Rippon and the Baptists
(SBHT vol. 12)

A leading exponent of the new moderate Calvinism which brought new life to many Baptists, John Rippon (1751–1836) helped unite the Baptists at this significant time. His many writings expressed the denomination's growing maturity and mutual awareness of Baptists in Britain and America, and exerted a long-lasting influence on Baptist worship and devotion. In his various activities, Rippon helped conserve the heritage of Old Dissent and promoted the evangelicalism of the New Dissent

2004 / 1-84227-193-8 / xviii + 340pp

Peter J. Morden
Offering Christ to the World
Andrew Fuller and the Revival of English Particular Baptist Life
(SBHT vol. 8)

Andrew Fuller (1754–1815) was one of the foremost English Baptist ministers of his day. His career as an Evangelical Baptist pastor, theologian, apologist and missionary statesman coincided with the profound revitalization of the Particular Baptist denomination to which he belonged. This study examines the key aspects of the life and thought of this hugely significant figure, and gives insights into the revival in which he played such a central part.

2003 / 1-84227-141-5 / xx + 202pp

Peter Naylor
Calvinism, Communion and the Baptists
A Study of English Calvinistic Baptists from the Late 1600s to the Early 1800s
(SBHT vol. 7)

Dr Naylor argues that the traditional link between 'high-Calvinism' and 'restricted communion' is in need of revision. He examines Baptist communion controversies from the late 1600s to the early 1800s and also the theologies of John Gill and Andrew Fuller.

2003 / 1-84227-142-3 / xx + 266pp

Ian M. Randall, Toivo Pilli and Anthony R. Cross (eds)
Baptist Identities
International Studies from the Seventeenth to the Twentieth Centuries
(SBHT vol. 19)

These papers represent the contributions of scholars from various parts of the world as they consider the factors that have contributed to Baptist distinctiveness in different countries and at different times. The volume includes specific case studies as well as broader examinations of Baptist life in a particular country or region. Together they represent an outstanding resource for understanding Baptist identities.

2005 / 1-84227-215-2 / approx. 350pp

James M. Renihan
Edification and Beauty
The Practical Ecclesiology of the English Particular Baptists, 1675–1705
(SBHT vol. 17)

Edification and Beauty describes the practices of the Particular Baptist churches at the end of the seventeenth century in terms of three concentric circles: at the centre is the ecclesiological material in the Second London Confession, which is then fleshed out in the various published writings of the men associated with these churches, and, finally, expressed in the church books of the era.

2005 / 1-84227-251-9 / approx. 230pp

Frank Rinaldi
'The Tribe of Dan'
A Study of the New Connexion of General Baptists 1770–1891
(SBHT vol. 10)

'The Tribe of Dan' is a thematic study which explores the theology, organizational structure, evangelistic strategy, ministry and leadership of the New Connexion of General Baptists as it experienced the process of institutionalization in the transition from a revival movement to an established denomination.

2006 / 1-84227-143-1 / approx. 350pp

Peter Shepherd
The Making of a Modern Denomination
John Howard Shakespeare and the English Baptists 1898–1924
(SBHT vol. 4)

John Howard Shakespeare introduced revolutionary change to the Baptist denomination. The Baptist Union was transformed into a strong central institution and Baptist ministers were brought under its control. Further, Shakespeare's pursuit of church unity reveals him as one of the pioneering ecumenists of the twentieth century.

2001 / 1-84227-046-X / xviii + 220pp

Karen Smith
The Community and the Believers
A Study of Calvinistic Baptist Spirituality in Some Towns and Villages of Hampshire and the Borders of Wiltshire, c.1730–1830
(SBHT vol. 22)

The period from 1730 to 1830 was one of transition for Calvinistic Baptists. Confronted by the enthusiasm of the Evangelical Revival, congregations within the denomination as a whole were challenged to find a way to take account of the revival experience. This study examines the life and devotion of Calvinistic Baptists in Hampshire and Wiltshire during this period. Among this group of Baptists was the hymn writer, Anne Steele.

2005 / 1-84227-326-4 / approx. 280pp

Martin Sutherland
Dissenters in a 'Free Land'
Baptist Thought in New Zealand 1850–2000
(SBHT vol. 24)

Baptists in New Zealand were forced to recast their identity. Conventions of communication and association, state and ecumenical relations, even historical divisions and controversies had to be revised in the face of new topographies and constraints. As Baptists formed themselves in a fluid society they drew heavily on both international movements and local dynamics. This book traces the development of ideas which shaped institutions and styles in sometimes surprising ways.

2006 / 1-84227-327-2 / approx. 230pp

Brian Talbot
The Search for a Common Identity
The Origins of the Baptist Union of Scotland 1800–1870
(SBHT vol. 9)

In the period 1800 to 1827 there were three streams of Baptists in Scotland: Scotch, Haldaneite and 'English' Baptist. A strong commitment to home evangelization brought these three bodies closer together, leading to a merger of their home missionary societies in 1827. However, the first three attempts to form a union of churches failed, but by the 1860s a common understanding of their corporate identity was attained leading to the establishment of the Baptist Union of Scotland.

2003 / 1-84227-123-7 / xviii + 402pp

Philip E. Thompson
The Freedom of God
Towards Baptist Theology in Pneumatological Perspective
(SBHT vol. 20)

This study contends that the range of theological commitments of the early Baptists are best understood in relation to their distinctive emphasis on the freedom of God. Thompson traces how this was recast anthropocentrically, leading to an emphasis upon human freedom from the nineteenth century onwards. He seeks to recover the dynamism of the early vision via a pneumatologically-oriented ecclesiology defining the church in terms of the memory of God.

2006 / 1-84227-125-3 / approx. 350pp

Philip E. Thompson and Anthony R. Cross (eds)
Recycling the Past or Researching History?
Studies in Baptist Historiography and Myths
(SBHT vol. 11)

In this volume an international group of Baptist scholars examine and re-examine areas of Baptist life and thought about which little is known or the received wisdom is in need of revision. Historiographical studies include the date Oxford Baptists joined the Abingdon Association, the death of the Fifth Monarchist John Pendarves, eighteenth-century Calvinistic Baptists and the political realm, confessional identity and denominational institutions, Baptist community, ecclesiology, the priesthood of all believers, soteriology, Baptist spirituality, Strict and Reformed Baptists, the role of women among British Baptists, while various 'myths' challenged include the nature of high-Calvinism in eighteenth-century England, baptismal anti-sacramentalism, episcopacy, and Baptists and change.

2005 / 1-84227-122-9 / approx. 330pp

Linda Wilson
Marianne Farningham
A Plain Working Woman
(SBHT vol. 18)

Marianne Farningham, of College Street Baptist Chapel, Northampton, was a household name in evangelical circles in the later nineteenth century. For over fifty years she produced comment, poetry, biography and fiction for the popular Christian press. This investigation uses her writings to explore the beliefs and behaviour of evangelical Nonconformists, including Baptists, during these years.

2006 / 1-84227-124-5 / approx. 250pp

Other Paternoster titles relating to Baptist history and thought

George R. Beasley-Murray
Baptism in the New Testament
(Paternoster Digital Library)

This is a welcome reprint of a classic text on baptism originally published in 1962 by one of the leading Baptist New Testament scholars of the twentieth century. Dr Beasley-Murray's comprehensive study begins by investigating the antecedents of Christian baptism. It then surveys the foundation of Christian baptism in the Gospels, its emergence in the Acts of the Apostles and development in the apostolic writings. Following a section relating baptism to New Testament doctrine, a substantial discussion of the origin and significance of infant baptism leads to a briefer consideration of baptismal reform and ecumenism.

2005 / 1-84227-300-0 / x + 422pp

Paul Beasley-Murray
Fearless for Truth
A Personal Portrait of the Life of George Beasley-Murray

Without a doubt George Beasley-Murray was one of the greatest Baptists of the twentieth century. A long-standing Principal of Spurgeon's College, he wrote more than twenty books and made significant contributions in the study of areas as diverse as baptism and eschatology, as well as writing highly respected commentaries on the Book of Revelation and John's Gospel.

2002 / 1-84227-134-2 / xii + 244pp

David Bebbington
Holiness in Nineteenth-Century England
(Studies in Christian History and Thought)

David Bebbington stresses the relationship of movements of spirituality to changes in their cultural setting, especially the legacies of the Enlightenment and Romanticism. He shows that these broad shifts in ideological mood had a profound effect on the ways in which piety was conceptualized and practised. Holiness was intimately bound up with the spirit of the age.

2000 / 0-85364-981-2 / viii + 98pp

July 2005

Clyde Binfield
Victorian Nonconformity in Eastern England 1840–1885
(Studies in Evangelical History and Thought)
Studies of Victorian religion and society often concentrate on cities, suburbs, and industrialisation. This study provides a contrast. Victorian Eastern England—Essex, Suffolk, Norfolk, Cambridgeshire, and Huntingdonshire—was rural, traditional, relatively unchanging. That is nonetheless a caricature which discounts the industry in Norwich and Ipswich (as well as in Haverhill, Stowmarket and Leiston) and ignores the impact of London on Essex, of railways throughout the region, and of an ancient but changing university (Cambridge) on the county town which housed it. It also entirely ignores the political implications of such changes in a region noted for the variety of its religious Dissent since the seventeenth century. This book explores Victorian Eastern England and its Nonconformity. It brings to a wider readership a pioneering thesis which has made a major contribution to a fresh evolution of English religion and society.
2006 / 1-84227-216-0 / approx. 274pp

Edward W. Burrows
'To Me To Live Is Christ'
A Biography of Peter H. Barber
This book is about a remarkably gifted and energetic man of God. Peter H. Barber was born into a Brethren family in Edinburgh in 1930. In his youth he joined Charlotte Baptist Chapel and followed the call into Baptist ministry. For eighteen years he was the pioneer minister of the new congregation in the New Town of East Kilbride, which planted two further congregations. At the age of thirty-nine he served as Centenary President of the Baptist Union of Scotland and then exercised an influential ministry for over seven years in the well-known Upton Vale Baptist Church, Torquay. From 1980 until his death in 1994 he was General Secretary of the Baptist Union of Scotland. Through his work for the European Baptist Federation and the Baptist World Alliance he became a world Baptist statesman. He was President of the EBF during the upheaval that followed the collapse of Communism.
2005 / 1-84227-324-8 / xxii + 236pp

Christopher J. Clement
Religious Radicalism in England 1535–1565
(Rutherford Studies in Historical Theology)
In this valuable study Christopher Clement draws our attention to a varied assemblage of people who sought Christian faithfulness in the underworld of mid-Tudor England. Sympathetically and yet critically he assess their place in the history of English Protestantism, and by attentive listening he gives them a voice.
1997 / 0-946068-44-5 / xxii + 426pp

July 2005

Anthony R. Cross (ed.)
Ecumenism and History
Studies in Honour of John H.Y. Briggs
(Studies in Christian History and Thought)
This collection of essays examines the inter-relationships between the two fields in which Professor Briggs has contributed so much: history—particularly Baptist and Nonconformist—and the ecumenical movement. With contributions from colleagues and former research students from Britain, Europe and North America, *Ecumenism and History* provides wide-ranging studies in important aspects of Christian history, theology and ecumenical studies.
2002 / 1-84227-135-0 / xx + 362pp

Keith E. Eitel
Paradigm Wars
*The Southern Baptist International Mission Board
Faces the Third Millennium*
(Regnum Studies in Mission)
The International Mission Board of the Southern Baptist Convention is the largest denominational mission agency in North America. This volume chronicles the historic and contemporary forces that led to the IMB's recent extensive reorganization, providing the most comprehensive case study to date of a historic mission agency restructuring to continue its mission purpose into the twenty-first century more effectively.
2000 / 1-870345-12-6 / x + 140pp

Ruth Gouldbourne
The Flesh and the Feminine
Gender and Theology in the Writings of Caspar Schwenckfeld
(Studies in Christian History and Thought)
Caspar Schwenckfeld and his movement exemplify one of the radical communities of the sixteenth century. Challenging theological and liturgical norms, they also found themselves challenging social and particularly gender assumptions. In this book, the issues of the relationship between radical theology and the understanding of gender are considered.
2005 / 1-84227-048-6 / approx. 304pp

David Hilborn
The Words of our Lips
Language-Use in Free Church Worship
(Paternoster Theological Monographs)
Studies of liturgical language have tended to focus on the written canons of Roman Catholic and Anglican communities. By contrast, David Hilborn analyses the more extemporary approach of English Nonconformity. Drawing on recent developments in linguistic pragmatics, he explores similarities and differences between 'fixed' and 'free' worship, and argues for the interdependence of each.

2006 / 0-85364-977-4

Stephen R. Holmes
Listening to the Past
The Place of Tradition in Theology
Beginning with the question 'Why can't we just read the Bible?' Stephen Holmes considers the place of tradition in theology, showing how the doctrine of creation leads to an account of historical location and creaturely limitations as essential aspects of our existence. For we cannot claim unmediated access to the Scriptures without acknowledging the place of tradition: theology is an irreducibly communal task. *Listening to the Past* is a sustained attempt to show what listening to tradition involves, and how it can be used to aid theological work today.

2002 / 1-84227-155-5 / xiv + 168pp

Mark Hopkins
Nonconformity's Romantic Generation
Evangelical and Liberal Theologies in Victorian England
(Studies in Evangelical History and Thought)
A study of the theological development of key leaders of the Baptist and Congregational denominations at their period of greatest influence, including C.H. Spurgeon and R.W. Dale, and of the controversies in which those among them who embraced and rejected the liberal transformation of their evangelical heritage opposed each other.

2004 / 1-84227-150-4 / xvi + 284pp

Galen K. Johnson
Prisoner of Conscience
John Bunyan on Self, Community and Christian Faith
(Studies in Christian History and Thought)
This is an interdisciplinary study of John Bunyan's understanding of conscience across his autobiographical, theological and fictional writings, investigating whether conscience always deserves fidelity, and how Bunyan's view of conscience affects his relationship both to modern Western individualism and historic Christianity.
2003 / 1-84227- 151-2 / xvi + 236pp

R.T. Kendall
Calvin and English Calvinism to 1649
(Studies in Christian History and Thought)
The author's thesis is that those who formed the Westminster Confession of Faith, which is regarded as Calvinism, in fact departed from John Calvin on two points: (1) the extent of the atonement and (2) the ground of assurance of salvation.
1997 / 0-85364-827-1 / xii + 264pp

Timothy Larsen
Friends of Religious Equality
Nonconformist Politics in Mid-Victorian England
During the middle decades of the nineteenth century the English Nonconformist community developed a coherent political philosophy of its own, of which a central tenet was the principle of religious equality (in contrast to the stereotype of Evangelical Dissenters). The Dissenting community fought for the civil rights of Roman Catholics, non-Christians and even atheists, on an issue of principle which had its flowering in the enthusiastic and undivided support which Nonconformity gave to the campaign for Jewish emancipation. This reissued study examines the political efforts and ideas of English Nonconformists during the period, covering the whole range of national issues raised, from state education to the Crimean War. It offers a case study of a theologically conservative group defending religious pluralism in the civic sphere, showing that the concept of religious equality was a grand vision at the centre of the political philosophy of the Dissenters.
2007 / 1-84227-402-3 / x + 300pp

Donald M. Lewis
Lighten Their Darkness
The Evangelical Mission to Working-Class London, 1828–1860
(Studies in Evangelical History and Thought)
This is a comprehensive and compelling study of the Church and the complexities of nineteenth-century London. Challenging our understanding of the culture in working London at this time, Lewis presents a well-structured and illustrated work that contributes substantially to the study of evangelicalism and mission in nineteenth-century Britain.
2001 / 1-84227-074-5 / xviii + 372pp

Stanley E. Porter and Anthony R. Cross (eds)
Semper Reformandum
Studies in Honour of Clark H. Pinnock
Clark Pinnock has clearly been one of the most important evangelical theologians of the last forty years in North America. Always provocative, especially in the wide range of opinions he has held and considered, Pinnock, himself a Baptist, has recently retired after twenty-five years of teaching at McMaster Divinity College. His colleagues and associates honour him in this volume by responding to his important theological work which has dealt with the essential topics of evangelical theology. These include Christian apologetics, biblical inspiration, the Holy Spirit and, perhaps most importantly in recent years, openness theology.
2003 / 1-84227-206-3 / xiv + 414pp

Meic Pearse
The Great Restoration
The Religious Radicals of the 16th and 17th Centuries
Pearse charts the rise and progress of continental Anabaptism – both evangelical and heretical – through the sixteenth century. He then follows the story of those English people who became impatient with Puritanism and separated – first from the Church of England and then from one another – to form the antecedents of later Congregationalists, Baptists and Quakers.
1998 / 0-85364-800-X / xii + 320pp

Charles Price and Ian M. Randall
Transforming Keswick
Transforming Keswick is a thorough, readable and detailed history of the convention. It will be of interest to those who know and love Keswick, those who are only just discovering it, and serious scholars eager to learn more about the history of God's dealings with his people.
2000 / 1-85078-350-0 / 288pp

Jim Purves
The Triune God and the Charismatic Movement
A Critical Appraisal from a Scottish Perspective
(Paternoster Theological Monographs)

All emotion and no theology? Or a fundamental challenge to reappraise and realign our trinitarian theology in the light of Christian experience? This study of charismatic renewal as it found expression within Scotland at the end of the twentieth century evaluates the use of Patristic, Reformed and contemporary models (including those of the Baptist Union of Scotland) of the Trinity in explaining the workings of the Holy Spirit.

2004 / 1-84227-321-3 / xxiv + 246pp

Ian M. Randall
Evangelical Experiences
A Study in the Spirituality of English Evangelicalism 1918–1939
(Studies in Evangelical History and Thought)

This book makes a detailed historical examination of evangelical spirituality between the First and Second World Wars. It shows how patterns of devotion led to tensions and divisions. In a wide-ranging study, Anglican, Wesleyan, Reformed and Pentecostal-charismatic spiritualities are analysed.

1999 / 0-85364-919-7 / xii + 310pp

Ian M. Randall
One Body in Christ
The History and Significance of the Evangelical Alliance

In 1846 the Evangelical Alliance was founded with the aim of bringing together evangelicals for common action. This book uses material not previously utilized to examine the history and significance of the Evangelical Alliance, a movement which has remained a powerful force for unity. At a time when evangelicals are growing world-wide, this book offers insights into the past which are relevant to contemporary issues.

2001 / 1-84227-089-3 / xii + 394pp

Ian M. Randall
Spirituality and Social Change
The Contribution of F.B. Meyer (1847–1929)
(Studies in Evangelical History and Thought)

This is a fresh appraisal of F.B. Meyer (1847–1929), a leading Free Church minister. Having been deeply affected by holiness spirituality, Meyer became the Keswick Convention's foremost international speaker. He combined spirituality with effective evangelism and socio-political activity. This study shows Meyer's significant contribution to spiritual renewal and social change.

2003 / 1-84227-195-4 / xx + 184pp

Geoffrey Robson
Dark Satanic Mills?
Religion and Irreligion in Birmingham and the Black Country
(Studies in Evangelical History and Thought)
This book analyses and interprets the nature and extent of popular Christian belief and practice in Birmingham and the Black Country during the first half of the nineteenth century, with particular reference to the impact of cholera epidemics and evangelism on church extension programmes.
2002 / 1-84227-102-4 / xiv + 294pp

Alan P.F. Sell
Enlightenment, Ecumenism, Evangel
Theological Themes and Thinkers 1550–2000
(Studies in Christian History and Thought)
This book consists of papers in which such interlocking topics as the Enlightenment, the problem of authority, the development of doctrine, spirituality, ecumenism, theological method and the heart of the gospel are discussed. Issues of significance to the church at large are explored with special reference to writers from the Reformed and Dissenting traditions.
2005 / 1-84227330-2 / xviii + 422pp

Alan P.F. Sell
Hinterland Theology
Some Reformed and Dissenting Adjustments
(Studies in Christian History and Thought)
Many books have been written on theology's 'giants' and significant trends, but what of those lesser-known writers who adjusted to them? In this book some hinterland theologians of the British Reformed and Dissenting traditions, who followed in the wake of toleration, the Evangelical Revival, the rise of modern biblical criticism and Karl Barth, are allowed to have their say. They include Thomas Ridgley, Ralph Wardlaw, T.V. Tymms and N.H.G. Robinson.
2006 / 1-84227-331-0

Alan P.F. Sell and Anthony R. Cross (eds)
Protestant Nonconformity in the Twentieth Century
(Studies in Christian History and Thought)

In this collection of essays scholars representative of a number of Nonconformist traditions reflect thematically on Nonconformists' life and witness during the twentieth century. Among the subjects reviewed are biblical studies, theology, worship, evangelism and spirituality, and ecumenism. Over and above its immediate interest, this collection provides a marker to future scholars and others wishing to know how some of their forebears assessed Nonconformity's contribution to a variety of fields during the century leading up to Christianity's third millennium.

2003 / 1-84227-221-7 / x + 398pp

Mark Smith
Religion in Industrial Society
Oldham and Saddleworth 1740–1865
(Studies in Christian History and Thought)

This book analyses the way British churches sought to meet the challenge of industrialization and urbanization during the period 1740–1865. Working from a case-study of Oldham and Saddleworth, Mark Smith challenges the received view that the Anglican Church in the eighteenth century was characterized by complacency and inertia, and reveals Anglicanism's vigorous and creative response to the new conditions. He reassesses the significance of the centrally directed church reforms of the mid-nineteenth century, and emphasizes the importance of local energy and enthusiasm. Charting the growth of denominational pluralism in Oldham and Saddleworth, Dr Smith compares the strengths and weaknesses of the various Anglican and Nonconformist approaches to promoting church growth. He also demonstrates the extent to which all the churches participated in a common culture shaped by the influence of evangelicalism, and shows that active co-operation between the churches rather than denominational conflict dominated. This revised and updated edition of Dr Smith's challenging and original study makes an important contribution both to the social history of religion and to urban studies.

2006 / 1-84227-335-3 / approx. 300pp

David M. Thompson
Baptism, Church and Society in Britain from the Evangelical Revival to *Baptism, Eucharist and Ministry*
The theology and practice of baptism have not received the attention they deserve. How important is faith? What does baptismal regeneration mean? Is baptism a bond of unity between Christians? This book discusses the theology of baptism and popular belief and practice in England and Wales from the Evangelical Revival to the publication of the World Council of Churches' consensus statement on *Baptism, Eucharist and Ministry* (1982).
2005 / 1-84227-393-0 / approx. 224pp

Martin Sutherland
Peace, Toleration and Decay
The Ecclesiology of Later Stuart Dissent
(Studies in Christian History and Thought)
This fresh analysis brings to light the complexity and fragility of the later Stuart Nonconformist consensus. Recent findings on wider seventeenth-century thought are incorporated into a new picture of the dynamics of Dissent and the roots of evangelicalism.
2003 / 1-84227-152-0 / xxii + 216pp

Haddon Willmer
Evangelicalism 1785–1835: An Essay (1962) and Reflections (2004)
(Studies in Evangelical History and Thought)
Awarded the Hulsean Prize in the University of Cambridge in 1962, this interpretation of a classic period of English Evangelicalism, by a young church historian, is now supplemented by reflections on Evangelicalism from the vantage point of a retired Professor of Theology.
2006 / 1-84227-219-5

Linda Wilson
Constrained by Zeal
Female Spirituality amongst Nonconformists 1825–1875
(Studies in Evangelical History and Thought)
Constrained by Zeal investigates the neglected area of Nonconformist female spirituality. Against the background of separate spheres, it analyses the experience of women from four denominations, and argues that the churches provided a 'third sphere' in which they could find opportunities for participation.
2000 / 0-85364-972-3 / xvi + 294pp

Nigel G. Wright
Disavowing Constantine
Mission, Church and the Social Order in the Theologies of John Howard Yoder and Jürgen Moltmann
(Paternoster Theological Monographs)

This book is a timely restatement of a radical theology of church and state in the Anabaptist and Baptist tradition. Dr Wright constructs his argument in dialogue and debate with Yoder and Moltmann, major contributors to a free church perspective.

2000 / 0-85364-978-2 / xvi + 252pp

Nigel G. Wright
Free Church, Free State
The Positive Baptist Vision

Free Church, Free State is a textbook on baptist ways of being church and a proposal for the future of baptist churches in an ecumenical context. Nigel Wright argues that both baptist (small 'b') and catholic (small 'c') church traditions should seek to enrich and support each other as valid expressions of the body of Christ without sacrificing what they hold dear. Written for pastors, church planters, evangelists and preachers, Nigel Wright offers frameworks of thought for baptists and non-baptists in their journey together following Christ.

2005 / 1-84227-353-1 / xxviii + 292

Nigel G. Wright
New Baptists, New Agenda

New Baptists, New Agenda is a timely contribution to the growing debate about the health, shape and future of the Baptists. It considers the steady changes that have taken place among Baptists in the last decade – changes of mood, style, practice and structure – and encourages us to align these current movements and questions with God's upward and future call. He contends that the true church has yet to come: the church that currently exists is an anticipation of the joyful gathering of all who have been called by the Spirit through Christ to the Father.

2002 / 1-84227-157-1 / x + 162pp

Paternoster
9 Holdom Avenue,
Bletchley,
Milton Keynes MK1 1QR,
United Kingdom
Web: www.authenticmedia.co.uk/paternoster

July 2005

www.ingramcontent.com/pod-product-compliance
Lightning Source LLC
Chambersburg PA
CBHW071230290426
44108CB00013B/1362